OTHELLO

SHAKESPEARE CRITICISM
Philip C. Kolin, *General Editor*

OTHELLO
NEW CRITICAL ESSAYS

EDITED BY PHILIP C. KOLIN

ROUTLEDGE
NEW YORK AND LONDON

Published in 2002 by
Routledge
270 Madison Ave,
New York, NY 10016

Published in Great Britain by
Routledge
2 Park Square, Milton Park,
Abingdon, Oxon, OX14 4RN

Routledge is an imprint of the Taylor & Francis Group.

Transferred to Digital Printing 2006

10   9   8   7   6   5   4   3   2   1

Cover photo: Laurence Olivier as Othello, 1964. Photograph by Angus McBean.
© The Harvard Theatre Collection. The Houghton Library.

Library of Congress Cataloging-in-Publication Data

Othello: new critical essays / edited by Philip C. Kolin.
    p. cm.—(Shakespeare criticism; v. 28)
    Includes bibliographical references and index.
    ISBN 0–8153–3574–1 (acid free paper)
    1. Shakespeare, William 1564–1616. Othello. I. Kolin, Philip C. II. Series
    PR2829 .O855 2001
    822.3'3—dc21   2001019475

ISBN10: 0–8153–3574–1 (hbk)
ISBN10: 0–415–41101–7 (pbk)

ISBN13: 978–0–8153–3574–0 (hbk)
ISBN13: 978–0–415–41101–1 (pbk)

**For Kathleen and John Curley,
with my love**

Contents

Acknowledgments

Iago may have been wrong on most things, but he was unequivocally clear on this: "Good name in man and woman . . . Is the immediate jewel of their souls." In gathering, preparing, and introducing this volume of original engaging criticism on *Othello,* I was greatly assisted by the following souls whose reputations are like valuable jewels to me.

First off, I owe an immense debt of gratitude to my 20 contributors, whose essays expand the horizons from which we see and yet recoil from the power and terror that is *Othello.*

I also would like to thank the many theatre companies who responded so generously to my requests for information on their productions of *Othello.* In particular, I am grateful to Derrick Ricketts at the Shakespeare Festival of Dallas, Amy Richards at the Oregon Shakespeare Festival, Jane Edmonds at the Stratford Festival of Canada, Sara Danielsen at Shakespeare Santa Cruz, Marsha Arado of the Utah Shakespeare Festival, Dennis Behl of the Guthrie Theatre, and Sara Gruber at the Shakespeare Theatre. Special thanks goes to Kent Thompson, the Artistic Director of the Alabama Shakespeare Festival, for kindly granting me the interview that appears at the end of this volume.

I also thank Allen Hale at the University of Illinois and Annette Fern at the Harvard Theatre Collection for their kind assistance in helping me locate several of the photos for this volume.

To my editors at Routledge—Anne Davidson, Angela Kao, and Henry Bashwiner—I say a hearty thank you for your cooperation and advice.

At the University of Southern Mississippi, I continue to record happily my gratitude to the following individuals who support my research—Vice President for Research Donald Cotten, Glenn T. Harper, Dean of the College of Liberal Arts and my patron, and Chair of the Department of English, Michael Salda. Karolyn Thompson, Inter-Library Loan Librarian, worked very hard with characteristic kindness and dispatch to find items for me. To my graduate students who have assisted me in countless ways over the last two years, I say a special prayer of thanks for Terri Ruckel, Christina Hunter, Christopher Reese, and Rick Warner; to Shanna Linder goes extra Paters and Aves for her superlative keyboarding skills. Most significantly, I am thankful for the Aubrey and Ella Lucas Grant which enabled me to prepare this volume and to purchase *Othello* films for the University of Southern Mississippi's Cook Library.

I am also grateful to my many friends in Hattiesburg who have assisted me with their kindness and prayers—Sister Carmelita Stinn, SFCC, Deacon Ralph and Mary Torelli, Father G. Ed Lundin, Father Tommy Conway, Russell and Debbie Dukette and Vicki Breazeale. To my spiritual parents— Margie and Al Parish—go my heartfelt thanks for counsel, trust, and their special love. I am also grateful to Abbot Cletus Meagher, OSB, at St. Bernard's Monastery, for his love and counsel.

Finally, I thank God for my sweet and beautiful children—Kristin Julie, Eric, Theresa, and Evan Philip, and their love and patience. And I embrace John and Kathleen Curley and my beautiful wife to be Maureen Curley, God's greatest gift to me, with prayers and love for all our new tomorrows.

January 2001

General Editor's Introduction

The continuing goal of the Shakespeare Criticism Series is to provide the most significant and original contemporary interpretations of Shakespeare's works. Each volume in the series is devoted to a Shakespearean play or poem (e.g., the sonnets, *Venus and Adonis, Othello*) and contains 18–25 new essays exploring the text from a variety of critical perspectives.

A major feature of each volume in the series is the editor's introduction. Each volume editor provides a substantial essay identifying the main critical issues and problems the play (or poem) has raised, charting the critical trends in looking at the work over the centuries, and assessing the critical discourse that has linked the play or poem to various ideological concerns. In addition to examining the critical commentary in light of important historical and theatrical events, each introduction functions as a discursive bibliographic essay citing and evaluating significant critical works – books, journal articles, theatre documents, reviews, and interviews—giving readers a guide to the vast amounts of research on a particular play or poem.

Each volume showcases the work of leading Shakespeare scholars who participate in and extend the critical discourse on the text. Reflecting the most recent approaches in Shakespeare studies, these essays approach the play from a host of critical positions, including, but not limited to, feminist, Marxist, New Historical, semiotic, mythic, performance/staging, cultural, and/or a combination of these and other methodologies. Some volumes in the series include bibliographic analyses of a Shakespearean text to shed light on its critical history and interpretation. Interviews with directors and/or actors are also part of some volumes in the series.

At least one, sometimes as many as two or three, of the essays in each volume is devoted to the play in performance, beginning with the earliest and most significant productions and proceeding to the most recent. These essays, which ultimately provide a theatre history of the play, should not be regarded as different from or rigidly isolated from the critical work on the script. Shakespeare criticism has often been informed by or has significantly influenced productions. Over the last thirty years or so Shakespeare criticism has understandably been labeled "The Age of Performance." Readers will find information in these essays on non-English speaking productions of Shakespeare's plays as well as landmark performances in English. Editors and contributors also include photographs from productions around the world to help readers see and further appreciate the ways a Shakespearean play has taken shape in the theatre.

Ultimately, each volume in the Shakespeare Criticism Series strives to give readers a balanced, representative collection of the most engaging and thoroughly researched criticism on the given Shakespearean text. In essence, each volume provides a careful survey of essential materials in the history of criticism of a Shakespearean play or poem as well as cutting-edge essays that extend and enliven our understanding of the work in its critical context. In offering readers innovative and fulfilling new essays, volume editors have made invaluable contributions to the literary and theatrical criticism of Shakespeare's greatest legacy, his work.

Philip C. Kolin
University of Southern Mississippi

Blackness Made Visible
A Survey of *Othello* in Criticism, on Stage, and on Screen

PHILIP C. KOLIN

In what must be the most egregious understatement in *Othello* criticism, William Hazlitt wrote in 1817 that the play "excites our sympathy in an extraordinary degree." Exceeding Hazlitt's enthusiasm, A. C. Bradley announced in 1904 that "Of all Shakespeare's tragedies *Othello* is the most painfully exciting and terrible" (*Shakespearean Tragedy,* 140). For centuries, though, the play had been terrifying readers and audiences. Dr. Johnson confessed that he could not bear to read or see the last act performed. Audience responses—like those of Hazlitt, Bradley, and Johnson—are a prolegomenon to any discussion of the critical heritage or stage history of the play. Audience reactions crystallize the major anxieties *Othello* has raised in its 400 year history. At the emotional center of the play—the vortex of its web—are some of the most inflammatory issues confronting early and late modern audiences alike: (a) miscegenation—a black man marrying a white woman; (b) adultery—openly incensing Othello yet based upon Iago's tissue of flimsy clues; (c) violence—directed toward both women and men; (d) sexuality/desire—narrated through violent fictions but horribly physicalized as well; (e) jealousy—the curse of marriage and military office undermining faith and trust; (f) loss of reputation—for Desdemona, Cassio, Othello; (g) class warfare—Iago, the underdog, Othello, the outsider. Inescapably, *Othello* is a cultural seismograph, measuring the extent and force of gender, racial, or class upheavals in any society that performs the script.

Historically, audiences have inscribed themselves in the text: *Othello* has been unpacked in their discomfitures. Propelled into the play, audiences have been imperilled in the web of its magic, and perplexed through its magic web of tangled uncertainties and implausible outrages. No other Shakespearean play seems to have invoked such pained and/or recriminatory audience/reader response as has *Othello*. As criticism of the play reveals, audiences have been ejected from the safety of readership/spectatorship and press-ganged into

1

collaboration with or against the characters. In 1930, G. Wilson Knight declared an essential truth—*Othello* affects us because of its "outstanding differences" *(Wheel of Fire,* 80). Recent studies by Jean Howard, E. A. J. Honigmann *(Shakespeare: Seven Tragedies)*, and Stephen Greenblatt all trace how Iago, Othello, Emilia, and even Desdemona employ dramaturgical strategies to recruit audiences into an *Othello* constituency, exploding expectations into anxiety, contradictions, and resistance. With timorous accent and dire yell, readers have advanced interpretations as if they were as strong a proof as holy writ. As Edward Pechter, one of the most perceptive *Othello* readers, repeatedly cautions, "It is not uncommon for *Othello* critics to claim that their interpretations are not just valid but true, yet another piece of evidence for the special pressures the play puts on us" *(Othello,* 18). Persistently, the epistemology of *Othello* criticism resides uncomfortably in the "contradictory energies of the play" *(Othello,* 164).

The fact that *Othello* has been repeatedly censored in production further documents an audience's demand to have their worst anxieties calmed, and quieted through excision. What editors and actors have tried to quarantine has erupted into pain and anger for audiences over the centuries. Marvin Rosenberg documents several instances where bowdlerization in *Othello* was exceeded by *plumptrianization,* a radical example of textual cautery performed by the nineteenth-century editor, the Rev. James Plumptre. Edwin Booth, for example, refused to utter any *Othello* vocabulary of assignation/copulation—*sheets, bed, lie* and so on. Yet the *Othello* text, if left to unfold in its most elemental, most unguarded shape, turns into an envenomed weapon against the audience's composure, destablizing their emotional status quo. At the end of the twentieth century, Edward Pechter argues that the play graphically projects the reader's revulsion of sexual fluids; the "slime" of the deceitful deed has its verbal roots in sexual secretions *(Othello,* 104; see also Pechter, "Sex and Sexual Stories"). *Othello* is a riotous text disturbing readers'/spectators' peace of mind, frustrating their desire for closure. Speaking to this point, Peter Davison aptly quotes Susan Sontag's essay "Against Interpretation": "Real art has the capacity to make us nervous." And as Davison further notes, "What is certain is that *Othello* is not a comfortable play: neither is its style, its construction, or its matter comfortable; and it ought to make us uneasy, a little nervous" *(Othello,* 5).

Desdemona's murder, for example, has provoked feverish agony in audiences. In 1610, Henry Jackson described a contemporary spectator's pained response to the play performed at Oxford's Corpus Christi College:

> They also had tragedies, which they acted with propriety and fitness. In which [tragedies], not only through speaking but also through certain things, they moved [the audience] to tears. But truly the celebrated Desdemona, slain in our presence by her husband, although she pleaded her case very

effectively throughout, yet moved [us] more after she was dead, when lying on her bed, entreated the pity of the spectators by her very countenance. (*Riverside Shakespeare,* 1852)

Other scenes have also evoked pity and terror. Richard Steele in the *Tattler* (2 May 1710) recorded the impact Thomas Betterton's Othello had on early eighteenth-century audiences: the actor "betrayed in his gesture such a variety and vicissitude of passion as would admonish a Man to be afraid of his own heart, and perfectly convince him that it is to stab it to admit that worst of daggers, Jealousy." In 1776, the power of the Moor's horrible deed put audiences of Ludwig Schroeder's adaptation of *Othello* in a state of turmoil. This spectacle on stage:

> . . . exceeded by far what the nerves of the men of Hamburg, and even more those of the women...could bear. The closer the performance approached the catastrophe, the more uneasy the audience grew. "Swoons followed upon swoons," reports an eyewitness. "The doors of the boxes opened and closed. People left, or when necessary, were carried out; and, according to trustworthy reports, the miscarriages suffered by various prominent ladies were the result of seeing and hearing the overly tragic play." (quoted in Habicht, 5)

Sixteen years later, when the great French tragedian François-Joseph Talma murdered Desdemona in Jean-François Ducis's adaptation (1792), the audience sent up:

> . . . a universal tumult. Tears, groans, and menaces resounded from all parts of the theatre; and what was still more demonstrative, and more alarming, several of the prettiest women in Paris fainted in the most conspicuous boxes and were publicly carried out of the house. Ducis was alarmed for his tragedy, for this fame, and for his life. (Rosenberg, 32)

Seeing Edmund Kean as Othello, an actor who sent "flashes of lightning" into the audience, "Byron wept sobs" (Rosenberg, 61), and recalling Kean's horrific performance in Act 3.3 demanding blood, John Keats claimed it was "direful and slaughterous to the deepest degree, the very words appeared stained and gory...His voice is loosed on . . . [audiences] like the wild dog on the savage relics of an Eastern conflict" (quoted in Rosenberg, 65). Especially noteworthy, too, was the manner in which Kean delivered Othello's "farewell speech" (3.3)—audiences were "reduced . . . to tears" (Cowhig, "The Importance of Othello's Race," 158).

Yet audiences have not been content merely to be wailing walls of pity or frozen columns of terror. *Othello* is so explosive that it has uprooted audiences from their stunned and seated anonymity to become vocal rhetors of protest and rage and, on some occasions, even defenders of character. Watching

Othello about to put out the light of a sleeping Desdemona, a woman in nineteenth-century Charleston, South Carolina stood up to rebuke the actor, "She did not do it." In another instance of audience entrapment in the world of the play, Pechter points out that:

> Perhaps the most striking instance of such bizarre overinvolvement comes in an anecdote transcribed in Stendhal of an 1822 performance in Baltimore, during which a soldier on guard duty, "seeing Othello . . . about to kill Desdemona, shouted: 'It will never be said that in my presence a confounded Negro has killed a white woman!'" whereupon "he fired his gun and broke an arm of the actor who was playing the Moor. (*Othello*, 12)

Conversely, when the Russian actor Alexander Ostuzhev (1874-1953) voiced Othello's bloody threats in his last speech, a man in the audience shouted: "It wasn't his fault: his kind of love could burn up a city." This last incident raises one of the most crucial questions for readers/audiences about the play. Is Othello a criminal, or simply a man who loved not wisely but too well?

Contemporary feminist critics analogize Desdemona's (and Emilia's) plight to that of post-millennial battered wives who too often suffer (murderous) spousal abuse; Sheryl Craig, for example, studies the battered wife syndrome in *Othello*. Yet diarist Samuel Pepys recorded in the1660s that "a very pretty lady sat by me and called out to see Desdemona smothered," an early alarming response to violence in the play. Thomas Rymer minimized the violence in *Othello* by framing it as an etiquette lesson for ladies to be more careful in disposing of their dirty linen. We may look back with smug humor today at Rymer's displaced morality or Pepys's "pretty lady," but have audiences really come that far from Restoration moralities? As Ania Loomba and others have pointed out, audiences have witnessed spousal cruelties inflicted on women for far less serious offenses than losing handkerchiefs (*Gender*). Sending even more into the docket of the guilty, Ruth Vanita claims that "Desdemona is killed not only by Othello and Iago but by all those who see her humiliated and beaten in public, and fail to intervene" ("'Proper Men' and 'Fallen Women,'" 3). Hugh Macrae Richmond explores the audience and *Othello* later in this volume.

Audience reaction to Othello's race has also evoked vitriolic and contradictory responses, mapping oppositional currents in the play that tug and pull at spectators' loyalties, exposing their prejudices. In the early 1930s, Paul Robeson declared that "*Othello* won't play in Memphis," because segregation and prejudice stood at the footlights with pickets. Corroborating Robeson's fear, a story in the *New York Times* for 22 May 1930 ran this title: "Negro Who Kisses White Girl on London Stage Would Expect Protest in America." In this story, Robeson was quoted as saying: "If any one does object to our [his and Peggy Ashcroft's Desdemona's] love making, the objection almost certainly will have to come from America." In 1979, Paul Winfield received hate mail for kissing a white Desdemona (Lower, 221). Yet the range of responses to Othello and the fair Desdemona also includes that of "a refined and lovely young lady" who, upon seeing Edwin Forrest's virile nineteenth-century *Othello*, confessed that "if that is the way Moors look and talk and love, give me a Moor for a husband" (quoted in Pechter, *Othello,* 12). And G. K. Hunter, quoting from the *Variorum*, analyzes a comment from a nineteenth-century Maryland lady who outlandishly stated, "In studying the play of *Othello* I have always imagined its hero a white man" ("Othello and Colour Prejudice"). No less outlandish was Peter Zadek's postmodern parody in 1976 in Hamburg where Ulrich Wildgruber's Othello, dressed in a King Kong costume with a black "paper-maché mask," had "deliberately pull[ed] up Desdemona's night-gown to expose her nude posterior to the audience." In turn they "laughed and shouted at him [while] Wildgruber shouted back . . . [in a] pandemonium of comic terror" (Kennedy, *Looking at Shakespeare,* 269).

On the other hand, examining *Othello* from the perspective of the O. J. Simpson case, audiences have seen the play as something "To haunt us as an uncanny projection from the past, of our conflicted present," as Mitchell Greenberg points out (quoted in Pechter, *Othello,* 7). Exploring *Othello* from the contemporary perspective of race relations and prejudice, Germaine Greer contends that the play is "an authentic and sensitive portrait of a black hero in a white society" ("Old Black Ram," 24), and Ruth Cowhig similarly concludes that Othello's tragedy is that of "a black man whose humanity is eroded by the cunning and racism of whites" ("Blacks in English Renaissance Drama," 7). Beyond a doubt, *Othello* has been exploited as a mirror of the times.

These contradictory reactions—from prejudiced outrage to fascination over sexual crimes—document "our willingness, even eagerness, to engage with the play's disturbing sexuality" (Pechter, *Othello,* 19). Terror gives way to expectation. As Lynda Boose perceptively claims, we want to see, gaze upon the ocular proof of Cassio tupping Desdemona and yet recoil in horror at the very thought of such an act ("'Let it Be Hid'"). Even more boldly implicating audiences in their desire to participate in the play, David Polland asserts that:

> We the audience, share in its exciting pathology. Our instincts healthily repressed or sublimated under compulsion from the reality principle, we do not shrink, like the self-tormented and emotionally violent Dr. Johnson, from the play's finale. Rather, we release the libidinal energies of our own scopophilia as we join vicariously Othello and Iago in Desdemona's bedroom. Thus do we indulge our own sadomasochistic fantasies in the aesthetically pleasing mayhem on the heroine's wedding sheets as it unfolds before our view. *Othello* thereby becomes the focusing instrument for complex and collusive "communal" aggression. ("Iago's Wound," 95–96)

Energized by race and sex, *Othello* audiences have engaged in a multivocal dialogue with the characters, liberating Othello (and Desdemona, too) from stereotype. In the process, *Othello* criticism has moved from erasure to emancipation.

Yet *Othello* is a paroxysm of paradoxes. The play resists the therapeutic and the cathartic. It eschews synthesis. John Bayley is only partially right: "The whole tendency of *Othello* is to make us partisan . . . to underline the incommensurability of opposed emotional states" (quoted in Pechter, *Othello,* 29). In point of fact, however, by declaring partisanship audiences fall into a trap of culpability. The history of *Othello* on stage might conveniently be seen as a continuing question of whose play is it— Othello's? Iago's? Iagothello's? Playing in repertoire, actors have often switched roles, one night taking Othello, the next Iago, as Edwin Booth and Henry Irving did in the nineteenth century, and as Richard Burton and John Neville did at the Old Vic in 1956, de-monstrating how quickly actors themselves are recruited into and yet unmoored from partisanship. But partiality in *Othello* breeds dissonance. If we side with Othello, we run the risk of valorizing and vindicating his unthinkable deeds. Confronting the anxieties of allegiance, Alexander Ostumov, the celebrated nineteenth-century Russian actor, put his finger on this very problem noting that he had to act "the part so as to make people love Othello and forget he is a murderer" (quoted in Cowhig, "The Importance of Othello's Race," 159). Differentiating the hero's fate from an audience's sympathy for him, Anthony Gerard Barthelemy aptly pointed out:

> Our sympathy for Othello, however, is sympathy for his struggle to escape his fate, not sympathy for what he is fated to be. For that there is no sympathy. Thus Brabantio can sympathize with Othello until he sees only the typical stage Moor, the man who bewitched his daughter. Those who sympathize see Othello as a brave warrior in control of his own destiny. Is not this the moral of his tale to Desdemona, who he says "lov'd me for the dangers I had pass'd" (I, iii, 167)? Brabantio himself was once beguiled by Othello's ability to overpower fate. (*Black Face, Maligned Race,* 70)

On the other hand, If we heed Iago too greedily, we court still other discomfitures. As Ania Loomba contends, the ensign is the agency for indicting the audience, the catalyst for its own undoing:

> Iago has often been seen as related to the Vice figure in a morality play. Unlike the morality Vice, however, he does not simply challenge accepted morality but is also the spokesperson for racist and patriarchal platitudes. His position is a sort of mediator between audience and action and his oft-commented upon role as producer of the play within the play is crucial. He undoubtedly articulates many of the viewers' common sense attitudes, and hence even while his plot offends them, it seeks their complicity. (in Barthelemy, *Critical Essays,* 182–83)

Similarly, Pechter warns about the nefarious implications of listening to Iago:

> The ascendance of Iago is a major triumph of *Othello* criticism. Our ability to acknowledge the extent of which Iago speaks for us and to produce his voice have added immeasurably to the energy of interpretive response to the play.... The privileges of membership in Iago's sophisticated club are not gratis; we have purchased power over the play at the cost of the play's power over us. Modern criticism of *Othello* is turning out to be a mixed blessing, maybe even a poisoned gift. (*Othello*, 28–29)

Pechter's characterization of contemporary views of *Othello* as a "poisoned gift" disturbingly, though no less accurately, captures the dilemma the play puts audiences in and through. A powerful Iago has ensnared audiences, not to mention Othello and Desdemona. However, a weak Iago hurts both Othello and the play. Reviewing such a production of *Othello* in 1954, starring Anthony Quayle as the Moor and Raymond Westwell as Iago, Richard David zeroed in on the delicate balance that exists between the two characters:

> Perhaps the Othello could have dared to be stronger if the Iago had been so. Raymond Westwell had most of the essential: the mask of camaraderie dropped at once when there was no need to charm, as with Emilia, or Roderigo dismissed with a viciously contemptuous "Nay, get thee gone"; the hesitant opening gambit, with the inner hate and sadism coming through ever more strongly as the operator becomes more confident of his power; the progressive risks taken with a mixture of circumspection and bravado, the cutting word—"lie," "gape on," "fond"—held back, but as soon as taken turned exultantly in the wound. Yet there was something lacking. "Not enough subtlety," said my neighbour; but to me it seemed more a question of size. There was a pettiness about this waspish Iago, his destruction of Othello an act of mere personal spite. The "Credo in un Dio crudel" that Boito added to the part, for Verdi, may often appear no more than melodramatic clap-trap; but Boito's feeling was right—unless there is something demoniac about Iago he is an insufficient explanation for the catastrophe, and he is scaled down so Othello too is diminished. (388)

Iago and Othello rise and fall together.

THE CRITICAL CANON

The canon of *Othello* criticism is expansive and complex, taking readers into gender studies, post-colonial protests, and postmodern semantics. The following comments do not propose to survey all *Othello* criticism; they are meant only to highlight, to categorize, and to elaborate upon what many critics and theatre historians have already unearthed. An impressive starting point

is Margaret Lael Mikesell's survey of *Othello* criticism from 1940 to 1985 in
the "Introduction, Part 1" of *Othello: An Annotated Bibliography* (xi–xxv).
Horace Howard Furness's *Variorum* edition of *Othello* in 1886 (1963) reprints
useful excerpts from many significant critical documents on the play. Helen
Gardner (1968) has reviewed major critical issues, and Peter Davison's slender but valuable volume surveys various critical approaches to the play (*Othello* in The Critical Debate Series). Yet these overviews pale in comparison to
the book-length survey of criticism and stage history by Joan Lord Hall (*Othello: A Guide to the Play*) and the 941-page *Othello: An Annotated Bibliography, 1940–1985*, compiled by Margaret Lael Mikesell and Virginia Mason
Vaughan. Hunter also traces the changes in the Moor's fortunes, especially the
resistance to and the reaction against his character. The most recent (and perhaps most perceptive) attempt to assess *Othello* criticism is Edward Pechter's
Othello and Interpretive Traditions (especially his Chapter 1, "Othello in Theatrical and Critical History"). Especially valuable, too, are anthologies of *Othello* criticism, including those which reprint classic texts and those that
contain only new essays: Leonard Dean (1961), Kenneth Muir (1967), John
Wain (1971), Richard Marienstras and Dominique Guy-Blanquet, *Autour
d'Othello* (1987), Susan Snyder (1988), Virginia Mason Vaughan and Kent
Cartwright (1991), Linda Cookson and Ben Loughrey (1991), Anthony Gerard
Barthelemy (1994), and Mythili Kaul (1999).

    The following discussion surveys major critical responses to Othello,
Desdemona, and Iago; and Emilia, Bianca, and Roderigo indirectly.

Othello

    Perhaps the most problematic presence in *Othello* is the Moor himself.
His very place in the script is uncertain and unstable. Michael Billington asks
an oft-heard question in *Othello* criticism: "But who is the central figure? Othello, fatally flawed by his mixture of self-regard and insecurity? Or Iago, the
active embodiment of evil?" ("Review"). Pechter notes: "*Othello* is the only
tragedy in which the protagonist does not have the most lines to speak. This
distinction belongs to Iago, who speaks almost one-third more lines than Othello" (*Othello*, 24–25). Such calculation, of course, raises the question of
whether Othello is the subject or object of the tragedy? W. H. Auden sardon-
ically noted:

> Any consideration of the tragedy of *Othello* must be primarily occupied, not
> with its official hero but with its villain. I cannot think of any other play in
> which only one character performs personal actions—and all the others
> without exception only exhibit behavior. In marrying each other, Othello and
> Desdemona have performed a deed, but this took place before the play
> begins. (*Dyer's Hand*, 251).

Othello's identity is another thorny issue. Who is he—racially? cultur-ally? politically? Is he a white Venetian, an Arab, or a blackamoor? Is he as much a Spaniard as an African, as Barbara Everett maintains ("'Spanish' Oth-ello," 101)? Later in this collection, James Andreas traces Othello's Judaic roots. Is Othello's hybridism a garland of distinction or a stigma of shame?

How much can we take Othello's words at face value? Do they enshrine or erase him? Does he, like Iago, swear by Janus? His admissions indict or even interdict him for critics. Does Othello tell the truth when he claims that he "loved not wisely, but too well" or does he know the truth? Has he let jeal-ousy storm his reasoning? He claims in Act 1.3 that he knows his cue, but does he always heed the cues society or his wife gives him? Why does he not inter-rogate Iago more? Lodovico claims that "passion could not shake" Othello (4.1.265), yet he is engulfed in a seething ocean of passions. Summing up some of the critical contraries in which Othello is caught, Edward Pechter questions if he is "the noble vs. the feeble Moor; a protagonist of 'perfect soul,' whose disintegration is puzzling and painful, or one who is anxiously vulnerable and radically flawed from the beginnning,' proceeding inevitably to utter collapse" (*Othello,* 107). Who causes the tragedy—Iago, Desdemona, Othello, or a disapproving white Venetian society? Perhaps the ultimate ques-tion about Othello is what does his (or the others') tragedy signify? Harley Granville-Barker simply abandoned that search: "It is a tragedy without mean-ing, and that is the ultimate horror of it" (*Prefaces*). These questions, some of them given more recent emphasis, set the stage for a review of the Moor's for-tunes among the critics.

For nearly 300 years, Othello enjoyed a reputation as the "noble Moor." Dr. Johnson praised him as "magnanimous, artless, and credulous, boundless in his confidence, ardent in his affection, inflexible in his resolution, and obdu-rate in his revenge" (quoted in Gardner, 4). Equally effusive, Coleridge hon-ored Othello as "noble, generous, open-hearted; unsuspicious and unsuspecting" (Raysor, *Coleridge's,* 227.) In fact, the nineteenth century apotheosized Othello. Jan Kott pointed out that "*Othello* turned out to be Shakespeare's most 'nineteenth-century play.' Not only was it the most roman-tic of the plays, *Othello* fitted all nineteenth-century theatres: it was a play, an opera, a melodrama. *Othello* had local colour, portrayed great characters and passions, was an historicial, psychological, realistic play. It was indeed Shake-speare's best stage play" (101).

Indebted to Coleridge, A. C. Bradley's character analysis has been a cen-tral, though very much contested, assessment of *Othello*. Bradley excessively glamorized the Moor as a romantic figure:

> Othello is, in one sense of the word, by far the most romantic figure among
> Shakespeare's heroes; and he is so partly from the strange life of war and

adventure which he has lived from childhood. He does not belong to our
world, and he seems to enter it we know not whence—almost as if from won-
derland. There is something mysterious in his descent from men of royal
seige; in his wanderings in vast deserts and among marvellous peoples; in his
tales of magic handkerchiefs and prophetic Sibyls; in the sudden vague
glimpses we get of numberless battles and sieges in which he has played the
hero and has borne a charmed life; even in chance references to his baptism,
his being sold to slavery, his sojourn in Aleppo. (*Shakespearean Tragedy,* 153)

But Bradley's valorization of Othello has not been endorsed in subsequent
decades. In the twentieth century, Othello's detractors have angrily outvoiced
his supporters, deconstructing the Bradleyan romantic and tragic Moor. An
unheroic, unflattering Moor replaced Bradley's romantic icon for critics. In the
1920s and 1930s, Othello succumbed as the hostile foe of critics such as T. S.
Eliot and F. R. Leavis. In "Shakespeare and the Stoicism of Seneca" (1927),
Eliot accused Othello of brutal selfishness and deep dishonesty. Analyzing
Othello's last speech ("Soft you, a word or two before you go"), Eliot declared:

What Othello seems to me to be doing in making this speech is cheering
himself up. He is endeavouring to escape reality, he has ceased to think about
Desdemona, and is thinking about himself. Humility is the most difficult of
all virtues to achieve; nothing dies harder than the desire to think well of
oneself. Othello succeeds in turning himself into a pathetic figure, by adopting an aesthetic rather than a moral attitude, dramatising himself against his
environment. He takes in the spectator, but the human motive is primarily to
take in himself. I do not believe that any writer has ever exposed this
bovarysm, the human will to see things as they are not, more clearly than
Shakespeare. ("Shakespeare and the Stoicism," 110)

Attacking Bradley, and through him Othello, F. R. Leavis excoriated Othello
in his 1937 essay, "Diabolical Intellect and the Noble Hero." Most particularly,
he faulted Othello's "habit of self-approving self-dramatization," his "self
pride . . . and insane and self-deceiving passion." In attacking Othello's pride,
Leavis claimed that "Othello's noble lack of self-knowledge is shown as
humiliating and disasterous." Leavis added that "Othello's inner timbers begin
to part at once, the stuff of which he is made begins at once to deteriorate and
show itself unfit" (144). Consequently, Othello's pride and lack of "awareness"
made him a sure target for Iago. "The essential traitor is within the gates,"
declared Leavis.

In destroying the Moor's legacy to integrity and nobility, Eliot and Leavis
ushered in a new age of *Othello* criticism, resulting in "the ascendancy of Iago
as major triumph of . . . [that] criticism" (Pechter, *Othello,* 28). Eliot and
Leavis have had many followers. D. A. Traversi, for example, maintained that
Othello "being unable to cope with the complicated business of living" delivered a final speech revealing "The dupe's attempt at self-justification in an

irrelevant pose . . . a splendid declamation [which] . . . is largely beside the point" (148–149). Expanding upon Eliot's premise, Carol McGinnis Kay asserted that Othello was "an adult personality . . . manifesting the classic signs of an underdeveloped ego" (265), "a man of low self-esteem who will snatch at any straw to shore himself up" (267). Neither Leavis nor Eliot, of course, escaped censure. A. P. Rossiter took Leavis to task (and Bradley, too) for ignoring the complexity of the play, as does Pechter. In her "Introduction: Perspectives on Othello: Old and New," Virginia Mason Vaughan helpfully concluded, "Whether critics saw Othello as Bradley's noble Moor, or Leavis's and Eliot's simple-minded egotist, or somewhere in between, they implicitly analyzed him as if he were a real person" (*Othello: New Perspectives,* 17). Undeniably, though, Bradley, Eliot, and Leavis have profoundly influenced the direction *Othello* criticism has taken.

Exploring the antecedant opinions of Bradley, Eliot, and Leavis, Estelle W. Taylor argues that they were all "neoRymers." Their "notions of Othello are . . . the link with Thomas Rymer that for too many of our respected and oft-quoted twentieth-century critics share" (132). Rymer's racist views, claims Taylor, have infected, "in open and in subtle ways," "the attempts to . . . denigrate the play and at the same time to diminish the stature of black Othello as a 'Shakespearean' tragic hero" (122). Kent Cartwright, however, studies Othello in "his double role as both Bradleyan victim and Leavisian victimizer" ("Audience Response and the Denouement of *Othello,*" 167). A post-structural critic, Christopher Norris ingeniously suggests that "the difference of views between Leavis and Bradley becomes oddly intertwined with the drama played out between Othello and Iago" ("Post-Structuralist Shakespeare," 59). Mark Gauntlett argues that the Bradleyean reader is like a performer, yet his lecture on *Othello,* "exemplifies the extent to which notions of 'theatre' and 'performance' in fact serve to sustain but at the same time destabilize certain literary approaches to dramatic texts" (71).

Othello's "occupation" as a soldier/warrior is at the heart of many problems both character and play raise. The mythos of a heroic warrior is strongly conveyed in acts 1, 2, and 5. Othello himself makes much of his military prowess and background, especially in 1.3, 2.3, and 3.3, where his tragedy is powerfully linked to the loss of his career. In fact, recent productions of the play foreground the military life/world in which, and because of which, Othello's tragedy occurs. Othello has in large measure been determined—or undermined—by the actor's physical presence as a strong military commander, a man of valor. Early studies such as those by Henry J. Webb and Paul Jorgensen confirmed Shakespeare's knowledge of the military life, its rituals and ranks. Yet more recently, Julia Genster has explored the problematic role of lieutenancy and its implications for Othello's undoing, sexually and politically. Totally committed to the heroic world, Othello speaks the language of chivalry and honor, key ideas explicated in Norman Council's *When Honour's at the*

Stake and in Chapter Two of Vaughan's *Othello: Contextual.* Yet these ideological props are pulled from underneath Othello leading to his downfall. As
Council notes, at the start of the play Othello's honor is a virtue, noble and
strong, but in his desire to murder an adulterous Desdemona, it changes to an
"a moral compulsion to revenge the affront to his 'honour'" (127). Similarly,
Vaughan hears in Othello's words to and about Desdemona the devotion of a
knight before his "fair damsel."

Othello's career, once the source of his strength and composure, is the
cause of his undoing. E. E. Stoll's contention that Othello dies as a noble hero
—this downfall being attributed to the "convention of the calumniator credited"—has not been in vogue (*Othello,* 6). As Helen Gardner observed, "Othello's absolute soldiership is the symbol of his entire masculinity"
("Retrospect," 6), and when he loses his command, chaos comes. Numerous
critics have pointed out that the martial skills that distinguished Othello before
the Senate in act one are the detriments that defeat him in his civil/married life.
An early essay by C. F. Burgess shows how Othello's demands for proof and
loyalty do not help him see or act honestly with Desdemona. Michael Neill
insightfully notes that with Iago usurping both Desdemona's and Cassio's
places, Othello himself become's "occupied territory" ("Changing Places in
Othello,"129). The noble Moor, the defender of Venice, becomes by his own
accusation a "malignant and turbanned Turk," whom he "smote . . . thus" (5.2.
351–53). Stripped of his sword twice and his command—in effect, cashiered
as Cassio had been—Othello suffers a painful punishment—the indignities of
the loss of command. Gone is the pride of self control. Harley Granville-
Barker offered a conventional reading of Othello's closing lines:

> No longer cruel tears; and the crude horror of the deed done already tem-
> pered a little—Nature's healing sadness would be at work. But not in him.
> He knows better than they can tell him or Venice decide what is due to an
> Othello, traitor to his Christian self, from him who is now that self again; and
> this they shall see. (*Prefaces,* 213)

Because of the ontologies of his military world, Othello is transformed into the
enemy, the infidel. Lisa Hopkins interrogates Othello's final words in light of
the narrative modes by which they are represented:

> This is a story that obviously means a lot to Othello: he dies uttering it, giv-
> ing it the talismanic force habitually attached to last words, and he is anxious
> that those hearing it should, in their turns, recount it. It is, however, unclear
> how exactly this relation relates to him. Initially, Othello is the hero of his
> own tales: has he now become the villain? Both the "I" and the "him" of the
> story . . . he is himself both Turk and not-Turk, subject and object of his own
> narration. Perhaps, however, even to think in such terms is in itself to com-
> mit one of the most common . . . of all interpretative errors: to read the self

into the text. On a thematic and psychological level, of course, it obviously is a *roman á clef;* I am not saying that I cannot see the extraordinary symbolic force of having Othello at this crucial moment presented to us as that most demonized of others, the Turk. Mention of Turks may also, however, remind us of their abrupt disappearance for the narrative (if not the thematic) structure of the play at the opening of act 2, when all the narrative competence we possess encouraged us to expect them to form a major part of the story. It thus underlines the problematics and containing structures of the narrative mode itself. (170)

The representation of Othello's race/ethnicity has been the central issue in the critical history and performance of the play. It is also one of the most problematic issues as well. Reviewing a 1993 production starring Paul Winfield, Jayne M. Blanchard asked: "Is Othello another example of the Mandigo Syndrome, in which a black man is ruined by his fatal attraction for a white girl? Or is it racism in robes, with Othello, the heroic noble savage, exploited by his melanin-deficient chief officer, Iago, a mean-spirited realist who is as worldy as his master is gullible?" ("Out-of-Towners"). These contemporary reactions should be compared with eighteenth-and-nineteenth-century views of Othello's color, as collected in Furness's *Variorum* (389–96). Some excellent recent studies that focus on race and racial issues in *Othello* are Anthony Barthelemy's *Black Face, Maligned Race;* Ania Loomba's *Shakespeare and Race*; Eldred Jones's *Othello's Countrymen*; *Shakespeare and Race*, edited by Catherine Alexander and Stanley Wells. See also vol. 26 of *Shakespeare Studies* (1998) which is devoted to "Race and the Study of Shakespeare." Elliot Butler-Evans's "'Haply, for I am black': *Othello* and the Semiotics of Race and Otherness" in Kaul (139–50) explores the issue of race, and concludes that Othello's status as the Other is neither stable nor consistent. Patrick C. Hogan claims that Othello is the victim of racism and suffers from "racial despair," or that his "skin is too black for anyone to accept—to forget or 'forgive'— [and] that one's skin blots out one's soul" (431). Ironically, Hogan maintains, "the most devastating tragedy is that, in the end, Othello himself comes to believe Brabantio" (447). (Barthelemy similarly claims that Barbantio's dream comes true ["Introduction," *Critical Essays,* 10]). In discussing Othello's "self-hatred," Patrick Hogan comes close to Eliot but vindicates Othello providentially. God has "spared" Othello and thus "God has judged on religious not racial grounds" (447).

Othello's race, of course, is irretrievably tied to his ideology of heroic honor. Casting a black actor in the role, according to Pechter, raises major problems for audiences: such an actor "simply transfers the problem [of heroism] to an audience for whom heroic blackness may now be as much of an impossibility (though for very different reasons) as it was for the nineteenth-century" (*Othello,* 111). Pechter elaborates upon those "very different reasons":

> Anxiety and a guilty conscience about race are likely to cut across all con-
> stituencies of the current theatrical audience, and although anxiety and guilt
> are entirely appropriate responses to the play (to say nothing of enduring his-
> tory of racialist belief), the problem is the context of liberal sensitivity within
> which these emotions are expressed. Theatrical audiences can't be expected
> (and are thus not asked) to make the leap of historical imagination by which
> they can enter into the overt contempt of Iago at the beginning. The magni-
> tude of Othello's own powerful presence may depend on this identification
> and its suprising subsequent discomfirmation, but a diminshed Othello
> seems a better fit with contemporary taste. (*Othello*, 215–16, note 40)

In academic terms, an abject Othello becomes the basis for solidarity with the
marginalized and dispossessed. Cowhig thus argues that "However great Othello's confidence, his colour makes his vulnerability plain" ("Blacks," 9). Yet
the white actor "can become one with the victim, black like him—a reversal
and repetition of Mary Preston's notorious claim that he was white like her . . .
The uphill struggle for black representation in elite culture, and perhaps more
crucially, for recognition of the capacity of people of African ancestry to
engage in mimetic performance, should not be underestimated" (Callaghan,
"Othello was a White Man," 214). So, too, with Othello's honor. Peter Erickson
explores the cultural interpretations of white/black in the play and in art later
in this collection.

Some critics have overlooked Othello's ancestry to view him as a universal protagonist. Robert B. Heilman, for example, asserts "*Othello* is not a treatise on mixed marriages, but a drama about Everyman, with the modifications
necessary to individualize him" (*Magic,* 138). Yedida Itzhaki studies Othello
in light of Aristotle's *Poetics* as a tragic hero. Yet race undeniably has been a
pulsating dynamic in the script and in theatre economies. Othello's roles as
Other/Outsider, warrior, and victim are inextricably tied to his racial ancestry
and diverse representations of it. Summarizing the conventional wisdom about
Othello's color, Julie Hankey pointed out that "blackness on the stage was
moral and religious rather than racial and geographical. Black was the colour
of the devil . . . Anyone going to a play about a Moor in the early seventeenth
century would have expected the worst from the apparition" ("Introduction,"
13–14). Shakespeare's audience, therefore, conceivably brought unmitigated
racial prejudice with them to the playhouse. See also John Draper's *The Othello of Shakespeare's Audience* for a further examination of conventional Elizabethan reactions to Moors.

Othello's differences notwithstanding, a leading goal of contemporary
Othello criticism has been to challenge readers'/viewers' cultural narrow-
ness, to dislodge them from dichotomous racial ontologies holding character and play captive. As Edward Pechter correctly observes, *Othello* is a
"cultural artifact" and "the way Renaissance audiences perceived race may
be far more complex than stereotypes indicate" (23). Historically, it has been

all too easy to demonize Othello racially. Even though Queen Elizabeth issued an order banishing blacks, because "great numbers of Negars and Blackamoors" were taking jobs away from her citizens, the Elizabethan social situation was not indisolvably categorical, black versus white. Some Elizabethans knew about and appreciated Moorish culture, which of course relates to Othello's character. Leo Africanus, one of the "most widely translated and reprinted" authors in Europe (Parker, "Fantasies," 84), was a converted Moor as was Othello. Politically, too, according to Pechter, intricate alliances compacted between the Elizabethan court and the Moors drew the two cultures closer by fighting their common (Catholic) enemies—Spain and Italy. Martin Orkin has even argued that during the Renaissance anti-racist sentiments were voiced, especially by Montaigne, thus mitigating a universal attack against people of color (*Shakespeare Against Apartheid,* 71). Patrick C. Hogan goes so far as to claim: "Shakespeare, it seems, was not only aware but deeply critical of racial hatred and related forms of exclusion and oppression. He was pained by brutality of the majority toward minority groups. But his empathy was not our multicultural empathy. It was, rather, thoroughly Christian" (446).

The theatre and visual arts likewise offered a less rigid, perfunctorily negative response to race, further mediating Othello's character. As Anthony Barthelemy points out:

> . . . in plays, masques, and pageants by Shakespeare's contemporaries from Jonson to Webster, black characters appear in greater numbers than many initially would believe. Variously called "Negroes," "Moors," "Black-amoors," "Ethiops," and/or "Africans," in most of those works the black characters hold high social positions, and in the plays, most marry white women. Although black characters such as Aaron in *Titus* are frequently negatively portrayed, not all were. In fact, not until the economics of chattel slavery began to shape all mercantile enterprise in England did black characters appear as slaves. ("Introduction," *Critical Essays,* 7–8)

Inescapably, black characters were very popular on the Elizabethan/Jacobean stage. Jones and Barthelemy study the importance of more than 40 black characters who appear in Elizabethan and Jacobean plays and masques. "Moreover, an appealing, exotic aura had long been associated with Moors in England" (Rosenberg, 199) where "blackmoor" was a sign for both "strange wonder" (e.g., Jonson's *Masque of Blackness*) and generosity. A play with a black protagonist like Othello did not deter audiences from the theatre. Quite to the contrary, *Othello* was one of the most popular plays of the age, and its popularity continued as the first Shakespearean work to be staged on the Restoration stage. Othello—general and husband, traveler and instrument of the Venetian state, fair and black—needs to be seen and re-seen in light of these multivalent cultural codes and symbols.

Desdemona

Desdemona, "the fair devil," is caught in the play's verbal epilepsy. Like the script itself, she has been polarized, valorized as a saint or vilified as a strumpet. "Just about every character misunderstands her," claims Honigmann (*Othello*, 42), which can be said about many of the critics' views as well. W. D. Adamson rightfully declares that "Very few readers have been able to contemplate Desdemona with anything like true balance" (169). Inevitably, Desdemona has been incorporated into the overall perplexities of the play. As S. N. Garner puts it:

> Desdemona's character is neither simple nor any more easily defined than Iago's or Othello's. Any effort to describe it must take into account all of what she says and does as well as what other characters say about her and how their views are limited by their own personalities and values. Though Shakespeare does not give Desdemona center stage with Othello, as he gives Juliet with Romeo and Cleopatra with Antony, he does not keep her in the wings for most of the play, as he does Cordelia or Hermione. She is often present so that we must witness her joy, fear, bewilderment, and pain. What happens to her matters because we see how it affects her as well as Othello. The meaning of the tragedy depends, then, on a clear vision of her character and experience as well as those of Othello and Iago. (235)

Central to the mystery of *Othello*, Desdemona has been identified as both the problem and the solution by critics. Pechter isolates the basic conflict Desdemona raises as it is manifested in the murder scene and her compliance (or lack thereof) in her own tragedy: "This question focuses on character, the effect of Desdemona as a developing consciousness within the dramatic action and effective economy of the play" (*Othello*, 126). As John A. Williams maintains, "Discussions of the play as a racial-sexual tragedy focus on Othello, however, rather than on Desdemona. Seeming contradictions in his behavior strike us, whereas those in her pass unnoticed. Yet Desdemona is more crucial than Othello to a 'black' perspective on the play" (15). Earlier critics such as A. C. Bradley or E. E. Stoll sentimentalized Desdemona as helplessly passive. "She can do nothing whatever. She cannot retaliate even in speech" (Bradley, 147). Yet in contemporary productions actors have frequently empowered her through bold deeds and even bolder words, recouping for her greater participation in the tragedy. In Trevor Nunn's production in 1990 in Stratford, Desdemona was a veritable scrapper:

> The murder scene was a violent struggle, Desdemona and Othello shouting at each other across the bed, she making frantic attempts to run away, crashing into a locked door, then a chase, their scramble across the bed before he seizes her, flinging her onto the bed and clambering on top of her; then the

> convulsive rhythmic tightenings of the strangulation: it grows as she resists, and then it stops as she goes limp and he rolls off her. (Smallwood, 113)

Reviewing Harold Scott's Shakespeare Theatre production of *Othello* at the Folger Library in 1990, Bob Mondello found that an overwhelmed Othello too early in the play created a greatly magnified, far different Desdemona than conventional readings have promulgated:

> It had never occurred to me that *Othello* could be seen as the Moor's wife's tragedy—we never get to know her well enough. But let Brooks [Othello] fall by the wayside too early, and you're left with a tale about a matter-of-fact woman beset on all sides by men she can't trust. Though she's done nothing wrong, the fates seem to be conspiring against her, almost as they would in Greek tragedy. As Jordan Baker plays the tall, flaxen-haired beauty, she's straightforwardly in love and utterly perplexed by the storms swirling around her honeymoon. The part as written is simply reactive, so she can't carry the play's second half, though she can give it a focus. ("Grand Othell")

Giving Desdemona an even stronger voice in resisting the patriarchy, Ania Loomba appropriately coordinates her struggles with Othello as his ally:

> The "central conflict" of the play, then, if we must locate one, is neither between white and black alone, nor merely between men and women—it is both a black man and a white woman. But these two are not simply aligned against white patriarchy, since their own relationship cannot be abstracted from sexual or racial tension. Othello is not merely a black man who is jealous, but a man whose jealousy and blackness are inseparable. Similarly, Desdemona's initial boldness and later submission are not discordant in the context of her position as a white woman. There is thus a tripartite and extremely complex relationship between black man, white woman, and the state. (in Barthelemy, *Critical Essays*, 172)

Loomba concludes, "Desdemona's desire is especially transgressive because its object is black" (179). Yet Alan Sinfield labels her "selfless love" as "subversive," since it counters the codes of wifely obedience found in marriage manuals (126). In her multiple roles as daughter, wife, Venetian citizen, counselor/friend, feminine confidante, martyr, and even seductress Desdemona challenges and provokes. Adamson conveniently labels Desdemona's critics as "allegorizers," "psychoanalyzers," and "anti-feminists" ("Unpinned or Undone?").

Historically, Desdemona has been enshrined in the annals of hagiography as a holy presence; a courageous, charitable, and obedient wife. (See Sara Deats's discussion of marriage and Desdemona in her essay found later in this collection.) A. C. Bradley proclaimed that she was "ardent with the courage and idealism of a saint" and that "her nature is infinitely sweet and her love absolute" (45). In the last act, her unselfishness even in death led Heilman to assert that she "becomes . . . the saint," the reincarnation of "the world of spirit" (*Magic*, 218). Alfred Harbage heard Cassio's greeting Desdemona to Cyprus as "a prayer to the Virgin" (351). For Robert G. Hunter, Desdemona is "a natural embodiment of grace apparently untainted by original sin (136). Carroll Camden lauded Desdemona for her conjugal virtues: "Shakespeare has been at some pains to set forth Desdemona as an exemplary ideal wife" ("Iago on Women," 70), and Alvin Kernan believes that she presents a "life force that strives for order, community, growth, and light" as opposed to Iago's "anti-life force that seeks anarchy, death and darkness" ("*Othello*: An Introduction," 80). (Clifford Ronan explores Desdemona's spiritual presence in light of Renaissance mythologies later in this volume.) S. N. Garner identifies the reason for the glorification of Desdemona: "Many critics and scholars come to Shakespeare's play with the idea that Desdemona ought to be pure and virtuous and, above all, unwavering in her faithfulness and loyalty to Othello. The notion is so tenacious that when Desdemona even appears to threaten, they cannot contemplate her character with their usual care and imagination" (234). Yet Ann Jennalie Cook cautions that "an obviously all-virtuous heroine would make Othello look like a fool for doubting her and would radically cut into any sympathy for him" ("The Design for Desdemona," 193–94).

Yet, Desdemona's fractious naysayers have assailed her for a host of wrongdoings, including disobeying her father; backchatting with Iago in act 2.1; lying to Othello about the handkerchief; pressing Cassio's suit with unflattering ardour; admiring Lodovico as a "proper man" in act 4.1; and absolving Othello of her death in act 5.2. Several critics cite Desdemona for violating Elizabethan/Jacobean law and propriety by denying her father and running off with the Moor. As Brabantio warns, "Look to her, Moor, if thou has eyes to see/She has deceived her father, and may thee" (1.3.292–93). Georges Bonnard branded her "a rebellious child" (183). No less a great one than President John Quincy Adams faulted Desdemona severely for this crime: "Who can sympathize with Desdemona?" he asked. "She falls in love and makes a runaway match with a blackamoor . . . She not only violates her duties to her father, her family, her sex, and her country, but she makes the first advances" (quoted in Rosenberg, 207); for Adams she "was little less than a wanton." Ironically, contemporary critic Lucille Fultz concurs: "In fact, Othello's rehearsal for the scene (1.3) clearly reveals that Desdemona, not he, was the seducer" ("Devouring Discourses," 196). Barbara Arnett Melchiori attacked Desdemona for lying and thus reinforces "Shakespeare's own reading of the female character—prone to duplicity and deception" (44). Though Davison applauds Desdemona for her honest sexuality and readily admits men's sensual attraction to her, he accuses her and Othello of the same "error of judgement" that "can be traced back to the manner of their marriage . . . " Running off as they did was, for Davison, "reprehensible" on Othello's part and "foolish" on hers. "All else," claims Davison, "is set in train by their error of judgment" (*Othello*, 78). Patrick C. Hogan accuses Desdemona of a "worse" type of racism than that of the Duke. In her speeches about Othello (called more often by the racial categorization "The Moor"), Desdemona "simultaneously confirms that, in Venice, or among Venetians, [Othello] will never be considered anything other than an instance of that race" ("*Othello*, Racism, and Despair," 441–42).

Besides being cast as an ungrateful and rebellious daughter, Desdemona, as Fultz and President Adams attest, has been excoriated as an adulteress, regardless of the double time clocks that beat in her favor (see Jay Halio's discussion of the composition of the play in this volume). Again, her "backchat" (Ridley) with Iago is read as a sign of her lascivious nature by some critics. Jan Kott spies "something of a slut in her" (118), and W. H. Auden similarly indicted Desdemona for putative sins of the flesh:

> It is worth noting that, in the willow-song scene with Emilia, she speaks with admiration of Lodovico and then turns to the topic of adultery....It is as if she had suddenly realized that she had made a *mésalliance* and that the sort of man she ought to have married was someone of her own class and colour like Lodovico. Given a few more years of Othello and of Emilia's influence and she might well, one feels, have taken a lover. (269)

But Desdemona's sexuality is a hotly contested issue. Adamson summarizes the critical debate over it:

> Where the earlier critics sentimentalize innocence and tend to suppress Desdemona's apparently contradictory sexuality, the newer ones often see her innocence as a neurotic defense mechanism, or even at one extreme a "life-destroying" characteristic, the epitome of "the sexual unreality the race longs for." Criticism thus goes on a progress from the desexualizing idolaters through the cynics and "humanizers" and eventually comes out close to where it began, with some readers who see Desdemona as a sexually repressed zombie (the modern equivalent of a sexless saint?). But all are mistaken, Shakespeare implies; Desdemona's innocence coexists with a rich sexuality, and the conspicuous expression of her innocence is her vital exuberance, including the hot, moist hand of sexual vitality. ("Unpinned or Undone," 179–80)

The erotics of staging key scenes with Desdemona, especially closet scenes before the bed in acts 4.3 and 5.2, have localized her desire for audiences. Michael Neill finds that early illustrations of the play, for example in Boitard (1709), Metz (1789), Leney (1799), repeatedly focused on Desdemona's bed, its curtains partially drawn to reveal her naked breast ("Unproper Beds"). In Leopold Jessner's Expressionistic *Othello* at the Straats Theatre in

1921 Berlin, "the major visual symbol . . . was the bed, placed and drapped with expansive white curtains. A white stand for the lamp, the white gowns of the actors, the white bedclothes, all were designed to contrast with Othello's [Fritz Kortner's] black face" (Kennedy, *Looking at Shakespeare,* 90). Studying "Transvestism and the 'Body Beneath,'" Peter Stallybrass argues that casting a boy actor as Desdemona, who undresses ("unpins") in act 4.3, leaves an audience "unsettled" ("Transvestism," 73) about closure, "radically uncertain" (77) about what they do and do not see on the transvestised Renaissance stage. "On the one hand, the clothes themselves—the marks of Desdemona's gender and status—are held up to our attention; on the other, we teeter on the brink of seeing the boy's breastless but 'pinned' body revealed" (77). Playgoers are caught in "contradictory fixations . . . precisely because the site of the audience's sexual fixation is so uncertain" (78).

Desdemona has not even been allowed to die "a guiltless death" amid the tragic loading of her bed. She has been maligned by critics who search for her culpability to the end. Not all readers are content to see her as a patient Griselda, as David Farley-Hill did. Julian C. Rice, for instance, issues this blanket (no pun intended) condemnation of Desdemona—"she shares the responsibility for her own murder," since "all men share the responsibility for the acts of any individual being" ("Desdemona Unpinned"). Stephen Reid interprets Desdemona's death as an expression of her guilt for betraying her father and, simultaneously, a punishment for Brabantio's opposing her marriage (242). Other readers contend that Desdemona is only partially responsible for her fate. Janet Overmeyer, surprisingly, blames Desdemona for not being more shrewd and worldly. Margaret Loftus Ranald finds Desdemona "innocent yet indiscreet," but pronounces her guilty nonetheless. Desdemona's "partial responsibility" (139) would have been obvious to Shakespeare's audience, claims Ranald, because her actions countered the rules of "feminine behavior" found in "homilies, broadside ballads, and courtesy books." "No wonder," Ranald continues, that Desdemona's actions are capable of deliberate misinterpretation by an Iago who can jocularly list the characteristics of a perfect woman to be found in such works" (128). According to this view, then, Desdemona enables Iago to destroy her by deliberately contradicting the courtesy books. Absolving Desdemona, Ruth Vanita claims that her "death blow . . . is made possible by the collusion of a number of others who act on the assumption that husband-wife relations are governed by norms different than those that govern other human relations" (341):

> Desdemona is killed not only by Othello and Iago but also by all those who see her humiliated and beaten in public and fail to intervene. The presumption that husband and wife, even when literally in a public space, metamorphically inhabit a private space wherein violence is somehow different from the violence of one man on another fosters the development of

a continuum of violence that escalates from abuse to beating to killing. Lodovico's role, as a Venetian and a kinsman, is crucial in the play's exposure of this pattern. (356)

Othello in general and Desdemona in particular have been the subject of judicious feminist criticism. Many critics, but especially feminists, have studied Desdemona in light of sexual politics, gender roles, and stereotypes. Several collections of essays focus on Desdemona, Emilia, Bianca, and Barbary as well—in volumes edited by Margaret Ferguson, Maureen Quilligan, and Nancy Vickers; and Peter Erickson and Coppelia Kahn, to cite only two. Desdemona is the victim of patriarchy (her father's, Othello's, the Duke's her culture's). Carol Thomas Neely usefully sketches in the critical response to this important element of *Othello* (105–109). As we have seen, Iago capitalizes on the tradition of misogyny that stereotypes women as dangerously lascivious and unfaithful. (See, for example, Valerie Wayne's "Historical Differences: Misogyny in *Othello*.") Moreover, as James Calderwood insists, Desdemona is victimized by "a proprietary husband claiming absolute title to his wife's body" ("Properties," 270).

Feminists are not alone in focusing on the political elements of Desdemona's body. Kenneth Burke analyzes Othello's relationship to Desdemona in terms of property: she represents "ownerships in the profoundest sense of ownership, the property of human affections, as fetishistically localized with object of possession, while the possessor is himself possessed by his very engrossment" (166). Peter Stallybrass also examines Desdemona in terms of patriarchal rights whereby owning herself she is free to give her honor away to whom she pleases ("Patriarchal Territories," 137). Paul Yachnin concludes that Desdemona is fetishized into "the treasure of land....as solid and valuable . . . Desdemona's body shines out wonderfully as the promised land forever out of reach" (207). And John Drakakis physicalizes Desdemona's body as "a storehouse, a geographical space, and . . . as an aberration of nature" (74) and even as Othello's demonized "Other."

Desdemona's plight is thus at the forefront of problems of identity, honesty, gender, and marriage in the play. Several contemporary women playwrights have rewritten Shakespeare's script to redress the abuses directed against women, especially Desdemona. For example, Anne-Marie MacDonald has written *Goodnight Desdemona (Good Morning Juliet)* and Paula Vogel has done *Desdemona*. For a study of these two different adaptations of Shakespeare's play see Marianne Novy's recent essay in *Transforming Shakespeare*. Devoting a chapter to marriage in *Othello*, Mary Beth Rose concludes that the feats of an earlier tragedy of action, symbolized by Othello, clash with the new private heroics of marriage represented by Desdemona (131–56). According to Rose, *Othello* reveals a dual mentality at work, which "simultaneously exalts and degrades women" (131). Even though Desdemona is the "heroine of marriage," her "predicament can be located at the contra-dictory terms in which female identity is constructed" (148). Studying cour-tesy books and conduct manuals, Catherine Belsey explicates views of marriage (Othello's to Desdemona) according to the Law of the Fathers, in which desire was to be contained and regulated.

The way Othello sees himself determines how we see Desdemona, according to many critics, feminists and post-structuralists alike. Othello "is in an ambivalent category by virtue of his marriage to the Venetian Desde-mona. As a Moor, he has married well above his rank, making him virtuous as a Venetian, but the very fact that Desdemona was 'open' to him endangers her status as his spiritual enclosure, the impermeable container of his honor" (Stallybrass, "Patriarchal Territories," 77–78). Richard P. Wheeler ironically points out that to become Othello's partner in his marriage bed, Desdemona must "unwittingly undermine the very heroic identity he has invested in her" ("'And my loud crying still'"). Wheeler investigates Othello's "suspended male sexuality" in light of the conflicting values of male autonomy, female sexuality, and nurturing. Also exploring identity issues, James Calderwood finds Othello transforming Desdemona into "an aggrandized version of his own I," thus robbing her of her own personhood. Because Othello possesses the only I, excluding Desdemona from the narrative and making her a third person, she "even more than Othello...seems the outsider in the first act" ("Appalling Property," 360). As Othello's "metaphorizing mirror," Desdemona looks through his blackness scrubbing it away with her words. If Calderwood sees Desdemona making Othello white, Patricia Parker conversely sees Des-demona becoming black:

> The play produces a series of powerful chiastic splittings. Desdemona the white Venetian daughter becomes, as it proceeds, the sexually tainted woman traditionally condemned as "black," part of the representational schema that gives ironic resonance to the choice of the name "Bianca" ("white") for the character most explicitly linked to that taint and that releases the "demon" within her own name. "Desdemon" (as she is called by Othello in V.ii.25) sings . . . of a "maid call'd Barbary" (IV.iii.26) while Othello the Moor, the "Barbary horse" (I.i.111) and "erring barbarian (I.iii.355) of the opening act, comes to occupy the perspective of wronged Venetian husband, executing judgment of a "blackened erring wife" (III.iii.387–88), "now begrim'd and black/ As mine own face." ("Fantasies," 95)

Desdemona's language, even her silence, has occupied many critics, some of whom use her own words to erase her. Pechter laments that "The interpre-tive tradition has been generally unwilling or unable to hear Desdemona singing her own song. During the period between Coleridge's claim that 'Des-demona has no character at all' and Sinfield's that 'Desdemona has no char-acter of her own' we have been consistently replacing Desdemona's voice with silence and transforming her presence into absence" (*Othello*, 130). Madelon Gohlke, for example, maintains that in the light of the "rhetorical fate" of the female characters in the tragedies, Desdemona, like Ophelia and Lady Macbeth, "retreats into a kind of speech which she herself cannot interpret" (165). Avoiding sexual language, Desdemona unintentionally uses ambiguity which Othello turns against her. Unlike the manipulative men—Iago or Othello—Desdemona "never gives any indication that she herself is aware of the interpretive possibilities contained in her speech" (166). Having to admit the "femininity of his own consciousness, as expressed through his ambiguous language, Othello fears losing his "honest masculinity" (172). R. S. White contends that Desdemona's "central trait" is to cover up her feelings in public; she has a strong desire for peace. Like Ophelia, she is "forced to speak her feelings obliquely" (72). Still, White insists, it is wrong to see her as a "stereotype of feminity" (71). The world around her forces her to "prevaricate" (13). An essential article on Desdemona's language is Eamon Grennan's "The Women's Voices in *Othello*: Speech, Song, and Silence" which maintains that Desdemona's speech is perfectly balanced between reason and passion, logic and feeling, thus showing that she is not the naive innocent. Her speech, "itself the moral act of her identity" (287), expresses her freedom to love. Unlike Othello's fantasies about her adultery, Desdemona's language is anchored in reality, the physical present. Though Othello extinguishes her speech, Desdemona is protective and generous even in silence.

The handkerchief that Othello transfers to Desdemona is undoubtedly the central icon in the play, yet there's critical diversity in the web of it. Referenced more than 30 times in the script, and variously represented on stage, the handkerchief is vital to the play's dramatic structure, and to Desdemona's relationship to Othello, Iago, Cassio, and even Emilia and Barbary. It surely reflects an audience's awareness of marriage customs. Harry Berger assesses the handkerchief in light of jealousy and marriage. Tracing the iconography of the handkerchief, Lynda E. Boose explicates how Shakespeare dynamically fuses "handkerchief and wedding sheets, the sanctified union promising life and the tragic union culminating in death" ("Desdemona's Handkerchief"). Clearly, the handkerchief is, as James Hodgson affirms, "an emblem of her reputation." This fetishized object is idealized as well as the longed-for virgin-stained bed sheets. For T. G. A. Nelson and Charles Haines, it is "a talisman . . . of the taking of Desdemona's virginity." One of the most controversial articles on the handkerchief, and on Desdemona, is Edward Snow's Freudian reading of *Othello* in light of male anxiety and as an attack on the "stability of the male world" (393). The cause of the tragedy for Snow resides in the "pathological male animas toward sexuality" (389). The wedding sheets represent the "lust's blood" of Desdemona's "orgasmic discharge" as well as Othello's own blood convincing him to suppress Desdemona's sexuality. The handkerchief thereby contains male fantasies about maternal betrayals. Peter Stallybrass argues that

Othello equates it with a symbol of his family's honor, and with Desdemona's
chastity and bodily functions, making it a symbol of both private and public
actions ("Patriarchal Territories"). Naomi Scheman posits that the handkerchief is really a shifting signifier, at first symbolizing Desdemona's power over
Othello, a maternal sign, and then becoming a paternal sign in act 5.

Two more recent articles intriguingly look at the handkerchief and Desdemona in terms of material culture, most notably, the Jacobean textile industry. Paul Yachnin analogizes this central signifier to the "operations of
commodity fetishism" (206) found in the theatre. "The play's stake in the
handkerchief registers the theatre's participation in English society's fetishized
trade in textiles" (202). The properties of the handkerchief—"reproducible,
exchangeable, and [its] cash value"—all apply to Desdemona as both object
and subject, woman of desire and wife/chattel. The handkerchief's properties
are, for Yachnin, "continuous with the properties love" (203). Like the handkerchief, Desdemona is "calculable," and her body actually "replaces the
handkerchief" (206). In fact, "the play trades the handkerchief for Desdemona's body" (206), thus creating the "wonder" on which theatres commer-
cially capitalize.

Susan Frye also examines the handkerchief as a "register of women's his-
toric connections to textiles" (221). The "use of the purse, the wedding sheets,
and most important, by the strawberry embroidered handkerchief [draw] on the
powerful visual semiotic of the connections textiles expressed and enforced
between men and women" (222). Traditionally, the domain of women, "who
owned, washed, and certainly managed" (226) these textiles, the industry in the
play comes under control of the men (Iago and Othello). "Their taking of interpretive control of these domestic textiles from Desdemona and Emilia coincides with the minimizing and invalidating of women's speech" for Frye (226).
She explains the strawberries on the handkerchief variously as "the potential
for the fruition of . . . marriage," "spots of adulterous lust," and religious allusions to the Blessed Mother (226). The purse, symbolizing Desdemona's
vagina, is also subsumed into male control. Although the purse lewdly suggests
that "Desdemona's vagina opens and closes every time 'money' is figuratively
'put' in it, in the play it is a largely homoerotic textile in that it produces male-
to-male exchange across Desdemona's continually deferred body" (228).
Appropriated into the homosocial order, these textiles, through "mimicking"
women's bodies, replace a "feminized reading" with a tragic male one.

Iago

Iago is "our usher into the action of the play," proclaims Pechter (*Othello*,
37). He draws audiences intimately into his plan through ingratiating and intimate soliloquies and asides. "The play makes sure that Iago is injected into us
right from the beginning, undiluted, not just before we know what is happening but as the way we know it is happening" (Pechter, *Othello*, 69). The epis-

temology—and disease—of the play comes from Iago. In his battle with Othello, he contends for supremacy over our wills and wit. As Harold Bloom aptly observed, "It is Othello's tragedy but it is Iago's play" (433). *Othello* dramatizes intense polarities (skepticism vs. belief, determinism vs. agency, pragmatism vs. idealism), and Iago is always on the left side of the field of combat. Yet he cannot easily be labeled as one-sided, for that implies a consistency his character neither possesses nor to which it aspires. In large part because of Iago, *Othello* bristles with contradictions, paradoxes, seeming truths and seeming lies. "Iago both subtends and determines belief" (Pechter, *Othello*, 75). Everywhere he verbally "plume[s] up [his] will in double knavery" (2.1. 392–93), advocating the very view he assaults. His speech is lethal. Barbara Irene Kreps explores Iago's manipulations through language, and Joseph A. Porter argues that "Iago more than any other character in *Othello* . . . seems concerned to problematize potentially comforting distinctions between speech directed to other onstage characters on the one hand and to audiences through soliloquy and aside on the other" (75). Moreover, Ruth Vanita claims that Iago's "villainy is as successful as it is because he speaks to the lowest common denominator, the most widely accepted prejudices." Peter Stallybrass similarly notes that "Iago's is the voice of 'common sense,' the ceaseless repetition of the always-already 'known,' the culturally 'given'" ("Patriarchal Territories," 139).

Trying to fix Iago is impossible. He leaves us in mysterious silence. John Bayley resolutely affirmed that "Iago maintains to the end the dreadful integrity of his own innocence—in spite of—or perhaps because of—the revelation of Desdemona's ignorance. . . . " and Othello's "agnonzied incomprehension. . . . " (129). Iago thrives in evolutionary flux. Dr. Johnson maintained that "the character of Iago is so conducted that he is from the first scene to the last hated and despised" (quoted in Honingmann, 38). Yet such a comfortably secure view is impossible in light of production history and critical debate. Much controversy swirls around Colderidge's assessment that Iago is caught up in "motiveless malignity." Pechter, for one, decanonizes Coleridge's hallowed pronouncement. Not surprizingly, Iago's amorphous, indeterminate status is the subject of a myriad of critical views about who he is and why he delights in villainy.

Iago has won many accolades in the twentieth century. In 1999 and 2000, Trinity Rep (in Providence, Rhode Island) audiences saw a jolly, gleeful Puck-like Iago, nullifying the moral certitude of Dr. Johnson's view of him. Iago has imploded the critical history that seeks to explain and contain him. Ironically, he is the only Shakespearean villian to survive the evil he engineers. Appropriately, Brian Bedford's 1994 production at the Stratford, Ontario Festival ended with the lights on Iago, not on the tragic loading of the bed. As Alan C. Dessen concluded, "The preferred choice today is, therefore, to treat Iago rather than the figures on the bed as the object of that poisonous sight and to direct him to be 'hid' or taken offstage. Bedford, who had no bed curtain, chose this approach and kept a handcuffed, smirking Iago as an offstage observer of Othello and Desdemona still visible on the bed" ("'Let it be hid,'" 7).

Critics have seemingly identified as many roles for Iago to play as he concocts motives to support them. Much critical attention has centered on who Iago is in the world of the play, situating him politically, socially, and domestically. In fact, any survey of criticism on Iago obligatorily concentrates on his role-playing. Earlier studies of a given Iago's role have been recycled in later criticism, redefining what had once been monolithically defined. Stanley Edgar Hyman's book on Iago identifies no less than six roles that have been the subject for much reinvestigation (*Iago*). And Hyman is by no means alone. Iago's genealogy has been tracked vigorously by a host of critics. He numbers his ancestors among the diabolic and the villainous. Modeled after *Othello* and with a nefarious character named Malignii, a "relative" of Iago's, Thomas Porter's play *The Villain* (1662) is "the earliest dramatic commentary on Iago in the Restoration" (Vander Motten). Bernard Spivack's *Shakespeare and the Comedy of Evil* located Iago's heritage in the figure of the Vice, declaring that Iago needs to be positioned in terms of theological/moral categories, and the way in which these categories lead to hybrids. E. E. Stoll likened Iago to the Weird Sisters (*From Shakespeare*). But as several critics have more persuasively announced, "If Iago were a straightforward villain he would arouse little feeling in audiences, yet of course he is anything but straightforward" (Honigmann, *Othello*, 38). An allegorical Iago just does not convince; audiences are intrigued by the pulsating drives of this most ingenious human being. Closely linked to the Vice for Elizabethan audiences was the stage Machiavel, the master of policy, deceit, and anti-Reformationism. Iago as Machiavel was the subject of Wyndham Lewis's *The Lion and Fox*.

But Iago is also the blunt, lower-class soldier, exemplified through his battlefield experiences, his views on women, and, of course, his ribaldry. Julia Genster studies military order, rank, and duties in light of Iago as the unpromoted ensign who is a "dealer in signs and emblems" and Cassio whose lieutenancy provokes anxiety as "a cipher in his captain's presence, a power in his absence," a source of Othello's jealousy by "standing in for him militarily and sexually" (788). William Empson's sociological reading portrayed a lower-ranking Iago as the victim of upper-class privilege, the underdog who bristles with class resentment because he has been denied the benefits of rank. In 1964, John Wain likewise emphasized Iago's plebian and military *modus vivendi*:

> A good many studies of Iago's character have been written to prove he was a fiend incarnate, a superhuman figure against whom neither Othello nor anyone else could have stood a chance...In fact, anybody who has ever been in the army or worked in a factory or just generally knocked about has met Iago. He is the sadistic sergeant who makes the men's lives miserable while

cultivating dozens of little arts which win the confidence of his superior officers. He is clever and quick-witted, within his limitations; he knows what it
behooves him to know; he has the skill that makes for survival and coming
out on top. (*Living Word*)

More recently, Emily Bartels observed that the socially inferior Iago attacks
blacks and women to feel superior ("Making More of the Moor"). Modern
stage history confirms such a reading. When *Othello* was performed in Russia in 1938, "the role of Iago was updated to include the racist tendencies of
'these days when chauvinism is again on the loose, preached by the medieval
fanatics in the Fascist countries and also in some bourgeoise-democratic countries of the capitalist world'" (quoted in Stribrny, 200).

In the domestic sphere, Iago has been tarred as the jealous husband himself, the lustful misogynist, who traiterously desires Desdemona. Patricia
Parker appropriately links Othello's "traveler's history" with a voluptuous Iago
who emphasizes opening or unfolding a new world with the "simultaneously
visual and close 'dilations' of [his] domestic informing, pruriently, even
pornographically exposing a hidden 'chamber' to the eye." Iago opens Desdemona's "hidden female place" to Othello's jealous gaze ("Fantasies," 92). As
we saw, feminist critics such as Carol Thomas Neely and Coppelia Kahn have
denounced Iago's attacks on women as reflections of an oppressive patriarchy.

But Iago also crosses strict homosocial lines for some critics as the
aggrieved homoerotic partner in act 3.3.213 and especially in the his oath-
taking "marriage" contract at the end of act 3.3. "I am your own forever," he
swears to Othello (476). Earlier work by Martin Waugh and Gordon Ross
Smith, for example, investigated the conduct and consequences of a homosexual Iago. The following more recent studies have explored and explicated
homosexuality in *Othello*: Patricia Parker, "Preposterous Events," *Shakespeare Quarterly* 43 (1992); Bruce Smith, *Homosexual Desire in Shakespeare's England* (1991); and Nancy Guitierrez, "Witchcraft and Adultery in
Othello: Strategies of Subversion" (1991). Robert Matz, "Slander, Renaissance
Discourse of Sodomy, and *Othello*," reformulates and amplifies the presence
of homosexuality in *Othello*. Stanley Edgar Hyman and, later, Peter Stallybrass
deduced that Iago even "plays" Desdemona in describing Cassio's dream to
Othello in act 3.3 419–31. "Iago constructs the narrative of Desdemona's
betrayal so that Othello can approach the 'grossly gaping' of her being 'top-
p'd.' He does it by casting himself in the role of Desdemona . . . Desdemona
and/as Iago" (Stallybrass, "Transvestism," 77–78). Like so many of Iago's
roles, his homoerotic presence has been countered with opposition, for example, by Jonathan Dollimore (*Sexual Dissidence*). In production, a gay Iago
does not always work, as Laurence Olivier learned when he countered Ralph
Richardson's Othello in 1937 with a fandango of homoerotic behaviors that
London audiences neither understood nor approved.

Beyond doubt, though, Iago is mired in things of the body, diseases and poisonous philtres; he is corrupt himself. Pechter labels him a "paranoid psychopath" (62), which in no way intereferes with "his extraordinary power to engage us with his point of view" (62). Mary Lux's essay included later in this collection examines Iago in light of physiological imperatives in the script. Robert B. Heilman earlier analyzed "Dr. Iago and His Potions," and Don Cartwell identified Iago as a shaman because of his doctoring, his cures and his diseases. Philip C. Kolin has situated Iago within the tradition of anti-doctors in Renaissance drama (*Elizabethan Stage Doctor*).

One of Iago's most fruitful roles—or an amalgam of related roles—emphasizes his talents as a creative artist, the "demonic playwright," according to Sidney Homan (*Theater*, 112). Unquestionably, Iago creates scripts, orchestrates plots, and boldly directs plays-within-a-play. *Othello* starts with an Iago-scripted dialogue between Brabantio and Roderigo, an exchange that continues, less successfully, in the confrontation in act 1.2 between Othello and the officers of the night. Acts 2.3, 4.1, and 5.1, though, are Iago's most energetic and fruitful "staged" performances where he skillfully and fortuitously develops fictions that ensnare his enemies. Iago's control over Roderigo's lines and action is studied by John Ford in his essay in this volume. In keeping with Iago's role as artist, Pechter characterizes him as the "master narratologist" (85) for his reportage of Cassio's dream and Desdemona's stolen hours of lust. Iago can also perform comedy routines marvelously well, according to Susan Synder who contends that *Othello* contains the vestigia of the comic turning tragic—Iago is the "clown without humor" (79–80). Emrys Jones identifies further comic techniques in Shakespeare's tragedy. No doubt Iago's stand-up humor links him to such bitter contemporary satirists as Mort Sahl, Jackie Mason, and Lenny Bruce.

Iago has also been identified with his creator—Shakespeare. Hazlitt provides an early instance of this association:

> The character of Iago is one of the superogations of Shakespeare's genius. Some persons have thought his whole character unnatural, because his villainy is without sufficient motive. Shakespeare...knew that love of power is natural to man . . . . Iago belongs to a class of character, common to Shakespeare and at the same time peculiar to him, whose heads are so acute and active as their hearts are callous. Iago is an extreme instance of the kind, that is to say of diseased intellectual activity, with perfect indifference to moral good or evil . . . He is an amateur of tragedy in real life; and instead of employing his invention on imaginary characters, or long forgotten incidents, he takes the bolder and more desperate course of getting up his plot at home, casts the principal parts among his nearest friends and connections, and rehearses it in downright earnest, with steady nerves and unabated resolution. (quoted in Furness, *Variorum*, 411)

In his Dickensian-like analysis, A. C. Bradley likewise linked Iago's cunning to Shakespeare's intuitive sense of character:

> Evil has nowhere else been portrayed with such mastery as in the character of Iago . . . He illustrates in the most perfect combination the two facts concerning evil which seem to have impressed Shakespeare most. The first of these is the fact that perfectly sane people exist in whom fellow-feeling of any kind is so weak that an almost absolute egoism becomes possible . . . The second is that such evil is compatible with exceptional powers of will and intellect. (*Shakespearean Tragedy*)

Harold Goddard stated that Shakespeare bestowed on Iago "the highest intellectual gift" (quoted in Honigmann, 40). Even more boldly, Stanley Edgar Hyman claimed that Iago "is a merciless self-portrait [of Shakespeare] as artist-criminal . . . and a therapeutic symbolic action of purging away the guilt of Shakespeare's Faustian craft" ("Portraits of the Artist," 18). Mark Rose even more stridently concluded that Shakespeare "through Iago represent[s] something like [Shakespeare's] own role in plotting the disintegration of the absolute world" ("Othello's Occupation," 300). Further recognizing Shakespeare's investment in Iago, Cedric Watts commended Iago as a semiotician, and William E. Bennett personified Iago as the "Kierkegaardian aesthete." Hyman has also analyzed Iago in terms of aesthetics ("Iago").

Of continuing importance to critics has been Iago's relationship with Othello, studying the two characters in light, or in the shadow, of each other. Honigmann asserted that "For many years critics have treated Othello and Iago as somehow equal and opposite" (31), though this is no longer the case. Wilson Knight long ago pointed out that as Iago gains mastery over Othello, the Moor adopts the ensign's imagery and predatory world view. Richard Marienstras contends that Othello is metamorphosized into Iago (*Le Procho*). Focusing on the metaphoric and spiritual concepts of color, G. K. Hunter insightfully weighed the balance between white Iago and black Othello:

> The relationship between these two is developed in terms of appearance and reality. Othello controls the reality of action; Iago the appearance of talk about action; Iago the Italian is isolated (even from his wife), envious, enigmatic (even to himself), self-centered; Othello, the "extravagant and wheeling stranger," is surrounded and protected by a network of duties, obligations, esteem, pious to his father-in-law, deferential to his superiors, kind to his subordinates, loving to his wife. To sum up, assuming that soul is reality and body is appearance, we may say that Iago is the black man with the white soul. ("Colour," 151)

There are many other links between the Moor and his ensign—both are outsiders, unenfranchised in Venetian society; both tell elaborate narratives;

both suffer from jealousy; both engineer the death of Cassio; both carry a lantern of revenge and dress in nightshirts in act 5.2.; and both kill their wives. Maud Bodkin argued that Iago is the darker side of Othello, a view which demands comparison with Janet Adelman's, that Iago's racism is really a projection of his own disease onto Othello. Apropos, the Folger Theatre production in 1990 cast a black man (André Braugher) as Iago, thus fusing the Moor and his enemy racially. Conversely, Marguerite Waller declared that Iago gives Othello a chance to escape the role of "licentious and inferior" black man (13) and to "participate actively and passionately in the emotions and jealousies, and vengeance of full-fledged Venetian male selfhood" (18). Ronald Draper, however, concentrates on how Iago's social inferiority propels him toward dominating Othello ("Unholy Alliances"). Thomas F. Connolly paints Othello as a "double man" whose insanity of evil comes from his alter ego, Iago, the "prime mover" of the Moor's world. As Connolly insists, Iago "is the sardonic half of Hamlet running rampant in Othello" (33). Rob Wilson finds that Othello and Iago are indeed "fraternal doubles . . . reconciled only through the sacrificial annihilation of their common female victim Desdemona." Focusing on psychic kinships as well, Kenneth Muir advocates that "the two main characters exemplify opposing principles which together constitute the human psyche." Comparing Othello and Iago, F. R. Leavis almost vindicated Iago by blaming the entire problem on the Moor: "We should see in Iago's prompt success not so much Iago's diabolic intellect as Othello's readiness to respond." So we have come full circle—Iago as not so evil and Othello as purely culpable.

OTHELLO IN PERFORMANCE

The following discussion of *Othello* on stage/film/television is highly selective and perfunctorily brief. For a thorough stage history of the play, however, consult these major works:

Carol J. Carlisle. *Shakespeare from the Greenroom: Actors' Criticisms of Four Major Tragedies.* Chapel Hill: University of North Carolina Press, 1969.

Julie Hankey, ed. *Othello: Plays in Performance.* Bristol: Bristol Classical Press, 1987.

Errol Hill. *Shakespeare in Sable: A History of Black Shakespearean Actors.* Amherst: University of Massachusetts Press, 1984.

Samuel L. Leiter, ed. *Shakespeare Around the Globe: A Guide to Notable Postwar Revivals.* Westport, CT: Greenwood, 1986.

Gino J. Matteo. *Shakespeare's 'Othello': The Study and the Stage, 1604–1904.* Salzburg: Institut für Englische Sprach und Literatur, 1974.

Lois Potter. *Othello in Performance.* Manchester: Manchester University Press, 2002.

Marvin Rosenberg. *The Masks of Othello.* Berkley: University of California Press, 1961.

Charles Shattuck. *Shakespeare on the American Stage: From the Hallams to Edwin Booth.* Vol. 1. Washington, DC: Folger, 1976.

James R. Siemon. "'Nay, That's Not Next': *Othello*, V.ii in Performance, 1760–1900." *Shakespeare Quarterly* 37 (1986): 38–51.

Arthur Colby Sprague. *Shakespeare and the Actors: The Stage Business in His Plays (1660–1905).* Cambridge: Harvard University Press, 1945.

Martin L. Wine, ed. *Othello.* Text and Performance Series. London: Macmillan, 1984.

Richard Burbage, the first Othello, played the role in blackface, no doubt to capture the assonance of the part. Virginia Mason Vaughan's *Othello: A Contextual History* sensitively explores Jacobean representations of *Othello.* Quite possibly, "English sailors may have played *Othello* on the African coast in the seventeenth century" (Kennedy, "Introduction," 2). Throughout the Restoration and eighteenth century, actors continued to portray Othello as comfortably black, stressing his African origins and customs. Interestingly, "there is no record of any controversy over the type of Moor intended by Shakespeare until late in the eighteenth century" (Cowhig, "The Importance of Othello's Race," 160). Restoration and early eighteenth-century actors captured a Europeanized but nonetheless gentlemanly black Moor reflecting, as Vaughan maintains, the military careers of several notable actors. In physicalizing Othello, David Garrick "chose an African in whose being circulated fire not blood" (Rosenberg, 40) and even added a turban to the Moor's costume to stress his exotic heritage.

Satirically pointing to Garrick's blackamoor make-up, rival actor James Quin compared him to the slave in the William Hogarth painting: "Othello . . .Psa! no such thing! There was a little black boy, like Pompey attending with a tea kettle, fretting and fuming about the stage; but I saw no Othello" (quoted in Rosenberg, 42). Quin himself "projected a large, heavy, slow-moving Moor whose surface seemed ideal for the times . . . an imposing, spectacular figure —a big Black Moor all in white: white wig, white British officer's uniform, white gloves, a famous piece of business was his slow peeling off of one pale glove to remove a black hand" (Rosenberg, 38–39). Quin's Othello, however, elicited laughter from some of his audience, though not because of his black make-up. He came on stage "in a large powdered . . . wig, which, with the black face, made such a magpye appearance of his head, as tends greatly to laughter" (quoted in Kaul, "Background," 3). Years later, even though Charles Fetcher appeared in blackface, he offered audiences an ethnically different Othello, a "Frenchified Moor" (Rosenberg, 73).

Edmund Kean, regarded as the nineteenth century's most memorable Moor, significantly departed from a blackfaced Othello when he opened at Drury Lane on May 16, 1814. "In the second decade of the nineteenth century, Kean abandoned blackface for light brown makeup . . . Kean's new makeup corresponds to a critical innovation usually said to originate with Lamb and Coleridge, claiming that Othello must be a tawny Moor rather than a black African" (Pechter, *Othello*, 15). Coleridge's famous dictum—"It would be something monstrous to conceive the beautiful Venetian girl falling in love with a veritable Negro" (Raysor, *Coleridge's*, 302)—helps to explain Kean's choice of make-up as do the even more racist sentiments of Charles Lamb who, so offended by the image of "the old black ram," insisted that Shakespeare's play should only be read, never staged. For Lamb there was "something extremely revolting in the courtship and wedded caresses of Othello and Desdemona; and whether the actual sight of the thing did not overweigh all that beautiful compromise which we make in reading" (97). Both writers lionized the racial imperative of the age in their stereotypical thinking. As Errol Hill rightly observed, "Othello's noble qualities and bearing did not fit the black stereotype" (9). Coleridge and Lamb's American counterpart in racist interpretations, John Quincy Adams, similarly maintained: "The great moral lesson of the tragedy of *Othello* is that black and white blood cannot be intermingled in marriage without a gross outrage upon the law of Nature . . . and that in such violations, Nature will vindicate her laws" (quoted in Kaul, "Background," 10). Continuing Kean's legacy at the end of the nineteenth century, Henry Irving played Othello in 1876 "'slightly tinged with walnut brown' according to the Edmund Kean precedent, so much applauded by Colderidge" (Cowhig, "The Importance of Othello's Race," 160).

Paul Robeson, one of the most renowned Othellos of the twentieth century, sketched in the cultural reasoning behind Kean's change of make-up.

> Shakespeare meant Othello to be a 'black moor' from Africa, an African of the highest nobility of heritage. From Kean on, he was made a light-skinned Moor because Western Europe had made Africa a slave center, and the African was seen as a slave. English critics seeing a black Othello—like my Othello—were likely to take a colonial point of view and regard him offhand as low and ignoble. (quoted in Rosenberg, 195)

A review of Ira Aldridge's *Othello* in England in 1846 further exemplifies the colonial prejudices that descended to Robeson. Although the reviewer for the *Manchester Examiner* (4 July 1846) praised Aldridge's acting, he could not forgive the color of the actor's skin, which he saw as a liability in effectively capturing the role:

> The Africanus Roscius made his appearance on Monday night at the Queen's Theatre in the character of Othello. This in our opinion is the most finished performance in the tragic line of this remarkable man. Throughout it is a most elaborate piece of acting; it gives indication of a cultivated mind and of good taste; it is nowhere marred by extravagance or rant; but still marvellous to say, the native African cannot depict as well as phlegmatic Englishmen

have done, the fiery-souled, noble-minded, suspicious Moor. The outward embodiment is there in perfectitude; the ordinary emotions are easily and well simulated; the act of the rhetorician combined with earnestness in manner, good gesticulations and attitudes give effectiveness to a large portion of the part; but the sable actor cannot depict the workings of a tossed, troubled, doubting mind. (quoted in Cowhig, "Ira Aldridge," 245–46)

Culture decided make-up. According to Vaughan, when Othello was staged in the postbellum South, he was "whitened" because of the fear of miscegenation (*Othello: Contextual*, 160). As Empire and anti-miscegenation become further entrenched, the gulf between the blackamoor and his white Venetian masters deepened. A spirited essay by Charles B. Lower, however, takes issue with those who have promulgated the idea of a light-skinned Kean. Lower maintains that Kean's Othello was a dark-skinned African based upon contemporary representations of the actor, and further argues that many antebellum Othellos were portrayed the same way, demonstrating the triumph of art over regional politics/prejudices. In retrospect, however, Kean's legacy cost more than one actor a high price for a lightened facade of negritude. Margaret Webster, who directed Paul Robeson in 1943, explained why a fairer-skinned Othello did not work:

It is true that many of the cultured gentlemen, reluctantly and faintly disguising from us their familiar features under a layer of becoming coffee-colored grease paint, rather as if they had recently returned from Palm Beach, have seemed to us possessed of far too much intelligence, restraint, and self-control ever to be swept by an uncontrollable passion which is not from the mind at all and only a little from the heart, but principally from the bowels. (234)

As if validating Webster's point of view, Anthony Hopkins's minimally tanned Othello for the BBC *Othello* in 1981 was speedily rejected by the critics. Ironically, Janet Suzman in her 1998 BBC *Othello* historically reversed Kean-Coleridgian colonialism by casting black actor John Kani to play opposite a white Iago in Apartheid South Africa.

Two of the most famous nineteenth century actors—Edwin Booth and Tommaso Salvini—represented Othello as more tawny than ebony. Combining various ethnic characters, Booth played Othello as a "dark poet," yet also as a "modest simple-hearted Gentleman" (Rosenberg, 82). Unlike the tempestuous Salvini, Booth represented a grieved Othello, filled with dignity and anguish. Still, as Rosenberg points out, he emphasized Othello's "oriental imagery in his make-up" (83), emotionally and physically. Regarding Booth's looks, M. E. Sherwood in the *New York Times* for January 20, 1875 commented: "That . . . proud beautiful . . . dark face, to which the Eastern robe was so becoming, seemed at once to be telling its mighty story of adventure and conquest. Desdemona was not worthy of it" (quoted in Rosenberg, 83). Booth's tawny visage accompanied his more tender, tearful Othello, the type of Moor that was more racially acceptable to the high Victorian audiences Booth strove to please.

Salvini played an Italian Othello in ways that were vehemently lauded or loathed by the critics. Even though he offered "the darkest Othello seen on the American stage" during the later part of the nineteenth century (Kaul, "Background," 11), Salvini still looked like a tawny Moor. He modeled his appeareance after Moors whom he had seen in Gilbralter and Rome. As Salvini pointed out in his autobiography, one Moor he emulated in particular had a "color [that] was between copper and coffee, not very dark, and he had a slender mustache, and scanty curled hair on his chin" (quoted in Vaughan, *Othello: Contextual*, 163). Clara Morris, a nineteenth-century actor, commented directly on Salvini's ability to capture African racial attributes: he "fiercely swept into his swarthy arms the pale loveliness of Desdemona . . . Passion choked, his gloating eyes burned with the mere lust of the 'sooty Moor' for the white creature in Venice" (quoted in Carlisle, 205). Because of his violent passion, Salvini readily embodied Othello's strong emotions. "In this respect, Salvini's heir was Olivier, who also performed the part with an aggressively sexual and . . . assertively foreign body" (Pechter, *Othello*, 99).

Yet Salvini's own ethnic identity—his "foreign body"—bled through his Othello, contributing to and reinforcing the critics' xenophobia. Salvini was attacked as an Italian butcher, a barbarian, a thirsty villain, dangerously emotional on stage. Significantly enough, the very "rage of an African" that Henry James had admired in Salvini (quoted Rosenberg, 115) became the racial/ethnic charcteristic that was responsible for the actor's own failure for many critics. His Italian ethnicity became the vehicle for assailing his passionate African representation of Othello. Opening at Drury Lane in 1875, Salvini spoke his lines in Italian (as he had done throughout his career) while the other actors delivered theirs in English. Paradoxically, Othello's race was being both represented and displaced through the actor's own unmediated ethnicity—race prejudice fading into anti-Italian suspicion and hatred. Pechter appropriately cites an attack on Salvini and other Italian actors by racist critic William Winter because of their "polyglot representations with which the American stage has been disfigured" (*Othello*, 227, note 10). The cachet of Empire was the pale, the myopic, and the homogeneous.

Twentieth-century Othellos have appeared in many hues—black, tawny, near white, and absolute white. Whether Othello should be seen as a blackamoor or an Arab has been a central dilemma for directors representing Othello on stage during the last century. Dympna C. Callaghan discourses on "the politics of representing a black man with white discrepancy between the cultural signs, a performance of alterity . . . and its lived condition . . . as a function of the representational systems required by an emergent capitalism"

("Othello was a White Man"). Francesca P. Royster also examines the politics of color underlying film/stage productions of *Othello*. The currency of representation has been varied in a post-Empire capitalistic society. In 1940, Donald Wolfit "rejected the light brown color of his predecessors and represented Othello as a curly-haired savage but noble north African" (Kaul, "Background," 19). Anthony Quayle played a dark-skinned and fearsome African Othello in 1954; he interpreted another blackamoor, Aaron, as dark in Peter Brook's distinguished film production of *Titus Andronicus* in 1955. Richard Burton's Moor at the Old Vic in 1956 also was deeply darkened opposite Rosemary Harris's fair white Desdemona. Olivier's Othello on the London stage in 1964 was coal black, and when some of his make-up came off in touching the snow-white Desdmona, played by Maggie Smith, critics questioned whether any white actor should ever take the role again. Figure 1 shows Olivier's blackamoor Othello lying next to Smith's Desdemona.

Peter Zadek's production in 1976 in Hamburg "made typological mockery" the "central issue" of *Othello* as Ulrich Wildgruber's Othello deliberately deconstructed and parodied a classical view of the Moor by appearing as a Negro minstrel. He "dressed in an absurd King Kong costume, his uniform jacket inside

FIGURE 1. Laurence Olivier as Othello and Maggie Smith as Desdemona, 1964. Photograph by Angus McBean. © the Harvard Theatre Collection. The Houghton Library.

out, carrying a mandolin, and put on a carnival paper-maché mask of a stereotyped African over his already blackened face . . . Ridiculously, and yet most movingly, as Wildgruber kissed and hugged Desdemona's dead body, his black make-up smeared more and more on his cheeks, rubbing onto Desdemona's white face" (Kennedy, *Looking*, 269). Zadek's postmodern spoof aside, "white actors have reverted to presenting him as black" (Kaul, "Background," 12).

But there are exceptions. Not all white actors followed Quayle and Olivier as dark-skinned Africans. Though Orson Welles's Othello in 1951 was described by the *Spectator* as "Very large, very black, very sonorous [but] insufficiently volcanic" (quoted in Rosenberg, 148), in point of fact he was not nearly as dark as eighteenth-century Othellos had been. In his 1952 film version, Welles's Othello was "a very light-complexioned, not at all rude or exotic in speech or manner, [with] little emphasis given to lines that evoke his strangeness or cultural alterity" (Donaldson, 118). Similarly, Abraham Sofaer, who played Othello in the 1930s, claimed that the Moor was "not a 'colored' man in the American sense of the word but a noble Arab—probably a Christianized Spanish Arab who found employment as a military man in Venice after the fall of the Spanish-Arab Empire . . . " (quoted in Rosenberg, 195). More recently, Ferial J. Ghazoul has also argued for Othello's unalloyed Arabization:

> No work of Shakespeare touches chords of Arab sensibility and identity so much as the tragedy of *Othello*. For one thing, the hero is a Moor and therefore an "Arab." Furthermore, he is not simply an Arab character in an Arab context; he is an Arab in Europe, necessarily evoking all the complex confrontations of Self/Other in a context of power struggle. (1)

Many white Othellos stretch across the twentieth century. In 1902, Forbes Robertson played Othello as nearly white. Interpreting Othello for Canadian television in 1953, Lorne Greene appeared only a few shades darker than actors portraying white Venetians; "his make-up showed his complexion darker than others (but not Negroid, so that most references to the 'black' Othello were omitted")" (Griffin, 335). Figure 2 shows Greene in the role. The ultimate "white" Othello, though, was Patrick Stewart's in Washington, DC, in 1997, in the less-than-celebrated "photo-negative " production where he and Bianca were Caucasian while the rest of the cast was black. Sujata Iyengar studies this production, and offers appropriate photographs, in her essay for this volume.

As a rule, directors have avoided casting a Caucasian as Othello, believing that a white man should not usurp a black man's play. As Vanessa Thorpe points out, "Colour is at the heart of a growing row about racism in casting as directors face the accusation that even the traditionally liberal world of the theatre is institutionally racist" (8). Seeing Paul Robeson at the Stratford-Upon-Avon Festival, John Dover Wilson expressed a sentiment contemporary

FIGURE 2. Lorne Greene as Othello with Josef Furst as Iago in the Canadian Broadcasting Corp. production, 1953. Courtesy of the Canadian Broadcasting Corporation.

directors have enthusiastically validated: "I felt I was seeing the tragedy for the first time. The performance convinced me . . . that a Negro Othello is essential to a full understanding of the play" (quoted in Rosenberg, 151). Margaret Webster explained why it was so important for Othello to be a black man:

> It is very apparent, and vital to the play, that Othello himself was very conscious of these same considerations—his black ancestry— and quiveringly aware of what the judgment of the world would be upon his marriage. It is one of the most potent factors in his acceptance of the possibility of Desdemona's infidelity. And she herself loses much in the quality of her steadfastness and courage if it be supposed that she simply married against her father's wishes a man who chanced to be a little darker than his fellows, instead of daring a marriage which would cause universal condemnation among the ladies of polite society. To scamp this consideration in the play is to deprive Othello of his skill and judgment, Emilia of a powerful factor in her behavior both to her master and her mistress, and Venice itself of an arrogance in toleration which was one of the principal hallmarks of its civilization—a civilization which frames, first and last, the soaring emotions of the play. (239)

In point of fact, since the early 1970s theatres have cast black actors in the role to foreground issues of racial identity and to disrupt cultural/conventional discourse. Adhering to such a policy, the Oregon Shakespeare Festival, which has staged *Othello* nine times since 1948, has featured black actors in the lead role since the 1970s when Ernie Stewart projected a "proud and imposing physical presence" (Carey, 439). As Paul Winfield observed, *Othello* has become "the classic play for black actors" (quoted in Mike Steele, 2.E). The accomplishments of leading black actors in the role have been carefully documented and analyzed, especially by Hill, Vaughan, and Kaul. Lois Potter's forthcoming *Othello in Performance* (Manchester University Press, 2002) also promises to be a significant study of the contribution of black actors in *Othello*, particularly Robeson, James Earl Jones, and Laurence Fishburne.

A history of black actors in the title role before Robeson properly begins with Ira Aldridge who performed *Othello* often and successfully in his European tours in Britain, Ireland, Berlin, Stockholm, St. Petersburg, and Constantinople, extending from the 1820s through the 1860s. Aldridge was the first black actor to become associated with *Othello*; Ignatius Sancho excepted. But it is highly likely that Sancho, a friend of Garrick's, refused the part on stage. Seeing Aldridge's performance in St. Petersburg in 1863, Theophile Gautier exclaimed that the actor's interpretation was "Othello himself, as Shakespeare has created him . . . quiet, reserved, classic and majestic," quite unlike Kean's more "fiery" approach. One German reviewer regaled Aldridge's *Othello* with hyperboles: "After this Othello it would be an anticlimax to have seen an ordinary Othello again. What abandonment, passion, beauty, greatness, sense . . . A Negro from Africa's Western coast had come to show me the real Othello" (quoted in Hankey, 81). Yet Aldridge was marginalized by being included only as a visiting artist in permanent all-white theatre companies and, unlike Salvini, spoke his lines in English while the other actors delivered theirs in native tongues. In England, Aldridge encountered bristling racist bias, even though he received kudos for his Othello, and enjoyed Edmund Kean's patronage. Ruth M. Cowhig's "Ira Aldridge in Manchester" evaluates the actor's reception in England. After Aldridge in importance is J. A. Arneaux (1855–?) who founded the Astor Place Company of Colored Tragedians, and played Iago as well as Othello several times. Also creating a powerful Moor, black actor John Hewlett (fl. 1820–1831) brought his success as a boxer to the stage in this country as well as in Europe.

Undeniably, Paul Robeson's Othello set a high standard for all subsequent actors, black as well as white. Seeing Robeson in March 1944, Tennessee Williams exclaimed, "Robeson as 'Othello' made my blood run cold . . . what majesty. All the rest here [on Broadway] is piffle" (Devlin and Tischler, *Letters,* 520). The fullest discussion of Robeson's contributions can be found in Vaughan's Chapter 9, "'The Ethiopian Moor': Paul Robeson's *Othello*" (*Othello: Contextual*) and in Hill (121–30) as well as in biographies by Martin

Duberman, Scott Ehrlich, and Paul Robeson, Jr. played Othello in three major productions spread over 30 years—(a) against Peggy Ashcroft's Desdemona and Ralph Richardson's Roderigo in 1930 at London's Savoy, (b) with José Ferrer's Iago and Uta Hagen's Desdemona in the 1943–1944 Theatre Guild production on Broadway, directed by Margaret Webster, and (c) at Stratford-upon-Avon in 1959, making Robeson the first black actor to play there. He brought enormous physical and psychological resources to the role—the strength and stature of a heroic soldier, the sonorous voice of an accomplished opera star, and, perhaps most important of all, pride in being black. According to Robeson in a 1930 interview, race and Othello were indivisible: "The problem [of *Othello*]," he asserted, "is the problem of my own people. It is a tragedy of racial conflict, a tragedy of honor, rather than jealousy" (quoted in Hill, 7). He continued: "It is because he is an alien among white people that his mind works as quickly, for he feels dishonour more deeply" (quoted in Vaughan, *Othello: Contextual*, 187). Robeson superimposed the suffering of his own segregated race onto Othello's tragedy. Yet he paid a dear price in 1930, as Vaughan points out:

> . . . despite some generous praise, the reviewers reveal that although Robeson hoped his appearance would overcome at least one barrier of racial prejudice [i.e. the theatre], his performance confirmed racial stereotypes embedded in traditional literary criticism and cherished by his white British audience. (*Othello: Contextual*, 190)

Robeson's biased London critics thought he looked too primitive and so evoked caricature, a charge earlier leveled at Aldridge. Herbert Farjeon saw Robeson as "being a member of a subjected race, still dragging in the chains of his ancestors [he] was not noble enough . . . The fact that he is a negro did not assist him . . . Shakespeare wrote the part for a white man to play" (quoted in Kaul, "Background," 15). Yet by 1943 Robeson's Othello was revered as a model. "No white actor could meet the fundamental requirement"—so powerful was the strength and dignity of a black Othello (Vaughan, *Othello: Contextual*, 195). From the vantage point of the 1990s, Bob Mondello attributed Robeson's popularity in part to the fact that he starred in the play "when simply seeing a black man on stage was a novelty" ("Grand Othell"). Nonetheless, as Vaughan rightly emphasizes, "Paul Robeson's interpretation of Othello had tremendous repercussions for the twentieth century's understanding of the play and the title role. It not only influenced the efforts of black actors such as James Earl Jones . . . but also white actors such as Sir Laurence Olivier" (*Othello: Contextual*, 197).

Since Robeson's Othello, many major black actors have triumphed in the role. A necessarily short stage history bears this out. Like Ira Aldredge before him, Earle Hyman contributed signficantly to *Othello* on stage, at home and abroad. Beginning with the Antioch Shakespeare Festival's "Shakespeare under the Stars," he appeared as Othello Off-Broadway in 1953 and continued his success, several times, including at the American Shakespeare Festival in Stratford, Connecticut 1957. He later toured Scandinavia until he returned to the Roundabout Theatre in New York in 1978. As many black actors had done, Hyman received high marks for his "cool wrought performance" (Atkinson, "Othello"), though his Othello was not as powerful as critics preferred. Unfortunately, reviews of Hyman's 1957 *Othello* were for the most part only mildly complimentary. Directed by John Hobbeman, and with a setting replete with Venetian blinds by Rouben Ter-Arutunian, this production was "crisp and swift without looking cultural" (Atkinson, "Shakespeare Festival Opens"). Francis Herridge claimed that Hyman was "well on his way to being one of the best Othellos around" (quoted in Leiter, 533), and Caldwell Titcomb lauded the actor for having the height and voice for the part (quoted in Leiter, 534).

What most critics found lacking in Hyman's interpretation, however, was fire and passion. As Atkinson claimed, "Hyman . . . is hardly the 'Noble Moor' whose . . . majesty overwhelms everyone he meets" ("Shakespeare Festival Opens"). His delivery was "thick" and he played the Moor "as a patient simple-minded Othello" (Atkinson, "Othello"). Claire McGlinchee concurred: "Earle Hyman's interpretation was powerful yet somehow lacked the essential nobility of the Moor," adding that "There was too much black in the costumes." For critics wanting an Othello large in statue and as overpowering as Robeson, Hyman did not meet the bill. Nevertheless, he demonstrated once more how realistically and powerfully a black actor could portray the Moor. For an overall appraisal of Hyman's acting, see Glenda E. Gill's work.

In June 1970, Moses Gunn (who starred in *Shaft*; *The Great White Hope*; and *Ragtime*, the film) played Othello for the first time in his career at the Festival Theatre at Stratford, Connecticut, and then at the ANTA Theatre in New York, directed by Michael Kahn. While the actor was generally praised for his interpretation, Gunn's race became an issue for some critics. Shockingly, Clive Barnes admitted that he did "not really approve of black actors playing Othello—it is too obvious," though they were in his estimation fine in *Lear* or *Hamlet*. Barnes nonetheless located the strength of Gunn's interpretation in his blackness, and unintentionally forecasted a dominant casting tradition:

> Othello was written for a white actor in blackface. Mr. Gunn plays him black —plays him from the deliberate position of black consciousness. Even in its simplicity this portrayal is gratifyingly complex. It has layers to it. There are new black actors now. For no very certain reason I got a fugitive and perhaps false impression that Mr. Gunn was possibly the first black actor to be asked to play Othello who was amused rather than flattered. He gives the part magnificently, but gives it on his own terms and at his own distance. ("Simplicity," 43)

Barnes further noted, "This is an Othello making it in a white world, wary of acceptance, disdainful . . . " However, Jerry Tallmer added: "I had read that Mr. Gunn provided the first Othello ever 'played black' in the contemporary sense of term. Not so. He 'plays it black' for one slow-building half of the first act. Then all the stops let out and it is something else." Gunn intentionally set himself apart. As Peter Smith observed, Gunn's "Othello is terribly out of place; he is the only one of his kind, not just in color but in style, in bravery, in simplicity; perhaps he should look and sound like a figure from another era" (453). Gunn was proud, assured, very much the confident warrior, "a giant Moor in a whorled orange robe that a tiger would feel at home wearing" (Kerr, "*Othello*"). Gunn's delivery also distinguished him from the rest of the cast, especially Roberta Maxwell's Desdemona, "a lovely sexual child" (Tallmer). Critics compared him to an opera star and, in fact, the *New York Times* christened him "the singing Othello." Referring to Gunn's melodious recounting of Othello's early life, Walter Kerr appropriately remarked: "We know, in the moment, that we are listening to an aria. We also realize . . . that *Othello* is in very large part composed of arias." Though called a "virtuoso" by Barnes and Kerr, other critics (e.g., John Simon and Jerry Tallmer) faulted Gunn. Simon harshly compared him to "a karate instructor" because instead of walking he will "shuffle, lope, or titubate," and stressed that his "madly quavering voice sounds like a theremin solo played during an earthquake."

Among the most distinguished actors to play Othello, James Earl Jones took the role seven times, the first when he was 38 at the New York Shakespeare Festival, a production that later moved to the Martinique Theatre Off-Broadway in July 1964. Jones's first Othello exhibited both the strengths (voice, stature, presence) and short-comings (unbelievable change of emotions) that would characterize his later performances. The most notable of these was in 1982 at the Winter Garden Theatre, starring Christopher Plummer as Iago and Dianne Wiest as Desdemona, and directed by Peter Coe later joined by Zoe Caldwell. Understandably, Jones's work was favorably compared with Robeson's. Richard Coe of the *Washington Post* claimed that Jones's interpretation "is seen as our finest since Paul Robeson's World War II performance." (Appropriately, too, Jones starred in a one-actor production of Robeson's life in 1978.) Like Robeson, Jones had the necessary prerequisties for the role—he was a black man with a heroic stature and a magnificent voice. Joel Siegal of WABC-TV applauded "the incredible . . . power of James Earl Jones."

Drawing impressively upon his African heritage, Jones was very much in touch with Othello's blackness. Charles Michener expressed what was rapidly becoming received opinion about black actors doing the role: "That Shakespeare's noblest tragic victim should be played by a black man seems imperative today. Othello's blackness is at the heart of his blindness (for all his towering authority, he is the lone outsider in an alien society), and blackface, however brilliantly Olivier and others have put it on, won't really do." Frank Rich identified the African subtext in Jones's Othello: "Mr. Jones's ease and authority as a military commander seem his by birthright, even as he maintains the uneasy aloofness of an outsider. Later on, his base, chest-thumping emotions upon summoning up his 'black vengeance' shake through both his body and the house like tribal exorcisms" (C15). Jones's sense of being as a black man was of course tied to his tragic relationship to Desdemona. As T. E. Kalem pointed out, Jones's "Othello regards every aspect of Desdemona's being as an extension of his personal honor." Yet his "massive mountain of strength is reduced to so much dust in his smothered Desdemona's boudoir" (Rich). Jones wore flowing African robes in the early and middle parts of the play but appeared in a monk's white habit in act 5.2 when he came to murder Desdemona.

Critical opinion maintained that Jones was overshadowed by Plummer's Iago, an interpretation that Walter Kerr hailed as "quite possibly the best single Shakespearean performance to have originated on this continent in our times" ("Jones-Plummer," 2). Jones's Othello, it was thought, was too easily outmanoeuvered and outsmarted by Plummer's cunning and "intellectual ferocity" (Barnes, "A Noble Othello"). Portraying Iago as a blunt, incisive master sergeant, Plummer even had "hair and a moustache . . . [that] were as sharp as porcupine quills" (Rich). Jones's towering presence weakened next to Plummer's hot, impassioned Iago. Jones "plays the warrior who is great of heart in such a quiet, offhanded way; he is almost in constant danger of disappearing," claimed Dennis Cunningham, expressing the most bitter disapproval of Jones's Othello yet. But Cunningham raised once again the central and chronic problem of "whose play *Othello* is it anyway?" If Jones's Othello was seen as too tentative before Plummer's too forceful Iago, he nonetheless captured through tears and gentle horror Othello's deepest emotions. Praising Jones's interpretation, Kerr pointed out: "Most productions, and most performances of the role, are so entirely concerned with making us believe step by step in the Moor's distrust of his wife that they quite forget his love for wife . . . But these two things coexist . . . and the tension of the play's climax depends upon their coexistence" ("Jones-Plummer").

In July, 1982 Morgan Freeman starred in an *Othello* at the 11th Shakespeare Festival in Dallas at an outdoor stage in the Fair Park bandshell. Directed by Dale A. Rose, this *Othello* featured Valerie Mahaffey as Desdemona and Mark Blum as Iago. Though Freeman won great praise for his interpretation of Coriolanus at the New York Shakespeare Festival earlier, his Othello is less well known. But clearly his presentation was powerful and apt, as can be discerned in Figure 3. He had "the stature, the gift for larger than life gestures necessary for Othello. He projected a warmth and generosity in the opening scenes that contrast well with the jealous husband, the maddened bull of the final scenes" (Hurlbert). Diane Wertz likewise praised the actor's stage presence: "Freeman makes a dramatic figure; he carries himself eloquently in his flowing robes . . . his gestures are soft and rolling in comparison with the sharpness of those around him, and his vocal tones are round and full" (1C). But she found Morgan too reserved, with the effect that he "allow[ed] Blum's Iago to steal away with the audience's attention and affections . . . " An ingratiating Iago has always been the audience's worst friend, however. Accompanying Freeman's expansive rage was some innovative concluding stage business—"Banners hanging about the set plunge[d] to the ground, as though a single cord had been cut . . . [with] the sense of momentum building toward doom" (Hurlbert), dramatically orchestrating Othello's downfall.

Playing Othello eight times in his career, Paul Winfield rivals James Earl Jones in the number of appearances in the role. Among his two most memorable productions were those at the Alliance Theatre in Atlanta in 1979, where the house was sold out for four weeks, and at the Guthrie in Minneapolis in 1993. Issues of black pride and politics were intertwined with these productions. "Winfield's presence provided the Alliance with the crucial leverage for the (black) city government of Atlanta to fund two free 'in the park' performances of *Othello*, drawing over 30,000. Much in the Othello characterization depended wholly on Winfield's being black"—rituals, robes, his "own elemental yet rich racial heritage" (Lower, 219–20). Kaul concluded that Winfield "Africanized" Othello ("Background," 19). Of course, that heritage included the ravages of racism: "a handful of hate letters" came in after Winfield kissed Dorothy Fielding's white Desdemona. But, overall, the audience's responses was not "crude or

FIGURE 3. Morgan Freeman as Othello and Valery Mahaffey as Desdemona— Shakespeare Festival of Dallas. Courtesy of the Shakespeare Festival of Dallas.

censorious. When Othello and Desdemona first kissed, there were audible gasps testifying to the depth of audience involvement" (Lower, 221).

Fourteen years later, Winfield played Othello for the thirtieth anniversary season at the Guthrie, which, surprisingly enough, had not mounted the play before. Reviewers again commented that a black actor strengthened the production. Additionally, Bianca was played by a black actor (Shawn Judge) as was one of the Venetian officers (James A. Williams). Winfield's 1993 Othello, however, was far different from the one he performed in Atlanta in 1979. Audiences at the Guthrie saw "a human sized loving older man exhilarated by his good fortune in marrying the daughter of a Venetian senator" (Bunke). Believing that Desdemona was unfaithful, Winfield's Moor turned violent, as captured in Figure 4. Winfield expressed the kind of stereotypical thinking about Othello that once unjustly excluded black actors from the role: "He's a general and he's married a senator's daughter. That's probably as high as he, a black man, can get socially" (quoted in Mike Steele, 2E). Taking a broader view, Winfield cautioned, "It's about race, of course, and about outsiders who have to live up to different standards. This is something I understand. But it also transcends race. It looks into love and the lack of love is overwhelming. It's a great part for any actor. It just

FIGURE 4. Melissa Bowen as Desdemona and Paul Winfield as Othello at the Guthrie Theatre, November 1993. Photograph by Michal Daniel. Courtesy of Michal Daniel.

doesn't have to be the only part for a black actor" (quoted in Steele). Not every reviewer validated Winfield's interpretation, however. Winfield "reverts to a kind of voodoo expression to rationalize his emotional feelings," announced Steele ("Othello"). Father John Malone similarly observed that the "Christian symbolism . . . is reduced to an almost black magic celebration."

Race almost worked against Winfield's Moor who projected moral grace, but "played Othello as a weighty, burdened, even tired man out of place. He's far from self assured in the world not only because he is black but because he believes in ethical behavior" (Steele). Winfield may have tapped the benefit of his racial heritage but he appeared too restrained for the critics. Father Christopher Trussel, for example, complained that Winfield's "befuddled manner does not give the impression he is an heroic general . . . even his madness is retrained." According to Jayne Blanchard, Winfield was perhaps too old for the role, displaying in "the Moor a Falstaffian generosity of spirit."

Though lacking Winfield's or Jones's experience, Charles S. Dutton starred in a Yale Rep production of *Othello* in March 1986. (Earlier, Dutton had won acclaim on Broadway in *Ma Rainey's Black Bottom*). Projecting a large Othello clad in Renaissance costume with a massive chain of entwined silver circles around his neck, Dutton looked exotic yet moving and fit for military command. Emphasizing the military ethos in the play, director Dennis Scott even choreographed the changing of the guard between acts (Markland Taylor). Mel Gussow praised Dutton's "visceral" interpretation and the envy that flowed from him ("Theatre: Charles S. Dutton"), but Steve Kemper recorded that Dutton was best in "physical moments but not those that required subtlety." Dutton was too self conscious. The reviewer for the *Journal-Courier* ("'Othello' Meets Unworthy") complained that Dutton "still has to acquire the range and depth" to play Othello "as the famed tragic hero." Markland Taylor expressed a similar opinion: the production "never attains genuine Shakespearean amplitude. It remains small-scale, almost suburban— Othello and Iago as the boys next door." Significant in *Othello*'s stage history, though, there was "neither a bed nor a pillow in Desdemona's chamber. Othello strangles her with his hands" (Gussow, "Dutton").

The Idaho Shakespeare Festival staged *Othello* in 1986 and again in 2000 —with black actors in the title role both times. In the 1986 *Othello*, director Vincent Murphy stressed the clash of cultures and interracial marriages, among other issues. The playbill noted: "The world we conjure for you . . . involves us with strong passions covered by smooth civilized surfaces." Murphy portrayed the "military world [of the play] where order is imposed but provides no defense against deliberate, devious evil from within its own ranks" (Ross). Steven Matt's muscular Othello was aptly described by Marie Devine Galyean as

> . . .the perfect foil to the evil Iago. Matt creates a strong, honest character who is slow to anger but passionate in his convictions. He is every inch the

professional soldier, respecting authority and performing his duty as he sees
it, even when it means executing his own wife as punishment for her supposed unfaithfulness. (*"Dynamic Drama"*))

Matt's background as a Phoenix cop, former boxer, and "part-time physical
trainer in Hollywood" (Judy McConnell Steele) equipped him well for one of
the most physical Othellos on record. Linking his own background to Othello's character, Matt commented: "I've solved problems by flattening people's
mouths . . . Othello's flaw is he doesn't know how to deal with social mores
. . . He's a mercenary soldier, hired to kick butt" (quoted in Judy McConnell
Steele). The motley costumes for the production, designed by Matt Schafer,
symbolized an omnibus military world of *Othello*: the men were clad in
doughboy hats and military jackets with ornate braiding while Desdemona
wore "lumpy 'high fashion' clothing and beehive hats" (Galyean). The Festival's 2000 *Othello* starred Allen Gilmore, a light-skinned African Othello,
reinforcing the Duke's response that the Moor was "far more fair than black."
Melanie Hoyt pointed out that Gilmore "endows Othello with a noble honesty.
His magnetism is reminiscent of the powerful charisma of actor Morgan Freeman on the screen. He brings a truth and complexity to Othello . . . " Rebecca
Prescott's Desdemona was "a perfect equal for this . . . Othello" (Hoyt), a
strong and realistic woman with a marvelous singing voice.

The Stratford, Ontario Festival, which has produced *Othello* several times,
staged two productions with prominent black actors who offered even more
variations on representation in the play. In August 1987, 38-year-old Howard
Rollins (*Ragtime*; *Soldier's Story*) interpreted the Moor, directed by John
Neville who in 1956 appeared as Othello opposite Richard Burton's Iago. With
his looks and physique, Rollins was admirably suited for the part; he was dash-
ingly clad in a nineteenth-century military uniform with heroic epaulettes and
golden braids. Laurence DeVine commented that Rollins looked "the strapping
Moorish general, descendant of Africans and Berbers." Yet because Rollins did
not have the power of a Robeson, critic Robert Reid faulted him. Seven years
later, another Hollywood black actor, Ron O'Neal (*Hill Street Blues*), tackled
the role at Stratford in a highly contextualized production. Director Brian Bedford modeled O'Neal's Othello after the first black general in the U.S. Army—
Benjamin O. Davis—to situate Othello's accomplishments within modern
black military history. Set in Washington, Bedford's *Othello* "transposed the
action to a 1940s USA, with period army uniforms, a big band sound, and auto-
mobiles, not to mention a cigarette-smoking Emilia in the style of Bette Davis
or Eve Arden and an act 2.2 proclamation delivered over a public address system in a manner reminiscent of M*A*S*H*" (Dessen, 6). Bedford painstak-
ingly evoked the times and temper of segregation by localizing racial prejudice.
Scott Wentworth's Iago, for instance, spoke with a Southern drawl.

Several productions from the 1990s strenuously reinterpreted the script without racial overtones for a postmodern society. In so doing, black actors have destabilized traditional productions anchored in absolute racial stereotypes. Shakespeare at Santa Cruz's *Othello,* for example, subordinated race altogether in 1990 when Ron Dortch (NBC's *Nasty Boys*) played the lead role set in contemporary America. In an update of the "tragic loading" of act 5.2, Desdemona is murdered on a queen-size bed in a tastefully decorated, stylish bedroom with Levellor blinds, reminiscent of a suite at the Marriott, as we can see in Figure 5. In August 1998, Robert Johnson offered an "elegant, refined, controlled" *Othello* at Santa Cruz. Admitting that a sympathetic Othello may have run counter to Elizabethan conventions, Rob Pratt noted that "it is the women characters who deliver the most compelling social message." Writing for *Critique*, Paul Parrish claimed that Johnson's *Othello* was not a "not a politically correct play. . . . The Romantic idealism that Othello and Desdemona share is out of fashion. In this contemporary production, Desdemona is likely to be seized on as a poster person for battered women, magnificent Othello reduced to a forerunner of O. J. Simpson." Yet Parrish applauded Santa Cruz and Johnson for "restoring" the balance and interpreting the sublime music of Othello as not all pomp and circumstance. *Othello* became a play about love not race at the end of a century that had witnessed profound changes in the ways society regarded race. Current social history gives credence to this interpretation: "A 1998 U.S. Census survey tallied more than 1.3 million racially mixed marriages in the United States . . . As the non-white population becomes more diverse, the number of interethnic marriages is fast increasing" ("Love Without Borders," 62). Since interracial marriages are

FIGURE 5. Camilia Sanes as Desdemona and Ron Dortch as Othello in the Shakespeare Santa Cruz 1990 production. Photograph by David Alexander. Courtesy of Shakespeare Santa Cruz.

rapidly becoming more common, couples of different racial and ethnic back-grounds are far less likely to be ostracized as strange, different, or radical, including the late-twentieth-century Othello and Desdemona.

One of the most daring productions of *Othello* in which racism was effec-tively diminished using black actors was staged at Shakespeare Theatre at the Folger Library in 1990–1991 where Avery Brooks (*Spencer for Hire*; *A Man Called Hawk*) as Othello starred opposite a black Iago, played by film star André Braugher (*The Court Martial of Jackie Robinson; Glory*), and a black Emilia (Franchelle Stewart Dorn), and directed by Hal Scott, himself an African American. Scott's nontraditional approach was provocative as it recast and interrogated traditions. Having a black Iago eliminated racism as one of the ensign's motives. Brooks's Othello, like Braugher's Iago, "belongs to the Moors. It is an African-centered realty" he inhabits (LaVerne Gill). In fact, Bob Mondello conjectured that a black Iago and Emilia might easily be seen as Othello's "Morish family . . . of his tribe." Braugher's Iago was propelled by jealousy and anger—not racial contempt—directed toward the general who refused to promote him. In an insightful review, Miranda Johnson-Haddad explored the "complex bonds between" a black Othello and a black Iago, con-cluding that because of casting, "there was a reason, a very basic one, for Oth-ello to trust Iago so unquestioningly in the first place" (478). In an interview in *Aside* (a Folger publication), Scott stressed that a black Iago coming out of Othello's past made the betrayal even more treacherous and tragic.

Scott linked the two men in costume (e.g., both wore Nigerian Tuareg headpieces in 2.1) and through other cultural associations (e.g., African talk-ing drums and trumpets). With both men portrayed as victims of cuckoldry, "Braugher's Iago and Brooks's Othello burn in the same hell" (Lloyd Rose). Given their shared racial pasts, the bonds between two black men—Iago and Othello—are even stronger in act 3.3 than in productions with a white Iago. Moreover, a black Emilia and Iago made Desdemona, not Othello, stand out as "the Other" (Johnson-Haddad, 478). In fact, a black Emilia frighteningly establishes that there is "someone more familiar with Othello's background and cultural context than Desdemona could perhaps ever hope to be" (Johnson-Haddad, 477). Lloyd Rose exclaimed, "With one stroke of nontradi-tional casting . . . Scott cuts *Othello* loose from racial melodrama and reestab-lishes it as pure tragedy." The Folger *Othello* was not the first time a black actor was cast as Emilia, however. In 1979, the Globe Playhouse of Los Ange-les featured Yahee as Emilia, though Iago, J. D. Hall, was white (Stodder and Wilds 233).

Scott's interpretation may have been "pure tragedy," but it was also dis-turbingly too modern for some reviewers. Deflecting such criticism, Scott explained, "All I've done is add a sociological rationale that makes what Shakespeare wrote more creditable for contemporary audiences" (quoted in Collins). Yet according to Collins:

The play does indeed look different. Given the current sociological climate, a black theatergoer might see it one way while whites might take it another. From my downtown white perspective, then, this is an *Othello* that brings to mind images from our city streets, although the production keeps to Shakespeare's Renaissance setting.

Collins further remarked, "Adding to the production's ghetto consciousness is the impression that the prncipal black figures are surrounded by a largely hostile white society." Some in the Folger audience no doubt saw the play exactly that way. LaVerne M. Gill reported:

This is an *Othello* just right for Washington's open dialogue on African-centered education. It is an *Othello* that uses the Euro-centric Shakespearean world to give us a glimpse of the Muslim world of the Moor. It raises some culturally different questions for this community. And answers them well. ("Shakespeare's *Othello*")

Yet there were some drawbacks to Scott's interpretation. While the "production's cultural complexity" erased one set of problems, it raised still others. "Sometimes it seemed merely that Iago had embraced a European identity more thoroughly than had Othello" (Johnson-Haddad, 478), but, even more seriously, Iago's motivation—through Braugher's acting—"made for several unsolved questions" (Johnson-Haddad, 479), such as his reactions to racist comments made in front of him. Nevertheless, Braugher won high praise for his fast-paced verbal manipulations and physical gyrations. "He makes Iago a street tough, copy-catting the language and gestures of a modern-day street-corner criminal. You'll also detect in his wheedling and bullying of his wife, the sweet-talk/contempt dichotomy of a pimp" (Mondello). Mike Giuliano, however, complained that this *Othello* "wallops us with the tragedy's visceral power at the expense of its poetry" ("Too Tough: Othello"). Johnson-Haddad noticed that Brooks becomes even more violent at the end of act 5.2 by carving a cross in Iago's chest, thus making the villain and not the tragic loading of the bed the climatic focal point for an audience. (Recall that Brian Bedford also deflected attention away from the bed in his 1987 Stratford *Othello*). Further stressing Brooks's terrifying physicality, Giuliano confessed, "One almost fears that in his jealous rage Othello will grab you and accuse *you* of sleeping with his wife." Blonde Jordan Baker's Desdemona's, too, departed from tradition. She was tall (the same height as Brooks), lustier, and far more physical than previous Desdemonas had been; for example, she attacked Othello ferociously with her fists in 5.2., and she was truly shocked by Othello's change in 4.3. Yet as Lucia Anderson pointed out, "Othello and Desdemona [were] always color-coordinated to the end in costume," earmarking them as a fashionable, blended family for the 1990s.

At the Oregon Shakespeare Festival, LeWan Alexander (1997) and Derreck Lee Weeden staged new Othellos, again with diminished emphasis and anxiety on race. Weeden (who played Othello at the Alabama Shakespeare Festival in 1994 and Montano at the OSF in 1992) appeared in a OSF production directed by Berkeley Rep artistic director Joe Taccone who "recentered Othello in the play" giving the Moor, not Iago, the prominent place. In the process, Taconne made Weeden's Othello "a hero for our multi-cultural times." Barry Johnson describes this new *Othello* as:

> a sympathetic, intimate reading that opens Othello to us and explains him in crucial ways and restores the real tragedy of his story. Strangely, it also diminishes the racial tension that has dominated thinking about Othello for the past few hundred years since slavery was institutionalized by the planta-tion systems in the New World. Past practice has made Othello either mon-strous and inhuman or light-skinned depending on the prevailing thinking about race. Taccone's Othello is African, sure, and Iago uses racial slurs against him. So does Desdemona's father. But this Othello isn't surround by overt racism, and he doesn't slaughter Desdemona because of racial hatred. ("Othello in Love")

Weeden's Othello is "the most attractive potent man on stage, and because he's so integrated into the production, the racial difference seems a small matter—especially in a late '90s American production. Why wouldn't he win the love of fair Desdemona? Why wouldn't Sidney Poitier get the girl in 'Guess Who's Coming to Dinner?'" (Barry Johnson). Misha Berson agreed that "Taccone swings the pendulum back" toward Othello in not making him Iago's dupe and found that Weeden is "a most impressive figure of innate nobility, poise, and charisma" (M1). But Berson vehemently opposed critics like Johnson who saw race being distilled out of the script. As Berson emphasized, when critics "call this 'the first post-racial *Othello*,' I disagree. The issue of Othello's African Otherness is embedded in the text. Just note how often the word 'slave' arises. That Taccone doesn't belabor the point, but focuses on a multi-dimensional portrait of a man often perceived only by his race and gullibility is one of this flawed but provocative production's strongest suits" (M2).

One of the most noteworthy *Othello*s of the 1990s was mounted by Sam Mendes (who also directed *Cabaret*) at the Royal National Theatre at the Cottesloe in June 1997, and then for a short run (six performances) at the Brooklyn Academy of Music in April 1998. Ben Brantley hailed this *Othello* as "spellbinding" ("A Down to Earth Iago," B7). John Peter observed that Mendes's *Othello* was one of those "rare production[s] in which Othello and Iago were evenly matched" ("The Touch of Evil"). It starred David Hare-wood as Othello, though, surprisingly enough, little mention was made of his race, Simon Russell Beale as Iago, and Claire Skinner as Desdemona. Even though Harewood's black heritage did not surface in the reviews, a sense of race nonetheless infused Mendes's production. He created an "almost film-noir *Othello*," according to Matt Wolf. Mendes transformed a Jacobean play set in Renaissance Venice into the Fascist military world of the 1930s where Venetian senators wore business suits and Cyprus was translated into "a stuffy, racist colonial outpost complete with wicker furniture, floor pillows, slowly revolving fans, men in khaki." *Othello* "becomes a story of the Raj" (Lyons).

In the process, however, Mendes transcended colonial polarities to focus more on "psychological imprisonment" (Kingston, 38), where both Harewood's Othello and Beale's Iago suffer. Interestingly, "after Iago has convinced the Moor of Desdemona's unfaithfulness, alone on stage he becomes physically sick, gagging on his own malevolence" (Core, 447). And Harewood's Othello, his encroaching madness physicalized in a whirling ceiling fan, bangs his head against a wicker chair during an epileptic fit (Daniels, 55). This Othello was trapped in a modernist warp. Mendes, however, was praised for not separating "the text from the director's version of it" (Brantley, "Down to Earth"), thus concentrating on the universal human emotions of distrust, envy, and rage. Sex was far more prominent than race in this *Othello.*

In casting a young Harewood as Othello, Mendes also departed from the more conventional practice of seeing the Moor as older (more a contemporary of Brabantio's than of Cassio's). Wolf claimed Mendes did this "to enhance the play's sexual potency." According to Mendes, "I wanted a believable sexual relationship between Othello and Desdemona . . .which I'd somehow never seen before. Othello is always treated as a father figure, whereas I wanted to feel electricity in the embryonic relationship which is destroyed" (quoted in Wolf, 9). Unquestionably, Harewood gave a charged performance—"in rage, Mr. Harewood thrills," although Lyons found him occasionally "bombastic and pompous." Peter discerned two separate Othellos in Harewood's performance—a solemn rhetor and an impassioned lover, and used the following graphic metaphor to describe the actor's agility: "It is as if Harewood's face opened up like a wound both tightening with anger and softening with agony." Overall, Harewood offered " a magnificent monumental simplicity."

Even with such power, Harewood's Othello was overcome by Iago. Lyons declared that this *Othello* "belongs to Beale's Iago." Core found that "his smooth slyness is at once mesmerizing and insidious." According to Brantley, Iago is "the ultimate disgruntled employee, a military version of the fabled postal worker who suddenly erupts into homicidal violence after a lifetime of servitude" ("Down to Earth"). He is jealous because he has been passed over and so is denied the good life with fine cigars and wines. Robert Daniels brilliantly described Beale's interpretation of an Iago for audiences in the 1990s: "Iago . . . is a most perfidious villain. The squattish brainwashing ensign revels in his unscrupulous scheming. Beale has a sly, impish, and triumphant grin that makes one's flesh creep. Short and bullish, his malevolent cunning brings to mind that classic villainy of Charles Laughton."

Dressed in a black evening gown in act 3 and in "silvery pajamas" in acts 4 and 5 (Daniels), Skinner's Desdemona intriguingly aroused the soldiers in a steamy Cyprus, yet she "gives us a girl whose truth of feeling never departs from her" (Kingston). "The thrashing of her lithe young body as she struggles for life under the weight of the vengeful Moor is . . . numbing" (Daniels).

Another presumably non-racial, yet covertly political, *Othello* was presented by the Royal Shakespeare Company in Stratford-upon-Avon in May 1999, directed by Michael Attenborough and starring Ray Fearon as Othello and Zoe Waites as Desdemona. Fearon, aged 31, was only the second black actor, after Robeson, to appear at Stratford-upon-Avon. According to Katherine Duncan-Jones, "neither Iago's resentment nor his attraction seem much connected explicitly with Othello's racial difference. There may be good reason for this. In 1999, aware of such men as Nelson Mandela and Kofi Annan, we are starting to take it for granted that 'white' wars may require 'black' moderators. The Venetian state's need for Othello seems now almost a truism, not a paradox" (13). Fearon's savvy Othello is nonetheless hoodwinked by Iago who exults in the Moor's "collapse into disordered thinking and manic violence with terrifying cogency" (Duncan-Jones).

Overall, Fearon's performance was "subtle and convincing" though "perhaps a little quieter than he could have afforded to be" (Jackson, 220). As other black actors did, Fearon impressively took the part of a commanding general, which was especially important in this production set on a "late-nineteenth century" military post, a *mise-en-scene* fast becoming a convention for stage and film directors. Act 2.3, for example, takes place "in a mess-hall" in the middle of a "drinking ritual." Richard McCabe's Iago, according to Jackson, delivered the "most commanding performance" with act 3.3 "end[ing] in a gesture of blood brotherhood" with Othello (221). Rather than hiding behind a pillar or leering from an upstairs room, Fearon's Othello watched the events in act 4.1 behind "vertical curtains of a Robbe-Grillett-like cream-colored fabric" upstage near the proscenium arch (Jackson, 221), physicalizing the contrast/barrier between his ethnicity and Desdemona's.

Another production which seemingly swept aside "most of the more problematic issues of racial and gender stereotypes" (Mirlani) was the Trinity Rep *Othello* for 1999–2000, starring John Douglas Thompson (*Malcom X*; *Secret Film*) and directed by 26-year-old Amanda Dehnert. This *Othello* was intensely military—Thompson, with a shaved head, was outfitted in a Marine ribbed jersey, green beret, combat boots, and with a knife hanging from his belt, a picture-perfect commando. He led a very tough bunch of soldiers "clad in post-punk paramilitary garb and sporting mohawks and other weird haircuts . . . [they] were very loud, wild and wanton, particularly when drunk" (Donahue, F3). Though Othello, Iago, Montano, and Cassio were "boot-camp honed" (Clay, 10), Lodovico, the Duke, and Brabantio wore smart business suits. Emphasizing Thompson's suitability for the role, Sam Coale observed he was a "superb Othello. His lean athletic body embodies Othello as a military hero and warrior, and he uses it instinctively, looping arms reaching up to the sky that is falling. He begins self-assured and almost cocky, a military general in command of his life and wife" (27). Although Trinity Rep wanted to move toward a post-racial *Othello*, it may not be possible for audiences to overlook Othello's distinctive, impressive African heritage. Terry Byrne, for example, still saw Thompson's Othello as the "Other":

> He was a wonderfully complex man: a commanding general, who tempers his self-confident control of his men with a tender vulnerability for his bride. Thompson is as sweet and boyish with her as he is tough and demanding of his men. Her love for him seems to be the last obstacle between his outsider status in the white world of Venice. But the many differences between them can only help foment his fear she might not truly love him.(Trinity's, *Othello*)

Even though Dehnert did not foreground race, contemporary racial politics were inherent in the set, casting, and circumstances of the production. Reviewers could not help but compare Thompson's Othello with a black man who once was America's leading general—Colin Powell. Highly instructive, for instance, was Peter Cassels's observation that: "The play is subtitled 'The Moor of Venice' because Othello is a successful black military man in a white world. He's no Colin Powell, and had none of his insecurities. However, I'm sure Powell has to deal with backstabbing politics and jealous Pentagonians just as the Moor did." In this regard, Dehnert's *Othello* demands comparison with Brian Bedford's production at Stratford in 1987 where Othello was modeled after black general Benjamin O. Davis. In keeping with a non-racial *Othello*, Eric Tucker's Iago was less the evil bigot plotting the Moor's destruction than an almost fey ensign, "boyish giddy, passionate, gleeful . . . He is downright frolicsome . . . he rides the sinews of his demonic scenario with such buoyancy that, in comparison to the more serious others, we almost root for him. Until we see what he has wrought" (Coale, 27). Iago as Puck—a new twist!

ETHNIC PRODUCTIONS OF *OTHELLO*

Ethnic actors/troupes also shed light on Othello's role as "the Other." Closer to tawny than black, distinguished Hispanic actor Raul Julia played Othello opposite Richard Dreyfuss's Iago, directed by Wilfred Leech, at the New York Shakespeare Festival in Central Park in 1979. This production raised subtle ethnic/racial issues. Amid Renaissance sets, costumes, and weapons, Julia received hearty praise for his interpretation of an Othello ignited by passion. In fact, as Mel Gussow confessed, "Julia's Moor is a man of passion as well as a man of action. He is the most romantic Othello within my memory, one who could charm a city of Desdemonas" ("Stage: Raul Julia"). At times, Julia "overdramatizes himself" (Gussow), but "sensual currents" ran between him and Frances Conroy's Desdemona. Julia's passion could be equally destructive. He forced a kiss on Desdemona and then threw her to the floor— a physicalization of his attitude of her as both "whore" and wife (act 4.2. 91–92). Though Dreyfuss lost some of Iago's lines, he presented a different, even non-traditional Iago—he "is not diabolical. There is no feeling of exultation when his plot works and when he is finally exposed, there is no adder's hiss" (Gussow).

A dark-skinned, mustachioed Julia played Othello again in June of 1991 at the Delacorte Theatre of the New York Shakespeare Festival, under the guidance of director Joe Dowling, and opposite a trendy Iago interpreted by Christopher Walken who dominated the performance. Frank Rich admitted that though Julia "has the physical and vocal authority of a military leader," he did not portray "the shattered soul" of the Moor. Instead, through Dowling's direction, the performance foregrounded jealousy, betrayal, slander. Again, race apparently did not play a major role for the critics. Yet Julia was characterized as a "Caribbean deity," speaking in a "lilting" way "far more evocative of a gentle Caribbean island than fierce Mauritania" (Rich, C:1). Julia's intimacy with Kathryn Nasle as Desdemona, as in his earlier 1979 Othello, won kudos. Unlike a white or black Othello, Julia offered a Hispanic Moor, big on eros but short on interaction with Iago. According to Frank Rich, the production "refused to see *Othello* as a piece in part about racism"; he did claim "honor and evil are the warring forces at work here not whites and blacks, and certainly this is a legitimate view of a seventeenth-century play that was not necessarily envisioned by its author as the ur-text of *Jungle Fever*" (C:1). Audiences disagreed, however. W. J. Weatherby reported that a student in the audience tried to convince his girlfriend that "*Othello* was like Spike Lee's *Jungle Fever* set hundreds of years ago," even though "Nothing . . . could be less like *Jungle Fever* than *Othello* with Raul Julia."

Walken played Iago as "mostly comic" from whom audiences received not invidious apothegms but "raspy Brandoish inflections." Having his soliloquies "isolated in harsh white light," Walken "emerged as the most memorable figure" of the production (Sterritt, 12). David Richards agreed that Walken's Iago, whose "skin is a bloodless white . . . his hair in a punk cut, dyed maroon," looked like a "motor cycle hoodlum" with line delivery reminiscent of "Jackie Mason." There was no distinction between an inner evil core and an external charming Iago. Tellingly, then, Iago's evil was sickly white. His style was "punk Renaissance."

When *Othello* has been staged in non-Western countries, or by non-Western theatre troupes in this country, the codes and signifiers of race have changed radically. As D. J. R. Bruckner profitably cautioned, "Remove the appearance of sharp racial differences from *Othello* and the difference in the play is so striking that it makes you wonder how many other stories have been distorted in our imaginations by our historical obsession with race" (E:5). In an Indian *Othello*, produced by the Theatre Group at Siri Fort in New Delhi, 30–31 March 1991, for example, Othello was "an Islamic Moor . . . whose Islamic past [was] the source of his original self, alienated from the present . . . [His attachment] comes to the fore in the second half of the play, when the Moor turns 'schizophrenic,'" according to director Alyque Padamsee (quoted in Chopra, 41). Yet the danger of such ethnic emphasis was that "perhaps the excessive concerns for the Islamic character undid the magic" (Chopra, 42). An Indian Desdemona (Nikki Vijakar) was, as required in Islamic law, under-played, subdued, docile, and not nearly as forceful as some contemporary American and British Desdemonas have been.

Othello's blackness disolves into other kinds of cultural representations in East Asian productions where, for example, race is filtered through native political (and theatrical) conventions. The history of *Othello* in Japan is illus-trative. Essential reading is *Shakespeare and the Japanese Stage*, edited by Takashi Sasyama, J. R. Mulryne, and Margaret Shewring. Many Japanese pro-ductions have destabilized Western assumptions. Although the first *Othello* in Japan was performed in English by a British touring troupe—the Miln Com-pany—in May of 1891, subsequent productions/adaptations document the continuing popularity of this Shakespeare tragedy transformed through East Asian adaptations. Though not as popular as *Hamlet*, *A Midsummer Night's Dream*, or even *Romeo and Juliet*, *Othello* has been performed regularly and successfully in twentieth-century Japan. An invaluable reference is Ryuta Minami's "Chronological Table of Shakespeare Productions in Japan, 1866–1994," included in *Shakespeare and the Japanese Stage* (257–331). The earliest Japanese adaptation of *Othello* was staged in 1903 by Kawakami Oto-jiro's Company. In March of 1917, "Kabuki actor Matsumoto Koshiro played the title role with shingeki actors" (Minami, 267), inaugurating a samurai Oth-ello, not a blackamoor mercenary in the service of white patrician Venice. Over the years Kabuki adaptations of *Othello* have been respected greatly in Japan, especially Onoe Shoruku's in 1969. As on the Jacobean stage, a Kabuki *Othello* in Nagoya cast a male actor as Desdemona. Robert Hapgood enthusi-astically applauded these Asian transformations:

> It is the spectator who must connect the chanter's voice with the puppets and in Kabuki transform an onnagata (male performer of female roles) into a beautiful maiden. The latter transformation, I confess, has yet to happen for me. Tamasaburo Bando is the exception that can help to clarify my general difficulty. One of the world's best actors, he has never in my experience failed in his depiction of women . . . In Kabuki-style *Othello* in Nagoya, I saw this Japanese man successfully impersonate an Italian lady of the Rennaisance. Unlike a "female impersonator," Tamasaburo does not exaggerate conven-tionally female characteristics. His portrayal of a woman is not basically dif-

ferent from that done by an actress . . . he distills an essence of beauty that is
more purely and concentratedly feminine than that of a real woman. ("A
Playgoers Journey," 249)

Another highly respected Kabuki Othello was done in the United States
in January–February 1988. Shozo Sato, artist in residence at the University of
Illinois's Krannert Center for the Performing Arts, conceived, designed, and
directed a Kabuki *Othello*, following an English script written by playwright-
actor Karen Junde. Sato's *Othello* first played at the Krannert Center and then
moved to Chicago's Wisdom Bridge Theatre. His goal was "to recreate an
American Kabuki for an American audience with American actors" (Gratton,
21). Figure 6 shows Othello, Desdemona, and Iago in the Kabuki *Othello*. Previously, Sato had done a Kabuki *Macbeth* and *Dr. Faustus* at the University of
Illinois. Beginning with Shakespeare's script and chief source (Cinthio's

FIGURE 6. Kabuki *Othello*. Courtesy of the Illinois Kabuki Theatre, Krannert Center
for the Performing Arts, University of Illinois at Urbana-Champaign.

novella), Sato incorporated elements of Kabuki's "stylized grandeur" (play-bill)—dance movements, costumes (kimonos, helmets, breastplates, wigs), marionette-like koken (or silent, black-clad stage hands)—to create a non-Western *Othello*. Lighting director John Boesche transposed "images once transparent for the screen" with shadow figures behind the screen, reminiscent of Asian theatre techniques (Bevington, 212). Shakespeare's words were sung in high "Kabuki fashion," too (Springer, 4).

Sato satisfyingly incorporated the spectacle of Kabuki into Shakespeare's tragedy. To emphasize Othello's "Otherness," Sato creatively represented the Moor (played by Paul Friedman) as a white-faced Ainu, one of the indigenous Caucasian people of Japan, thus incorporating Japanese cultural codes and signs in a Western play. The color white took on associations of black, a reversal of Western color symbolism. The motivation of Othello's cruel, arch-enemy Iago (Mark Smith) was stinging lust for Desdemona (Anne Tremko), a desire fetishized Kabuki-syle by two koken holding burning candles, or poles, at the end of the platform as Iago soliloquized about his desire for her (Springer, 3). To symbolize Desdemona's death, Sato buried her alive under "yards of her own hair, extended poetically by the koken from the platform" (Springer, 2–3). Textually, too, Sato opened the script to Eastern theology and philosophy. As Christine Schaak observed:

> Sato succeeds in emphasizing the paradox that is intrinsic to the performance, and it's largely the contrast between the two very different cultures . . . There are numerous references to Buddha and Karma, rather than Shakespeare's Christian God, as the sources of Desdemona's and Othello's tragedy. (3)

Nōh *Othello*s have been popular as well. Munakata Ueda has been instrumental in translating *Othello* into Noh. He created the first English Shakespeare Nōh play—*Hamlet*—in 1982 and subsequently turned to *Othello*. In 1986, he supplied Nōh scripts in English with musical notations to be used in a performance by the Nōh Shakespeare Group in Tokyo. He created a Nōh *Othello* in English in 1987 for the National Nōh Theatre in Tokyo and for the East-West Fusion Theatre at Harvard University in 1988. Another Nōh *Othello* was done in 1989 and directed and adapted by Kuniyoshi Munakata. See also Jeffrey Kahan's interview with Kuniyoshi Munakata on Nōh translations of Shakespeare. And a radically altered/adapted *Othello* was performed in Kyogen, a highly stylized Japanese theatrical style, in the 1980's by Onsui Emi (Sasyama et al., 215).

The National Asian-American Theatre Company, where "all the actors are of Asian descent—Korea, China, Japan, the Philppines"—performed *Othello* at the Connelly Theatre in New York in 2000, directed by Jonathan Banks. Though Bruckner found some of the acting "excessive," there was no doubt that colorblind casting was telling. Joshua Spafford was "a great warrior who is largely innocent of the manipulative malice . . . around him" while Joel de la Fuente's Iago was frightening. Acting like a powerful samurai, Spafford's Othello lifted Tina Hari's Desdemona "18 inches off the floor with his hands around her throat" (Bruckner).

Chinese *Othello*s are also instructive in terms of how Otherness is represented in a non-Western culture. Coming to China much later than it did to Japan, *Othello* was adapted for audiences at the Shanghai International Shakespeare Festival on 19–26 September 1994, and directed by Lei Guohua at the People's Art Theatre. She "interpreted *Othello*, as an allegorical tragedy in which common human weaknesses are carried to their worst extreme" (Lingui, 79). Yet both the director and the adapter (Li Rong) "detected some typical concerns of contemporary Chinese people and tried to put such feelings into their production" (Ruru, 361). Chief among these concerns was economic injustice and the "economic competition that resulted in an obsession about fairness" (Ruru, 361). According to director Lei, Iago, who vied with Othello for audience's sympathy, was portrayed as a man whose jealousy was rooted in "the injustice and unfairness to be found in society" (Ruru, 360). Heavily cut, this Chinese adaptation deleted Shakespeare's first act as well as Bianca's and Lodovico's parts.

Othello and Desdemona were often featured in "a paired pose," further reflecting Chinese theatre conventions. He Wei's Othello was an "impudent credulous Moor" (Lingui). Yet this Chinese production still emphasized Othello as an outsider—"a racial Other"—by presenting him "with a short black beard and mustache, a long gown, and large black leather boots" (Stanley, 72). Othello's rage and jealousy were represented through familiar Chinese stage symbolism. As the audience witnessed thunder and lightning, "strange, dark forceless creatures . . . writhed in the background" (Stanley, 76). In dramatizing the eavesdroping scene (act 4.1), the director had Othello "cover himself in a red velvet cloak while Desdemona passed by with a sheet-sized handkerchief covered with large strawberry shapes resembling blood" (Stanley, 76). This is Shakespeare writ large indeed! Ultimately, this Chinese *Othello* with its singing and dancing more closely resembled Verdi's opera *Otello* than a Jacobean tragedy.

OTHELLO ON FILM

Othello has been an extremely popular subject for film. While not receiving as many cinematic interpretations as *Hamlet* or *Romeo and Juliet*, *Othello* has been adapted to the screen at least twenty times, beginning with seven silent films. The first filmed *Othello* was in German in 1907, directed by Franz Porten; an Italian *Otello* was done the same year, directed by Mario Caserini; an American *Othello*, also known as *Jealousy*, followed in 1908, directed by William Ranous. In 1909 and 1914 the second and third Italian silent *Otello*s were made, and in 1918 another German *Othello*—directed by Max Mack—

and still another German version in 1922, directed by Dimitri Boukhoyietski, were released. Robert Hamilton Ball's *Shakespeare on Silent Film* is an excellent guide to these early *Othellos*. The play's success on stage has been repeated in popular entertainment showcasing a variety of famous directors and stars in film and television versions from the 1940s to the present, including Sebastian Cabot as Iago in a 1946 *Othello,* directed by David MacKane; Andre Morell in 1950; Orson Welles in 1951; Sergei Yutkevich's Russian *Othello* in 1955; Laurence Olivier in 1965; Yaphet Kotto in 1980; William Marshall in 1981; and Laurence Fishburne in 1995.

The three most famous *Othello* films, however, include those starring Orson Welles, Laurence Olivier, and Laurence Fishburne. Significant books devoted to Shakespeare on film include Douglas Brode, *Shakespeare in the Movies: From the Silent Era to Shakespeare in Love*; Peter S. Donaldson's *Shakespeare on Film and Shakespearean Film Directors;* Kathy M. Howlett's *Framing Shakespeare on Film*; Roger Manvell's *Shakespeare and the Film*; Robert Willson's *Shakespeare in Hollywood, 1929–1956*; and Jack Jorgens's *Shakespeare and Film*. Moreover, highly regarded collections of essays on Shakespeare and film have been edited by Anthony Davies and Stanley Wells, and Lynda E. Boose and Richard Burt (1997). *The Shakespeare on Film Newsletter,* another valuable resource, was subsumed by *The Shakespeare Bulletin*. A useful web site is the "Film History of *Othello*" at http://hubcap.clemson.edu/ ~rosea/filmhist.htm.

Released in 1952, and restored and reissued in video in 1992 by Castle Rock, and now available only in DVD, Orson Welles's *Othello* is considered an "unforgettable filmic experience" (Davies, "'Othello,'" 209). Starring in and directing this highly innovative *Othello*, Welles cut the playing time to 90 minutes, eliminating and rearranging many scenes in Shakespeare's play. As he emphasized, "In *Othello* I felt I had to choose between filming the play or continuing my own line of experimentation in adapting Shakespeare quite freely to cinema form . . . *Othello* the movie, I hope, is first and foremost a motion picture" (quoted in Bent, 360). Years later, Welles made *Filming Othello* (1978) in which he meticulously assessed what he tried to accomplish in the film and how he did it. A complete transcript of the film and an interview with cinematographer Gary Graver and Welles by Laurence French is available online at http://film.tier-ranet.com/dirctors/o.welles/fothelloe.html.

Filmed on location in Venice and Portugal in black and white (symbolically non-chromatic), Welles's *Othello* won the Cannes Film Festival Award in 1952. His filmic work was hailed as a "visual opera" (Davies, "'Othello,'" 209), a triumph of the camera over psychology or fidelity to the script. Jack Jorgens succinctly summarized the importance—and liabilities—of Welles's adaptation: "Welles's *Othello* is one of the few Shakespeare films in which the images on the screen generate enough beauty, variety, and graphic power to stand comparison with Shakespeare's poetic images. His visual images compensate for the inevitable loss of complexity and dramatic voltage accompanying heavy alterations in the text" (175). Among Welles's many "alterations" were cutting Desdemona's willow song, the Venetian emissaries in act 4, and Iago's last speech. Welles's emphasis was not on characterization but on cinematic imagery, which was his major contribution to interpreting and expanding Shakespeare's verbal text.

Welles created a nightmare montage through highly innovative settings and daring camera work. His film opens and closes with a cage suspended high in the air on a tree limb, imprisoning the foul Iago, a reminder of his ever-present danger, and with a funeral procession where cowled monks carry biers of Othello and Desdemona to the sound of ritualistic chants. Within this framework Welles contrasted unhindered views of St. Mark's Cathedral and flowing canals in act 1 with the claustrophobic parapets on the fortress and the elaborate geometric enclosures in Cyprus (really Portugal). Acts 2–5 are embedded in a seemingly endless labyrinth of shadowy corridors, vaulted chambers, circling stairways, latticed windows, mirrors, grates, and intimidating arcades as if Othello were trapped in the very architecture that he supposedly commands. Welles's sets radically departed from Shakespeare's script to reveal Roderigo murdered in a Turkish bathhouse, Othello rushing madly among a herd of goats while a swarm of gulls circled above him, and Othello kissing the murdered Desdemona through the sheets.

Jorgens labeled Welles's *Othello* a "flawed masterpiece" (175), and Donaldson maintained that the film "cannot go beyond its own revelations, its own collapses . . . psychologically and politically [it is] caught in its own evocation of entrapment" (122). In discussing Welles's *Othello,* Kathy Howlett argued that "getting back to the original Shakespeare" is both "impossible" and contrary to "Renaissance theatre practice" (7). While the settings were brilliantly imaginative, the acting and Welles's concept of character were found wanting. Eric Bentley quipped that Welles's Othello "never acts, he is photographed" (236). Envisioning Othello as "sympathetic" and "melodramatic," Welles portrayed the Moor as "the victim of impersonal fate rather than of personal failing . . . [he] opts for a heroic Othello and consequently plays down the racial aspects of the character" (Bent, 363). Vaughan likewise claimed that Welles "minimized race as an issue" (*Othello: Contextual*, 199). Iago, too, underwent a profound transformation in Welles's film; he had "savagery drained from his character" (Jorgens, 180). Michael MacLiammoir recorded his experience playing Iago in *Put Money in Thy Purse: The Filming of Orson Welles's Othello*. Welles conceived of Iago's brand of villainy as "workmanlike," dispelling the mystery of evil that has surrounded Shakespeare's character for centuries. Describing to MacLiammoir the way Iago should be interpreted, Welles insisted that:

> No single trace of the Mephistophelean Iago is to be used: no conscious villainy; a common man, clever as a wagonload of monkeys, his thought never

on the present moment but always on the move after the move after next; a
business man dealing in destruction with neatness, method and a proper
pleasure in his work. (quoted in *Put Money*)

No wonder MacLiammoir's Iago was icy cold. Suzanne Cloutier's Desdemona
"did little more than read her lines" for Bent while according to Jorgens she
"show[ed] little evidence of humanity, or an inner life" (180).

Peter B. Donaldson's Chapter 4, "Mirrors and M/Others: The Welles
Othello," masterfully studies camera angles, "complex visual design," and
an undulating destructive materialism pervading Welles's film. Bent like-
wise examines the architectural design of Welles's imagery, which he
divides into the two main categories of "confinement and aerial perspec-
tive." Especially useful, too, are chapter-length studies by Barbara Hodgson
("Race-ing *Othello*: Re-engendering White-Out") and Vaughan ("Kiss Me
Deadly: or the Des/Demonized Spectacle," in Vaughan and Cartwright).
Vaughan also analyzes the cinematography in light of "male subjectivity and
Welles's female objectification" ("Patriarchal Eye," *Othello: Contextual*).
Maintaining that Desdemona is "the object of masculine sexuality anxiety,"
Vaughan argues that through Welles's camera work—lighting, reverse angle
shots, phallic pillars, mirror images—her body is fetishized by a voyeuris-
tic patriarchal gaze. Vaughan believes that the camera actually is "the sub-
stitution . . . for the patriarchal eye" ("Patriarchal Eye," 207). She concludes,
as does Hodgson, that these elements were already "deeply embedded in
Shakespeare's text" (216).

A second highly influential film version was the John Dexter/Stuart Burge
Othello in 1965, starring Laurence Olivier. Olivier received exemplary
reviews, many of which Tynan collects as he offers his own useful commentary. Peter Rainer said Olivier's Othello is "regarded by many critics and actors
as the greatest performance of the 20th century." And Geoffry Bent lauded
Olivier's film as "the most famous and controversial *Othello* in this century"
(363). Unlike Welles's highly innovative cinematic interpretation, though, the
Olivier *Othello* recorded an actual performance based on his earlier 1964
National Theatre production, which cut only 600 lines from Shakespeare's
play. The film, with camera work done by Burge, employed the same actors,
sets, and costumes as those for the London stage. Seeing Olivier at the
National Theatre the previous year, Alexander Anikst extolled his performance, which carried over into the film:

Olivier is the first of the great twentieth-century British actors who has created a brilliantly original interpretation of Othello . . . [Olivier's] Othello is
a man of gigantic stature but he is not a man of titanic thought; and by no
means is he an "umo universale," a man of many-sided character, typical of
the Renaissance. This Othello came into the world from a less civilized soci-

ety. He is very close to nature, to the earth. He has had no time to absorb the
culture of the new world surrounding him. With all its glitter, this world is in
fact trivial and mean . . . Othello's simple soul makes him vulnerable to the
pretty contrivances of the environment. A civilization that is false and untrue
kills the simple minded man . . . This is what Olivier, the actor, shows us. (in
Tynan, *"Othello": National Theatre Production,* 108).

Jorgens carefully contrasts the Welles and Olivier film versions in style,
theme, and affect (191–95), as does Bent. Cinematically, however, the Olivier
Othello was faulted for the following reasons: "Too often the camera is in the
wrong place, the editing thoughtless, the lighting and make-up shoddy" (Jorgens, 206). Davies likewise pointed to the "film's failure to satisfy in terms of
cinematic drama" (198) because of its restricting "two-dimensionality" (197)
and "selective" camera work that filters out the necessary contextual clues
(199). Undeniably, though, Burge's close-ups of Olivier were riveting.

Technical problems aside, Olivier offered "the most dominating Othello
of recent years" for John Russell Brown (xvii). Olivier scripted a fundamentally different, more faithful *Othello* than did Welles. In Welles's film, Othello
was a mythic Everyman, a victim of violated trust. In the Burge-Dexter *Othello,* controlled by Olivier, the Moor is caught in the net of jealousy. Jorgens
distinguished "the meticulous naturalistic details of the performance in Burge
and Dexter's film, giv[ing] it a realistic texture" (193) from the "formalism" of
Welles's film which gave it "an artificial feeling." In such a highly realistic
context, Olivier's Othello was far more erotic, physical, flamboyant, and proud
than was Welles's. Adopting the looks and mannerisms of the West Indies,
Olivier with his blackened and mustached face, striped flowing African robes
(magnificently portrayed on the front cover of this collection), scimitar, and
ankle bracelets cast a hypnotic spell over audiences. As Geoffrey Bent
quipped, "No Arabic evasions here, no Victorian gentleman in cocoa butter
declaiming pretty verse while holding a silken pillow over his wife. Olivier's
Othello is as African as Lake Tanganyika" (364). Of course, several critics
protested that Olivier (this white actor in blackface) came close to caricature,
rolling his eyes and smacking his pink lips. Othello's "errors, misperceptions,
then seem racially motivated" (Bent). Alice V. Griffin offered this useful summary of Olivier's achievement: "Laurence Olivier's interpretation of Othello,
which caused such sensation (pro and con) when it appeared on the English
stage, was an excellent choice for filming, a medium well suited for the story
and the realism of Sir Laurence's acting" (383).

But Olivier's Othello rose above stereotype, turning the Moor's excesses
into theatrical virtues. Though Dexter claimed to base his interpretation on F.
R. Leavis's view of Othello as a self-dramatizing and proud non-hero who
never reaches tragic insight, Olivier offered a far more complex and tragic figure. As Jorgens again observed, "Olivier's triumph is that he liberates film

audiences from trivial, demeaning images—and allows us a glimpse into a splendid, more Shakespearean image of an earlier age." Olivier "reaches for a grand, breath-taking presence lost to an audience since the nineteenth century" (194). To be sure, he unleashes savagery and is the victim of his own arrogance, blind to unfolding events. He suffers from a grievous tragic flaw. In one interview, Olivier commented that when "Othello swears he's 'not easily jealous,' it's the most appalling bit of self-deception. He's the most easily jealous man that anybody's ever written about" (quoted in Tynan, *National Theatre*). But Olivier's Othello is chastened into humility and wisdom in act 5.2. Audiences were spellbound by the actor's howling as he embraced the dead Desdemona. As Robert Hapgood explained:

> At this point something alarming happened. Suddenly both Sir Laurence and his imitated African were gone; and Othello himself was at large, not a person but a force as demonic as Oedipus—a black titan raging dangerously about the stage. There was nobility about this figure as he held his wife to him while delivering his final speech: self-pity now transmuted to an appeal for understanding; sensuality now transmuted to a union at once sexual and timeless. But above all was his unjudgeable force, whose compulsive course, like to the Pontic Sea, carried all before it. ("Two Othellos," 32)

Equally memorable was Olivier's stage business signifying Othello's downfall. Audiences saw Othello's romantic, even effeminate side as Olivier smells a rose and later blows petals off, as if it were a dandelion, to discern if Desdemona is indeed true. Much of the staging from act 3.3 forward, for instance, concentrated on stripping Othello of his rank, honor, peace of mind, and love. In act 3.3, he tears a large ornate cross, the symbol of his service to white Venice, off his neck. Olivier also disrobes to just his stark military tunic, removing the white caftan and shinny scimitar, visually affecting a comparison with the nondescript, plainly-clad Iago (Frank Finlay). The weaponry in act 4.1 also symbolizes Othello's downfall. While Othello is in his trance, Iago places the hilt of a dagger between Olivier's teeth, one of the most homoerotic symbols in the film. Moreover, the act "figuratively fit[s] him with the pointed tongue of the devil" (Jorgens 200). And in the quintessential instance of pairing these two men, Othello and Iago kneel and swear allegiance to each other on a sword with the point up and the handle down. As Harland Nelson aptly observed, this "would mean something to Olivier's Othello"—"a reversed cross" invokes "the power of darkness" (19).

If Olivier's Othello was large, imposing, and eloquent, Frank Finlay's Iago (seen in Figure 7) was the common man spurned, a short, squat malcontent. His hatred was directed toward the upper-classes, symbolized by a vain Cassio (played by a very young Dereck Jacobi), and toward an overreaching black Othello. Seething with racism, Iago's prejudice fueled his ire and forged his

plots. His contempt of Othello's "Otherness" motivated his treachery as much
as Othello's pride in being black helped to undermine the Moor. "As [Olivier]
grew to a great beast, Finlay shrunk beside him, clinging to his shoulder like
an ape, hugging his heels like a jackal" (Ronald Bryden quoted in Tynan,
National Theatre, 106). Unlike MacLiammoir's Iago, Finlay's was aggressively physical, even bordering on the homoerotic. He enfolded himself passionately in Othello's embrace in act 3 and subserviently wiped the foam from
his general's tongue during the trance in act 4.1. Finlay's Iago was precipi-
tously lewd, brooding, far more treacherous than MacLiammoir's.

A young but mature Desdemona—Maggie Smith—responded with passion to Olivier's touch. (Bent even accused Smith of being suspiciously "flir-
tatious.") Each encounter between them was electrified with sexual energy,
passion, desire. When Olivier came to murder her, Smith at first begs for
mercy but then puts up a spirited struggle. Like Salvini in the nineteenth cen-

FIGURE 7. Laurence Olivier as Othello and Frank Finlay as Iago, 1964. Photograph by
Angus McBean. © The Harvard Theatre Collection. The Houghton Library.

tury, Olivier's Othello confronted a crying and shocked Desdemona who was determined not to be a passive victim. Joyce Redman's Emilia was a loyal and loud defender of her mistress Desdemona.

The ultimate Hollywood *Othello* was directed by Oliver Parker in 1995 with box-office attractions Laurence Fishburne and Kenneth Branaugh. According to Janet Maslin, Fishburne was "the first black actor to play the role in a major film," overlooking William Marshall's earlier achievements. More correctly, Francesca T. Royster pointed out that "Fishburne was the first African American to be cast as Othello in a mainstream production" (65). Fishburne, who played "an unusually hot blooded Othello" (Maslin), had starred in 1993 as the volatile Ike Turner in *What's Love Got to Do With It*. Doubtless Parker took advantage of this previous association by casting Fishburne, "every inch the warrior sex symbol" (Delingpole, 24). Since Parker's film emphasized the "physical Othello," it is not surprising that "Fishburne's Othello is most evocative of a cultural figuration of the American black male in the 1990s" (Royster, 66). Extolling Fishburne's *Othello*, Amanda Haertling delighted to see a black man in the role:

> Laurence Fishburne played Othello as he should be portrayed as an honorable, strong, dignified man who is deceived by an evil and devious man, rather than as a weak man who was out of control in the first place. His performance alone is enough to make this movie a milestone in Shakespearean film production. (quoted in Leiter)

Branaugh's credits as a seasoned and respected Shakespearean actor were many, and although Fishburne did not have an extensive background in theatre, the two were well matched nonetheless.

Building on Fishburne's passion and the beauty of Irene Jacob's Desdemona, Parker developed a highly erotic *Othello*. His film was incontrovertibly rated "R." The way Parker interpreted Shakespeare's script evocatively foregrounded the sensual. Severely cutting and rearranging scenes in Shakespeare's play, Parker's film is rich in flashbacks, many of them highly graphic, intensely erotic. We see Othello giving Desdemona a long, passionate kiss during their wooing; where Shakespeare leaves us wondering about the time and place of the consummation, Parker's camera transports us back to the wedding night as the Moor crawls into a bed strewn with roses to take his naked bride; and later in the film we watch as Cassio dances suggestively with Desdemona. While under Iago's spell in act 3.3, Othello hallucinates that Desdemona and Cassio are naked in bed. As Bent argues, a naked Desdemona gives the role "a new dimension"—for "a sexual Desdemona can create sexual worries." Further physicalizing only suggestions in Shakespeare, Parker actually shows Iago having intercourse with Emilia, tupping for the camera. Parker's film thus exploits and expands the verbal and the unseen to create a series of sexual fantasies that surround Shakespeare's script, further contributing to Othello's undoing. Overall, Parker's Othello was praised for its ingenuity, though Ben Brantley complained that the film:

> . . . tends to go for the obvious. And with its labored images of Iago coolly
> studying the figures on a chessboard, its casting of the beautiful French star
> Irene Jacob as Desdemona, who can't begin to get her mouth around the lan-
> guage, and its Zeffirelli-esque bed scenes, the film can seem unintentionally
> kitschy. ("Mesmerizing," 25)

Indisputably, Fishburne offered a substantially different Othello from Olivier's in heightened blackface or Welles more formal, reserved portrait. For one thing, Fishburne was a much younger Othello than they were (or than Shakespeare's script indicates). Moreover, he gloried in his racial heritage. Wearing a hand brimming with rings, a pearl earring, and changing into various African robes, including a yellow one in act 4.1 to denote jealousy, the shaved-headed Fishburne took pride in his racial difference; he was not the outsider but, instead, was empowered because of his racial strengths. He "delivers dialogue as if it were street talk and is particularly effective convey-ing racial and sexual tensions" (Brantley, "New Video Releases," D19). Despite the Ike Turner (and putative O. J. Simpson) connections, Fishburne did not play a wild or savage Othello, though at times his responses were ter-rifyingly swift as when he held Branaugh's head under the waves crashing on the shore at the end of act 3.3 to insist on ocular proof. Another effective (and bloody) piece of business occurred in the temptation scene as Fishburne and Branaugh pierce their palms and join hands as blood brothers united in the same cause of revenge. Unlike Olivier, Fishburne cried real tears long before act 5.2, particularly in denouncing "the pity of it."

While Janet Maslin acclaimed Fishburne's performance for "its pathos and power," some critics found his interpretation wanting, in particular because his voice lacked Olivier's range and resonance. Bent judged Fish-burne a "monolithic Moor" who too rarely showed suffering. Yet in a percep-tive analysis of Fishburne's "ambiguously located Moor" who is an officer of Venice, Francesca Royster examined the film in terms of Frederick Jameson's libidinous historicism, concluding that in "the replication of past images of black masculinity" Parker enters the postmodern and "presents an alternative of blackness for a media perhaps too weary of the cultural specifics of black villains" (67). Imposing swift punishment on himself—without the prolonged trial of an O. J. Simpson—Fishburne's Othello "presents a racial menace to society that can ultimately be controlled" (Royster, 67). The benefit of Parker's *Othello* is that it "illustrates that this very act of racial erasure has its link to a history of racist strategies of containment of the other" (Royster, 67).

Trying to accommodate Fishburne's intense physicality and respond appropriately, Branaugh's Iago was constantly ingratiating himself with the Moor. Calling Branaugh's Iago a "seductively colloquial character," Maslin identified one of his key traits—believability. His concern and his compassion for his friends—Cassio, Roderigo, Desdemona, Othello—seemed honest, including the tears he shed. Branaugh's treachery was, therefore, all the more terrifying, yet he did not dispel the mystery of Iago. He was "a mask without a face behind it" (Bent).

Parker's film—like Welles's—entered cinematic history for its innovative additions to and alterations of *Othello*, the opening scene in particular. As the film begins, Othello, wearing a white mask, glides down a Venetian canal in a gondola, and as the mask is removed audiences see a black Othello, the wooer and the soldier who will eventually be tricked into thinking that everyone except him and Iago wear masks. The film ends unconventionally, too—not with the "tragic loading of the bed"—but with the bodies of Desdemona and Othello dropped in the canal, each symbolically wrapped in a white shroud and each destined for a separate journey—peaceful heaven or fiery hell. Parker creatively used symbolic settings, incorporating Welles's lattice work, bars, and shadow motifs from the 1952 film. Staging act 3.3 in two locations —indoors to outdoors—was a sign of Parker's involvement in the script. He began the temptation scene in the bowels of the fortress but then moved to the seashore with waves crashing all around, an ominous prelude to the nefarious pact between Othello and Iago and the looming threat to Desdemona's and Cassio's lives. Yet, ironically enough, Parker discarded the storm announcing Othello's and Desdemona's arrivals on Cyprus in act 2.1.

Other noteworthy *Othello*s on film include those directed by Liz White and by Frank Melton. Liz White's *Othello* is a significant but inaccessible cultural icon. It was the first film to employ an all-black cast, crew, cinematographer, and director. Not available for commercial distribution, White's *Othello* can be found in the Howard University archives in Washington, DC. White had originally directed the play in 1960, receiving high praise in the *Manchester Guardian* for Dec. 15, 1960. The film was actually shot over four years, from 1962 to 1966, but did not premiere until 1980 at Howard University. White's son, Richard Dixon, played Iago and his wife Audrey Dixon was Desdemona while White herself interpreted a Jamaican Bianca. A young but erotic Yaphet Kotto portrayed a strong and stately Othello.

The only in-depth assessment of White's achievement is in Donaldson. While the film celebrated black pride, it also was grounded in "color prejudice," much as was the all-black cast of the Howard University production of *Streetcar Named Desire* in 1988 where darker skin actors contrasted politically with lighter ones (Kolin, *Williams: Streetcar,* 141). Kotto's Othello was a dark-skinned African dressed in flowing robes while Iago and the Venetians were presented as lighter, urban American blacks. As Donaldson correctly observed, "conflicts and self-negotiations whose origins lie in the absent white culture emerge" (130). As a result, black can be the sign of "oppression" as well as "ethnic kinship" (133) between Othello and Iago. Again, as Donaldson pointed out, "The film's historical subtext, its concern with black ambivalence toward an African heritage, works finally to enrich the psychological and family dynamics of the play . . . " (143). These issues primarily resided in "the failure of father-son relationships, a failure that allows social and Oedipal conflicts . . . " (138–39). Dixon's Iago becomes a vulnerable son longing for a father and Othello sees another father figure—Brabantio—when he looks in the mirror and finds Desdemona's father looking back at him in one of the most memorable scenes in the film. Donaldson praised White for her innovative, bold film techniques—masking half of a character's face through side lights; cutting act 1 entirely only to re-incorporate it later in the film through flashbacks and quotations; and using space (high/low) to physicalize authenticity/truth and deception/lies.

In 1985, Frank Melton's *Othello,* released by Bard Productions, Ltd., featured William Marshall as the Moor and Jenny Agutter as Desdemona, with Ron Moody as Iago. (Marshall, of course, had played Othello much earlier than 1985.) This *Othello* was intended primarily as an educational film to be shown in schools, and so, not surprisingly, followed Shakespeare's text faithfully. Yet even though they appealed to the same markets, the Bard production of *Othello* never gained the publicity of the BBC televised *Othello* (1981). Beyond doubt, though, Marshall looked and acted the role of a self-controlled general, a mercenary but distinguished-looking blackamoor in the service of the Venetian government. While some critics complained that Marshall was wooden, and not as successful as Olivier had been, his majestic height and deep, melodic voice—clearly projecting an American Othello, though—at once separated him from the rest of the cast. Agutter spoke standard British English while Moody's patois was that of the underclasses—again, more American than British.

TELEVISED OTHELLOS

Othello has been no wheeling stranger to television audiences. The BBC aired several renditions of *Othello* from the 1940s through the 1980s. A successful 1950 BBC *Othello* for TV starred André Morell as Othello with Laurence Harvey as Cassio, Joan Hopkins as Desdemona, and Stephen Murray as Iago. In America, a "special two-hour television version," considerably shortened from a concurrent "live" production at the Great Lakes Shakespeare Festival, was broadcast on an Ohio station in 1962 (Shedd, 559–60).

One of the most daring televised *Othellos* appeared on Canadian TV (CBC) in 1953, starring Lorne Greene (the Cartright father on *Bonanza*) as Othello and Patrick McNee as Iago, and directed by David Greene. Josef

Furst's Iago's heavy accent did not hinder his villainy. The CBC's "first attempt at Shakespearean drama" ("Othello," *The Telegram*), this *Othello* was severely truncated for television, running less than ninety minutes, and shot in a studio only 15 by 73 feet. Alice Venezky Griffin praised the "camera work . . . to establish relationships, to reveal subtle reactions through close-ups, and to focus on significant detail" (335). This Canadian production, as indicated earlier, presented a minimally darkened Greene, hardly a blackamoor. Towering over the rest of the cast, Greene was "impressive as a figure of dignity with his rich-toned voice"; his Othello, "with his simple nobility, gained and curiously held the sympathy" of the viewers (335). Herbert Whittaker claimed Greene "did not disappoint . . . [His] deep plunging voice, the powerful physique and leonine head created a wonderfully satisfying Othello" (12), though Greene did "sacrifice subtlety of necessity." Even in his epileptic fit, Green's Othello possessed majestic strength. Peggi Loder, an innocent Desdemona, was "overshadowed by Othello's roaring strength" (Poulton). Curiously enough, Greene strangled Desdemona with the handkerchief.

One of the most significant *Othello*s made for TV was broadcast as part of the BBC's Shakespeare Series, which showed all 37 plays from 1979 to 1984. The BBC *Othello* was first seen on 12 October 1981 in a highly controversial production directed by Jonathan Miller, who also oversaw *Antony*, *Troilus*, and several other plays in the series. Three important books discuss the history, scope, and success of the BBC Shakespeare: Susan Willis, *The BBC Shakespeare Plays: Making the Televised Canon*; Henry Fenwick, *The BBC Shakespeare Plays;* and J. C. Bulman and H. R. Coursen, *Shakespeare on Television*. In his "Epilogue," Martin Wine also examines this BBC *Othello*. Lynda Boose's "Grossly Gaping Viewers and Jonathan Miller's *Othello*" is certainly helpful, as, of course, are Miller's own assessments included in his *Subsequent Performances*. Among those who endorsed Miller's work enthusiastically, Boose pinpointed the director's innovations:

> [His] *Othello* manages to work with rather than (as is too often the case) against the medium for which it was made . . . it represents a noteworthy instance of transferring/transforming Shakespeare to video. The Miller *Othello* has used the very constraints of the medium to generate some of its most inspired suggestions about not only the genesis of sexual violence and the complicity of the world coded in this play as civilized and normative (i.e., "Venice") but, finally, about the relation between the bedroom tableau to which the play leads and its voyeuristic viewers. ("Grossly Gaping," 186)

Yet despite this triumph, Miller was attacked for viewing Othello not as a tragic hero or larger-than-life African outsider but as an ordinary man who weakly succumbs to his own passions, the view of F. R. Leavis that Miller closely followed. J. C. Bulman summed up the main opposition to Miller's approach to the play and to the character: "Miller opted to do two things that made a mockery of Shakespeare's play. The first was to tone down Othello's passion, the rhetoric of tragedy, and to have Anthony Hopkins speak soliloquies *sotto voce*, reducing them to a domestic, intimate style. The second was to deny the importance of Othello's blackness" ("The BBC Shakespeare and 'House Style,'" 58). According to Miller, *Othello* was not a play about blackness but about jealousy, asserting that "blackness was 'the myth of performance over text.'" Wearing a thin veil of make-up, Hopkins looked white, "a slightly dusky Moor dressed in dandified Venetian clothing, a vision much closer to Ronald Colman than to Laurence Olivier" (Simone). (Interestingly enough, the BBC *Merchant* also presented a fairer skinned Prince of Morocco whose appearance belied Porta's curt farewell—"Let all of his complexion choose me so"). According to John J. O'Connor, "Hopkins play[ed] Othello the noble Moor as an Arab, an exotic figure plucked from a painting by Velazquez" (1981). Miller confessed that for him Othello was "a Hashemite warrior, drilled in British army manners" (159). Bulman disapprovingly pointed out "that his diminutive model for Othello was King Hussein of Jordan" ("House Style," 58).

Hopkins neither looked like a soldier nor talked like one; he was "too slight and pale" for G. M. Pearce. He wore an unfortunate (and unflattering) codpiece and a plumed helmet that detracted from his manliness. In stature, Hopkins did not project the epic hero, the noble Moor, as Paul Robeson or Laurence Fishburne did; his physique was more Prufrockian than Olympian. Hopkins was also one of the most lachrymose Othellos on film or in television —sobbing in the brothel scene and weeping in response to Iago's painful rendition of Desdemona's nights of stolen lust. O'Connor quipped: "When Mr. Hopkins explodes emotionally he seems to slide incomprehensibly into the accent of his native Wales."

Though far from being universally praised, Hoskins's Iago undoubtedly was the star of the BBC *Othello*. "Jonathan Miller wanted a play called Iago," remarked Simone. Miller envisioned Iago as a "working class sergeant under much stress because of social frustration" (*Subsequent*, 60). Hoskins easily deceived Desdemona, Cassio, Othello and even the audience through his credible and intimate asides and soliloquies. The audience rapidly sensed that Hoskins's Iago valued friendship above all else. Yet Dave Richards of the *Washington Post* ("Moor's the Pity") declared Hoskins's Iago to be "loutish, vulgar . . . appear[ing] to have no neck and a dumpy body, which suggests [together with] his sniggling laugh, that Iago is the eighth dwarf—Nasty." Hoskins's laughter was the focal point of much attention from the reviewers. Cast as a "practical joker" (Miller), Hoskins's Iago is not cruelly cold or removed from the suspecting souls he wants to destroy; instead, he is the arch railer, the mocker whose laughter terrorizes at the most painful spaces of the play, as when Hoskins laughs in act 5.1 while the bloody deeds he has engineered unfold before him and the audience, and his mocking laughter, not obdurate silence, frame his exit. Russell Davies succinctly panned Hoskins's Iago—he was "brutish and short, and making Iago a giggling psychopath reduced the tragedy to victimization." Nonetheless, Hoskins's physicality was powerful; when he swears allegiance to Othello at the end of act 3.3, he grabs the Moor's neck in a terrifying death grip, the two of them in a collaborative desire for murderous revenge.

Miller's camera work reflected both the strengths and limitations of a televised script. Seeing *Othello* as a "closet play," Miller avoided outdoor shots, as were used by Welles, Olivier, or Fishburne. During the storm scene (act 2.1), for example, audiences caught only a glimpse of the sea through a window. Like Welles, though, Miller centered much of his action in a maze of rooms and hallways within the fortress. The effect was suffocatingly claustrophobic, another sign of the "domestication of Othello" (Simone). Eavesdropping was a vital part of the architecture of Miller's *Othello;* there was no escaping. Accordingly, Miller's camera often single-mindedly centered on Othello, fixed in a given scene; inviting, pushing the audience into the Moor's psyche. Yet in the most intimate scene in the play (act 5.2), Miller deprived BBC audiences of "the tragic loading of the bed" and instead zoomed in on a "laughing Iago in place of the site of desire" (Boose, "Grossly Gaping").

An acclaimed televised version of *Othello* was done in 1989 by Trevor Nunn (who also directed *Cats*, *Les Miserables*, etc.). This *Othello* has been analyzed at length by Vaughan (*Othello: Contextual*) and by Holland. The former artistic director of the Royal Shakespeare Company, Nunn televised an *Othello* production he had earlier overseen at the RSC's sparse and intimate stage—The Other Place—to create the claustrophobic, insular world in which Iago fells Othello. Peter Holland precisely identified the reason for Nunn's success:

> Nunn's *Othello* moved effortlessly from the Other Place to the television, its domesticity of scale and fascination with the social interaction of the characters in a social circumstance far more detailed, far more realistic than the conventions of theatrical Shakespeare. The sustained close attention of the stage-version was conceived for small spaces in which the audience is, in theatrical terms, as close to the action as to a television screen. It translated perfectly to television. (52)

Holland concluded: "Nunn's *Othello* is much more than a record of a stage production; it is a perfect example of filming Shakespeare theatrically" (53). Olivier's cinematic translation from the stage was not nearly as successful as Nunn's to the television screen. Important discussions of Nunn's *Othello* can be found in Barbara Hodgson ("Race—ing *Othello*")*, and* Vaughan's "*Othello* for the 1990's: Trevor Nunn's 1989 Royal Shakespeare Company Production" in *Othello: A Contextual History*, and Richard Burt in Boose and Burt, (32–34). An extremely valuable interview with Nunn can be found at http//www.achievement.org/autodoc/page/nun0int-2.

Hodgson analyzes Nunn's accomplishments in terms of a post-colonial critique of the Empire. The set for Nunn's *Othello* was reminiscent of a U.S. Civil War fort or a nineteenth-century colonial outpost that might be anywhere in Britain's Empire (25). It was a world of Victorian white supremacy, the racist creeds upon which the Empire was founded and promulgated. Like Janet Suzman's *Othello* in 1988, Nunn's work "evokes particular colonialist locale" of the Empire (Hodgson, 31). Act 1 was set in a Victorian Venice, where gentlemen senators discussed politics over brandy, plentifully available in handsome decanters. Brabantio was a stern but loving patriarch who despairs at the thought of a black son-in-law. Ingeniously, Clive Swift who played Brabantio also doubled as Gratiano, another reminder of the omnipresent Victorian father. Acts 2–5, on a military post, are consumed with barracks life, rituals and rivalries. Because Nunn wanted to capture the drill by which the Empire ruled, his televised *Othello* was attuned to military rituals of saluting, clicking heels, sounding bugle calls, and straightening beds. Ian McKellen's Iago is a buttoned-down regimental man given to "obsessive tidiness" (Hodgson, 32). He scrupulously cleans and straightens up throughout the play; for example, he washes out a basin in which Cassio vomits in act 2. McKellen goes by the book and chaffs having to serve under black Othello. Audiences saw McKellen's Iago sitting on the edge of Cassio's cot in act 2.3 consoling him and overhearing his restless talk as the lieutenant sleeps, which becomes matter for Cassio's betrayal dream that Iago reported to Othello in act 3.3.

Nunn's choice of Willard White to play Othello was enthusiastically applauded. A Jamaican-American, White had the stature and voice to play a brave and dignified Othello. An opera singer, White used his sonorous baritone voice and large impressive frame (he was over six feet) to project physically the sway of Othello's power. According to Barbara Hodgson, White's Othello "ocupp[ies] two alien categories" (31)—"The Black Other" and the actor whose name is eponymously White. The actor played "a very English Othello whose exotic origins and sexuality are buttoned up and whose assimilation seems (comfortably) complete" (31). White wore a waistcoat, and epaulettes adorned his stiff, formal military tunic. He was very much the gentlemanly Moor. In the temptation scene, for instance, White sat at a writing desk and, as Iago's poison spews out, ripped up the papers he was working on, only to have McKellen's Iago try to reassemble them, a stage business reminiscent of Fechter's and Salvini's nineteenth-century Othellos. In act 4.1, White's Othello eavesdrops through slats in an upper window rather than hiding tremulously behind a post or a prop on stage. Presenting a much more controlled Othello than other film or television versions, White was neither histrionic (as Olivier) nor erotic (as Fishburne). In fact, one criticism of his performance was that "Othello's sexuality is absent from the representation until the close" (Hodgson, 33). But, ironically, White's murder of Desdemona in act 5.2 might be recorded as the most erotic to date. After he suffocates her and inflicts his own death wound, White mounts Desdemona as if for inter-course, writhes on top of her, and then dies.

McKellen's Iago was a martinet, "tightly reined in . . . an inscrutable, smiling psychopath with a Fuhrer moustache, dead eyes and officious man-ners who is consumed by sexual and professional jealousies" (Hodgson, 31). McKellen's concept of Iago doubtless spilled over into his representation of Richard III years later. McKellen's Iago was a robust spokesperson for colo-nial privilege. Among the most private Iagos, McKellen portrayed a repressed, neurotic villain whose cleanliness and military hairsplitting concealed a deep hatred for a black general and for women, too. He spoke with crisp military diction, giving orders in act 2.1, for instance, or at the end of acts 2.3 and 5.1, with drill sergeant precision and authority. Yet the hate built up in his Iago had been physically repressed by circumstances. He actually believed Emilia cuckolded him and seethes when Cassio kisses her in act 2.1. Unlike many previous Iagos, McKellen barely touched Othello, though he was no stranger to other characters—Cassio or Roderigo. At the end of the play, McKellen nei-ther smiled nor laughed but folds his arms, coldly staring at the audience as if he had just completed a military assignment and was waiting for new orders, new opportunities for villainy. Provocatively, Iago controlled the camera with "framing . . . that stresses his omnipresent voyeurism" (Hodgson 32). Close-ups of McKellen brought home how masterfully penetrating Iago's evil was.

The role of women in Nunn's barracks setting was perilous. Misogyny raged. Imogen Stubbs's Desdemona was a pristine and ebullient girl who viewed marriage to Othello as a way to see the Empire, but she was too easily swept into the turmoil of Iago's calumny. When she was "actually felled by Othello's blows it stop[ed] one's breath" (Davies, 209). Emilia, played by Zoe Wannamaker, was classified a "battered wife" by Coursen ("The Case for Black Othello," 159); Iago was always cruel to her, even in his lovemaking. Sean Baker's Cassio behaved like an upper-class snob who disdained too much contact with those of lesser rank. Interestingly enough, he gives Desde-mona a box of chocolates which she hurriedly conceals from Othello in act 4. Cassio's callous treatment of Bianca, played by an actor of color, further rein-forced Nunn's message about the racial and gender economics of colonialism. Michael Grandage captured a gullible Roderigo, dressed in a dandy's suit, complete with bow tie, and a thriving, feminized presence. He was dependent on Iago's advice and touch, for McKellen was constantly massaging, bandag-ing, or thumping him. Later in this volume John Ford assesses Roderigo in light of gender and racial roles.

OTHELLO IN OTHER MEDIA

Othello has been transformed to other types of media. Perhaps the most famous adaptations of *Othello* are the operas by Rossini, produced in Naples in 1816, and by Verdi for La Scala in Milan, 1887. With a libretto by Arrigo Boito, Verdi's *Otello* departs significantly from Shakespeare's plot, but contains a haunting, frenzied, and at times enchanted musical score. *Othello* has also been adapted for the ballet many times. Limon did "The Moor's Pavane" in 1949 and Kirk Peterson performed an *Othello* in 1985. In 1997–98 Lar Lubovitch's *Othello* was jointly performed by the American Ballet and the San Francisco Ballet. It starred Yuri Possokhov, formerly of the Bolshoi Ballet in Moscow, as Othello and Yan Chen as Desdemona with Parrish Maynard as Iago. It was scored by Elliot B. Goldenthal. Lubovitch's work has been highly praised. Octavio Roca, for example, exclaimed:

> Lubovitch speaks his own language and speaks it persuasively, with a strong American accent. His "Othello" is traditional in that it aims at enriching the canon rather than rejecting it. But it is also a radical dance, both in its negation of fashionable Balanchinean abstraction and its unembarrassed embrace of the theatrical values of modern dance. Inspired at every step by Goldenthal's music, Lubovitch achieves archetypal ideals. He explores the universal themes of Shakespeare's tragedy with sympathy and clarity through movement that is always drenched in dramatic truth. ("Everything and Moor")

Among less serious transformations of Shakespeare's tragedy is a cartoon version in *Shakespeare's Animated Tales*, broadcast on Showtime in 2000, increasing *Othello*'s appeal to a mass market audience. There is even an "updated" *Othello* (2000) with an all-teen cast http://www.us.imdb.com/ Title?0184791. Oscar Zarate created "a full-text comic book version of the play" analyzed in detail by James P. Lusardi who notes: "Zarate's *Othello* is replete with scenes that appropriate the techniques of stage director and filmmaker. While continuing to notice these, [Lusardi] concentrate[d] on effects that are special to the comic-book medium of production." Finally, a spoof of both the "Newlywed Game," hosted by Bob Eubanks, and Shakespeare's play is found in Carly Sommerstein (130–31). "What a pity that we can call these delicate creatures ours / And not their appetites!"

WORKS CITED

Adamson, W. D. "Unpinned or Undone? Desdemona's Critics and the Problem of Sexual Innocence." *Shakespeare Studies* 13 (1980): 169–86.

Adelman, Janet. "Iago's Alter Ego: Race as Projection in *Othello*." *Shakespeare Quarterly* 48 (1997): 125–44.

Alexander, Catherine and Stanley Wells, eds. *Shakespeare and Race*, Cambridge: Cambridge Univ. Press, 2001.

Anderson, Lucia. "Othello." *Free-Lance Star* [Fredrickburg, VA], 15 Dec. 1990.

Anikst, Alexander. "Review of Olivier's Othello." *Sovetskaya Kultura* (1964); rpt. in Kenneth Tynan, ed. *"Othello": William Shakespeare: The National Theatre Production.* New York: Stein and Day, 1967. 108.

Atkinson, Brooks. "Othello." *New York Times,* 30 June 1957:2: 1.

———. "Shakespeare Festival Opens with *Othello.*" *New York Times* 24 June 1957: 19:2.

Auden, W. H. "The Joker in the Pack."*The Dyer's Hand and Other Essays.* New York: Random House, 1962. 246–72.

Ball, Robert Hamilton. *Shakespeare on Silent Film.* London: Allen and Urwin, 1968.

Barnes, Clive. "A Noble Othello." *New York Post* 4 Feb. 1982.

———. "Simplicity Underlines Play's Direction." *New York Times* 22 June 1970: 43.

Barthelemy, Anthony Gerard. *Black Face, Maligned Race: The Representation of Blacks in English Drama From Shakespeare to Swinburne.* Baton Rouge: Louisiana State University Press, 1987.

———. *Critical Essays on Shakespeare's "Othello."* New York: G.K. Hall, 1994.

Bartels, Emily. "Making More of the Moor: Aaron, Othello, and Renaissance Refashioning of Race." *Shakespeare Quarterly* 41 (1990): 433-54.

Bayley, John. *The Characters of Love: A Study of the Literature of Personality.* London: Constable, 1960.

Belsey, Catherine. "Desire's Excess and English Renaissance Theatre: *Edward II, Troilus and Cressida,* and *Othello.*" *Erotic Politics: Desire on the Renaissance Stage.* Ed. Susan Zimmerman. New York: Routledge, 1992. 84–102.

Bennett, William E. "Shakespeare's Iago: The Kierkegaardian Aesthete." *Upstart Crow* 5 (Fall 1984): 156–59.

Bent, Geoffrey. "Three Green-Eyed Monsters: Acting as Applied Criticism in Shakespeare's *Othello,*" *The Antioch Review* 56 (Summer 1998): 358–73.

Bentley, Eric. *What is Theatre.* New York: Atheneum, 1968.

Berger, Harry, Jr. "Impertinent Trifling: Desdemona's Handkerchief." *Shakespeare Quarterly* 47 (1996): 235–50.

Berson, Misha. "Shakespeare Fest: Aiming Big at Ashland." *Seattle Times* 12 March 1998: M1, M6.

Bevington, David. "Kabuki *Othello* at the Wisdom Bridge Theatre, Chicago." *Shakespeare Quarterly* 38 (1987): 211–14.

Billington, Michael, "Review of Sam Mendes *Othello.*" *The Guardian* 18 Sept. 1997.

Blanchard, Jayne M. "Othello Stereotypically Shakespeare." *Saint Paul Pioneer Press* 17 Oct. 1993: E1

———. "The Out of Towners." *Saint Paul Pioneer Press,* "Showtime," 10 Oct. 1993: E:1.

Bloom, Harold. *Shakespeare: The Invention of the Human.* New York: Riverhead Books, 1999.

Bodkin, Maud. *Archetypal Patterns in Poetry: Psychological Studies of Imagination.* Oxford: Oxford, University Press, 1934.

Bonnard, Georges. "Are Othello and Desdemona Innocent or Guilty?" *English Studies* 30 (Oct. 1949): 175–186.

Boose, Lynda E. "Othello's Handkerchief: The Recognition and Pledge of Love." *English Literary Renaissance* 5 (1975): 360–74.

————. "Grossly Gaping Viewers and Jonathan Miller's *Othello.*" *Shakespeare and the Movie: Popularizing the Plays on Film, TV, and Video.* Eds. Lynda E. Boose and Richard Burt. New York: Routledge, 1997. 186–97.

————. "'Let it Be Hid': Renaissance Pornography, Iago, and Audience Response." *Autour d'Othello.* Ed. Richard Marienstras and Dominque Guy-Blanquet. Paris: ERLA è Institut Charles V, 1987. 135–43.

Bradley, A. C. *Shakespearean Tragedy:Lectures on Hamlet, Othello, King Lear, and Macbeth,* (1904), rpt. New York: Meridian Books, 1955.

Brantley, Ben. "A Down to Earth Iago, Evil Made Ordinary." *New York Times* April 1998: B7.

————. "Mesmerizing Men of Ill Will." *New York Times* 21 Jan. 1996: 2:1.

————. "New Video Releases." *New York Times* 26 Feb. 1996: D: 19.

Brode, Douglas. *Shakespeare in the Movies: From the Silent Era to Shakespeare in Love.* New York: Oxford University Press, 2000.

Brown, John Russell, ed. *Shakespeare's Othello.* New York: Harbrace Theatre Edition, 1973.

Bruckner, D. J. R. "New Clarity from a Colorblind 'Othello.'" *New York Times* 2 Feb. 2000: E5.

Bryden, Ronald. "*Othello.*" *New Statesman* (1964); rpt. in Kenneth Tyanan, ed. *Othello: The National Theatre Production.* New York: Stein and Day. 1967.

Bulman, J. C. "The BBC Shakespeare and the 'House Style.'" In J. C. Bulman and H. R. Coursen. *Shakespeare on Television.* Hanover, NH: University Press of New England, 1988. 50–60.

————. and H. R. Coursen. *Shakespeare on Television: An Anthology of Essays and Reviews.* Hanover, NH: University Press of New England, 1988.

Bunke, Joan. "Star Power Fuels Guthrie's Othello." *Des Moines Register* Apr. 12, 1993.

Burgess, C. F. "Othello's Occupation." *Shakespeare Quarterly* 26 (1975): 208–11.

Burke, Kenneth. "*Othello*: An Essay to Illustrate a Method." *Hudson Review* 4 (1951): 165–207.

Butler-Evans, Elliot. "'Haply, for I am black': *Othello* and the Semiotics of Race and Otherness." *Othello: New Essays by Black Writers.* Ed. Mythili Kaul. Washington, DC: Howard University Press, 1997. 139–50.

Byrne, Terrry. "Trinity's *Othello* is a Monster of a Production." *Boston Herald* 18 Sept. 1999.

Calderwood, James. "Appalling Property in *Othello.*" *University of Toronto Quarterly* 57 (1988): 353–75.

————. *The 'Properties' of Othello.* Amherst: University of Massachusetts Press: 1989.

Callaghan, Dympha. "'Othello was a White Man': Properties of Race on Shakespeare's Stage." *Alternative Shakespeare.* Ed. Terence Hawkes. 2nd ed. London: Routledge, 1996. 192–215.

Camden, Carroll. "Iago on Women." *JEGP* 48 (1949): 57–71.

Carey, Robin B. "Oregon Shakespeare Festival." *Shakespeare Quarterly* 24 (Autumn 1973): 439.

Carlisle, Carol J. *Shakespeare from the Greenroom: Actors' Criticisms of Four Major Tragedies.* Chapel Hill: University North Carolina Press, 1969.

Carmin, Christine. "Tainted Love." *Sentinel* [Santa Cruz], "Spotlight," 7 Aug. 1998:9.

Cartwell, Don. "Iago as Shaman." *Theatre Southwest* 12 (October 1985): 25–30.

Cartwright, Kent. "Audience Reponse and the Denouement of *Othello.*" *Othello: New Perspectives.* Eds. Virginia Mason Vaughan and Kent Cartwright. Rutherford, NJ: Fairleigh Dickinson University Press, 1991. 160–76.

Cassels, Peter. "*Othello.*" *Bay Windows* 17 (Sept. 23 1999).

Chopra, Vikram. "*Othello.*" *Shakespeare Bulletin* 12 (Winter 1994): 41–42.

Clay, Carolyn. "Sound and Fury." *Providence Phoenix* 17 Sept. 1999.

Coale, Sam. "Trinity Presents Powerful Othello." *East Side* (Oct. 1999): 3, 27.

Coe, Richard. "Great Roles that Measure Players." *Washington Post* 4 April 1982. G1.

Collins, William B. "A Contemporary *Othello* at the Folger." *Philadephia Inquirer* 7 Dec. 1990.

Connolly, Thomas F. "Shakespeare and the Double Man." *Shakespeare Quarterly* 1 (1950): 30–35.

Cook, Ann Jennalie. "The Design for Desdemona: Doubt Raised and Resolved."*Shakespeare Studies* 13 (1980): 187–96.

Cookson, Linda and Ben Loughrey, eds. *William Shakespeare. Othello.* Longman Critical Essays Series. Harlow: Longman, 1991.

Core, Susan. "Life on the London Stage." *Sewanee Review* 105 (Summer 1997): 447.

Council, Norman. *When Honour's at the Stake.* London: Allen and Unwin, 1973.

Coursen, H. R. "The Case for Black Othello." *Shakespearean Performance as Interpretation.* Newark: University of Delaware Press, 1992. 152–62.

Cowhig, Ruth. "Blacks in English Renaissance Drama and the Role of Shakespeare's *Othello.*" *The Black Presence in English Literature.* Ed. David Dabydeen. Manchester: Manchester University Press, 1985. 1–25.

———. "Ira Aldridge in Manchester." *Theatre Research International* 3 (1986): 239-48.

———. "The Importance of Othello's Race." *Journal of Commonwealth Literature* 12, no. 2 (1977): 153–61.

Craig, Sheryl. "'Shakespeare Abused': The Battered Wife Syndrome in *Othello.*" *Publications of the Missouri Philological Association* 23 (1998): 1–11.

Cunningham, Dennis. "*Othello.*" WCBS. *New York Theatre Critics Reviews,* 3 Feb. 1982: 377.

Daniels, Robert. "*Othello.*" *Variety* 20 April 1998: 55.

David, Richard. "Stratford 1954." *Shakespeare Quarterly* 5 (Autumn 1954): 385–94.

Davies, Anthony. "'Othello' and "King Lear' on Film." *Shakespeare and the Moving Image: The Plays on Film and Television.* Eds. Anthony Davies and Stanley Wells. Cambridge: Cambridge University Press, 1994. 196–210.

Davies, Russell. "How Bizarre to Meet Mr. Carson." *London Times.* 11 Oct. 1981: 39.

Davison, Peter B. *Othello.* The Critics Debate Series. Atlantic Highlands, NJ: Humanities Press International, 1988.

Dean, Leonard. *A Casebook on Othello.* New York: Crowell, 1961.

Delingpole, James. "Upstaged by the Bad Guy." *London Daily Telegraph* 16 Feb. 1996.

Dessen, Alan C. "'Let it be hid': Re-Scripting Shakespeare in 1994." *Shakespeare Bulletin* 13 (Winter 1995): 7 –13.

DeVine, Laurence. "Spiritless 'Othello' Provides a Real Letdown." *Detroit Free Press* 9 Sept. 1987: 4C.

Devlin, Albert J. and Nancy M. Tischler, eds. *The Selected Letters of Tennessee Williams.* Vol. 1. 1920-1945. New York: New Directions, 2000.

Dollimore, Jonathan. *Sexual Dissidence.* Oxford: Oxford University Press, 1991.

Donahue, Ann Marie. "Riveting Thompson Leads Pack in Trinity High-Energy *Othello.*" *Boston Globe* 11 Sept. 1999: F3.

Donaldson, Peter B. "Mirrors and M/Others: The Welles *Othello.*" *Shakespearean Films/Shakespearean Directors.* Boston: Hyman, 1990. 97–107.

Drakakis, John. "The Engendering of Toads: Patriarchy and the Problem of Subjectivity in Shakespeare's Othello." *Shakespeare Jahrbuch* 124 (1988): 62-80.

Draper, John. *The Othello of Shakespeare's Audience.* Paris, 1952; rpt. New York, Octagon, 1966.

Duberman, Martin. *Paul Robeson: A Biography.* New York: New Press, 1995.

Duncan-Jones, Katherine. "Circling the Square." *TLS* 14 May 1999: 13.

Ehrlich, Scott. *Paul Robeson: Singer and Actor.* New York: Chelsea House, 1988.

Eliot, T. S. "Shakespeare and the Stoicism of Seneca" (1927); rpt. in *Selected Essays of T. S. Eliot.* New York: Harcourt, 1960.

Erickson, Peter, and Clark Hulse, eds. *Early Modern Visual Culture: Representation, Race, and Empire in Renaissance England.* Philadelphia: University of Pennsylvania Press, 2000.

———. and Coppelia Kahn, eds. *Shakespeare's "Rough Magic": Renaissance Essays in Honor of C. L. Barber.* Newark: University of Deleware Press, 1980.

Evans, G. Blakemore, et. al, eds. *The Riverside Shakespeare.* Boston: Houghton Mifflin, 1997.

Everett, Barbara. "Spanish Othello: The Making of Shakespeare's Moor." *Shakespeare Survey* 35 (1982): 101–112.

Farjeon, Herbert. *The Shakespearean Scene: Dramatic Criticism.* New York: Hutchinson, 1949.

Farley-Hill, David. *Shakespeare and the Rival Playwrights.* London: Routledge, 1990.

Fenwick, Henry. *The BBC Plays.* London: BBC, 1981.

Ferguson, Margaret W., Maureen Quilligan, and Nancy S. Vickers, eds. *Rewriting the Renaissance: The Discourse of Sexual Difference in Early Modern Europe.* Chicago: University of Chicago Press, 1986.

Frye, Susan. "Staging Women's Relationist Textiles in Shakespeare's *Othello and Cyberline.*" *Early Modern Visual Culture: Representation, Race, and Empire in Renaissance England.* Eds. Peter Erickson and Clark Hulse. Philadelphia: University of Pennsylvania Press, 2000.

Fultz, Lucille. "Devouring Discourses: Desire and Seduction in *Othello.*" *Othello: New Essays by Black Writers.* Ed. Mythili Kaul. Washington DC: Howard University Press, 1997. 189–204.

Furness, Horace Howard. *Othello: A New Variorum Edition.* Philadelphia: Lippincott, 1877.

Galyean, Marie Devine. "Dynamic Drama Features Powerful Performances." *Idaho Press Tribune* 20 July 1986.

Gardner, Helen. "*Othello*: A Restrospect, 1900–1967." *Shakespeare Survey* 21 (1968): 1–11.

Garner, S. N. "Shakespeare's Desdemona." *Shakespeare Studies* 9 (1976): 233–52.

Gauntlett, Mark. "The Perishable Body of the Unpoetic: A. C. Bradley Performs *Othello." Shakespeare Survey* 47 (1994): 71–80.

Genster, Julia. "Lieutenancy, Standing In, and *Othello*." *ELH* 57 (1990): 785–809.

Ghazoul, Ferial J. "The Arabization of *Othello*." *Comparative Litearture* 50 (1998): 1–31.

Gill, Glenda E. "The Triumphs and Struggles of Earle Hyman in Traditional and Non-Traditional Roles." *The Journal of American Drama and Theatre* 13 (Winter 2001): 52–72.

Gill, LaVerne. "Shakespeare's Othello, the Moor's Play." *National Chronicle* 7 Dec. 1990.

Giuliano, Mike. "Too Tough: Othello." *Columbia Flier* 20 Dec. 1990.

Gohlke, Madelon. "'All that is spoke is marred': Language and Consciousness in *Othello*." *Women's Studies* 9 (1982): 157–76.

Granville-Barker, Harley. *Prefaces to Shakespeare.* Vol. IV. Princeton: Princeton University Press, 1946.

Gratton, Claudio. "Kabuki Instructor Translates Tradition to West." *The Daily Illionian* [University of Illinois] 3 Feb. 1988: 21–22.

Greenblatt, Stephen. *Renaissance Self Fashioning from More to Shakespeare.* Chicago: University of Chicago Press, 1980.

Greer, Germaine. "Black Ram: Germaine Greer on Othello as Nigger." *Times Educational Supplement* 3328 (1980): 24.

Grennan, Eamon. "The Women's Voices in *Othello*: Speech, Song, and Silence." *Shakespeare Quarterly* 38 (1987): 275–92.

Griffin, Alice Venezky. "Shakespeare Through the Camera's Eye." *Shakespeare Quarterly* 17 (1953): 334–36.

Guitierrez, Nancy. "Witchcraft and Adultery in *Othello*: Strategies of Subversion." *Playing with Gender: A Renaissance Pursuit.* Eds. Jean R. Brink and Maryanne C. Horowitz. Urbana: University of Illinois Press, 1991. 3-18.

Gussow, Mel. "Stage: Raul Julia Portrays Othello." *New York Times* 9 Aug.1979: C: 15.

———. "Theatre: Charles S. Dutton 'Othello' at Yale." *New York Times* 2 March 1986: I: 64.

Habicht, Werner. *Shakespeare and the German Imagination.* Hartford: Stephen Austin, 1994.

Hall, Joan Lord. *Othello: A Guide to the Play.* Westport, CT: Greenwood, 1999.

Hankey, Julie, ed. *Othello: Plays in Performance.* Bristol: Bristol Classical Press, 1987.

Hapgood, Robert. "A Playgoer's Journey: From Shakespeare to Japanese Classical Theatre and Back." *Shakespeare and the Japanese Stage.* Eds. Takashi Sasyama et. al. Cambridge: Cambridge University Press, 1998.

———. "Two Othellos." *Drama Critique.* (Winter 1965): 32.

Harbage, Alfred. *William Shakespear: A Reader's Guide.* New York: Farrar, 1970.

Hazlitt, William. *Characters of Shakespeare's Plays. Complete Works of William Hazlitt.* Ed. P. Howe. London: Dent, 1930.

Heilman, Robert B. "Dr. Iago and His Potions." *Virginia Quarterly Review* 28 (Autumn 1952): 568–84.

———.*Magic in the Web: Action and Language in Othello.* Lexington: University of Kentucky Press, 1956.

Hill, Errol. *Shakespeare in Sable: A History of Black Shakespearean Actors.* Amherst: University of Massachusetts Press, 1984.

Hodgson, Barbara. "Race-ing *Othello*: Re-engendering White-Out." *Shakespeare, the Movie: Popularizing the Plays on Film, TV, and Video.* Eds. Lynda E. Boose and Richard Burt. New York: Routledge, 1997. 23–44.

Hodgson, James. "Desdemona's Handkerchief as an Emblem of Her Reputation." *Texas Studies in Language and Literature* 19 (1977): 312–22.

Hogan, Patrick C. "*Othello,* Racism, and Despair." *College Language Association Journal* 41 (1998): 431–51.

Holland, Peter. "Two Dimensional Shakespeare: *Othello* and *King Lear* on Film." *Shakespeare and the Moving Images: The Plays on Film and Television.* Eds. Lynda Boose and Richard Burt, Cambridge: Cambridge University Press, 1994.

Homan, Sidney. "Iago's Aesthetics: *Othello* and Shakespeare's Portrait of an Artist." *Shakespeare Studies* 5 (1970): 141-48.

———. *When the Theatre Turns to Itself.* Lewisburg, PA: Bucknell University Press, 1986.

Hopkins, Lisa. "The Representation of Narrative: What Happens in *Othello.*" *Journal X* 1 (Spring 1997): 159–74.

Honigmann, E. A., ed. *Othello.* 3rd ed. The Arden Shakespeare Walton-on-Thames: Nelson, 1997

———. *Shakespeare: Seven Tragedies: The Dramatists Manipulation of Audience.* London: Macmillan, 1976.

Howard, Jean. *Shakespeare's Art of Orchestration: Stage Techniques and Audience Response.* Urbana: University of Illinois Press, 1984.

Howlett, Kathy M. *Framing Shakespeare on Film.* Athens: Ohio University Press, 2000.

Hoyt, Melanie. "Shakespeare Festival Offers Tragedy." *Idaho Press Tribune* 11 Aug. 2000: 40.

Hunter, G. K. "Othello and Colour Prejudice." *Proceedings of the British Academy* 53 (1967): 139–63.

Hunter, Robert G. *Shakespeare and the Mystery of God's Judgments.* Athens: University of Georgia Press, 1976.

Hurlbert, Dan. "All is not well under the stars: 'Othello' Works, 'All's Well' Doesn't." *Dallas Morning News* 12 Sept. 1982.

Hyman, Stanley Edgar. *Iago: Some Approaches to the Illusion of His Motivation.* New York: Atheneum, 1970.

———. "Portraits of the Artist: Iago and Prospero." *Shenandoah* 21 (1970–71): 18–42.

Itzhaki, Yedida. "Othello and Woyzeck as Tragic Heroes According to Aristotle and Hegel." *Strands Afar Remote: Israeli Perspectives on Shakespeare.* Ed. Avraham Oz. Newark, DE: University of Delaware Press, 1998. 204–31.

Jackson, Russell. "Shakespeare at Stratford-upon-Avon: Summer and Winter, 1999-2000." *Shakespeare Quarterly* 51 (Summer 2000): 217-29.

Johnson, Barry. "Othello in Love." *The Sunday Oregonian* 17 March 1999.

Johnson-Haddad, Miranda. "The Shakespeare Theatre at the Folger." *Shakespeare Quarterly* 30 (Spring 1990): 472–84.

Jones, Eldred. *Othello's Countrymen: The African in English Renaissance Drama.* Oxford: Oxford University Press, 1965.

Jones, Emrys. *Scenic Form in Shakespeare.* Oxford: Oxford University Press, 1971.

Jorgens, Jack. *Shakespeare and Film.* Bloomington: Indiana University Press, 1977.

Jorgensen, Paul. "Military Rank in Shakespeare." *Huntington Library Quarterly* 14 (1950): 17–41.

Kahan, Jeffrey. "Nōh Shakespeare: An Interview with Kuniyoshi Munakata." *Shakespeare Bulletin* 14 (Winter 1996): 26–28.

Kahn, Coppelia. *Man's estate: Masculine Identity in Shakespeare.* Berkeley: Univ. of California Press, 1981.

Kalem, T. A. "KoEd in Venice." *Time.* 15 Feb. 1982.

Kaul, Mythili, ed. *Othello: New Essays by Black Writers.* Washington, DC: Howard University Press, 1997.

———. "Background: Black or Tawny? Stage Representations of Othello from 1604 to the Present." *Othello: New Essays by Black Writers.* Ed. Mythili Kaul. Washington DC: Howard University Press, 1997.

Kay, Carol McGinnis. "Othello's Need for Mirrors." *Shakespeare Quarterly* 34 (Autumn 1983): 261–70.

Kemper, Steve. "Middling Moor." *New Haven Advocate* 5 March 1986: 27

Kennedy, Dennis. "Introduction: Shakespeare Without His Language." *Foreign Shakespeare.* Ed. Dennis Kennedy. Cambridge: Cambridge University Press, 1993. 1–18.

———. *Looking at Shakespeare: A Visual History of Twentieth-Century Performance.* Cambridge: Cambridge University Press, 1995.

Kernan, Alvin. "*Othello*: An Introduction." *The Tragedies.* Ed. Alfred Harbage.Englewood Cliffs, NJ: Prentice-Hall, 1964.

Kerr, Walter. "The Jones-Plummer *Othello* is Twice Blessed." *New York Times* 14 Feb. 1982: 2:1.

———. "*Othello*." *New York Times* 28 June 1970: 2: 1.

Kingston, Jeremy. "Dark Reeds Played to Thrill." *London Times* 18 Sept. 1997.

Knight, G. Wilson. *The Wheel of Fire.* London: Metheun, 1949.

Kolin, Philip, C. *The Elizabethan Stage Doctor as a Dramatic Convention.* Salzburg: Institut für Englische Sprache und Literatur, 1974.

———. *Williams: A Streetcar Named Desire.* Plays in Production Series. Cambridge: Cambridge University Press, 2000.

Kott, Jan. *Shakespeare Our Contemporary.* New York: Doubleday, 1966.

Kreps, Barbara Irene. "The Failure of Reason in *Othello:* A Study of Iago's Subversive Technique." *RLMC* 38 (1985): 145–73.

Lamb, Charles. *Works of Charles and Mary Lamb.* Ed. E.V. Lucas. London: Metheun, 1903.

Leavis, F. R. "Diabolical Intellect and the Noble Hero; or The Sentimentalist Othello." 1937; rpt. in *The Common Pursuit.* Harmondsworth: Peregrine, 1952.

Leiter, Samuel L. *Shakespeare Around the Globe: A Guide to Notable Postwar Revivals.* Westport, CT: Greenwood, 1986.

Lewis, Wyndham. *The Lion and the Fox.* London: Metheun, 1951.

Lingui, Yang. "1994 Shanghai International Shakespeare Festival." *Shakespeare Newsletter* 44 (Winter 1994): 79.

Loomba, Ania. *Gender, Race, and Renaissance Drama.* Manchester: Manchester University Press, 1989.

———. *Shakespeare and Race.* Oxford Shakespeare Topics. London: Oxford University Press, 2001.

"Love Without Borders." *Newsweek* 18 Sept. 2000: 62–63.

Lower, Charles B. "Othello as Black on Southern Stages, Then and Now." *Shakespeare in the South.* Ed. Philip C. Kolin. Jackson: University Press of Mississippi, 1983. 199–228.

Lusardi, James P. "Icon Shakespeare: Oscar Zarate's *Othello.*" *Shakespeare Yearbook* 11 (2000): 136–53.

Lyons, Donald. *"Othello." Wall Street Journal* 17 April 1998: W12.

Malone, Father John. "Wrong for Othello but Guthrie Effort Possible." *Catholic Bulletin* [Minneapolis] 4 Nov. 1993.

MacLiammoir, Michael. *Put Money in Thy Purse: The Filming of Orson Welles's Othello.* London: Metheun, 1952.

Manvell, Roger. *Shakespeare and the Film.* New York: Praeger, 1971.

Marienstras, Richard. *Le Procho et le liotan: Sur Shakespeare, le drame elisabethian Et l'ideologie anglaise au XVIIe sreches.* Paris: Editions de Minuit, 1981.

———. and Dominque Guy-Blanquet. *Autour d' Othello.* Paris, ERLA Institut Charles V, 1987.

Maslin, Janet. "Fishburne and Branaugh Meet Their Fate in Venice." *New York Times* 14 Dec. 1995: C11.

Matteo, Gino J. *Shakespeare's "Othello":A Study and the Stage, 1604–1904.* Salzburg: Institut für Englische Sprache und Literatur, 1974.

Matz, Robert. "Slander, Renaissance Discourse of Sodomy, and *Othello.*" *ELH* 66 (1999): 261–76.

McGlinchee, Claire. "Stratford, CT Shakespeare Festival, 1957." *Shakespeare Quarterly* 8 (1957): 507–10.

Melchiori, Barbara Arnett. "Desdemona's Two Lies." *Universita Degli Studi di Milano* 42 (1985): 41–49.

Michener, Charles. "A Triumphant Iago." *Newsweek* 15 Feb. 1982: 92.

Minami, Ryuta. "Chronological Table of Shakespeare Productions in Japan, 1866-1994." *Shakespeare and the Japanese Stage.* Eds. Takashi Sasyama et. al. Cambridge: Cambridge University Press, 1998. 257–331.

Mikesell, Margaret Lael and Virginia Mason Vaughan, comps. *Othello: An Annotated Bibliography, 1940–1985.* New York: Garland, 1990.

Miller, Jonathan. *Subsequent Performances.* London: Faber, 1986.

Mirlani, Bob. "News Release for Trinity Rep." Find. RI.com. 1999.

Mondello, Bob. "Grand Othell." *City Paper* [Washington, DC] 14 Dec. 1990.

Muir, Kenneth, ed. *Othello.* Harmondsworth: Penguin, 1968.

Neely, Carol Thomas. *Broken Nuptials in Shakespeare's Plays*. New Haven: Yale University Press, 1985.

Neill, Michael. "Changing Places in *Othello*." *Shakespeare Survey* 37 (1984): 115-31.

———. "Unproper Beds: Race, Adultery, and the Hideous in *Othello*." *Shakespeare Quarterly* 40 (1989): 383–412.

Nelson, Harland. "Othello." *Film Heritage* 2 (1966): 19.

Nelson, T. G. A. and Charles Haines. "Othello's Unconsummated Marriage." *Essays in Criticism* 33 (1983): 1–18.

Norris, Christopher. "Post-Strucuralist Shakespeare: Text and Ideology." *Alternative Shakespeare*. Ed. John Drakakis. New York: Methuen, 1985. 47–66.

Novy, Marianne, ed. *Transforming Shakespeare: Contemporary Women's Re-Visions in Literature and Performance*. New York: St. Martin's, 1999.

O'Connor, John J. "Miller Directs '*Othello*.'" *New York Times* 12 Oct. 1981: C:24.

Orkin, Martin. *Shakespeare Against Apartheid*. Craighall: Donker, 1987.

"Othello." *Minneapolis Spokesman* 2 Oct. 1993: F4.

"Othello." *The Telegram* [Toronto] 14 Feb. 1953: 8.

"Othello Meets Worthy, Mediocre Fate." *New Haven Journal-Courier* 25 Feb. 1986: 42.

Overmeyer, Janet. "Shakespeare's Desdemona: A Twentieth-Century View." *University Review* 37 (1971): 304–305.

Park, Roy. *Lamb as Critic*. Lincoln: University of Nebraska Press, 1980.

Parker, Patricia. "Fantasies of 'Race' and 'Gender': Africa, *Othello*, and Bringing To Light." *Women, "Race," and Writing on the Early Modern Period*. Eds. Margo Hendricks and Patricia Parker. New York: Routledge, 1994. 84–100.

———. "Preposterous Events." *Shakespeare Quarterly* 43 (1992): 207–209.

Parrish, Paul. "*Othello*." *Critique* Aug. 1998: 55.

Pearce, G. M. "Shakespeare's Tragedies, Especially *Othello*." *Cahiers elisabethaines* 24 (1983): 84–85.

Pechter, Edward. "'Have you not read of some such thing?' Sex and Sexual Stories of Othello." *Shakespeare Survey* 49 (1996): 201–216.

———. *Othello and Interpretive Traditions*. Iowa City: University of Iowa Press, 1999.

Pepys, Samuel. *The Diary of Samuel Pepys*. Vol 1. Ed. John Warington. London: Dent, 1953.

Peter, John. "The Touch of Evil." *Sunday London Times* 21 Sept. 1997. II:18.

Polland, David. "Iago's Wound." *Othello: New Perspectives*. Eds. Virginia Mason Vaughan and Kent Cartwright. Rutherford, NJ: Fairleigh Dickinson University Press, 1991.

Porter, Joseph A. "Complement Extern: Iago's Speech Acts." *Othello: New Perspectives*. Eds. Virginia Mason Vaughan and Kent Cartwright. Rutherford, NJ: Fairleigh Dickinson University Press, 1991. 74–89.

Potter, Lois. *Othello in Performance*. Manchester: Manchester University Press, 2002.

Poulton, Ron. "See-Hear." *Telegram* [Toronto] 14 Feb, 1953.

Pratt, Rob. "Tragedy of Deception." *Good Times* 6 Aug. 1998.

Rainer, Peter. "Olivier's Othello." *Los Angeles Times* (1991).

Ranald, Margaret Loftus. "The Indiscretions of Desdemona." *Shakespeare Quarterly* 14 (Spring 1963): 127-39.

Raysor, Thomas. ed. *Coleridge's Shakespearean Criticism.* London: Dent, 1960.

Reid, Robert. "Bloodless Othello Stratford Let Down." *K-W Record* 1 Aug. 1987.

Reid, Stephen. "Desdemona's Guilt." *American Imago* 27 (Fall 1970): 245-62.

Rice, Julian C. "Desdemona Unpinned: Universal Guilt in *Othello.*" *Shakespeare Studies* 7 (1974): 209-226.

Rich, Frank. "Walken as Iago in an 'Othello' in the Park." *New York Times* 28 June 1991: C: 1.

Richards, Dave. "Moor's the Pity." *Washington Post* 12 Oct. 1981: D:12.

Richards, David. "For *Othello* the Fault Lies in the Stars." New *York Times* 7 July 1991: 2: 1.

Ridley, M. R., ed. *Othello.* New Arden Edition. London: Metheun, 1962.

Robeson, Paul, Jr. *The Undiscovered Paul Robeson: An Artist's Journey, 1898-1939.* New York: Wiley, 2001.

Roca, Octavio. "Everything and Moor: S. F. Ballet's 'Othello': A Spectacular Blending of Traditional and Radical Dance." *San Francisco Chronicle* 2 Apr. 1998: E1.

Rose, Lloyd. "*Othello*: The Two Faces of Tragedy: At the Folger, A Black Iago Makes All the Difference." *Washington Post* 5 Dec. 1990: C1.

Rose, Mark. "Othello's Occupation: Shakespeare and the Romance of Chivalry." *English Literary Renaissance* 15 (1985): 293–311.

Rose, Mary Beth. *The Expense of Spirit: Love and Sexuality in English Renaissance Drama.* Ithaca: Cornell University Press, 1988.

Rosenberg, Marvin. *The Masks of Othello.* Berkley: University of California P, 1961.

Ross, Jeanette. "*Othello* Producers Seek Purity." *Idaho Statesman* 25 July 1986.

Rossiter, A. P. *Angel with Horns.* London: Longman, 1961.

Royster, Francesca T. "The End of Race and the Future of Modern Cultural Studies." *Shakespeare Studies* 26 (1998): 59–69.

Ruru, Li. "Shakespeare on the Chinese Stage in the 1990s." *Shakespeare Quarterly* 50 (1999): 355–67.

Sasyama, Takashi, J. R. Mulryne, and Margaret Shewring, eds. *Shakespeare and the Japanese Stage.* Cambridge: Cambridge University Press, 1998.

Schaak, Christine. "When Cultures Meet." *Daily Illini* [University of Illinois] 29 Jan–4 Feb. 1988.

Scheman, Naomi. "Othello's Doubt/Desdemona's Death: The Engendering of Skepticism." *Power, Gender, and Values.* Ed. Judith Genova. Edmonton: Academic Press, 1987. 113–33.

Shattuck, Charles. *Shakespeare on the American Stage: From the Hallams to Edwin Booth.* Vol.1. Washington, DC: The Folger Shakespeare Library, 1976.

Shedd, Robert G. "The Great Lakes Shakespeare Festival in Lakewood, Ohio: Reaching New Audiences." *Shakespeare Quarterly* 13 (Autumn 1962): 559–60.

Siegal, Joel. "*Othello.*" *New York Theatre Critics Review, 1982.* 376.

Siemon, James. R. "'Nay, That's No Next': *Othello,* V.ii in Performance, 1760–1900." *Shakespeare Quarterly* 37 (1986): 38–51.

Simon, John. "Othello." *New Yorker* 28 Sept. 1970.

Simone, R. Thomas. "*Othello.*" *Shakespeare on Film Newsletter* Mar. 1982.

Sinfield, Alan. *Faultlines: Cultural Materialism and the Politics of Dissident Reading.* Berkeley: University of California Press, 1992.

Smallwood, Robert. "On *Othello,* Directed by Trevor Nunn at the Other Place, Stratford-upon-Avon." *Shakespeare Quarterly* 41 (1990): 110–14.

Smith, Bruce. *Homosexual Desire in Shakespeare's England.* Chicago: University of Chicago Press, 1991.

Smith, Gordon Ross. "Iago and the Paranoic." *American Imago* 16 (Summer 1959): 155–67.

Smith, Peter. "The 1970 Season at Stratford, Connecticut." *Shakespeare Quarterly* 21 (Autumn 1970): 451–55.

Snow, Edward. *Rewriting the Renaissance: The Discourse of Sexual Difference in Early Modern Europe.* Chicago: University of Chicago Press, 1986.

———. "Sexual Anxiety and the Male Order of Things in *Othello.*" *English Literary Renaissance* 10 (1980): 384–412.

Snyder, Susan. *Critical Essays on Othello.* New York: Garland, 1988.

Sommerstein, Carly. "The Cast of *Othello* Goes on the Newlywed Game." *Whole Earth Review* (Fall 1987): 130–31.

Sprague, Arthur Colby. *Shakespeare and the Actors: The Stage Business in His Plays (1605–1905).* Cambridge: Harvard University Press, 1945.

Springer, P. Gregory. "'Kabuki Othello' Has Something for Everyone." *Champaign-Urbana News-Gazette* 5 Feb. 1988: 1–4.

Stallybrass, Peter. "Patriarchal Territories: The Body Enclosed." *Rewriting the Renaissance.* Eds. Margaret W. Ferguson, Maureen Quilligan, and Nancy J. Vickers. Chicago: University of Chicago Press, 1986.123–42

———. "Transvestism and the 'Body Beneath': Speculating on the Boy Actor." *Erotic Politics: Desire on the Renaissance Stage.* Ed. Susan Zimmerman. New York: Routledge, 1991. 64–83.

Stanley, Audrey. "The 1994 Shanghai International Shakespeare Festival." *Shakespeare Quarterly* 47 (Spring 1996): 72–80.

Steele, Judy McConnell. "The Role of a Lifetime: LA Actor Realizes Dream Playing Othello." *Idaho Statesman* 26 July 1986: D2.

Steele, Mike. "*Othello.*" *Minneapolis Star Tribune* 15 Oct. 1993: 2E.

Sterritt, David. "The Jealous Moor in the Park." *Christian Science Monitor* 12 July 1991: 12.

Stodder, Joseph H. and Lillian Wilds. "Shakespeare in Southern California." *Shakespeare Quarterly* 30 (Spring 1979): 233.

Stoll, Edgar Elmer. *From Shakespeare to Joyce.* New York: Doubleday, 1944.

———. *Othello: An Historical and Comparative Study.* 1915; rpt. New York: Guardian, 1967.

Stribrny, Zdenek. *Shakespeare and Eastern Europe.* Oxford: Oxford University Press, 2000.

Tallmer, Jerry. "Mr. Gunn in New York." *New York Post* 15 Sept. 1970: 26.

Taylor, Estelle. "Unmasking *Othello* Criticism." *Shakespeare Worldwide* 13 (1991): 117–39.

Taylor, Markland. "Yale Rep's *Othello.*" *New Haven Register* 23 Feb. 1986.

Thorpe, Vanessa. "Theatre Cast as a Villain by Black Actors." *Observer* 2 May 1999: 8.

Traversi, D. A. *An Approach to Shakespeare*. 1938. Rev. ed. New York: Doubleday, 1959.

Trussel, Fr. Christopher. "Othello Lacks the Guthrie's Usual Luster." *St. Cloud Visitor* 28 Oct. 1993.

Tynan, Kenneth, ed. *"Othello": The National Theatre Production*. New York: Stein and Day, 1967.

———. "The Actor: Tynan Interviews Olivier." *Tulane Drama Review* 11 (1966): 71-101.

Vander Motten, J. P. "Iago at Lincoln's Inn Fields: Thomas Porter's *The Villain* on the Early Restoration Stage." *SEL, 1500–1900* 24 (1984): 215–28.

Vanita, Ruth. "'Proper' Men and 'Fallen' Women: The Unprotectedness of Wives in *Othello,*" *SEL, 1500–1900* 34 (Spring 1994): 341–56.

Vaughan, Virginia Mason, and Kent Cartwright, eds. *Othello: New Perspectives*. Rutherford: Fairleigh Dickinson University Press, 1991.

Vaughan, Virginia Mason. *Othello: A Contextual History*. Cambridge: Cambridge University Press, 1994.

———. "Kiss me Deadly: or the Des/Demonized Spectacle." *Othello: New Perspectives*. Cranbury, NJ: Fairleigh Dickinson University Press, 1991.

Wain, John. *"Othello": A Casebook*. Rev. ed. London: Macmillan, 1994.

Waller, Marguerite. "Academic Tootsie: The Denial of Difference and the Difference It Makes." *Diacritics* 17 (1987): 2–20.

Watts, Cedric. "The Semiotics of *Othello.*" *William Shakespeare. Othello*. Eds. Linda Cookson and Bryan Loughrey. Longman Critical Essays. Harlow: Longman, 1991. 33–42.

Waugh, Martin. "*Othello*: The Tragedy of Iago." *Psychoanalytic Quarterly* 19 (1950): 202–12.

Wayne, Valerie. "Historical Differences: Misogyny in *Othello.*" *The Matter of Reference: Materialist Feminist Criticism of Shakepeare*. Ithaca: Cornell University Press, 1991. 153–175.

Weatherby, W. J. "Othello." *The Guardian* [London]: 18 July 1991.

Webb, Henry J. "The Military Background in *Othello.*" *Philological Quarterly* 30 (1951): 40–52.

Webster, Margaret. *Shakespeare Without Tears*. New York: McGraw-Hill, 1942.

Welles, Orson. *Filming Othello* http://film.tier-ranet.com/directors/o.welles/fothelloe.html. (1978) 2001

Wertz, Diane. "There's a whole lot to Shakespeare goin' on." *Dallas Morning News* 12 July 1982: 1C, 2C.

Wheeler, Richard P. "' . . . And my loud crying still': The Sonnets, the *Merchant of Venice* and *Othello.*" *Shakespeare's "Rough Magic": Renaissance Essays in Honor of L. C. Barber*. Eds. Peter Erickson and Coppelia Kahn. Newark, DE: University Delaware Press, 1980.

White, R. S. *Innocent Victims: Poetic Injustice in Shakespearean Tragedy*. Newcastle-Upon-Tyne: Tyneside Free Press, 1986.

Whittacker, Herbert. "Show Business." *The Globe and Mail* [Toronto] 13 Feb. 1953.

Williams, John A. "Who is Desdemona?" *Othello: New Essays by Black Writers*. Ed. Mythili Kaul. Washington, DC: Howard University Press, 1997.

Willis, Susan. *The BBC Shakespeare Plays: Making the Televised Canon*. Chapel Hill: University of North Carolina Press, 1991.

Willson, Robert F., Jr. *Shakespeare in Hollywood, 1929-1956*. Madison: Fairleigh Dickinson University Press, 2000.

Wilson, Rob. "Othello: Jealousy as Mimetic Contaigon." *American Imago* 44 (1987): 213–33.

Wine, Martin L., ed. *Othello. Text and Performance*. London: Macmillan, 1984.

Wolf, Matt. "London Maverick Arrives for First (and Second) Time." *New York Times* 1 Feb. 1998: 2: 9.

Yachnin, Paul. "Magical Properties: Vision, Possession, and Wonder in *Othello.*" *Theatre Journal* 48 (1996): 197–208.

Zimmerman, Susan, ed. *Erotic Politics: Desire on the Renaissance Stage*. New York: Routledge, 1991.

The Audience's Role in *Othello*

HUGH MACRAE RICHMOND

Modern theatrical technology has brought live theatre to a point at which it can often attempt to duplicate the lighting, acoustics, and locational resources of the cinema, so that we may lose sight of the crucial distinction between stage and screen: a live performance is the unique result of the interaction of a particular audience and a group of performers, in which the audience is an active determinant of the outcome through its sustained communication with the actors. The uncertainty of each outcome of a live performance is what gives the theatre its excitement, perhaps verging on the uncertainty, even apprehension, with which we watch the acrobatics of trapeze artists. The divergences between successive performances of the same production of a play confirm the decisive role of the audience in a successful outcome, often to the discomfiture of critics and reviewers, not to mention actors and directors. *Othello* has always been one of Shakespeare's most popular and often performed plays (as its frequent seventeenth-century reprinting as a single-play quarto indirectly confirms). This success suggests an exceptional impact in the play's effect on audiences, making it a plausible example of the intersection of the roles of actors and audience.

From early performances of drama, this defining status of the audience was implicitly recognized by the terms used in Aristotle's *Poetics* to identify the emotional impact of ancient Greek tragedy. His term "catharsis" was applied to the consequences of audience identification with a positive hero-figure on stage, whose mistakes and misfortunes excited sympathy and personal application, usually translated as "pity" and "fear." Aristotle's observations, largely based on the *Oedipus* of Sophocles, have found sympathetic modern echoes. Freud's description of "identification", as abstracted by Norman Holland in *Psychoanalysis and Shakespeare*, is "based upon the possibility or desire of putting oneself in the same situation as another" because "one ego has perceived a significant analogy with another" which "may arise with any new perception of a common quality shared with some other person."[1] One example of this kind of audience affinity with a role is identified in the dramatic form of comedy by Bertrand Evans in *Shakespeare's Comedies*, where he has shown in detail how Shakespearean audiences empathize with the best-informed character on stage and relish the feeling of mastery resulting from awareness of dramatic irony involving the actions of less well-informed characters.[2] In the mixed dramatic forms of Shakespeare, various feelings about characters may coexist in the audience, as with our initial identification with Richard of Gloucester's manipulative domination of his unwitting and somewhat guilty victims in *Richard III*, which ultimately leads to our rueful detachment from the later role of Richard, when we see its high costs to innocents such as the princes in the Tower (for fuller discussion, see *Critical Essays on Shakespeare's Richard III*).[3] This distinctive catharsis gives that play its unique and powerful "affect" which has insured its continued stage success, and I believe it will also prove helpful in clarifying that of *Othello*.

I would argue that every successful performance of a play has such a distinctive emotional interaction between actors and audience, though not necessarily exactly those specified by Aristotle, Freud, and Evans. The determination of just what this interaction might be in some broadly representative performance of a specific play defines the distinctive operation of drama criticism, and indeed of the professional motivation for the performers themselves. A basic account of a dramatic script focuses ultimately not on its purely literary character but on its characteristic emotional "affect" in performance, which must be its primary justification as a play, and is far more physiological than the silent reading of nondramatic literature which concerns such "reader-response" critics as Stanley Fish. This live group experience also necessarily differs from that of a silent private reading even of a playscript, which has its own, different nature and values, perhaps more akin to that of reading a conventional novel than to a performance. The publication of Shakespearean quartos like those of *Othello* proves that Elizabethans did consider such reading rewarding, unlike the literary censure implicit in the inaccessibility of most modern television and film scripts. Nevertheless, insofar as the genre of Elizabethan drama has its own unique aesthetic, this aesthetic can only properly apply to the audience's experience of a script in live performance. Reading of a published script is normally a consequent of its performance success. Readers necessarily undergo crucially different experiences from this dynamic activity, as we perceive instantly in the gains and losses of attending the staging of a dramatized novel, which is no less significantly distinct from a film or television version. The shared experience evokes an immediacy of empathy for which there is scarcely any equivalent outside live theatre.

Thus, for me, the formative experience in defining the uniqueness of *Othello*'s impact came in the 1949 production at Stratford-upon-Avon in which Godfrey Tearle (1884–1953) played Othello to Antony Quayle's Iago. Like his actor father, "a man of natural elegance and dignity," (Grebanier)[4] Tearle was a grandiloquent and monumental actor in the old, mellifluous tradition surviving in John Gielgud's Shakespearean vein, against which Quayle mustered a believable jaded military authenticity founded on his own front-line army service in World War II. The stylistic tension between the archaic Edwardian romanticism of Tearle's Othello and the wry expertise of Quayle's war-weary Iago had an immediacy and pathos which still resonates vividly with my own experience of military service, set against the simultaneous experience of the last surviving vestiges of the prelapsarian world shattered by World War I. As it progressed, the production rang the changes in mourning for Othello's heroic image, declining like that of mythic England, as modern expediency ground it down. The audience responded instinctively to this cumulative loss of legendary status by the hero from moment to moment in a way I have rarely experienced as reviewers noted: "Othello may be at a height of self-torment; the actor is unstrained; and works on our sympathy as he will." (London *Times*, 20 June, 1949). This archetype of heroic decline provided a performance with an audience impact "not equalled by any other actor of our time," as reaffirmed by Marvin Rosenberg's *The Masks of Othello*.[5] The experience depended not simply on the script but on its unique power to evoke two authentic temperaments in an historical confrontation relevant to the condition of the audience at that moment. In 1989, a very similar unique tension occurred at a New York performance of *The Merchant of Venice*, when Dustin Hoffman played Shylock in intuitive Method style for Peter Hall's production, against the grain of more formal British acting of the rest of the cast, and before a largely Jewish audience recruited for that performance by Sam Wanamaker in support of his restoration of the Globe Theatre.

In the *Poetics*, Aristotle hypothesized in rather more general terms than these that dramatic structure requires analysis of a script's progressive intersection with an audience's experience. While such broad ideas as exposition, complication, climax, reversal, and resolution have relevance to basic theatrical progressions in audience experience, they are not precise enough to define the emotional affects of staging *Othello* from moment to moment. Take the issue of exposition. This opening phase of any drama establishes a situation, ideology, context, and characterization, but such terms do not in themselves differ absolutely from the requirements of most genres from lyric to novel. What is distinctive is how this exposition impacts on the feelings of the audience by the physical impressions created on the stage. In *Fiction and the Shape of Belief*, Sheldon Sacks has plausibly argued that the opening of any literary text involves the negotiation of an aesthetic contract with its audience about the conventions and texture of the communication: for example, is it to be laboriously documentary, allegorically stylized, flippant, or intense, and so on. This negotiation is accomplished by "signals which influence our attitudes toward characters, acts, and thoughts represented."[6] Sacks goes so far as to assert that writers' "ethical beliefs, opinions, and prejudices are expressed as the formal signals which control our response to the characters, acts, and thoughts represented." (231)

However, we can more properly begin to appreciate the opening procedures in *Othello* by comparing them with those of similar plays not novels. Sometimes Shakespeare goes so far as to establish these attitudinal considerations by a prologue laying out the relevant groundrules for the subsequent performance, like the sonnet rather laboriously opening the self-professed love tragedy of *Romeo and Juliet*, or the exact reverse anticipations for mockery of fated love established before we are exposed to the merry tragedy of *Pyramus and Thisbe*. These signpostings are relatively primitive, to ensure they are accurately registered. For, like all introductions of a key character, the opening lines of most plays establish clearly the audience's role and point of view: "the kinds of critical discriminations we can make are rigidly controlled by our initial preconceptions" (Sacks, 3). In the Prologue to *Henry VIII*, for example, we are firmly instructed that we are to concentrate empathetically on the misfortunes of Katherine of Aragon, in what the author considers to be a distinctively "feminine" mode. In complete contrast, the *macho* opening of *Richard III* establishes the audience's initial relationship to the plot as that of an involuntary confidant of the omniscient and masterly Richard of Gloucester, from which "insider" role we are progressively detached, and ultimately completely alienated. The audience's initial association with Richard is achieved by the nature of his opening soliloquy, which invites the actor to address himself directly to the audience as recognized observers, who are therefore "compromised" or "involved" involuntarily, whatever the moral issues. The catharsis of the play lies in the purgation of this initial synchronization of audience perspective with Richard's superior insights. By contrast, the Induction to *The Taming of the Shrew* establishes the artifice both of the frame story and of the plots contained within it about Katherina and Bianca. We certainly do not sympathize with the drunken lout Christopher Sly. If we identify at all, it is with the controlling intelligence of the Lord and his actors, later inherited to a considerable degree by the dramatist's manipulative surrogate in the play-within-the-play, the puppet master Petruchio.

In this context of establishing expectations, the opening of *Othello* proves more sophisticated than most of these precedents, as it blends many of their options, establishing the artifice of the plot initially through Iago's avowals, which (like Richard of Gloucester's) invite involuntary association with the manipulative intelligence of Iago as the stage manager of the action. Like the Lord in the Induction of *The Taming of the Shrew*, in *Othello*'s opening scene Iago emerges progressively as the manipulative intelligence controlling his dupes, Roderigo and Brabantio, but our identification with Iago's point of view is sealed only by his soliloquy near the end of the opening scene. I believe it is Shakespeare's recurring skill as a dramatist to ensure by the device of soliloquy that we identify with the outsider, the excluded, however wicked he may be (as we do with both Falstaff and Macbeth, not to mention Hamlet). In the course of the audience recognition implicit in Shakespearean soliloquy, the actor playing Iago can acquire audience domination, so that we perceive Othello from the outside when he appears.

The audience identification with the cynical manipulator is largely attributable to the stage effect of soliloquy, which readily allows the speaker the unique relation to the audience of acknowledging its existence, as in the queries which Iago implicitly addresses to his audience:

> And what's he that says I play the villain,
> When this advice is free I give, and honest,
> Probal to thinking, and indeed the course
> To win the Moor again? (2.3, 336–39)[7]

and:

> How am I then a villain,
> To council Cassio to this parallel course,
> Directly to his good? (2.3, 48–50)

The other characters are given no opportunity to recognize the artifice of Iago's performance and this leaves them in a lesser condition of awareness of their own artificial identity and situation. It is probable that this direct appeal to spectators was initiated by the Devil and Vice figures of medieval drama, with which characters such as Richard of Gloucester, Falstaff, and Iago are traditionally bracketed (as Bernard Spivack has shown in *Shakespeare and the Allegory of Evil*)[8]. This device of direct address to an acknowledged audience is classically attributed to diabolic forces: they know themselves, because they understand the universal nature of evil in themselves and others (a classic Reformation obligation). Their didactic display of self-awareness is another inviting attribute in the ancient tradition of the admonition: "Know thyself." This skill in self-exposition persists in Milton's Satan in *Paradise Lost* and *Paradise Regain'd*, recurring later in *The Brothers Karamasov* (Book IX, Chapter IX), where Dostoevsky allows the forces of evil to defend themselves candidly as the catalyst of all knowledge, "the indispensible minus."

By Bertrand Evans' criteria, if the Devil is traditionally self-aware, we are bound not only to see the action from his perspective but inevitably to prefer his seeming initial mastery to the doomed unawareness of his naive victims. The resulting device of discrepant awareness (as Evans calls it) or dramatic irony (in more traditional terminology) takes shape in our perception of the ignorance of the other characters and victims of the self-aware hero or villain. Such superior alertness is a crucial source of audience involvement, inducing a self-flattering sense of one's superiority to the other, unaware characters on the stage. The resulting complacency may well be one of the sources of *Othello*'s popularity, for Evans observes that the play is among those with the highest "proportion of scenes during which we hold significant advantage over participants, and the number of participants over whom we hold advantage." (Evans, *Shakespeare's Tragic Practice*)[9] This condition is the defining perspective which Shakespeare maintains throughout *Othello*, so that we continually refract our views of Roderigo, Cassio, Othello, and even Desdemona, through the lens of Iago's soliloquies. This point of view is established immediately, as Evans notes of the play's opening: "It tells us unmistakably that Iago is not what he seems to others in his world. During the course of subsequent action, and always as a result of specific practices contrived by Iago, numerous incidental discrepancies arise between the participants' awareness and ours." (Evans, *Shakespeare's Tragic Practice*, 116) All these others are innocent in all senses of the word: inexperienced, naive, unaware, and self-destructively idealistic. This displacement of audience perspective from the victims' point of view certainly justifies Aristotle's idea of pity as a classic emotional response to tragedy: we are sorry to see well-meaning personae destroyed by their own credulity. But we cannot identify with either their ignorance or their moral simplicity.

In *Othello* Aristotle's other asserted audience "affect" of fear could perhaps be derived from anxiety whether we might be so trapped as the hero, but this has never been a basic response to Othello by critics or audiences, who tend to censure the victims' credulity rather than empathize with it. This Brechtian view is reinforced not only by conservative critics such as Thomas Rymer and T. S. Eliot, but also by many radical feminists and African Americans. Far from identifying with Desdemona as a victim of *machismo*, both reactionary and progressive thinkers despise her, from Thomas Rymer's sarcasm about her poor housekeeping skills in his *Short View of Tragedy* (1693), through James Baldwin's contempt for her dependency (in the Shakespeare anniversary issue of *Le Figaro Littéraire*, in 1964), down to modern feminist attacks on her self-sacrifice: "Desdemona's moral development is arrested at the level of altruistic self-denial." (Diane Dreher in *Domination and Defiance*).[10] Shakespeare systematically reinforces this detachment from the victims' perspective by the repeated soliloquies assigned to Iago alone, which serve, like those of Richard of Gloucester, to continue the audience entrapment in the superior awareness of the manipulator.

One outcome of this approach to the script is to greatly enhance the status of the role of Iago. It is already the longest part in the play (1,094 lines to Othello's 879, according to Stanley Wells, *Dictionary of Shakespeare*,[11] and the third longest in all of Shakespeare (after Hamlet and Richard III). Perhaps a more accurate title for the play would be *Iago*, acknowledging that, because of our superior knowledge of the plot, we can never identify fully with Othello's overtly mistaken point of view. Like the somewhat rigid virtue of Brutus, Isabella, or Timon, the "goodness" of Desdemona and Othello is the object of dispassionate psychological investigation: they are ruthlessly tested to destruction by the dramatist, as with Bosola's treatment of the Duchess of Malfi. Iago is the dominant toreador, Othello the simpler, albeit heroic victim in a sacrificial rite of doomed primal innocence. We are not required to share the mental condition of the sacrificed at any point. For example, the stupefied paralysis of the toreador's baffled victim matches the momentary catatonic fit of Othello (4.3. 35–59). This pathological episode is distanced by Iago's cold diagnosis of Othello's sickness, like Caesar's comparable deafness and epilepsy, which we perceive similarly, through Casca's eyes, as symptoms of Caesar's megalomaniac excess and insensitivity which invite his assassination (*Julius Caesar*, 235–75).

The comparably detached state of mind of the audience during the most intense scenes of *Othello* thus resembles that which I believe is intended during the storm scenes in *King Lear*. We are clinically fascinated by Lear's excessive emotion but not sharers of it, since its initiation occurs with Lear's monstrous and truly pathological curse against Goneril. (For fuller discussion of these issues, see Hugh M. Richmond, "A Letter to the Actor Playing Lear".) If this is true, one must reject the idea that entropy constitutes the climax of the plays in the misguided rages of Othello or Lear, which too many actors see as their optimum opportunity for "acting." The emotional climax of both plays is not merely this midpoint entropy of megalomaniac resentment in the principal characters, but the infinitely subtler sequels in which they finally begin to escape from this "mad" condition: Lear's new humility, Othello's increasing doubt of the appropriateness of brutal "justice." Only at these truly climactic points of discovery is audience empathy with the hero made possible. Unlike our more modern identification with madness as seen in Ginsberg's *Howl,* in *Shakespeare's Tragic Heroes, Slaves of Passion*, Lily B. Campbell has stressed that Shakespeare approaches intense feeling as a dispassionate pathologist, even when exploiting the voices of the Gravediggers to review the theological implications of Ophelia's merely effervescent state of mind, with which we are not expected to empathize. By deliberate contrast, Hamlet's subtler character is expressed directly to the audience through his recurring soliloquies, which irresistibly invite us to appreciate his skeptical views. He proves more aware than the other characters of the dangers of high feeling, as Lily B. Campbell's title reminds us.[13]

This verdict against entropy overlaps with the modern theatre issue of casting, in which paradoxes have evolved. One is the supposed preferability of race-and gender-neutral casting. A version of the latter deliberately replaces the "boy playing a girl" convention with its opposite: a female Richard II, Falstaff, Lear, or Prospero. This reversed impersonation of men by women is far less plausible physically and vocally than what we hear of the Elizabethan boys' impersonation of young women, so that it may become a distractingly overt gesture of "political correctness." Such openly forced casting contrasts with the other modern tendency to cast Othello and Shylock from actors with the same ethnic character as the roles (as in Peter Hall's use of Dustin Hoffman as Shylock in the *Merchant of Venice* previously mentioned), presumably because other races would be seen as condescending in their portrayal. The irony is that such casting invites a non-aesthetic identification with the actors as truly representatives of the historical victims of just such condescension, which is potentially at odds with the author's more objective intent, to display the tragic fact that racism may distort its victims' own behavior. Just as we might be less immediately troubled by Petruchio's treatment of Katherina because we have been reminded that she is played by a male, so we might identify less with the emotional extravagance of Othello if we know he is not acted by someone of actual African descent. Similarly, Lear should not (indeed, normally cannot, if he is to carry Cordelia's dead weight) be played on stage by a literal octogenarian, so that we do not involuntarily feel the sympathy for age which might approve Lear's hysteria, but which he learns to transcend, earning our proper sympathy thereby. As with the wasteful energies of Victorian steam engines, entropy is never admirable, however picturesque the steam and smoke in Turner's paintings and those of the Impressionists who followed his lead. They indicate waste and pollution.

Another crucial issue involving detailed Elizabethan and modern audience reactions to *Othello* is how they diverge in responding to a female role such as Desdemona's. One basic concern is discovery of the Elizabethan audience affect of having boys play women's roles, which is something which it seems we have barely become able to understand. Seventeenth-century Londoners were probably completely at ease with the convention, as Samuel Pepys revealed in describing a Cockpit performance of *The Loyal Subject* (by John Fletcher, Shakespeare's colleague), in which "one Kynaston, a boy, acted the Duke's sister, but made the loveliest lady that I ever saw." (F. E. Halliday, *A Shakespeare Companion*)[14] Such evidence is confirmed by our most recent discoveries at the restored Globe Theatre. In reviewing the implications of experience in the Globe, Pauline Kiernan has noted, in *Staging Shakespeare at the New Globe*, how recently "studies have focused on what is perceived to have been the homoeroticism of the boy actor in the original staging of the plays when women were forbidden from acting on a public stage in England."[15] Putting on one side the more specialized minority reaction that sees boys in themselves as objects of sexual excitement on or off the stage, it appears that most Elizabethans did not see boys on stage as primarily exciting on homosexual grounds, or even as disturbing challenges to sexual identity. Such a response reflects primarily a late twentieth-century anxiety about gender (contrasting with early treatments of the youth of Achilles, or Hercules with Omphale, etc.).

Fortunately, as Kiernan notes, the normal heterosexual response has been effectively validated by Toby Cockerell in the role of Princess Katherine in the *Henry V* of the restored Globe (1997), in which the pathos of the Princess' situation was not deflected through homosexual responses but heightened by the male actor's genuine empathy with his role's feminine anxieties. His awareness made us understand the persona's tension between political constraint, social propriety, and the historical original's compulsive sexual attraction to Henry, which is the often ignored subtext of the script, however deftly veiled. Like his seventeenth-century predecessors, Toby Cockerell demonstrated his understanding so well that he was much courted off-stage, not by gay men but by nubile women, in a triumph for the sensitive heterosexual. Kiernan concludes "from the experience of seeing a young man in the part of Katherine in *Henry V*, it would seem that some recent scholarship's evidence on the homoerotic effects on the original audience (apparently taking its cue from certain antitheatrical pamphleteers of the period who railed against the provocative effects on male playgoers of boys dressed up as women on the public stage) may have to be reassessed." (55)

In this sense we must radically question the current acute hostility to Desdemona's devotion to Othello as necessarily at odds with the exact conditions of performance. Just as a non-Jew playing Shylock with laborious "Jewishness" might be considered offensive on the modern stage, so a boy playing a woman contemptibly would necessarily offend the substantial female element of Shakespeare's audience, of which we know he was intensely aware because of his epilogues to *As You Like It* and *Henry VIII*. Hence comes Celia's bitter commentary on just such a potentially offensive phase in Rosalind's misogynistic exposition to Orlando: "You have simply misus'd our sex in your love-prate. We must have your doublet and hose pluck'd over your head, and show the world what the bird hath done to her own sex." (*As You Like It*, 4.1. 200–203) Paradoxically, the reference to stripping indicates that the audience recognize that, after all, it is a boy actor who has spoken lines against women, who is therefore a tainted authority.

In his development of Desdemona's presentation, Shakespeare ultimately requires the boy actor to identify Desdemona's bold courage and independence, but only through the veil of her initial conventional "femininity." As with so many other Shakespearean heroines the role requires creation of a plausible female posture, which is then modified by a heroic if modestly expressed autonomy of judgment. Whether we talk of Rosalind, Cordelia, Imogen, or Hermione, we must observe in the staging of each a deliberate progression from propriety to enforced and highly reluctant rebellion. It is this paradox which makes Shakespeare's female roles so vital and attractive to women in the seventeenth-century audiences (as reflected throughout the pages of *The Shakespere Allusion-Book*): there is a continuous tension between the boy actor's efforts to evoke a conventional feminine manner, while allowing for an unexpected heroic autonomy to subvert it. Desdemona's behavior illustrates this fascinating paradox throughout: she carries her commitments beyond the bounds of plausibility, as her father Brabantio establishes for us:

> A maiden, never bold,
> Of spirit so still and quiet that her motion
> Blush'd at herself: and she, in spite of nature,
> Of years, of country, credit, every thing,
> To fall in love with what she fear'd to look on!
> It is a judgment maim'd, and most imperfect,
> That will confess perfection so could err
> Against all rules of nature, and must be driven
> To find out practices of cunning hell
> Why this should be. I therefore vouch again
> That with some mixtures pow'rful o'er the blood,
> Or with some dram (conjur'd to this effect)
> He wrought upon her. (1.3. 94–106)

These lines amount to authorial directions for the boy actor: he should perfect his attractively feminine presentation (as illustrated by Pepys' view of Kynaston) as a foil to a subsequent and surprising negation of it. Shakespeare continues to ensure audience attention to his female characters from moment to moment by defying our expectations, because he introduces abrupt divergences from a successful impersonation of traditional femininity. From such a desire to subvert expectations comes the amazing reversal of the dying Desdemona's assertion that she herself is guilty of her own death. The boy actor has simply to enunciate the statement to astound the audience, just as does Cordelia's abrupt refusal to flatter Lear, or Lady Macbeth's assertion that she could dash out her child's brains. Such statements can only have their intended shocking effect on the audience in a context of performance which has established an absolutely plausible femininity. "Camping" of the roles by modern males cast as Shakespeare's women may amuse some critics, but it falsifies the scripts.

In this sense the feminist and racial critics have misunderstood and misrepresented a distinctive theatrical experience in Shakespeare: the shock of reverse psychology dependent, for example, on the establishment of a conventionally ideal feminine persona which is then subverted by one significant choice. There may even be re-reversals, with consequent further subversive effects, as in Kate's final speech in *The Taming of the Shrew*, or Katherine of Aragon's ultimate acceptance of her unkind fate in *Henry VIII* and of the genuineness of the salvation of her enemy Wolsey by the end of that play. The repentance of Edmund in *King Lear* is another case in point, which so offends modern rigidity of mind that it is often cut by directors such as Peter Brook in his film as too shocking for modern sensibilities to bear. These reversals offend "political correctness" in favor of theatrical surprise, but validate Aristotle's sense of the intrinsic stage relevance of his concept of "reversal"—that the shock of the unexpected is an essential part of theatrical affect. In the face of academic criticism in the vein of Sidney's preference for boring consistency in *The Apology for Poetry*, Shakespeare follows the practices of his equally successful contemporaries, Lope de Vega in Spain, and Cinthio Geraldi in Italy, by preferring the reversals of tragicomedy to the staid consistency of neoclassical tragedy which ensured its theatrical failure as a genre in these three countries. Typically, Lope is obliged to defend his "melodramatic" practice by ironically blaming barbarous audience responses, in *Arte nuevo de hacer comedias en esto tiempo.*

Obviously, an exhaustive analysis of the affect of every scene in *Othello* in these terms would require far more space than the illustrations selected here. However, my conclusions about *Othello* can already be adequately distilled for consideration. First, no local critical comment is valid which does not establish the probable context of audience experience to each successive moment in the staging of the script. Furthermore, any staging which does not overtly and systematically consider and assimilate this progression into the interpretation is likely to be ineffective. All successful performances involve the audience as an active participant in the actors' articulation of their roles, as Antony Sher discovered in his first performance in a Shakespeare production, of *Richard III*, which he only began to understand after he could observe audience reactions. He found that, in terms of preparation, "previews are almost the most valuable in the whole process. The audience teaching us what does and doesn't work." (*The Year of the King*,)[16] By this criteria the modern fashion of excessive rehearsal is self-defeating: achieving only a rigid conditioning which may well defy the audience's role, in contrast to the near improvisation typical of Elizabethan production of scripts, which assures response to audience input.

In terms of interpretation of *Othello*, my conclusions are that Iago must be seen as the pivotal role, with Othello as subsidiary and not to be credited with excessive sympathy during his emotional extravagances, which are not the core of the play; that Desdemona should appear as the conventional heroine, but should periodically subvert the intrinsic texture of her own performance by radical reversals of expectations about her both on and off the stage, reversals which must be clearly punctuated to ensure recognition. These terms of reference can be applied to discontinuities in other characters, as in the double reversal in the status of Cassio, or the paradoxes in his sexual vagaries from idealist to rake; or in the unexpectedly fluent feminism of Emilia, leading to her ultimate moral authority in judging all the characters—all redeployments which should be heightened to the point of audience provocation, rather than offered as marginalia to a central "grande passion." Through excessive ratiocination about the potential logic of Shakespeare we have forgotten the element of surprise, the deliberate discontinuities which are essential to vital dramatic performance. We are still Romanticists enough to want the consistency of self-indulgent feeling, which is not able to survive the challenge of fluctuating circumstances. Indeed, we tend to censure Shakespeare's deliberate contrivance of innumerable reversals as overly elaborate, as is indicated by condescending comments about the elaborate discontinuities which he sustains from his writing of *The Comedy of Errors* to that of *Cymbeline*'s notoriously tortuous last act, which the rationalist George Bernard Shaw felt constrained to rewrite. Audience participation in performances is subtler.

NOTES

1. Norman Holland, *The Dynamics of Literary Response* (New York: Oxford University Press, 1968), 278.
2. Bertrand Evans, *Shakespeare's Comedies* (Oxford: Clarendon Press, 1960).
3. For fuller treatment of these issues see the Introduction to *Critical Essays on Shakespeare's "Richard III,"* ed. Hugh Macrae Richmond New York: G. K. Hall,1999).
4. Bernard Grebanier, *Then Came Each Actor* (New York: David MacKay), 336.
5. Marvin Rosenberg's *The Masks of Othello* (Berkely, University of California Press, 1961), 149.
6. Sheldon Sacks, *Fiction and the Shape of Belief* (Berkely: University of California Press, 1964), 230
7. All quotations are taken from *The Riverside Shakespeare*, ed. G. Blakemore Evans (Boston: Houghton Mifflin, 1997).
8. See Bernard Spivak's *Shakespeare and the Allegory of Evil* (New York: Columbia University Press, 1958).
9. Bertrand Evan's *Shakespeares Tragic Practise* (Oxford: Clarendon Press, 1979), 115.
10. Diane E. Dreher, *Domination and Defiance: Fathers and Daughter's in Shakespeare* (Lexington: University of Kentucky, 1986), 90, 180.
11. Stanley Wells, *Dictionary of Shakespeare* (Oxford: Oxford University Press, 1998), 228—29.
12. See Hugh Richmond, "Letter to the Actor Playing Lear" in *Illuminations*, ed. Jay Halio and Hugh M. Richmond (Newark: University of Delaware Press, 1998), 110-30.
13. Lily B. Campbell, *Shakespeare's Tragic Heroes: Slaves of Passion* (Cambridge U.K: Cambridge University Press, 1930).
14. F. E. Halliday, *A Shakespeare Companion, 1564–1964* (Harmondsworth: Penguin, 1964), 269.
15. Pauline Kiernan, *Staging Shakespeare at the New Globe* (London: Macmillan, 1999), 55.
16. Antony Sher, *The Year of the King* (London: Hogarth, 1985), 240.

WORKS CITED

Campbell, Lily B. *Shakespeare's Tragic Heroes: Slaves of Passion.* Cambridge, U.K.: Cambridge University Press, 1930.

Critical Essays on Shakespeare's "Richard III." Ed. Hugh Macrae Richmond. New York: G. K. Hall, 1999.

Dreher, Diane E. *Domination and Defiance: Fathers and Daughters in Shakespeare.* Lexington: University of Kentucky, 1986.

Evans, Bertrand. *Shakespeare's Comedies.* Oxford: Clarendon Press, 1960.

————. *Shakespeare's Tragic Practice.* Oxford: Clarendon Press, 1979.

Grebanier, Bernard. *Then Came Each Actor.* New York: David MacKay, 1975

Halliday, F. E. *A Shakespeare Companion, 1564-1964.* Harmondsworth: Penguin, 1964.

Holland, Norman. *The Dynamics of Literary Response.* New York: Oxford University Press, 1968.

Kiernan, Pauline. *Staging Shakespeare at the New Globe.* London: Macmillan, 1999.

Richmond, Hugh M. "A Letter to the Actor Playing Lear" in *Illuminations.* Ed. Jay Halio and Hugh M. Richmond. Newark: University of Delaware Press, 1998.

Rosenberg, Marvin. *The Masks of Othello.* Berkeley: University of California Press, 1961.

Shakespeare, William. The Riverside Shakespeare. Ed. G. Blakemore Evans, Boston: Houghton Mifflin, 1997.

The Shakespere Allusion-Book. Ed. C. M. Ingleby, *et al.* Freeport N.Y.: Books for Libraries, 1970.

Sacks, Sheldon. *Fiction and the Shape of Belief.* Berkeley: University of California Press, 1964.

Sher, Antony, *The Year of the King.* London: Hogarth, 1985.

Spivack, Bernard. *Shakespeare and the Allegory of Evil.* New York: Columbia University Press, 1958.

Wells, Stanley. *Dictionary of Shakespeare.* Oxford: Oxford University Press, 1998.

White Faces, Blackface
The Production of "Race" in *Othello*

SUJATA IYENGAR

> *To the English, from Othello to Sancho the big—we are*
> *either foolish—or mulish—all—all without a single*
> *exception.*
> —IGNATIUS SANCHO, PROBABLY THE FIRST BLACK
OTHELLO ON THE ENGLISH STAGE

Ben Okri remarks, "If *Othello* is not a play about race, then its history has made it one" (563): but does this mean that we can cheerfully chorus with Ruth Cowhig, "I only want to see black actors in the part" (25)? Does the presence of a black actor automatically ensure political engagement, or could a white actor potentially highlight the intersections of race, class, sexual politics, and translation? Eric Lott calls the almost symbiotic relationship between black and white American working-class culture in the nineteenth century a sequence of "love and theft," culminating in the minstrel show, the stolen kisses of whites performing a mannered "blackness":

> to put on the cultural forms of "blackness" was to engage in a complex affair of manly mimicry . . . To wear or even enjoy blackface was literally, for a time, to become black, to inherit the cool, virility, humility, abandon, or *gaité de cœur* that were the prime components of white ideologies of black manhood. (52)[1]

This desire for appropriation explains why there have been so few black[2] Othellos in the official stage history of the play; black*face* becomes the safety net of a secondhand narration, while "tawniness" (a term I am borrowing from Cowhig) blanches the play of political content and context, fading an entrenched, institutional and collective racism into the "motiveless malignity" of an individual, essentially evil Iago and sporadic personal insults from Roderigo and Brabantio.

Judith Butler argues in *Gender Trouble* that the body is:

> not a "being" but a variable boundary, a surface whose permeability is polit-
> ically regulated, a signifying practice within a cultural field of gender hier-
> archy and compulsory heterosexuality . . . consider gender, for instance, as
> *a corporeal style*, an "act" as it were, which is both intentional and perfor-
> mative, where "performative" suggests a dramatic and contingent construc-
> tion of meaning. (139)

If "political color rather than precise shade of non-whiteness is what matters" (Loomba, 50) and "black" is a political color, then can directors and performers use strategies of "passing" and the over-determination of blackface to
destabilize the categories of "race" and the racial body in the way that Butler
and Marjorie Garber (in *Vested Interests*) argue that "drag" performs and jeop-
ardizes the notion of gender? Butler's later work, *Bodies That Matter*, further
questions the received psychoanalytic view that sexual difference precedes
and thus becomes the mold in which other kinds of difference is cast. What
would happen, she asks, if we were to regard the division of human beings into
distinct sexes "not only through a heterosexualizing symbolic with its taboo
on homosexuality, but through a complex set of racial injunctions which operate in part through the taboo on miscegenation" (167)? How can a psycho-
analysis which incorporates (the bodily metaphor is deliberate) an awareness
of racial and economic factors and their psychic consequences helpfully
inform our reading or viewing of *Othello*?

It is important to distinguish between reading and viewing at the outset
because, historically, critics and editors have tended to neglect *Othello* in performance for *Othello* in the library, a preference that allowed them to ignore
Othello's race and its implications if they so desired.[3] Charles Lamb praised
the written text over the performed, while, as recently as 1958, an Arden editor quoted a woman from Maryland, who always "*imagined* the hero a *white*
man," in order to justify his vision of an Othello with "noble" European features to mitigate the effect of his dark skin (Ridley, li, original emphasis). Performance, however, compels critics and directors, actors and audiences, to
encounter Othello as a *black* man. The important work begun by Ruth Cowhig,
Errol Hill, Herbert Marshall and Mildred Stock, and continued most recently
by Mythili Kaul ("Background"), and Joyce Green MacDonald, has recovered
black Othellos for theater history; this paper extends, and, to a certain extent,
critiques this process of recovery. Okri argues against a black Othello, claiming that a black Othello may convince us of his "nobility . . . but not [his] rage"
(Okri, 564), his personal but not his political tragedy, and thus "[continue] to
be white underneath" (563). In the second half of the twentieth century, critics and directors have tried to bring out *Othello*'s racial dynamics in a number
of ways, ranging from the crude symbolism of Leslie Fiedler (where Othello

and Iago slowly strip off masks to show that Othello is "really" white under-neath and Iago, black), to Sheila Rose Bland's provocative suggestion that we turn the play into a "minstrel-show":

> I would cast the show entirely with white males, having Othello played by a white male in blackface. White males dressed in female clothing would play Desdemona, Emilia and Bianca. I would allow the white male homoerotica [sic] to be played for both humor and titillation.
> In fact, I would treat the entire production as a white male fraternity ini-tiation skit. (29)

Bland argues that the play is a comedy—even a farce—and is "actually about Iago"; she claims that her production would return to the "original" condi-tions of casting, in which Othello himself "was never meant to be more than a caricature" (31). While Bland's proposed performance would certainly repli-cate a few of the original conditions of production, two of her primary assumptions, first, that *Othello* is a comedy of exclusion, and second, that female impersonation and racial impersonation, both on the early modern and on the post-modern stage, are somehow *essentially* comic, are clearly flawed. At least one seventeenth-century audience was moved to tears by *Othello* (Sanders, 38), and recent theatrical experiments both with cross-dressing (such as Cheek By Jowl's 1991 *As You Like It*, or the London Globe's 1999 *Antony and Cleopatra*) and with racial masquerade (such as the Shakespeare Theater's "photo-negative" *Othello*, a production we will consider at length later) have demonstrated that actors do not need to share either the sex or the race of their characters to represent them on stage in a moving, convincing, and illuminating way.[4]

This essay recounts a brief performance history of some black Othellos and Othellos as black, in particular, the performances of Ira Aldridge, Paul Robeson, Willard White, Laurence Olivier, and Patrick Stewart, in order to argue that, under certain specific conditions, the use of a white actor in what I call "strategic blackface" can foreground the fact that the category of "race" itself is "the figment of a white man's imagination" (Kee, 106)—and that the development of these imaginary categories constitutes the greatest tragedy. Stewart's un-blacked, "photo-negative" performance with an almost entirely African American cast belongs with the black Othellos for reasons that will become clear: Jude Kelly's performance text retained the color of insult ("black ram," "black devil"), while reversing the color of its actors. The photo-negative *Othello* detached the sign (physical appearance) from the signified (the social division of race), and in so doing challenged its viewers' assump-tions about identity, race relations, sexual politics, class mobility, and the ethics of adapting Shakespearean texts for the theater.

Ira Aldridge may not, contrary to received theater history, have been the very first black man to play Othello. Errol Hill argues that the very first

Othello of African descent in Britain was Ignatius Sancho (Hill, 10–11).[5] Born
and christened "Charles Ignatius" during the infamous Middle Passage, when
his mother died of disease and his father committed suicide in preference to
slavery, the orphaned Ignatius was given to three English ladies who surnamed
him Sancho because they thought he looked like Don Quixote's squire. The
ladies believed that keeping slaves ignorant was the only way of keeping them
peaceable, a course which drove Sancho to run away repeatedly to the Duke
of Montague, who encouraged him to read. Upon the Duke's death, Sancho
escaped once more and appealed to the Duchess, who initially rejected him
but finally hired him, first as her butler, then as the young Duke's valet. Sancho married an Afro-British woman, Anne Osborne, and fathered seven children; when "a constitutional corpulence" made it impossible for him to remain
in service, the second Duke set him up in a grocer's shop, where he dispensed
tea, pickles and literary criticism until his death in 1780 (Jekyll, 7; Carretta,
xiv). Hill argues that Sancho played Othello in 1760, shortly after coming to
work for the Duchess; Peter Fryer, however, finds no evidence that Sancho
ever in fact performed Othello on a public stage, although he evidently
enjoyed a tremendous liking for both *Othello* and *Oronooko* in performance,
traveling to London to see Garrick play the lead roles (Fryer, 94). The discrepancy between Hill's and Fryer's accounts results, I believe, from an
ambiguous phrase in Joseph Jekyll's "Life of Ignatius Sancho," a memoir prefacing Sancho's *Letters* (published in 1782, two years after Sancho's death).
Jekyll comments on Sancho's love of the theater and adds:

> He had even been induced to consider the stage as a resource in the hour of
> adversity, and his complexion suggested an offer to the manager of attempt-
> ing Othello and Oroonooko [sic]; but a defective and incorrigible articula-
> tion rendered it abortive. (Jekyll, 7)

Jekyll's word "abortive" could mean either that the manager rejected Sancho's
offer without even allowing him to take the stage, or, equally, that the manager agreed to cast Sancho; Sancho tried to play, but failed to attract audiences. It seems likely that Sancho attempted at least a few performances; it is
also probable that the supposed speech impediment was not the only cause for
the failure of Sancho's acting career (remember that customers came into his
shop for advice as well as tea, so his "articulation" was at any rate not incomprehensible). As we shall see, the complaint that black Othellos could not
enunciate Shakespeare's text correctly because of inherited, "incorrigible"
flaws was to become a charge leveled repeatedly at Aldridge, Robeson, and
even White.

There would not be another black Othello on stage until the debut of Ira
Aldridge, who began his theatrical career in Britain under the name of "Mr.
Keene, the African Roscius" in 1824. The pseudonym was perhaps not solely

an attempt to benefit from Edmund Kean's famous name; Kean was the first actor to use blackface make-up to *detach* Othello from his blackness, playing Othello as "tawny" or light-skinned rather than as a dark-skinned sub-Saharan African because he believed that a paler skin would enhance the character's nobility. Aldridge was attempting to contradict the racial implications of Kean's tawny performance. The London reviewer from the *Morning Post* commented that the actor's "sable brethren" would greatly benefit from Aldridge's portrayal,

> inasmuch as [he has] afforded a powerful illustration that blacks as well as whites may be equally fashioned by education—and that to education, principally, is to be ascribed that mental superiority which the latter have too often endeavored to persuade themselves that they exclusively enjoy. (quoted in Marshall, 68)

The Times, however, insisted that "owing to the shape of his lips it is utterly impossible for him to pronounce English in such a manner as to satisfy even the unfastidious ears of the gallery" (quoted in Marshall, 62). Despite the adverse reviews, Aldridge was enormously popular and his engagement was extended for four weeks. After a variety of "Negro" roles, including *The Revolt of Surinam* and Aphra Behn's *Oronooko*, at the London Coburg, Aldridge began to play Shakespearean parts, including Othello and Aaron in *Titus Andronicus*, in the provinces in 1825, spending many years on tour. Aldridge altered *Titus Andronicus* considerably, omitting the rape and mutilation of Lavinia, legitimizing the bond between Aaron and Tamora, turning Shakespeare's villainous Moor into a "noble and lofty character" (*The Era*, quoted in Marshall, 172) and emphasizing the tragic death of Aaron's son. An eyewitness reported that Aldridge even incorporated a scene from *Zaraffa, the Slave King*, a play written specifically for him, into his *Titus* (Marshall, 170–74); Aldridge was already beginning theatrically to criticize the institution of slavery with increasing momentum, as we shall see in his performances as Othello.

Aldridge's *Othello* was enthusiastically received in the provinces, particularly in Hull, but after his debut in Covent Garden (a challenge in any case, since he was following the immensely popular Kean who had collapsed suddenly while playing the role) in 1833, *The Times* lambasted him:

> We could not perceive any fitness which Mr. Aldridge possessed for the assumption of one of the finest parts that was ever imagined by Shakespeare, except, indeed, that he could play it in his own native hue, without the aid of lampblack or pomatum . . . Mr. Aldridge's Othello, with all the advantages of *hic niger est* [here is the black man], wanted spirit and feeling. His accent is unpleasantly, we would say, vulgarly, foreign . . . well might Desdemona's father imagine that sorcery, and not nature, had caused his daughter to listen to such a wooer. (quoted in Marshall, 121)

Marshall and Stock speculate that Hull, (where Aldridge first experimented not only with Othello but with other leading Shakespearean roles like Lear and Macbeth) enjoyed a more congenial political environment than London since, as the hometown of William Wilberforce, it had a local interest in the anti-slavery movement. It is also possible that there were fewer black people in the provinces than in London (as, indeed, is the case now and was in the seventeenth century), so the economic and sexual threat of the "black man" was less potent. London reviewers were also notoriously hard-to-please, blasé and snobbish; the London *Athenaeum* manages to conflate cultural anxieties about gender, class, race, and "art" in one meaty paragraph:

> It is impossible that Mr. Aldridge should fully comprehend the meaning and force or even the words he utters, and, accordingly, the perpetual recurrence of false emphasis . . . shows distinctly that he does not. In the name of common sense we enter our protest against an interesting actress and decent girl like Miss Ellen Tree being . . . pawed about by Mr. Henry Wallack's black servant; and finally . . . we protest against acting being any longer dignified by the name of art. (Marshall, 127)

FIGURE 8. Ira Aldridge as Othello, Constantinople, 1866. Reproduced by kind permission of the Raymond Mander and Joe Mitchenson Theatre Collection, The Mansion, Beckenham, Kent. The age of this photograph (which is possibly taken from a newspaper clipping) explains its poor quality. Still visible, however, are Aldridge's Moorish costume with gold embroidery, his jewelled bracelet, and his curved scimitar.

In response to complaints like these, the theatre was closed down for five days on the pretext of illness, and Aldridge's two nights at Covent Garden were also his last. He continued, however, with enormous success on the Continent and, notably, in Russia, where Théophile Gautier was amazed by his intelligence and skill. Aldridge seems to have played Lear with more than a little irony in his presentation, "whiting up" with evident glee:

> A flesh-coloured headpiece of papier mâché, from which hung some silvery locks of hair, covered his woolly thatch and came down almost to his eyebrows like a helmet; an addition of wax filled in the curves of his flat nose. A thick coat of grease paint covered his black cheeks, and a great white beard enveloped the rest of his face and came down over his chest . . . That Aldridge had not whitened his hands was a caprice which is easily comprehensible, and they showed below the sleeves of his tunic. (Gautier: Marshall, 230)

Marshall and Stock disagree with Gautier's interpretation, finding in Aldridge's clean hands a plea for understanding; they "do not believe it was 'caprice' . . . that prompted Aldridge to play with unwhitened hands. It would seem rather that he was trying to say to the audience, "Let me remind you, I am still a Negro!" (Marshall, 231). We might ask ourselves what Gautier means by "flesh-coloured"; we might also want to compare this account to Olivier's own blow-by-blow description of his make-up as Othello:

> Black all over my body, Max Factor 2880, then a lighter brown, then Negro Number 2, a stronger brown. Brown on black to give a rich mahogany. Then the great trick: that glorious half yard of chiffon with which I polished myself all over until I shone . . . The lips blueberry, the tight curled wig, the white of the eyes, whiter than ever, and the black, black sheen that covered my flesh and bones, glistening in the dressing-room lights. (Olivier, 109)

Aldridge in whiteface differs from Olivier in blackface both in intention and in effect. Aldridge, claims Gautier, left only his hands unbleached from "caprice" or whimsy; Olivier's *entire* impersonation, in contrast, is a self-proclaimed "great trick" or whimsical masquerade with a "glorious half yard of chiffon." Aldridge's aim is to represent Lear, *a* particular white man; Olivier's, to be Othello, *the* characteristic black man. Aldridge's make-up, elaborate though it seems, characterizes Lear not only as a "white" man but also as an old man ("silvery locks"), a powerful man ("headpiece . . . like a helmet"), and a representation of suffering that is all the more moving because it is just that—a representation (the unwhitened hands). Olivier's description fetishizes blackness ("brown on black"), the physical characteristics stereotypically associated with Africans ("the tight curled wig, the white of the eyes") and the collapse of personality into mannerism ("the black . . . sheen that covered my flesh and bones"). Aldridge's unwhitened hands emphasized the limits of role-playing and asserted his own personhood (an especially important political move, as will become clear), but Olivier's performance struck Kenneth Tynan as, more than anything else, a "closely studied piece of physical impersonation" (5), as if the painstaking imitation of an ideal "black" body could more convincingly bring to life an imaginary black character on the stage.

As Marshall and Stock point out, Théophile Gautier's essay on Ira Aldridge was the only omission from the twenty-four volume Harvard translation of Gautier's *Complete Works*, Published in 1900 (229); its erasure was only one of many such "sins of omission" they found when they first published their biography in 1958. They argue that not only the history of *Othello* in performance, but also its critical history and the reviews of those few productions starring black actors have been ones of racism, both witting and unwitting, and give as examples Aldridge's absence from scholarly studies purporting to discuss the dramatic criticism of Gautier, and from *The Annals of Covent Garden Theatre*. Marshall and Stock's biography has itself been reprinted (in 1968 and 1993) and Aldridge has finally been granted his place in received theater history.[6]

Aldridge's reception in Russia had political reverberations for its audience that the British and North American press perhaps could not face. Aldridge arrived in St. Petersburg in November 1858, less than a year after Alexander II had published a bill for liberating Russian serfs. Aldridge himself easily made the connections between African American slavery and Russian serfdom, incorporating Russian folk-songs into his performances of the farce *The Padlock*, with which he invariably followed *Othello*. As Mythili Kaul observes ("Background"), for Zvantsev, Aldridge's Russian biographer, Aldridge became a symbol of black oppression; Zvantsev felt that all the whites around Othello, even Desdemona, were implicated in his guilt:

> Seeing before one the tamed Othello in the net of the tamer, . . . one involuntarily thinks of the many generations of black people suffering under the whip of American slave-traders . . . All this has been represented by Shakespeare so truthfully, so powerfully, that, without the slightest exaggeration, one risks hating all his white heroes . . . not excluding, possibly, even Desdemona herself. It is a pity that even she is not black! (Zvantsev: Marshall, 232)

Zvantsev's "it is a pity [Desdemona] is not black!" is of course ironic, since her whiteness and the sexual charge that this interracial marriage generates help to precipitate the tragedy. Furthermore, it is Othello's isolation as the *only* man or woman of color that brings out the social implications of presenting "race" on stage. This enforced textual isolation is why, for all its amazing tragic force, Trevor Nunn's production of *Othello* at The Other Place in 1989 turned the play into a domestic tragedy-of-love, rather than one "about" racial prejudice; Bianca was played by a black actress, so that Othello's (Willard White's) race did not visually and emotionally brand him in the way that Aldridge, Robeson and even Olivier were marked. The play on her name, "white," becomes a

FIGURE 9. Willard White as Othello and Imogen Stubbs as Desdemona, dir. Trevor Nunn, Royal Shakespeare Company, Stratford-upon-Avon, 1989. Reproduced by kind permission of the Shakespeare Centre, Stratford-on-Avon. This production emphasized Othello's size and Desdemona's fragility: this shot contrast's Desdemona's "too little" handkerchief with the sturdy sailor's cravat knotted around Othello's neck.

sarcastic comment not only on her purity (as it would if she were played as white) but on her skin color. In American productions during the 1990s, it became fashionable to have a black actress play Bianca; one reviewer surmises that directors did this because of Bianca's "low social status" (Johnson-Haddad, 10), so that she becomes Othello's foil, a sign of how far Othello has traveled and how far he can fall, a sign of the limits that race draws around individuals. This has an especially strong resonance in North America, but it is not Shakespearean: Shakespeare's Othello, is, crucially, a solitary stranger abroad, not a member of a particular, distinct, domesticated minority group.

Cowhig points out that it was not until the late eighteenth century that the degree of Othello's blackness came into question and suggests that the historical strength of the abolition movement at this time made spectators uncomfortably aware of the position of slaves in America; Charles Lower makes a similar point when, arguing against received theatre history, he asserts that Othello was played as black as possible on stage in the American South, because

> Antebellum southern audiences regarded theatrical performance as Art, quite distinct from life . . . Shakespeare was consummate Art and thus was part of a city's coming of age culturally. *Othello* . . . was a superb actor's

vehicle, its "act 3" being frequently selected for potpourri benefits . . . It was
a story (safely) far away and long ago particularly because it *was* 'Shakespeare.' (218)[7]

In other words, the presence of blackness is only tolerable as a masquerade or
as a mask with a "white" man underneath; even as recently as 1979, an interracial kiss between the first black Othello in the South and the white Desdemona "prompted a handful of hate letters . . . [and] audible gasps" (221).[8]

The 1930 London production starring Paul Robeson as Othello was,
according to *The Times*, "a freakish production [with] a grotesquely maimed
text" (St. Clare Byrne, 551); the director, Ellen ("Nellie") Van Volkenburg, was
patronizing and, in Peggy Ashcroft's view, "a racist" who cut the text in order
to introduce dances and sailor songs, even suggesting that Othello should land
at Cyprus singing (Duberman, 135). Ashcroft called her experience of the play
"an education in racism"; Robeson himself moved during his career from
being fairly neutral on the question of Othello's "Moorishness" or "blackness"
in 1930 to a firm conviction by the Broadway *Othello* in 1943 that "Moors"
and "blacks" were one and the same in Shakespeare's mind. Robeson's 1959
appearance at Stratford was critically acclaimed; even the right-wing *Daily
Express*, which had condemned Robeson's politics in no uncertain terms,
called his performance "strong and stately" (Duberman, 477). Robeson's Iago
in 1959 was Sam Wanamaker, whose daughter Zoë played Emilia in the 1989
Royal Shakespeare Company production starring Willard White, and Ira
Aldridge's second daughter befriended Robeson in 1925 (one hundred years
after her father's debut at the Coburg Theatre), sending him the earrings her
father had worn as *Othello* and her wishes that Robeson should inherit the part
(Duberman, 91); the three black Othellos in Britain to receive widespread critical attention were therefore familiarly and theatrically linked.[9]

Unlike Robeson's performance, Tony Richardson's "over-clever production" (St. Clare Byrne, 551) was the object of critical scorn, ostensibly because
of its unconventional text. The reviews turned the play text into a fetish.
"Fetish" is, of course, an anthropological term for a small object that comes,
often through a metaphoric or metonymic relationship, to represent something
else, something larger. In the reviews of Robeson's Othello, the uncut text,
identified with an "authentic Shakespeare" (to borrow Stephen Orgel's phrase)
became a fetish for not only the ideal of "Shakespeare" or "high culture," but
also for the transcendence of character itself as written *by* Shakespeare and, by
extension, for the essential nature of the viewing subjects. This position has
been challenged by scholars, directors and teachers in the past thirty years, but
remains current. Recent advocates include Edward Pechter, who asserts that
Othello fails as a tragedy unless we understand the tragic hero as the "author
of his actions" (190), and that certain kinds of tragic performance are "authorized . . . by the words in the script" (9); and Harold Bloom, who argues that

Shakespearean texts create the idea of personality, or "the human," for early modern spectators.

Margreta de Grazia, Orgel, Gary Taylor, Randall McLeod and others have challenged conceptions of an essential or authentic Shakespeare on two grounds: first, on the instability of Shakespearean texts and the collaborative, contingent activity of Elizabethan printing (since texts themselves are so fluid, identifying any one version with Shakespeare's authorial intention or with a prior character or narrative is foolish); second, on the conclusions of post-structuralist theories of identity, such as those of Foucault or Derrida, that emphasize differences between groups of people, and the tensions between individual will and social or cultural forces (since identities or characters are not fixed or eternal, we should think of them not as states of being but as processes of negotiation, responsiveness, and change). De Grazia argues that Malone's burning desire to return to "Shakespeare Verbatim" represents an impossible ideal, and one which necessitates, for example, turning the 1609 sonnets from a collection of lyrics without a coherent story or subject-position into a narrative emphasizing the development of a Shakespearean soul and enshrining Shakespeare at the center of English culture. Gary Taylor argues that our culture's emphasis on Shakespeare as a figure who transcends history and context, like "a god," leads us not only to neglect other dramatists (in both the early modern period and the twenty-first century) but also to suffer from "a schizophrenic criticism, mixing abasement and appropriation" (411). McLeod examines the moralizing terms applied to texts of varying origins— "good" and "bad" quartos—to argue that, in dismissing so-called bad quartos, we ignore a rich mine of information about the early modern stage and obscure the material conditions of text and performance (the voice of the actor, the hand of the printer).[10]

These material conditions necessarily include, in *Othello*, the representation of race. As Kaul remarks, most of the reviews of Robeson's performance "focused on the quality of his performance and, in so doing, sidestepped the question of race" ("Background," 15). Criticism of the play itself from the same era often similarly imagined a transcendent, Shakespearean text that could never be fully realized in performance because of the obfuscating fact of race: Rosenberg, for example, devotes an entire book to the description of previous Othellos, Iagos and Desdemonas and to explanations of how they failed to penetrate beyond "the mask of Othello" to the "essence" of the Moor underneath (subtitle; introduction, *passim*). This idealized conception of the Shakespearean hero is also reflected in the concern for diction which we see in reviews of not only Aldridge and Robeson but also of the more recent black Othello, Willard White, and indeed in Ignatius Sancho's "defective and incorrigible articulation."

The three black actors, Aldridge, Robeson and White, whom I have hitherto discussed are thus also linked by the burden of proof, of showing us what

Othello was "really" like: Robeson and White equally suffer from the twentieth-century insistence on "unexpurgated" or uncut texts as an anachronistic enshrining of the Shakespearean text, as "bardolatry" in its worst form. Stanley Wells argues:

> With a short interval [Trevor Nunn's 1989 *Othello*] lasted over four hours. (Were these texts really played in full to audiences of Shakespeare's time? And if so, must they not have formed some of the most intelligent, thoughtful, attentive, imaginative and intellectually receptive audiences ever to have peopled the theatre?) (191)

Performance texts reflect this change, which is usually not to Othello's benefit. In nineteenth-century productions Othello's "trance" was usually cut altogether, along with the entire eavesdropping scene, since it was seen as beneath Othello's dignity (Lower, 222); if eighteenth- and nineteenth-century directors considered that the "fit" would diminish the dignity of a white man playing a black Othello, why should we assume that it is eminently suitable for a black man in the same role to be reduced to grotesque convulsions? I use the passive voice deliberately; as Okri observes, Shakespeare gives Othello "nobility . . . not rage," a malleable passivity of which the epileptic fit, if played as such, becomes an unnecessary emblem.

    Paul Winfield, the Othello of the Atlanta production discussed by Lower, refused to play the "trance" scene, replacing it with a "ritual chant" because the text "'disturbed [him] a lot'" (220). He was right to feel "disturbed." Burton writes in *The Anatomy of Melancholy* that "a black man is a pearle in a faire woman's eye" (3.83), but she should beware, since "Leo Afer [sic] telleth incredible things almost of the lust and jealousie of his countrymen of Africke": the trance, if played as a fit, conveniently slots into the supposed structure of the jealous black man's progression "from suspition to hatred, from hatred to frensie, madnesse, injury, murder and despair" (Burton 3: 273 –304). Both Olivier and Hopkins, however, play Othello's trance as a full-blown "epileptic"[11] fit, rolling their eyes and jerking spasmodically. Olivier

> Pulls out all the stops . . . the long, shuddering breaths; the head flung back; the jaw thrust out are painstakingly [painfully?] reproduced; and when he falls thrashing to the ground like a landed barracuda, Iago shoves the haft of a dagger between his teeth to keep him from biting off his tongue. (Tynan, 10)

The beastly analogy is apt; playing the trance as a "fit" (for which in any case we have only Iago's word), also reinforces the play's running equation of Othello with the very "Goats and monkeys!" by whom he swears. In the BBC/Time-Life production, directed by Jonathan Miller, Hopkins foams at the mouth and bites his lip, for all the world like a "Barbary horse."[12] Aldridge apparently once tried to imply a medical history for Othello's "fits" by feigning a trance-like state on Iago's "For nothing can'st thou to damnation add / Greater than that," where it was customary for Othello to launch a physical attack on Iago, so that there would be truth in Iago's statement that "he had [a fit] yesterday." Unfortunately neither audience nor reviewers realized what he was attempting and he never made a similar innovation again (Marshall, 68). In this context the BBC's and Olivier's retention of the trance as a "fit" provides yet another example of the involuntary racism not of audiences but of producers and directors. Of course, Nunn, who directed Willard White, is far from being a racist; he insists on the need for a black Othello,

> Not only for political reasons, but for reasons of integrity to the play, and sheer theatrical practicality. A play that's so overwhelmingly about male-female relationships needs a physical relationship between Othello and Desdemona. And with a white actor in black make-up that's the one thing you can't have. If they touch each other, Othello comes off on Desdemona. (*The Independent*: Thursday 17th August 1989)

Nonetheless, he shares critical assumptions about the sanctity of the culture text and, rather like the nineteenth-century *Othellos* in the American South, the name of "Shakespeare" confers an instant blessing on any performance, however lengthy. Nunn's real innovation was in his emphasis on "naturalism" in speech rather than applying the received Royal Shakespeare Company wisdom of "correct" verse-speaking technique. The result was that "the play sounds as if it is being new-minted as it goes along" (Coveney, 1128), although *The Spectator* claimed that "the phrasing of all [Othello's] major speeches is leaden" (Edwards, 1124). As we have seen, this last is a familiar complaint; even as he praises Robeson's epoch-making performance, John Dover Wilson pays lip service to the fallen idol of "technique":

> [T]he crowning proof of Othello's race is that I once had the good fortune to see him played by a Negro—that great gentleman with the golden voice, Paul Robeson: and I felt I was seeing the tragedy for the first time, not merely because of Robeson's acting, which despite a few petty faults of technique was magnificent, but because the fact that he was a true Negro seemed to floodlight the drama . . . The performance convinced me, in short, that a Negro Othello is essential to the full understanding of the play. (quoted in Cowhig, 22)

Dover Wilson is willing ultimately to sacrifice "technique" to a fuller understanding of the play. Note the terms of his praise, however: Robeson's "golden voice" is singled out as part of what makes his performance authentic, part of what makes him "a true Negro," as if all Africans or African Americans are musicians. There seems to be in traditional stage histories an ideal of pure Shakespearean production, the integral text, versus what is seen as somehow miscegenating the text, corrupting it for overt and crude political agendas, as if "politics" and "art" were two separate terms, enabling, for example, Sanders to suggest that:

> Most of his admirers noted the consciousness of race in Robeson's perfor-
> mance, which for some gave it a seriousness of purpose that made all others
> seem trivial, but for others militated against the tragic sense of the original. (47)

At stake, then, in the reviewers' dislike of textual experimentation hides a notion of an essential Othello who will somehow transcend the vagaries of both text and production, and even "race."

"Tragedy" is, of course, another "pure" form that is violated by *Othello* and another area in which black Othellos are seen as deficient. If we, like *The Gaurdian's* Michael Billington, define Shakespearean tragedy in Bradleian terms, with a hero whose "fall" is determined by an innate, fatal "flaw," then no wonder that a black Othello mitigates "the tragic sense of the original" or "ultimately misses the sound we long for in tragedy: the agonized cry of a cornered human soul" (Billington, 1129), since the circumstances of historical existence and of social interactions outweigh the failings of an inherent "personality" in determining the catastrophe. Olivier's Leavisite Othello is infuriating not even so much because of the grotesque make-up but because of its resolute assignation of consistent motive or of a fatal flaw to Othello. As a theatrical experiment, this could be a chance to give Othello the rage that Okri finds missing; in this case, however, character is divorced from history so that Othello's self-absorption is not a reaction to others' perception of him nor to his colonial past but a feature of his royalty, his blackness and his insensitivity. Tynan notes:

> Olivier displays the public mask of Othello: a Negro sophisticated enough to
> conform to the white myth about Negroes, pretending to be simple and not
> above rolling his eyes, but in fact concealing (like any other aristocrat) a
> highly developed sense of racial superiority. (5)

In some ways this performance was a brave attempt to factor in the element of class and to provide a way of centering the play around Othello rather than, as so often happens, Iago; unfortunately Olivier's own egotism rather than Othello's is what remains with us of his performance—the image of Olivier bouncing on the balls of his feet, turning up his eyes to heaven, rolling his words around his mouth, cocking his head on one side to drink in Iago's voice.

The tension between Iago and Othello in performance is, in many ways, a version of the tension Karen Newman finds in the play between aural/oral and scopic drives; Iago's lies and Othello's attention parallel Othello's story-telling and Desdemona's "greedy" listening, but the demand for "ocular proof" both supersedes and fulfills the events set into motion by tale-telling and listening. During the "eavesdropping" scene, Othello can see both Cassio and Bianca clearly, but his hearing is muffled: at the same time, visual patterns, like the strawberries on the handkerchief, become obscure or even removed, as Cassio asks Bianca to unpick the work on the napkin and as Othello destroys the "cunning'st pattern" of the sleeping Desdemona. Othello himself can rely on neither his eyes nor his ears, a disability that the play explicitly connects to race and to spectatorship.

Recent black feminist criticism has focussed on the problem of "the gaze" in mainstream cinema and, critiquing Laura Mulvey's work, has concentrated on the suggestion of an "oppositional gaze" through which black women can articulate a position which neither colludes in an active scopophilia nor passively identifies with the image of objectified white womanhood on display:

> Black female spectators actively chose not to identify with the film's imaginary subject [both narrating and narrated] because such identification was disenabling . . . Looking at films with an oppositional gaze, black women were able to critically assess the cinema's construction of white womanhood as object of phallocentric gaze and choose not to identify with either the victim or the perpetrator. (hooks, 122)

Emotionally detached from the white women on screen because of their race, hooks argues, black women can question what it means, culturally, to be female, and reject the traditional constraints of gender; viewing pleasures, for black women, include intellectual critique and a sense of community, stemming from estrangement from the white majority on the one hand, and identification with an imagined group of similar, alienated black women on the other. I would add a third oppositional pleasure to hooks' list: if black women "actively cho[o]se" not to identify with white femininity on screen, they are also free to choose "actively" to *share* those identifications if they so desire. These identifications would be performative, in Butler's sense, in that they would be crucially, temporally, limited, lasting only for the duration of the film.

Theorizing the spectator is important because, as Butler points out, it is the context of drag which renders it subversive: a team of rugby players who habitually plunder their girlfriends' wardrobes for skirts when they are the worse for alcohol are not necessarily "performing gender" in the way that a parade on San Francisco's Castro Street may be. It seems to be the cultural position of the gay or transgendered man as marginalized or oppressed subject (as opposed to the rugby player) which interrogates "gender,"[13] while the rugby player's position as (in my example) privileged heterosexual middle-class white male uses drag to reinforce a kind of male solidarity at the expense of women. In the same way, Laurence Olivier playing Othello in elaborate make-up at the height of his career in order to celebrate the centenary of the National Theatre might have nothing in common with a seventeenth-century production where "the boy who impersonated Desdemona 'moved [the audience] especially in her death' " (Sanders, 38).

Crudely put, there needs to be more than one element of so-called subversion in order to destabilize gender or race. There is also the possibility that drag works precisely because viewers may speculate that the "queen's" biological gender is (usually) empirically and biologically determinable, where they can have no such certainty about "race," which can disappear after a couple of generations and is more firmly legislated.

Performance artist Adrian Piper, accused of "passing for black" in order to qualify for scholarships and quotas, analyzes the "one-drop" rule, which

> uniquely characterizes the classification of blacks in the United States in fact even where no longer in law. So according to this longstanding convention of racial classification, a white who acknowledges any African ancestry implicitly acknowledges being black—a social condition, more than any identity, that no white person would voluntarily assume, even in imagination. This is one reason that whites, educated and uneducated alike, are so resistant to considering the probable extent of racial miscegenation. (291)

Piper argues that "white resistance to the idea that most American whites have a significant percentage of African ancestry increases with the percentage suggested." While her most obvious target is the American white, she also quotes studies finding a degree of African ancestry present in the genes of "British whites" as well. Audiences encounter, I believe, other difficulties, when a production may star a black actor yet nonetheless naïvely reinforce white ideologies of "blackness": by retaining the trance in Iago's terms, as an "epilepsy"; by encouraging Iago to upstage Othello by refusing to prune his speeches, making Othello look foolish; by cutting the "willow-scene" (4.3) and Desdemona's bawdy, racial banter during the landing at Cyprus (3.1) thus relegating her to the status of a pawn. Despite Robeson's magnificent performance, Tony Richardson's 1959 production, for example, cut most of the willow-scene and kept Othello entranced on the floor until he rose on a devout, "O, thou art wise, I know't." Texts need cutting, as I have said all along, but invariably removing the women's lines in preference to all others denies *Othello* its full range of tragic expression, as Irene Dash and others have observed. This *is* a text in which I see "manly mimicry" (in Lott's phrase) or sexual difference expressed not prior to but at the same time as racial identity. Textual interpolations can serve as "an education in racism," in Ashcroft's words (as in Nellie Van Volkenberg's production); cutting the text can diminish the play's complex relationships, (as in Tony Richardson's production); leaving the play intact can turn Othello into a racialized buffoon (as in Jonathan Miller's production).

Jude Kelly's self-described "photo-negative" production of *Othello* at the Shakespeare Theater in 1997, however, combined controversial issues of textual integrity and strategic blackface. The production starred Patrick Stewart

FIGURE 10. Ron Canada as Iago and Patrick Stewart as Othello, dir. Jude Kelly, The Shakespeare Theatre, Washington D.C., 1997-1998. Reproduced by kind permission of Carol Rosegg and the Shakespeare Theatre, Washington, D.C. Photo credit: Carol Rosegg. Othello's tattooed scalp and "tribal" jewelry were some of the ways in which Kelly's production attempted to "race" Othello's whiteness.

as a white Othello in a black republic; the cast was predominantly African American, but Othello, Bianca, Montano and a couple of other roles were played by white actors. In this production, it was not make-up or cutting that drew critical attention—or opprobrium—but the decisions to avoid doing either, by having Stewart play Othello as a white man, but without reversing the binaries of "black" and "white" in the language of the play. Many critics praised Stewart's performance, but disliked the production's "high concept" of racial reversal, objecting in particular to its retention of Shakespeare's text without altering the "color" of the racial slurs.

The production drew a substantial amount of media attention on both sides of the Atlantic, not only because of its concept but also on account of the fiery star power of classically trained British actor Patrick Stewart, fresh from the syndicated science-fiction franchise, *Star Trek: The Next Generation*. In general, the British press dismissed the concept of photo-negativity as "an irrelevance," asking "whether the photo-negative device is merely a ruse to allow Stewart to play a long-coveted part without blacking up" (Gardner), and claiming,

[i]n a play only part of whose subject is racial prejudice it makes little difference whether it is a white regarding a solitary black with suspicion or vice

versa. (To hammer home the point the servants and the prostitute Bianca are played by white actors too.) In this context, "black" is merely synonymous with "alien" or "outsider." (Spencer, Interview)

Charles Spencer here articulates a view frequently found in the British press that *Othello* is not a play about race, but, as Lynn Gardner argues, a "domestic tragedy," "so much more a play about love, jealousy and the blindness of male machismo than it is about race," as if the play would need an apologist if it *were* found to be "about race." British reviewers, on the whole, took Stewart's performance as another opportunity to cavil against what Jeremy Kingston called "the PC factor [that] has denied a generation of white actors the chance to play the Moor." Spencer and Kingston apparently still believed that African American and Afro-Caribbean actors were fully-employed; Spencer argued that, "when it is regarded as highly desirable for black actors to play conventionally white roles, it is absurd, even hypocritical, that white actors can no longer play Othello" (Interview). Kingston even accused directors of giving roles to black actors because of "funding dependent on doing the PC thing."

FIGURE 11. Patrick Stewart as Othello and Patrice Johnson as Desdemona, The Shakespeare Theatre, Washington, D.C., 1997-1998. Reproduced by kind permission of Carol Rosegg and the Shakespeare Theatre, Washington, D.C. Photo credit: Carol Rosegg. This photograph brings out the "photo-negative" aspects of the production's staging; the scattered books upon the table, and the physical closeness between Othello and Desdemona seem to mirror Trevor Nunn's production above, but the actors' skin colors are reversed.

In fact, cross-racial casting had become a *canard* for the right-wing British press even before Stewart's production opened: in August 1997, David Harewood, a black British actor, played Othello at the National Theatre in the first performance of the play there since 1980. He received some good notices from the press but also many complaints about "unfair" casting rules, and "reverse discrimination." Geoffrey Wheatcroft, in the *Daily Telegraph*, compared theaters' reluctance to cast white actors as Othello to anti-Semitism in Vienna in the 1930s, and suggested a campaign: he recommended that a white actor should audition for the part, and then "sue under the Race Relations Act" if denied it. David Lister's complaint about the allegedly inexperienced Harewood in *The Independent* was that "no white actor with a similar background would be playing the lead in a Shakespeare tragedy at the NT." Perhaps this reluctance to recognize both the importance of race in the play and the implications of the photo-negative approach stemmed from a more general failure in Britain to recognize the effects of racism both in everyday life and in the theater. Ironically, Lister's article denying the presence of racism in the theater appeared just one week after the Home Secretary established an inquiry into racism in British life, particularly in the police force.[14]

The North American responses to the Stewart/Kelly *Othello*, in contrast, focussed upon the racial reversal, even if they hated the concept or thought it did not work. Peter Marks, writing for the *New York Times*, began by insisting that "the racial turning of the play . . . tends to take the racial issue off the table," but contradicted himself a few lines later by spelling out the specific ways in which the photo-negative concept did indeed bring the "racial issue" to the fore:

> when Othello is a white military leader—what more recognizable authority figure exists in Western culture?—it's hard to feel particularly sorry for him. It's an instance in which race reversal does not jibe with an audience's sense of the way the world beyond the theater works. (Marks)

Surely this unexpected fissure between the "world" and the "theater" is a "racial issue" of its own, and perhaps one which is closer to Shakespeare's mighty, military Moor than the victim for whom we "feel . . . sorry." If Othello is consistently played as only a victim, as Iago's stooge, as a minstrelized parody of the effects of racism, then casting a black actor would be as offensive as casting a white one, blacked up—both of them would, like Olivier, be attempting to portray an originary or essential "black experience" rather than the intersections between individual experience and the collective experience of prejudice.

The popular daily *USA Today* called the production a "disaster," complaining that the modern setting made the production's "feminist" emphasis anachronistic and "hyper-emotive." The reviewer failed to be convinced by the "confusing" photo-negative approach, asking, "who could expect a predominantly black cast to be comfortable when they've been assigned the play's most racist lines?" (Stearns) But why (as the writer implies) might a predominantly *white* cast be "comfortable" uttering racial slurs? If the blackness of the cast did indeed make the insults more incomprehensible, perhaps Stewart and Kelly succeeded in their intention

> to say what a conventional production of *Othello* would say about racism and prejudice . . . in a more intense and possibly provocative way by reversing the usual racial characteristics. To replace the black outsider with a white man in a black society will . . . encourage a much broader view of the fundamentals of racism, and perhaps even question those triggers—color of skin, physiognomy, language, culture—that can produce instant feelings of fear, suspicion and so forth. (Stewart, quoted in Amanda Kelly)

In other words, Stewart was hoping to interrogate the North American definition of "race" itself and its dependence upon supposedly fixed physical characteristics. That this is a challenge that needs to be made is clear from the unintentional racism of even enthusiastic reviewers. Toby Zinman commented in *American Theatre* that "many of the play's nuances strike the ear as ludicrous: Desdemona's skin is decidedly not 'alabaster' nor is Stewart a 'black devil' with 'thick lips.'" Let's leave aside the question of whether these are "nuances" or gross epithets, and ask instead whether *any* Othello, white or black, is "decidedly" a "'black devil' with 'thick lips.'" If Othello *were* played by a black man, would he then really be the "black devil" that Emilia vilifies? Are we to take the description of Othello with "thick lips" as a stage direction, and if so, how "thick" would a supposedly Othello's lips have to be? Finally, surely the writer does not imagine that European women naturally have skin that is chalk-white or "alabaster"?

The *Atlanta Journal and Constitution* likewise objected to the unchanged language of the play, claiming that when "the Scotsman [sic] . . . intone[d], 'I am black' . . . the line was greeted with titters" (Hulbert, Review). Dan Hulbert argued that "*Othello* . . . is . . . not about some abstract 'other,' but about a black man as seen through the prejudices of Shakespeare's time." He seemed to imply that the play itself panders to those "prejudices," by casting "the black man" as a "sexual threat" a guileless dupe, and a "slave to emotion" (Hulbert, Review). But, if this interpretation is correct, then Sheila Rose Bland is on target to call the play a "minstrelized comedy," and there is no place for a black actor in the role. In a later article about non-traditional casting, Hulbert made his preferences clearer:

> the Stewart *Othello* . . . can't decide which type of nontraditional effect it seeks: the type in which viewers are supposed to remain aware of the racial mismatch, for ironic effect, or they're invited to look past the actor's skin, to the soul. (Hulbert, "Shakespeare classic isn't the same")

In fact these two imagined reactions are not opposite, but similar: they both depend upon a sense of racial identity that is fixed, related in a coherent way to our world outside the theater, to the world on stage, and to the personality or "soul" of the actor. But it seems as though Stewart and Kelly's ideal was for audiences to respond in neither of these ways, but instead to question the nature of racial difference and ask themselves *whether* race is defined by physical difference, social position or anything else, and *whether* they can separate "the skin" and "the soul." In particular, the production asked questions about race in America, and the limits and stereotypes associated with blackness.

More helpful analyses, like Robert King's in the weekly periodical *The North American Review*, discuss this challenge to racial stereotype with specific examples:

> When Roderigo tells Brabantio that his "fair daughter" is in "the gross clasps of a lascivious Moor," Iago faces front in a half squat, sways, swings his drooping arms before him and whoops like a chimpanzee. This offensive stereotype is undeniably racist, yet it is enacted by and for a black man. If it is meant to mirror the white audience's prejudices, it is little more than reverse racism, arrogant in its sweeping assumptions. Perhaps it is meant to be symptomatic of racism learned and absorbed by its victims. (King)

King offers two interpretations of this "chimpanzee" dance: first, the director and cast have arrogantly assumed that the predominantly white audience shares Iago's belief in ethnic stereotyping, and the players are trying to startle or shock the audience out of applying these prejudices to the predominantly black cast; second, the black characters in their fictional African republic have internalized the stereotypes that the Western world applies to them and use them to dominate other groups. Both explanations make a certain sense, but they are not the only logical interpretations. There is no intrinsic connection between chimpanzees and blackness, any more than between chimpanzees and whiteness, and Iago's mocking dance makes a point that recent scholarly work on early modern race has suggested: the associations of blackness with inferiority, animal behavior, servitude and so on came about because of specific historical conditions and economic factors—it was necessary to dehumanize a particular group of people in order to enslave them (see, for example, Theodore Allen's argument in *The Invention of the White Race*).[15] Jude Kelly did not claim that Othello, or Stewart, was ever a non-specific "abstract other," as Hulbert complained (Hulbert, Review), but that "Patrick [Stewart] isn't playing a white man—he's playing a black man, although he's white . . . It is the audience that has to make the adjustment" (Kelly, quoted in Kuchwara, "Patrick Stewart's Othello"). Perhaps it might help to recall Patrick Stewart's television show, *Star Trek: The Next Generation*, where the crew occasionally found themselves in "parallel" or quantum universes: in such universes, the

Earth occupies the same position in space-time and is populated by human beings, but human history, and its consequences, are radically different. In the alternative universe of the Stewart/Kelly *Othello*, the group of people that were becoming enslaved during Shakespeare's lifetime were light-rather than dark-skinned.

The opposite of "black" for an early modern audience is not "white" but "fair," and "fair," as Kim Hall points out, is a comparative term. Does it therefore matter that the first recipient of the racial insults, Othello himself, is in the Stewart/Kelly production that we now call white? The metaphor of blackness is a powerful statement of the imbrication of language and racism. But what can we do about it? Can we detach the two relationships? We need to continue to denaturalize the association of "black" or dark skin and black deeds, black days, black thoughts, and black moods. What we might call Stewart's strategic, rather than literal, blackface uncouples race and skin color. In reverse-casting while retaining the color of insult, the Stewart/Kelly production emphasized the arbitrariness of racial classification and the interweaving of politics and art.

NOTES

I would like to thank Anita Loomba, Alan Sinfield, Frances Teague and Philip Kolin for comments on earlier drafts of this essay.

1. If we consider many white youths' fondness for rap and hip-hop and the associated clothing as a kind of "black-face," this is perhaps still the case; Lott writes: "every time you hear an expansive white man drop into his version of black English, you are in the presence of blackface's unconscious return" (5).

2. I am using the word "black" not, I hope, in an insensitive, essentializing and reductive manner but as a political designation for actors "of color" who are visually marked as "other" in the theatrical space. I do not include "Arabian" Othellos (like, for example, the 1987 Royal Shakespeare Company production with Ben Kingsley as Othello) for historical reasons; as Cowhig points out, the arguments in favor of a "tawny" Othello stem from a reluctance to acknowledge people with "African" features and/or descent as fully human. For example, the published prompt-book of *Othello: As Presented by Edwin Booth* (New York: Francis Hart, 1881) contains an appendix that claims, "It used to be the practice of the stage to paint the Moor quite black—to present him, in fact, as a Negro . . . But, . . . since to make Othello a Negro is to unpoetize the character, and to deepen whatever grossness may already subsist in the subject of the tragedy . . . [t]he Moor should be painted a pale cinnamon color, which is at once truthful and picturesque" (7:121). Perhaps within the next twenty years attitudes will change enough to permit me to modify my own.

3. A recent statement of this preference can be found in Pechter's wide-ranging study, which he describes as "grounded almost wholly in a text-centered interpretation" (9).

4. On the Cheek By Jowl tenth anniversary production of *As You Like It*, see Dusinberre; Gussow; Ko; Morris; Nightingale, "As You Like It"; Rutherford; Spencer,

"Gender-Benders in Arden." On the London Globe *Antony and Cleopatra*, see Bassett; Billington, "Comedy of Lovers"; Hewison, "Playing Fast and Loose"; Holden; Macaulay; Nightingale, "'Antony and Cleopatra. Shakespeare's Globe"; Taylor, "Delectable Mark Finds Cleopatra's Sensitive Soul."

5. Errol Hill's account of Sancho appears in *Shakespeare in Sable* (10–11), and Sancho is mentioned briefly by William Torbert Leonard in his history of whites in blackface, *Masquerade in Black*.

6. Gautier's comments on Aldridge may have been missing from the standard Gautier edition in 1900, but they did, however, appear in 1905 in *Russia Observed*, translated by Florence MacIntyre Tyson, in a two-volume set that was reprinted in one volume in 1970.

7. Compare Levine's analysis of the Shakespearean playlet which the "King of France" and "Duke of Bilgewater" put on in a small southern town in Twain's *Huckleberry Finn*; Levine argues that, for nineteenth-century American audiences, Shakespeare *was* popular culture, ripe for appropriation and export, a kind of common currency.

8. The first interracial *screen* kiss in the United States was for years thought to have been a clinch between Lieutenant Uhura and Captain Kirk in an episode of *Star Trek* in 1964; recently, however, William Shatner [Kirk] acknowledged in his memoirs (excerpted in *TV Guide*) that the "kiss" was an illusion. The camera tracks around them, creating the illusion of a prolonged embrace. Their lips do not actually meet. The reason for this was the producer's fear that the Southern television stations would not accept the episode unless they were assured that labial contact had not, in fact, occurred.

9. Married, like Aldridge, or Othello himself, to a white woman, in 1930 Robeson had an affair with Peggy Ashcroft; like Desdemona, she loved him for the dangers he had passed (Duberman 138).

10. To emphasize his point about arbitrary, contingent Elizabethan printing practices, McLeod published this essay under the anagrammatic pseudonym "Random Cloud," the result of a contemporary equivalent of the confused compositor—the spell-check function on a word-processor.

11. I put "epileptic" in "scare quotes" because physicians tell me that, again contrary to myth, most epileptics *don't* thrash around and foam as actors do but tend to lie there quietly until helped.

12. Ironically, the BBC had originally wanted the well-known black American actor, James Earl Jones, to play Othello, but was thwarted by British Equity's insistence that a British actor should be chosen for the role, even if (as was the case) no black British actor could be found.

13. There are, obviously, feminists who find drag degrading. Carole-Anne Tyler offers a helpful summary:

> Judith Williamson writes that men in drag undermine "female characteristics" and therefore women because they parody "the feminine form" instead of adopting a "natural" feminine style. And in a similar vein, Erika Munk argues that female impersonators are currently "no more subversive" than whites in blackface were when minstrel shows were popular (41).

14. The investigation was set up on 31 July 1997 to inquire into the vicious, racially motivated murder of black teenager Stephen Lawrence nearly five years previously, "in order particularly to identify the lessons to be learned for the investigation and prosecution of racially motivated crimes" (Lawrence Inquiry, 3.1). Lawrence was waiting at a bus stop when he was "engulfed" by a group of white youths who called "What, what nigger?" before stabbing him twice "to a depth of about five inches on both sides of the front of his body to the chest and arm" (Lawrence Inquiry, 1.3; 1.7). The Lawrence Inquiry would eventually conclude that the murder was an "unmotivated racial attack" and that the killers had been acquitted because of "institutional racism" throughout the Metropolitan Police Service (MPS), whose "first investigation was palpably flawed and deserves severe criticism" (Lawrence Inquiry, 2.10). Given that it took a five-year campaign by Lawrence's articulate, intelligent parents before the MPS admitted to racism within its ranks, critics' dismissal of the importance of race on stage, in their responses both to Harewood in August and to Stewart in November, seems in retrospect a sinister, if well-intentioned, move.

15. Recent critical work on "race" in the early modern period, such as Ania Loomba's *Gender, Race, Renaissance Drama*; Patricia Parker and Margo Hendricks' collection of essays, *Women, "Race" and Writing in the Early Modern Period*; or Kim Hall's *Things of Darkness*, have broken down many assumptions about early modern race. First of all, Loomba counters the arguments of earlier critics, such as G. K. Hunter, that there were no black people in Britain; far from being an inevitable or "natural" response to the unfamiliar, or the natural consequence of church teachings associating blackness and the devil, Loomba argues, racism in the Renaissance arises as the reflection of rapidly-changing economic and social conditions, most notably colonial expansion (encounters abroad) and the black presence in Britain (encounters at home). Parker and Hall's anthology contains not only essays, like Lynda Boose's "The Getting of a Lawful Race," discussing theories of Africans' blackness as an hereditary contamination but also articles, like Dympna Callaghan's, that analyze the subtle relations between different foreign groups such as Moors and Jews. Most recently, Kim Hall has insisted that, while we cannot *prove* the existence of a large African presence in early modern England, such a diaspora is not necessary for the analysis of the Renaissance imagery of "dark" and "light" that she takes as central to the later developments of racism. Black, as an insulting epithet, is applied both to racially white and black and brown people. *Othello* itself is full of this punning, as we can see from Othello's and Iago's strictures on Desdemona's chastity; "black" is a term used to describe unchaste women, whatever their skin-color.

WORKS CITED

Allen, Theodore W. *The Invention of the White Race*. 2 vols. London: Verso, 1994.

Bassett, Kate. "Role Reversal As Actor Steps Into Cleopatra's Shoes." Review of *Antony and Cleopatra*. *The Daily Telegraph*. 31 July 1999. 7. On-line. Lexis-Nexis. University of Georgia. 24 February, 2000. Keywords: Antony and Cleopatra, Globe, London.

Bayley, John. "*Love and Identity:* Othello." Wain 169–198.

Billington, Michael. Review of *Othello. The Guardian.* 26 August 1989. Rpt. in *London Theatre Record.* 13–26 August 1989.

———. "Comedy of Lovers." Review of *Antony and Cleopatra. The Guardian.* 2 August 1999. 12. On-line. Lexis-Nexis. University of Georgia. 24 February, 2000. Keywords: Antony and Cleopatra, Globe, London.

Bland, Sheila Rose. "How I Would Direct *Othello.*" Kaul 29–41.

Bradley, A. C. *Shakespearean Tragedy.* Wain 57–68.

Burton, Richard. *The Anatomy of Melancholy.* 1621. Ed. Thomas Faulkner, Nicholas Kiessling, Rhonda Blair. 5 Vols. Oxford: Clarendon, 1989–1994.

Butler, Judith. *Gender Trouble: Feminism and the Subversion of Identity.* London: Routledge, 1990.

———. *Bodies That Matter: On the Discursive Limits of "Sex."* London: Routledge, 1993.

Carretta, Vincent. "Introduction." *The Letters of Ignatius Sancho, an African.* Harmondsworth, Middx.: Penguin, 1998. ix–xxxii.

Cloud, Random [Randall McLeod]. "The Marriage of Good and Bad Quartos." *Shakespeare Quarterly* 33.4 (1982): 421–31.

Coleridge, Samuel T. "*Marginalia on* Othello, *and Report of a Lecture at Bristol.*" Wain 51–56.

Conan, Neal. Interview with Patrick Stewart. *Talk of the Nation.* National Public Radio. 16 December 1997. Transcript 97121601-211. Transcribed by Federal Document Clearing House, Inc. On-line. Lexis-Nexis. University of Georgia. 22 May 1999. Keywords: Othello and Patrick Stewart.

Coveney, Michael. Review of *Othello. Financial Times.* 26 August 1989. Rpt. *London Theatre Record.* 13–26 August 1989.

Cowhig, Ruth. "Blacks in English Renaissance Drama and the Role of Shakespeare's Othello." In *The Black Presence in English Literature.* Ed. David Dabydeen. Manchester: Manchester University Press, 1985.

Dash, Irene. *Wooing, Wedding and Power: Women in Shakespeare's Plays.* New York: Columbia University Press, 1981.

De Grazia, Margreta. *Shakespeare Verbatim: The Reproduction of Authenticity and the 1790 Apparatus.* Oxford: Clarendon, 1991.

Duberman, Martin Bauml. *Paul Robeson.* New York: Alfred Knopf, 1988.

Dusinberre, Juliet. "As *Who* Liked It?" *Shakespeare Survey* 46 (1993): 9–21.

———. "Women and Boys Playing Shakespeare." As You Like It: *Essais critiques.* Ed. Jean-Paul Debax and Yves Peyre. Toulouse, France: Presse Universitaire du Mirail, 1998. 11–26.

Edwards, Christopher. Review of *Othello. The Spectator.* 2 September 1989. Rpt. *London Theatre Record.* 13–26 August 1989.

Fanon, Frantz. "The Man of Color and the White Woman." *Black Skin, White Masks.* 1968. New York: Pluto, 1986.

Fiedler, Leslie A. "The Moor as Stranger: or 'Almost damned in a fair wife . . . .' " *The Stranger in Shakespeare.* Frogmore, Herts.: Paladin, 1974. 117–64.

Garber, Marjorie. *Vested Interests: Cross-dressing as Cultural Anxiety.* London: Routledge, 1992.

Gardner, Lynn. Review of *Othello*. *The Guardian*. 25 November 1997. 9. On-line. Lexis-Nexis. University of Georgia. 1 March 1999. Keywords: Othello and Patrick Stewart.

Great Britain. The Home Department. *The Stephen Lawrence Inquiry*. Comp. Sir William Macpherson of Cluny. London: HMSO. February 1999. On-line. North-East Georgia Internet Access. 23 May 1999. /http://www.official-documents.co. uk/document/cm42/4262/4262.htm/

Gussow, Mel. "'As You Like It' in its Native Language." Review of *As You Like It*. *New York Times*. 26 July 1991. C18. On-line. Lexis-Nexis. University of Georgia. 24 February 2000. Keywords: As You Like It and Cheek By Jowl.

Hall, Kim. *Things of Darkness: Economies of Race and Gender in Early Modern England*. Ithaca: Cornell University Press, 1996.

Hewison, Robert. "Playing Fast and Loose With a Queen." Review of *Antony and Cleopatra*. *Sunday Times*. 8 August 1999. Features. On-line. Lexis-Nexis. University of Georgia. 24 February 2000. Keywords: Antony and Cleopatra, Globe, London.

Hill, Errol. *Shakespeare in Sable*. Amherst, MA: University of Massachusetts Press, 1984.

hooks, bell [Gloria Watkins]. *Black Looks: Race and Representation*. Boston: South End, 1992.

Holden, Anthony. "Drag Queen Barges On." Interview with Mark Rylance. *The Observer*. 25 July 1999: 9. On-line. Lexis-Nexis. University of Georgia. 24 February 2000. Keywords: Antony and Cleopatra, Globe, London.

Hulbert, Dan. Review of *Othello*. *Atlanta Journal and Constitution*. 19 November 1997: 8B. On-line. Lexis-Nexis. University of Georgia. 22 May 1999. Keywords: Othello and Patrick Stewart.

———. "Shakespeare classic isn't the same with a white Othello." *Atlanta Journal and Constitution*. 23 November 1997: 3K. On-line. Lexis-Nexis. University of Georgia. 22 May 1999. Keywords: Othello and Patrick Stewart.

Hunter, G. K. "*Othello* and Color Prejudice." 1967. Vol. 53 of *Proceedings of the British Academy*. London: British Academy/Oxford University Press, 1968.

Jekyll, Joseph. "The Life of Ignatius Sancho." Sancho 5–9.

Johnson, Samuel. "*General Remarks on* Othello." Wain 49–50.

Johnson-Haddad, Miranda. "The Shakespeare Theatre *Othello*." Review. *Shakespeare Bulletin* 16.2 (1998): 9–11.

———. "Patrick Stewart on Playing Othello." Interview. *Shakespeare Bulletin* 16.2 (1998): 11–12.

Kaul, Mythili, ed. Othello: *New Essays By Black Writers*. Washington, DC: Howard University Press, 1997.

———. "Background: Black or Tawny? Stage Representations of Othello from 1604 to the Present." Kaul 1–19.

Kee, Robert. Review of *Othello*. *New Statesman*. Tynan 106–7.

Kelly, Amanda. "Star Trek skipper to play white Othello." *The Independent*. 15 November 1997: 2. On-line. Lexis-Nexis. University of Georgia. 1 March 1999. Keywords: Othello and Patrick Stewart.

King, Robert. "The Seeing Place." Review of *Othello. North American Review* 283.1 (1998): 36–39. On-line. EBSCO index. University of Georgia. 21 May 1999. Keywords: Othello and Patrick Stewart.

Kingston, Jeremy. "Skin-deep *Othello* misfires." Review of *Othello. The Times.* 25 November 1997. On-line. Lexis-Nexis. University of Georgia. 1 March 1999. Keywords: Othello and Patrick Stewart.

Ko, Yu Jin. "Straining Sexual Identity: Cheek by Jowl's All-Male *As You Like It.*" *Shakespeare Bulletin* 13.3 (1995): 16-17.

Kuchwara, Michael. "In Washington, Patrick Stewart's 'Othello' in Black and White." Review of *Othello. Buffalo News.* 30 November 1997: 3E. On-line. Lexis-Nexis. University of Georgia. 22 May 1999. Keywords: Othello and Patrick Stewart.

———. "'Picard' explores bold new Othello." Review of *Othello. The Toronto Sun.* 1 December 1997: 43. On-line. Lexis-Nexis. University of Georgia. 22 May 1999. Keywords: Othello and Patrick Stewart.

Lacan, Jacques. *The Four Fundamental Concepts of Psycho-Analysis.* Trans. Alan Sheridan. 1977. London: Penguin, 1986.

Leavis, F. R. "Diabolic Intellect and the Noble Hero." Wain 123–46.

Leonard, William Torbert. *Masquerade in Black.* Metuchen, NJ: Scarecrow, 1986.

Levine, Lawrence W. *Highbrow/Lowbrow: The Emergence of Cultural Hierarchy In America.* Cambridge, MA: Harvard University Press, 1988.

Lister, David. "Can it be wrong to 'black up' for Othello?" *The Independent.* 7 August 1997. On-line. Lexis-Nexis. 22 May 1999. Keywords: Othello and black.

Loomba, Ania. *Gender, Race, Renaissance Drama.* Manchester: Manchester University Press, 1989.

Lott, Eric. *Love And Theft: Blackface Minstrelsy and the American Working Class.* Oxford: Oxford University Press, 1993.

Lower, Charles B. "Othello as Black on Southern Stages, Then and Now." In *Shakespeare in the South.* Ed. Philip C. Kolin. Jackson: University Press of Mississippi, 1983.

Macaulay, Alastair. "Rylance's Cleopatra Fails to Match His Female Peers." Review of *Antony and Cleopatra. Financial Times.* 3 August 1999: 14. On-line. Lexis-Nexis. University of Georgia. 24 February, 2000. Keywords: Antony and Cleopatra, Globe, London.

MacDonald, Joyce Green. "Acting Black: *Othello, Othello* Burlesques, and the Performance of Blackness." *Theatre Journal* 46 (1994): 231–249.

Marks, Peter. "The Green-Eyed Monster Fells Men of Every Color." Review of *Othello. New York Times.* November 21 1997: E5.

Marshall, Herbert, and Mildred Stock. *Ira Aldridge: The Negro Tragedian.* New York: Macmillan, 1958.

Randall McLeod [Random Cloud]. "The Marriage of Good and Bad Quartos." *Shakespeare Quarterly* 33.4 (1982): 421–431.

Morris, Tom. "The Man as a Woman as a Man as a Woman." Review of *As You Like It.* The Independent. 24 November 1991: 29. On-line. Lexis-Nexis. University of Georgia. 24 February 2000. Keywords: As You Like It and Cheek By Jowl.

Mulvey, Laura. "Visual Pleasure and Narrative Cinema." 1975. Rpt. in *Art after Modernism: Rethinking Representation.* Ed. Brian Wallis. Boston: New Museum of Contemporary Art/David R. Godine, 1991.

Newman, Karen. "'And wash the Ethiop white': Femininity and the Monstrous in *Othello.*" *Fashioning Femininity and English Renaissance Drama.* Chicago: University of Chicago Press, 1991. 71–94.

Nightingale, Benedict. "As You Like It." Review of *As You Like It. The Times.* 5 December 1991: Features. On-line. Lexis-Nexis. University of Georgia. 24 February 2000. Keywords: As You Like It and Cheek By Jowl.

Okri, Ben. "Meditations on *Othello.*" *West Africa.* 23 March 1987: 563.

Olivier, Laurence. *On Acting.* London: Weidenfield and Nicolson, 1986.

Parker, Patricia and Margo Hendricks, ed. *Women, "Race," and Writing in the Early Modern Period.* London: Routledge, 1994.

Pechter, Edward. Othello *and Interpretive Traditions.* Iowa City: Iowa University Press, 1999.

Piper, Adrian. "Passing For White, Passing For Black." *Transition* 58 (1992): 4–32. Rpt. *Out of Order, Out of Sight.* 2 Vols. Vol. 1: *Selected Writings in Meta-Art 1968–1992.* Cambridge, Mass.: MIT Press, 1996. 275–307.

Richards, David. "Patrick Stewart, Inside a Murderous Mind." Interview with Patrick Stewart. *Washington Post.* 12 November 1997: D1. On-line. Lexis-Nexis. University of Georgia. 1 March 1999. Keywords: Othello and Patrick Stewart.

Ridley, M. R., ed. *Othello.* 1958. Arden Shakespeare. Second series. London: Routledge, 1990.

Rosenberg, Marvin. *The Masks of Othello.* Berkeley: University of California Press, 1961.

Rutherford, Malcolm. Review of *As You Like It. Financial Times.* 6 December 1991: 15. On-line. Lexis-Nexis. University of Georgia. 24 February, 2000. Keywords: As You Like It and Cheek By Jowl.

Sancho, [Charles] Ignatius. *Letters of the Late Ignatius Sancho, an African.* 1782. Ed. Vincent Carretta. Harmondsworth, Middx.: Penguin, 1998.

Sanders, Norman, ed. *Othello.* New Cambridge Shakespeare. 1984. Cambridge: Cambridge University Press, 1987.

Spencer, Charles. "Gender benders in Arden." Review of *As You Like It. Daily Telegraph.* 6 December 1991: 14. On-line. Lexis-Nexis. University of Georgia. 24 February, 2000. Keywords: As You Like It and Cheek By Jowl.

———. "Othello? Isn't he meant to be black?" Review of *Othello. Daily Telegraph.* 21 November 1997: 25. On-line. Lexis-Nexis. University of Georgia. 22 May 1999. Keywords: Othello and Patrick Stewart.

St. Clare Byrne, M. "Shakespeare at Stratford and the Old Vic." *Shakespeare Quarterly* 10:1 (1959): 545–567.

Stearns, David Patrick. "'Othello' cast not wisely nor too well." Review of *Othello. USA Today.* 18 November 1997: 1D. On-line. Lexis-Nexis. University of Georgia. 1 March 1999. Keywords: Othello and Patrick Stewart.

Taylor, Gary. *Reinventing Shakespeare: A Cultural History* from the *Restoration to the Present.* New York: Weidenfeld, 1989.

Taylor, Paul. "Delectable Mark Finds Cleopatra's Sensitive Soul." Review of *Antony and Cleopatra. The Independent.* 31 July 1999: 7. On-line. Lexis-Nexis. University of Georgia. 24 February, 2000. Keywords: Antony and Cleopatra, Globe, London.

————. "Meeting the Boys in Lieu." Review of *As You Like It. The Independent.* 6 December 1991: 13. On-line. Lexis-Nexis. University of Georgia. 24 February, 2000. Keywords: Antony and Cleopatra, Globe, London.

Tyler, Carole-Anne. "Boys Will be Girls: The Politics of Gay Drag." In *Inside/Out: Lesbian Theories, Gay Theories.* Ed. Diana Fuss. London: Routledge, 1991. 32–70.

Tynan, Kenneth, ed. *Othello: The National Theatre Production.* London: Rupert Hart-Davis, 1966.

Tyson, Florence MacIntyre, trans. *Russia Observed.* By Théophile Gautier. Philadelphia: International/John Winston, 1905. 2 Vols. Rpt. New York: Arno/New York Times, 1970. 1 Vol.

Wain, John, ed. *Othello: A Casebook.* London: Macmillan, 1971.

Wells, S. W. "Shakespeare Production in England." *Shakespeare Survey* 43. Cambridge: Cambridge University Press, 1990. 183–203.

Wheatcroft, Geoffrey. "Sorry, sweetheart, but whites need not apply." Editorial. *Daily Telegraph.* 21 September 1997. On-line. Lexis-Nexis. University of Georgia. 22 May 1999. Keywords: Othello and black.

Zinman, Toby. "Beam me up, Patrick Stewart." Interview with Patrick Stewart. *American Theatre* 15.2 (1998): 12–15. On-line. EBSCO Index. University of Georgia. 21 May 1999. Keywords: Othello and Patrick Stewart.

Images of White Identity in *Othello*

PETER ERICKSON

The present essay continues the inquiry in my contribution to the Routledge volume on *Hamlet*. The two essays were planned as interconnected parts of the same overall project—namely, to rethink the transition from *Hamlet* to *Othello* by concentrating on race and thus expanding my earlier focus on gender in *Patriarchal Structures in Shakespeare's Drama* (1985). The general problem that the study of race in Shakespeare confronts is how to move beyond a narrow approach restricted to black characters. In quite different ways, both *Hamlet* and *Othello* offer opportunities for broadening the scope of the analysis of race.

In the case of *Hamlet*, the issue is whether the element of race exists at all in the play—hence my title posed the question, "Can we talk about race in *Hamlet*?" With its obvious racial dimension, *Othello* presents a different challenge. Here the question I would ask is: How should we talk about race in *Othello*? Because *Othello* is the one Shakespeare play with an undeniably central black character, it is too easy to settle for a narrowly formulated account of the problematics of Othello's black identity and to avoid direct focus on the problematics of white society itself. *Othello* thus requires a different kind of effort to broaden the conceptual range within which race is defined and assessed. To pursue this expanded framework, I propose to shift the emphasis to the play's representations of "white self-fashioning" (Erickson, "'God for Harry'"). My goal is to examine what Joyce Green MacDonald describes as "the places where the apparently marmoreal surface of whiteness splits to reveal the operating mechanisms just beneath," especially as awareness of these mechanisms impedes the smooth "performance of racial authority" and prevents "absolute racial closure" (MacDonald, 205–206).

I. NEGOTIATING RACE IN DUTCH ART

I would like to establish some terms for the investigation of whiteness by considering two paintings, Christiaen van Couwenbergh's *The Rape of the Negro Woman* of 1632 (Figure 12) and Rembrandt's *Baptism of the Eunuch* from 1626 (Figure 13). In both cases, the formal organization relies on a marked black-and-white color scheme in which the reciprocal interaction between the two colors makes whiteness as visible as blackness: we can't see one without registering the other. In Van Couwenbergh, the contrast is stark not only because of the depth of the woman's black coloring but also because of the large areas of whiteness. The intertwined limbs of the white man and black woman on the bed serve as a cue that brings our attention to the white expanses of the man's body and half-removed shirt on the left, and of the sheets and pillow on the right.

The black-white contrast is more modulated in Rembrandt but nonetheless central. The division between the light sky in the background and the earth tones of the river bank in the foreground is echoed and mediated by the pair of horses on the right; the placement of the white horse in the back associates it with the sky, while the darker horse closer to us correlates with the earthen color in the front. Blackness is strongly conveyed by the striking triangle of three African faces, whose eyes are intent with concentration, and they stand out even more contrasted with the indistinctness of the corresponding triad of faces in the back. Equally strong is the impression of whiteness made by the face, beard, and clothing of Philip as it merges with the eunuch's garment.

The basic distinction between baptism and sexual violation is plain enough, though the very naming of Van Couwenbergh's painting has caused difficulty. In his recent survey of Van Couwenbergh's work, Wolfgang C. Maier-Preusker calls the painting *Die Mohrenwäsche* (196). But the appeal this designation makes to the epigram concerning the impossibility of washing the Ethiop white is convincingly rejected by Albert Blankert on the grounds that visual evidence is lacking: "there are no toilet articles, and the main scene is set on a bed not in a bath" (158). Yet Blankert's substitution of the blandly neutral *Three Young White Men and a Black Woman* is also unsatisfactory because it avoids naming the central sexual drama, which includes the possibility of orgasm for the completely undressed white man sitting on the bed from whose lap the black woman is trying to free herself. Hans Werner Debrunner's use of the succinct title *The Rape of the Negro Woman* more accurately addresses the physical action (61).

The difference between the sexually assaulted black woman whose unavailing struggle to escape is portrayed as an occasion for white humor in Van Couwenbergh and the black man whose voluntary religious submission is met with white acceptance in Rembrandt could not be clearer. In both paintings, the positioning of the hands dramatizes the emotional transaction. In Van Couwenbergh's *Rape*, the languid pointing finger of the white man on the left

FIGURE 12. Christiaen van Couwenburgh. *The Rape of the Negro Woman.* 1632.
(Musée des Beaux-arts de Strasbourg.)

sets in motion the tone of mockery that travels through the array of white
hands. To show that the man's left hand knows what his right hand is doing,
his other hand loosely gathers the long shirt that has been pulled both down
and up around the waist; it can easily be released to complete his disrobing and
to expose his genitals. The upraised hands of the one fully clothed white man
in the middle adds to the derogatory treatment: his melodramatic gesture conveys only mock horror, and the helplessness expressed by his hands cruelly
echoes that of the black woman's outstretched right arm and flailing hand.

In Rembrandt's *Baptism,* by contrast, the hands are crossed over the chest
of the kneeling black man, and the right hand of Philip reaching out and above
communicates calmness and gentleness. Black and white converge at the
painting's center, as the ritual motion of the white hand enters the pictorial
space of the black man's head. While I agree that this touching is genuinely
different in spirit from the rough tactility portrayed in Van Couwenbergh's
Rape, the contrast is relative rather than total. The basis for qualifying the positive treatment in Rembrandt is its invocation of the Christian tradition that
presents conversion and baptism as a purification in which the black man's
soul is washed white (Courtès; Bruyn, 102–103).

FIGURE 13. Rembrandt. *The Baptism of the Eunuch*. 1626. (Museum Catharijnecon-vent, Utrecht.)

This process creates an awkward split that generates tension between exterior blackness and inner whiteness because the latter tends to devalue the former. Other artists such as Pieter Lastman (Trümpel) and Aelbert Cuyp (Slive) draw on this popular religious motif, but Rembrandt's painting is notable for the way it gives the spiritual idea a visual embodiment in the black man's ermine coat and white belt. Rembrandt thus emphasizes the transformative power of whiteness at the moment of baptism by wrapping the black man in white. Given the climate implied by the palm tree in the upper left and the orientalist cast of the three background figures, the fur coat becomes even more conspicuous, as though Rembrandt were literalizing the image of washing the soul as white as snow (Schama, 235). Becoming spiritually white is understood as the equivalent to location in the privileged space of Northern Europe; hence the need to be prepared for cold weather.

From the perspective of these two visual examples, Othello might be described as someone who moves from the serenity of Rembrandt's *Baptism* to the violence of Van Couwenbergh's *Rape*. The Christianized Othello's humble appeal to the status of symbolic eunuch is blocked because the play disallows his claim to be a desexualized black man: "Vouch with me, heaven, I therefore beg it not / To please the palate of my appetite, / Nor to comply with heat, the young affects / In me defunct" (1.3.262–65). Pressured by his implication in sexuality, Othello plays out the aggression in Van Couwenbergh's bedroom scene with the racial roles reversed, but also with the further difference that he retains the religious awe and reverence of the Rembrandt baptismal scene.

My purpose in juxtaposing the two paintings, however, is not to locate exact analogues for Othello, but rather to provide a larger context in which to reconsider the simple contrast they appear to offer between positive and negative versions of white response to blacks. In Rembrandt's *Baptism,* the encroachments on the eunuch's black identity required by the Christian premium on whiteness as the ultimate priority give his positive inclusion a complicating twist. Because the Rembrandt has its problematic side, we must replace the idea of an absolute contrast between positive and negative with a more supple interpretive sense of relative gradations along a spectrum. I propose applying the latter critical model to *Othello* with a view to avoiding a simplified either/or division into hostile and favorable white attitudes towards Othello.

II. WHITE SOCIETY AS A LANGUAGE COMMUNITY

At the very outset *Othello* plunges us so forcefully into a tumult of racial contempt keyed to visible physical features—Roderigo's "the thicklips" (1.1.65), Iago's "old black ram" "tupping your white ewe" (1.1.87–88), Brabantio's "sooty bosom" (1.2.70) said right to Othello's face—that we are in danger of seeing this vicious rhetoric as the whole story of race in the play. By contrast with the overt racial prejudice of this subgroup, other characters' gestures of inclusion and acceptance look quite positive. Yet, in a longer view, Iago's group is not an isolated aberration in an otherwise unprejudiced white society. Because there are problems with the "positive" side represented by Desdemona and the Duke of Venice, a better working method is to assume a more nuanced model of crude versus subtle versions of prejudice along a spectrum of prejudicial white views.

Squarely placing the focus on white racism in the play, Janet Adelman's cogent study demonstrates the vested interest whites have in the production of discredited blackness and the lengths they will go to achieve it. Her intensive close interpretation shows how much analytical depth a single-character account can attain. Yet white racism does not reside in one character or subgroup, no matter how crucial, but rather depends on a more comprehensive network of white motivational patterns, each a part which actively contributes to the overall outcome. A complete picture of racism in the play therefore involves a survey of the full range of white positions. In particular, Othello's vulnerability to Iago is explained not only by his own inner doubts and deficiencies but also by equivocations in the support he receives from others.

To pursue this thesis, I adopt Harry Berger's concept of "language community": "the characters of a play do not speak its language; the language speaks the characters. One language speaks, or circulates through, all the characters, one community *langue* speaks all the *paroles*" ("Text Against Performance," 53). Berger has applied this critical approach to Desdemona's role ("Impertinent Trifling"), yet his analysis makes minimal reference to the ways in which racial issues shape the marital conflict. Like Berger, I focus on complicity, but with race as the primary concern. Like Adelman, I focus on white complicity in racial tension, but with the central power structure embodied in the Duke of Venice as the principal indicator.

Despite the fast pace of preliminary actions designed to guarantee a collision course, the conflict is not actually joined until almost fifty lines into scene three when Brabantio and Othello enter to present their competing claims to the Duke of Venice, whom both contestants regard as the highest political authority and final arbiter. Recognizable as the stock type of the aggrieved father who feels betrayed by his daughter's independence, Brabantio is like Egeus coming before Theseus at the beginning of *A Midsummer Night's Dream*. Even with the additional overlay of racial anxiety, Brabantio's behavior is predictable and transparent to the point of cliché.

The real interest lies in the question of the Duke's response, the issue being less what decision he makes than how he makes it. The focal point is thus the Duke's mode and style of adjudication, and it is important to note that Iago is silent during the proceedings, his improvisational energy put out of play. The Duke's formulations are not invented by or derived from Iago, but are entirely his own expressions as the voice of the state. The Duke makes three statements about his decision, each of which is calculated to assuage and reconcile Brabantio (1.3.172–75, 200–210, 289–91). The Duke projects his authority in a pithy, sententious style that leans heavily on the proverbial. The canned quality of his eloquence is indicated by its failure to move Brabantio, who sarcastically throws the Duke's rhetoric back at him rhyme for rhyme (211–220).

The Duke's most important contribution is his final attempt to achieve closure: "Good-night to everyone. And, noble signior, / If virtue no delighted beauty lack / Your son-in-law is far more fair than black" (1.3.289–91). This brief concluding remark, the Duke's first and only reference to Othello's race, introduces a note of ambivalence. Though addressed to Brabantio, the comment glances at Othello in a way that bears direct relation to Desdemona's earlier declaration and explanation of her love: "I saw Othello's visage in his mind" (253). Both assertions draw on the contrast between exterior and interior that we have seen in the conventional Christian idea about the black African's capacity for attaining a whitened soul. The visage/ mind and black/fair counterpoints set up a tension whose unintended but unmistakable effect is to call attention to the negative aspect of these endorsements: acceptance is contingent on overlooking or sidestepping the outer blackness. Since even Othello's admirers have implicitly qualified and hedged their responses, Othello has something less than full support from the very beginning, and this is what makes it necessary to talk about a comprehensive white language community.

When, after uttering the final two lines regarding Othello, the Duke exits the play, he himself has helped to establish a mood of irresolution because his remark can be heard in different ways. The formal devices of the rhyming couplet and the bracketing with "If" may be interpreted favorably. The single rhyme has an authoritative, aphoristic ring that conveys a decisive finality that settles the matter, while the use of the word *if* has the spirit of Touchstone's conviction that "Your If is the only peacemaker." Yet the sense of the lines is so shifting that they open themselves to an alternate reading. The concision enabled by rhyming creates a terseness that seems not only cryptic but evasive. The insertion of *if* changes an ostensible declaration of belief into a conditional statement that withholds belief and instead makes an experimental proposition. This latter reading is consistent with the otherwise unaccountable warning with which the first senator immediately follows the Duke's conclusion: "Adieu, brave Moor, use Desdemona well" (1.3.292). One didn't know that there was any doubt in the senate's mind on this score. Well before Iago speaks and even before Brabantio delivers his rhymed curse (293–94), the culmination is heavy with uncertainty and postponement. The Duke has made a clear-cut decision, yet his resolution leaves much unresolved.

The proximity between the Duke of Venice's compressed couplet and Iago's loquacious elaboration in the very next scene (2.1.117–61) suggests a continuum rather than a total gap. Iago is a master at placing pressure on social and linguistic stress points, yet the black/fair word play does not originate with him, but is rather a cultural site he shares with the Duke. Iago's exposure of the Duke's circumspection mimics the Duke's strategic use both of rhyming and of the term *if*. Iago gleefully recycles the interracial "beast with two backs" which he had earlier evoked to arouse Brabantio (1.1.115): "If she be black, and thereto have a wit, / She'll find a white that shall her blackness fit" (132–33). By the time Iago has finished his rhetorical gyrations, he has brought out the racial burden latent but available in the Duke's opposition of black and fair.

Harry Berger's conception of language community has two crucial advantages. First, although all the characters use the same *langue*, this does not mean that they each speak exactly the same set of *paroles*. The concept of a shared language does not erase distinctions among individual speakers and make them completely equivalent. The salient point is that the Duke of Venice and Iago are on the same page, even though they are not saying the same thing or using the same tone. Second, the idea of a structure of language with a built-in racial bias allows us to avoid automatically jumping to the worst possible construction of a character's intentions. When analyzing the Duke's speech, for example, we need not infer deliberate malevolence on the Duke's part. To say that the Duke's words mean more than he is able or willing to grasp is not to relieve him of responsibility but rather to place responsibility at a deeper, more complex level. To generalize Othello's final appeal—"Nothing extenuate / Nor set down aught in malice" (5.2.340–41)—we can define the goal as avoiding the critical extremes of extenuation and malice, concentrating instead on an unstinting analysis of the difficulties in which a character is enmeshed that preserves the possibility of sympathetic acknowledgment of how intractable those difficulties are.

A further benefit of an approach based on the play's overall language community is that it suggests a new understanding of Othello's particular dilemma. Given that Iago neither exclusively creates nor entirely controls the society's discourse on race, it becomes possible to see Othello's entrapment in part as the product of more impersonal linguistic forces. From this perspective, Othello appears less isolated in the sense that what he has in common with the other characters is participation in the same community language. The difference is that the cost is greater for Othello because the language works against black identity. For example, the haunting resonance of Othello's desperate phrase "ocular proof" (3.3.363) comes from its double meaning. Othello intends it to refer to Desdemona's imagined sexual betrayal. But the phrase enacts a boomerang effect by reinforcing instead a second, incontrovertible meaning of ocular proof as Othello's own visually evident blackness.

Another instance of linguistic slippage is traceable to the inadequacy of Desdemona's original formulation, "I saw Othello's visage in his mind" (1.3.253). In the immediate circumstances, Othello completes the exchange with a parallel statement of desire: "to be free and bounteous to her mind" (266). Because the underlying implication that Othello's literal visage is an awkward problem is not addressed, it lingers as a point of weakness that is subject to others' manipulation—an opening that Iago eagerly exploits in act three, scene three. Having insufficient cultural resources to offer an alternative definition of his black face, Othello readily gravitates toward the pejorative view that his face makes him "begrimed": "Her name, that was as fresh / As Dian's visage, is now begrimed and black / As mine own face" (3.3.389–91). Through this outburst, Othello breaks a tension and a taboo. He not only finds at last a context in which he is encouraged to speak about his actual face but —inasmuch as he redirects the negative image of his face by projecting it onto Desdemona—he can also vent his anger against her polite avoidance that diverted him from addressing this facial reality earlier. Though this new avenue is self-defeating, it appears to be the only one available.

Color is not only ocular but also verbal proof against Othello because his language uncontrollably "turns Turk" (2.3.166) against him. The play's loaded vocabulary of color acts as a switch point that converts sexual meanings into racial signifiers. At the very moment that Othello seeks to condemn Desdemona as blackened by her presumed sexual duplicity, his own language recirculates racial connotations. Othello's agonized appeal to his former view of her purity—"Who art so lovely fair" (4.2.69)—frames his approach in racial terms because the key word "fair" is already firmly linked to the idea of racial whiteness through the Duke of Venice's juxtaposition of fair and black (1.3.291). This defining moment resonates as a reference point for the play's myriad uses of "fair," especially as an adjective applied to Desdemona as exemplified by Othello's greeting "O my fair warrior!" (2.1.180).

In act four, scene two Othello's repetition of "fair" continues this racial context:

> Was this fair paper, this most goodly book
> Made to write "whore" upon? . . .
> I should make very forges of my cheeks
> That would to cinders burn up modesty
> Did I but speak thy deeds. (72–73; 75–77)

The implied images of black ink on white paper as well as the burnt cinders replacing chaste whiteness escape the intended target of Desdemona's sexual transgression and reinforce a white-black racial dynamic. Othello's accusatory language inadvertently becomes a self-indicting rhetoric. So wrought is the racial and linguistic shuttle bearing down on Othello that white and black are finally split apart. Desdemona's "fair paper" is preserved as an unmarred field of pure whiteness—"Yet I'll not shed her blood / Nor scar that whiter skin of hers than snow" (5.2.3-4)—while Othello's blackness is sealed off in the image of "a malignant and a turbaned Turk" whose elimination is acted out in his suicide (351).

III. "STATE AFFAIRS"

In conclusion, I would like to return to the Duke of Venice and his relationship with Othello. Their encounter is conducted with elaborate politeness on both sides—Othello's "Most humbly therefore, bending to your state" (1.3.236) is matched by the Duke's inclusion of "such things else of quality and respect /

As doth import you" (283–84). Protocol aside, however, the structure of power is clear: the Duke's prerogative is to command, Othello's role is to obey. Othello is entirely dependent on this structure for his validation, and the Duke immediately complicates their power relations by injecting a racial dimension into this process of legitimation with his observation that Othello is "far more fair than black" (291). The Duke, not Othello, is the one in the position to define Othello's racial makeup and to judge the degree of its acceptability. The comparative form of this pronouncement begs questions about the standard of measurement: how much is "far more"? Where is the midpoint where the balance tips?

The Duke's evasiveness in setting up a situation and then withdrawing is reminiscent of Duke Vincentio's initial action in *Measure for Measure*. Unlike Vincentio, the Duke of Venice never reappears. Yet his presence is nonetheless felt through three elements: the entry of his surrogate Lodovico, the circulation of written communication, and the abstract force of the state with which he is closely identified. Lodovico's connection to the Duke is strongly signaled as he arrives: "'Tis Lodovico, this, comes from the duke" (4.1.213), "The duke and senators of Venice greet you" (217). Lodovico's choric function must be viewed from two different angles. His outcry—"Is this the noble Moor whom our full senate / Call all in all sufficient?" (264–65)—registers genuine shock at Othello's change. Yet "all in all sufficient" also implies an exaggerated innocence because it forgets that Othello's send-off concluded with a judgment that approved his racial identity as tolerable and perhaps even adequate, but definitely not ideal.

The exchange of written documents begins with the Duke's "commission" to be sent after Othello (1.3.282), and continues with Othello's letters reporting back along with his "duties to the Senate" (3.2.1-2). The circuit is completed by the letter brought by Lodovico from the Senate, which Othello receives with a flourish: "I kiss the instrument of their pleasures" (4.1.218). Of the contents we hear only the one-line snippet Othello speaks aloud: *"This fail you not to do, as you will—"* (228). In sharp contrast to the more gracious earlier moment of Othello's appearance before the Senate, here without warning politeness is dropped and the brusque tone strips the command structure to its basic bare-bones core: "they do command him home" (235), "I am commanded home" (258). The gist is clear but, because the full message is not revealed, the reasoning remains unknown and the Duke's motives obscure and unresolvable.

This uncertainty is the issue: we can imagine a positive explanation that Othello is needed elsewhere, but we can equally imagine that his recall represents a gratuitous withdrawal of support. Faced with this vacuum, Desdemona supposes that Brabantio's sentiments may have prevailed in the long run: "If haply you my father do suspect / An instrument of this your calling back" (4.2.45–46). This version of the behind-the-scenes politics need not be correct; the important point is that, under the circumstances, it is plausible. It may or may not be disconfirmed by the subsequent information about Brabantio's death: "Thy match was mortal to him, and pure grief / Shore his old thread in twain" (5.2.203–204). Nevertheless, the person who provides this elegiac news is Brabantio's brother Gratiano, to whom Lodovico will soon award Othello's inheritance: "seize upon the fortunes of the Moor / For they succeed to you" (364–65). This restoration of order tacitly enacts a closing of the ranks of white kinship.

The operations of state power are also conveyed by the heft of the term "state" in and of itself. Of the instances of the word in the play as a whole, nine occur in the first act, while seven occur in the second half when the word reenters with special force. In a concentration at the very end, the word is used four times in a space of thirty-three lines. Othello's final negotiation of his relationship with the Duke is conducted in terms of his relationship with the state. Although the Duke is absent, his role in act one as the representative of state authority allows us to make the connection between the state and the Duke here. Upon receipt of the letter commanding him home, Othello manages to assume his characteristic posture of obedience: "Sir, I obey the mandate / And will return to Venice" (4.1.259–60). However, disobeying for the first time, he does not return. Paradoxically, this disobedience is cast as a retrospective summary of his acts of obedience. Yet the irony is deeper and more critically honed than the interpretive explanation of a mere compromise formation would indicate.

Othello gives himself permission to speak by starting with a direct appeal to the state: "I have done the state some service, and they know 't" (5.2.337). We underestimate the emotional timbre if we read this as a humble or depressed monotone because the tonalities are more significantly multiple. The second clause especially suggests not only a general anger toward the state power he has served but also a more sharply targeted ironic edge. Despite his apparent dismissal of the topic—"No more of that" (338)—Othello circles back to it with a vengeance:

> And say besides that in Aleppo once,
> Where a malignant and turbaned Turk
> Beat a Venetian and traduced the state,
> I took by th' throat the circumcised dog
> And smote him—thus! (350–54)

The ironies cut in several directions at once. The vengeance is directed against himself in self-inflicted punishment for his murder of Desdemona. Yet at the same time he acts out an ironic parody of his state service that critically exposes the racial double bind in which his commitment to the defense of white society placed him.

In its primary effect, this moment expresses neither celebration of, nor nostalgia for, past heroism. Pulling us up short, "thus!" brings us back into the immediate present, where, in taking his life, Othello now portrays the emptiness of his career. Othello's action is not a simple defense—"I am still far more fair than black"—or a simple reversal—"I am far more black than fair." Rather, he now implicitly rejects the entire racial formulation on which his career was based. The bed curtain is pulled to hide the sight of the interracial couple, and thereby achieves white closure, yet the impact of Othello's revision remains. At the cost of death, he takes back the power to define his own identity.

WORKS CITED

Adelman, Janet. "Iago's Alter Ego: Race as Projection in *Othello*." *Shakespeare Quarterly* 48 (1997): 125–44.

Berger, Harry, Jr. "Impertinent Trifling: Desdemona's Handkerchief." *Shakespeare Quarterly* 47 (1996): 235–50.

———. "Text Against Performance: The Gloucester Family Romance." *Making Trifles of Terrors: Redistributing Complicities in Shakespeare.* Stanford: Stanford University Press, 1997. 50–69.

Blankert, Albert. *Dutch Classicism in Seventeenth-Century Painting.* Rotterdam: Museum Boijmans Van Beuningen, 1999. 156–59.

Bruyn, J., et al. *A Corpus of Rembrandt Paintings.* Vol. 1. The Hague: Nijhoff, 1982. 94–103.

Courtès, Jean Marie. "The Theme of 'Ethiopia' and 'Ethiopians' in Patristic Literature." *The Image of the Black in Western Art.* Vol. 2, Part 1. Ed. Jean Devisse. Houston: Menil Foundation; Cambridge: Harvard University Press, 1979. 9–32.

Debrunner, Hans Werner. *Presence and Prestige, Africans in Europe: A History of Africans in Europe before 1918.* Basel: Basler Afrika Bibliographien, 1979.

Erickson, Peter. "Can We Talk about Race in *Hamlet*?" *New Critical Essays on Hamlet.* Ed. Arthur F. Kinney. New York: Routledge, 2001.

———. "'God for Harry, England, and Saint George': British National Identity and the Emergence of White Self-Fashioning." *Early Modern Visual Culture: Representation, Race, and Empire in Renaissance England.* Ed. Peter Erickson and Clark Hulse. Philadelphia: University of Pennsylvania Press, 2000. 315–45.

———. "Maternal Images and Male Bonds in *Hamlet, Othello*, and *King Lear*." *Patriarchal Structures in Shakespeare's Drama.* Berkeley: University of California Press, 1985. 66–122.

MacDonald, Joyce Green. "Black Ram, White Ewe: Shakespeare, Race, and Women." *A Feminist Companion to Shakespeare.* Ed. Dympna Callaghan. Malden: Blackwell, 2000. 188–207.

Maier-Preusker, Wolfgang C. "Christiaen van Couwenbergh (1604–1667): Oeuvre und Wandlungen eines holländischen Caravaggisten." *Wallraf-Richartz-Jahrbuch* 52 (1991): 163–236.

Schama, Simon. *Rembrandt's Eyes.* New York: Knopf, 1999.

Shakespeare, William. *Othello*. Ed. E. A. J. Honigmann. Walton-on-Thames: Thomas Nelson, 1997.

Slive, Seymour. "*Saint Philip Baptizing the Ethiopian Eunuch* by Aelbert Cuyp." *The Menil Collection: A Selection from the Paleolithic to the Modern Era.* Newly updated ed. New York: Abrams, 1997. 106–10.

Tümpel, Christian. "Pieter Lastman en Rembrandt." *Pieter Lastman: Leermeester van Rembrandt, The Man Who Taught Rembrandt.* Astrid Tümpel and Peter Schatborn. Zwolle: Waanders, 1991. 54–84.

"Words and Performances"
Roderigo and the Mixed Dramaturgy of Race and Gender in *Othello*

JOHN R. FORD

In the summer of 1997 at the reconstructed Globe theatre in London, I was part of an audience that shaped and was shaped by a performance of *Henry V*. We were groundlings huddled up against the front of the stage. It was cold and raining in the yard when Henry (Mark Rylance) addressed his troops. He looked up into the rain and then into our eyes as his words addressed themselves to *both* the imaginary army we represented and the "real" shivering spectators we actually were: "Old men forget; yet all shall be forgot, / But he'll remember with advantages / What feats he did that day" (*Henry V*; 4.3.49–51). And we *have* remembered what we did that day—no doubt with advantages. We were in three places at once. We were watching an imaginative play; we were part *of* that play—Henry's troops in France; and finally we were in the yard at the Globe, just across the river from St. Paul's, gawking at both the real and painted heavens, negotiating with a mobile crowd, and having a conversation with Mark Rylance about how great we were going to feel tomorrow.

Such a blest description may seem too wondrous for critical discourse, where, of course, we work by wit and not by witchcraft. In fact, my description could read suspiciously like the mystification of that massive commercial project known as the restoration of Shakespeare's Globe Theatre. And *that* project, which can sometimes look suspiciously like both the mystification and the reification of whatever "ineluctable commodity" the term "Shakespeare's Globe" suggests to us, is as much an experiment in capitalistic as in aesthetic wonder.[1] Can the world buy such a jewel? Yea, and a case to put it into.

But there's more in it. That production never asked us to forget the materiality of what we saw and heard; and it certainly made little effort to conjure us into suspending our disbelief. Indeed, the performance from first to last was determined to make the audience sharply aware of the *constructedness* of the illusions it offered, to teach us how to suspend our suspension of disbelief. Mistress Quickly and Katherine were both played by male actors, whose transvestite skills were consciously and playfully evident. The afternoon wind and rain made our physical discomfort quite literally rub elbows with our imaginary puissance. The stage could indeed hold both the vasty fields of France *and* the English scenes largely because it turned out to be neither, but a beautiful space with wooden pillars painted like marble, richly detailed hanging tapestries, and a ceiling aglow with painted sun, moon, and stars, so that it seemed "fretted with golden fire." Our imaginations were rooted in skepticism. As groundlings, we most assuredly had our feet firmly on the ground. Standing just across the river from St. Paul's, if we could not see, we could at least hear, a church by daylight.

Yet the effect of this production's success in making visible and audible the processes that constructed this play was hardly to take down the pegs that made its music. Rather, its material emphasis, with its ever-attendant skepticism, helped awaken one's belief in something we could not see. And yet we were hardly in "possession" of this play, certainly not in the way Peter Donaldson describes "the viewer of a great Renaissance painting . . . a master of what is displayed" (93).[2] Nor was it quite the comfortable, equally possessive, control over a literary experience Paul Yachnin has in mind when he speaks of the "Shakespearean wonder" available not so much to auditors at a performance but to "readers who owned the text" (201).

Instead, there was at the center of my pleasure and consciousness as an audience member something other than pleasure and beyond the customary borders of my thoughts. It was more like a quick recognition, a hint of mere otherness: a surprising, limited, even "unnatural" expansion of consciousness, hardly "probal to thinking," that nonetheless glimpsed with astonishing clarity and suddenness the sheer contradictory disjunctions and differences that can reside in a thought, a body, a gesture, a "character," or a space. I was allowed, for a moment, to get outside my own habits of constructing and recognizing experience, to "see things with parted eye" (*A Midsummer Night's Dream*, 4.1.186).

This inclusive moment is made especially powerful in performance, when this response is shared by hundreds, if not thousands, of other spectators and auditors, who, except for this extraordinary intimacy, share little in common. Moreover, it is a particularly dynamic and interanimating experience. An audience is using theatrical conventions to construct a play text at the same time that the actors, as well as the language and conventions they use, are constructing an interpreting audience.

Perhaps the pleasurable freedom of escaping the limits of one kind of theatrical construction only to discover yet another, as well as the fears and suspicions that lurk within those pleasures, may have something to do with the powerful and contradictory involvement audiences have always had with *Othello*, a play that consistently requires the audience to judge and interpret. Yet this is a play equally determined to disable, or at least make darkly problematical, the very theatrical conventions we rely on to interpret. Kent Cartwright has argued that "[t]he great problem in responding to *Othello* is not simply what to think but rather *how* to know what to think" (139–40). Moreover, in *Othello, dramatic* conventions, wherein an audience is instructed to project or "read" meaning onto an empty stage, a body, a gesture, a stage property, clothing, the spatial relationship that blocking enforces, are disturbingly twinned with those *social* and *cultural* conventions that project meaning into clothing, gesture, skin color, or property to construct gender, race, or class. Such a vexed relationship among conventions may account for what Peter Davison has observed as a personal acrimony marking interpretive differences: "We are accustomed to wondering whether newspaper critics have attended the same opening nights, so diverse can be their responses. What is surprising, perhaps, is the degree of acrimony, *personal* acrimony, betrayed by some critics towards one another or even towards Othello" (10). Similarly, Paul Yachnin writes of the play's mixed signals that both create and dismantle a sense of wonder. That the play "is both wonderful in itself and critical of how 'magical' properties can seduce the eye and mind" (197) defines a critical axis on which can be plotted whole generations of quarreling "Othello" and "Iago" critics.[3] I am especially interested in the relations between the ways these theatrical conventions work in this highly self-conscious play to construct and define space, stage properties, character, and the uncomfortably similar mechanisms by which social and cultural conventions—what Iago refers to as "my country's disposition"—construct and define space, identity, race, gender, and relation. Those theatrical and social designs are made to so interanimate one another that, for the audience, the very act of employing our "imaginary puissance" to construct the play *Othello* deeply implicates us in the demeaning social codes of race, gender, and class that make up not only the play's "disposition" but that of the audience. This is true even though the play powerfully critiques the—our— racist and misogynist constructions of Venice by making its codes and conventions so visible to the audience.

The disturbing power of this play both to require and to disable an audience's capacity to "know" Othello may root itself in what Kent Cartwright defines as "the divided spirit of *Othello*" (x), its power to provoke in the audience a disorientating "double response" of sympathetic or "heroic" engagement and detached or "unheroic" understanding (165). Our interpretive dilemma as an audience, then, is that we are simultaneously required to participate in processes of "wit" as well as "witchcraft," to use Iago's uncomfortable terminology. Both processes, whether employed by characters in the play or by the audience, are vulnerable to parodic distortion: the reductive materialism of the one or the sentimental idealization of the other. Carol Thomas Neely has argued that audiences be open to a plurality of interpretive designs. *Othello*'s rich and multiply constructed language, Neely points out, allows, even conditions, an audience to experience what Neely calls the "mestizo" wonder in the otherness of race and gender that marks this play's "extravagant and wheeling stranger[s]" ("Circumscriptions," 303–305). Michael Goldman's term for this multiplicity is "exoticism," an expansive inclusiveness that must hold together the rich and dangerous contrarieties that simultaneously define Othello, the actor who plays him, and the audience who imagines him. It is "a power to relate divergent expressive elements—a structure of expression secure enough, controlled and spacious enough, to wear the exotic as a badge of security" (60). There is a rich mixture in Othello's—and *Othello*'s—language that woos us with the possibility that we can be larger than we are. This tale would win us, too.

But we are also smaller than this. Such a process of sympathetic engagement, as enlarging and enriching as it may be, may involve us in theatrical constructions eerily similar to the engaged imaginative process of "witchcraft" by which Othello constructs and reconstructs a narrative of self, or the way Cassio idealizes the mysterious and "divine Desdemona." Even worse, the very disengaged, analytical processes of "wit," through which this play invites its audience to demystify or deconstruct the elaborate mechanisms of racist and misogynist judgements, at times implicate us in habits of thought too close for comfort to Iago's own peculiar style of cultural materialism. To remind ourselves of the material source of those codes of race, gender, and class that make up this playworld's "disposition" requires something of the detached wit that Iago employs to remind Roderigo about Desdemona's disposition: that the wine she drinks is made of grapes. We know our price. I'd like to pursue some of the ways that *Othello* in performance requires an audience to recognize its own multiply constructed presence, an odd collaboration of the theatrical conventions of the play and the social conventions of the play world. I am particularly interested in how one of the play's more modest features—the character of Roderigo—facilitates our implication and perhaps our qualified release from those habits of thought that define the "pitchy" constructions of race and gender in this play.

Roderigo is often discussed merely as Iago's "gulled gentleman" and dull implement, a foil for both Iago's manipulative skills and for Othello's unmaking. He's not even mentioned in Cinthio, Shakespeare's source. And while Shakespeare clearly felt a need to create this character, neither critics nor directors have much shared that urgency. Roderigo's stage history, as Julie Hankey observes, is not particularly noteworthy: variously conceived but invariably reduced to one stock role or another to swell a scene or two. In the eighteenth century, the role, in Francis Gentleman's words, "require[d] nothing but smartness of figure, airiness of deportment and pertness of expression. The addition of a vacant cast of features must be of advantage" (quoted in Hankey, 138). In fact throughout the nineteenth century the character was so consistently seen as interrupting the main action of the play that the pressures of audience impatience "degenerated [Roderigo] into a 'low' comedian's part"

(Hankey 138–39). Only in the twentieth century has the role been taken with any seriousness, as in Peter Hall's 1980 National Theatre production in which Michael Gambon played the role. In that production, as Julie Hankey observes, Roderigo portrayed, in the words of one critic, "an implacable, almost honourable stupidity," which linked Roderigo to all the male lovers in this play (139).[4] In Trevor Nunn's 1989 production, Roderigo (Michael Grandage) was allowed a certain physical attractiveness that not only made him less distinguishable from the other men, but troubled the audience's complacent superiority over Roderigo, threatening whatever "sport and profit" we might hope to gain from "such a snipe."[5] H. R. Coursen, describing the Trevor Nunn "barracks" scene early in 2.3, notes a momentary confusion, both destabilizing and ironic, between Roderigo and Cassio (Sean Baker). "The cashiered Cassio in his white planter's outfit, with straw fedora and string tie, suddenly resembles Roderigo, who is now wearing Union blue. That each is a 'reflector' of the other, in a Jamesian sense, is nicely suggested by their change, exchange of outfits" (*Watching Shakespeare*, 151). Indeed, Roderigo's few appearances are nonetheless so timely that he becomes invaluable to the audience's alternating acceptance and mastery of the play's theatrical and social codes, even as we grow smugly superior to this "gulled gentleman."[6] Roderigo is an important and dangerous guide for the audience. Deeply implicated in the racist and misogynist values that animate this play world, Roderigo will instruct us in the social and theatrical conventions that will first implicate the audience in Venetian values and, later, allow us alternative, if limited, multiple constructions of race, gender, and class that will enable us to confront our own "disposition," if not entirely to escape it. At the same time, my purpose here is not to claim that *only* Roderigo can instruct us in the complex relationship between theatrical and social codes in this play. Rather my point is that in *Othello* the relationships between theatrical conventions and the social codes of race, gender, and class are *so* entangled, *so* volatile, that *even* Roderigo can set them off.

Othello has a history of provoking powerful and contradictory audience response. Michael Goldman has written that "*Othello* is probably, of all tragedies, the one in which the audience comes closest to intervening in the action" (46). Its stage history is replete with audience members so moved that they have forgotten all the conventions of theatrical fiction making, and in some cases have even intervened into the theatrical world. Citing such repeated instances, Edward Pechter speculates that "[i]t is as though this 'overly tragic' play does not allow for the distance we normally associate with dramatic representation" (12). And yet, as Pechter and others have noted, *Othello* also invites its audiences into one of Shakespeare's most self-consciously constructed worlds. Repeatedly we are required to watch ourselves watching as this play leads us into concentric circles of fiction making, where characters obsessively re-fashion themselves and others, using the resources of theatre to do so: language, gesture, iconography, blocking, stage properties, and space. Paul Yachnin speaks of how the play, by foregrounding its own strategies of mystification and construction, helps condition the audience into a resisting awareness that allows them to "deploy a strategic resistance to the play's sublimity" (198). But Yachnin's "strategic resistance," essential as it may be for all interpreters of *Othello*, whether on- or offstage, is not by itself sufficient. It is required, as Paulina will insist in another play, that we awake our faith. Merely to resist *Othello* 's "sublimity" may be as dangerous and as limiting as merely to accept it. Such unalloyed detachment, which is nothing if not critical, would place us too close to Iago's wit and judgement—and that of the legion of "Iago critics"—for comfort. Again, our central dilemma with *Othello* is that both the resistance and the faith we need to understand its world are deeply infected.

How does Shakespeare's Venice understand itself? The Venice of *Othello*, like the Venice of *The Merchant of Venice* is a place of indeterminate values, where identity and status are never fixed but must be continually negotiated. Moreover, in both Venices any sense of the homogeneity of community and place must be simultaneously fixed and destabilized by uneasy intercourse with strangers. In *The Merchant of Venice,* Antonio knows that, despite the communal hatred of "the Jew," the Duke must accommodate Shylock's

> course of law
> For the commodity that strangers have
> With us in Venice, if it be denied,
> Will much impeach the justice of the state,
> Since that the trade and profit of the city
> Consisteth of all nations. (3.4.26–31)

Similarly, in *Othello*, Iago realizes that whatever the racial, sexual, and cultural fears Othello may awaken in Venice, the Moor is paradoxically essential if the city is to insulate itself from "the general enemy Ottoman," for "[a]nother of his fathom they have none / To lead their business" (1.3.48; 1.1.149–50). The "business" of Venice, then, requires an intimacy with the strangers it fears and hates. Even the analysis of the "malignant and . . . turbaned" Turks' war strategy is conceived in merchant's terms:

> We must not think the Turk is so unskillful
> To leave that latest which concerns him first,
> Neglecting an attempt of ease and gain
> To wake and wage a danger profitless. (1.3.27–30)

Despite, or more properly *because of,* such a world of fluid and negotiated values, it is not surprising that characters are inclined to define place and property—and by implication themselves—in fixed, even immutable terms.

When, for example, Roderigo warns Brabantio that his daughter and his property have been violated, "from the sense of all civility," by the black stranger Othello, Brabantio dismisses Roderigo in language that rests on geographic and economic certainty: "What tell'st thou me of robbing? This is Venice; / My house is not a grange" (1.1.12–13). Significantly, when the play transplants these Venetians to a new geography in Cyprus, even though they have lost the very ground of their self-definitions, nevertheless they will urge the old links among self, sexuality, race, and property all the more insistently.[7] Lodovico's response to Othello's public violence against Desdemona fuses value and geography on two levels: by reminding his on- and offstage audiences that Othello's behavior is linked to his "travel's history" (1.3.38), and by re-affirming the geographical and ethical frontiers of his own home. "This would not have been believed in Venice, / Though I should swear I saw't" (4.1.242–43). That last clause has a second sting, glancing at the credulity of Othello's earlier narrative. In Venice, Lodovico says, credulously, we are not so credulous. Critics such as James Calderwood have associated the play's emphasis on place and property with a nostalgia for the secure values of land at a time of aristocratic crisis marked by "an extraordinary reorganization of property lines" brought about by the "many sales of manorial holdings" (15).

Given such widespread cultural anxiety, Roderigo's own behavior is revealing. To purchase Desdemona, whom Iago has described as a "land carrack" (1.2.49), Roderigo will "sell all my land" and, following Iago's instruction, "fill [his] purse with money" (1.3.373).[8] Such social behavior works as a theatrical cue, prompting an audience to demean Roderigo's status in a society that values land over money (Calderwood, 15). But Roderigo's foolish behavior also gives the lie to the very basis of Venice's sense of spatial superiority. Roderigo's "travel's history" is merely Venice's cultural history writ small. Venice's most valuable commodity is to be found in the trash of purses, "the trade and profit of the city."

What are we to make of Roderigo's purse? How are we to know it? That purse is a piece of property in a double sense: both an object to be possessed and a stage prop to be interpreted. As such, it is almost as overdetermined with contesting readings as Desdemona's handkerchief. In fact, the two props bear a curious relationship. For Roderigo the purse and its contents represent the practical source of his capacity to purchase the saint-like Desdemona and the feminine mysteries and powers encoded in her handkerchief. But the purse is also a more mysterious assurance of his social status and his sexual prowess, qualities that for Roderigo are intimately linked.

But as Calderwood and Yachnin point out, Roderigo's fiscal strategy procures just the opposite results, establishing both his economic and sexual inadequacy. "Roderigo is a Venetian gentleman and appropriately therefore a landowner" (Calderwood, 16). And in Venice land is encoded with the language of sexual and marital possession. "The virtue of land is that it is truly private property, reliably bound to its owner by contract. Money, on the other hand, is common . . . a strumpet; and the quick cash transaction at the brothel epitomizes the casual relationships it provokes" (16).

But Roderigo's purse is also linked—often through antithesis—to other kinds of exchanges and value. It is particularly related linguistically to the linked resources of knowledge and good name. Desdemona, of course, would rather lose her "purse / Full of crusadoes" (3.4.25–26) than lose her handkerchief and all the mysterious knowledge and power woven into it.[9] And Iago will opportunely argue against himself when he makes a distinction between the "trash" of his purse and the more authentic value of his reputation. Roderigo's purse, then, becomes associated with that "commodity of good names" that Falstaff so eagerly desired to purchase.

Roderigo's purse is associated with other kinds of knowledge as well. Joel B. Altman points out that *Othello*'s many references to money work differently than they might in plays like *Volpone* or *Bartholomew Fair*, where "gold, jewels, or coins" are actually "chang[ing] hands" (108). For Altman, "[s]omething less material and perhaps more interesting is going on here. In this play Roderigo's purse is the metaphoric source of all the activities of gathering, collating, and imparting verbal intelligence" (108–09). Not only will this promiscuous circulation of knowledge work within the social conventions that mark the fictional world of *Othello*, where characters may "unlace . . . and spend [one's] rich opinion" (quoted in Altman, 109), but such exchanges of knowledge will also operate on a theatrical and metatheatrical level, distributing to the audience the pieces of information we need to fashion interpretation, and to secure our rich opinion of our own critical judgement. "[I]f Roderigo's purse holds potential value for Iago," Altman continues,

> that wealth will be expended not on commodities but on interpretations—choral commentaries of ostensible value to him . . . . Iago is the chief dispenser of poetic deception, and the audience is privileged to observe how he distributes and fashions his goods. When his deceits are finally revealed to his victims and he is punished, Shakespeare's auditors are confirmed in their belief that they have all along—unlike most of the characters in the play—enjoyed an untampered vision of reality. (109)

Iago's final challenge will haunt an audience: "What you know, you know" (5.2.300).

But if social assumptions can infect an audience's independent power to interpret, the very instability of theatrical conditions has its own unruly potential to undermine the very grounds on which those social and cultural fictions rest. Given the minimalist stage conditions of the Globe, practices increasingly reprised in the late twentieth century, *Othello*'s capacity to destabilize its own conventions, particularly those that map out its economic and racial geography,

is further evidenced by the open and presentational conventions of Shakespeare's stage, where every space is here and everywhere. Just as the practice
of male actors impersonating women, by calling attention to the various theatrical strategies of gender construction, might vex conventional definitions of
men and women, and just as the mere presence of changeable costumes might
foreground the arbitrariness of sumptuary laws, so too an open stage that could
now be Venice, now Cyprus, now Brabantio's private property, now the
entrance to Bianca's dwelling, calls into question any sense of proprietorial
ownership, or land as a fixed, *essential* sign of self or status. In a play, at least,
all property is common. As Viola, who knows something of the dizziness of
theatrical conventions puts it, "[s]o thou mayst say the king lies by a beggar, if
a beggar dwells near him; or the church stands by thy tabor, if thy tabor stand
by the church" (*Twelfth Night*, 3.1.8–10). Although Roderigo appears in only
six scenes, his presence plays an important—if often unconscious—role in the
play's theatrical deconstruction of these social and spatial conventions.

Othello begins with Roderigo knocking or shouting at a closed interior
door. Julie Hankey speculates that "[a]t the Globe, Brabantio would have
probably appeared in the little gallery over the doors of entrance at the back of
the stage" (Hankey, 141). Standing on the bare, undifferentiated stage of the
Globe theatre, Roderigo's first act, then, would be to redefine the actors' tiring
room into Brabantio's house, thereby undermining Brabantio's confidence in
his own geographical possessions and the central feature of Venetian social
identity. When Brabantio proclaims that "[t]his is Venice! My house is not a
grange!" the audience, even as it uses the metonymy of language and props to
construct that dwelling, is free to note the irony: that the very property that
defines Brabantio's identity and status is no more than a fluid space of theatrical metamorphosis: the actors' tiring house.

Performance choices can of course intensify the subversive energies of
theatrical constructions. In some recent productions of *Othello*, including the
1997 Royal National Theatre and 1999 Royal Shakespeare Company productions, the space where Othello encaved himself in 4.1 was the same backstage
area we had earlier identified as Brabantio's house. Similarities of space and
blocking allowed the audience to perceive an unlikely semblance between this
Venetian landowner and an extravagant and wheeling stranger of here and
everywhere, especially as these two scenes were performed on a relatively
bare stage free from fixed, illusionary detail. The mirrored scenes reminded
the audience that Iago's "awakening" of Othello to Cassio's theft of his wife
resembled Roderigo's awakening of Brabantio to Othello's threat, expressed
in similar terms of thievery. Moreover, as Othello interprets the bits and pieces
of Cassio's words and gestures—sometimes even creating dialogue where
none exists—in order to fit Othello's own sexual fears, we might remember
Brabantio's similar construction of Roderigo's and Iago's fragments of evidence: "This accident is not unlike my dream" (1.1.141).

Finally, that Othello and Brabantio share the same theatrical space and participate in the same interpretive codes, allows the audience a metatheatrical mirror of its own processes of "knowing." However, that self-conscious detachment, paradoxically, does not lead to an Iago-like cynical skepticism but to our *engagement* as we participate in an Emilia-like discovery about "these men." Such "twinning" exposes and links the shared rhetoric of racism and misogyny. Othello's misogynist reshaping of Desdemona is not at all the result of some foreign or racial passion, as Brabantio, Iago, and some critics may think. To the contrary, Othello's thoughts are all too Venetian, all too much the consequence of a habit of mind "[w]hereto we see in all things nature tends" (3.3.231). Othello's misogynist construction of Desdemona, then, is indistinguishable from Brabantio's racist construction of Othello.

Moreover, even as these mirrored and metatheatrical conventions allow the audience the detachment it needs to demystify the codes that limit racial and gender identity, those same conventions implicate the audience in a shared process of thinking. Like Othello and Brabantio in their scenes, we are watching a performance. And like them we have learned to "piece out the imperfections" of the "thoughts" embedded in the theatrical conventions of performance. But this is also the very metonymy of racial and gender hatred: the thick lips and sooty bosoms we need to create a racial caricature "not unlike our dreams"; or the moist and liberal hands we need to change female sexuality into whoredom.

These are the "satisfying reasons" required by Roderigo and by some audiences and critics who must choose between the sentimental mystifications of Cassio and the "apt" thinking of Iago and Roderigo. But Carol Thomas Neely has argued for a more inclusive critical vocabulary, one that risks its own coherence and unity by *mixing* multivalent terms, thus eluding the play's "binary traps" ("Circumscriptions," 303): black *or* white, Venetian *or* Turk, gender *or* race. Instead, for Neely, "the categories of gender, race, and sexuality are inseparable, unstable, disunified, and mutually constitutive" (303). Othello, then, is multiply, even incoherently constructed, "constituted by, shot through with, different and contradictory cultural formations: African and European, slave and General, non-Christian and Christian, wanderer and defender of Venice" (305). Desdemona too is multiply constructed: an obedient and maidenly "insider who chooses 'by downright violence and scorn of fortunes' (1.3.249) to break out of her house, her milieu, and her country" (305). These pluralistic contradictions help shape subjectivities for Othello and Desdemona that Neely terms "mestizo" or "mestizola."

Such pluralistic constructions, beyond the reach of "wit," are not at all akin to the sentimental language of magic and mystification that Paul Yachnin warns against. On the contrary, such critical language is the result of a self-conscious coincidence of engagement and detachment. At the same time such a conception of subjectivity works along principles quite opposed to the metonymy of conventional social and theatrical constructions. Rather than reduce a whole to the certainty of a single identifying part, such "mestizo" readings will disintegrate a whole character into the uncertain multiplicity of autonomous elements. While such multiplied readings are certainly possible within a single reading of a play and especially in a single performance, it is the mysterious capacity of a playtext to keep renewing, reinventing itself in multiple performances that offers the best realization of Neely's argument.

Some late-twentieth-century productions of *Othello* have attempted to discover these contradictions, "the magic in the web" that weaves the plural subjectivities of Othello and Desdemona, by mixing together a number of discrete, even contending, theatrical and social codes. The 1987 South African production of *Othello,* directed by Janet Suzman and later reproduced as a video, is a case in point. That production seemed at first to ratify Roderigo's definitions of both feminine idealization and racial otherness. Desdemona's "blessed condition" was defined by her blond hair and fair and delicate complexion. When Brabantio insisted to Othello that only African magic could compel Desdemona "to the sooty bosom / Of such a thing as thou" and to reject "[t]he wealthy curled darlings of our nation" (1.2.70–71; 68), Brabantio gestured unmistakably toward Roderigo. But in subsequent scenes, Suzman used a variety of theatrical conventions, properties, and blocking techniques to create for the audience much more elusive representations of both Othello and Desdemona. Desdemona (Joanna Weinberg) was especially adept at creating the mysterious theatricality of her own feminine desire, as remote from Venetian definitions of gender as Othello's was from their ideas of race. In the scene at the quay, Desdemona had masked her anxieties about Othello by inviting, and in one instance pretending to cooperate in, Iago's reductive definitions of femininity. When Iago praised a "deserving" woman as one who, "being angered, her revenge being nigh, / Bade her wrong stay, and her displeasure . . ." he stopped at "displeasure" and looked expectantly at Desdemona, who playfully supplied the rhyme: "fly." But when Othello arrived, at the top of a movable flight of stairs that remained upstage for much of the play, and began his descent, Desdemona exploded Iago's definitions as she declared her love. Here was a Desdemona who defied the borders of all attempts to construct her. She was indeed "framed as fruitful / As the free elements" (2.3.308 –309). In a brilliant improvisational gesture, she appropriated Cassio's sword, as if to invert Cassio's (and Roderigo's) Petrarchan image of both themselves and her, and held it high as she rose to meet the descending Othello (John Kani). Othello's "O my fair warrior" became charged with a private sexuality as mysterious as it was transgressive. Their performance baffled all onlookers and, for one brief, magnificent moment, established Desdemona and Othello as partners far beyond the reach of anyone's definitions.

But it is a part of the "disposition" of Venice, and of most audiences, to disable these "mestizo" constructions by erasing the contrarieties,[10] reducing them back to the homogeneous, material, and ocular certainty of conventional metonymy: satisfying reasons. We work by wit and not by witchcraft. Janet Suzman staged the handkerchief scene with blocking that seemed to mirror the scene at the quay. Again, Othello appeared at the top of the stairs while Desdemona looked up from the bottom. When Desdemona asked, "How is't with you, My lord?" Othello rapidly descended as Desdemona arose. As they met, they joined hands in a ceremony that would "unmarry" them, largely through the force of Othello's new, Iago-like definition of female sexuality, a more impoverished iconography that will guide, not just Othello's, but the audience's thinking. In fact, Othello's language would mimic Iago's earlier verbal instructions to Roderigo and the audience in the art of unpacking the theatrical codes of Cassio's "courtesy": "Didst thou not see her paddle with the palm of his hand? Didst not mark that? . . . an index and obscure prologue to the history of lust and foul thoughts" (2.1.240–41; 243–44). Othello's inquisition completes the "reading" implicit in Iago's "prologue":

OTHELLO:	Give me your hand. This hand is moist, my lady.
DESDEMONA:	It yet hath felt no age, nor known no sorrow.
OTHELLO:	This argues fruitfulness and liberal heart.
	Hot, hot, and moist. This hand of yours requires
	A sequester from liberty. . . (3.4.32–36)

Desdemona's "frank" hand, no less than the multiply woven handkerchief, must be reinterpreted according to "the sense of all civility" (1.1.130) before it can become yet another example of the "knowledge" that haunts and infects this play's unfathomed faith. Suzman's mirrored blocking and gestures, then, require us to partake of two quite different "readings" of the same space and actions: one that enables us to get beyond the conventional and limiting codes that define both Desdemona's sexuality and Othello's racial otherness, and another that enforces our participation in those stereotypes. If our contrary readings implicate us in the virulent habits of "thinking" that animate this world and its social codes, they also allow us a glimpse of the fragility, the arbitrariness, of those codes.

Perhaps that is one reason why so many recent productions of *Othello* have set the play in periods where political and economic conceptions of space, either as property, territory, or as national boundaries, are undergoing violent redefinition, if not disintegration. The 1989 Trevor Nunn *Othello* takes place in an unspecified but deeply suggestive nineteenth-century setting that reminded some critics of the latter days of British colonialism and others of the American Civil War era (Smallwood, Review 307).

Similarly, the 1997 Royal National Theatre production of *Othello*, directed by Sam Mendes, was set in a 1930s Europe caught in the undefined space between two world wars that would together violently redraw the boundaries of the world. Like the world of Nunn's *Othello*, as Robert Smallwood has observed, Mendes's Europe nervously tried to evoke "the general suggestion of a colonial world" as well as its "details": "the sound of cicadas, the cane furniture, the jug of 'real' lemonade on Desdemona's table, the sense of a gentleman's club about the Venetian senate—cigars, brandy, old oak desks . . ." ("Shakespeare," 253).

And in the 1999 Royal Shakespeare Company production, Michael Attenborough's Edwardian milieu linked assumptions about colonialism and empire with anxieties about racial and sexual disorderliness. According to one reviewer, "[t]he production brilliantly uses the militaristic maleness of its Edwardian, last-days-of-empire milieu to suggest undercurrents of slightly disturbed sexuality that implicitly highlights the great imaginative daring and sanity of the racial divide-leaping love between hero and heroine" (Taylor, 14).

What is especially relevant here is that all of these productions established a highly volatile interdependence between the theatrical conventions the audience needed to create these imaginary places, and the social conventions that made them recognizable to the audience. All of these productions took place on relatively uncluttered, if not bare, stages. That meant that each of those particularized spaces had to be invented by audiences practiced in the art of eking out imperfections with their minds. But such imaginary puissance also suggests the instability, the queasy integrity of such a world, where, on the one hand, identity and status depend on fixed and "essentialist" definitions of space, as well as racial and sexual otherness, and yet where, on the other hand, *any* place, with its particular associations with identity, race, gender, and social status, can be so easily erased, rewritten, or made to mirror its very antithesis. So a Venetian house, wherein a white citizen can articulate his fears of a black stranger's sexual predilections, can become the Cyprian "cave" from which Othello can "bewhore" Desdemona, rereading her free elements as sexual promiscuity, of here and everywhere.

One scene that, throughout *Othello*'s production history, has disturbed directors with its spatial ambiguity is 4.2 in Desdemona's private room, specifically from the moment Roderigo enters to confront Iago to the end of the scene, when Roderigo insists that Iago supply "further reason" to support the murder of Cassio. Julie Hankey writes that some productions of *Othello*, including one with Edwin Booth as Othello, were so concerned with the social and dramaturgical impropriety of Roderigo's presence in a space so intimately associated with Desdemona and her sexuality that they created a separate scene and location for the Roderigo-Iago confrontation (291).[11]

But both the spatial ambiguity and the impropriety of Roderigo's presence seem to work here. Roderigo enters Desdemona's room in 4.2 just after Iago has "comforted" a distraught Desdemona after the "brothel" scene (Hankey, 291). It is interesting that at this moment Roderigo and Iago should "invade" this feminine and aristocratic space—and allow us to redefine it as well. This is the first time the two have appeared in Desdemona's space. Yet throughout the play both Roderigo and Iago are depicted as social interlopers, "strangers," who for one reason or another are allowed to visit domains not entirely "proper to themselves."[12] So this scene in Desdemona's room might mirror Roderigo's invasion of the masculine and military space in 1.3, especially in productions by Nunn, Mendes, and Attenborough. Moreover, in all three productions, but especially Nunn's and Mendes's, that space is further inscribed with the clear social markings of a gentlemen's club. In Nunn's version of the senate council scene, when Iago and Roderigo remain after all else exit, both of them enjoy playing with forbidden properties, sitting in the Duke's chair or drinking his brandy or stealing his cigars. In Sam Mendes's production, Roderigo (Crispin Letts) also usurps himself into Cyprus (2.1) quite literally hidden in the portable property that Iago opens after the stage clears. As Iago opens the hinges of the trunk, out pops Roderigo.

The effect of such "violations" creates an ambivalent irony. Roderigo, and in some cases Iago, becomes marked as an outsider in spaces encoded with social and masculine markings. And yet the very presence of Iago and Roderigo in these spaces, as they imitate the behavior of their superiors and play with the signs and symbols that mark their exclusion, is inherently subversive of the very social codes that give meaning to such spaces, the way the Marx Brothers, as they sweep indecorously and incompetently through the coded world of an aristocratic dinner party, leave both the party and the codes that mark it in shambles.

Roderigo's presence in Desdemona's room, as the emendations of Edwin Booth and others attest, is also a dramaturgical impropriety. In fact, Roderigo's very reproach to Iago has a metatheatrical slipperiness to it, identifying not just a character's failure to match his words with deeds but an actor's failure to suit the action to the word: "I have heard too much; for your words and performances are no kin together" (4.2.180–81). Trevor Nunn's 1989 production, at least in its video format, exploited the theatrical awkwardness to great effect. Roderigo's behavior here will require an audience to reinterpret a number of earlier scenes it thought it "knew," as well as this one. Here, Roderigo's and Iago's violation of Desdemona's space both mirrors and re-writes Othello's earlier presence in the scene, especially in performance. Trevor Nunn especially complicates Roderigo's influence on the audience's definition not only of space but of Othello, for whom that space was once "home," but who now is become an alien intruder. As that scene begins, we see Othello furtively move into Desdemona's room, trying to unlock Desdemona's vanity, seeking perhaps letters or other ocular proof of Desdemona's sexual contamination as a silent and horrified Emilia looks on. Later, when Roderigo enters, we see him from Iago's point of view, sneaking into the room and, like Othello before him, attempting to enter Desdemona's locked cabinet, perhaps looking for the jewels that "would half have corrupted a votarist" (4.2.185). Here, not only does Nunn's blocking fuse Roderigo and Othello into a single image of a sexual predator, even a rapist, intruding first into Desdemona's room and then attempting to force open a locked interior space, but both Roderigo and Othello cooperate to redefine the nature of that space, just as an audience must do. Here the mirrored actions of Roderigo and Othello, by turns attempting to take possession of Desdemona's theatrical and social space, transform that space from Desdemona's fixed, personal geography to the portable "common" property that makes up the contents of both Desdemona's cabinet and Iago's purse —"'twas mine,' tis his" (3.3.159)—and finally to a stage property.[13]

Again, the effects of Nunn's mirrored blocking on an audience are complex. Since, at least in the video version, the audience sees Roderigo from Iago's point of view, we become complicit in the Othello-Iago-Roderigo construction of Desdemona. At the same time Nunn's practice increases the audience's self-conscious understanding of a process of thought and judgement that would otherwise be mysterious, unknowable, and unthinkable. It is as if we saw acted out before us the pantomime of our own thought processes. Our interpretive acts convict us. What we know, we know.

I would like to conclude by raising some questions about the history of performing Othello's race. How closely have the theatrical codes of racial construction reinforced the social semiotics so clearly outlined by Roderigo and Iago? And to what extent can the actor's business of impersonating race purposefully or unintentionally undermine this social "disposition"? What we first knew, or thought we knew, of Othello's racial identity was shaped by the shared vocabulary of Roderigo and Iago. The very evolution of their diction recapitulates a semiotics of racist construction. We never learn Othello's name until well into the third scene of the play, when the Duke greets the "[v]aliant Othello" (1.3.46). Until then our vague fears of some unnamed threat are coaxed along by the vaguest of verbal referents: "this," "him," "he," then resting momentarily in the usefully ambiguous epithet, "his Moorship," until those fears finally root themselves in racial metonymy: "thick lips," "black ram," a nightmare "Barbary horse" who could transform and enclose the "fair" Desdemona to become "the beast with two backs" (1.1.3, 7, 11, 33, 67, 89, 111, 116).[14]

Whatever the disruptive or subversive energies within the mixed theatrical conventions of *Othello* that might destabilize or at least make visible the social codes of racial construction, the actual performance history of the play seems to tell another story. Neither Coleridge nor Lamb, otherwise sensitive critics of Shakespeare, could even *imagine* the play in performance, where a reader's imaginative editing strategies were powerless to prevent the "monstrous" visual image of a black Othello embracing a white Desdemona (Hawkes, 169).

Of course, even in such a nightmare performance as Lamb or Coleridge might fear,[15] the Othello the audience saw was almost always white, and had been so since Burbage. Virginia Mason Vaughan writes that, with the exception of the American black actor Ira Aldridge, who would later be barred from London and American stages for his offense, there were simply no African Othellos on major stages until well into the twentieth century. She adds, "[i]t wasn't until 1930 that a black American actor, Paul Robeson, would play Othello to a London audience in a major theatre, and only in 1943 was the color barrier broken on Broadway; both of these firsts featured Paul Robeson" (181–82). After Robeson's brief return to the Royal Shakespeare Company in 1959 to reprise his role, it would take thirty years for the Royal Shakespeare Company to cast another black actor as Othello: Willard White in Trevor Nunn's 1989 Royal Shakespeare Company production. Some directors and scholars have even argued for non-black representations of Othello on the basis of textual references that seem to associate Othello not with Africa, but with Spain, or Morocco, or, more vaguely, the Arab world, while downplaying or rereading the play's more specific racially charged terms, like "thick lips," "sooty," and so on.[16]

But what if these "contradictory" markers in Shakespeare's text are not contradictory at all: not inconsistent representations of Othello but *complementary* representations of two cultural strategies for constructing race? The first is to isolate and caricature those physical features that mark the difference between a dominant culture and a particular "other." These features, while "real" in a limited sense, really work as the site of the dominant culture's fears and fantasies. As those fears grow wilder and more threatening, so must the caricatures. On the other hand, Shakespeare's blurred references to "moors" and "strangers" represent not so much Othello but a second strategy to isolate and semantically control such an extravagant and wheeling stranger. If the first strategy demonizes "real" features of a particular other, the second strategy blurs all particular distinctions into overdetermined phrases that link one group, and the fears associated with it, to a range of groups, who become the locus for a range of otherwise inarticulate and "unknowable" fears, or what Karen Newman refers to as the "monstrous." Othello remains Othello. To those who must construct him, however, he is *both* black and "moor," specifically African and, more vaguely, an extravagant and wheeling stranger of here and everywhere.

Similarly, the long and unhappy tradition of white actors playing Othello in blackface may have resulted in destabilizing the very social practices such a "tradition" clearly endorsed. Listen to Laurence Olivier describe his theatrical caricature of Othello's racial identity:

> Black all over my body, Max Factor 2880, then a lighter brown, then Negro No. 2, a stronger brown. Brown on black to give a rich mahogany . . . . The lips blueberry, the tight curled wig, the white of the eyes, whiter than ever, and the black, black sheen that covered my flesh and bones, glistening in the dressing-room lights . . . I am Othello . . . but Olivier is in charge . . . Oth-

ello is my character—he's mine . . . He belongs to me. (quoted in Hodgdon, 158–59)

Clearly, as Barbara Hodgdon has pointed out, here is an actor consciously defining the essential qualities of Othello in terms of the cosmetics of race (26 –27). But theatrical conventions are nothing if not volatile. I would suggest that Olivier's theatrical caricature of Othello's racial identity may articulate a profoundly, if unintended, subversive commentary, uncovering the arbitrary and artificial social codes that invisibly construct our racism and our misogyny. Olivier's description of his creation of Othello describes both a white man imagining a black man and an actor describing his craft. In fact, much of the play's verbal evidence that clearly establishes Othello as African also evokes an actor's dressing table: "sooty bosom," or, as "begrimed and black / As mine own face" (3.3.388–89). These are metatheatrical moments, intended or not, that simultaneously create a character and deconstruct an actor's craft. The implications are more than a little subversive, inviting the audience to recognize as culturally constructed the very "essentialist" features that both racism and misogyny require.

Given these destabilizing energies, latent within both performance conditions and Shakespeare's text, it is quite possible to imagine that even the most racist intentions an actor or director might have could betray themselves by foregrounding the artificial dynamics of social and theatrical construction. After all, the Elizabethan practice of boys ventriloquizing women's parts, whatever the misogynist fears behind *that* practice, often had the ironic effect of making visible and theatrically felt the artificial process of creating gender. Thus, when a boy playing Viola/Caesario confesses that "[a] little thing would make me tell them how much I lack of a man" (*Twelfth Night*, 3.4.355–56), or when Olivier as Othello speculates that "[h]aply for I am black" (3.3.265), what we see is neither gender nor race but the social and artistic enactment, the *words* and *performance,* of both.[17]

Any play consists of an argument of voices. But *Othello*, as Virginia Mason Vaughan has eloquently and forcefully argued, is an especially "multivocal" play.[18] All too often, however, it has been subjected to univocal interpretation. In fact, the many discordant strands of *Othello* criticism seem naturally to define themselves according to particular voices in the play: Othello critics, Iago critics, and Emilia critics. The title of this paper notwithstanding, I'm not sure that what is needed now is a legion of Roderigo critics. But, as Carol Thomas Neely insists, interpretive response to this play must discover a critical vocabulary sufficiently mixed or "contextual" to articulate that plural language. For it is precisely this play's rich, multivocal sounds that encircle and expose the reductive voices of racial and sexual hatred that *Othello* both embodies and subverts. That wild multiplicity grows even more unruly as the play keeps rediscovering itself through performance. As Virginia

Mason Vaughan observes in her contextual history, "[e]very time the play is produced, debated in critical periodicals and conferences, taught in school, or read privately for pleasure, the text is reinscribed with a new and unique set of attitudes and values. Awareness of such multivalence will open up the text" (237). It is the magic in the web of it.

NOTES

1. Paul Yachnin, for example, speaks of the "commodity" of "literary wonder" (201).
2. Donaldson is contrasting the ways in which conventions of Renaissance painting, particularly laws of perspective, place the viewer's eye in a special position of authority, as arbiter of the painting's meaning, with the disorientating cinematics of Orson Welles's *Othello* film.
3. For helpful summaries and analyses of these and other critical positions on *Othello*, see especially Davison, Neely (*Broken Nuptials, 105–08*), Pechter, and Rosenberg.
4. Hankey is citing the *TLS* review of 28 March 1980.
5. Michael Coveney, for example, writing in *The Financial Times* (26–27 August 1989) praises Grandage's performance of a "finely judged, non-buffoonish Roderigo" (32).
6. Edward Pechter is especially interested in Roderigo's effect on an audience's culpability for the "tragic loading" that weighs down the play's concluding scene. Our very willingness to join with Iago in the gulling of so easy a mark does not speak well of us. In Pechter's words, "it's a free ride" (70). Moreover, our readiness to participate in Iago's rhetoric of gulling further involves us in the criminal thoughts that mark this play: "Roderigo and Othello are both (with Cassio) made fools of by Iago. If we laugh at the process in one case, we are guilty by association with the other, so that when Lodovico tries to concentrate responsibility onto Iago at the end—'This is thy work'—we have to acknowledge our share" (70).
7. Ralph Berry sees the "small, military-social group" established in Cyprus as "a microcosm of Venetian society" (112). Virginia Mason Vaughan notes that in the Trevor Nunn production, "[t]he switch from Venice to Cyprus is marked only by the removal of a carpet from the bare floor" (218).
8. See Calderwood, (15–17) and Yachnin (206–07).
9. For thoughtful and extended analyses of the handkerchief's multiplicity of meanings, see especially Boose, Neely (*Broken Nuptials*, 127–31), Newman (55–57), and Teague (182–84).
10. The term evokes Norman Rabkin's invaluable work, in *Shakespeare and the Problem of Meaning* and *Shakespeare and the Common Understanding*, on the problems of "meaning" and "common understanding" in Shakespearean texts that require our recognition of "absolute values even though they are contradicted by other values that paradoxically turn out to be equally absolute" (*Shakespeare and the Common Understanding*, 9).
11. Booth's editing here is consistent with what Marvin Rosenberg has observed as a "tenderness" that shaped the "excessively restrained text" of that production, which not only eliminated "the actual striking of Desdemona before Lodovico"

(86) but also any verbal hint of physical or sexual violence: "such words as 'sheets,' 'bed,' and 'body,' changing 'whore,' 'bawdy,' 'strumpet,' and obscuring the details of sexual relationship" (87).

12. Ralph Berry notes that in the very first scene in Cyprus, Iago's social exclusion is marked by an aside. Speaking of Iago's long description of Cassio's "courtesies" with Desdemona, Berry argues that "[s]ince nothing of this can conceivably be spoken in the company's hearing, the speech must be an aside. It is so long, however, that 'aside' cannot denote, as it usually does, a momentary turning away from the stage company so that the actor can address the audience directly. Iago is therefore set apart from the other actors on stage. There is nothing in the dialogue to suggest that Iago has turned away from the others. The others have turned away from him . . . . Behavior appropriate to rank often looks like bad acting to those of lesser station, placed as audience" (115).

13. Julie Hankey mentions that Charles Fechter's Othello (perf. 1861), after he had done his "course" with Desdemona, "threw a purse on the table before departing, and this was probably the tradition at the time" (285).

14. Edward Pechter writes persuasively of the impossible semiotics of the play's opening exposition. "In no other play of Shakespeare's except maybe *Hamlet* do we have to work so hard and over such a sustained period in order to determine what the play is about" (31). Karen Newman argues that "the delay undoubtedly dramatizes Othello's blackness and the audience's shared prejudices which are vividly conjured up by Iago's pictorial visions of carnal knowledge" (151).

15. Coleridge's racial fears continue to inhabit audiences' responses. In 1943 Paul Robeson, along with director Margaret Webster and Uta Hagen, who played Desdemona, was very apprehensive about white audiences reacting to a black actor kissing a white actress (Vaughan, 193). And well they might. According to Elliot Norton, who reviewed Robeson's Cambridge, Massachusetts, performance in 1943, "I remember when Paul Robeson bent down for the first time to kiss his Desdemona, there was a thrill of excitement in the theatre. No black actor, believe it or not, had ever kissed a white actor on the American stage before that time" (quoted in Hill, 126). More than fifty years later, H. R. Coursen would report that "[w]hen [Oliver Parker's *Othello* film] was shown at a school in Louisiana in February 1996, a white woman covered her eyes as Othello and Desdemona kissed (*Teaching Shakespeare*, 126).

16. See H. R. Coursen's "The Case for a Black Othello" (*Watching Shakespeare*, 126–62). As late as 1981, Jonathan Miller, producer of the BBC *Othello*, could argue that "[w]hen a black actor does the part, it offsets the play, puts it out of balance. It makes it a play about blackness, which it is not (. . . The trouble is, the play was hijacked for political purposes" Barnet, 285).

17. For H. R. Coursen, the sense of performing blackness in the Olivier/Burge *Othello*, both theatrical and film versions, is an intentional strategy. "In the Burge film," Coursen argues, "Olivier plays at stereotype, savoring the fascinated response of the Venetian senate. This sets his Othello up neatly for Iago's insistence on the female stereotype of Venice" (*Teaching Shakespeare*, 130). See also Wine (49–51).

18. In *Othello: A Contextual History*, 6.

WORKS CITED

Altman, Joel B. "'Prophetic Fury': *Othello* and the Economy of Shakespearean Reception." *Studies in the Literary Imagination* 26 (1993): 85–114.

Attenborough, Michael, dir. *Othello*. Perf. Ray Fearon. Royal Festival Theatre, Stratford-upon- Avon. 25 June 1999.

Barnet, Sylvan. "*Othello* on Stage and Screen." *The Tragedy of Othello, The Moor of Venice*. Ed. Alvin Kernan. The Signet Classic Shakespeare. New York: Signet, 1963, 1986. 270–86.

Berry, Ralph. *Shakespeare and Social Class*. Atlantic Highlands, NJ: Humanities Press International, 1988.

Boose, Lynda. "*Othello's* Handkerchief: 'The Recognizance and Pledge of Love.'" *English Literary Renaissance* 5 (1975): 360–74. Rpt. in *Critical Essays on Shakespeare's Othello*. Ed. Anthony Gerard Barthelemy. New York: Hall, 1994. 55–67.

Calderwood, James L. *The Properties of Othello*. Amherst: University of Massachusetts Press, 1989.

Cartwright, Kent. *Shakespearean Tragedy and Its Double: The Rhythms of Audience Response*. University Park: Pennsylvania State University Press, 1991.

Coursen, H. R. *Teaching Shakespeare with Film and Television: A Guide*. Westport, CT: Greenwood, 1997.

———. *Watching Shakespeare on Television*. Rutherford, NJ: Fairleigh Dickinson University Press, 1993.

Coveney, Michael. "A monumental Othello." Review of *Othello*, dir. Trevor Nunn. The Other Place, Stratford-upon-Avon. *Financial Times* 26 Aug. 1989: 32.

Davison, Peter. *Othello*, The Critics Debate. Atlantic Highlands, NJ: Humanities, 1988.

Donaldson, Peter S. *Shakespearean Films/Shakespearean Directors*. Boston: Unwin, 1990.

Goldman, Michael. *Acting and Action in Shakespearean Tragedy*. Princeton: Princeton University Press, 1985.

Hankey, Julie, ed. *Othello*. By William Shakespeare. Plays in Performance. Bristol: Bristol Classical, 1987.

Hawkes, Terrence, ed. *Coleridge's Writings on Shakespeare*. New York: Putnam, 1959.

Hill, Errol. *Shakespeare in Sable: A History of Black Shakespearean Actors*. Amherst: University of Massachusetts Press, 1984.

Hodgdon, Barbara. "Race-ing *Othello*, Re-engendering White-out." *Shakespeare, The Movie: Popularizing the Plays on Film, TV, and Video*. Eds. Lynda E. Boose and Richard Burt. London: Routledge, 1997. 23–44.

Mendes, Sam, dir. *Othello*. Perf. David Harewood, Simon Russell Beale. Cottesloe Theatre, London. 2 Aug. 1997.

Neely, Carol Thomas. *Broken Nuptials in Shakespeare's Plays*. 1985. Urbana: University of Illinois Press, 1993.

———. "Circumscriptions and Unhousedness: *Othello* in the Borderlands." *Shakespeare and Gender: A History*. Eds. Deborah E. Barker and Ivo Kamps. London: Verso, 1995. 302–15.

Newman, Karen. "'And wash the Ethiop white': Femininity and the Monstrous in *Othello.*" *Shakespeare Reproduced: The Text in History and Ideology.* Eds. Jean E. Howard and Marion F. O'Connor. New York: Methuen, 1987. 143–62.

Nunn, Trevor, dir. *Othello.* Royal Shakespeare Company. Video, 1989.

Olivier, Richard, dir. *Henry V.* By William Shakespeare. Shakespeare's Globe, London. 18 July 1997.

Pechter, Edward. *Othello and Interpretive Traditions.* Studies in Theatre History and Culture. Iowa City: University of Iowa Press, 1999.

Rabkin, Norman. *Shakespeare and the Common Understanding.* New York: Free Press, 1967.

———. *Shakespeare and the Problem of Meaning.* Chicago: University of Chicago Press, 1981.

Rosenberg, Marvin. *The Masks of Othello: The Search for the Identity of Othello, Iago, and Desdemona by Three Centuries of Actors and Critics.* Berkeley: University of California Press, 1961.

Shakespeare, William. *Henry V.* Ed. Andrew Gurr. The New Cambridge Shakespeare. Cambridge: Cambridge University Press, 1992.

———. *The Merchant of Venice.* Ed. M. M. Mahood. The New Cambridge Shakespeare. Cambridge: Cambridge University Press, 1987.

———. *A Midsummer Night's Dream.* Ed. R. A. Foakes. The New Cambridge Shakespeare. Cambridge: Cambridge University Press, 1984.

———. *Othello.* Ed. Norman Sanders. The New Cambridge Shakespeare. Cambridge: Cambridge University Press, 1984.

———. *Twelfth Night.* Ed. Elizabeth Story Donno. The New Cambridge Shakespeare. Cambridge: Cambridge University Press, 1985.

Smallwood, Robert. Review of *Othello,* dir. Trevor Nunn. The Other Place, Stratford-upon-Avon. *Shakespeare Quarterly* 41 (1990): 110–14. Rpt. in *Shakespeare in the Theatre: An Anthology of Criticism.* Ed. Stanley Wells. Oxford: Clarendon, 1997. 307–13.

———. "Shakespeare Performances in England, 1997." *Shakespeare Survey* 51 (1998): 219–55.

Suzman, Janet, dir. *Othello.* Othello Productions. Video, 1988.

Taylor, Paul. Review of *Othello,* dir. Michael Attenborough. *The Independent* 10 Jan. 2000. Rpt. in *Theatre Record* 20.1–2 (16 Feb. 2000): 14–15.

Teague, Frances. "Objects in *Othello.*" *Othello: New Perspectives.* Eds. Virginia Mason Vaughan and Kent Cartwright. Madison: Fairleigh Dickinson University Press, 1991. 177–87.

Vaughan, Virginia Mason. *Othello: A Contextual History.* Cambridge: Cambridge University Press, 1994.

Wine, Martin L. *Othello: Text and Performance.* London: Macmillan, 1984.

Yachnin, Paul. "Magical Properties: Vision, Possession, and Wonder in *Othello.*" *Theatre Journal* 48 (1996): 197–208.

The Curse of Cush
Othello's Judaic Ancestry

JAMES R. ANDREAS, SR.

Speak of me as I am . . . of one whose hand,
Like the base Judean, threw a pearl away
Richer than all his tribe; . . .
I took by the throat the circumcisèd dog,
And smote him, thus. (5.2.351–365)[1]

The Quarto (1622) and Folio (1623) title of the play we now know simply as *Othello* was *The Tragedy of Othello, the Moore of Venice*. Scholars have searched for the elusive *Love's Labors Won* as the companion play to *Love's Labor's Lost*. We know Shakespeare loved sequels and prequels enough to produce three *Henry VI* plays which extend ultimately backwards and forwards to produce his ten play historical cycle on the English monarchy. Similarly, Shakespeare's plays can be divided into cycles: the Roman plays, the Greek comedies, the medieval romances. The interest provided in these textual clusters is the insight one play provides for the companion play or plays. In that context then, what does the earlier *Comical History of the Merchant of Venice*, also known as *The Jew of Venice*, tell us about the later Moor of Venice? Certainly the plays share a location, but what might considering them as a unit tell us about the fate of aliens in that foreign location, and is there a commonality between Jew and Moor in the Early Modern period that needs further investigation?

The matters of ethnic and religious differences were associated under the dubious category of race—or "complexion," the marker for race in the Elizabethan mind—on the stage of the early modern period and in two of Shakespeare's most controversial plays, *The Merchant of Venice* and *Othello: The Moor of Venice*. Kwame Anthony Appiah argues that the racial stereotypes which arose in the sixteenth and seventeenth century to justify the economic and social manipulation of native populations both inside and outside Europe

169

were predicated on religious rather than genetic differences: "The stereotypes were based on an essentially theological conception of the status of both Moors and Jews as non-Christians; the former distinguished by their black skin, whose color was associated in Christian iconography with sin and the devil; the latter by there being, as Matthew's account of the crucifixion suggests, 'Christ-killers'" (Appiah, 277–78). And yet, V. G. Kiernan tells us that "Color, as well as culture, was coming to be a distinguishing feature of Europe," in the seventeenth century (quoted in Orkin, 167). To refine that sentiment, color, or what Shakespeare calls variously "hue" and "complexion," was coming not only to define ethnicity but also cultural attitudes, objectives, and behaviors toward ethnic and religious difference. "Complexion," both masking and marking religious difference, is the thematic linchpin of these two controversial plays: the first delineating the ethnic source for the racial conflict in the other.

Given the infrequently noted subtitle of *Othello*, "The Moor of Venice," we are invited by Shakespeare to look carefully at the political and thematic similarities between these companion plays—bookends on the alien question for the Europe of the time—that are linked by locus, focus, and *mythos* or plot. In fact, the first recorded allusion to *Othello* before the publication of a quarto in 1622 and the first Folio in 1623 was to "The Moor of Venis" by "Shaxberd" performed on November 1, 1604, and the subtitle appears in both Quarto editions and the Folio. Both of these plays take place in Venice, a "cosmopolis" where ethnic minorities or "aliens" are tolerated and even encouraged for the "service" they provide to the state—lending money and military expertise to its exploits—but whose social and especially sexual interaction with native Venetians is tightly circumscribed. In both plays a father witnesses the "theft" of his daughter in a marriage that is complicated as a miscegenous relationship by racial and religious factors. In both plays the alien is safely expelled from the city by play's end, one by ostracism and the other by suicide. What really distinguishes the two plays in addition, however, is the sympathy that is somehow generated for the two aliens, Shylock the Jew and Othello the Moor, even as they are being violently extirpated from Venice—read Europe. But most importantly, the two Venetian plays, *The Jew* and *The Moor of Venice*, link Jewish and African matters in novel ways that mirror the rising cultural attitudes toward aliens and the peculiar institution of slavery in the West that exploited them. The link is race, often denoted in the plays by "complexion," the visual marker that was, as Kim Hall, Joyce MacDonald, Peter Erickson, and others have shown, coming to distinguish ethnic and even national difference among Elizabethan people.[2]

I want to ask a number of questions about these two plays which have always generated controversy but which are at the center of cultural materialist and new historicist agendas today. Why does Shakespeare include two black characters in *The Merchant of Venice*—the Prince of Morocco and the offstage "Negro" mistress of Lancelot Gobbo—the presence of whom reinforces the themes of miscegenation which resonates menacingly in the subsequent Venetian play?[3] Secondly, why was Shakespeare's Venice a safe harbor for speculation about the possibilities of interaction between racial and ethnic constituencies, an interaction that stops considerably short of tolerating miscegenation or race "mixing," seen as the contamination of both complexion and essence by early modern Europeans. And finally, why are there references to Shylock as being "black as jet" in the former, and to Othello as the "base Judean" and "circumsisèd dog" in the latter play?

The fortunes of Jews and Blacks were linked sociologically and economically throughout the Early Modern period. Jews were banished by edict from England as early as 1290. Although the occasional Jew was allowed to live and work in England during the early modern period, the prohibition was not not officially lifted until 1655 under the insistence of Oliver Cromwell. Queen Elizabeth, on the other hand, issued two edicts expelling the "Blackamoors" in 1596 and again in 1601, both for reasons of scarcity of resources and gainful employment in England. "Those people"—the blackamoors in the 1596 edict—are banished because their service was considered superfluous in a realm "so populous and [sic] numbers of able persons, the subjects of the land and Christian people, that perish for want of service, whereby through their labor they might be maintained" (McDonald, 296). In the second edict, promulgated in 1601, the Queen is anxious, even "highly discontented" about "the great numbers of Negars and Blackamoors which (as she is informed) are crept into this realm since the troubles between Her Highness and the king of Spain, who are fostered and relieved here to the great annoyance of her own liege people that want the relief which those people consume" (quoted Jones 1971, 20). Iago might agree that Blackamoors were, certainly in his case, snatching up the prize jobs, at least in the ranks of the military. Jews and Blacks are linked then by the suspicion that they were consuming resources and providing services that should be reserved for the English as a white and "Christian people." They were also linked by association as infidels.

What then of Jews or Moors who convert, like Othello, or are forced to renounce their heathen ways, like Shylock? In the Venetian plays, such efforts at conversion are plainly fruitless—at least for black and Jewish males—because Jews and "Negars" are marked as aliens not simply by their religion or ethnicity but by their "race," in other words, by their natures (Shapiro, 72). Like Othello, the Queen's Jewish physician Roderigo Lopez was tried and convicted of a plot to poison Elizabeth and executed in 1594 in spite of the fact that he was, according to Gabriel Harvey, "descended of Jews, but [is] himself a Christian" (73). The religions and even ethnic convictions of the male alien might change then, but his color and ethnicity cannot, the color which marks his "race" for perfidy and the treachery of which Shylock is accused and Othello punished. "You can't," as Karen Newman explains, "wash the Ethiop white."

In *Shakespeare and the Jews*, James Shapiro demonstrates that Jews were marginalized in European society not only for their religious practices and ethnic distinction, but for their racial difference. In the Elizabethan age Jews were not identified by their religious beliefs and ethnic character alone but by national and racial affiliation as well. Similarly, African Moors or "Blackamoors" were visually identified by their complexions and their ethnic and religious differences as a "race" distinct from Whites. Blacks and Jews constituted a conspicuous if not numerous minority, numbering four or five per cent of London's 250,000 residents in the late sixteenth century. As aliens, however, they were allowed to practice their carefully prescribed professions—usury and mercenary warfare in the case of Shylock and Othello—but, at least in Shakespeare's broad representation of ethnic minorities, only within the confines of the mysterious "cosmopolis" of Venice. Venice, after all, had a virtual lock on English trade up through the early part of the sixteenth century, so the island was not unfamiliar with dark-skinned or exotic people. Local aliens for the English—the Spanish, the French, and the Irish—are mildly satirized in Shakespeare's domestic comedy, *The Merry Wives of Windsor*, or the history plays like *Henry V*, but Venice was a continent away from England and was close to the Middle East and Africa, the home of Semites and Blacks. Whatever xenophobia might be attributed to the Elizabethan audience who would have enjoyed the taunting and baiting of the Merchant and the the Moor of Venice, the Venetian plays take place on Italian, not English ground. After all, Portia, an Italian Lady, lumps the English prince in with other distasteful aliens in her wholesale rejection of foreigners in *The Merchant of Venice*.

Jews were often linked with Blacks not only in terms of complexion or skin color, but as idolaters and stealthy thieves and murderers. Leo Africanus catalogues the similarities of these two distinct ethnic groups in his prologue to *A Geographical Historie of Africa* (1600):

> About the fountaines of Nilus some say, that there are Amazones or women-warriers, most valiant and redoubted, which use bowes and arrowes, and live under the governement of a Queene: as likewise the people called Carfir or Cafates, being as blacke as pitch, and of a mightie stature, and (as some thinke) descended of the Jewes; but not they are idolaters, and most deadly enimies to the Christians; for they make continuall assaults about the Abassins, dispoiling them both of life and goods: but all the day-time they lie lurking in mountaines, woods, and deepe valleies. (19)

This "blacke as pitch" African tribe, the Cafir, is not only "descended of the Jewes" in ways that shall be explained below, but associated with the matriarchy of the "Amazones" or "women-warriors" Theseus conquers in Chaucer's "Knight Tale" and in Shakespeare's *A Midsummer Night's Dream*. Contemporary Jewishness, we know, is inherited from the mother which makes the defection of Jessica all the more heart-rending to her father, Shylock. The association of Jessica with the ring of faith observed in *The Merchant of Venice* reaffirms the power and influence of women in Judaism. We might also mention Othello's preoccupation with his mother in his tragedy, particularly in the association once again of fidelity in the "web" of the infamous hand-kerchief. Furthermore, Leo declares that "in past times Ethiopia was governed by queens only" (396). What we would call ethnicity today could and was extended to include racial classification and even gender attributes in the Early Modern period.

However, in the mind of the Early Modern "Ethiopian"—as Africans were often called in the period—the connection between African and Jew was claimed as a birthright through the union of Solomon with the Queen of Sheba as narrated in the Old Testament. Leo Africanus reports: "Whereupon we reade in the history of the old testament, that the Queen of the south came to King Salomon from Saba, to heare his admirable wisedome, about the yeere of the world 2954. The name of this Queen (as the Ethiopians report) was Maqueda." Solomon courted Maqueda with his wealth and wisdom, wherefore,

> The Ethiopian kings suppose, that they are descended from the lineage of *David*, and from the family of *Salomon*. And therefore they use to terme themselves the sonnes of *David*, and of *Salomon*, and of the holy patriarkes also, as being sprung from their progenie. For Queene *Maqueda* (say they) had a sonne by *Salomon*, whome they named *Maleich*. But afterward he was called *David*.

At twenty years of age David was sent to his father, Solomon, "that he might learn of him wisedome and understanding."

> Which so soone as the said *Meilech* or *David* had attained: by the permission of *Salomon*, taking with him many priests and nobles, out of all the twelve tribes, he returned to his kingdome of Ethiopia, and tooke upon him the government thereof. As likewise he carried home with him the law of God, and the rite of circumcision. (396–97)

Leo Africanus, then, makes much of the tradition, heritage, and ances-try of "Jewry" among Africans, concluding, "These were the beginnings of the Jewish religion in Ethiopia." So deep were the roots that "even to this present none are admitted into any ministry or canonship in the court, but such as are descended of their race that came first out of Jewry." (397) Else-where Leo continues that the Jews were dispersed throughout Africa, par-ticularly in sub-Saharan Africa, after the reign of Solomon and the Ethiopian David: "they not onely filled Abassia, but spread themselves likewise all over the neighbour provinces. . . . Cosmographers set downe a province in those quarters, which they call The land of the Hebrewes, placed as it were under the equinoctiall, in certaine unknowne mountains, between the confines of Abbassia, and Congo." (379).

Such is the Ethiopian or African explanation of the sacred blood relationship between Jews and Africans in the Early Modern period. Europeans, however, devised another radically pejorative genealogy tracing that relationship back not only to explain the origin of blackness but to justify the "peculiar institution" of slavery which was in full force by the composition of *The Jew of Venice* and *The Moor of Venice*, both of which, as we shall see, touch on the issue. Since it could not be proved that Morocco and Othello were black simply because of the climate they inhabited, European Christians conjectured that the kinship between Jew and African was due to the sin of Ham who inadvertently discovered his father, Noah, drunk on his own vintage and naked after the flood. His brothers, Shem and Japhet, turned away from their father's exposure, but Ham looked. Ham himself was not cursed directly. The sin of the father was visited on Canaan and Cush, the sons of Ham who were cursed with a life of eternal servitude. As the only male inhabitants of the planet, Shem, Japhet, and Ham divided the earth between them and repeopled it. Ham inherited Africa. Joseph Glanvill even attempted to trace the ancestry of chimpanzees back to Ham, but it was generally agreed that the progeny of Ham were turned black because of his sexual transgression against his father (Allen, 118–19).

Of interest for our focus is the fact that Ham's sin was considered to be not only sexual but transgressive and incestuous. Don Cameron Allen informs us that "Von der Hardt, a late seventeenth century exegete, evolves the theory that to 'look on the nakedness' of one's father is to have incestuous relations with one's mother; so Canaan was the child of Noah's wife and Ham" (Allen, 78 n. 69). But how exactly did Cush become black? "Torniellus thinks that Ham's wife's mind was either on something black at the time of Cush's conception or else she was afflicted with a longing for black during his gestation" (Allen, 119). Finally, rabbinical scholars conjectured that Ham's sin amounted not simply to voyeurism, but to the castration of the father. "The rabbinic sages of the Midrash and Talmud generally agreed that Noah was castrated in the tent. In reconstructing the incident, some rabbis pictured Canaan, Ham's little son, entering the tent, looping a cord around his grandfather's exposed testicles, and castrating him by drawing it tight" (Cohen, 13). Whatever the theological conjecture, the crime of Ham was considered primal and from it Europeans deduced, apes, Africans, and Negroes were thought to have evolved. Even Leo Africanus mentions the curse of Ham but claims quite logically that it extends only to Jews who inhabit Africa, "thought to be descended from *Cham* the cursed son of *Noah*" (6).

Winthrop D. Jordan argues in his National Book Award Study of 1969, *White Over Black: American Attitudes Toward the Negro 1550–1812*, that in the early centuries of slavery, including the seventeenth, Ham's curse was used to justify the enslavement of Africans. Jordan sums up the story as follows:

Ham looked at his father drunk and naked in his tent while his brothers, Shem and Japheth, covered his nakedness. When Noah learned of Ham's insubordination, he cursed one of his sons, Canaan, saying that he would become a "servant of servants" to his brothers. The curse was linked to color because the word Ham was thought to denote "dark" and "hot" by the Church fathers including St. Jerome and St. Augustine. In Talmudic and Midrashic commentaries on the passage Ham was described as "smitten in his skin." Noah, the sources say, told Ham, "your seed will be ugly and dark-skinned" (Jordan, 18).

The narrative continues, as folk legends are wont to do. In 1578 George Best published a discourse on the habitability of all parts of the world where he expressed another commonly held suspicion about the origins of the black race in Jewish sin. Noah and his wife were "white," as were all precursors of the great flood, and "should have begotten . . . white children." However, in the course of the flood, Noah commanded his sons, Ham among them, to abstain from sexual intercourse with their wives, a commandment Ham disobeyed. To punish this disobedience, God proclaimed that "a sonne should bee born whose name was Cush, who not only it selfe, but all his posteritie after him should bee so blacke and lothsome, that it might remain a spectacle of dis-obedience to all the worlde. And of this blacke and cursed Cush came all these blacke Moores which are in Africa" (41). Cush thus became "the notorious world-darkener" according to Jordan.

Jews, Prudencio de Sandoval writes in 1604, passed on the ignorance and ingratitude inherent in their race to their posterity just as surely as Negroes passed on blackness to their own progeny. "Who can deny that in the descen-dants of the Jews there persists and endures the evil inclination of their ancient ingratitude and lack of understanding, just as in negroes [there persists] the inseparability of their blackness? For if the latter should unite them[selves], even a thousand times with white women, the children are born with the dark color of the father" (quoted in Shapiro, 37). Blackness of complexion is the marker, in the Elizabethan mind, of both Jewish and Negro inferiority, treach-ery, inconstancy, and sexual promiscuity. And blackness, like "optical proof," in the eyes of Elizabethans at least, is passed on by the father. White women, therefore, must be protected from genetic and social contamination by inter-course with a male of another race or alien ethnicity, while white Christian men are free to pursue the exotic alien because they can only pass on their own normative and clearly superior characteristics to an inferior race. The curse of Ham and Cush not only linked Africans and Jews scripturally, but suggested there was a genetic link as well: a link by origin and complexion that deter-mined the cultural destiny, enslavement, and diaspora of Jews and Blacks that Shakespeare chose to portray from a decisively Western perspective and bias in his twin Venetian plays. The bias, of course, continues to resonate tragically and idiotically in Ku Klux Klan ideology and xenophobic behavior all over the Western world to this very day.

How does this dangerous but convenient genealogy play out in *The Jew* and *The Moor of Venice*? When, according to Shapiro, Shylock swears to Tubal and Cush as "his countrymen" that he would rather have a pound of Antonio's flesh than twenty times the sum of the bond (*The Merchant of Venice*, 3.2.284), the name of Cush would have been "immediately recognizable to Elizabethan audiences as the progenitor of all Black Africans" (Shapiro, 172). In this passage Shylock admits he is of the tribe of Ham and Cush, Jews who by their sexual transgressions were transformed into Blacks for eternity. Ham and Cush are the causes and progenitors of blackness, a trait shared by Jews and Africans alike, and their progeny are condemned to justifiable servitude in perpetuity. What remains for us to pursue here is how these distorted biblical views play out in the various miscegenous relationships, the issue of slavery, and the ostracism of the dangerous alien in, respectively, *The Jew* and *The Moor of Venice*.

The Merchant of Venice is marked by distinctive biracial relationships—transgressive sexual intrigues—that come into stark and catastrophic focus in *Othello*. How these relationships are judged dramatically and ethnically is determined largely by gender. To begin with the relationships from the perspective of the European and ethnic males: an African prince and Moor, Morocco, courts an Italian Christian, Portia. Lorenzo, a white Christian, courts, converts, and marries Jessica, a "black" Jew who is redeemed and "cleansed" by her marriage to a Venetian Christian. Lancelot Gobbo, the clown, is allowed to poke fun at his "Negro" mistress whom he has impregnated. And finally, in the most famous of all biracial relationships in Western literature, Othello, Shakespeare's third and ultimate blackamoor after Aaron and Morocco, marries—with predictable and catastrophic sexual results given the European disposition—Desdemona, a Venetian Christian. These cases of transgressive Venetian sexuality might well resonate tragically with the sexual history of Noah and his sons. In every case patriarchal—read Noah's—"authority" is threatened by alien intrusion and intermarriage with what Stephen Greenblatt calls the "threatening Other—heretic, savage, witch, adulteress, traitor, Antichrist" (Greenblatt, 9).

The Prince of Morocco is permitted to deliver a stunning celebration of his heritage—like Aaron's "is black so base a hue" speech and Othello's "unvarnished tale" of his African past—relating his accomplishments and his appeal to women of his own region. None of the other suitors, the dozen or so who are rejected on ethnic grounds out of hand by Portia, Aragon, or even Bassanio, is allowed the *apologia* promulgated center-stage by Morocco. The robust poetic speech of Othello is anticipated in the defense of Morocco. Realizing he will be judged primarily by his skin color, the Prince disarms an audience who will, like Portia, "mislike" him for his "complexion," which, he says is a product simply of "the shadowed livery of the burnished sun" rather than the curse of Cush.[4] Anticipating Othello, who will also have to justify his courtship and marriage to Desdemona, Morocco pleads his case based on internal "color"—if not character as Othello will insist—the color of his blood: "let us (rival suitors) make incision for your love / To prove whose blood is reddest, his or mine" (2.1.6–7). His "aspect," what she sees, may have frightened his "valiant" enemies, but "The best-regarded virgins of our clime / Hath loved it too" (10–11). Like Aaron the Moor and Shylock the Jew, if not Othello, Morocco remains proud of his color and heritage, but would renounce it for her preference: "I would not change this hue, / Except to steal your thoughts, my gentle queen" (11–12).

Interestingly Portia replies in the "ocular" terms that resonate so menacingly with the racial cues of black skin in the Venetian plays. (Recall Othello's tragic insistence on having "ocular proof" of Desdemona's perfidy from Iago.) "In terms of choice I am not soley led / By nice direction of a maiden's eyes" (13–14). But she is, of course. She has clearly responded to Morocco's open defense of his "hue," but is compelled to defer to the lottery which he father has set in place, a lottery which forbids judging content and character by appearance and facade. Morocco's choice of the golden casket precipitates the moral that is not so much a reflection of the Prince's character as it is Portia's. After all, he chooses the casket not because he arrogantly, like Aragon, assumes gold is the color that best denotes his own worth, but that gold complements the beauty of Portia. "Never so rich a gem" as Portia, he muses aloud, "Was set in worse than gold" (2.7.54–55). The scroll, the moral within the golden casket reads: "All that glisters is not gold" (65), suggesting that one should not judge the inside, souls or scrolls that signify, by outside appearance, the mere signifier. Of course that is exactly what Portia does in expelling the alien from Belmont: "A gentle riddance. Draw the curtains, go. / Let all of his complexion choose me so" (78–79). Even more damning, Portia had already made up her mind about Morocco before his arrival and attempt at the lottery prescribed by her father when she confides her color bias to Nerissa and, presumably, a racially sympathetic audience. Anticipating Morocco's arrival she says, "If he have the condition of a saint and the complexion of a devil, I had rather he should shrive me than wive me" (1.3.128–30). "Shrive" and "wive" is a fine Chaucerian rhyme indeed, but it suggests something rather ominous about Portia, that she is well aware there is something she needs redemption for.

As the white Christian male, Lorenzo is, of course, also committing miscegenation, but the racial-religious effects are reversed. Solanio, drawing on the accepted association of Jews and Blacks coming from a single race marked by complexion, taunts Shylock about his daughter's defection from her "tribe" in marrying Lorenzo, a Christian. He says to the Jew, "There is more difference between thy flesh and hers than between jet and ivory" (3.1.34), metaphorically recalling the racial taint Jews pass on to Africans. Solanio is here referring to Jessica's "complexion," which was symbolically "jet" or black before her marriage to Lorenzo, but has been whitened to "ivory" by her conversion to Christianity. She has, in her defection from her father, undone the genetic and ethical damage of Ham and Canaan, and redeemed herself and presumably her children. Her marriage to a Christian is considered a kind of conversion not only of the spirit, but of the flesh, specifically of the complexion. Unlike Portia who dismisses the Prince of Morocco for his skin color—"Let all of his complexion choose me so" (2.7.79)—Jessica, as a Jewish woman, is an "Ethiope washed clean" after all by her marriage and conversion.

Lancelot Gobbo doubles the plot motif of race-mixing comically. In 3.5 he comes on stage in Belmont articulating our theme to Jessica: "Yes, truly; for look you, the sins of the father are to be laid upon the children." Her best hope, "a bastard hope," is that she is "not the Jew's daughter" (3.5.6–11). She retorts, however, that she "shall be saved by her husband" (15), echoing Corinthians 7:14, in that "He hath made me a Christian." When Lancelot teases that Jessica's conversion will raise the price of pork because it is in demand by Christians, Lorenzo retorts "I shall answer that better to the commonwealth than you can the getting up of the Negro's belly. The Moor is with child by you, Lancelot!" (31–33). The startling revelation elicits a snide response from Lancelot: "It is much that the Moor should be more than reason; but if she be less than an honest woman, she is indeed more than I took her for" (34–36). Lancelot, whose name itself means betrayal in the English-speaking world, is punning on Moor and more, suggesting that Moorish women are easily impregnated, probably because of their in-bred lascivious nature. This is the only instance of the word "Negro" in the works of Shakespeare and the only mention of a black woman in all of the plays. However, the mistress is black, female, pregnant, and offstage, in other words unrepresented.

There are four women who are confronted with choices involving miscegenation in the Venetian plays: two white Christian women, Portia and Desdemona; a Jew, Jessica; and an appropriately unnamed "Negro" courtesan. Portia, anticipating Desdemona in the Moorish play, is constrained in her choices of a suitable mate by her European Christian father who sets the rules in the lottery of the caskets. But unlike Brabantio, the father of Desdemona who seems genuinely interested in Othello as a man and a general but is clearly put off by his race, Portia's father commands his daughter to judge her men by the "content of their character" rather than external appearance or wealth.

Jessica knows she has been contaminated by her father's blood which she will remedy by marriage to a Christian. Desdemona, on the other hand, is blackened by her marriage to and sexual intercourse with Othello, a "blackamoor." Her crime in marrying an alien, her father Brabantio says, is a "treason of the blood" (*Othello*, I. i. 171), a crime not only against the family (which he would rouse to arms against Othello) in choosing her own mate, but in blackening the blood of the posterity of the clan—once again reminiscent of the curse of Cush or, at the very least, the transgression of Ham's wife who had her mind on "something black" when she conceived Cush. Desdemona's union with the alien, as opposed to Jessica's with the Christian, is "monstrous" and is caricatured variously by Iago to Brabantio as "an old black ram . . . tupping your white ewe" (1.1.88–89)—which resonates racially with Shylock's interpretation of the Jacob/Laban story of the speckled sheep (Merchant, 1.3.67–91)[5]—and that his "daughter (is) covered with a Barbary horse" so that he will "have your nephews neigh to you" and "have coursers for cousins and jennets for germans" (1.1.112–14). Unlike Jessica's relationship with Lorenzo, where the female is rescued from her tainted "blood" by marriage to a Christian, Desdemona, the white European woman, is coarsened and defiled by her marriage to Othello, the Moor, "such a thing," says Brabantio, she was taught "to fear, not to delight" (1.2.72). In the European mind-set, Desdemona lives up to her name which suggests she is "of the demons" in submitting to a bestial union with a "devil (that) will make a grandsire" of Brabantio, her father (1.1.91).

In most productions of *Othello* in the last twenty years, Bianca is played by a black actress. While this may be considered a matter of non-traditional casting, just an arbitrary choice Cassio makes for a passing affair or the availability of a black actress for the part, it does introduce racially complicating variables in this particular play. A black Bianca throws the relationship of Othello and Desdemona into bold relief and illustrates how dramatically different the contexts and impacts of those relationships are. What is good for the gander in this case, Cassio, as the white male, is not good for the goose, Desdemona. While there is no real indication in the play that Bianca is a whore, she is certainly treated like one by Cassio, particularly for show before his military colleagues, especially Othello. In the Royal Shakespeare Company production which opened at the Young Vic in 1989, Trevor Nunn deliberately cast a black woman as Bianca to show, "Cassio's double standard in sexual matters —he idealises the divine Desdemona, but relieves himself with a harlot," a black harlot he might have added (quoted in Vaughan, 229). The effect was to double the "monstrous" sexual relationship between black and white. If the woman is white, she has something to lose in the relationship with a black mate: purity, the respect of her race, family, and nation, and control of her progeny which will be automatically black, racially inherited in the paradigm from the black male, recalling the curse of Cush. If the woman is black, no loss: her progeny is already black with all the corruptions and aspersions implicit in that complexion. Bianca's function was to play the whore that Iago would have her be in the "ocular" spectacle she plays out for Othello who eavesdrops on the scene. She is the woman of easy virtue whom Cassio frequents which would, in Othello's mind, now include Desdemona, the "supersubtle Venetian" and "whore of Venice" who has taken up with an "erring barbarian."

The transgression of Ham condemns his sons, Canaan and Cush, to perpetual slavery and Cush to perpetual negritude. Slavery is an important issue for comment by the alien in both of the Venetian plays. In the courtroom scene where Shylock, the Jewish outsider, has the audacity to challenge the state of Venice, he scores a "palpable hit" in arguing that his Venetian superiors have constructed a legal system which condones the ownership of human beings as chattel slaves to do with as they please—to buy and sell, exploit sexually and manually, torture, and murder—all with impunity, even with a sense of moral superiority. And yet these same officials would deny him his simple pound of flesh which his legal bond demands.

> You have among you many a purchased slave
> Which, like your asses and your dogs and mules,
> You use in abject and in slavish parts
> Because you bought them. Shall I say to you
> "Let them be free, marry them to your heirs.
> Why sweat they under burdens? Let their beds
> Be made as soft as theirs, and let their palates
> Be seasoned with such viands"? You will answer,
> "The slaves are ours." So do I answer you:
> The pound of flesh which I demand of him
> Is dearly bought, is mine, and I will have it.
> If you deny me, fie upon your law:
> There is no force in the decrees of Venice.
> (*The Merchant of Venice*, 4.1.89-101)

Is not Shylock provided by Shakespeare here with an irrefutable argument, given the arbitrary nature of all laws and their strategic execution on behalf of those who have the power to articulate and wield them? What neither Shylock nor Othello realize, of course, is that they, as aliens, are at once the instrument—as usurer and general—and the victim of the laws that were at the time slowly but surely institutionalizing chattel slavery in the West. Othello, of course, was "taken by the insolent foe / And sold to slavery" before "redemption" (*Othello*, 1.3.136-37), but is still, under "the decrees of Venice," an outsider marked by the complexion which is the sign of the curse of Ham to suffer a lifetime of servitude. Shylock may have legal logic on his side, but remains the alien to be exploited and discarded by the system he would appeal to for justice. The European system of chattel slavery was predicated on a few brutally simple economic realities, among them the expenditure of Jewish capital for Negro slaves. Clean European hands all the way around. In sum, slavery is the system that provides the underpinning and the unarticulated argument for both the Venetian plays which anticipate and rehearse the most devastating crimes of the Early and the Late Modern period, the four-hundred-year scourge of European and American slavery and the Nazi holocaust.

Considered as dramatic rituals with authoritative political overtones, the Venetian plays share a single structure: the manipulation, exploitation, and eventual expulsion of useful but dangerous aliens. Shylock's money, and the religious tradition that not only tolerates but encourages the "use" and growth of capital through loans at interest, is not only essential to Antonio to validate his friendship with Bassanio, it is crucial to the prosperity of Venice if it is to pursue its destiny as the leading mercantile power in the Mediterranean. But the church and European custom will not allow the practice of moneylending. Shylock is fully aware of his own "use" to the Venetians and would limit his contact with natives to business dealings. He makes this perfectly clear to Bassanio who invites him to dinner on the Rialto as he sounds him out about the loan: "I will buy with you, sell with you, talk with you, walk with you, and so following; but I will not eat with you, drink with you, nor pray with you" (1.3.29–32). Shylock will also not tolerate contact between his daughter and the Christians, locking Jessica away especially during the riotous moments of Christian holiday, for reasons that are made obvious in the play.

Othello, however, as an African general on Venetian turf, seems perfectly assimilated in his own "mind's eye," as Desdemona says, to the customs of the state and its culture. A "Turk"—or even a Jew—once removed by Christian conversion, he too has, as he says prefacing his confession to the murder of Desdemona, "done the state some service, and they know't" (*Othello*, 5.2.348). In the eyes of the Senate at the beginning of the play, he is probably little more than a mercenary for temporary hire to drive out the Turks. Its leniency may be interpreted as expedient when one of its members, Brabantio, brings severe and predictable charges against him: the "treasonous" theft of and monstrous union with his daughter. Othello, more surprised than his superiors at the violence of Brabantio's reaction—"Call up all my people! . . . Call up my brother. . . . Get weapons, ho!" (1.1.142, 176, 182)—takes the time to reason with Brabantio and the Senators. The bemused reaction of the Duke to the marriage—"I think his tale (Othello's) would win my daughter too" (1.3.170)—may well be more a strategic ploy to secure the services of Othello, his chief in the battle against the Turks, than an honest acceptance of the Moor on terms so equitable that intermarriage is tolerable.

Once, however, services are rendered—the loan is made, the Turks expelled—the alien law is mysteriously produced in *The Merchant of Venice* by, appropriately enough, Portia; the alien Jew is expelled, and Othello, as ultimate authority on the island of Cyprus, executes himself for having murdered a Venetian. Both Shylock and Othello stand accused of having, in fact, "traduced the state," by plotting violence against a member of the Venetian community—Antonio and Desdemona (5.2.363). The inevitable consequence of the transgression of housing an alien within that community—it is implied—

is violence against one of its members. After ritual excoriation by Gratiano and others as Jews, Shylock is basically stripped of his wealth and then of his religion by the state to which he replies, "I am content," an assertion not even the Nazis could have believed. Othello, on the other hand, having been fully assimilated by the host culture, objectifies himself, recognizing, sentencing, and finally executing the alien enemy of the state that he now represents.

The language Othello uses to narrate his story brings us full circle in the argument against the alien. Characterizing himself as a "base Judean" in the first Folio reading, the text most often adopted by editors, he narrates his own execution by objectifying himself as blackamoor and "Judean." He insists in telling his story—in other words, narratively rehearsing the ritual of alien expulsion—"Nothing extenuate, / Nor set down aught in malice," but speak:,

> . . . of one whose hand,
> Like the base Judean, threw a pearl away
> Richer than all his tribe; . . .
>   . . . Set you down this
> And say besides that in Allepo once,
> Where a malignant and a turbaned Turk
> Beat a Venetian and traduced the state,
> I took by th' throat the circumcisèd dog
> And smote him thus. (5.2.351, 355–57, 360–65).

Of course the base "Judean"/"Indian" controversy continues to rage unresolved in edition after edition of the play. "Judean" is the reading in the Folio edition of the play, "Indian" in the Quarto. In the most recent edition by Stephen Greenblatt which follows the Oxford edition, "Indian is used" but justified in a note that confirms the obvious choice of "Judean" above in the context of this paper.

In his final speech, Othello, Greenblatt reasons, evokes an uncivilized "'Indian' unaware of the value of a pearl. Compare this reading from the Quarto with the Folio's 'Judean' which may suggest malice rather than ignorance by alluding to Judas (betrayer of Christ) or perhaps Herod (who killed his wife Marianne out of jealousy). 'Judean' also anticipates 'circumsizèd' (364) and hence an identification of Othello with Jews" (5.2.357, n. 1). In the text Greenblatt follows the editorial tradition with "Indian"; in the note, he confirms the thematic preference for "Judean." After all, as the representative of martial law on the island, not to mention commander and chief and Christian convert, Othello executes "a turbaned Turk" who "Beat a Venetian and traduced the state," a "circumcisèd dog," clearly a Jew in the tradition of Cush, at once defiled by his blackness and his Judaic heritage.

There is, of course, a certain sympathy that is generated for Shylock and Othello of Venetian fame that we do not feel for Barabas in *The Jew of Malta* or Aaron the Moor in *Titus Andronicus*. The apologias of Shylock, Morocco, and Othello invite empathy for human beings living at the margin who nevertheless feel pain, love, anger, humiliation, and loss. These are aliens who, because of their professional utility in sustaining and promoting the objectives of the dominant culture, assume momentary status as "subjects," politically but also ethnically. Of course, as human beings they see themselves as subjects existentially and ethically wherever they reside. Shakespeare provides us with more than the alien objects. He gives us human beings, viewing themselves as perceiving, sensitive subjects in the process of serving their social function to the state. However, they are returned to objective status by play's end as aliens to be disposed of with legal and military pomp and circumstance. What resonates in our mind, though, is their imprecation to onstage and offstage audiences that they be regarded as subjects with histories, families, temperaments, and most of all, feelings that differentiate themselves from their marginal compatriots—simple "Moors" and "Jews" in the minds of a European audience. Shylock, at the nadir of his humiliation in Venice, just as he is about to learn of the defection of Jessica and the sale of Leah's wedding "turquoise" for a monkey, states, "I am a Jew. Hath not a Jew eyes? Hath not a Jew hands, organs, dimensions, senses, affections, passions . . . subject to the same diseases, healed by the same means, warmed by the same winter and summer as a Christian is" (*The Merchant of Venice*, 3.1.49–54). As the allegory of the caskets invites us to do, in this speech we cannot but look into the life of the alien to share the pains of his exclusion and the righteousness of his anger, in short, to empathize with him fully as a fellow human being.

Similarly, if Othello ultimately objectifies himself as a "base Judean" and "circumsizèd dog" to be liquidated at the end of his Venetian parable, at the beginning, after he has been excoriated as the "black ram," "Barbary horse," and the "extravagant and wheeling stranger," he appears onstage in his full and impressive status, exhibiting none of the physical characteristics or outrageous behaviors ascribed to him in act one, scene one. To demonstrate that Shakespeare was more than capable of reifying such biased judgments in the actual physical characteristics of his aliens, we need only to look to Caliban's first appearance onstage in most productions as a scaly, reptilian monster. Othello, on the other hand, is allowed to deliver an inspired *apologia* for his life and his successful, legitimate courtship of Desdemona. He is extended—by the Senate and by Shakespeare—the opportunity of "speaking for myself" (*Othello*, 1.3.89), of representing his own experience and position as alien within the Venetian community, a rare insight indeed in any age. He speaks of "most disastrous chances," "moving accidents by flood and field," of "hair-breadth scapes," and being "sold to slavery" and of his "redemption," referring to his emancipation but also possibly to his conversion to the religious tradition of his host country (1.3.133, 134–35, 137). He "nothing extenuates" in his description of African "cannibals that each other eat, / The Anthropophagi, and men whose heads / Do grow beneathe their shoulders," exotic and horrifying details that would at once confirm the prejudicial view of Africans that Europeans were developing at this time and evoke the intense empathy for Othello that Desdemona, the senators, and the audience itself must feel by the end of the speech (142–44). "She gave me for my pains a world of sighs. . . . She loved me for the dangers I had passed" (158, 166).

Othello's crime against his innocent wife ranks perhaps as the most offensive, horrifying deed in all of Shakespeare. It is certainly prepared for most meticulously with Desdemona's long dressing scene, the willow song, and the extended, passionate exchange between husband and wife just prior to the strangling. After all, even Macbeth never considers murdering Lady Macbeth, no matter how dangerous she becomes in her madness to their mutual conspiracy. It is unimaginable that Romeo would murder Juliet, or Antony, Cleopatra, for any reason, and that is precisely the heinous crime Othello commits in the play. And yet audiences feel compassion for this murderer, a compassion carefully prepared for by a master playwright who, in the process of constructing what Harold Bloom celebrates as the notion of human identity in Western culture, excluded no single hero in his plays from that inclusive rubric, not even the aliens who were to serve the questionable needs of a now expanding European empire.

NOTES

1. All references to the plays are taken from *The Norton Shakespeare*.
2. The growing bibliography of such studies includes Emily Bartels' "Making More of the Moor: Aaron, Othello, and Renaissance Refashionings of Race;" Anthony Barthelemy's *Black Face Maligned Race: The Representation of Blacks in English Drama from Shakespeare to Southerne*; Ruth Cowhig's "Actors Black and Tawny in the Role of Othello—and Their Critics," and "Blacks in English Renaissance Drama;" David Dabydeen's The Black Presence in English Literature; Jack D'Amico's *The Moor in English Renaissance Drama*; Peter Erickson's "Race in Renaissance Art" and "Representations of Blacks and Blackness in the Renaissance;" Henry Louis Gates' "Writing, 'Race,' and the Difference It Makes," Kim Hall's "Refashionings of Race,"*Things of Darkness: Economies of Race and Gender in Early Modern England*," "'Troubling Doubles: Apes, Africans and Blackface in Mr. Moore's Revels," "Beauty and the 'Beast' of Whiteness: Teaching Race and Gender," and "Culinary Spices, Colonial Spaces: The Gendering of Sugar in the Seventeenth Century;" Eldred Jones' *The Elizabethan Image of African and Othello's Countrymen: The African in English Renaissance Drama*; Ania Loomba's Gender, Race, Renaissance Drama; Joyce Green MacDonald's *Race, Ethnicity and Power in the Renaissance*, Karen Newman's "'And wash the Ethiop white': Femininity and the Monstrous in *Othello*;" and Elliot Tokson's *The Popular Image of the Black Man in English Drama*, 1550–1688.

3. Although "miscegenation" is a nineteenth-century term, the conception of race-mixing which determined color consciousness and classification by complexion was commonplace in the sixteenth century.
4. Many editors gloss "complexion" as a trait of "temperament" rather than skin color. In this and the plays under discussion here, the operative definition is obviously "hue" or color, as Morocco indicates when he talks about his skin as "burnished" by the sun.
5. Shylock uses the story of Jacob and Laban told in Genesis 30:25–43 to justify the taking of interest when money is lent:

> Mark what Jacob did.
> When Laban and himself were compromised
> That all the eanlings which were streaked and pied
> Should fall as Jacob's hire, the ewes, being rank,
> In end of autumn turned to the rams;
> And when the work of generation was
> Between these woolly breeders in the act,
> The skilful shepherd peeled me certain wands,
> And, in the doing of the deed of kind,
> He stuck them up before the fulsome ewes,
> Who, then conceiving, did in eaning time
> Fall parti-colour'd lambs; and those were Jacob's.
> This was a way to thrive, and he was bless'd:
> And thrift is blessing, if men steal it not.

Breeding sheep is taken as a sign of God's approval of making money off of money, of, as Shylock calls it, "breeding" money (1.2.93). Shylock's language is blunt and sexual. Also, the example highlights the color, specifically black and white, of the sheep, and the mixing of these colors—all of which would seem to relate to the attribution of sexual transgression and cross-breeding to the Venetian aliens under investigation here.

WORKS CITED

Africanus, Leo Johannes. *A Geographical Historie of Africa*. London, 1600. Reprinted in Facsimile, Amsterdam: De Capo Press, 1969.

Allen, Don Cameron. *The Legend of Noah: Reniassance Rationalism in Art, Science, and Letters*. Urbana: University of Illnois Press, 1963.

Appiah, Kwame Antony. "Race," in *Critical Terms for Literary Study*, Ed. Frank Lentricchia and Thomas McLaughlin. Chicago: University of Chicago Press, 1990. 274–287.

Bartels, Emily. "Making More of the Moor: Aaron, Othello, and Renaissance Refashionings of Race." *Shakespeare Quarterly* 41 (1990): 433–54.

Barthelemy, Anthony. *Black Face Maligned Race: The Representation of Blacks in English Drama from Shakespeare to Southerne*. Baton Rouge: Louisiana State University Press, 1987.

Bloom, Harold. *Shakespeare: The Invention of the Human.* New York: Riverhead Books, 1998.

Cohen, H. Hirsch. *The Drunkenness of Noah.* University, Alabama: University of Alabama Press, 1974.

Cowhig, Ruth. "Actors Black and Tawny in the Role of Othello—and Their Critics." *Theatre Research International* 4 (1979): 133-46.

———. "Blacks in English Renaissance Drama." *The Black Presence in English Literature.* Ed. David Dabydeen. Manchester, UK: Manchester University Press, 1985. 1–26.

Dabydeen, David. *The Black Presence in English Literature.* Manchester, UK: Manchester UP, 1985.

D'Amico, Jack. *The Moor in English Renaissance Drama.* Tampa, Florida: University Press of South Florida, 1991.

Erickson, Peter. "Race in Renaissance Art." *The Upstart Crow: A Shakespeare Journal* 18 (1998): 2-9.

———. "Representations of Blacks and Blackness in the Renaissance." *Criticism* 35 (1993): 499–527.

Gates, Henry Louis, Jr. "Writing, 'Race,' and the Difference It Makes."*Loose Canons: Notes on the Culture Wars.* New York: Oxford University Press, 1992.

Greenblatt, Stephen. *Renaissance Self-Fashioning: From More to Shakespeare* Chicago: University of Chicago Press, 1980.

Hall, Kim. "Refashionings of Race," *Shakespeare Quarterly* 41 (1990): 433–54.

———. *Things of Darkness: Economies of Race and Gender in Early Modern England.* Ithaca and London: Cornell University Press, 1995.

———. "'Troubling Doubles': Apes, Africans and Blackface in Mr. Moore's Revels." *Race, Ethnicity and Power* in the Renaissance. Ed. Joyce Green MacDonald. Totowa, NJ: Fairleigh Dickinson University Press, 1997.

———. "Beauty and the 'Beast' of Whiteness: Teaching Race and Gender." *Shakespeare Quarterly* 47 (1996): 461–75.

———. "Culinary Spices, Colonial Spaces: The Gendering of Sugar in the Seventeenth Century." *Feminist Readings of Early Modern Culture: Emerging Subjects and Subjectivities.* Eds. Lindsay Kaplan, Valerie Traub, and Dympna Callaghan. Cambridge: Cambridge University Press, 1996. 168–90.

Jones, Eldred. *The Elizabethan Image of African.* Charlottesville: University Press of Virginia, 1971.

———. *Othello's Countrymen: The African in English Renaissance Drama.* London: Oxford University Press, 1965.

Jordan, Winthrop D. *White Over Black: American Attitudes Toward the Negro 1550–1812.* Chapel Hill, NC: University Press of North Carolina, 1969.

Loomba, Ania. *Gender, Race, Renaissance Drama.* Manchester, UK: Manchester University Press, 1989.

MacDonald, Joyce Green, ed. *Race, Ethnicity and Power in the Renaissance.* Totowa, NJ: Fairleigh Dickinson University Press, 1997.

McDonald, Russ. *The Bedford Companion to Shakespeare: An Introduction with Documents.* New York: St. Martin's Press, 1996.

Newman, Karen. "'And wash the Ethiop white': Femininity and the Monstrous in *Othello.*" *Shakespeare Reproduced: The Text in History and Ideology.* Ed. Jean E.

Howard and Marion F. O'Connor. Methuen: New York and London, 1987. 143–63.

Orkin, Martin R. "Othello and the 'plain face' of Racism." *Shakespeare Quarterly* 38 (1987): 166–88.

Shakespeare, William. *The Norton Shakespeare, Based on the Oxford Edition*. Eds. Stephen Greenblatt, Walter Cohen, Jean E. Howard, Katharine Eisaman Maus. Norton, New York, 1997.

Shapiro, James. *Shakespeare and the Jews*. New York: Columbia University Press, 1996.

Tokson, Elliot. *The Popular Image of the Black Man in English Drama, 1550–1688*. Boston: G. K. Hall and Co., 1982.

Vaughan, Virginia Mason. *Othello: A Contextual History*. Cambridge: Cambridge University Press, 1994.

Relating Things to the State
"The State" and the Subject of *Othello*

THOMAS MOISAN

> *Yea and some forrain men and strangers haue beene*
> *adopted into this number of citizens, eyther in regard*
> *of their great nobility, or that they had beene*
> *dutifull towardes the state, or els had done unto them*
> *some notable seruice.* (CONTARENI, 18)

> *Men in Great Place, are thrice Seruants: Seruants*
> *of the Soueraigne or State; Seruants of Fame; and*
> *Seruants of Businesse. So as they haue no Freedome;*
> *neither in their Persons; nor in their Actions; nor in*
> *their Times.*
>
> (BACON, "OF GREAT PLACE," 42)

From "honest" to "dilate," from "what's the matter?" to "My husband?" *Othello* has been shown to be home to a number of aurally and thematically resonant expressions, expressions that ramify in significance even as they impress themselves reiteratively upon the ear, contributing to what G. B. Shaw, writing of *Othello*, termed "the splendor of its word music" (135).[1] One is reminded of such expressions by the collocation whose occurrence, and recurrence, draw the attention of this essay, namely, "the state." On the face of it, to be sure, the interpretative possibilities annunciated by "the state" seem modest. Lacking the ironic power that builds in the numerous variations we hear on the word "honest," and less susceptible to the revealing paranoumasic dissonances that Patricia Parker has heard in "delate" and "dilate," references to "the state" seem to be what their contexts suggest: collectively an ellipsis for Venice the city-state, metonyms for the Venetian polity, for Venice in its governing authority and power. Indeed, context would seem to render it difficult to hear in the phrase a reference to "state" as "condition"; we do not hear anyone complain that there is something rotten in, or with, the state of Venice. Nor is the word "state" paired off against its etymological and phonological kin, "estate," which does not occur in the play. Instead, with the long vowel of its iamb giving it insinuatingly easy *entree* to the rhythms and sound of both prose and verse,[2] references to "the state" make the domain and claims of public affairs audible and rather talismanic presences in the opening act of the play and in its closing minutes: the claims of "the state" set the geographical agenda of the play; the recollection of service done "the state" brings the play to its "bloody period"; the intent to "relate" what has happened to "the state" brings the play to its smoothly rhyming close.

"The state" occurs more frequently in *Othello* than in *Hamlet*, with its princely protagonist and "statist" preoccupations; it occurs more often than in Shakespeare's earlier "Venetian" play, *The Merchant of Venice*, where a spate of references to "the state" clustered in the "trial" scene intones what Venice is legally exacted to permit and what it is legally permitted to exact (4.1.222, 312, 354, 365, 371, 373; also, 3.2.278; 3.3.29).[3] Indeed, references to "the state" occur more frequently in *Othello* than in any other of Shakespeare's plays except *Coriolanus,* a coincidence that would seem anomalous. For, however one assesses the various topical political readings that have been offered for *Coriolanus*, *Coriolanus* is still a play whose fable centrally concerns "the state," something that would seem less self-evidently true about *Othello*. In *Coriolanus* "the state" of Rome is part of the focal agon of the play, making Coriolanus and undoing him quite, its presence sustained and citations of it evenly distributed over the five acts of the play; in *Othello*, on the other hand, the role of "the state" and the Venice it represents seem thematically relegated to the margins they help spatially and aurally to define, the public sphere they evoke in acts 1 and 5 muted in and displaced by the domestic and claustrophobically private action of acts 2, 3, and 4. In short, "the state" seems integral to the subject of *Coriolanus,* but not to that of *Othello.*

Or so at least we might infer from Verdi and his librettist, Boito, who, locating the operatic center of the play in, in fact, the heavily domestic and claustrophobically private action on Cyprus, effectively mute references to "the state" by excising Shakespeare's entire first act along with Venice and "the state." In doing so, however, Verdi and Boito are only subtracting what Shakespeare appears to have added, at least if we follow Geoffrey Bullough's lead in taking as the principal source for *Othello* Cinthio's story of the "Moorish Captain." In Cinthio Shakespeare would have found references to the Signoria (Bullough, 242; 252)—which he absorbs (1.2.17)—but not to "the state." What difference does the addition of "the state" make? Most obviously, the presence of "the state," with its foreign strategic concerns and its debate over whether it is Rhodes or Cyprus that is likely to be in danger, brings into the discourse of the play the threat of the Turk, "the angrie Turke" whom "of all others," Richard Knolles wrote (1603) "that understanding and provident State" of Venice "most dread" (Bullough, 262). How potent was the fear of "turning Turk" or forced conversion to the infidel for an early modern English audience has been interrogated recently by Daniel J. Vitkus ("Turning Turk in *Othello*"), and it may have had an especial immediacy for the original audience of *Othello*, who, as Virginia Mason Vaughan has suggested, were likely to have known about the fall of the historical Cyprus to the Turk some years before the play, and might have seen in the ruination of Venice's chosen general an admonition for the Christian West (34). Less obvious, perhaps, is the effect the presence of "the state" has upon the definition of the general himself. At the very least, to make Othello the most significant servant of the *mysterium* of Venetian power invests Othello and his story with a tragic *gravitas* that his counterpart in Cinthio's fiction—a fiction that evokes those steamy "enchantments of Circe" Roger Ascham derides in Italian *novelle* (67–68)— simply does not have. The repeated reference to Venice in act 1 as "the state" elevates Othello from mere employee of the city to savior of the nation—or at least part of its commercial empire— someone so vital that "the state" "[c]annot," as Iago remarks, "with safety cast him" (1.1.148).

Yet references to "the state" do more than provide a courtesy upgrade to this tragedy without a crowned head. Rather, in what is to follow I would suggest that "the state" and Othello are tied to each other in a relationship both mutually exploitative and mutually revealing, one that leads Othello to define himself by his reading of "the state," and that makes "the state" an interested participant in Othello's tragedy. Moreover, even as a number of recent analyses have invaluably drawn our attention to the culturally charged images in the play of disclosure, to the darknesses that whet the obsession within the play with "ocular proof" (Patricia Parker, *Shakespeare from the Margins;* Michael Neill, "Unproper Beds: Race, Adultery, and the Hideous in *Othello, Issues of Death*, 141–67; and Arthur L. Little, Jr.), a consideration of the role of "the state" complicates our appreciation, not simply of the discursive in the play, but of the sense in which the play draws attention to discourse, and to its medial and ultimately repressive relationship with the visual. It is for "the state" that certain accounts get delivered; it is with the intent of "relating" things to "the state" that the stage is cleared and the sight blocked off of "the tragic loading" of the bed. Indeed, though Richard Helgerson's caution against reading the early modern notion of "state" through anything even as little removed in time as a Hobbesian lens (295) makes us cautious in treating "the state" as an abstraction of political theory, still, the discursive interaction of protagonist and "state" in *Othello*, with "the state" vetting discourse and Othello shaping discourse on "cue," evokes the relationship of two powerful institutions whose negotiation was an ineluctable reality of Shakespeare's existence: the state—or the crown with which the state was identified—and the theater.

But what is "the state" in *Othello*, and would a contemporary audience have heard in the term anything but a transparent marker for Venice? Though it is unlikely that the audience would have felt invited to ponder the term as an abstraction, surely even an early Jacobean audience was not unfamiliar with efforts to describe the workings of "the state," or its equally familiar—if less prosodically commodious—synonym, "the commonweal." "Amongst many the great and deepe deuices of worldly wisedome, for the maintenance and preseruing of human societies (the ground and stay of mans earthly blisse) the fairest, firmest, and the best, was the framing and forming of Common-weales . . ." So Knolles alliteratively opines at the outset of a work he pro-duced not long after his *The Generall Historie of the Turkes,* his translation (1606) of Jean Bodin's *The Six Bookes of a Commonweale* ("To the Reader," iv). Still, in *Othello* the reiterated appearances of "the state" have the effect of underscoring Venice in the exercise of its governing power and leaving unstated anything that would suggest that large complex organism Bodin and Knolles thought of as the "commonweal"; when, after all, Othello refers to "the state" as anything but "the state" or Venice he chooses a transliteration for the Venetian version of an executive council, "the signiory" (1.2.17).

And, to be sure, in this case any hint of mystery and abstraction that builds in the repetition of "the state" may well have reminded the audience how lit-tle they understood Venice itself. After all, as editors have observed, it is not clear that the playwright himself had fully mastered the *technicalities* of vari-ous Venetian governmental offices (Saunders, 64; n. 1.2.14; Honigman 128, n. 1.2.13–14)—perhaps a reason in itself for referring to matters of state as often as possible by the umbrella term. . . . "the state"! Nor if, as has been frequently suggested, the playwright looked at Lewis Lewkenor's translation of Gasparo Contareni's *The Commonwealth and Gouernment of Venice* (1599), would he have found the picture it presented of the intricate formulation of the Venetian system of government uniformly lucid, either in the model of government pro-duced, or in the means that produced it.[4] "Shakespeare saw Venice as part of his world," A. J. Honigmann has observed, "but not so Cyprus" (11), a valid distinction if on no other grounds than that by the time of the play Cyprus had succumbed to Ottoman invasion, while Venice was still at least in the Christ-ian orb. And the sense that Venice, for all its celebrated, or notorious, opulence was nonetheless culturally familiar has been helpful to a reading of the play that would parse it in culturally oppositional terms, with Othello the "out-sider" and "extravagant and wheeling stranger" and Venice, or "the state," the establishment, indeed, a reading to which Brabantio, Roderigo, and Iago all in various ways find it convenient to subscribe: "This is Venice; / My house is not a grange" (1.1.105–106). Still, a glance at the commentary Lewkenor pro-vided at the outset of his translation suggests that for this Englishman at least, unblushing purveyor, as Vaughan has noted, of the myth of Venice (17), "the state" of Venice was best appreciated as an exciting, "culturally broadening" conundrum. From the preface "To the Reader" to Lewkenor's translation of Contareni it is Venice itself that emerges as the "extravagant and wheeling stranger." Recalling that Homer especially praises Ulysses for the breadth of his travels, for the fact that *"Multorum mores vidit & urbes"* (Ad), Lewkenor —who might have agreed with the Duke that Othello's adventurous "tale would win my daughter too"—offers a paean to the difference that is Venice in which two notes predominate: the "strangeness" of everything connected with Venice—its history, its government, its prosperity, its physical situation; "wonder" at having observed these things. Venice, the veritably floating signifier? Lewkenor signifies the intensity of his wonder at the thought by employing as an adverb of "otherness" a word we hear repeatedly in *Othello* to suggest moral hideousness: "what euer hath the worlde brought forth more monstrously strange, then that so great & glorious a Citie should be seated in the middle of the sea. . . . ?" (A3v).[5]

Not, of course, that "the state" remains an abstraction throughout the play, and, indeed, it is in its selective moments of demystification that "the state" and the Venice it represents come to be drawn into the play as actors, at least as proximate occasions, in the circumstances that shape Othello's tragedy. In no scene are the officers and workings of "the state" rendered more humanly recognizable than in the momentous council scene (1.3), and particularly in the first forty-five lines, where we come upon the Duke and two senators attempting to puzzle out the sense of conflicting reports they have received on the Turks' intentions (1–43), a scene that seems especially demystified when compared with the description of the Great Council of three thousand described by Lewkenor, that body which deliberates so efficiently, and with so divine a peaceableness, and so without all tumult and confusion," Lewkenor gushes, "that it rather seemeth to bee an assembly of Angels, then of men"(A2d). Decidedly more sublunary, the effort of the three officers of "the state" at disambiguation puts "the state" in the business of reading signs and thus gives "the state" something in common with numerous enigma-pondering characters throughout the play, with the notable difference that the Duke and his colleagues actually manage to reason their way to a correct answer.[6] Nor is it the only time in the play at which "the state" turns out to refer to personages or collectivities. In an instance we noted earlier, Iago, who has already displayed a knack for demystifying august Venetian institutions— parrying Brabantio's charge, "Thou art a villain," with "you are a Senator" (1.1.117)—and can always be relied upon to "demystify" anyone or, in this case, thing by attributing to it a recognizably humanly self-serving motivation, and follows hard upon Roderigo's hendyadic invocation of "the state" as some abstract guarantor of justice— "the justice of the state" (91.1.139) to predict, correctly, that "the state" will find Othello too valuable to "cast him" (1.1.147). Brabantio, anxious to assert his importance at a moment when that importance seems to have been disregarded, makes the state a fraternity to which he belongs, certain that the Duke or any of his "brothers of the state" would feel his grievance (1.2.96). And in its most impersonated form, "the state" "becomes a "they," when Othello reminds those about to lead him away that he had "done the state some service, and they know't" (5.2.354).

Still, when read in the diverse contexts in which it is cited, "the state" as an entity appears something of a chimera, less a thing or concept with definable terms than a rhetorical inflection. We encounter it as an affiliative tag-on that enables Brabantio both to flash his influence and ground his personal outrage and complaint in a presumption of socio-political empathy: "The Duke himself, / Or any of my brothers of the state, / Cannot but feel this wrong as 'twere their own" (1.2.95–7). We hear it invoked to justify why something is to be done, not done, or done later; a piece of allusion and illusion central to praeteritive devices of which Iago is only the most malevolent, not the sole, practitioner. "What if I do obey?" asks Othello, of course rhetorically, when Brabantio orders him to prison. "How may the Duke be therewith satisfied, / Whose messengers are here about my side / Upon some present business of the state / To bring me to him?" (1.2.87–91). And having enabled Othello to elude detention at the beginning of the play, the discourse of "the state" serves Othello at the end as well in the literally breathtaking praeterition with which Othello takes his leave, putting his "bloody period" to a lively demonstration of the sort of service to "the state" that he had begun this nineteen-line, "word or two" speech by reminding the assembled emissaries of the state that he would not continue to remind them of: "I have done the state some service, and they know't—No more of that" (5.2.339–40). "The state" occupies the final rhyme and image of the play, but its concluding centrality as the authority offstage to which Lodovico will "[t]his heavy act with heavy heart relate," not to mention the nature of the report it is likely to receive, are complicated by the image onstage of the tragically loaded bed, the "object" which "poisons sight," and which Lodovico orders to be "hid." In the final piece of praeterition perpetrated in the play "the state" is kept in shadow: the audience is invited to pass over what it has seen and is not likely to forget; to look forward to a report it will never hear to an entity it cannot see; instead of enjoying a privileged position as the repository of what has happened, "the state" is relegated to an alternative realm of report, a realm and report rendered necessarily more shadowy in the degree to which they are to be denied the fullness of sight, a realm and report associated through the words of Lodovico with suggestions of repression and censorship.

Shadowy as the representation of "the state" may be, things still get done in its name; indeed, it is an insight of the play into the paradox of Venetian power, and perhaps the power of states in general, that we never discern the power of Venetian authority so much as when we do not see it. When, for example, Lodovico exercises his authority to announce to Othello after his murder of Desdemona has been discovered that "Your power and your command is taken off, / And Cassio rules in Cyprus" (5.2.331–32), we may initially feel that we are in the presence of Venetian justice, until we recall that what sound like penalties meted out to Othello for his crime are performative statements of administrative actions that "the state" had already taken, news of which, it is supposed, Lodovico had brought to Othello in the letter from Venice (4.1.225). Since Othello had only arrived in Cyprus in act 2, clearly "the state" had wasted no time, or, rather, operated offstage and by its own "dilatory" time to remove the Moor once, presumably, it had somehow ascertained that the military threat to Cyprus had passed. Othello's transgression only allowed "the state" to give a punitive articulation and formality to actions intended to be muted in the silences of the epistolary form.

Yet as the visit of Lodovico to Cyprus can by itself only hint, the nature of "the state" in *Othello* is most fully on display in the complexities of its relationship with its "all in all sufficient" general. That Shakespeare seems to have conned the notion that aliens were permitted, even encouraged, to contribute their talents and services, artisanal, commercial, or military, to the Venetian state is evident, and A. D. Nuttall makes a useful observation when he declares that for Shakespeare Venetian tolerance, indeed, use of the exotically different would merely have been a reflection in its political culture of the exoticism and difference that defined Venice's physical environment. "Venice," Nuttall remarks, listing just a bit towards the *coloratura*, "is for Shakespeare an anthropological laboratory. Itself nowhere, suspended between sea and sky, it receives and utilizes all kinds of people" (141).

That Shakespeare was aware that the Venetian state *received* "all kinds of people," at least as business traders, was clear in *The Merchant of Venice* (3.3.27). His sense—and his character Othello's sense—of how Venice *utilized* "strangers" could only have been complicated by exposure to Contareni, who at once celebrates the welcome aliens received, while giving clues of the limits the Venetian state placed on its inclusiveness, particularly in its relationship with aliens it retained to address its military affairs. In Lewkenor's translation of Contareni one finds, for example, an accounting of the special legal processes instituted to expedite suits brought by "strangers," with the ostensibly benign rationale that they "should not be molested and lingred off with long delayes, but quickly come to an ende of their suites" (105). Implicit, of course, in the very attention paid to the benign and genuinely more than just treatment of "strangers," is the fact that aliens normally remain aliens and outside the citizenship reserved for "Venetians," natives of "the state," and far from all of those. One thinks of the norm when Contareni duly notes a significant exception, an exception for merit, one that echoes memorably in Othello's parting *apologia*—even in its association, by proximity, of "the state" with a plural pronoun. It happens, Contareni observes, that "some forrain men and strangers haue beene adopted into this number of citizens, eyther in regard of their great nobility, or that they had beene dutifull towardes the state, or else had done vnto them some notable seruice" (18). "[S]ome notable seruice," naturally, could refer to the deeds done by those mercenary generals who tend to Venice's military foreign policy, by the likes of Othello and, perhaps, the as yet unidentified Marcus Luccicos, for whom the Duke sends along with "the valiant Moor" (1.3.45–8). Yet a scan of Contareni's comments on the attitude of "the state" towards affairs and personages military reveals an ambivalence that would render any mercenary general's hold on public esteem precarious. With an early modern nod to the policy of preparedness, leaders are encouraged to cultivate "the offices of warre," but only "for the cause of peace" (9), while a historical aside reminds the reader that the founders of "the state" "alwaies with greater regard and reckoning applyed their minds to the maintenance of peace then to glorie of warres" (15). So much for "the plumed troop, and the big wars / That make ambition virtue"(3.3349–50); to thrive in Venice Othello's occupation might indeed be gone, or rather, the cast of mind that could find "content" (348) in battle might well be distrusted. That distrust surfaces, as it were, in a Venetian law that gives ancient Roman practice a nautical twist and prohibits any returning "Generall, Legate, or Captaine of a nauie" from bringing his war gallies into the city of Venice, and obliges him to disband at a point about a hundred miles away from Venice. And though, as Honigmann reminds us (7), Lewkenor's translation mentions that the "Captaine Generall" of the Venetian army is always a "straunger," the text adds the significant qualification that the "Captaine Generall" "hath no authority to doe or deliberate any thing without the aduice of the Legates," the political officers "who neuer stirre from the side of the Captaine Generall" (132). In *Othello* this anti-militarism attributed to the Venetian state goes unvoiced, conveniently displaced by the threat posed by the Turk, not to Venice itself, but to a colonial and commercial vital interest, and a threat not unacknowledged. Yet the cultural anxieties that, as Emily Bartels has shown, a Western audience was likely to have brought towards a Moorish protagonist may only have been reinforced by the peculiar symbiosis of Venice and its military factotums. Read in this context, the determination arrived at offstage by "the state" to have Othello replaced for unspecified reasons by Cassio—a change that seems all the more peremptory to an audience that has not been given any reason to believe that a substantial amount of time has elapsed in the play—seems merely to give dramatic emphasis to the uncertain position of the warrior and the stranger in Venice recorded in Contareni and Lewkenor.

That Othello reflects the uncertainty of the soldier's and stranger's position in the Venetian state helps, of course, to define the vulnerability that is his undoing with Iago in act 3. My concern here, however, is not to revisit the psychic dynamics of that scene, and ask why Othello falls or falls so rapidly in it, but to consider the role "the state" has in shaping the vulnerable self that Othello exhibits in the play, in the beginning and at the end. We observed above that Othello's memorable protest, at "the end," that "I have done the state some service—and they know it" recalls closely the section in Lewkenor's translation that describes how "forrain men and strangers" can attain citizenship by

"Notable seruise," by merit and deeds. The recollection is worth noting because Othello's outcry very much sounds like the protest of injured merit, or of merit unrecognized, or, rather, of someone who believes that "the state" about to cart him away would be susceptible to arguments from merit—"and they know it." The particular line Othello employs here to buy time with which to dictate his statement and do away with himself is interesting. For one thing, we had not been acutely aware that Othello was suffering the pangs of injured or unrecognized merit, and the circumstances seem hardly propitious for raising questions of merit. On the other hand, however, the tack Othello takes here reminds us of Othello's first appearance in the play, when Othello dismisses the concerns Iago so helpfully raises about the harm the enraged Brabantio may do, on the grounds that "[My services which I have done the signiory / Shall outongue his complaints" (1.2.18–19). Michael Neill has referred to the "civil self" of Othello from which Iago strips away the fabric to expose the "dark" secrets Iago "has taught the audience to expect" (*Issues of Death*, 167). In Othello's comment to Iago in this first appearance we get a hint of what the fabric of that "civil self" may consist. Othello stakes his survival and advancement on the very Venetian notion of a meritocracy; that is, he defines himself according to what he believes "the state" will recognize and reward. In doing so, however, he chooses to suppress another part of himself, or, indeed, another version of himself, that part "Tis yet to know," the lineage of "royal siege," of which, in the first piece of praeterition in which he engages in the play, he at once brags while claiming he will not brag of it until bragging is in vogue (1.2.19–23). Praeterition it is, but it is a piece of praeterition that ultimately gets nullified, in that that other self Othello claims he will suppress for awhile actually stays suppressed. "Men in Great Fortunes", Bacon claims in the essay that provides one of the epigraphs to this essay, "are strangers to themselves" (42). Othello has not defined himself by his fortune, but he follows the path Bacon sees men "Of Great Place," who are enslaved to "the state," following to self-alienation. Small wonder that in his final speech, just when he has ensured himself a captive audience and can say anything he might want to say about himself, his sense of subjectivity should lead him to reenact an episode from his *vita* and subsume, indeed, extinguish himself in deeds done for "the state."

Still, as Othello tells Iago, it is not exactly his deeds that Othello claims will redeem him with "the state," but the ability of his deeds to "outongue" Brabantio's complaints. At a glance one might take this to be Othello's appeal to meritocracy and a deprecation of rhetoric, an assertion that his deeds "speak for themselves," or that "actions speak louder than words." Yet as the scene in the council meeting unfolds, "outongue" proves, of course, to be less metaphoric, or closer to personification than one at first supposes. For rather like "the state" itself, Othello's deeds in the play exist as rhetorical fodder, allusions to accomplishments designed to make points for or about Othello. It is not, we know, Othello's deeds as such that lead the Duke to "think" that "this tale would win my daughter too" (1.3.171), or even the tale itself, but a meta-tale, Othello's telling of how he had been accustomed to telling it, or as James Calderwood has described it, "a voice telling about himself telling about himself" (294). In approving that voice, "the state" does more than vet the rhetoric in which Othello fashions himself; rather, "the state" helps to define that self as rhetorical.

And well might "the state" claim some authority at judging rhetoric, since "the state" itself proves attentive to rhetoric, if ultimately transparent at its use, when it serves its interests. Nowhere is this more on display than in the council scene, where Shakespeare gives "the state" its fullest personification in the play and gives most audible voice to the celebrations of Venice's deliberative wisdom he might have found in Contareni and Lewkenor. That "the state" has interests is dramatically underscored when its spokesmen come to perceive those interests to be threatened, when in rapid succession the Duke and the senators deduce the threat to Cyprus only to hear Brabantio bring charges of witchcraft against their best hope at resisting that threat. "We are very sorry for't," the response of "All" to Brabantio's accusations (1.3.73) is heartfelt, even though the sentiment it embodies probably transcends fraternal regard for the injury suffered by their "brother of the state," Brabantio. And, indeed, it is a measure of their moral sense, or at least of their desire to live up to the moral reputation of the Venetian state, that its representatives on stage should feel an ethical dilemma at the possibility that defending Cyprus and avenging Brabantio might not be compatible goals, a dilemma that is made all the more embarrassing by the firm pledge of judicial severity the Duke issues—"yea, though our proper son / Stood in your action" (1.3.69–70)—immediately before he learns who the accused is. When "the state" is spared the necessity of condemning its military champion, it is, of course, still left with the dilemma of reconciling itself, and Brabantio, to the marriage of the fair skinned-Desdemona and the dark-skinned Moor. Wooed by Othello's own rhetoric and bound by Venice's reputation of toleration towards strangers, especially strangers that are to help it defend its possessions against the Turk, "the state" in the cloying balm of the Duke's rhymed couplets, employs a trope to deny the seemingly undeniable fact of skin color, in the process endorsing the sort of color-coded metaphysics that, as Neill has demonstrated, ultimately enables Othello to demonize Desdemona by demonizing himself (*Issues of Death*, 144-44):

> If virtue no delighted beauty lack,
> Your son-in-law is far more fair than black. (1.3.289–90)

What the Duke so fecklessly does here, Lodovico will much more effectively do later, in fact ending the play in the process. That is, both align the authority of "the state" and rhetorical discourse to deny nothing less than the evidence of sight: the Duke formally bolsters the authority of his rank with the authority of rhymed couplets to claim that black can really be white; Lodovico, as we have noted before, forcibly averts everyone's glance from the sight-poisoning bed and diverts attention to a narrative to come, the narrative to be "related." In the process, the invention of "the state," its extrapolation on Shakespeare's putative source in Cinthio, provides a vehicle by means of which *Othello* appears to tame the narrative it has staged, devising strategies of domestication, familiarization, and ultimately recuperation while calling attention to the ways in which that narrative ultimately eludes control. Indeed, we get a hint of this in the scene in the council meeting when the Duke first calls for and then blesses Othello's account of how he used to account for his past and its adventures. Again, what wins Othello sympathy in this speech, before Desdemona arrives to exonerate him formally, is as much the performance of the speech as its content, its collection of wild and unfamiliar things and experiences harnessed within Othello's recognizably and sonorously attractive delivery. The Duke's prompt, "Say it, Othello" (1.3.126), or what Honigman calls an unusual turn of phrase" (143, n.1.3.128), does not so much command Othello to speak as cue him to perform, and exemplifies both the way in which "the state" domesticates Othello's "extravagant strangeness" and part of the "service" through which Othello ingratiates himself with "the state."[7] In "Othello Furens" Robert S. Miola has charted a number of instances in which Othello's language is suffused with recollections of Seneca's *Hercules Furens*, a possible source of the argot that Iago claims is laden with "bumbast circumstance / Horribly stuff'd with epithites of war"(1.1.13–14). Invested with a familiarly theatrically wild, heroic language that, much to Iago's stated chagrin, is part of the winning persona Othello wears in "the state," Othello and "the state" demonstrate the terms of their peculiar, mutually cultivating, mutually exploitative relationship. Indeed, that moment so central to Othello's need for ocular proof, the scenario Iago stages with Cassio for Othello's benefit (4.1.103–68), only demonstrates the way in which the imposition of a conventional dramatic form can hide sight and misinform, since Othello becomes enraged, less at what he sees than by the words he thinks he hears, the script from familiar plays he is imaginatively writing into what he sees before him, with Cassio a swaggering stage Roman: "Do [you] triumph, Roman? Do you triumph?" (4.1.118).

Finally, Lodovico's determination at the end of the play to hide the bed and what it reveals and his announcement of his intention to "relate" what had happened to "the state" enlist "the state" in a recuperative strategy that attempts to rewrite what has happened in familiarly, manageably, and conventionally tragic terms, terms that exempt us from having to pose or cope with the harder questions the events onstage force. To Iago, now conveniently demonized as "O Spartan dog" (5.2.361), incomprehensibly evil but, then, beyond the need to comprehend because undeniably inhuman, is shifted all of the responsibility for "the tragic loading of this bed; / This is thy work" (5.2.363–64). Simultaneously Othello emerges as a tragic icon and victim: his suicide provides a theatrically familiar demonstration that "he was great of heart" (5.2.361), and spares "the state" the burden of having to learn from his own testimony "the nature of [his] fault." In the degree to which the recuperative strategy doesn't work, leaving in our sight the bed and the questions it provokes, underscoring as a strategy of denial the narrative Lodovico will present to "the state," and affiliating "the state" itself with the agency of censor, *Othello* presents as an undomesticatable form drama itself.

NOTES

1. See Granville-Barker, 130; Moisan; Parker, "Shakespeare and Rhetoric: 'dilation' and 'delation' in *Othello*, 54–74, *Shakespeare from the Margins* 229–72; Shaw.
2. So "the state" slips seems to slip formulaically into the rhythm of an editorial gloss by Kittredge on the name Marcus Luccicos, who Kittredge surmises is "[d]oubtless some foreigner in the service of the Venetian state" (16, n.1.3.44).
3. Unless otherwise stated, references to Shakespeare's text are from *The Riverside Shakespeare*, ed. G. Blakemore Evans, 2d ed. (Boston: Houghton Mifflin, 1997). References to "the state" are not affected by the notorious variations between Folio and Quarto.
4. So, for example, we have Contareni's account of Venice's "great counsell"—the Duke's voting powers on which Shakespeare has been said to have misrepresented —wherein "the shew of a popular estate" is seasoned, somehow, by just enough of "entermixture of the gouernment of the nobility" to ensure a meritocracy, a salutary hybridity that draws the marginal gloss, "The commonwealth of Venice is neither a popular estate, nor an Olygarchy, but a wel tempered gouernment betweene both" (33–4).
5. Kenneth Muir (187) has detected resemblances between Lewkenor's language and the language of the play in the Council Scene (.3), including the parallel between the modesty *topos* with which Othello prefaces his defense against Brabantio's accusation (1.3. 81–2)
6. Vaughan (20–21) cites speculation, or as she dubs it, "wild surmise," that the representation of the deliberations of the Venetian Senate in 1.3 could have had a topical significance and coincided with a visit by Venetian ambassadors to the English court around the time when *Othello* was first performed.
7. Indeed, as the play unfolds, Othello's standing with "the state" continues to be, in modern bureaucratic parlance, "performance based," but his "performance" is measured by criteria other than his military prowess, which, after all, becomes moot once nature intervenes to destroy the Turkish fleet. When Lodovico s arrival in Cyprus triggers Othello's outburst against Desdemona, Lodovico's indignant question, "Is this the noble Moor whom our full Senate / Call all in all sufficient" (4.1.264–5), suggests that "the state" reserves the right to define "sufficiency" by a number of criteria, including the decorum of one's public behavior. When

Lodovico rebukes Othello for striking Desdemona by invoking Venice as an arbiter, "this would not be believ'd in Venice" (4.1.242), "the state" emerges as much as an aesthetic and theatrical critic as a moral censor.

WORKS CITED

Bacon, Francis. *Essays*. London. Oxford University Press, 1966.

Bartels, Emily C. "Making More of the Moor: Aaron, Othello, and Renaissance Refashionings of Race." *Shakespeare Quarterly* 41 (1990): 433–54.

Bodin, Jean. *The Six Bookes of a Commonweale: A Facsimile Reprint of the English Translation of 1606. Ed. And Introduction by Kenneth Douglas McRae*. Cambridge. Harvard University Press, 1962.

Calderwood, James L. "Speech and Self in *Othello*. *Shakespeare Quarterly* 38 (1987): 293–303.

Contareni, Gasparo. *The Commonwealth of Venice*. Trans. Lewis Lewkenor (1599) Amsterdam: De Capo Press, 1969.

Granville-Barker, Harley. *Prefaces to Shakespeare*. 2. Princeton: Princeton University Press, 1947.

Helgerson, Richard. *Forms of Nationhood: The Elizabethan Writing of England*. Chicago: The University of Chicago Press, 1992.

Little, Jr, Arthur L. "'An essence that's not seen': The Primal Scene of Racism in *Othello*." *Shakespeare Quarterly* 44 (1993): 304–24.

Miola, Robert S. "Othello *Furens*." *Shakespeare Quarterly* 41 (1990): 49-64.

Moisan, Thomas. "Repetition and Interrogation in *Othello*: 'What needs this Iterance?' or, 'Can anything be made of this?'" *Othello: New Perspectives. Ed.* Virginia Mason Vaughan and Kent Cartwright. London: Associated University Presses. 48–73.

Muir Kenneth. *The Sources of Shakespeare's Plays*. New Haven: Yale University Press, 1978.

Neill, Michael."Unproper Beds: Race, Adultery, and the Hideous in *Othello*." *Shakespeare Quarterly* 40 (1989): 383–412.

———. *Issues of Death: Mortality and Identity in English Renaissance Tragedy*. Oxford: Oxford University Press, 1997.

Nuttall, A.D. *A New Mimesis: Shakespeare and The Representation of Reality*. London: Methuen, 1983.

Parker, Patricia. *Shakespeare from the Margins: Language, Culture, Context*. Chicago: The University of Chicago Press, 1996.

Parker, Patricia, and Geoffrey Hartman. Ed. *Shakespeare & The Question of Theory*. New York: Methuen, 1985.

Shakespeare, William. *Othello*. Ed. George Lyman Kittredge. Rev. Irving Ribner. New York: John Wiley & Sons, 1969.

———. *Othello: The New Cambridge Shakespeare*. Ed. Norman Sanders. Cambridge: Cambridge University Press, 1984.

———. *Othello: The Arden Shakespeare*. Ed. E. A. J. Honigmann. 3rd Edition. London: Thomas Nelson & Sons, 1997.

————. *The Riverside Shakespeare.* Ed. G. Blakemore Evans. 2nd Edition. Boston: Houghton Mifflin, 1997.

Shaw, John. " 'What is the Matter' in *Othello?*" *Shakespeare Quarterly* 17 (1966): 157 –61.

Vaughan, Virginia Mason. *Othello: A Contextual History.* Cambridge: Cambridge University Press. 1994.

Vitkus, Daniel J. "Turning Turk in *Othello:* The Conversion and Damnation of the Moor." *Shakespeare Quarterly* 48 (1997): 145–76.

Venetian Ideology or Transversal Power?
Iago's Motives and the Means by which Othello Falls

BRYAN REYNOLDS AND JOSEPH FITZPATRICK

This essay presents a new perspective on the means by which Othello falls from his position of high status both within Venetian society and in the eyes of the play's audience. By examining the pertinent critical history of *Othello*, especially criticism accounting for the effects on Othello of Iago's machinations, this analysis explores the social and ideological relations between Iago and Othello through the lenses of several different critical approaches, including new historicist and cultural materialist. Our aim is to reveal the contradictions and limitations in this critical history that encourage an examination of the play in light of a more inclusive approach that we call "transversal theory," which will be explained as the analysis progresses.[1] In doing this, we hope to emancipate the critical history of *Othello* from the delimiting analytical parameters that have characterized it and to show the transversal ways in which Iago paradoxically opposes and reifies Venetian state ideology.

CRITICAL TRADITIONS

In order to situate our transversal analysis in terms of the critical discourse on *Othello*, we will begin with G. K. Hunter's "Othello and Colour Prejudice" because it was groundbreaking in examining how racial issues inform Othello's fall, and because it was keenly aware of its own intervention in *Othello* criticism. Hunter shows "how mindlessly and how totally accepted in this period was the image of the black man as the devil" (39).[2] Yet, according to Hunter, Shakespeare's Moor defeats this prejudice of the Elizabethan audience as soon as he appears on stage in act I, scene 2: "This is no 'lascivious Moor,' but a great Christian gentleman, against whom Iago's insinuations break like water against granite. Not only is Othello a Christian; moreover, he is the leader of Christendom in the last and highest sense in which Christendom existed as a viable entity, crusading against the 'black pagans'" (45).

Following this passage, we may infer that the audience's acceptance of Othello, if Hunter is correct and Othello was accepted, stemmed less from his redeeming personal traits than from his association with the two dominant sociopolitical institutions of the period: Church ("Christendom") and state (the government and military).[3] Thus, the paganism and demonism associated with Othello because of his race would have been largely dismissed by the audience once they learned of his conversion to Christianity.[4] And much of the antipathy that the Elizabethans might still have felt toward Othello, not specifically as a black man, but more generally as an obvious non-European, is mediated by the position of authority he has earned in the Venetian military.

It is generally accepted that as the audience's potential prejudices against the black protagonist are reversed in the play's first act, because Othello is identified as worthy by both the Venetian state and one of Venetian society's prized possessions (Desdemona), a simultaneous reversal in the opposite direction reveals the unexpected vileness of the white, Venetian antagonist.[5] Hunter describes the situation in powerful terms: "We might say that Iago is the white man with the black soul while Othello is the black man with the white soul" (Hunter, 46).[6] Janet Adelman advances this reading, noting that "This trope [of Iago as "monstrous progenitor" (1.3.401–402)] makes the blackness Iago would attribute to Othello—like his monstrous generativity —something already inside Iago himself, something that he must project out into the world" (130). This "blackness" that is transferred to Iago is accompanied by the designation of "devil." Iago repeatedly refers to himself as the devil, and is joined in doing so by those who recognize his villainy in like terms. Thus a chiasmic double reversal occurs within the first act: the suspicious "outsider" Othello becomes, for the audience especially, a respected member of Venetian society, an "insider," and the outwardly "honest" Iago is unveiled as a villain. The relationship between Othello and Iago is therefore reduced by these critics, to different degrees, to symmetrical antithetism: the semblance of wholeness or totality is constructed methodologically through the binary oppositions (light/dark, white/black, insider/outsider, self/Other, good/evil) either cited from or imposed onto the text to give an explanatory coherence to their relationship and to the play overall. We call this analytical strategy, which is characteristic of most dialectical argumentation, the "dissective-cohesive mode."

As an alternative, transversal theory insists on the "investigative-expansive mode" of analysis.[7] Like the dissective-cohesive mode, the investigative-expansive mode requires that the subject matter of interest be divided up and partitioned into variables in accordance with the selected parameters of the investigation. But unlike the dissective-cohesive mode, whose goal is to reconstruct the variables as a coherent whole, the investigative-expansive mode examines both the internal connectedness of the variables (among themselves) and the external connectedness of the variables (to other forces, such as the play's critical history) in coordination with a fluid openness to reparameterizing as the analysis progresses—in response to the emergence of unanticipated problems, information, and ideas. Thus, the purpose is not to assemble a fully accounted for whole, but to better our comprehension of the subject matter's changing relationships to its own parts, as well as to the environments of which it is a part. The subject matters of the present analysis are *Othello* and its critical history; the chosen variables include the characters Iago and Othello and various readings of the play: and the greater environment of concern is the hermeneutic space in which the play and its criticism resides and across which they will continue to travel.

To review, we have seen that critics who focus on the play's first act reveal the chiasmic double reversal, which is accentuated, as Adelman notes, by the act's concluding soliloquy in which Iago forms his fiendish scheme: "Hell and night," Iago exclaims, "Must bring this monstrous birth to the world's light" (1.3.402). Furthermore, we have shown how critics have found ample fodder in this act for dissective-cohesive formalizing. What happens in the following four acts, however, is an issue of much debate. Hunter and Adelman both claim that "the dark reality originating in Iago's soul spreads across the play, blackening whatever it overcomes and making the deeds of Othello at last fit in with the prejudice that his face at first excited" (Hunter, 55).[8] Hunter contrasts this reading with what he calls "a powerful line of criticism on *Othello*, going back at least as far as A.W. Schlegel, that paints the Moor as a savage at heart, one whose veneer of Christianity and civilization cracks as the play proceeds, to reveal and liberate his basic savagery: Othello turns out to be in fact what barbarians *have* to be" (55).[9] This line of criticism might be best represented in the twentieth century by Bloom and Jaffa in *Shakespeare's Politics*: "Shakespeare's Moor . . . returns at the end to the barbarism that the audience originally expected. The first, primitive prejudice against Othello seems to find justification in the conclusion" (Bloom and Jaffa, 43).[10] In terms of the earlier transfer of the role of "devil" from Othello to Iago, the two major critical traditions might be summarized thus: The Schlegel, Bloom and Jaffa line of criticism claims that Othello and Iago were *both* devils from the beginning; just as Iago hides his identity from the play's other characters, so does Othello hide his own identity from the other characters, the audience, and himself. Hunter and Adelman's alternative line of criticism considers the original role reversal valid, but have the devil Iago corrupting the virtuous Othello, and thereby transforming him into the fiend the Elizabethans assumed him to be.

Alan Sinfield offers what amounts to a revision of Bloom and Jaffa's reading from a critical perspective that is potentially capable of avoiding the racist implications that Bloom and Jaffa see in the play. As Sinfield writes, "In the last lines of the play, when he wants to reassert himself, Othello 'recognizes' himself as what Venetian culture has really believed him to be: an ignorant, barbaric outsider—like, he says, the 'base Indian' who threw away a pearl.

Virtually, this is what Althusser means by 'interpellation': Venice hails Othello as a barbarian, and he acknowledges that it is he they mean" (31). Sinfield introduces the Althusserian vocabulary of ideology that informs much new historicist and cultural materialist criticism to explain Othello's transformation. Notwithstanding his high position within what Althusser would call the "Repressive State Apparatus" of the military, Othello fails to adopt sufficiently the proper Venetian ideology, falling victim instead to a contrasting "barbarian" ideology that hauntingly informs his characterization and is actualized. This reading is in effect similar to Schlegel's, but without the suggestion that Othello is somehow inherently *defective* in his Otherness.[11] Yet Sinfield's approach to this line of criticism leaves us with a number of questions including: Where and when is Othello indoctrinated with this "barbarian" ideology? And why does he recognize himself as being like the "base Indian" only long after he has apparently succumbed to the "barbarian" ideology?

Even though this type of ideological interpretation jibes well with the action of the play,[12] Sinfield does not follow through with this interpretation. Instead, he leaves it stranded just a step away from the old reversion-to-savagery interpretation, separated from Bloom and Jaffa's and Schlegel's readings, one might argue, by a veneer of Althusserian jargon. It seems, though, that Sinfield has keenly pointed to the need for an understanding of how Othello's initial status in Venice and his subsequent actions throughout the play are ideologically formed.

A TRANSVERSAL DISJUNCTION

At this point, we will turn from considering an ideological reading of *Othello* to discussing these critical limitations. If the negating of one's subjectivity is a path to empowerment—even greatness (as Bradley would have it)—in the world of the play, Desdemona's final self-effacing declaration, "Nobody, I myself" (5.2.125), is a fluke: she dies powerless. If Iago does use empathy as a means of accessing Othello's psychology and thereby manipulating him, as Greenblatt persuasively argues, then Iago cannot possibly be outside of ideology, but rather moving between ideologies and across their boundaries. It appears, then, that personal empowerment is obtained not through self-negation alone, however provisionally negated, but more effectively through imagining oneself outside of one's self or through the active acknowledgment that we are not limited to a singular constant self. In fact, Iago thrives within a conceptual framework of identity multiplicity. He reveals this to Roderigo: "our bodies are gardens, to the which our wills are gardeners, so that if we will plant nettles, or sow lettuce, set hyssop, and weed up thyme . . . why, the power, and corrigible authority of this, lies in our wills" (1.3.320—26). Iago seizes the "power" and "authority" to create and shape his own identity by placing the burden of its formation entirely upon himself, his "will." As noted

above, the language Iago uses in an earlier conversation with Roderigo anticipates this revelation: "It is as sure as you are Roderigo, / Were I the Moor, I
would not be Iago: / In following him, I follow but myself" (1.1.56–58).
"Be[ing] Iago" denotes an ability to play many different roles rather than signifying a static identity. His statement that following Othello is equivalent to
following his own desires suggests a connection and an identification with
Othello that would make empathy, and therefore manipulation, possible.

Put in transversal terms, empathy enables people to venture beyond their
own conceptual and emotional boundaries, to think and feel as others do or
might, and thus expand or transcend their own "subjective territories." We call
this process "transversal movement." "Subjective territory," as Bryan
Reynolds explains, "refers to the scope of the conceptual and emotional experience of those *subjectified* by the state machinery or any hegemonic society"
(146). Specifically, "subjective territory is delineated by conceptual and emotional boundaries that are normally defined by the prevailing science, morality, and ideology. . . . [It is] the existential and experiential realm in and from
which a given subject of a given hierarchical society perceives and relates to
the universe" (146–47). Transversal movements occur when one entertains
alternative perspectives and breaches the parameters of their subjectification.
Such movements require engagement with, and, at the very least, a passing
through "transversal territory," which is "the non-subjectified region of one's
conceptual territory [of one's imaginative range]" (149). Thus, transversal territory is entered through the transgression of the conceptual and emotional
boundaries of subjective territory.

The ease with which Iago accesses transversal territory enables him to
enter freely into the subjective territories of others where he can readily comprehend their sensibilities and idiosyncrasies. He then uses this information to
force them into transversal movements across the emotional and conceptual
spaces of alternative ideologies. Transversal theory, however, accepts the
premise that humans exist in, and are influenced by, ideology inasmuch as they
are social beings. Hence, Iago can never be totally outside of ideology unless
he becomes psychotic or his consciousness is somehow shattered. Moreover,
because humans are social, the "scientific objectivity" suggested by Althusser
is only possible insofar as humans can experience unmediated access to social
events, which is impossible.

MOVING BEYOND THE DISSECTIVE-COHESIVE MODE

We have demonstrated that Othello's acceptance into Venetian society depends
on his Christianity.[13] Yet, as the Schlegel line of criticism shows, Othello's jealous actions throughout the later portions of the play are antithetical to both the
Christian ideology and the broader social norms enforced by the overarching
Venetian state ideology. They reflect his movement, propelled by Iago, beyond

the officially-sanctioned parameters for living and operating in the world. Iago's subversion of Othello's Christianity is powerfully manifested in Othello's final acts. Indeed, murdering Desdemona, revenging himself upon Iago, and then taking his own life flout the most fundamental precepts of Christian ideology including "Thou shalt not kill." More subtle but no less telling of his departure from Venetian state ideology is his transgression of the essential Christian imperative to "temper justice with mercy." Othello strangles Desdemona in the marriage bed, which she allegedly defiled, because, for him, "the justice of it pleases" (4.1.205). At the moment when Othello is prepared to mete out that justice, Desdemona appeals to the Christian mercy she believes is still in him:

> OTH.   Thou art to die.
> DES.   Then Lord have mercy on me!
> OTH.   I say, amen.
> DES.   And have you mercy too! (5.2.57–60)

Operating now outside of the Christian ideology, Othello can acknowledge Christian values without believing in them. He can wish the Lord to have mercy on Desdemona without feeling any imperative to grant such mercy himself. Indeed, he responds to Desdemona's plea by renewing his accusations and finally by carrying out his threat.

Iago's method in toying with and eventually reversing Othello's Christian beliefs can best be seen by looking closely at act 3, scene 3, where Iago sets to work on Othello. Iago begins by playing dumb to Othello's question of whether Cassio is "honest," causing Othello to remark, "By heaven, he echoes me, / As if there were some monster in his thought, / Too hideous to be shown" (3.3.110–12). Iago continues to stall, bluff, and insinuate, until finally Othello bursts out, "By heaven I'll know thy thought" (3.3.166). The phrase "by heaven" is repeated, a simple and no doubt unconscious exclamation that comes naturally to the Christian Othello. In both cases, though, it suggests that heaven alone knows what Iago is thinking. Iago picks up on this usage, and quickly twists it to his own purpose, warning Othello: "I know our country disposition well; / In Venice they do let God see the pranks / They dare not show their husbands" (3.3.205–207).[14] Here Iago refers explicitly to his status as an insider, as someone who understands Venice in a way that Othello never will. His claim regarding Venetian practices rouses Othello's jealousy, but also plants certain associations in his mind. It suggests that the man who catches his unfaithful wife has seen what was meant for God's eyes only; and it also implicates God as a silent witness to cuckoldry, telling Othello that the God in Venice is content with letting adulterers go unpunished, cuckolds unrevenged. That Othello has picked up on these meanings is clear when he says, "If she be false, O, then heaven mocks itself" (3.3.282). Othello has already made the link between Desdemona's alleged falsehood and the injustice or even perversity of a God that would allow this to happen. By the end of the scene, Othello has knelt down with Iago and vowed his revenge, "Now by yond marble heaven" (3.3.467).[15] Later in the play we do not see "heaven mocking itself," but rather Othello mocking heaven: he perverts the sacrament of confession first in dialogue with Iago, in which Cassio's confession leads not to forgiveness but to damnation—"To confess, and be hanged for his labour" (4.1.37)—and then later with Desdemona, when he tries to make her confess so that he will feel more justified in killing her.

There is evidence, then, that Othello's relationship to Christian ideology has been subverted and altered by Iago. But what about his relationship to Venetian ideology? In act 1, scene 3, we see Venetian ideology at work in the pseudo-legal proceedings initiated by Brabantio against Othello. Implicit in this scene is the assumption that those involved are living within the same Venetian state ideology; there does not appear to be any dissent beyond Brabantio's initial vehemence and lingering bitterness. Hence, this scene revealingly contrasts Othello's shifting system of values in later acts. In the "temptation scene," for instance, as Iago is just beginning the processes of indoctrination, he offers Othello "imputation and strong circumstances, / Which lead directly to the door of truth" (3.3.412–13). Of course, it is "imputation" and "circumstantial" evidence which Brabantio brings before the Duke to support his case against Othello. Yet, while the Duke finds this kind of evidence against Othello insufficient in court, it is here being offered by Iago as the best proof available, and Othello appears willing to accept it. In the next scene, Othello questions Desdemona about the handkerchief, and we find yet another inverted parallel with the earlier court scene. Othello describes the allegedly "charmed" handkerchief and its mystical history. He claims that the handkerchief was to "subdue" his father "entirely to [his mother's] love," but would have the opposite effect if lost or given away, so much so that, "To lose, or give't away, were such perdition / As nothing else could match" (3.4.65–66). This strange fetishism recalls Brabantio's earlier argument in which he accuses Othello of witchcraft:

> I therefore vouch again,
> That with some mixtures powerful o'er the blood,
> Or with some dram conjur'd to this effect,
> He wrought upon her. (1.3.103–106)

Once again the speaker, this time Othello, masks his unreasonable expectations in a supernatural discourse, accepting this mysticism as a part of his own righteous justice. Even more blatant, however, is Othello's outright refusal to grant Desdemona the same due process that saved *him* from Brabantio's accusations. Othello was allowed to speak his case, and to send for the one witness who could resolve the problem peacefully and justly: "I do beseech you, / Send for the lady to the Sagittar, / And let her speak of me before her father"(1.3.114–16).

Under Iago's influence, Othello never confronts Desdemona with the actual accusation of adultery until he has already passed sentence on her. The exact point in the play when we can see Iago retraining Othello comes in act 2, scene 3. Pouring out liberal helpings of alcohol, Iago manages to orchestrate a brawl between Montano and Cassio. But it is only after Othello has stopped the fight and demands an explanation that we see the wicked brilliance of Iago's plan: the two combatants, drunk and wounded, are unable to present Othello with a clear narrative of what has happened, and must defer to Iago to explain everything. Whatever his affiliation with the Venetian state, whatever his belief in civil law, Othello is operating at this point in a military capacity that allows him to make unilateral decisions based on the best information he can gather. Iago uses this situation to insinuate himself further into Othello's trust, planting in Othello's mind the idea that Iago's word should count as legal proof. This idea takes hold more and more as Iago weans Othello from Christian and Venetian state ideologies. At the end of the play, as Othello prepares to kill her, Desdemona begs him to let Cassio explain the situation: "Send for the man and ask him" (5.2.50). Othello refuses her; he has already ordered Cassio killed. Proof therefore is pursued and authorized not through justice but through rash retribution.

IAGO'S MOTIVES?

> I hate the Moor,
> And it is thought abroad, that 'twixt my sheets
> He's done my office; I know not if 't be true . . .
> Yet I, for mere suspicion in that kind,
> Will do, as if for surety. (1.3.384)

If we choose to take at face value Iago's own professed motives, he himself operates according to what one might describe as a subset of Venetian ideology, that of the cuckold, a perspective that opposes cuckoldry's threat to patriarchal hierarchy. Because Iago is an organ of Venetian state power, he condemns cuckoldry; however, Iago exceeds state-prescribed subjective territory and enters transversal territory when his condemnation becomes pathological in its violation of the Venetian state's judicial process. Iago circumvents the Venetian state's legal system when he acts from a sensitivity to what is "thought abroad" about him, and dismisses the procedure requiring burden of proof demonstrated in the trial scene, acting "as if [with] surity" without searching for proof beyond "mere suspicion." As we have seen, Iago is not *trapped* within either this cuckold ideology or a particular subjective territory. The nonsubjectivity of "I am not what I am" permits him to move transversally beyond the ideology and view it *as* an ideology. Nevertheless, this self-negating phrase, "I am not what I am," is Iago's *modus operandi* only in the actual processes of empathizing and disseminating his ideology. But Iago's function as a representative of Venetian state power, manifest in spreading his repudiation of cuckoldry, transgresses subjective territory when he skirts that same state ideology's legal standards. Iago's movement into transversal territory, then, challenges the Venetian state because it flouts its judicial codes. However, Iago's transversally-inspired actions can be interpreted as paradoxically reinforcing Venetian state power, even while they undermine that power through the destruction of Othello.

This brings us back to Sinfield, and what he calls "the 'entrapment model' of ideology and power, whereby even, or especially, maneuvers that seem designed to challenge the system help to maintain it" (39). This model, also known as the new-historicist "subversion/containment paradigm," uses a dissective-cohesive mode of analysis in that it insists that all social phenomena work to produce a singular sociopolitical system or dominant power structure.[16] According to this model, Iago's subversion of the ideologies that have created Othello as a leader of Venice's military appears to "challenge the system" but, in actuality, would "help to maintain it." The transversal movement that Iago demonstrates by taking the Venetian state's repudiation of cuckoldry too far makes suspicion count as proof and posits the cuckold himself (and not the state) as the executioner, and destroys both Iago and Othello. While the state is clearly better off without the mercilessly self-serving Iago, the benefit of destroying Othello may not be obvious, until we turn to F. R. Leavis's interpretation of Othello's character.

Leavis critiques what he considers to be the sentimental idealizing of Othello's character by critics such as A. C. Bradley, arguing instead that Othello only succumbs to Iago's insinuations because his character—self-important, self-deceiving, and sentimental—is inherently prone to the jealousy that Iago suggests. For Leavis, it is "Othello in whose essential make-up the tragedy lay" (151). This reading makes Othello's downfall truly *tragic* and not merely the lamentable result of Iago's demonic machinations. In this case, rather than undermining the order of the state's military apparatus, Iago has done the state a service, albeit inadvertently: he exposes Othello's tragic flaw in a time of peace. This is especially fortunate for the state given that the consequences of this flaw surfacing while at war would be unpredictable and potentially disastrous. Hence, Iago's vindictive measures play directly into Sinfield's entrapment model.

Yet this reading supposes that Iago really acts from the motives he cites in his concluding monologue of act I. What are we to make, then, of the fact that Iago himself lays out a completely different set of motivations in his act I, scene i, dialogue with Roderigo? In lines 8 through 33, Iago explains that he was passed over for promotion by Othello, and that his job was instead given to Cassio, who, unlike Iago, "never set a squadron in the field, / Nor the devision of a battle knows, / More than a spinster" (1.1.22). Iago's motive is therefore revenge: revenge against the military general who did not promote him, against the captain who, lacking his qualifications, got his place, and against the system that permitted it. Put differently, Iago seeks revenge against an unjust and capricious hierarchical institution of the state by causing the destruction of the institutor of hierarchical order (symbolized by Othello) and of its nepotistic beneficiary (Cassio). More than in the jealousy scenario in which Iago indirectly challenges the Venetian state, Iago is here seen as directly attacking it. But it is still easy to see the entrapment model at work. By directing his revenge primarily against the representative of state hierarchy (Othello), Iago not only causes the elimination of himself and Othello, but he also carelessly allows Cassio to live. Since Iago's machinations necessarily brought out the flaws in Othello's character, it is reasonable to assume that at the end of the play Cassio stands an excellent chance of being restored to his official position before he was cashiered by the Othello that Venice now sees was deluded by jealousy. Iago's attempts at revenge, it seems, have in the end done no substantial harm to his hated rival Cassio, and have even potentially *helped* him by creating an open position further up in the military hierarchy.

The problem with the subversion/containment paradigm in both cases, however, is that it does not account for the complexity of the situation. As Reynolds argues, "It is especially significant that this paradigm, as it is often applied, precludes or ignores micro-subversions, or small revolutionary changes" (148). In the two scenarios discussed here, the immediate impact on the morale and organization of the state is not considered. For instance, Iago can be seen as scoring a small victory against state order in that his vigilantism challenges the ability of the military leader to make unilateral decisions regarding his inferiors without fear of violent retribution. It is also entirely likely that Iago's subversive activity will affect how the state is likely to treat converted Moors in the future. Moreover, the parameterization behind these entrapment scenarios is dissective-cohesive and state-centered; as a result, the analysis does not consider such questions as: What happens to Iago, Cassio, and the state at the play's conclusion? Where did Othello and Iago come from in the first place? What impact will Desdemona's murder have on her family and friends and, therefore, the state? And how might the audience respond to the play's action?

In order to foreground this transversal analysis it is helpful to go beyond Althusser and look instead to Gilles Deleuze and Félix Guattari.[17] They accept an essentially Althusserian model of the state, dividing the state apparatus into "two heads: the magician-king and the jurist- priest" (Deleuze and Guattari, 351). These "heads" of the state "are the principal elements of a State apparatus that proceeds by a One-Two, distributes binary distinctions, and forms a milieu of interiority" (352). In this "milieu of interiority," the state apparatus creates an ordered, "striated," hierarchical society, organized by the state-imposed system based on supposedly absolute categories and binary opposi-tions. Opposed to this state apparatus is the "war machine," a "pure form of exteriority" (354), that operates outside of the state apparatus. The war machine opposes the state's rigid hierarchy, its order, its "striation," its binary oppositions, its stasis: "the war machine's form of exteriority is such that it exists only in its own metamorphoses" (360). Yet while the war machine is defined in opposition to the state, as "a form of pure exteriority," it can become involved in the state system when it is "appropriate[d] . . . in the form of a mil-itary institution" (355) and in the relation between the two "heads" of the state apparatus: "One would have to say that it is located between the two heads of the State, between the two articulations, and that it is necessary in order to pass from one to the other. But 'between' the two, in that instant, even ephemeral, if only a flash, it proclaims its own irreducibility" (355). While the war machine can surface within the state apparatus, its presence is problematic because by its nature it lies outside of the state's control.

If Iago is attacking the military order that passed him over for promotion, then he can be seen as a manifestation of Deleuze and Guattari's war machine. Iago originates in the state's military institution, appropriates the war machine, and moves insidiously into the state apparatus. He subverts in Othello both Christian ideology and Venetian state ideology as they are manifested in judi-cial codes; these two ideologies are aligned with the "jurist-priest" head of the state, characterized as "the clear," "the calm," "the weighty," and "the regu-lated" (Deleuze and Guattari, 351). What Iago turns Othello into resembles more closely the "magician- king" head of the state as described by Deleuze and Guattari: "the obscure," "the violent," "the quick," and "the fearsome" (351). Thus, "'Between' the magical-despotic State and the juridical State containing a military institution, we see the flash of the war machine, arriving from without" (353). From here we can understand Iago's relationship to the Venetian state's ideological machinery as an almost ironic reversal of Deleuze and Guattari's statement that the state supporter "can only appropriate [a war machine] in the form of a military institution, one that will continually cause it problems." Iago, the "problematic" part of the military war machine that the Venetian state has appropriated, attacks the state hierarchy by appropriating and transversalizing the methods of Venetian state ideology.

In order to reveal further Iago's transversal relationship to Venetian state ideology—that is, his movements in and out of subjective and transversal ter-ritories—it is necessary to review the two motivations which Iago gives for his actions, either as a cuckold or as an undervalued military official. Turning to the play, we see that the latter explanation is highly dubious. Bradley cautions us against believing Iago too readily: "One must constantly remember not to believe a syllable that Iago utters on any subject, including himself, until one has tested his statement by comparing it with known facts and with other statements of his own or of other people, and by considering whether he had in the particular circumstances any reason for telling a lie or for telling the truth" (198). By these well-justified standards, Iago's conversation with Roderigo must be considered suspect. The only statement he makes in that dialogue which can be verified by recourse to facts within the play is that Cassio is Othello's lieutenant. There is no evidence that Othello passed Iago over for the promotion or that Iago was ever even considered for it. Iago's own statements do not support this motivation anywhere else in the play, and his subsequent monologue at the end of act I, scene iii, offers a completely different motivation without mention of Cassio's promotion. Iago would certainly benefit from lying to Roderigo: he has to offer some sort of motivation, and this is one that Roderigo would easily understand and believe, without the condescension he might feel towards a cuckold.

Perhaps, then, Iago really does believe he has been cuckolded. There does not seem to be any reason for him to tell lies in a monologue directed to the audience; moreover, there appears to be support for this motive in Emilia's lines, "Some such squire he was, / That turn'd your wit, the seamy side without, / And made you to suspect me with the Moor" (4.2.147–49). This support, Ridley says, "disposes of any idea that Iago's suspicions of Othello (1.3.385; 2.1.290) were figments, invented during momentary 'motive-hunting' and dismissed. They have been real, and lasting, enough for him to challenge Emilia" (159). Even if Iago's suspicions were real and lasting, however, this does not prove that they are in fact the motivating force behind his actions, a fact which becomes clear upon closer examination of Iago's language in the act 1, scene 3, monologue. In this speech Iago first states his motivation of cuckoldry in the following words: "I hate the Moor, / And it is thought abroad, that 'twixt my sheets / He's done my office" (1.3.384–86). This is supposedly a statement of motivation, of cause and effect. Yet the sentence is not constructed on the logical model of "A then B," but rather on the model of a different Boolean operator, on "A *and* B": "I hate the Moor, / *And* it is thought abroad . . ." (our emphasis). On the most basic level of language and of symbolic logic, Iago is not stating a motive; he is merely listing two separate facts which are simultaneously true. Here we can see why Coleridge labeled this monologue "the motive-hunting of motiveless malignity" (49). Iago knows only that he "hates the Moor"; he puts this together with his belief that "it is thought abroad . . .", and realizes that this is sufficient motive to act on his preexisting, "motiveless" hatred of Othello.

If Iago does represent this "motiveless malignity," where does that leave him in relation to Venetian state ideology? If he does not work as a normal agent of the state, fully inculcated in one of its minor ideologies (that of the cuckold), and does not work against the state, as a war machine that appropriates the methods of state ideology, then how *does* he work? In act 3, scene 3 (right before the temptation scene in which Iago interpellates Othello as cuckold), Othello makes the prophetic statement in his apostrophe to Desdemona: "Excellent wretch, perdition catch my soul, / But I do love thee, and when I love thee not, / Chaos is come again" (3.3.91–93). Even proponents of the entrapment model would have to admit that Iago brings some degree of "chaos" into the functioning of the state; and those, like us, who dismiss the idea of him as a true mechanism of the state may see this as the primary result of his actions. Without ascribing to the Iago-as-war-machine model, then, we may still believe that his effects are very much like those of a war machine, breaking down the hierarchical order of the state apparatus, turning the violence inherent in a military man such as Othello against the state's ordered society. What is needed, however (once we have dismissed his act I, scene i, motive of revenge against the military system) is a model that does not rely on the aggression toward the state which Iago does not seem to possess.

Such a model can be found in our concept of "transversal power." Transversal power is any force (physical or metaphysical) that causes movements in or through transversal territory. As Reynolds puts it, "transversal power induces people to transversally cut across the striated, organized space of subjectivity—of all subjective territory—and enter the disorganized yet smoothly infinite space of transversal territory" (150). Like the war machine of Deleuze and Guattari, "Transversal territory invites people to escape or deviate from the vertical, hierarchicalizing and horizontal, homogenizing assemblages of any organizational social structure" (149). Iago enters the "non-subjectified" (once again, "I am not what I am") transversal territory outside of the conceptual boundaries set on him by the state. Without just cause, and separate from any existing suspicion of cuckoldry, Iago hates his commanding officer and desires the "chaos" of Othello's downfall. As would the war machine, Iago appropriates the form of the Venetian state official, and recreates Othello's subjective territory in a manner that reveals—relative to the subjective territories created by the state—transversal movement; Othello's conceptual and emotional boundaries are reconfigured under the influence of Iago's transversal power. Thus, from the "motiveless" irruption of transversal power into Iago's subjective territory we see a chain of events that lead inexorably to "chaos."

There may be some danger of implying with this interpretation that *Othello* should be read as a reactionary text, condemning all subversive action because of the results of Iago's. Of course, this reactionary conclusion could never actually be reached from the evidence given in the above analysis: the power that Iago wields over Othello demonstrates the frightening power that the state itself can wield if its ideological mechanisms and institutions are not constantly questioned and challenged. Yet this raises an important point, which is the inadequacy of all interpretations that attribute to Shakespeare's works a didactic moral, whether reactionary or "progressive." Bloom and Jaffa summarize the moral of *Othello* with the following formula: "*Othello* appears . . . to leave us with this choice—a mean life based on a clear perception of reality or a noble life based on falsehood and ending in tragedy" (66). An Althusserian reading of the play, if it accomplishes nothing else, at least shows the error of Bloom and Jaffa's moralizing oversimplification. Othello's downfall is not simply a matter of being mistaken about the facts; it is rather a result of an entirely different way of relating to the world around him which is developed in him by Iago. Othello is indoctrinated with an ideology which does not require the same degree of proof of wrongdoing as does Venetian state ideology, and which is harsher in its punishment than the Christian faction of that ideology. Both the old ideology of the Venetian state and the new minor ideology of the cuckold are "based on falsehood" in the sense that they are "imaginary" (in Althusser's definition) and mutually contradictory. Othello's tragedy comes from his indoctrination into an ideology that encourages him to ignore (or at least distort) the facts and act swiftly, "justly," and without mercy.

TOWARDS INVESTIGATIVE-EXPANSIVENESS

Having moved from critical history to ideological indoctrination, from Schlegel and Hunter to Althusser and Iago to Deleuze and Guattari, our transversal analysis defies the sort of holistic conclusion that is characteristic of the dissective-cohesive mode of analysis. More important, though, our view of the role that transversal power plays in Iago's machinations leads us to believe that a dissective-cohesive conclusion, that seeks to explain Iago or to explain *Othello* itself, would necessarily misrepresent the play. *Othello*, as we have noted, breaks the world into binary oppositions and encourages us to use these oppositions to categorize its characters, its plots, and its themes: thus, as Hunter tells us, the black foreigner turns out to be a good Christian, while the white Venetian is quickly seen to be an evil man who masks his true self with a veneer of honesty. Nevertheless, when we use these oppositions to assemble a holistic view of the play, we arrive at contradictions. Where Hunter sees the black man with a white soul being corrupted by the white man with a black soul, Schlegel sees a black foreigner who masquerades unsuccessfully as a Venetian before reverting to his original barbaric state. These readings use the binary oppositions found in the play to describe each character at each point in the play (and beyond the play, during events we may assume took place before the beginning of the play), and then they use these definitions to determine how the characters get from point to point. By contrast, our analysis is concerned primarily with this movement; the process of change rather than the initial and final states. Iago is postulated as an Althusserian state supporter only because the action of the play suggests ideological indoctrination; we accept Althusser's designation of objectivity as the opposite of ideology only because Iago's transversal movement out of his own subjective territory, symptomatically revealed when he exceeds the state- prescribed position on cuckoldry, requires some concept of exteriority. While *Othello* lays out a system of interrelated binary oppositions, it exists neither in nor between them, but in its own movement through them. To use an example from Hunter's essay, the play is not built on categorizations such as that of Othello as the black man with the white soul and Iago as the white man with the black soul. Rather, it is built on such actions as the audience's realization that their expectations have been contradicted. It is a play neither of seeming nor of being, but of becoming. And the character who best represents the play is Iago, who shows us "motive hunting" rather than a motive, and whose transversal movements constitute the action of the play.

NOTES

1. For a more detailed explanation of "transversal theory," see Bryan Reynolds's work: "The Devil's House, 'or worse': Transversal Power and Antitheatrical Discourse in Early Modern England," *Theatre Journal* 49 (May 1997): 143–67; *Becoming Criminal: Transversal Performance in Early Modern England* (Baltimore: Johns Hopkins University Press, 2001); with Donald Hedrick, "Shakespace and Transversal Power," Hedrick and Reynolds, eds., *Shakespeare Without Class: Misappropriations of Cultural Capital* (New York: St. Martins Press/Palgrave 2000); with Joseph Fitzpatrick, "The Transversality of Michel de Certeau: Foucault's Panoptic Discourse and the Cartographic Impulse" *Diacritics* 29.3 (Fall, 2000): 63–80.

2. See also Karen Newman, "'And wash the Ethiop White': Femininity and the Monstrous in *Othello*," in *Fashioning Femininity and English Renaissance Drama* (Chicago: Chicago University Press, 1991).

3. Of course, Othello's relationships with these two institutions are themselves both interdependent and intertwined, leading, for example, Allan Bloom and Harry Jaffa to comment: "How is he able to make himself so Venetian? It is surely, in part, his Christianity that is responsible" (48).

4. Though the first conclusive textual evidence for his conversion comes at 2.3 161–163 ("Are we turn'd Turks, and to ourselves do that / Which heaven has forbid the Ottomites? / For Christian shame, put by this barbarous brawl"), Othello's Christianity is implied both by his references to heaven during the trial scene (1.3.163; 266) and in his initial dialogue with Iago, in which Iago implies that the supposed theft of Desdemona was a legal marriage (1.2.11).

5. Here we side with A. C. Bradley in calling Iago a Venetian. Bradley cites 3.3.201 and 5.1.89f as evidence, and reads Cassio's comment that "I never knew a Florentine more kind and honest" (3.1.42–143) to mean, "not that Iago is a Florentine, but that he could not be kinder and honester if he were one" (200). M. R. Ridley appears to agree with Bradley in his 1958 edition of the text, in which his annotation of the above line clarifies it as "i.e. *even* a Florentine (Cassio being from Florence)" (Ridley, ed., 92).

6. Hunter may be paraphrasing A.W. Schlegel here, who writes in an essay later alluded to by Hunter, "While the Moor bears only the nightly colour of suspicion and deceit on his visage, Iago is black within" (Schlegel, 196).

7. Bryan Reynolds and James Intriligator introduced this methodology in a paper entitled "Transversal Power," given at the Manifesto Conference at Harvard University on May 9, 1998.

8. In Adelman, see especially pages 129–31 and 137–44.

9. Schlegel writes: "What a fortunate mistake that the Moor, under which name a baptized Saracen of the Northern coast of Africa was unquestionably meant in the novel, has been made by Shakespeare in every respect a negro! We recognize in Othello the wild nature of that glowing zone which generates the most raging beasts of prey and the most deadly poisons, tamed only in appearance by the desire of fame, by foreign laws of honour, and by nobler and milder manners" (195).

10. An even more recent example would be Walter S. H. Lim's comment: "That Iago finds it easy to undermine the Moor's emotional stability reveals that Othello can never fully obliterate his African self when he fabricates his Venetian/white identity" (Lim, 62).

11. Julie Hankey has mentioned Marowitz's 1972 adaptation *An Othello* as an example of how a radically conceived reworking of the play (which Hankey herself labels "propaganda") demonstrates the deep rooted investment of Shakespeare's original in problems of ideology (Hankey 113–14).

12. For an in depth analysis of the power of storytelling in the play, see Greenblatt, especially pages 237–47.

13. Here we can explain in Althusserian terms Bloom and Jaffa's assertion quoted in note 4: it is because Othello has been inculcated in the state ideology through the "Ideological State Apparatuses" of religion (Christianity) that he is able to assimilate, to whatever extent, into Venetian society.

14. The explicit connection of the term heaven to Christian thought is even more clear in the Folio and Second Quarto texts, where "God" is replaced by "Heaven".

15. Oliver Parker's film version presents an interesting interpretation of this scene, breaking Iago and Othello's discussion into segments that occur in different settings at different times of the day, suggesting that the conversation is either repeated almost verbatim a number of times or dragged out for much longer than the audience is shown.

16. While Sinfield does not apply his "entrapment model" specifically to the type of interpretation given in this essay, he does note that, "entrapment . . . arises generally in functionalism, structuralism, and Althusserian Marxism" (39). For discussion of this subversion/containment paradigm, see, among other sources, Bryan Reynolds (148–149); Jonathan Dollimore, *Sexual Dissidence: Augustine to Wilde, Freud to Foucault* (Oxford: Clarendon Press, 1991), 81–91; Michael Bristol, *Shakespeare's America, America's Shakespeare* (London: Routledge, 1990), 189–211; and Louis Montrose, "Professing the Renaissance: The Poetics and Politics of Culture" in *The New Historicism*, ed. Aram H. Veeser (New York: Routledge, 1989), 20–24.

17. In fact, Althusser's system does not allow for such a creature as Iago, an ideologue who *opposes* the state, whose indoctrination of state citizens constitutes his own private *war* against the state.

WORKS CITED

Adelman, Janet. "Iago's Alter Ego: Race as Projection in *Othello*." *Shakespeare Quarterly* 48:2 (1997): 125–144.

Althusser, Louis. "Ideology and Ideological State Apparatuses (Notes towards an Investigation)." Trans. Ben Brewster. *Lenin and Philosophy*. New York: Monthly Review Press, 1972.

Bartels, Emily C., "Making More of the Moor: Aaron, Othello, and Renaissance Refashionings of Race." *Shakespeare Quarterly* 41:4 (Winter 1990): 433–54.

Bloom, Allan with Harry V. Jaffa. *Shakespeare's Politics*. Chicago: The University of Chicago Press, 1964.

Bradley, A. C. *Shakespearean Tragedy: Lectures on Hamlet, Othello, King Lear and Macbeth*. New York: Penguin Books, 1991.

Cavell, Stanley. *Disowning Knowledge in Six Plays of Shakespeare*. Cambridge: Cambridge University Press, 1987.

Coleridge, Samuel Taylor. *Coleridge's Shakespearean Criticism,* Vol. 1, Ed. Thomas Middleton Raysor. Cambridge: Harvard University Press, 1930.

Deleuze, Gilles, and Guattari, Félix. *A Thousand Plateaus: Capitalism and Schizophrenia,* Trans. Brian Massumi. Minneapolis: University of Minnesota Press, 1987.

Greenblatt, Stephen. "The Improvisation of Power." *Renaissance Self-Fashioning From More to Shakespeare*. Chicago: University of Chicago Press, 1980.

Hankey, Julie. "Introduction" in Shakespeare, William. *Othello*. Ed. Julie Hankey. Plays in Performance Series. Bristol: Bristol Classics Press, 1987.

Hunter, G. K. "Othello and Colour Prejudice." *Dramatic Identities and Cultural Tradition: Studies in Shakespeare and His Contemporaries*. New York: Barnes and Noble, 1978.

Knight, G. Wilson. "The *Othello* Music." *The Wheel of Fire: Interpretations of Shakespearian Tragedy with Three New Essays*. London: Methuen & Co. Ltd., 1949.

Leavis, F. R. "Diabolic Intellect and the Noble Hero: or The Sentamentalist's Othello." 1937; rpt. in *The Common Pursuit*. Harmondsworth: Peregrine, 1952.

Lim, Walter S. H. "Representing the Other: *Othello*, Colonialism, Discourse." *The Upstart Crow* 8 (1993): 57–78.

Little, Arthur L. Jr., "'An essence that's not seen': The Primal Scene of Racism in *Othello*." *Shakespeare Quarterly* 44:3 (Fall 1993): 304–24.

Newman, Karen. "'And wash the Ethiop White': Femininity and the Monstrous in *Othello*," in *Fashioning Femininity and English Renaissance Drama*. Chicago: Chicago University Press, 1991.

Reynolds, Bryan. "The Devil's House, 'or worse': Transversal Power and Antitheatrical Discourse in Early Modern England." *Theatre Journal* 49 (May, 1997): 143–167.

Schlegel, Augustus William. *A Course of Lectures on Dramatic Art and Literature, Vol. 2,* Trans John Black. London: J. Templeman and J.R. Smith, 1840.

Shakespeare, William. *Othello*. Ed. M. R. Ridley. London: Routledge, 1958.

Sinfield, Alan. *Faultlines: Cultural Materialism and the Politics of Dissident Reading* (Berkeley: University of California Press, 1992)

Stallybrass, Peter. "Patriarchal Territories: The Body Enclosed." *Rewriting the Renaissance*. Ed. Gerguson, Margaret Quilligan and Vickers, Nancy J. Chicago: Chicago University Press, 1986.

Othello: Portrait of a Marriage

DAVID BEVINGTON

> O curse of marriage,
> That we can call these delicate creatures ours
> And not their appetites! (3.3.284–86)[1]

"Why, what is this?" asks Othello, when Iago has first brought up the idea of jealousy. "Think'st thou I'd make a life of jealousy, / To follow still the changes of the moon / With fresh suspicions?" (3.3.190–93). Othello's first response seems fully in accord with the character we have come to know thus far in the play. He rejects the idea of jealousy with the firm determination of one who knows, as a military commander, how to settle a question. "To be once in doubt / Is once to be resolved." Othello believes of himself that he will test any suspicion carefully and rationally. He will "see before I doubt; when I doubt, prove; / And on the proof, there is no more but this—/ Away at once with love or jealousy" (204–206). This forthright course of decision making seems postulated, so far as we can tell, upon a complete faith in Desdemona's virtue. It allows for two possibilities, love or the rejection of love, but proceeds from the assumption that his love for Desdemona is unassailable.

Othello is indeed happily in love and happily married as he speaks. Shakespeare chooses to give him an eloquent and full explication of what it is to be happily married—perhaps the most insightful definition in all the canon. Othello seems to understand, at this moment, that love must be generous and inclusive, not fearful and possessive. He loves Desdemona in good part because he need not resent her warmth toward others or her attractiveness to other men:

> 'Tis not to make me jealous
> To say my wife is fair, feeds well, loves company,

221

Is free of speech, sings, plays, and dances well;
Where virtue is, these are more virtuous. (197–200)

Othello's supreme confidence in his marital bliss frees him to cherish what is so humanly characteristic of Desdemona: her appetite for pleasure. That appetite does not threaten him; even his awareness of his own "weak merits" cannot draw from him "the smallest fear or doubt of her revolt" (201–202). Desdemona is very much a woman in Othello's view of her, and that very womanliness is what he cherishes. Her accomplishments are those in which women are supposed to excel: music, gracefulness of conversation, physical attractiveness, and social elegance. She adorns his manly, military life with her feminine charms. Woman and man complement one another in the archetypal pattern of Venus and Mars: the beautiful woman and the soldier.[2]

Yet some eighty lines later, still in the same scene, Othello has become the stereotype of the anxious male beset by fears of womanly duplicity. The very things that have counted so heavily in Desdemona's favor—her openness and warmth of response to the tactile pleasures of physical existence—are now the basis of the most terrible indictment against her. "O curse of marriage, / That we can call these delicate creatures ours / And not their appetites!" (284–86). The fact that Desdemona has appetites is what makes her so threatening, from the point of view of males who assume that men have a right to own women (to "call these delicate creatures ours") but then find they cannot control that part of them, their appetites, which should "belong" to their husbands.

Simultaneously, Othello's calm assurance earlier that he need not fear his "own weak merits" has been translated into its precise opposite: a growing conviction that his presumed demerits in Desdemona's eyes are the cause of his having lost control over her appetites. He has lost her, it seems, because he is "black" and lacks "those soft parts of conversation / That chamberers have," and because he is "declined / Into the vale of years." The thought that he is not yet very old—"yet that's not much"—offers no consolation. "She's gone. I am abused, and my relief / Must be to loath her" (279–84).

How is it possible that so much has changed in the course of a single conversation in which no evidence has been produced against Desdemona? Readers often find the alteration too abrupt to be believable, and either blame Shakespeare for hasty writing or object to Othello himself as unworthy of tragic stature.[3] The contention of this essay will be that the shift is indeed breathtakingly rapid, but that it is prepared for in ways that make clear Othello's vulnerability and that connect him to other anxious males in Shakespeare's plays. We can see elements of Othello's possessiveness, and of his tendency to relegate women (especially Desdemona) to the status of being "delicate creatures" designed to promote male happiness, in the very nature of his courtship of her.

This is not to demean Othello or dismiss his marriage with Desdemona as lacking in greatness of spirit. To the contrary, their marriage is arguably, for a brief time, the most rich and compatible in the Shakespeare canon. Happy marriages are perhaps not an apt subject for dramatic treatment; conflict is essential for storytelling, and good-natured day-to-day management of a productive and symbiotic relationship can seem outwardly boring. Shakespeare's elegant portrayals of heterosexual love usually dwell on the agonies and ecstasies of courtship and end with a parade to the altar, not choosing to gaze too intently on what is to follow. The Capulets seem too caught up in their marriage designs for their daughter to share much of an inner life together. Henry VI's marriage to Margaret of Anjou is the beginning of England's century of civil war, much as the rape of Helen sets in motion the Trojan War. Paris and Helen are not married in *Troilus and Cressida,* and in any case their scene together is made to seem mawkish and sybaritic. Hector and Andromache end their last moments together in painful difference and the retreat of the long-suffering, obedient wife; Calpurnia and Portia both offer good advice to their husbands that is fatally ignored; Hotspur and Kate too, for all their moments of teasing fondness, are divided on the central issue that will lead to the husband's condescension toward his wife's counsel and to his subsequent death.

Similarly the marriages of Master Ford, Antipholus of Ephesus, Antony, Cymbeline, Posthumus Leonatus, Leontes, and still others are beset by jealousies imagined or real, infidelities, guilt, and every sort of failure. The queen in *Cymbeline* is a wicked witch out of a fairy tale, adept in the art of secret poisoning. Claudius in *Hamlet* is so besotted on Gertrude that he commits murder to have her. Perhaps the most intimate of marriages in all Shakespeare, that of Macbeth and Lady Macbeth, is also the most terrifying in its indictment of the "suffocating mother."[4] Increasingly in Shakespeare, the heroes are seen to have no wives, even when the sources suggest otherwise: King John, Henry IV, Brabantio, King Lear, Prospero. Other relationships, of parent to child, of friend to friend, of master to servant, take up the fulfilling complexities of mutual dependency that marriage in Shakespeare seems not to supply.

Othello and Desdemona are, for a time, happily married. They genuinely admire each other. They both take huge risks and make sacrifices in order to share a life together. The great difference that they sense in their heretofore separate lives is one that they embrace in its complementarity. They cherish each other for offering such new worlds that they can occupy jointly: Desdemona longs to know what it is to be a soldier, whereas Othello craves the domestic joys that Desdemona can provide. They both insist on Desdemona's accompanying her husband to Cyprus, where Othello is almost childishly eager to show her what a soldier's life is like. "O my fair warrior!" he greets her on his arrival in Cyprus (2.1.182). "Come, Desdemona," he says to her when she has been awakened by a night brawl among the soldiers. "'Tis the soldiers' life / To have their balmy slumbers waked with strife" (2.3.251–52). Iago knows how to turn this into an antifeminist joke: "Our general's wife is now the general," he confides to Cassio (2.3.308–309).

Othello wants to open his life up to Desdemona, and her only wish is to become a part of that world.

For all this mutuality and openness, nonetheless, the relationship of Othello and Desdemona is fraught with gendered differences that bode trouble. From the start, Othello speaks of her as of a person whose function is to complement his life and make him feel wonderful about himself. She is a perfect audience, as Othello describes her to the Duke and senators of Venice. Her acquaintance with Othello comes about when he is invited to her father's house to speak of his travels. Those travels are indeed remarkable, and Othello describes them eloquently—so much so that the Duke, and we as theatre audience, are all invited to respond as Desdemona does, with wonder and admiration. Desdemona's role, as Othello remembers it, is to listen when she can in the midst of her household affairs, catching the story "by parcels," not "intentively." This circumstance gives her occasion to be a petitioner, praying with "earnest heart" that he tell her all.

Othello's account of their conversations together dwells on the emotions of her response: her sighs, her declaration that "'Twas pitiful, 'twas wondrous pitiful," her wishing "That heaven had made her such a man" (1.3.147–64). We can hear in that ambivalent phrase, perhaps, a longing on her part both to have such a man as her husband, and to be able herself to be subsumed into Othello's gloriously active life—to become like him. Certainly that is what Othello hears, and he is immeasurably flattered by the thought. The storytelling is from his male point of view: he falls in love with a woman who wants him and wants to be like him. Her seeming forwardness in hinting that "a friend" who loved her could prevail as a suitor simply by telling such a story (166–68) is confirmation of what he needs to know, that the woman regards him as lovable and desirable.

Othello sums up his successful courtship in a way that stresses the differences between him and Desdemona, he as active warrior, she as supportive audience:

> She loved me for the dangers I had passed,
> And I loved her that she did pity them. (1.3.169–70)

One can think of other things that a man might have said: that the woman is intelligent, innovative, responsible, well educated, and so on. Instead, Othello's first and highest praise appears to be that he is privileged to enjoy her unhesitating admiration—an admiration made all the more keen by the great distance between her uneventful and constricted domestic life and the unlimited opportunity for adventure that he has enjoyed as a man. He finds her pity so gratifying because it dramatizes him as the protective male, the one who takes risks in good part to win the admiration of the fair sex. Othello's motive for falling in love, as he himself presents it, is one of self-regard. Desdemona makes him feel better about himself. The speech allows him to fashion his construction of Desdemona, before she has appeared onstage; and we see that he constructs her as a part of his own ego.

When we get a glimpse later in the scene of Desdemona's own sense of how she fell in love with Othello, the perspective is strikingly different. First of all, she makes no attempt to assess his motives for falling in love with her. She delights in his love for her, but she does not describe it as something brought into being by her own need to be admired. There seems to be no narcissism in her account of their falling in love; her interest is in describing what it was about Othello that made her love him. And here she gives us no reinforcement of what Othello has presumed to say about her motives, about her pitying him and loving him for the dangers he had passed. Instead, she ascribes her love to the inner qualities she has quickly come to admire in him. "I saw Othello's visage in his mind, / And to his honors and his valiant parts / Did I my soul and fortunes consecrate" (255–57). She readily defines the woman's role as one of subservience: she consecrates herself to Othello, and proclaims that "My heart's subdued / Even to the very quality of my lord." She does not, however, define her love for Othello as springing from any need for self-regard that can be supplied by his adoration of her.

The potential weakness of Othello's view of love is that it makes him fatally dependent on Desdemona's love for him. As he puts the case himself, he is happy with himself because she loves him. The corollary, present from the very start of the play, is that if she no longer loves him—or, just as dangerously, if he perceives that she no longer loves him—then he will no longer love her, and "Chaos is come again." That is his own expression; he says it (3.3.99–100) moments before Iago first bids him beware of jealousy. He means it in a playful and happy sense as he speaks, since he is still blissfully in love with Desdemona, and only means to say that she is everything to him, but the warning is there for us (and Iago) to hear. Paradoxically, in a play that depicts men as strongly masculine and powerful while women are dependent on men for their social being, the men, especially Othello and Iago, are at the mercy of their own fantasies about loss of control of women. Happiness and proper self-regard are impossible without the adoring approval of women, and male assurance of that approval is inherently unstable.

The evidence of that instability early in the play surrounds Othello, even while we hear him speak of his calm, assured love for Desdemona. Iago and Roderigo awaken Brabantio with horrid images of female wantonness, of Desdemona as a possession like money that can easily be robbed from the most watchful of fathers. Desdemona, in the nightmare that Iago and Roderigo conjure up for Brabantio, is imagined to be a violently sexual partner in a relationship that is diabolical, miscegenated, and sodomitical; her imagined partner is an old black ram, or a Barbary horse, or the devil himself, and the descendants of this unholy coupling will contaminate Brabantio's patrician family line with neighing nephews, "coursers for cousins and jennets for germans" (1.1.81–116). The saddest thing of all is that Brabantio, after an initial moment of resistance, believes everything that they say, and sees that they are merely confirming his own worst nightmare: "This accident is not unlike my dream" (146). The male imagination is all too ready to abuse itself with this most recurring of male fantasies, because that fantasy speaks to the deepest fear of all: the conviction in the male that he is ultimately unlovable, and that women are merely playing their game of deception to lure him into a situation where he will be cuckolded and thereby deprived of the self-image upon which his emotional well-being depends. The power of women to cuckold men is the power to deprive them of their sense of self assertion and male   omplishment. Without that sense of phallic power, men are ridiculous—in their own eyes, and in the supposed judgment of other men on whose good opinion they are also pathetically dependent.

The Othello of act one is a man who resists and refutes these insinuations, and one could argue that the portraits of male anxiety to which we are introduced—in Iago, in Roderigo, in Brabantio—serve by way of contrast to show the strength of Othello's self-esteem and the generosity of his love for Desdemona. Indeed, that sense of contrast is essential both to the creation of heroic stature for Othello and to the tragic fall that then follows. Othello is self-assured. He speaks of his marrying Desdemona as a loss of his own "unhousèd free condition"—a loss he has willingly incurred for her, but a sacrifice nonetheless. He is, after all, a prince in his own right, one who can justly claim that he fetches his life and being "From men of royal siege" (1.2.21–28). Why should his marrying her be viewed as any less a concession on his part than for her to marry a black man? His account of his military exploits is remarkable for its air of calm endurance of hardship. His remarkable oratory grows out of his extraordinary sense of self. He wins the hearts of the Duke and the the senators of Venice; the Duke advises Brabantio that "If virtue no delighted beauty lack, / Your son-in-law is far more fair than black."

Yet the vulnerability is there as well, because the entire hypothesis of male self-sufficiency, in Othello as in the other males, depends on an assumption that the needed adoration of the woman is genuine and unswerving. That assumption is under stress because of the elopement of Desdemona. "Look to her, Moor, if thou hast eyes to see," Brabantio warns Othello. "She has deceived her father, and may thee." Othello's self-assured reply, "My life upon her faith!" (1.3.292–97), bespeaks his trust in Desdemona, but it also implicitly restates the logical proposition that will undo him: if his faith in her love for him should somehow collapse, then his life will be at an end. The motif returns later as a haunting refrain: "Chaos is come again" (3.3.100), "O, now, forever / Farewell the tranquil mind," and so on (363–64). Even more explicitly, the argument that her elopement was a betrayal will return to plague Othello. "She did deceive her father, marrying you," argues Iago to Othello, "And when she seemed to shake and fear your looks, / She loved them most." To which Othello can only reply, "And so she did" (3.3.220–22). All that Iago need really do to poison Othello's mind is to induce him to internalize as his own the very arguments brought forward in act one as evidence of the perfidy of women and the unlovable weakness of men.

Painful indeed is the irony that Desdemona's brave and imprudent act of elopement, her gift of self to Othello, should thus be used as evidence of her changeability of affection and her deceptive ways, but such is the nature of the diseased male imagination in this play. Othello and Brabantio are alike in their vulnerability to this irrational fear. The irony is further intensified by the way in which Desdemona's elopement is presented to us as evidence not of her willfulness, but of her uncomplaining endorsement of a patriarchal world. Her argument to her father is that her mother left her own father to live with Brabantio, and that Desdemona must now choose to do the same, not setting off independently on her own but declaring that the unswerving obedience she once owed to her father now belongs to another man. She will call that man her "lord," just as previously Brabantio was her "lord of duty." She is responding without question to the way in which Brabantio has put the question to her: "Do you perceive in all this noble company / Where most you owe obedience?" She does not start by complicating the issue of obedience; she accepts as given the proposition that she, as a woman, owes obedience to her husband or a father (1.3.181–91).

The play as a whole confirms this wish in her to obey, to the point of her going to bed in act five to await the arrival there of a husband whom she knows to be irrationally angry at her and capable of physical violence. The only disobedience, prevarication, or managereal assertion of control of which she is "guilty" in the play is her determination to urge the reinstatement of Cassio at whatever cost to herself, and then her attempt to take the blame for her own death (5.2.128). She is the woman Othello wanted all along—the admiring, accepting, supportive wife—but he has lost, through a jealousy born of his own fears, any ability to sustain himself in that vision of her. She must be murdered because she represents to him the image of his own insufficiency as a man.[5]

Desdemona's view of what to expect in marriage is one that sustains her through her incredible suffering and being accused of being a whore. She does not need Othello to bolster her belief in herself as a virtuous woman. She certainly needs him in order to find the happy married union that evades them, but her sense of self-regard is not vulnerable in the way that his is. When Othello turns on her with his terrible accusations, her first and last response is to blame herself, as we might expect: she has angered him in some way that she did not intend; she has not been the supportive and loyal wife that he asked her to be (e.g. 4.2.72, 112–14). She does not, however, know how this could have happened, and she does not doubt her own goodness. She knows that she is unwavering in her love for Othello, and that she expresses fondness for other men without letting that threaten the singleness of her devotion to Othello.

Desdemona thus does not need Othello as an audience to confirm the goodness she knows to be in her. When he calls her "whore," she weeps, but does not wonder if she is a whore. "I do not know. I am sure I am none such," she says in reply to Iago's disingenuously asking why Othello has used such a term for her (4.2.130). Perhaps, she wonders, some news from Venice has disturbed Othello (3.4.142–45). She will not allow herself to accuse him of malice, and repeatedly expresses forgiveness for his erratic and violent behavior, however much it distresses her and accuses her unfairly. The point here is not simply that Desdemona is unassailably good, but rather that her emotional strength derives from the nature of what she expects from a marital relationship. She does not need Othello to know that she is virtuous, unlike Othello, who needs to sustain a perception of her as the adoring wife in order to believe in his own masculinity.

The men in *Othello* generally suffer from the same affliction that leads to Othello's tragedy. Even Cassio, the most amiable of the chief male characters, reveals under the influence of alcohol a dangerously macho side, and we come to realize that he solves his anxieties about women by radically bifurcating them into saints and whores, in much the same way that Freid's male patients behave in late-nineteenth-century Vienna.[6] Some women, like Desdemona, are to be worshipped. She is to Cassio "the divine Desdemona." He greets her upon her arrival at Cyprus as though she reminded him of the Mother of God: "Hail to thee, lady! And the grace of heaven / Before, behind thee, and on every hand / Enwheel the round!" (2.1.75–89). At other times, we see Cassio with Bianca, whose fondness for him he regards with amused condescension, and whom he would never think of marrying. Sexual pleasure and a genuine mutuality of admiration between men and women are not to be vested in one woman, as far as Cassio is concerned. The ideal of companionate marriage, at once erotic and spiritualized, that Othello and Desdemona find together for a brief time, and which Othello defines so aptly when he praises Desdemona for being a person of vital and legitimate appetites, is something that Cassio never seeks.

Iago's malignancy is incomparably worse, but it is of a similar nature. He is the catalyst for Othello's lapsing into the male fears that the men seem to share. Indeed, this sharing would appear to be at the heart of what we can understand about Iago's motive—bearing in mind Colderidge's famous conundrum that it is at bottom "motiveless."[7] Jealousy is seen in the play as at once incomprehensible and all too understandable. Emilia expresses beautifully this paradoxical idea. Men are jealous not for any rational cause, she says to Desdemona, "But jealous for [i.e. because] they're jealous." Her definition and analysis of jealousy are complete and self-enclosed: jealousy is itself. "Ironically enough, her husband agrees: jealousy "is a monster / Begot upon itself, born on itself" (3.4.160–63). What more is there to say? At the same time, the play makes much of the proverbial idea that "The devil loves company." The only way that Iago can seek temporary relief from the irrational jealousy that he suffers is to make Othello suffer too. At the same time, the jealous male is driven to seek vengeance on women, and especially on the one woman who seems to refute Iago's self-justifying contention that all human beings are the victims of their own appetites, insecurities, and desires.

Compelled by such a need to destroy, Iago's best vengeance is to convince Othello of what Iago and other men fear most: the wantonness of woman and the power she possesses to destroy male self-confidence. In the process, Iago wakens in Othello a deep anxiety about his own mother and the means by which she "subdued" her husband, Othello's father, by a handkerchief with "magic in the web of it" (3.4.57–77).[8] At the height of his misery, utterly persuaded (though without evidence) of Desdemona's guilt, Othello speaks of the loss of her as though he were experiencing once again the estrangement from the woman who gave him life and then abandoned him to live without her:

> But there where I garnered up my heart,
> Where either I must live or bear no life,
> The fountain from the which my current runs
> Or else dries up—to be discarded thence! (4.2.59–62)

The ambivalence of this remarkable passage that may describe either mother or wife bespeaks the image in this play of marriage as at once vitally necessary and yet so difficult for men to attain.[9] Perhaps too, then, this passage helps explain the underlying weakness of Othello's possessive love for Desdemona that makes wonderfully plausible what seems at first so hard for many readers to accept:[10] Othello's precipitous decline within some eighty lines of 3.3 from proud and trusting husband to one who can never be convinced again of his wife's virtue until he has snuffed out her life.

NOTES

1. Citations are from *The Complete Works of Shakespeare*, ed. David Bevington, 4th ed. updated (New York: Longman, 1997). I gave a version of this lecture as the nineteenth James Edwin Savage Lecture in the Renaissance at the University of Mississippi, Oxford, on March 26, 1991. I wish to thank my hosts there for their warm hospitality and generous response to my talk.
2. See Raymond B. Waddington, "Antony and Cleopatra: 'What Venus did with Mars,'" *Shakespeare Studies,* 2 (1966), 210–26.
3. As an instance of response of incredulity to the rapidity of Othello's change in the course of this one scene, I might cite classroom experience in a course entitled "The Renaissance as an Age of Discovery" (course number 303), in a program entitled Master of Liberal Arts, Continuing Studies, University of Chicago, Fall Quarter, 1995 and 1996.

4. Janet Adelman, *Suffocating Mothers: Fantasies of Maternal Origin in Shake-speare's Plays, "Hamlet" to "The Tempest"* (New York and London: Routledge, 1992). See especially chapter 6, "Escaping the Matrix: The Construction of Masculinity in *Macbeth* and *Coriolanus*," 130–64; and, as background for the discussion of *Othello* throughout this present essay, see Chapter 3, "'Is Thy Union Here?': Union and Its Discontents in *Troilus and Cressida* and *Othello*,". 38–75.

5. It must be conceded here that criticism of *Othello* does not lack those who, for their own reasons I suspect, take it for granted that Desdemona would soon have fulfilled Iago's obscene prophecies if she had been given time. Most notable among these is W. H. Auden, "The Joker in the Pack," in *"The Dyer's Hand" and Other Essays* (New York: Random House, 1948, reprinted 1962), 246–74, especially 268–69.

6. Sigmund Freud, "Über die Allgemeinste Erniedrigung des Liebeslebens" (1912), "The Most Prevalent Form of Degradation in Erotic Life," *Gesammelte Werke,* ed. Anna Freud et al., 18 vols. (Frankfurt am Main, 1940–68), 8.78–91, in *The Standard Edition of the Complete Psychological Works of Sigmund Freud,* trans. James Strachey, in collaboration with Anna Freud, assisted by Alix Strachey and Alan Tyson, 14 vols. (1953–74), 11.179–90, and in *Sexuality and the Psychology of Love,* ed. Philip Rieff (New York, 1963), 58-70.

7. S.T. Coleridge, *Lectures and Notes on Shakspere and Other English Poets,* collected by T. Ashe (London: G. Bell, 1902, Section IV, pp. 384–94, especially 388). See also Stanley Edgar Hyman, *Iago: Some Approaches to the Illusion of His Motivation* (New York: Athenaeum, 1970).

8. See Lynda E. Boose, "Othello's Handkerchief: The Recognizance and Pledge of Love," *English Literary Renaissance,* 5 (1975), 360-74, and Robert B. Heilman, *Magic in the Web: Action and Language in "Othello"* (Lexington: University Press of Kentucky, 1956).

9. Arthur Kirsch, *"Othello," The Passions of Shakespeare's Tragic Heroes* (Charlottesville: University Press of Virginia, 1990), 44–75, a revision of "The Polarization of Erotic Love in *Othello*," *Modern Language Review,* 73 (1978), 721–40, reprinted in *Shakespeare and the Experience of Love* (Cambridge: Cambridge University Press, 1981).

10. Audiences in the theatre do not often seem to have the same problem of being unpersuaded by Othello's sudden change—in good part, perhaps, because of the dramatic vitality and immediacy of the action when brought to theatrical life by skilled actors.

WORKS CITED

Adelman, Janet. *Suffocating Mothers: Fantasies of Maternal Origin in Shakespeare's Plays, "Hamlet" to "The Tempest."* New York and London: Routledge, 1992.

Auden, W. H. "The Joker in the Pack." *"The Dyer's Hand" and Other Essays.* New York: Random House, 1948, reprinted 1962.

Bevington, David, ed. *The Complete Works of Shakespeare.* 4th ed. updated. New York: Longman, 1997.

Boose, Lynda E. "Othello's Handkerchief: The Recognizance and Pledge of Love." *English Literary Renaissance* 5 (1975): 360–74.

Coleridge, S. T. *Lectures and Notes on Shakspere and Other English Poets.* Collected by T. Ashe, London G. Bell, 1902. Section IV, 384–94.

Freud, Sigmund. *The Standard Edition of the Complete Psychological Works of Sigmund Freud.* Trans. James Strachey, in collaboration with Anna Freud, Alix Strachey, and Alan Tyson. 14 vols. Trans. of "Über die Allegemeinste Erniedrigung des Liebeslebens" (1912), "The Most Prevalent Form of Degradation in Erotic Life," *Gesammelte Werke,* ed. Anna Freud et al. 18 vols. Frankfurt am Main, 1940–68.

Freud, Sigmund. *Sexuality and the Psychology of Love, ed. Philip Reif.* New York, 1963. 58–70.

Heilman, Robert B. *Magic in the Web: Action and Language in "Othello."* Lexington: University of Kentucky Press, 1956.

Hyman, Stanley Edgar. *Iago: Some Approaches to the Illusion of His Motivation.* New York: Athenaeum, 1970.

Kirsch, Arthur. *"Othello," The Passion of Shakespeare's Tragic Heroes.* Charlottesville: University Press of Virginia, 1990. Rpt. of "The Polarization of Erotic Love in *Othello." Modern Language Review* 73 (1978), 721–40. Rpt. in *Shakespeare and the Experience of Love.* Cambridge: Cambridge University Press, 1981.

Waddington, Raymond B. "Antony and Cleopatra: 'What Venus did with Mars.'" *Shakespeare Studies* 2 (1966): 210–26.

"Truly, an obedient lady"
Desdemona, Emilia, and the Doctrine of Obedience in *Othello*

SARA MUNSON DEATS

I.

The fourth act of *Othello* contains a scene of shocking brutality, in which the enraged hero of the tragedy publicly strikes his young wife in the presence of her kinsman Lodovico and her attendant and confidant Emilia. Trembling, humiliated, the young wife protests with dignity, "I have not deserved this" (4.1.244),[1] before docilely departing from her infuriated husband, murmuring, "I will not stay to offend you" (4.1.250). Othello's public attack evokes from Lodovico a shocked remonstration, "Truly an *obedient* lady / I do beseech your lordship, call her back" (4.1.252–53; emphasis added). Othello complies, gloating:

> Ay, you did wish that I would make her turn.
> Sire, she can turn, and turn, and yet go on
> And turn again; and she can weep, sir, weep;
> And she's *obedient,* as you say, *obedient,*
> Very *obedient* . . . (4.1.257–61; emphasis added)

Othello's cruelty, Desdemona's defenselessness, and the quadruple repetition of the word *obedient* graphically accentuate the abuse of power inherent in the dominant matrimonial ideology of the period, the precept of patriarchal supremacy and wifely subservience, a precept vitiating even the mutuality of the consensual, companionate marriage. However, contrary discourses circulating at this period, particularly the doctrine of conscience, challenged the ideology of unconditional patriarchal authority. Positioning itself within the contemporaneous debates on female agency, wifely subjection, and spousal abuse, this essay relates *Othello* to the conflict within early modern marriage between the doctrine of obedience and the doctrine of conscience, reading the play as a critique of uxorial violence and a trenchant interrogation of the venerated ideal of unconditional wifely obedience.

II.

The genesis in England of the ideal of the consensual, companionate marriage remains one of the most vigorously debated topics in early modern scholarship. Yet, whether they follow C. S. Lewis, who credits the Renaissance with transforming the romance of adultery into the romance of marriage; or William Haller and Malleville Haller, who locate amorous matrimony within the Puritan art of love; or Alan Macfarlane, who identifies consensual conjugality as emerging in the thirteenth century; or Jean H. Hagstrum, who praises the marriage of love as the signal achievement of the high middle ages; most scholars agree that this conjugal pattern, which unites "esteem" and "desire" in an amorous mutuality, had become the dominant social ideal, if not always the reality, by the late sixteenth century.[2] This matrimonial model affirmed individual choice as the soundest basis for marriage, with mutual support, companionship, and love as its primary goals. According to Catherine Belsey, a new orthodoxy emerged at this time in which romantic wedlock was celebrated as "a terrestrial Paradise," with the love between husband and wife pictured as an analogue for the love of God (20). A popular sixteenth-century pamphlet, *The Glasse of Godly Love*, paints the following portrait of the ideal husband, the Adam of this terrestrial paradise. The husband is the woman's ruler and protector; he owes her:

> most fervent love and affection, all gentle behavior, all faithfulness and help, all comfort and kindness, as to himself, his own flesh and body; so that under God there is no love, no affection, no friendship, no nearness of kin, to be compared unto this, nor any one thing under the Sun, that pleases God more than man and wife that agree well together, which live in the fear of God. (quoted in Macfarlane, 181)

It should be stressed, however, that although striving for mutuality, the consensual companionate marriage denied equality. Thus, the dominance of the husband over the wife, ratified in St. Paul's dictum that the husband should be head of the wife as Christ was head of the church, was axiomatic. Hortatory treatises of the period, like "A Homily of the State of Matrimony," emphasize the asymmetry of even the consensual, companionate marriage:

> You wives, be you in subjection to obey your own husbands. To obey is another thing than to control or command, which yet they may do to their children and to their family; but as for their husbands, them must they obey, and cease from commanding, and perform subjection. For this surely both nourishes concord very much, when the wife is ready at hand at her hus-

band's commandment, when she will apply herself to his will, when she endures herself to seek his content, and to do him pleasure, when she will eschew all things that might offend him. (242)[3]

Similarly, William Whately, in the popular domestic conduct book, *A Bride-Bush,* reminds the wife that if she proposes to be a good spouse and live comfortably, she must learn to accept that *"Mine husband is my superior, my better;* he hath authority and rule over me" (361). Even the legal language of the period reflects the asymmetry of marriage. Francis E. Dolan cites the example of the justice of the peace who succinctly explained that "a wife or servant who 'malitiously killeth' a husband or master was accused of treason while a husband or master who 'malitiously killeth' a wife or servant was accused of murder, 'for the one is in subject and oweth obedience, and not the other'" (quoted in Dolan, 21). Moreover, even though husbands might be encouraged to love and cherish their wives as their own flesh, much contemporary scholarship has painted a darker picture of early modern marriage.[4] And although husbands were strongly discouraged from battering their wives, such "correction" was legally allowed. Indeed, according to "the rule of thumb," a man might beat his wife almost to death as long as he wielded an instrument no thicker than that opposing finger; if death resulted, the husband could plead guilty of manslaughter rather than of murder if he could prove "only an intent to chastise, not to kill" (Blackstone, 4: 200). As these and other instances suggest, disobedience could be a dangerous business in the early modern family.

However, despite the many exhortations to obedience in the pamphlets, domestic conduct books, and sermons of the day, opinions favoring absolute submission of the wife to the husband were not unanimous. Indeed, as feminist scholars of the last two decades have alerted us, the role of women in marriage constituted a major site of contestation within early modern society. Moreover, although moralists unanimously proclaimed the subordination of the wife to the husband, even within the consensual, companionate marriage, the degree of compliance that the wife owed the husband was actively debated. Much of the controversy arose from the implications for the family inherent in the Puritan doctrine of conscience.

The Puritans of the period vigorously affirmed the right, indeed the obligation, of the devout Christian to place conscience above law and defy even the monarch if necessary to preserve Christian integrity. William Perkins, a leading spokesperson for the Puritan view, explicates the doctrine of conscience as follows: "God's authority binds conscience; Magistrates' authority is God's authority; therefore, Magistrates bind conscience properly" (*Treatise of Conscience,* 522). Perkins then draws upon the widely accepted analogy between the magistrate and the father:

> For there be sundry authorities ordained of God, as the authority of the father
> over the child, of the master over the scholar, which do bind conscience as
> the authority of God's law does. (522)

However, Perkins insists that the highest authority is always God, and since
kings and magistrates derive their power only from God, if rulers command
actions contrary to God's law, they abrogate their authority and the subject is
duty bound to disobey:

> But if it shall fall out that men's laws be made of things that are evil and for-
> bidden by God, then is there no bond of conscience at all, but contrariwise
> men are bound in conscience not to obey. . . . Moreover, in that man's law
> binds not but by authority of God's law, hence it follows, that God's law alone
> has this privilege, that the breach of it should be a sin. (524)

According to this doctrine, therefore, the king, although deserving reverence
and obedience in secular matters, ceases to be God's viceroy upon earth and
"all courts of men are inferior to conscience, the tribunal which God has
erected in every man's heart" (Hill, 315).

However, the doctrine of conscience sparked some vexing problems for
its adherents. On the one hand, it provided a moral rationale for the Puritan
resistance to many of what the reformers considered to be the "popish" practices of the Anglican church. On the other hand, it threatened to undermine
one of Puritanism's most sacrosanct precepts, the authority of the patriarch in
the nuclear family. For, given the analogue between the family and the state
ubiquitous at this period,[5] the doctrine of conscience, if carried to its logical
conclusion, would legitimate the disobedience of the wife to the unjust husband, *on the grounds of conscience,* even as it legitimated the defiance of the
subject to the tyrannical king on similar grounds. Many of the advocates of
this doctrine recognized its implications and did not shirk from extending the
doctrine of conscience to include defiance of the ungodly and unjust husband
as well as of the ungodly and unjust king.

Like most of the Puritan preachers of the period, Perkins found himself
confronting an ethical dilemma. He clearly wished to defend the sovereignty
of conscience, the litmus test of Puritan orthodoxy; however, at the same time,
he did not wish to adulterate the authority of the father in the patriarchal
nuclear family, another Puritan shibboleth. Ultimately, Perkins chose logical
consistency over male chauvinism, declaring that just as the subject must ele-
vate fidelity to God's law as revealed by the individual conscience above duty
to the king, so the wife should place her allegiance to God's law as discerned
by her conscience above her obligation to her husband:

> There is a double calling; the general, standing in the worship of God; the
> particular, as the calling of marriage, or of single life. When the two callings

cannot stand together, the latter must give place to the former. (*Christian Oeconomie*, 109)

A number of popular marriage guides of the period tackle the chafing problem of "how far the wife should obey," with the majority endorsing Perkins's distinction between male dominance in spiritual and mundane spheres. In "A Preparation to Marriage," Henry Smith anticipates Perkins' argument, admonishing the wife to submit unto her husband and regard his will as the Lord's will, with the proviso that just "as the Lord commands only that which is good and right, so she should obey her husband in good and right, or else she does not obey him as the Lord, but as the tempter" (28). He further asserts, "The husband says, that his wife must obey him, because he is her better, therefore if he let her be better than himself, he seems to free her from her obedience, and bind himself to obey her" (21). Similarly, Whately in *A Bride-Bush*, although affirming man's natural sovereignty over woman, also maintains conscience as the final arbiter between husband and wife, just as it is between magistrate and citizen, king and subject. Thus, Whately indicates that the wife may disobey an unlawful command: "The wife indeed should cast her eye only upon the lawfulness or unlawfulness of the thing, asking none other questions but whether it offend God, yea or no" (23). Finally, even that bastion of male supremacy, William Gouge, in his influential tome *Of Domestical Duties*, after a lengthy exhortation enjoining the wife to obey her husband at all times, grudgingly admits that, following the doctrine of conscience, there are times when a wife should disobey:

If God expressly commands the wife any duty, and her husband will not by any means give consent that she shall do it, but forbid her, she may and ought to do it without, or against his consent. (326)

By upholding the wife's prerogative to evaluate her husband's commands and act upon these judgments, the doctrine of conscience implicitly—and perhaps inadvertently—destabilizes the patriarchal positioning of woman as *femme covert*, subsumed under the identity of her husband, and instead establishes her as a subject capable of decision and agency.

Domestic conduct books and homilies also debate the degree to which chastisement of the wife by the husband should be permitted. Even so comparatively conservative a document as the Anglican "A Homily of the State of Matrimony" insists that a man should not beat his wife, "for that is the greatest shame that can be, not so much to her that is beaten, as to him that does the deed" (245). Similarly, the majority of the Puritan marriage guides deplore corporal punishment of the wife by the husband. Henry Smith absolutely forbids the husband to beat his wife, insisting that "the wife's cheeks were made for the husband's lips, not his fists" (23–24). John Dod and Robert Cleaver state emphatically that although a husband should admonish his wife often and give her good instructions, he should reprehend her seldom and "never to lay violent hands on her" (167). Whately, while counseling the husband to preserve his authority within the family, nevertheless also urges him to rule with gentleness, kindness, and diplomacy, not with force and rage, and never to correct by strokes (22, 27–28). Perkins agrees, denying that the husband may chastise the wife:

> Though the husband be the wife's head, yet it seems he has no power or liberty granted him in this regard. . . . He may reprove and admonish her in word only, if he sees her at fault. . . . But he may not chastise her either with stripes, or strokes. The reason is plain. Wives are their husbands' mates; and they two be one flesh. And no man will hate, much less beat his own flesh, but nourishes and cherishes it. (*Christian Oeconomie*, 127)

Furthermore, although maintaining that the wife should obey the husband in all things not contrary to God's law, Perkins also insists that if the husband is an unbeliever and breaks God's law himself (threatening his wife, striking her, or forsaking her), the wife is justified not only in disobeying her husband but also in leaving him:

> Again, if the husband threatens hurt, the believing wife may flee in this case and it is all one, as if the unbelieving man should depart. For to depart from one, and drive one away by threats, all is equivalent. (*Christian Oeconomic*, 107)

Rather surprisingly, this conclusion is anticipated in "A Homily of the State of Matrimony," which also insists that physical violence by the husband is not to be endured, because the law does discharge the wife "any longer to dwell with such a husband, as unworthy to have any further company with her that does smite her" (245). In judging the chastisement of the wife by the husband as an infraction of God's law, Perkins denies the belief, widely-accepted at this time, that the husband had the same authority over the wife as Christ over his church:

> As Christ does entirely love his church, so he may also chastise the same, because he is not only husband, but also absolute Lord and King of his church; so is not the husband absolute over the wife. But his authority over the wife is after a sort civil, as is the authority of the Magistrate over his people. (*Christian Oeconomie*, 128)

Therefore, according to many of the Puritan domestic conduct books, the doctrine of conscience not only grants the wife agency within marriage but also protects her, as a free subject, from physical abuse by her husband.

The drama of the period, simultaneously subversive and conventional, both a barometer and an initiator of social change, participates in the debate on the obedience of women in marriage. On the one hand, the early modern drama seems obsessed with the disastrous results of wifely disobedience and unfaithfulness. The crimes of unfaithful, even sometimes murderous wives are dramatized in at least three domestic tragedies: The anonymous *Arden of Feversham* (1592) and *A Warning for Fair Women* (1593–1599), as well as Thomas Heywood's *A Woman Killed with Kindness* (1603). On the other hand, counterpoised with these domestic tragedies are a group of comedies that ask the question so often posed in the homiletic literature, "Not whether she should obey, but how far"? (Whately, 42). A number of plays answer this query through their portraits of Patient Griselda figures whose steadfastness, obedience, and sexual fidelity lead to the regeneration of their husbands. One of the earliest of these Griselda comedies is *Patient Grissel* (1599), attributed to Thomas Dekker, Henry Chettle, and William Houghton, which is followed by four domestic comedies all written between 1600 and 1608:[6] *How a Man May Choose a Good Wife From a Bad,* usually attributed to Thomas Heywood, the anonymous *The Fair Maid of Bristow* and *The London Prodigal,* and Thomas Dekker and Thomas Middleton's *The Honest Whore, Part I.* The Griselda figures in these plays inevitably embody the qualities of the ideal wife, ironically enunciated in the opening scene of *A Woman Killed with Kindness* to describe Frankford's new bride Anne: "A perfect wife already, meek and patient . . . Pliant and duteous in your husband's love" (1.1.37, 41). Even plays apparently interrogating the asymmetry of early modern marriage frequently conclude with an affirmation of patriarchal domination and wifely subjection, as when Adriana's protest against the gender double standard in Shakespeare's *The Comedy of Errors* (2.1.10) is answered by Luciana's encomium to "natural" male supremacy:

> Why, headstrong liberty is lashed with woe.
> There's nothing situate under heaven's eye
> But hath his bound, in earth, in sea, in sky.
> The beasts, the fishes, and the wingèd fowls
> Are their males' subjects and at their controls.
> Man, more divine, the master of all these,
> Lord of the wide world and wild watery seas,
> Endued with intellectual sense and souls,
> Of more preeminence than fish and fowls,
> Are masters to their females, and their lords.
> Then let your will attend on their accords. (2.1.15–25)

Finally, of course, Shakespeare's fiery Kate offers the most hyperbolic paean to wifely obedience in early modern drama (*The Taming of the Shrew,* 5.2.140–83)—a paean that would probably have shocked many of the Puritan marriage counselors cited above. And whatever one feels about the much-debated irony of Kate's final speech in the play, one must admit that, at the very least, Kate has learned to play the marriage game. [7]

However, like the homiletic literature of the period, the dramatic texts present contradictory opinions concerning the unconditional obedience of the wife to the husband, a *heteroglossia* apparent even in some of the Griselda comedies. Although ostensibly celebrating the Griselda figure's fabled patience, Dekker, Chettle, and Houghton's *Patient Grissel*, through its exaggeration of the Marquese's grotesque torture of his much-maligned wife, actually renders the entire Patient Griselda legend ludicrous. Moreover, the play allows Grissel two uncharacteristic protests (4.1.191–93; 4.2.142–43) and puts into the mouth of the misogamist Julia a blistering indictment of the inequality of early modern marriage that produces either simpy Griseldas or raucous shrews (4.3.204-14; 275-83). *The London Prodigal* employs a similar strategy, allowing Delia, sister of the long-suffering Luce, a critique of marriage that parallels Julia's earlier denunciation (5.1.462–67).[8] John Marston's The Faun (1604), roughly contemporaneous with the Griselda comedies and probably written the same year as *Othello*, satirically treats the issues dramatized tragically in *Othello*. Marston's iconoclastic play bitingly satirizes the jealous husband Don Zuccone, who defames and seeks to divorce his innocent wife Zoya. Reversing the action of *Othello*, Zoya both tames and forgives her jealous spouse, evoking from the miscreant a promise to:

> adore thee more than a mortal, observe and serve you as more than a mistress, do all duties of a husband and offices of a man, all service of thy creature, and ever live in thy pleasure, or die in thy service. (5.1.344–45)

Elizabeth Cary's *The Tragedy of Mariam* (1603–1609), also closely contemporaneous with *Othello*,[9] similarly challenges the doctrine of unconditional wifely obedience, through the action of the play suggesting that under certain circumstances the virtuous wife—like Mariam, the hero of the tragedy—should practice a principled disobedience. Herod's brutal execution of his blameless wife, paralleling Othello's "sacrifice" of the innocent Desdemona, also foregrounds the potential cruelty inherent in the doctrine of patriarchal hegemony. Finally, *A Yorkshire Tragedy*, probably composed around 1605 and thus coeval with both *Othello* and *Mariam*,[10] dramatizes the heinous deeds of an abusive husband and father who, like Othello, defames his innocent wife as a whore and attempts to kill her, while also slaying two of his three children. Moreover, like Desdemona, the Wife (wounded but not slain) forgives her murderous spouse and displaying a wifely patience and obedience matching that of Griselda pleads for clemency for her dastardly husband.

Dolan argues that although "women and servants committed fewer acts of violence, the story of the murderous wife or murderous servant is far more frequently narrated and published than the story of the murderous husband or master" (25). Yet within approximately five years, the early seventeenth century produced three tragedies—*Othello* (1604), *A Yorkshire Tragedy* (1605), and *The Tragedy of Mariam* (1603–09)—dramatizing the violent physical abuse of wives by their husbands. These dramas, like the hortatory texts examined above, also call into question the doctrine of absolute patriarchal power. My essay seeks to situate *Othello* within this interrogative context.

III.

Even as the role of women in the early modern family has generated much critical debate, so the role of Desdemona, an individual woman in a very unconventional early modern marriage, has sparked considerable controversy. In her pioneering essay, "Women and Men in *Othello*," Carol Thomas Neely protests that during the past one hundred years or so critics of *Othello* have divided into two camps. The first of these camps consists of the Othello critics, who view the text through the Moor's eyes, not only accepting Othello's high estimate of himself but also idealizing Desdemona as Othello does at the beginning of the play. The second group contains the Iago critics, who take their cues from the Ancient, demeaning both Othello and Desdemona as Iago does. The hagiographic commentators depict a saintly Desdemona, with a passivity verging on catatonia; the demonizing commentators portray an overconfident Desdemona, with an aggressiveness approaching shrewishness. According to Neely, both sets of critics misrepresent not only Desdemona but all of the women in the play, effacing the gender issues the drama foregrounds (211–13). However, rallying to Neely's challenge, feminist critics of the past two decades have attempted to rescue particularly Desdemona, but also Emilia and even Bianca, from this metaphorical prison.[11]

Many of the problems arise from the disjunctive nature of the character of Desdemona. How can an audience explain the disparity between the courageous, unconventional, confident, articulate young bride of the opening scenes, who appears to challenge many of the mores of early modern marriage, and the dazed and defenseless wife of the denouement, who declines into complete submissiveness to her husband? Before addressing this crux, I posit another query: Just how unconventional would the Desdemona of the opening scenes have appeared to an early modern audience?

The Desdemona whom we encounter in the first acts of the play is a far cry from "the maiden never bold" (1.3.96) depicted by her myopic father. First, the clandestine wedding of Desdemona and Othello—performed at non-canonical hours, without proscribed banns or proper ceremony and without the presence or permission of parents or legal guardians—would certainly be considered unconventional.[12] Nevertheless, these irregular nuptials subvert custom, not law.

David Cressy speaks for majority scholarly opinion when he states:

> Conventionally, out of love and duty, in deference to age and authority, and
> no doubt with an eye to inheritance prospects, many young people took note
> of their elders' opinions. But they were not strictly beholden to their parents
> for matrimonial consent. No man or woman could lawfully be forced to a
> wedding, nor could they be prevented from marrying where they list so long
> as they were free from impediments of affinity and consanguinity, pre-
> contract, or insufficient age [14 for a male, 12 for a female]. (256)

Moreover, once a couple was married, albeit irregularly, there was little that
the authorities or the aggrieved families could do, provided it could be shown
that both parties had freely granted their consent (312–13). The centrality of
choice, stressed by law and custom, also dominates Othello's "trial" before the
senate, which emphasizes Desdemona's willing consent to the marriage as the
primary issue on which Othello's guilt or innocence is predicated.

In other ways as well, in the early acts of the play Desdemona deviates
from the ideal passive daughter and wife fetishized by the literature of the
period. Othello testifies to the degree to which she was half the wooer in their
courtship (1.3.147–72). She not only elopes with an exotic alien and participates in an irregular, secret ceremony, but she also boldly confronts the Venetian Senate to defend her love for Othello, insisting that she "did love the Moor
to live with him" (1.3.251). Later, on her arrival in Cyprus, Desdemona
exchanges with the misogynist Iago witty badinage that some commentators
have found too arch and sophisticated for the sequestered daughter of a Venetian nobleman. Still later, she is not only fondly assertive with her husband
(3.3.43–97), but promises Cassio to play the shrew if her husband does not
heed her suit:[13]

> My lord shall never rest.
> I'll watch him tame, and talk him out of patience;
> His bed shall seem a school, his board a shrift.
> I'll intermingle everything he does
> With Cassio's suit. (3.3.22–26)

Both Cassio and Iago also cast Desdemona as the "woman on top."[14] According to Cassio, she is "our great captain's captain" (2.1.76), who, claims Iago,
"may make, unmake, do what she list," with her husband (2.3.340). When
describing his wife to Iago, Othello further portrays a lively, gregarious Desdemona who "feeds well, loves company, / Is free of speech, sings, plays, and
dances well" (3.3.198–99). Finally, Othello's references to his wife's hot,
moist palm—a hand requiring "A sequester from liberty, fasting and prayer, /
Much castigation, exercise devout" (3.4.40–41)—suggest an erotic warmth

and sensuality in his marriage partner that perhaps arouses in the older man a fear of sexual inadequacy, or even, as some commentators suggest, a sexual revulsion.[15]

In the first acts of the play, therefore, Desdemona defies the shopworn cliches with which the men who love, laud, and lust after her attempt to incarcerate her. Instead of the "maiden never bold" (1.3.96) that her father misconceives her to be, we meet a woman of adventurous spirit, who threw away the book of gender etiquette as she wooed the man of her choice, who risked loss of status by eloping with a man outside of her accepted kinship group, and who courageously defends her right to choose her marriage partner before the Venetian Senate. Instead of the elevated courtly lady of Cassio's visions (2.1.62–75, 85–90), we encounter a woman of frank and open sensuality, who proudly proclaims the "violence" of her love and passionately asserts to the patriarchs of Venice, "That I did love the Moor to live with him" (1.3.251). Finally, instead of the subtle Venetian whore that Iago and Othello later construct (4.2.93–94), we confront a woman of astonishing constancy and devotion, who commits herself unequivocally to her husband, insisting "my heart's subdued / Even to the very quality of my lord" (1.3.253–54). In the first three acts of the play, therefore, Shakespeare has created in Desdemona an oxymoronic blend of boldness and docility, sophistication and naivete, sensuality and chastity, a formidable and independent woman who challenges the dominant feminine ideals of the period.

We must ask, What happened? How can we explain Desdemona's rapid disintegration from the lively, outspoken young woman of the opening scenes to the subdued, submissive wife of the play's catastrophe? Following Irene G. Dash, I suggest that Desdemona is never as unconventional as she first appears (119–20). Certainly, as Ann Jennalie Cook insists, Desdemona's marriage against her father's wishes and without his knowledge would have probably appeared to an early modern audience as a blatant transgression of expected daughterly obedience (189). Yet despite her defiance of her father and of social mores in wedding without parental consent a man so different from her in complexion, clime, and degree, her attitude toward matrimony at the beginning of the play is otherwise thoroughly conventional, reflecting the tenets of the consensual, companionate model. This conjugal pattern, while strongly encouraging parental approval in the selection of a mate, identified individual choice, personal attraction, and intellectual compatibility as the fundamental donnees of a successful marriage, although, of course, property considerations remained important (Wrightson, 82–84). Desdemona's public defense of her love, her desire to cohabit with her chosen mate, even her sensuality (implied in Othello's reference to her hot, moist hand), would all be sanctioned within this ideal of amorous interdependence.[16] Even her assertiveness can be seen as an index of her confidence in the mutuality of her relationship with her spouse, a reciprocity she affirms as she gently upbraids her husband (Dusinberre, 84):

> Tell me, Othello. I wonder in my soul
> What you would ask me that I should deny,
> Or stand so mammering on. . . . (3.3.74–76)

Yet, despite her assurance Desdemona seems fully aware that mutuality in marriage does not imply equality, and she decorously concludes her petition with the pledge, "Be as your fancies teach you; / Whate'er you be, I am obedient" (3.3.96–97).

Indeed, from the beginning of the play, Desdemona accepts her subordinate role in society and defines herself in relation to men, as either a wife or daughter, but not as an independent individual. Her triple reference to *duty* in her apologia to the Senate accentuates her acceptance of the subservient role mandated even by the consensual, companionate marital model, even as she simultaneously affirms her right to choose her own mate:

> My noble Father,
> I do perceive here a divided *duty*
> To you I am bound for life and education;
> My life and education both do learn me
> How to respect you. You are the lord of *duty;*
> I am hitherto your daughter. But here's my
>   husband,
> And so much *duty* as my mother showed
> To you, preferring you before her father,
> So much I challenge that I may profess
> Due to the Moor my lord. (1.3. 182–91; emphasis added)

Furthermore, Desdemona perilously internalizes the total identification between husband and wife intrinsic to the consensual, companionate marriage. Othello recalls that, during their courtship, Desdemona sighed, wishing "That heaven had made her such a man" (1.3.164). Through this double entendre, she reveals her desire to escape, if only vicariously, from the claustrophobic confines of woman's domestic role in marriage, even as she had neglected household tasks by listening to Othello's marvelous tales of adventure. Once they are married, Othello becomes for Desdemona not only her dearest friend but also an extension of her being; thus, she totally commits herself to her husband and submerges her identity in his:

> I saw Othello's visage in his mind,
> And to his honors and his valiant parts
> Did I my soul and fortunes consecrate. (1.3.255–57)

Moreover, even as Desdemona sees her husband as an extension of herself, so Othello also envisions his wife as a reflection of his martial image, his "fair warrior" (2.1.180), a view that Desdemona enthusiastically accepts. Throughout the play, Desdemona celebrates a "marriage of true minds" perfectly consonant with the companionate ideal that elevated matrimony as "a pleasing combination of two persons, onto one house, one purse, one heart, and one flesh" (Whately, 7).

Initially, Othello, like Desdemona, embraces this ideal of mutual amity, and despite his initial reluctance to sacrifice his free, unhoused condition to the limitations of the connubial state also commits himself totally to his marital partner, who becomes his "soul's joy" (2.1.182), the fountain from which his current runs or else dries up (4.2.61–62). At one point, he fondly promises Desdemona, "I will deny thee nothing" (3.3.91), and exults, in words rich in dramatic irony:

> Excellent wretch! Perdition catch my soul
> But I do love thee! And when I love thee not,
> Chaos is come again. (3.3.98–100)

However, in the middle of the play, Othello falls under the influence of the misogynist Iago and begins to accept a very different concept of the married state. This model favored arranged marriages based principally on social and economic factors (with the woman considered the possession of the father and the husband), and stressed the absolute domination of the patriarch in the family rather than the limited suzerainty approved in the Puritan version of the consensual, companionate marriage. Most historians consider this to be a minority pattern at this time, limited primarily to the aristocracy, gentry, and uban elite, although not always practiced even by these groups.[17] The woman hater Iago and the irate father Brabantio share this competing view of marriage. Iago seeks total mastery of his wife and demeans all women, viewing even the paragon of women delineated by Desdemona as good for nothing but suckling fools and keeping petty household accounts (2.1.160). Less misogynistic, certainly, but equally committed to patriarchal control, Brabantio regards his daughter as his property, his jewel (1.3.198), to be merchandized as he sees fit. As the play progresses, Othello vacillates between these two conjugal models, perceiving his wife not only as his "soul's joy" but also as a valued possession, his chrysolite, his pearl.[18] Inviting her to the nuptial bed, he employs the lexicon of commerce:

> Come, my dear love,
> The purchase made, the fruits are to ensue;
> That profit's yet to come, 'tween me and you. (2.3.8-10)

Later, possessed by the spirit of Iago, he laments in the language of patriarchal possession:

> O curse of marriage,
> That we can call these delicate creatures ours
> And not their appetites! (3.3.284–86)

Furthermore, in the "temptation scene," Othello echoes both Brabantio's words and his sentiments, "And yet, how nature erring from itself—" (3.3.243). These words reveal that Othello has begun to view Desdemona through her father's eyes, seeing her as an erring daughter who has deceived her parent and defied the fiats of the patriarchal family. Internalizing the values of this more rigorously patriarchal conception of marriage, Othello perceives Desdemona's alleged unfaithfulness as a defacement of his private property, not only a loss of love but also a loss of male honor. Finally, exceeding the masculine power granted in even the most patriarchal of matrimonial models, he unquestioningly affirms his prerogative not only to chastise, but even to execute his wife, and he never questions his right to kill her if she is unchaste, sanctifying her murder as a sacrifice.

Desdemona's attitude toward marriage also changes radically during the course of the play. Her commitment to her husband is so complete that when he inexplicably turns on her, she withdraws, stunned into passivity, denial, and helplessness. A child to chiding, who, as she explains to her husband, has "felt no age nor known no sorrow" (3.4.37), she is totally unprepared for the verbal and physical violence that Othello hurls at her. Thus, like her husband, she retreats from the ideal of heroic mutuality that she had earlier espoused, seeking emotional security in the more patriarchal model of absolute domination and subservience. Refusing to be inscribed as a whore, yet interpellated into the sexist patriarchal philosophy of the age—a sexist ideology vitiating even the idealism of the consensual, companionate marriage—Desdemona accepts her subordinate subject position, affirming her duty to obey her husband unconditionally. Rejecting the more liberated attitude endorsed by the Puritan marriage counselors, she affirms her husband's right to chastise her, even though she is unaware of her fault, and she never attempts to retaliate against Othello or expose him, even though she has premonitions of her impending death. Even after Othello has publicly humiliated her, striking her and demeaning her before Lodovico, vilifying her before Emilia, and accusing her of whoredom, she takes no steps to escape, as Perkins advises abused wives to do. She does not even try to defend herself until the very end of the play when the crazed Othello threatens her with death.[19] Instead, she responds to her husband's cruelty with love and forgiveness, protesting that "Unkindness may do much, / And his unkindness may defeat my life, / But never taint my love" (4.2.166–68). Embracing the role of the loving, self-denying wife, she seeks excuses for her violent husband, blaming herself:

> Nay, we must think men are not gods,
> Nor of them look for such observancy
> As fits the bridal. Beshrew me much, Emilia,
> I was, unhandsome warrior as I am,
> Arraigning his unkindness with my soul;
> But now I find I had suborned the witness,
> And he's indicted falsely. (3.4.150–56)

In direct contrast to Othello, who convicts his innocent wife, Desdeoma exonerates her guilty husband, demonstrating that it is she, rather than Othello, who "loved not wisely but too well" (5.2.354). Finally, she lies to protect her mate, with her dying breath asserting his innocence and her culpability. When Emilia demands, "O, who hath done this deed?" Desdemona murmurs, "Nobody, I myself" (5.2.127–28). Ultimately, therefore, Desdmona shrinks her vibrant personality to the Procrustean bed of a rigorously patriarchal marriage pattern, declining from a dynamic subject, possessing independence and agency, into the classic battered wife.[20] Dash sees the play as "the tragedy of a woman, of women, pummeled into shape by the conventions that bind" (104), a view supported by Edward Snow's assertion that Desdemona's "loss of self-confidence and forthrightness under the pressure of Othello's accusations only emphasizes a process intrinsic to the institution of marrriage in a patriarchal society" (408). Finally, David Bevington asserts that even as Othello is a victim of racism, so Desdemona becomes a victim of sexism, "lapsing sadly into the stereotypical role of passive and silent sufferer that the Venetian world expects of women" (1121). I agree with all of these statements, only adding, as I have indicated above, that some early modern moralists advocated a more liberated view of marriage, a view that Othello and Desdemona initially endorse, only ultimately—and tragically—to reject.

In my reading, therefore, the play presents a conflict between two contrasting matrimonial models: The first, the consensual, companionate model, the dominant marital ideal of the period; the second, a more sternly patriarchal model, a pattern confined primarily to the aristocratic strata of society. The rejection by both Othello and Desdemona of the heroic ideal of amorous mutuality enshrined in the first conjugal pattern, and their acceptance of the patriarchal ideology of absolute authority and subjugation affirmed in the second, serves as catalyst to the tragedy. Moreover, in my reading, *Othello* offers a trenchant critique of marital violence and of the patriarchal ideology of absolute domination and submission that undergirds it.

The play develops the critique through several strategies. First, the scene where the furious Othello publicly strikes and humiliates his wife serves to dramatize the potential brutality inherent in absolute patriarchal authority. The play foregrounds this focus by the quadruple reiteration of the word *obedient,* even as Desdemona's acceptance of her subservient role in marriage had earlier been punctuated by the triple repetition of the word *duty*. Lodovico's shocked response to Othello's violence, "What, strike his wife?" (4.1.277), and his questioning of Othello's sanity, "Are his wits safe? Is he not light of brain?" (4.1.274), indicate that spousal abuse of this type is not respectable in the Venetian society in which the play is set, nor, as the remarks of the Puritan marriage counselors cited above validate, in the early modern society in which it was written.[21] Indeed, Whately specifically condemns the foolish rashness of the husband who reproves, much less physically abuses, his wife before children, servants, or strangers (27).

The murder scene, of course, offers the most trenchant critique of the potentiality for violence endemic to unconditional patriarchal rule. In his own eyes, of course, Othello is not a murderer. As his reference to *justice* reveals ("O balmy breath, that doth almost persuade / Justice to break her sword!" [5.2.16-17]), Othello accepts the traditional correspondence between the patriarch within the family and the magistrate, or king, within the state. He thus persuades himself that the execution of his unfaithful wife is an act of proper governance necessary to maintaining the peace within the microcosmic commonwealth under his rule. Still later, he expands this analogy to compare himself not only to the magistrate governing the state but also to God governing the universe, as he laments, "This sorrow's heavenly, / It strikes where it doth love" (5.2.21-22).

Not only does the play highlight the corruptive potential intrinsic to absolute patriarchal dominance, but it also dramatizes the perils of unquestioning wifely submission. Indeed, the tragic catastrophe can be directly traced to the excessive compliance of two abused wives. In the first of these examples, Emilia filches the treasured handkerchief in a servile attempt to win favor with her conniving husband. In the second of these instances, Desdemona fails to defy, expose, or, at the very least, flee from her husband, even when she intuits his murderous intentions.[22] Although at the denouement of the play both wives belatedly defy their husbands—Desdemona pleads vigorously with her murderer to spare her life, while Emila sacrifices her own life to expose Desdemona's murderer—both acts of resistance come too late to prevent tragedy.

Finally, the play offers a contrasting female view of marriage—the perspective of Emilia. The play counterpoises two sets of marriages: one, a promising young nuptial, originally ardently committed to the ideal of the consensual, companionate marriage; the other, a weary, stale alliance, entrenched in the reactionary rut of dominance/subordination and routine abuse. In both cases, the husbands sooner or later violently mistreat their wives, and, in both cases, the excessive subservience of the wives to their husbands contributes to the tragic catastrophe. However, both Emilia's perspective on marriage and her progression from pathetically acquiescent wife to rebellious spouse contrast sharply with Desdemona's contrary trajectory. In the beginning of the play Desdemona is unusually articulate and bold, whereas Emilia is very much the browbeaten wife, but as Desdemona moves from articulateness to silence, Emilia progresses to brazen speech. Ultimately, unlike Desdemona, Emilia breaks the cycle of spousal abuse and speaks for dignity and equality between husbands and wives. Emilia's passionate indictment of the sexual double standard—something the Puritan marriage counselors also attacked[23]—reminds the audience, as Desdemona does not, that what is sauce for the goose is sauce for the gander (4.3.86–106). Emilia's censure of the inequality in early modern marriage also recalls the queries of Adriana in *The Comedy of Errors* and the denunciation of marriage by Julia in *Patient Grissel*. Later, Emilia defies her spouse and delivers an unvarnished narration of events. When Iago twice seeks to silence his wife and twice commands her to return home, she resists, invoking the doctrine of conscience even as she acknowledges her subjection, "'Tis proper I obey him, but not now" (5.2.203). At the end of the play, therefore, in the name of principled disobedience, Emilia violates three cardinal rules for the good wife: to be silent, to remain at home, and to obey her husband.[24] The sentiments on wifely obedience expressed in the Puritan conduct books cited above read like a gloss on Emila's declaration of limited independence. Emilia's lines also anticipate the question of the Separatist Katherine Chidley, "I pray you tell me what authority [the] unbelieving husband has over the conscience of his believing wife; it is true that he has authority over her in bodily and civil aspects, but not to be a lord over her conscience" (quoted in Thomas, 52). Ultimately, female bonding provides Emilia the courage to resist her bullying husband, and although her devotion leads to her death, she offers a standard of value in the play and a foil to Desdemona's submission.

At the denouement of the play, the marital model of amorous mutuality originally fervently endorsed by Othello and Desdemona is in shambles. Macfarlane argues that this matrimonial paradigm was originally unique to England and Western Europe. However, during the past five hundred years, this conjugal pattern has been exported to other countries and although still not universally accepted has been widely adopted throughout the world. Nevertheless, even in our comparatively liberated times, the consensual, companionate marriage, because still tainted by the patriarchal ideology of dominance and subordination, continues to produce battered wives and abusive husbands. Thus, the deplorable events occurring in *Othello*, operating on a much smaller scale and shorn of the play's glorious rhetoric and moving catharsis, continue to be replayed over and over, while a helpless, saddened society can only say with Othello, "O, . . . the pity of it" (4.1.196).

NOTES

1. All citations from Shakespeare are from David Bevington's 4th edition of *The Complete Works of Shakespeare*.

2. For a discussion of the Lewis-Haller view of the romanticizing of marriage in the early modern period, see Belsey, 19–20. David Cressy supports Macfarlane's early dating, insisting that "The ideal of companionate marriage based on 'mutual society, help, and comfort' was enshrined in the prayer book from its inception and was not the invention of seventeenth-century puritans or eighteenth-century modernizers. Puritans, however, were more likely to promote this ideal in their writings" (297). For a contrary view, see Lawrence Stone, who contends that although the nuclear, patriarchal family emerged in the Post-Reformation sixteenth century, it does not reach its fulfillment in "love marriage" until the late seventeenth century.

3. I have normalized the spelling and punctuation of all quotations from early modern texts, except when citing passages quoted by another critic, in which case I have maintained the spelling and punctuation of the cited commentator.

4. For vivid accounts of domestic violence in the early modern period, see Dolan and Lena Cowen Orlin.

5. For examples of this ubiquitous analogue, see Desiderius Erasmus, 170; Jean Bodin, 6; Sir Thomas Smith, 14–16; Sir Walter Raleigh, 156–60; Robert Mocket, 2; William Whatley, 16; William Gouge, 17–18; King James, 24, 272, 307. For a useful discussion of this analogy, see Susan Dwyer Amussen, 36–38.

6. I am here following the suggested dating of Viviana Comensoli (132).

7. For a survey of the critical debate evoked by Kate's praise of patriarchal supremacy and wifely subordination, see Hopkins, 42.

8. My examination of the Griselda figures in these plays, as well as my general discussion of early modern domestic tragedies and comedies, is deeply indebted to the enlightening analyses of Comensoli. See particularly 56–64, 132–36.

9. I follow Barry Weller and Margaret W. Ferguson (*Tragedy of Mariam*, 5–6), who date the play sometime after Elizabeth Cary's marriage to Sir Henry Cary in 1602 and before the birth of her first child Catherine in 1609.

10. I am here accepting the dating suggested by A. C. Cawley and Barry Gaines (*A Yorkshire Tragedy*, 1–2).

11. Other pioneering critics who treat Desdemona as a fully developed character rather than a patriarchal icon include S. N. Garner, 233–52; Gayle Greene, 16-32; W. D. Adamson, 169–86; Ann Jennalie Cook, 187–96; Carole McKewin, 117–32; and Irene G. Dash, 103–30. For a more recent, extremely insightful discussion of Desdemona, see Edward Pechter, 120–31. Eloquent apologists for Emilia include Neely, 211–13; Eamon Grennan, 275–92; Greene, 27–28; and Pechter, 113–20. Critics seeking to rehabilitate the much-maligned Bianca include Nina Rulon-Miller, 99–114; and Pechter, 131–40.

12. See Cressy on clandestine marriages and non-canonical hours, 318–29, and on espousals, betrothals, banns, and contracts, 267–81.

13. Lisa Hopkins (155) discusses the degree to which Desdemona plays the shrew.

14. See Michael Bristol's discussion of Desdemona as "the woman on top," 3–21.

15. Stephen Greenblatt (232–540) argues that Othello has internalized the Catholic fear of sexuality and views even marital eroticism as inevitably adulterous. For a survey of commentators supporting this reading, see Hopkins, 211 n. 36.

16. For a defense of sexuality within the consensual, companionate marriage, see Dod and Cleaver, 167; Hagstrum, 315–15; and Cressy, 290.

17. For a lucid explanation of these two marital models, see Keith Wrightson, 70-88. In discussing these two, conjugal models, I am referring to early modern England in which the play was written, not to Renaissance Italy where it is set, because I read the play as participating in the social controversies of Shakespeare's own social milieu.

18. Snow (386 n. 4) notes the recurrent association of women in the play with possessions: Brabantio's sense of his daughter as a jewel; Othello's view of his wife as a pearl; Cassio's reference to Bianca as a bauble. Lynda Boose (427–37) also analyzes the jewel motif in the play.

19. For a provocative contrary reading that portrays Desdemona as much less passive than I do, see Emily C. Bartels, 417–33.

20. In an earlier essay (Deats and Lenker, 87–90), I discuss the degree to which the portrait of Desdemona corresponds to that of the battered wife of contemporary clinical literature. Ruth Vanita (355 n.22) also situates Desdemona within contemporary narratives of battered women.

21. Dolan (115) adduces this scene as an example of the early modern tendency to represent violent, murderous husbands as not only a deviation from the norm but as actually insane.

22. Marguerite Waller (15) agrees with me that had both Desdemona and Emilia been more disobedient, they might have survived.

23. On Puritan protests against the sexual double standard, see Wrightson, 99–101.

24. On the importance of wifely silence, see Henry Smith, 29; Dod and Cleaver, 160, 164; and Whately, 40–41. On the necessity of the wife's remaining at home, see Henry Smith, 28. For the association of "babbling," "gadding," and "light behavior," see Dod and Cleaver, 166–67. For the definitive connection of silence, chastity, and remaining at home, see Peter Stallybrass, 123–42.

WORKS CITED

Adamson, W. D. "Unpinned and Undone? Desdemona's Critics and the Problem of Sexual Innocence." *Shakespeare Studies* 13 (1980):169–86.

Amussen, Susan Dwyer. *An Ordered Society: Gender and Class in Early Modern England.* Oxford: Blackwell, 1988.

Arden of Feversham. Drama of the English Renaissance. Vol.1: The Tudor Period. Ed. Russell Fraser and Norman Rabkin. New York:Macmillan, 1976. 411–38.

Bartels, Emily C. "Strategies of Submission: Desdemona, the Duchess, and the Assertion of Desire." *Studies in English Literature* 36 (1996): 417–33.

Belsey, Catherine. *Shakespeare and the Loss of Eden: The Construction of Family Values in Early Modern Culture.* New Brunswick: Rutgers University Press, 1999.

Bevington, David. Introduction to *Othello. The Complete Works of Shakespeare,* ed. Bevington, David. 4th ed. New York: HarperCollins, 1992.

Blackstone, William. *Commentaries on the Laws on England*. 4 vols. London: Weir, 1786.

Bodin, Jean. *Six Books of the Commonwealth*. Trans. M. J. Tooley. New York: Barnes, 1967.

Boose, Lynda. "Othello's 'Chrysolite' and the Song of Songs Tradition. *Philological Quarterly* 60 (1980): 427–37.

Bristol, Michael D. "Charivari and the Comedy of Abjection in *Othello*." *Renaissance Drama* 21 (1990): 3–21.

Cary, Elizabeth. *The Tragedy of Mariam: The Fair Queen of Jewery*. Ed. Barry Weller and Margaret W. Fergerson. Berkeley: University of California Press, 1994.

Comensoli, Viviana. *'Household Business': Domestic Plays of Early Modern England*. Toronto: University of Toronto Press, 1996.

Cook, Ann Jennalie. "The Design of *Othello*: Doubt Raised and Resolved." *Shakespeare Studies* 13 (1980): 187–96.

Cressy, David. *Birth, Marriage, and Death: Ritual, Religion, and the Life-Cycle in Tudor and Stuart England*. Oxford: Oxford University Press, 1998.

Dash, Irene G. *Wooing, Wedding, and Power: Women in Shakespeare's Plays*. New York: Columbia University Press, 1981. 103–30.

Deats, Sara Munson. "From Pedestal to Ditch: Violence Against Women in Shakespeare's *Othello*." *The Aching Hearth: Family Violence in Life and Literature*. Ed. Sara Munson Deats and Lagretta Tallent Lenker. New York: Plenum, 1991. 79–93.

Dekker, Thomas, Henry Chettle, and William Houghton. *Patient Grissel. The Dramatic Works of Thomas Dekker*. Vol. 1. Ed. Fredson Bowers. Cambridge: Cambridge University Press, 1953. 207–98.

Dekker, Thomas, and Thomas Middleton. *The Honest Whore, Part I. The Dramatic Works of Thomas Dekker*. Vol. 2. Ed. Fredson Bowers. Cambridge: Cambridge University Press, 1955. 1–130.

Dod, John, and Robert Cleaver. *A Godly Form of Household Government*. London: Thomas Man, 1612.

Dolan, Francis E. *Dangerous Familiars: Representations of Domestic Crime in England, 1500-1700*. Ithaca: Cornell University Press, 1994.

Dusinberre, Juliet. *Shakespeare and the Nature of Women*. 1975. London: St. Martin's, 1996.

Erasmus, Desiderius. *The Education of a Christian Prince*. Trans. Lester K. Born. New York: Norton, 1965.

The Fair Maid of Bristow. Ed. Authur H. Quinn. Philadelphia: University Press of Pennsylvania P, 1902.

Garner, S. N. "Shakespeare's Desdemona." *Shakespeare Studies* 9 (1976): 233–52.

Gouge, William. *Of Domestical Duties: Eight Treatises*. Facsimile of the 1622 edition. Amsterdam: Johnson, 1976.

Greenblatt, Stephen. *Renaissance Self-Fashioning: From More to Shakespeare*. Chicago: University of Chicago Press, 1980.

Greene, Gayle. "This That You Call Love: Sexual and Social Tragedy in *Othello*." *Journal of Women's Studies in Literature* 1 (1979): 16–32.

Grennan, Eamen. "The Women's Voices in *Othello*: Speech, Song, Silence." *Shakespeare Quarterly* 38 (1987): 275–92.

Hagstrum, Jean H.: *Esteem Enlivened by Desire: The Couple from Homer to Shakespeare.* Chicago: University of Chicago Press, 1992.

Haller, William, and Malleville Haller. "The Puritan Art of Love." *Huntington Library Quarterly* 5 (1942): 235–72.

Heywood, John. *A Merry Play Between John John the Husband, Tyb His Wife, and Sir John the Priest. The Dramatic Writings of John Heywood.* Ed. John S. Farmer. Facsimile of the 1905 edition. New York: Barnes, 1966. 3–25.

Heywood, Thomas. *How a Man May Choose a Good Wife from a Bad.* London: Mathew Law, 1608.

———. *A Woman Killed with Kindness. Drama of the English Renaissance.* Vol. 1: The Tudor Period. Ed. Russell A. Fraser and Norman Rabkin. New York: McMillian, 1976. 511–36.

"A Homily of the State of Matrimony." *Certaine Sermons or Homilies Appointed To Be Read in Churches, in the Time of Queen Elizabeth I (1547–71).* Facsimile of the 1623 edition. Gainesville: Scholars Facsimiles and Reprints, 1968. 239–48.

Hopkins, Lisa. *The Shakespearean Marriage: Merry Wives and Heavy Husbands.* St. Martin's Press, 1998.

James I of England. *The Political Works of James I.* Ed. Charles Howard McIlwain. 1918. New York: Russell, 1985.

Lewis, C. S. *The Allegory of Love: A Study in Medieval Tradition.* Oxford: Oxford University Press, 1942.

The London Prodigal. The Shakespeare Apocrypha. Ed. Tucker Brooke. Oxford: Clarendon Press, 1908. 191–218.

Macfarlane, Alan. *Marriage and Love in England: Modes of Reproduction, 1300–1840.* Oxford: Blackwell, 1986.

Marston, John. *The Faun.* Ed. Gerald A. Smith. Lincoln: University of Nebraska Press, 1965.

McKewin, Carole. "Counsels of Gall and Grace: Intimate Conversations Between Women in Shakespeare's Plays." *The Woman's Part: Feminist Criticism of Shakespeare.* Ed. Carolyn Ruth Swift Lenz, Gayle Greene, and Carol Thomas Neely. Urbana: University of Illinois Press, 1980. 117–32.

Mocket, Robert. *God and King.* 1615. London, 1663.

Neely, Carol Thomas. "Women and Men in *Othello*: 'What should such a fool do with so good a woman?'" *The Woman's Part: Feminism Criticism of Shakespeare.* Ed. Carolyn Ruth Swift Lenz, Gayle Greene, and Carol Thomas Neely. Urbana: University of Illinois P, 1980. 211–39.

Orlin, Lena Cowen. *Private Matters and Public Culture in Post-Reformation England.* Ithaca: Cornell University Press, 1994.

Pechter, Edward. *Othello and the Interpretative Traditions.* Iowa City: University of Iowa Press, 1999.

Perkins, William. *Christian Oeconomie.* London: Felix Kynyston, 1609.

———. *A Treatise of Conscience.* Cambridge, Eng.: John Legate, 1608.

Raleigh, Sir Walter. *The History of the World (1614).* Ed. C. A. Patrides. Philadelphia: Temple University Press, 1971.

Rulon-Miller, Nina. "Othello's Bianca: Climbing Out of the Bed of Patriarchy." *Upstart Crow* 15 (1995): 99–114.

Shakespeare, William. *The Complete Works of Shakespeare.* Ed. David Bevington. 4th ed. New York: HarperCollins, 1992.

Smith, Henry. "A Preparation to Marriage." *The Sermons of Master Henry Smith.* London: Thomas Man, 1594.

Smith, Sir Thomas. *De Republica Anglorum.* Facsimile edition. Amsterdam: Johnson, 1970

Snow, Edward A. "Sexual Anxiety and the Male Order of Things in *Othello.*" *English Literary Renaissance* 10 (1980): 384–412.

Stallybrass, Peter. "Patriarchal Territories: The Body Enclosed." *Rewriting the Renaissance: The Discourses of Sexual Different in Early Modern Europe.* Ed. Margaret W. Ferguson, Maureen Quilligan, and Nancy J. Vickers. Chicago: University of Chicago Press, 1986. 123–42.

Stone, Lawrence. *The Family, Sex, and Marriage in England 1500-1800.* New York: Harper, 1977.

Thomas, Keith. "Women and the Civil War Sects." *Past and Present* 13 (1958): 42–62.

Vanita, Ruth. "'Proper' Men and 'Fallen' Women: The Unprotectedness of Wives in *Othello.*" *Studies in English Literature* 43 (1994): 341–56.

Waller, Marguerite. "Academic Tootsie: The Denial of Difference and the Difference It Makes." *Diacritics* 17.1 (1987): 2-20.

A Warning for Fair Women. Ed. Charles Dale Cannon. The Hague: Mouton, 1975.

Whately, William. *A Bride-Bush or A Wedding Sermon.* Facsimile of the 1616 edition. Amsterdam: Johnson, 1975.

Wrightson, Keith. *English Society 1580-1680.* New Brunswick: Rutgers University Press, 1982.

A Yorkshire Tragedy. Ed. A.C. Cawley and Barry Gaines. The Revels Plays. Manchester: Manchester University Press, 1986

Morality, Ethics and the Failure of Love in Shakespeare's *Othello*

JOHN GRONBECK-TEDESCO

For the first twenty-nine pages of his masterful *Othello and Interpretive Traditions*, Edward Pechter reiterates in different ways just how painful it is to experience Shakespeare's play both on the page and the stage. It is precisely this pain that, according to Pechter, has helped sustain the play's "extraordinary power to affect audiences over four centuries" (21), and it is this pain that is at the very core of so many responses to *Othello* (8). In part, the "excruciating anxiety" upon which Pechter dwells has much to do with the "impossible demands of responding at once to Othello's and Iago's voices." And, it is these "impossible demands" that have produced a "record of grief, rage and resistance" across numerous interpretations of the play (8).

Of course, critics, directors, and actors have had their own versions of pain, each anchored to different views of the wild, colliding sympathies and antipathies induced by the conflict between Othello and Iago. Joan Lord Hall notes how Shakespeare's "tragedy touches on sensitive issues that have acquired fresh resonance in our own age: racial prejudice and fascination with the 'other,' the nature of sexual jealousy, and the difficulty of knowing anyone or anything definitively" (ix), to name only a few recent and not so recent interpretive directions in commentary and production.

My own version of Pechter's refined frustration lies in how impossible it is to interpret any of the characters without involving Iago as the crucial touchstone. Desdemona, Othello, Roderigo, Cassio, Emilia—all—become entangled in the presence of a villain who is the dominating interpretive crux of their dramatic careers. Whereas Iago speaks plainly to the audience about himself and for himself, the other characters speak in terms of what Iago makes of them as he goes about his murderous project. More insidiously, what Iago evokes from the audience is judgment, not only toward himself but toward the other characters, too. Emerging directly from Iago's position as the lens through which others are seen and judged, there comes

255

the central event which accumulates one beat at a time throughout the play. That event is the breach between morality and ethics that widens relentlessly and is never quite healed. By morality I mean an approach to managing human desire by a direct appeal to a transcendent source of value. In *Othello*, that source is the Judeo-Christian version of God as interpreted chiefly —but by no means exclusively—through the New Testament. Ethical systems, on the other hand, control desire by an appeal to custom and consensus. The dominant tradition in Christian theology grounds ethics in morality, so that customary procedural constraints on desire are legitimated by an appeal to moral maxims (or, in the idiom of medieval and Renaissance literature, *sententiae*). Ethics becomes, in effect, practical morality; that is, the conversion of the will of God into daily protocols that constrain human desire and its consequences.

It is precisely this traditional patristic relationship between morality and ethics that is the basis of Shakespeare's tragic vision in *Othello*, conservative in its theology, perhaps, but exploratory in its penchant for confronting the more intractable dilemmas challenging the human condition. Throughout the play, the relationship between ethics and morality unravels to a point where the latter becomes nothing more than stolid platitudes with little power to alter the situations in which they are uttered, and the former degenerates into a coarse social practice made up of manipulative agreements between villains and their cohorts or victims (Hardy). Yet, from this interpretive movement, grounded on the slippage between morality and ethics, comes an allegorical by-product, which I will develop later in the essay.

I

The theme of morality and its application to the human realm is clear from the beginning. In the first beats of the play, Iago indulges his discontent over Cassio's promotion to lieutenant over him in terms of the jealousy and self-aggrandizement that soon will blossom into a murderous game. Iago resents Cassio's "preferment" (1.1.36) because it is based on a system of merit determined by a regard for strategic and mathematical principles, rather than "by old gradation" (1.1.32), whereby rank was inherited through customs that honored experience couched in terms of seniority. Cassio wins rank because he understands the mathematics of modern gunnery. Iago must remain an "ancient" because he does not; nor can he understand the new system of merit that displaces age-old precedent. Iago's account of what he deems an oversight is his first guarantee to Roderigo that he can count on his help in dissolving Othello's relationship to Desdemona. In the next scene, the complex issues of custom, moral principle, and practical adjustment to circumstance remain in the foreground. Iago helps Roderigo incite Brabantio against Othello by accusing him and Desdemona of fornication. Iago's tactics are revealing. In his attack on Brabantio's equanimity, he mixes the diction of moral sensitivity with that of vulgar prejudice:

> Zounds, sir y'are robbed! . . .
> Your heart is burst; you have lost half your soul.
> Even now, now, very now, an old black ram
> Is tupping your white ewe. Arise, arise! (1.1.86–9)

Iago's attempt to "poison" Brabantio's "delight" (1.1.69) leads him to a seemingly inept rhetorical brew. His game is to incite Desdemona's father to practice against the very fairness Iago knows he pledges as a citizen and senator (Time): " . . . [Y]ou'll have your daughter covered by a Barbary horse; you'll have coursers for cousins, and gennets for germans" (1.1.110–13). The language intended to motivate base practice with moral sentiments is annoying and vulgar. "Old black ram," "tupping," and "Barbary horse" jar against a "heart" that is "burst," and the loss of a daughter who is "half" her father's "soul." Brabantio's response is pure reflex based no less on social class than on his paternal sensitivities. He calls Iago a "villain" (1.1.117) and promises retribution. Roderigo, himself a well-born Venetian, must drown out Iago's miscalculation with an elegant reconnection of moral appeal to rhetorical decorum:

> If it be your pleasure and most wise consent,
> As partly I find it is, that your fair daughter
> At this odd-even and dull watch o'th'night,
> Transported, with no worse nor better guard
> But with a knave of common hire, a gondolier,
> To the gross clasps of a lascivious Moor—
> If this be known to you, an your allowance,
> We then have done you bold and saucy wrongs;
> But if you know not this, my manners tell me
> We have your wrong rebuke. Do not believe
> That, from the sense of all civility,
> I thus would play and trifle with your reverence.
> Your daughter, if you have not given her leave,
> I say again, hath made a gross revolt,
> Tying her beauty, wit and fortunes
> In an extravagant and wheeling stranger
> Of here and everywhere. Straight satisfy yourself.
> If she be in her chamber, or your house,
> Let loose on me the justice of the state
> For thus deluding you. (1.1.119-38)

Roderigo's background as a courtier makes him Iago's able dupe. The sophistication of Roderigo's verse matches that of his argument which elides moral principles with appropriate ethical action. The moral principles are Desdemona's duty to remain chaste as part of the filial piety owed to her father, and Othello's responsibility to respect the sanctity of Brabantio's home. Part of the ethical practice is the form and content of Roderigo's report itself, which he claims he owes to Brabantio as a father and statesman. But Roderigo's lines raise another kind of relationship between morality and ethics—a complex connection between a narrator willing to take public responsibility for his words and the obligation of one who may benefit from those words even while doubting them. Roderigo's readiness to pay in court, should Brabantio search and turn up Desdemona asleep in her room, places the old senator under obligation to honor the younger man's sense of duty. Brabantio responds viscerally to Roderigo's complex coupling of morality to ethical protocol:

> Strike on the tinder, ho!
> Give me a taper! Call up all my people! . . .
> Light, I say! light! (1.1.139-41)

The spatial arrangement adds emphasis to the reading I have just offered. On the Elizabethan stage, Shakespeare could layer space and language so that they could suggest more together than either could alone, and so effect a strategy of rhetorical amplification unique to production (Dox, 182). Brabantio stands in front of the inner above, the space he occupies becoming the balcony of his home. He is framed by his own domestic order where his ethical office as *paterfamilias* is enfranchised by a moral code that connects his authority to that of god. Scattered downstage on a platform that juts into the audience are Roderigo and Iago. They occupy the *transversia*—the alleyway—between domiciles and full-fledged streets (Smail, 41). Their location is an unformed space suggested not so much by a scenic structure but by a stage area in concert with the language of intrigue. Thus positioned, they are interlopers who are in the shadows of those sorts of defined places that impart identity and normative social advantage. In the alley that is no place, Iago and Roderigo erect a kind of shadow ethics in which want and will collapse into one another, becoming appetite and obsession. Both characters muster cunning, conspiracy, false agreements, lies, and duplicity to compensate for their lack of authority.

How have Roderigo and Iago come to this space between places (Burroughs, 80–82) to embark upon an incendiary course of provocation and disruption that ends once in the Venetian Senate and then resumes more terribly on the island of Cyprus? Roderigo has been brought to the shadows in part by his own frustrations over the loss of Desdemona, and in part by the skillful manipulation of Iago who has promised his companion an annulment. But what of Iago? Shakespeare tells the back story of Iago's attempt to undo the laminations between ethics and morality in fits and starts through the chancy words of the villain himself. Moreover, the circumstances that incite his action against Othello include much more than the promotion of Cassio to lieutenant:

> . . . I hate the Moor;
> And it is thought abroad that twixt my sheets
> H'as done my office. I know not if 't be true;
> But I, for mere suspicion in that kind,
> Will do as if for surety. . . . (1.3.380–84)

Revenge, as Linda Anderson has pointed out (13–22), is a motivational crux in many of Shakespeare's plays and a lynchpin in the theory of tragedy, where it is placed both opposite and apposite to systems of public justice. In part, the reason for Iago's desire for a private revenge is precisely that he has no public way to redress the alleged violation of his marriage by his commanding officer who rules in a system quite the opposite of the Venetian version of oligarchic democracy.

Complicating Iago's problem is that he has no proof of Othello's transgression. Throughout *Hamlet* (written immediately before *Othello*), the moral basis for Hamlet's revenge is guaranteed by the testimony of his father's ghost fresh from the grave, by the mousetrap play, by Claudius's own words in a failed attempt to repent, and in Claudius's final effort to kill his nephew. All of this frames Hamlet's act as a means of reestablishing justice in a kingdom where "something rotten" threatens the public good. By contrast, Iago's practice of revenge is unacceptable because it has none of the guaranteed moral grounding at work in *Hamlet*. Iago is angry, spiteful, and obsessive. So too is Hamlet, but he is something more. Hamlet searches for an ethical practice to complement his moral cause. He kills as the only remaining legitimate head of state; he kills before officials of the state, in the place of divine authority where justice is customarily dispensed; and he kills only after Claudius has proclaimed his treachery by murdering Gertrude and Laertes before all eyes in a final and successful attempt to poison his nephew (Anderson, 13 ff.). Part of Hamlet's fabled delay comes from his obligation to orchestrate a complex act of justice that is public and clear, an act at which he fails at least once when he kills Polonius rashly and by mistake in Gertrude's private chamber. But Iago launches his revenge based on "mere suspicion" and abject jealousy. So, on two counts, Iago's accusation, like Iago himself standing in the no-man's-land of the *transversia*, has no place and no status as a public claim.

In *Othello*, Shakespeare repeats his concern for the official public demeanor necessary to separate personal revenge from a moral act of justice. In 1.3 he fills the stage with the Venetian Senate. The Duke most probably is in or just in front of the inner below with the rest of his entourage extending downstage left and right. The Senate is a deliberative and forensic space where public decisions are made based upon the rule of law. Iago's game is to cast

Brabantio as his own surrogate in the hope that Desdemona's father will seek a "legal" revenge from his peers for the transgression against his authority and his home. Moreover, Iago counts on the Senate to be guided by their own prejudices into complicity with Brabantio. Indeed, Brabantio charges Othello with abduction and rape:

> She is abused, stol'n from me and corrupted
> By spells and medicines brought of mountebanks,
> For nature so prepost'rously to err,
> Being not deficient, blind, or lame of sense,
> Sans witchcraft could not. (1.3.60–4)

And, indeed, the first words from the Duke seem in accord with Iago's fondest wishes:

> Whoe'er he be that in this foul proceeding
> Hath thus beguiled your daughter of herself,
> And you of her, the bloody book of law
> You shall yourself read in the bitter letter
> After your own sense; yea, though our proper son
> Stood in your action. (1.3.65–70)

What follows is one of the most remarkable scenes in the play for the way it orders the complex relationships between morality and ethics. The Senate abides by the rules of the space it inhabits. The Duke seeks evidence in the form of testimony from the alleged victim. The case turns not on the appeal of a father who has lost his daughter, but on the issue of love. When Desdemona professes her love for Othello in the lucid terms of the "duty" she now owes to the man who is her husband, the case against Othello comes to an abrupt end. In the Venetian Senate, love readjusts moral principle and ethical protocol to one another. The moral principle of a father's rights and a daughter's sanctity would normally find expression in a procedure of retribution. But all is reordered by Desdemona's love for Othello. (No one asks whether he loves her.) Quite simply, love actually serves as an overarching framework that determines which moral principles to invoke and which ethical practices to use. The difference between Othello as a usurper and Othello as a just suitor is precisely the love of Desdemona. And it is this very fact that Iago has forgotten in the heat of his dissatisfaction, suspicion, and jealousy. His hope that prejudice might prevail in place of the Senate's customary search for just solutions comes to naught. Brabantio himself, who has already pronounced against Othello's race and nationality in the name of nature, gives way instantly, albeit grudgingly, to the ordering effect of love in law. "God be with you! I have done" (1.3.189). His next deed is to surrender his daughter to

Othello in a public act:

> Come hither, Moor.
> I here do give thee that with my heart
> Which, but thou has already, with all my heart
> I would keep from thee. . . . (1.3.192–95)

In the body of the Senate, moral principle and procedural ethics drive a wedge between what Brabantio wants and what he wills, so that he ends up *willing* what is right as required by his place and status in that body; while, as a father, he continues to *want* something else entirely. The Senate is a heterotopic space (Dox, 182), where different kinds of scenes seem to be superimposed upon one another: a scene of personal resentment is also a scene of public rectitude; and a scene of judgment, and a scene of legitimate betrothal after the fact of matrimony. All cohere into a single dramatic event by means of a stage craft and a dramaturgy that make love and law somehow one. Just as the Senate is the place of Iago's undoing, so too is it the stage where Othello fashions himself as a son of the State. While Iago has forgotten the force of love in Venetian protocol, Othello has counted on it from the very first utterance of Brabantio's accusation:

Othello:

> I do beseech you,
> Send for the lady to the Sagittary
> And let her speak of me before her father.
> If you do find me foul in her report,
> The trust, the office, I do hold of you
> Not only take away, but let your sentence
> Even fall upon my life. (1.2.115-21)

Othello relies on the morality and ethics of the very people that will judge him: their sense of fairness and the way they respect one who is willing to submit to their procedures and scrutiny. In this moment, Othello's rhetoric is like Brabantio's in the alley, but with one important difference. Othello is in love with Desdemona, and she with him (Charney, 95–106). Moreover, in grounding his defense on Desdemona's love for him (1.3.125–70), Othello demonstrates how well he knows the mores of his audience.

In the final moment of act 1, Iago strives to recover the ground he has lost with Roderigo, who lives in the stagnant stillness of a plan gone bad. Iago's argument reverses the logic of grace underlying what the Senate has just accomplished. He denigrates love as "a lust of the blood and a permission of the will" (1.3.333–34) and claims to place reason above all human faculties. But since love is really lust to Iago, reason has no higher purpose than to satisfy the desire of the flesh, so that Iago ends up contradicting himself by installing lust ahead of reason even as he argues for the latter's primacy. Without love as a transcendent value, Iago's argument falls apart almost comically.

II

Cyprus is not Venice, and there is no Senate in a sacramental space to separate desire and volition by granting love superordinate authority. Cyprus is Iago's turf, his own game board on which he dishevels ethics and morality, turning himself into . . . what? Does Iago's explicit disconnection of social agency from moral principle find a precise analogue in Machiavelli's *Prince*, as others have argued (Hall, 30)? I think not. While Machiavelli may provide a general historical influence on the structure of Shakespeare's antagonist, Iago departs markedly from his textual relative. Iago, a twenty-eight-year-old ensign, has none of the responsibilities for managing and negotiating upper-class cadres of power, or for defeating multiple closet alliances organized for the purpose of undermining his own legitimate influence on a far-flung social system. Iago is simply not a civil ruler.

The word that best defines Iago's agency is *actor*. Iago is an actor played by an actor, the virtuosity of each coinciding and coalescing with the other. As such, Iago is the version of Plato's nightmare inherited by Elizabethan opponents of the theatre. In the idiom of that nightmare, when moral commitment and fundamental identity lose all connection to one another, social agency (the realm of ethics) becomes no more than one performance after another, a rhetoric of word, gesture, and alliance: otherwise known as lying.

After the return to Cyprus, *Othello* becomes, in part, an allegory on the morality and ethics of theatre approached through a *via negativa* provided by Iago in cahoots with the actor playing him. It is precisely this allegory that shows clearly as a residual of the action by which virtue and its procedures come undone. While Iago is the villain of the play, the actor playing Iago is most certainly the protagonist of the metatheatrical layer, for it is he who sponsors the positive regard for theatre that emerges so emphatically even as the character he plays moves relentlessly toward his evil purpose.

The allegorical dimension of the play comes forward aggressively in Iago's long exchange with Desdemona as she waits for Othello's return from battle. In style and rhythm, Iago openly takes on the role of the fool using turns of chop logic, puns and double meanings similar in form to the word games of Proteus, Launce, and Grumio, although Iago's are certainly more bleak. Moreover, Desdemona realizes Iago is performing, and he himself raises and counts on this awareness to keep her from taking his words literally. Throughout their repartee, Desdemona continues to regard herself as his audience, however active and engaged she may be. Her challenge that Iago bestow "praise" on a "deserving woman . . . one that in the authority of her merit did justly put on the vouch of very malice itself" (2.1.145–46) is a request for a performance. Unwittingly, she raises the very issue that Iago cannot abide: a system of merit based on personal traits that supersede tribal tradition and seniority. It is here that his acting almost disappears, and he nearly becomes visible to Desdemona as the villain he is. Ironically, Cassio steps in to excuse the near obscenity to which Iago stoops with the reminder "You must relish him more in the soldier than in the scholar" (2.1.164–65).

By clear contrast with the wit exchange between Iago and Desdemona, the next scenes between Othello and Iago strike important differences between lying and acting. After the reunion of the couple, Iago changes his plan, based largely on his assessment of the qualities he sees Othello display in his treatment of Desdemona:

> The Moor, howbeit that I endure him not,
> Is of a constant, loving, noble nature,
> And I dare think he'll prove to Desdemona
> A most dear husband. . . . (2.1.282-85)

The plan is no longer to discredit Othello directly but to get him to kill Desdemona by first driving him mad with jealousy. The madness Iago seeks to impart is precisely that which comes when an audience is not permitted to discern a pretense. Desdemona escapes anger and emotional upset on the beach because she believes Iago is acting and therefore not to be taken literally. But Iago prevents Othello from perceiving himself as an audience member who is outside the gambit of action erected by the actor. Instead, Iago erases any demarcation between the world he constructs and the world Othello inhabits. It is this refusal to mark a distinction by shifts in his style of communication that turns Iago's performance into a lie. On the beach, Desdemona divided the space into stage and audience through her own awareness of Iago as an actor, an awareness cultivated by Iago himself. But Othello is never afforded such a perspective. What Iago says and does issues a set of stakes and obstacles that Othello believes he must address with agency and participation that is coherent with Iago's own.

At this point, the play's metatheatrical discourse reverses the accusations against "playing" as a form of deception made by the likes of John Northbrooke (1577), Stephen Gosson (1579), and Philip Stubbes (1583) into an examination of audience responsibility. This reversal comes into focus just following Cassio's drunken act of violence against Montano when Iago's manipulative abilities are so powerfully evident. If Iago is such a successful liar, it is in large measure because of the way Othello, his principal audience in the scene, inhabits his own social role. On Cyprus, Othello is surrounded by the rigidities of military protocol, where egregious breaches in discipline incur consequences not subject to argument or interpretation. The problem is that Othello never questions his own habits of disciplinary retribution which always have served him so practically. Nor has he learned from his experience in the Venetian court where argument is permitted full sway. To move from incident to consequence rapidly, Othello must be willing to believe his subordinates and act on their words. No one understands military ways better than Iago. He relies on the direct relationship between words uttered in the chain of command and the actions of authority. It is this straightforward relationship, so important to military efficiency, that he uses to subvert Cassio in the eyes of Othello.

As a liar, Iago relies on the fact that Othello will never question himself or the ways he makes decisions in matters of "conduct unbefitting." Moreover, Iago knows the situation. A newlywed fresh from bed and a governor of a dicey community of soldiers and civilians, Othello wants quick closure without extended due process. Iago's intuition pays off. Called by noise and an alarm bell to quell Cassio's drunken violence, Othello initiates no systematic inquiry but orders Iago: "[S]peak. Who began this?" (2.3.168) The ensign's words will be sufficient. And, no one will usurp Iago's prerogative as the reporter, even after he seems to decline from giving the account Othello requests. What is more, Iago counts on this fact. His status and obligation are safe enough to allow him the time he needs to hesitate so as to force Othello to repeat his order, thereby making Iago look reluctant to perform what is, after all, only his duty. Iago, therefore, manages to appear to everyone as both a good friend and a good soldier. Once honor is earned in the once-upon-a-time of former distinction, it is assumed to remain. Unlike the Venetian Senate that finds ways to divine evidence even in the moment of deliberation, the military tradition, by which Othello acts against Cassio, uses Iago's reputation as the surrogate for evidence. The irony in all this will come later, when Othello shall try to abandon his traditional military habits and demand "ocular proof" for Iago's charges against Desdemona.

Indeed, on one level, Iago underscores the worst fears of Elizabethan critics of "playing," but, on another, he does so in a way that is inflected toward the audience and away from the actor. Within the allegorical dynamic, Othello has become the audience's surrogate. So, while Iago's success against Othello acknowledges the way an actor can manipulate an audience's most facile habits of mind and more, the actor, in performing Iago, points out these very habits and the complex vulnerabilities they create. Whereas in the world outside the theatre, falsehood and truth may mix and be confounded in ways that remain invisible, on the stage, this very comingling is revealed clearly before an audience that can then bear witness to what it recognizes to be false and true.

The demotion of Cassio displays the metatheatrical dimension of the play in yet another way. Iago's facility in betraying Cassio, while remaining in the good graces of all, is an epiphany.   He moves to and fro among his allegiances to Othello, Cassio, and Roderigo. Iago's free oscillation betwixt and between men who are his superior in rank or class is done in full view of all and demonstrates the grounds of his villainy. Iago refuses any stable place in the social system that surrounds him, and with his disregard comes the avoidance of any stable set of moral and ethical responsibilities and practices associated with place. What is curious is how Iago's continuous movement between social positions goes unnoticed by others. Through the second half of act 2, Iago acts in voices. First, he assumes the voice of a friend among friends ("friends all" [2.3.169]) when he first declines to give testimony against Cassio. Then he uses the voice of the good soldier that the wounded Montano exhorts to honorable conduct:

> If partially affined, or leagued in office,
> Thou dost deliver more or less than truth,
> Thou art no soldier. (2.3.208)

(The irony here is that Montano has fallen exactly upon Iago's game of affinement and leagues "in office.") The good-soldier act moves the protean game of voices forward to the impersonation of a brother counselor to the disreputed Cassio. Iago's voice comes full of maxims: " . . . You have lost no reputation at all unless you repute yourself such a loser" (2.3. 261).

Although a master of personae, his ability as a performer does not explain the extent of his success as an always socially mobile liar. In fact, Iago makes no attempt to excuse his refusal to abide firmly in the position of his rank. Neither can his success as a social dancer be attributed to some sort of general dramatic premise: "Iago's dupes do not see because that is the way Shakespeare wrote the play." Nor is it because villainy always entrances its victims before defeating them. The reason Iago's associates do not notice his failure to accept his place in the world is because they themselves exploit his capacity to slip between social boundaries and borders. Repeatedly, continually, Othello, Roderigo, Cassio, Montano—all—use him in their own social games, both pragmatic and internecine—even as he uses them. And, in order to exploit Iago, everyone must permit him to step out of place. A brilliant actor still must have a willing audience. And, none are more willing than those Iago pretends to serve. Iago's own title for *Othello* might be "The Revenge of the Good and Faithful Servant." The oxymoron is part of what makes Iago's identity an issue. Where is the social and moral point on which the "real" Iago stands and becomes visible and accountable? There is no such fulcrum. Iago is always the uses to which he is put by others. His exploitation of others becomes hidden under their exploitation of him. Moreover, he parts company with his precedent in Roman drama. Unlike the slippery comic slave, Iago does not seek to hide the fact of his social jig, but only his intentions.

Iago's continuous movement "betwixt and amongst" furthers Shake-speare's metatheatrical allegory in a way that merges even more snugly into the thematics of the play. On stage, the actor, like Iago, abandons the restrictions of class and place in order to claim the license to confront his betters in ways that would be disallowed in the streets and pavilions of the lived world. But the licence the actor claims can come only from the audience which is always responsible for the kinds of prerogatives it grants over its own responses. The audience must never relinquish the reasoned volition that is the unique gift which the theatre offers to human discernment. While the actor may stir desire, the will, grounded on moral precept, must remain ultimately in control. It is the practice of reasoned volition (i.e., the ethics of wanting) that becomes central to the audience's own role in the theatre. Spectators and readers too must resist the ascendency of desire over will which is so central to Iago's action upon Othello. In underscoring the power of the actor, the play reemphasizes the value of theatre as a specific kind of moral exercise. In *Othello*, the actor—using Iago—coaches the audience to distinguish keenly between appetites and faculties, where the former are goblin shadows of the latter. The audience has an advan-tage over the characters in that it can experience the play through the structures of drama and performance which Shakespeare has set in motion. The perspec-tive and distance afforded by these structures allow the audience to place its judgments in the right epideictic directions: toward searching out useful dis-tinctions between what is praiseworthy and what is contemptible in an enor-mously complex world. Shakespeare's drama rehearses the audience in a self-possession appropriate to all situations where uncertainty, confusion and emotional turmoil defy overt control.

Nowhere does the metatheatrical commentary of the play become more important than in the Temptation Scene. For Iago, the handkerchief is pre-cisely what it is for the audience in the theatre, a prop in a plot to madden Othello. But Othello insists upon it as forensic evidence of Desdemona's spir-itual state. The piecemeal empirical attitude that bestowed "preferment" on Cassio comes decisively into the play once again. Othello founders in the muddled transition from decisions based on custom to those based on induc-tion which he has only just begun to usher into his military command. Othello wants evidence that will speak for itself, issue its own narrative:

> Villain, be sure you prove my love a whore!
> Be sure of it; give me the ocular proof; . . .
> Make me to see't; or at least so prove it
> That the probation bear no hinge nor loop
> To hang a doubt on. . . . (3.3.359-60; 363-65)

Because he is both a creature in the theatre and of the theatre, Iago knows that evidence—no matter how concrete—seldom speaks for itself, especially in matters of the human heart. To make it an index of guilt, Iago speaks for and with the handkerchief, like a ventriloquist, creating the very story Othello must believe. Iago relies on the fundamental capacity of theatre: to spin a tale by means of interactive configurations of characters, actions, and contexts that change through time. In the moments surrounding Othello's request for visual confirmation, these configurations shift and re-form around Iago to create the need for the interpretation that he uses to impel Othello toward murder. Iago's narrative shenanigans are dizzying. He doubles back briefly to the history of the handkerchief in the courtship of Desdemona; which account comes only after he has feigned resistance to Othello's demand that Iago divulge the information he pretends to hold secret. Mention of the handkerchief in the possession of Cassio comes reluctantly when Othello threatens Iago in order to make him tell what he knows. But the threat itself is induced by Iago's account of Cassio's lascivious words and actions during a dream, the validity of which Iago himself denies even as Othello goes into shock and rage. The handkerchief does not stand alone, but rides the swirling eddies in a Romanesque narrative of dreams, jealousy, accidents and lies (Hardy). By the end of the scene, Iago still has not produced the handkerchief, but, by talking about it, he has earned Othello's belief nonetheless.

The double edge in the metatheatrical allegory is cunning. Iago does what terrifies those who mistrust the theatre. The core of his villainy is ontological. He rubs out the line between what seems to be and what is, and does so with something as trivial and incidental as a handkerchief. Yet, his action is revelatory when seen from a metatheatrical perspective. In an age when journeys of discovery supported the status and power of inductive reasoning, Iago's sleight of hand teaches the shortcomings of empiricism in its early throes. Iago's "ocular proof" is really a stunt performed for a man who thinks seeing is believing. The truth, upheld by the actor playing Iago, is that evidence rarely exists outside the influence of agents, acts, events, motives, decisions and settings. In *Othello*, evidence is entirely secular and carries no pure authority of its own.

After Iago "produces" in words the handkerchief that will not appear until several beats later, Othello moves from resistance to a full commitment to kill Desdemona in the space of not even half a scene. By the end of 3.3, he has advanced Iago to the rank of lieutenant with orders to murder Cassio. The compression in this region of the play gives the action a shocking momentum. The last third of the piece relies structurally on the inventional strategy of amplification; in this case, the amplification of sheer emotional anguish. After Othello finally does see the handkerchief in the hands of Bianca in 4.1, all the major characters proceed to inherit the future of pain prepared for them by Iago. Othello's anguish leaps to the level of physical fits. Desdemona's is first the anguish of confusion and torture; then, of waiting for her own death. Emilia, Cassio and the Venetian delegation: all become wrapped in the gyre of pain that defines the emotional ecology of the final two acts. The audience is included, I think. Their own anguish comes from the recognition that there can be no intervention or reversal of circumstance; that what has been set in motion has become somehow irretrievable.

During much of the last two acts, the metatheatrical allegory becomes less visible. This comes largely from Iago's efforts—only partially successful—to step back from the events that he has set in motion. As Iago allows his plan to run its course, Othello's agency becomes more central. Indeed, the theme of the calamitous fissure between morality and ethics returns to the foreground. Othello's words over the sleeping Desdemona in 5.2 are maddening and ironic. What the Venetian Senate could do on his behalf, he himself cannot do on behalf of Desdemona. Othello has no access to any procedure that will allow his love for her to influence moral judgment. Yet, this was precisely what the Duke and Senate were able to accomplish. Instead, Othello moves love outside the pale of morality, in the interests of what he considers justice:

> *He kisses her.*
> O balmy breath, that almost doth persuade
> Justice to break her sword! One more, one more!
>
> Be thus when thou art dead, and I will kill thee,
> And love thee after. . . . (5.2.17-20)

Morality first; love after. It is Othello's inability to coordinate morality and love, and then to translate them into a system for judging and acting that makes his deed inconsistent with the Venetian precedent in act 1. The entrance of the Venetian delegation toward the end of the play underscores this very contrast.

Having receded for a time, the metatheatrical layer emerges decisively in the last moments of the play when Shakespeare departs from the more conventional features of neoclassical tragedy and thereby calls attention to form. After Desdemona's death, the action does not slow into resolution but bustles with entrances and exits, testimony and confrontation, murder and attempted murder and finally an act of self-destruction. The proliferation of beats before the end of the play I take as an unsuccessful search for a just ending that can never occur. Instead, the final moment provides only the appearance of closure in the theatrical grammar of neoclassical tragedy with the bodies arranged in a tableau. The normal use of such tableaux, according to William Bache, is to evoke "recapitulation." In most of the tragedies, Shakespeare's formal display of the dead is a way of getting the audience to bring forward all the powerful responses the characters have evoked throughout the play into a final impression that creates a sense of emotional finality. But use of this technique in *Othello* cuts in the opposite direction because it emphasizes the impossibility of any kind of satisfying summary emotion. Instead, the ambivalence pointed out by Edward Pechter comes flooding back. The fissure between conventional form, on the one hand, and significance, on the other, mirrors the same fissure between morality and ethics. There is no formal practice that can restore justice to the universe of the play. Othello's love for Desdemona and hers for him do not suffice against evil. All that remains after Othello adds himself to the tableau of death is the mechanical promise that the penal system will punish Iago.

The tableau, because it is a formal device, cannot help but point to itself as a conventional structure and thereby continue the metatheatrical parable. Why does love fail to defeat evil? Is it because Othello's love is imperfect and because Desdemona's is too docile, and because Iago is too skillful an adversary? And . . . what? The string of possibilities grows longer with every critic who puzzles over the final moments of the play.

Here, I offer my own addition to the list. The theatre of community (here in the form of a domestic tragedy) is a genre that offers audiences exactly what its characters are not allowed to know or use; that is, a diverse abundance of moral distinctions and ethical strategies. In *Othello*, these opportunities become visible to an audience through the dense patterns of human interaction imbedded in kinetic contexts which ensnare and torture the characters. What the audience comes to know is that such antagonistic systems cannot be overturned by a single individual. It is love in the form of human collaboration and the abundance of actantial strategies such collaboration makes possible that is at the heart of the play's theatrical allegory. Love fails in *Othello* because the characters who strive to love do not understand how to sustain a collaborative bond against hostile and impenetrable social contexts. How could they? As characters, they have no access to their author's metatheatrical allegory. This has been reserved for those in the auditorium or study. And so, none of the characters can recognize the very thing Shakespeare's theatre teaches so eloquently: how to move hand in hand through a treacherous world without losing one's grip.

WORKS CITED

Anderson, Linda. *A Kind of Wild Justice: Revenge in Shakespeare's Comedies.* Newark, Delaware: University of Delaware Press, 1987.

Bache, William B. *Design and Closure in Shakespeare's Major Plays: The Nature of Recapitulation.* New York: Peter Lang, 1991.

Burroughs, Charles. "Spaces of Arbitration and the Organization of Space in Late Medieval Italian Cities." In *Medieval Practices of Space.* Eds. Barbara A. Hanawalt and Michal Kobialka. Minneapolis, Minnesota: University of Minnesota Press, 2000.

Charney, Maurice. *Shakespeare on Love and Lust*. New York: Columbia University Press, 2000.

Dox, Donnalee. "Theatrical Space, Mutable Space, and the Space of Imagination: Three Readings of the Croxton *Play of the Sacrament*." in *Medieval Practices of Space*. Eds. Barbara A. Hanawalt and Michal Kobialka. Minneapolis, Minnesota: University of Minnesota Press, 2000.

Gosson, Stephen. *School of Abuse*. 1579. New York: AMS Press, 1966.

Hall, Joan Lord. *"Othello": A Guide to the Play*. Westport, Connecticut: Greenwood Press, 1999.

Hardy, Barbara. *Shakespeare's Storytellers*. London: Peter Owen Publishers, 1997.

Northbrooke, John. *A Treatise against Dicing, Dancing, and Interludes. With Other Pastimes*. 1577. London: Reprinted from the Shakespeare Society, 1843.

Pechter, Edward. *Othello and Interpretive Traditions*. Iowa City, Iowa: University of Iowa Press, 1999.

Shakespeare, William. *Othello the Moor of Venice*. Ed. Gerald Eades Bentley. *William Shakespeare: The Complete Works*. Ed. Alfred Harbage. Baltimore, Maryland: Penguin Books, 1970 [1969].

Smail, Daniel Lord. "The Linguistic Cartography of Property and Power in Late Medieval Marseille." *Medieval Practices of Space*. Eds. Barbara A. Hanawalt and Michal Kobialka. Minneapolis, Minnesota: University of Minnesota Press, 2000.

Stubbes, Phillip. *Anatomy of Abuses*. 1583. Ed. Frederick J. Furniwall. Under the title, *Anatomy of Abuses in England in Shakespeare's Youth*. London: New Shakespeare Society: N. Trubner and Company, 1877.

Time, Victoria M. *Shakespeare's Criminals: Criminology, Fiction and Drama*. Westport, Connecticut: Greenwood Press, 1999.

Keeping Faith
Water Imagery and Religious Diversity in *Othello*

CLIFFORD RONAN

When *Othello* was mounted for Jacobean Oxfordians in 1610, one undergraduate recorded the audience's intense distress at the sight of the dead Desdemona: she "moved us," "entreat[ing] the pity of the spectators by her very countenance"(Henry Jackson, cited in Hankey, 18). Though a fictional representation, it touched their very being—just as, we can say, the artist's rendition of Troy's fall affected viewers in Virgil's *Aeneid,* when they succumbed to "tears for human, mortal things." Indeed, *Othello* is as effective as the *Aeneid* or Book of Job in revealing heroic mankind's vulnerability to forces greater than himself—in this case, biology, environment, upbringing, and what he perceives to be fate, stars, demons, and most important, gods. And like the *Aeneid* or Book of Job, it does not *prove* what the author's opinions were, let alone the existence of any supernatural dimension in life. But it does keep alive the importance of the choices the self must face courageously and humbly, at least according to Western traditions (cf. West, 342).

More fully than *Lear* or even *Hamlet, Othello* treats religion from a cosmopolitan and Christian-humanist perspective. Characters in *Hamlet* live variously also: by the codes of Machiavelli, aristocratic honor, humanistic learning, Catholicism, and Protestantism. The figures in *Lear* believe in a somewhat larger variety of entities: Nothing, Nature, the stars, the individual will, human bonds, supernal charity, providence, or malignant supernatural forces. But in *Othello* characters are differentiated even more by a mixed, diversified, and fluctuating collection of faiths. These figures believe not just in the *Lear* pantheon but also in Islam, Judaism, Fate, witchcraft, demonism proper, the old courtly-love worship, resurgent classical paganism, alchemy, the code of *reputatio* and manly/aristocratic honor, the apotheosis of the individual will, and a spectrum of Catholic and Protestant articles of faith. And to express this theme of human religious diversity, the dramatist employs at least two devices that will bear detailed examination: a multicultural setting and a crucial use of images of liquidity, particularly water, which by its very nature underlines the play's preoccupation with constancy and change, surface and substance.

Othello cries for a theological approach, if only because no other Shakespearean Folio work contains more references to "heaven." Criticism has long noted the tragedy's affinities to martyrology and to morality plays: the dialogue itself likens Desdemona to an "angel," and Iago is a self-confessed ally of the devil(1.3.358; cf. 2.3.345–48, 5.2.284–85). To judge from Iago's opening self-description—"I am not what I am"—he is an anti-type of the Creator, who identified himself as "I AM THAT I AM" (Ex.3:14; cf. *Lear*. 4.7.70). Every one of the play's scenes, in fact, warrants biblical parallels and glosses (cf. Shaheen, Milward, Noble).

Like all life conceived by the early modern imagination, the action of *Othello* transpires on both a temporal and an eternal stage. An obvious exemplar of this phenomenon is the concept of grace, which amphibiously moves between Christian and secular contexts. Deriving from the Latin *gratia*, which means favor and in favor, the medieval English word "grace" denoted Jesus' presence in any sacrament, including marriage (Lehmkuhl). Secularly, it became a signifier of high social rank (denoting members of the signiory in *Othello*). "Grace" is also the name of a simple attractive personal trait (Othello is in love with Desdemona's "parts and . . . graces"). And finally, "grace" can be an inner human excellence externally conferred upon *and/or* internally generated by a person. This last is part of what Iago has in mind when he speaks resentfully of the "daily beauty in [Cassio's] life," which renders Iago contemptible both in his own eyes and those of others (5.1.19–20). Cassio uses a particularly complicated allusion to grace when he prays for and to Desdemona:

> the grace of heaven,
> Before, behind thee, and on every hand,
> Enwheel thee round! (2.1.85–87)

To the extent that he sees her as a superlatively beautiful woman, he is acknowledging heaven's role in creating her earthly excellence. But insofar as he worships her in a quasi-religious fashion, he sees her as a manifestation of supernatural grace, and says it seems to emanate from her. Finally, his words can constitute not just a statement but an entreaty: a prayer that this fellow human will be surrounded by heaven's grace in all its protective capacity.

As befits so theological a dramatization of Christian marriage, the audience is encouraged to recall biblical injunctions and concerns. There are three prime virtues, St. Paul writes: "faith, hope and love," and "the chiefest" of these is love or charity, which "doeth never fall away" (1 Cor. 13:8,13). Love "Suffreth all things, "believeth all things," "hopeth all things," and "endureth all things." John, in fact, states that "God *is* Love" "and he that dwelleth in Love dwelleth in God, and God in him" (1 Jn. 4:8, 16; italics supplied). James and Peter add that Love covers and "hide[s]" a "multitude of sinnes " (1 Pet. 4:8; Jas. 4:20).

From classical pagan as well as Hebrew traditions, there developed the idea that Love is the organizing principle of the universe. Desdemona and, intermittently, her husband are of this opinion. Desdemona affirms a holiness in love, when she states, "That death's unnatural that kills for loving." At practically the last moment of her life, when she is about to meet her Maker, Desdemona quibblingly resorts to a lie, but a loving one, when she asks to be commended to her "kind lord" (5.2.123)—that is, not only to the Lord of heaven but also to her lord on earth, whose essential kindness she wishes to affirm, despite how his actions appear to contradict it. Although her final act on behalf of her husband contains a falsehood, she seems to be conforming to the spirit of Jesus' injunction:

> Love your enemies; bless them that curse you: do good to them that hate you,
> and praye for them which hurt you, and persecute you. (Matt. 5:44)

In dying she would save Othello from execution. Even after he slaps her and subjects her to verbal cruelty in public before her uncle, she sees his behavior as part of a post-honeymoon hiatus, pleading that husbands are not always "god," able to keep "such observancy / as fits the bridal" (3.4.149–51).

Othello, in turn, speaks of his relationship with Desdemona as the banishment of personal chaos, the condition of the "earth" when it was "without forme and voyde, and darknes was upon the depe" (Gen. 1:1–2):

> perdition catch my soul
> But I do love thee! and when I love thee not
> Chaos is come again. (3.3.90–92)

When he dissociates himself from this love, he speaks of blowing it back to heaven and plighting a troth in "hate" to snaky "hell" (3.3.446–53). It may well seem to some spectators that he has organized his whole being around love—a love that he associates with heavenly Love, even when he lachrymosely prepares to kill his wife:

> So sweet was ne'er so fatal. I must weep,
> But they are cruel tears. This sorrow's heavenly,
> It strikes where it doth love (5.2.20–22)

On Christian marriage, Paul's remarks, though chauvinistic and puritanical by today's standards, are carefully nuanced and were central to both Catholic and Protestant marital doctrine. Believing that the end of the world is near, Paul prefers that Christians not marry, for "he that is maried, careth for the things of the worlde, how he maie please *his* wife" (12 Cor. 7:33). Those who are married or wish to marry, however, he admonishes to comfort one another physically, the husband "lov[ing] their wives, as their own bodies," "nouris[hing] and cheris[hing] it" as if it "his owne fleshe," "even as the Lord *doeth* the Church" (Eph. 5:21–29). This view is, of course, a natural extension of the Hebrew metaphor of the chosen people as Yahweh's loved ones: worthy to be wooed, instructed, and, when necessary, forgiven.

The application of these teachings to the problems of Othello, Desdemona, and most of the minor characters would seem relevant to some early modern spectators as they watched Othello penitently kissing the beloved he has slain —or noticed Iago's lack of self-esteem, secular fidelity, and affectionate commitment. One deficiency implies another, for not only are heaven and earth implicated in each other, but so too are the virtues of each place. St. Paul, for instance, comes very close to seeing hope as a form of faith when he writes that:

> . . . we are saved by hope . . . [in] what we see not [and] . . . with patience
> abide for . . . (Romans 8:24–25)

To have hope in one's God, certainly, involves love and a large measure of faith. For Iago to have confidence in his ability to be loved by other human beings, he has to risk a faith in and love for them. We never see him venturing along any of these paths, nor does he show signs of regretting that he does not do so. Any love he has is murderously twisted; and any faith, restricted only to himself.

Highlighting the importance of faith and love are the allusions to the mesocosmic enemy, the Turk. Turks presumably lack the loving truth/troth that unify things of this earth with heaven. Although the infidel status of Islam as a rebellious offshoot of Judaeo-Christian faith is not made explicit in the dialogue, every spectator would be acquainted with this prejudiced assessment. What we do hear is that Turkishness is an attack on Love and/or Faith. For as Iago exclaims in his "honesty" disguise, "it is true, or else I am a Turk" (2.1.114). To "turn Turk" meant literally to be an blaspheming apostate, renouncing Christianity for Islam—or to become a sensualist (Vitkus 157) and as Othello seems to use the term, engage in un-Christian rebellion and internecine strife, the like of which stereotypically greeted, supposedly, any change of regimes in both Ottoman and Christian parts of the Middle East:

> Are we turned Turks, and to ourselves do that
> Which heaven hath forbid the Ottomites?
> For Christian shame, put by this barbarous brawl. (2.3.266–68)

> a malignant and a turban'd Turk
> Beat a Venetian and traduced the state. (5.2.350–51)

For Othello, an alien who never lived long in civilian Venetian society, the role of the Judaeo-Christian husband is an especially challenging one. After all, he is capable of taking seriously the idea that his noble bride and upperclass lieutenant are naked Adamites, practicing the Cathar-like *coitus interruptus* rumored prevalent in the Anglo-Dutch sect of the Family of Love[1]:

> In Venice they do let God see the pranks
> They dare not show their husbands; their best conscience
> Is not to leave't undone, but keep't unknown. (3.3.205–07)
> Or to be naked with her friend in bed
> An hour or more, not meaning any harm. (4.1.3–4)

The Familists' activities, it is perhaps significant to note, are sometimes thought to be reflected in Bosch's popular *Garden of Earthly Delights*. This astounding painting, well-known in sixteenth–century Hapsburg Europe, combines numerous scenes of nakedness, marked by highly erotic play among pairs and groups of whites, and whites and, oftenest, male blacks.

Othello's task of being a good Venetian Christian husband is rendered especially difficult because he seeks three diverse goals simultaneously: (1) a Pauline ministry to his wife's mind:

> Vouch with me, heaven, I therefore beg it not,
> To please the palate of my appetite,
> Nor to comply with heat, the young affects
> In me defunct, and proper satisfaction.
> But to be free and bounteous to her mind. (1.3.262–66)

(2) a Pauline service to her bodily being:

> Come, my dear love,
> The purchase made, the fruits are to ensue:
> That profit's yet to come 'tween me and you. (2.3.8–10)

and (3) a worshipful and communion-like consumption of her as the ultimate source of his being:

> where I have garnered up my heart,
> Where either I must live or bear no life,
> The fountain from the which my current runs. (4.2.58–60)

He places Desdemona in a role reserved for Christ alone, the genuine and eternal fountain of water; or as Revelation puts it, "the Lambe . . . shal leade them unto the livelie fountaines of waters" (Rev. 7:17).

What lexicon can possibly interpret for us Othello's final allegation that he truly "loved" the "pearl"–like Desdemomna "too well" (5.2.342, 345)?

> For what shal it profite a man though he shulde winne the whole worlde, if he lose his owne soule? Or what shal a man give for recompense of his soule (Matt. 16:26, cf. Mk 8:36–37)

Has he so *treasured* her that she has become for him an earthly thing more precious, as Iago claims, than the fountain of "baptism,/ All seals and symbols of redeemed sin" (2.3.338–39) (Redemption means buying back, a process which a onetime slave would not readily forget.) Has he failed to remember the verse that circulates below the surface when Emilia endorses an adultery that will purchase "the whole world" (5.2.78)

Othello dies still in love with Desdemona but a hopeless suicide, certain that he deserves whatever punishment that God, the state, or his own position in the state confers. Would it be right for either God or man to forgive such a man even for his deficiencies in faith and hope, just because he possesses love, even a dreadfully flawed love?

Because this tragedy is one of Shakespeare's most theological, spectators of all creeds peer out from God's judgment seat—as it were—at the last "compt" (5.2.271). A secret of the play's appeal is that to watch or read this fiction attentively becomes an innocent act of sacrilege and blasphemy. From our seats, we judge not only the characters' actions but also the theology of an inscrutable, even putatively cruel, Providence. This is often the God of the Book of Job (itself instanced in 4.2.47-54) or of Romans 9:18, which reiterates the Torah's harsh message that God "hathe mercie on whome he wil, and whome he wil, he hardeneth."

No reflective spectator would charge the Deity unforgivingly with Desdemona's undeserved death: the role of a worthy victim *is* to suffer without final loss of faith or hope or love, and to be forthwith rewarded in another life.

But that is not Othello's case. He is a man who rejects hope. Othello is a suicide as well as a murderer, and he does not plead for God's forgiveness (Bethell, Siegel, Hunt). But he does die expressing love for Desdemona, and faith in her, God, and justice. Is the emotionally insecure, culturally ignorant Othello rightly to be damned by God, who has tested him in the fires of Iago's hellishly sick intellect? Is it too much to expect God to act as mercifully to Othello as Desdemona had done, when she excused her murder almost as readily as she had excused his slap and verbal cruelty? She sees them all almost as mere post-honeymoon slips, maintaining that husbands cannot always be expected to imitate the "gods" and keep to "such observances /As fit the bridal" (3.4.151).

The sense of religious diversity during the age of exploration and colonialism is here implicated in the work's settings: Venice and Cyprus, and virtually, London. This last is evoked by references to or hints of predestination, the Family of Love, English folksongs, tavern songs, and references to military and sexual customs.

The religious diversity of commercial Venice and of the Mediterranean islands that she often protected was widely known to playgoers, if only from watching *The Merchant of Venice* or *The Jew of Malta*. Indeed, Venice was as pragmatic as any rich imperial and mercantile state must eventually be, and accommodated resident aliens of several colors, creeds, and nations. For a long while, she seemed to Protestant Northern Europeans the best hope in Italy of accommodation with Catholic Europe. The Venetian dependency on Cyprus periodically passed under Ottoman control, and connoted a world where Jew, Moslem, and Christian vied for power—a world, many spectators would remember, where Eastern Christianity met that of the West. The text explicitly reminds us that the currency here is the "crusad[o]" (3.4.26; Hecht, 64), commemorating the Roman Catholic expeditions against the Moslems, Jews—and fellow Christians of other stripes. Besides, in the old pagan faith, Cyprus was the haunt of foam-born ("Aphro-dite") Venus, who emerged from the sea where Zeus had thrown her father's severed genitals. The scholarly viewer might thus recall that the Cyprian shore on which Venus landed was the scene of Desdemona's own disembarking to a life of love—and death.

And at the first appearance of *Othello*, the port and city of London itself was beginning to assume the role of replacing Venice as one of the world's greatest business and colonial headquarters. A Moslem Moorish emissary had recently been in residence, the streets had numerous refugees—economic, ethnic, and religious—from such forces as that of Spanish religious persecution in the Iberian peninsula, northern Italy, the Low Countries and so forth. Catholic priests and nonconforming preachers of all sorts were coming to England. According to current estimates, the Catholic and radical Protestant contingency in the country was quite large. London, port and city, was taking on many of the qualities of imperial, mercantile Venice, with its diversity of aliens ethnically, racially, and religiously. The tone in London about 1601 is likely, however, to have been less hospitable than that in Venice: the Moorish ambassador departed with no treaty and a clutch of unpaid bills for his keep; and a "blackamoor" threat to native employment (and worse?) was addressed by the government, which rounded up free blacks and shipped them out of the kingdom by formal edict (Honigmann, 16, 29). Shakespeare's audiences knew that they were daily jostled in the London streets, and theaters, by people whom, however, their government and many fellow playgoers felt called upon to condemn as heretics or public nuisances. Altogether, the relative lack of tolerance of difference in England would have made the Other that they repelled on the street more romantic and manageable in the theater—a safer model to anatomize and to learn from.

We can never know the extent to which Shakespeare and his audience would consciously apply to the play what they already knew of the Mediterranean world. But the play does record obvious remarks about Turkish and Jewish(?) perfidy, Moroccan innocence and jealousy, African pagan barbarism, occultist spells and fortune-telling, cannibalism, and the like. Moreover, the Bible itself, not to mention the Koran, indicates the status of Middle-Eastern women in cases of sexual infidelity. Adulterers in Jesus' time could be stoned to death, and the Koran authorizes a wronged husband to immure an unfaithful wife and let her starve to death. Even today, public executions of adulterers are not unknown in the Islamic world, and several Arab countries grant *de facto* immunity to males who murder any female family member for dishonoring the household.

Creedal multiplicity in this play is increased by the fact that several characters have varied religious identities that they do not necessarily explicitly acknowledge, but that certain spectators cannot help but consider. Iago is a *self-confessed* ally of hell. Desdemona, it can be shown, is a type of Christ and Mary. Othello is connected not only with "pagan[s]" and "devil[s]" as his critics onstage maintain, but subtextually he could remind some spectators of the good gentile Balthazar, the Magus (Lupton, 77) or, conversely Ham, punished by discoloration after he broke sexual and religious taboos.[2] Othello is even associated with Jesus; both are repeatedly called lord/Lord, and when on trial are greeted with similar salutations: "Here is the man" (1.2.72), which may easily recall Pilate's "*Ecce homo,*" "Behold the man"*(*Jn. 19:5). Continual alternations and variations occur in the characters' religious identity and status. And as these changes are rung, early modern audiences are encouraged to contemplate how similar phenomena occur in their own worlds, and in their own beings.

Iago stands as a reminder that holding to Christian doctrines is no guarantee that a person is going to avoid evil for he, in effect, worships the devil, not God. Like a Catholic, he classifies sins by gradation, though his own system of measurement would not always meet with Catholic approbation, as when he claims that Othello and Cassio's supposed lusting after Emilia is exactly as sinful as Iago's own unnatural urge to bed Desdemona out of cold-blooded revenge (2.1.289–92). In Catholicism sins of the flesh are usually less heinous than those of hard reason.

Iago combines a faith in his own will and the power of fate and chance, as well as of hell:

> let me see now,
> To get [Cassio's] place and to plume up my will
> In double knavery: How? How? let's see:
> . . .

> I have't. It is engendred! Hell and night
> Must bring this monstrous birth to the world's light. (1.3.391–403)

In the matter of will, here he is close to a Pelagian (Battenhouse, 380–84; Hunter 128) or Stoic faith, even though he knows it does not really work. In preaching secular voluntarism to simple Roderigo, Iago shows such unusual vehemence that we may suspect that the ancient is himself a true believer: in "our wills" . . . "we have reason to cool our raging motions, our carnal stings, our unbitted lusts" (1.3.321, 330–32). Yet he shows no ability to control the burning poison of jealousy that he says is painfully within him.

Roderigo and his intellectual superior Brabantio are examples of upper-class Catholics who would embrace racism, murderous revenge, and suicide. By play's end Brabantio is judged as someone likely to have "curse[d] his better angel from his side" and through "desperate" suicide incurred "reprobance" or reprobation (5.2.205–207; Hunt, 352; cf. Milward, 107); words that pull us into a Calvinist more than a Catholic discourse: a world where a sinner's sudden loss of faith is forecast/predestined by a God, who, cognizant of all humans' perfidy, has, in his inscrutable wisdom, decided not to reverse or forgive this particular instance of sin

The most thoroughly Christian, subtype Catholic figure in the play is doubtless Brabantio's daughter. Though Desdemona can be accused of self-important nagging, presumption towards her husband, and tactlessness, she truly cares for both her husband and other human beings. She is adept in upper-class accomplishments and is almost unceasingly possessed of a good heart. Her husband admits that in the post-consummation relationship, her "chastity" has been "cold" (5.2.273–74) but that need not be the entire truth nor, if it is, a particularly damning admission. St. Jerome argued that "a husband who is too ardent a lover of his wife" is guilty of "adulter[y]" (Neill,140). Protetant views on sexual pleasure in marriage were somewhat less severe on husbands, but wives were especially cautioned to keep their native hypersexuality under control..

Some scholars have wondered whether Desdemona's behavior blasphemously presumes on her own innocence (Rice, 217–18) in the face of death (Hunt, 361–62)—the charge made against Job by his comforters. According to Protestantism, a person with a chance of being saved will sense his/her participation in universal human corruption and will know that self-accusation and abject surrender to God are the only appropriate sentiments with which to exit this world. Admittedly, Desdemona does not literally fulfill these requirements, but she does die expressing love. In addition, throughout her life, she is charitable, trying to placate her father, speaking with affectionate humility to Iago, and committing her safety and reputation to danger for the sake of Cassio and Othello alike. We sense that she would do anything for Emilia, so great is the love Desdemona inspires in the latter. As for marital fidelity,

Desdemona is so full of saintly innocence and commitment that she can barely imagine how women are unfaithful to their husbands (4.3.60–82). In this play with its double clock creating two sets of realities, there is an analogous sense in which Desdemona remains *spiritually* a virgin until the concluding moments of the play, when her blood is shed on the wedding sheets and she receives Othello's final kiss.

Although Desdemona never thinks of herself as a Mary figure, let alone a Christ figure (even if she resumes breathing and speech after apparent death), Cassio does grant her this status, and the dramatist gives her actions and lines in likely support of these symbolic identities. Unlike Catholicism and the Eastern churches, Protestantism denies any role in salvation to Mary and the other saints. For Jesus, reconciling God to man is the one intermediary between sinful man and the Father. Noteworthy, therefore, is Desdemona's language of advocacy of Cassio's pardon. Marian piety is fond of promising that the Mother of God is likely to persuade her Son to hear any moral human prayer that goes through her (Ashe). Desdemona's diction has a likely religious connotation when she avers, "If I do vow a friendship, I'll perform it / To the last article" "Good my lord,/If I have any *grace or power* to move you,/ [Cassio's] present *reconciliation* take (3.3, 21–22, 45–47, italics supplied). The language of this last speech continues in the Marian theme—Desdemona is a figure of "grace"—and anticipates Shakespeare's constellation of religious ideas in *The Tempest*, where he has a Christ-like Miranda beg her magician-father to save "fraughting souls," as she would "Had [she] been any god of power" (1.2.10–13)—a god-like action he had indeed taken on his own.

Emilia, in contrast to her husband, has a diversity of commitments rather than of faiths, a distinction captured in her fantasy of walking barefoot to Jerusalem for a sexual favor (4.3.37–38). Like Catholics and unlike strictest Protestants, she believes in purgatory and does not classify all sins as equal rejections of God's grace. Instead, she categorizes adultery as "a small vice," worthy only of "purgatory" (4.3.69, 76), a location whose existence is of course denied by Protestantism. Emilia is uninformed about the very Catholicism she professes: not only is adultery usually a grave sin but committing any serious sin in coldblood—here for a material reward to please her husband— would arrogantly presume on her God's Catholic mercy, which does not automatically provide occasions for timely and adequate repentance; a necessary condition for entry into purgatory.

By play's end, in her dying moment, Emilia arrives at a truer Christianity. Though retaining her anger at Othello and Iago, she affirms her love for Desdemona, and Desdemona's fidelity to her and to marital troth: "she was chaste, she loved thee, cruel Moor, / So come my soul to bliss as I speak true" (5.2.247 –48). Thus, with no Catholic thoughts about purgatory, Emilia dedicates her life to Desdemona's posthumous reputation on earth, and while doing so, affirms her own faith in a higher Christian eternity.

Othello and Cassio display even more theological complexity and diversity than the other characters do. Cassio's Catholicism is of a richly mixed sort. He has an *amour courtois* crush on his employer's wife, and somewhat blasphemously confers upon her the Catholic status of the Virgin Mary. Elsewhere he teeters on the Catholic-Calvinist breach in babbling drunkenly about redemption, predestination, and merit (Hunt, 346–51; cf. Coursen 197–98, Frye 147):

> I hold him to be unworthy of his place that [listens to frivolous drinking
> songs]. Well, God's above all; and there be souls must be saved, and there be
> souls must not be saved . . . I hope to be saved . . .; the lieutenant is to be
> saved before the ancient. (2.3.293–305)

Worse, Cassio affirms the unchristian belief that his "immortal" soul is identical with his reputation (2.3.255)—a premise that is but one of the many religiously suspect views that he voices throughout the play.

Like many of his even-Christians, Othello is also often open to multiple irreconcilable beliefs. But the sincerity of his conversion is beyond doubt. Othello's language is immersed in heartfelt Christian idioms and thought patterns, even if his mind merges the Creator with the created, Christ with Desdemona, as when he thinks of his life as a "pilgrimage," not to the Holy Land but to Desdemona's Christian Venice (cf. Manzanas Calvo, 233):

> [I] dr[e]w from her a *prayer* of earnest heart
> That I would all my *pilgrimage* dilate. (1.3.153–54,
> italics supplied)

In the final scene alone (5.2), he passionately affirms a faith in divinity, the last "compt," "fiends," and "soul[s]" "hurl[ed] from heaven." Earlier he swears angrily "by the worth of man's eternal soul"; he sees himself as tested more severely than Job; and when he calls oratorical skills a divine "blessing"("Rude am I in my speech, / And little bless'd with the soft phrase of peace"). More than other men, his experience of slavery encourages him to treasure both earthly and supernatural redemption. Though truth makes us free, as Jesus says, love encourages surrender of freedom in vows of sacred Christian troth—a risk he has faith enough to take. Though Othello acts irrationally in a horrendous way, he tries consciously to be a good Venetian general and governor, which means to be a Christian of at least as strong a religious orientation as Brabantio.

All the same, Othello is marked by the most diverse of faiths in this play. Awareness of Italian moral and theological outlooks sometimes sits shakily on the alien hero. Hence, as we have already seen, he can be persuaded that Venetian Catholic custom includes lying naked with a "friend" in bed and not intending intercourse. Doubtless, one of the most intriguing, sympathetic, and forgivable sides to Othello is the variety of religious experiences available to this vulnerable ex-prince, ex-slave from infidel Africa. For his exposure to a diversity of religious cultures make him as fascinating to audiences as he was in act 1 to Desdemona, Brabantio, and the Duke. Othello could "dilate" movingly on ancient or modern, familiar or exotic, true or legendary events and customs until nothing seems incredible to him.

The Moor's soul is a palimpsest or photomontage: whatever has been in it can arise again from a new trajectory into a new concatenation. He possesses the same fatalism that had been circulating in the Mediterranean since classical antiquity. Some "fate," he says is "unknown" (2.1.191); other, like the cuckoldry destined for "great ones," is all too predictable:

> Destiny unshunnable,like death:
> Even then this forked plague is fated to us
> When we do quicken. (3.3.279–81)

And like many Christians today, he somehow reconciles his religious faith with an astrology that denies free will; he argues that the path of the "moon" . . . "makes men mad," including him, as he proceeds towards murder (5.2.108–10). Also, he evinces his obsessive interest in North African animism and witchcraft. Even if a part of him does not believe in the powers that he claims to Desdemona inhere in his family's handkerchief (3.4.57-77), another part of him is so involved in his speech that he seems to become self-convinced of what he is saying, or at least can talk himself into speaking fanatically about it.

Most tragically of all, after he slays Desdemona, he loathes himself as a pagan "Indian" (Quarto, 5.2.345—from either the New World or the Asian subcontinent). Or else as a faithless "Judean"—that is, simultaneously a Judas and a Jew, rejecting Desdemona/Jesus, a "pearl" beyond price (Folio, 5.2.345; Matt. 13:46; Noble 91–93, Siegel, 1072). Furthermore, Othello believes himself worthy of punishment not just as a murderer and someone who has upset the military government of Cyprus but as an alien whose sins are compounded by his being a "circumcised" and "malignant" *Moslem* ("turbanned Turk," 5.2.351–53).

With great ease, Othello also projects himself beyond the three sister religions, the occult, and animism into a world of ancient Roman paganism (see Hecht, 68–84). He seems, in fact, to think of himself as more an antique Roman than a Moslem Moroccan. For instance, he has his household say that his native land is not Morocco but "Mauretania" (4.2.225), the long gone Roman province from which Morocco gets its name. Too, when he is angered to see Cassio, a Renaissance Florentine, bragging over sexual conquest, Othello pictures Cassio as a long-"nose[d]" ancient "Roman" engaging in an ancient "triumph" (4.1.119, 141). Here and elsewhere, Othello goes far beyond what is expected of someone with a Renaissance humanist education. The pagan pantheon is especially alive for Othello. Even though he stops short of seeing that he is playing Mars to her Venus in Cyprus, he is pleased to see her arrayed at dockside as a "warrior" (2.1.179)—the sort of court costume by which many a Renaissance princess could be transformed into Minerva Armata. More seriously pagan, however, is his exclamation that he no longer can be an earthly Jove, commanding the cannons of war as Jove does with the thunder and lightning:

> O you mortal engines, whose rude throats
> That th'immortal Jove's dread clamours counterfeit. (3.3.358–59)

The word "Jove" is not a simple substitute invented when Jacobean censors curtailed casual reference to the Deity in stage plays. Rather, this passage unmistakably shows that for the general, "immortal" Jupiter can be as vividly present as Jehovah is. Significant too is the fact that where most Catholics might think of Mary or chaste saints as models for Desdemona's purity, Othello's mind gravitates instead to "*Dian*'s visage" (3.3.390). It is revealing that he also sees himself as the victim of a professional Tyche, or fortune/fate beyond anything sanctified by Christianity. He is cuckolded, he says, by one who is charming enough to have lain by an "emperor's side" and "command[ed]" him(4.1.180–81)—an allusion that implicitly compounds *romanitas* from elsewhere in the play (for instance Iago's calling Othello's lieutenant a "soldier fit to stand by Caesar," 2.3.118). When talking of the antecedents for his cuckolding, he seems to think his life is simply lived in the pattern of the uxorious Roman Emperor Claudius. Desdemona is another Empress Messalina, the nymphomaniac who serviced great numbers of men in a given night. And thus it is not unthinkable that "the general camp, / Pioneers and all, had tasted her sweet body" (3.3.348–49).

Detail after detail directs *Othello* audiences to religious concerns, particularly to religious diversity. The final tableau of the richly furnished bed with its candles (lit or not) and its three victims of love, ironically parallels a Catholic altar, with its relics of those who imitated the God of Love. To preserve a sense of the uniqueness of Christ's saving death on the cross, Anglicanism forbad candles and rich accoutrements on the communion table during the commemoration of the Last Supper. Catholicism, by contrast, taught that the Mass is a bloodless re-enactment of the events on Golgotha, not just as a commemoration but itself a source of saving grace. The spectators at, and emotional participants in, this secular Mass are, of course, the theater audience.

Another device encouraging awareness of religious diversity is the play's references to liquids. The story is set on water, drowned in tears, and concerned with a man whom even baptism will not wash clean of original blackness—a cruel enactment of the old biblical proverb about the impossibility of washing an Ethiope. Try as he can to steer his bark aright, he ends with the "Bloody period" and "sea-mark" of suicide. Travel in the first of the play's settings is by "gondol[a] (1.1.123); ships take us to the second setting, beloved of foam-born Aphrodite, who emerged from the sea where her father's severed genitals were cast. Explicit fluids or fluid-related items are everywhere in this tragedy. Soldiers overindulge in alcohol, people refer to "drown[ing] cats and blind puppies," or being "Wash[ed]" in "gulfs of liquid [hell-]fire" (1.3.337,5.2.280) Handkerchiefs are dyed in virgins' mummified blood; characters meditate on touching the "filth[y]" "slime" that "sticks" to sexual deeds, or squirting enema water into the mouth, or viewing the spawning fluids of reptiles and amphibian polluting the characters' water cisterns (3.4.76; 5.2.146–47; 2.1.176; 3.3.274–77; 4.1.60–63).

The presentational images of explosives and the rattling of wind and thunder machines in 2.1 would make the storm at sea an unforgettable part of the play's liquid imagery. It is also a part that significantly expands and advances the sense of the play's religiously diverse perspectives. Whereas Shakespeare's source, Cinthio, explicitly states that the wedded couple sailed together over calm seas on their way to Cyprus (Honigmann, 373), Shakespeare introduces a horrendous tempest that foregrounds the issue of providence. God lets through the vessels of the Christian Venetians, but wrecks the ships of the Ottoman infidels (not to mention the lives of the newly wedded couple!). The characters' prayerful testimonials to God's intervention in Mediterranean politics must have triggered many thoughts in the original audience: memories of Biblical salvation from water in the time of Noah, Moses, Jonah, Paul; the saving of the apostles on the Sea of Galilee; and the wreck of the Spanish Armada, enlisted by the Pope to displace the Virgin Queen and reestablish Roman Catholicism in England. According to most English Protestants and some Catholics, the defeat of this invasion was like the drowning of Pharoah's army as it pursued God's people across the Red Sea. But an effect of Shakespeare's fictive event may have been to problematize such happenings for many spectators in their own lives. To create religious unease is to manufacture religious diversity.

In Cassio's eyes, however, the safe arrival of Iago, Emilia, and the General's wife is achieved by the "divine" . . . "beauty" of Desdemona herself, who can change the innate rebellious "natures" of storms, granting "most favourable and happy speed" to "barks."

> Tempests themselves, high seas, and howling winds,
> The guttered rocks and congregated sands,
> Traitors ensteeped to clog the guiltless keel,
> As having sense of beauty, do omit

> Their mortal natures, letting go safely by
> The divine Desdemona. (2.1.68–73)

What Cassio has done is to affirm two faiths—one Courtly and the other Marian-heading-in-the direction-of-Messianic. He implicitly casts her as The Lady that all courtly lovers worshipped from, supposedly, afar. And yet secondarily he also likens her to Our Lady, the model for the courtly lady. Eastern Orthodoxy and Roman Catholicism venerate Mary as the Mother of God, but stop short of granting to her an actual divinity, or salvific equality with the Son. Yet Cassio comes close to doing so, and even confers on Desdemona qualities of a pagan Eastern love-goddess who is marrying a "divine" king:

> Great Jove, Othello guard,
> And swell his sail with thine own powerful breath
> That he may bless this bay with his tall ship,
> Make love's quick pants in Desdemona's arms,
> Give renew'd fire to our extincted spirits
> And bring all Cyprus comfort! (2.1.77–82)

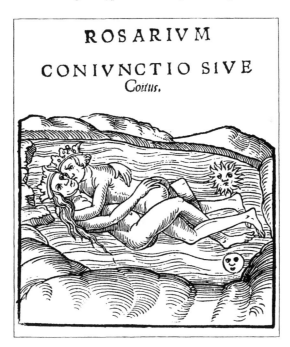

FIGURE 14. Consummation of Red King and White Queen in alchemical liquid. *Rosarium Philosphorum* (1550). Permission of Harry Ransom Humanities Research Center. University of Texas, Austin.

Cassio suddenly seems a believer in both Jove and Lord Othello's power to "bless," seeing the General's marriage not only as a communal ritual of solidarity, for which there is some scriptural and theological warrant, but also as a source of "spirit[ual]" enlightenment and invigoration for a whole population. How many in the audience would immediately grasp here a metaphor drawn not so much from Christianity as from pagan Middle Eastern dogmas about monarchy, the sort of belief that Shakespeare knew that Julius Caesar and Antony wanted to manipulate?

In Cassio's language, some spectators might also catch a whiff of alchemy when he describes the governor and his consort's initial act of love radiating warmth to the entire population of the island. According to Arnold of Villanova's influential *Rosarium Philosophorum* of 1550, a royal *"coitus"* in seawater is a visual symbol for the initial purifying stage in the transformation of lead into gold (Fig 14). This transformation is in turn, writes Lyndy Abraham, an image for the even more desirable *spiritual* transformation that the alchemist can facilitate, of "earthly man into the divine" through an androgynous union. This union is presided over by "sacrifice or death," and leads to personal integration and, ultimately, "pure love": "the perfect union of creative will or power (male) with wisdom (female) to produce pure love" (Abraham, 37).

Interestingly, the royal alchemical couple consists of a dark (red) sulphurous Sun King and his far paler Lunar Queen. In several portrayals, this royal female is denoted by the astrological/alchemical/chemical sign that is shared by Venus, femininity, and copper, the metal linguistically associated with Cyprus. In other portrayals, the Lunar Queen is associated with silver, the metal of the virgin-like "Dian," as is, of course, Desdemona.

Cassio worships Desdemona, and Iago and Roderigo highlight this procedure by discussing whether she is blessed. Roderigo claims that she is "full of most blest condition" while Iago scoffs, "Blest fig-end," . . . "Blest pudding," and maintains that her wine is simply physical and earthly, and that her choice of husband is less than holily inspired (2.1.248–51). Spectators of all creeds might indeed doubt that any aspect of her could still a storm—a trait that the synoptic gospels use to point to Jesus' superhuman status, saying "Who is this that commandeth bothe the windes and the water, and they obey him!" (Luke 8.25): But this is not Cassio's view when he exclaims,

> Ye men of Cyprus, let her have your knees.
> Hail to thee, lady, and the grace of heaven,
> Before, behind thee, and on every hand
> Enwheel thee round! (2.1.85–87)

In the context of the passage, the command to let Desdemona have one's "knees" goes beyond what the recent Arden editor suggests—namely a curtsy.

Conceivably there is a reference to a requirement in Protestant England that all kneel when the Virgin Queen passed on her way to the royal chapel. But certainly the main subtext for the kneeling reference is Paul's words on celebrating the name of Jesus in response to his kenosis. Though "equal with God," Jesus humbly took on humanity and suffered death:

> Wherefore God hathe . . . highly exalted him, and given him a Name above everie name, That at the Name of Jesus shulde everie knee bowe. (Philippians 2:5–10)

Cassio never quite applies to Desdemona the Marian epithet "Star of the Sea," "Queen of Heaven," or "Mother of God," but he surely depicts her as going beyond the human, "tir[ing] the inginer" to imagine or describe.

The Marian hyperboles in this scene must have called to some spectators' minds the divisions of faith in the very audience itself. Some spectators would sense here the litmus test of the Ave Maria. This medieval prayer, though based in part on words in Luke's gospel, was a battle cry of the wars of religion—an unsubtle reminder of religious diversity and for some spectators, of Cassio's otherness:

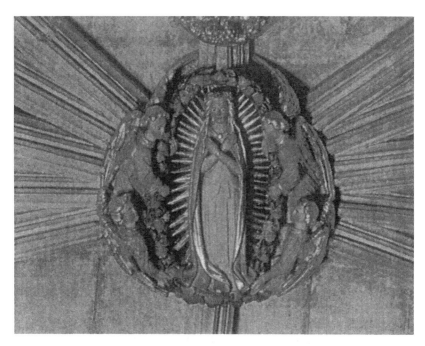

FIGURE 15. Rays in medieval Assumption boss, central arch in altar screen. York Minster. Permission of Pitkin Unichrome, by Sidney Newberry.

Hail Mary, full of grace. The Lord is with thee. Blessed art thou amongst women, and blessed is the fruit of thy womb, Jesus; . . . pray for us sinners now and at the hour of our death.

Cassio's notion of Desdemona's being "wheel[ed]" about with "grace" should be seen in a Marian context, where rays emanate from portrayals of Our Lady (and her cosmic prototype from the Book of Revelation)—rays visible in the Assumption that still crowns the arch of the medieval altar-screen in York Minster (*Visitors' Guide* and Figure 15).

Cassio goes far beyond humanist Pertrachism in making Desdemona "the riches of the ship," hinting that his "captain's captain" (12.3.83, 74) is a Noah and a Moses as well as a Mary. She is a "bark" (2.1.48) that implicitly contains —if we may make a quibble—the *ark* of a new covenant between God and man.[3] Because the final supplication in the "Hail Mary" is for the Virgin to "pray for us sinners now and at the hour of our death," Cassio's allusion to the prayer has at least two ironical applications. For one thing, Desdemona is a virgin who will indeed do a lot of 'praying' to her lord on behalf of Cassio himself. In another irony, Othello will soon crave 'the hour of his own death' right on the dockside, wanting to die after the couple's first Cyprian kiss. Desdemona, who begged not to be left at home and be deprived of her marital "rites" (1.3.259), is more a Venus than a Mary or Diana, and exclaims, "The heavens forbid / But that our loves and comforts should increase, / Even as our days do grow" (2.1.191–93).

Storms at sea, the water of a christening, perhaps even alchemical transformations would be familiar and significant to many early modern English audiences. So too would the notion of the power of God-involving love: including Othello's dying kiss for Desdemona, his *gestural* plea for loving kindness on earth and in heaven on behalf of his Jesus-and-Mary intercessor; the flesh by which he reenacted Christ's love for his church.

But what we may not immediately realize is that a simple glass of pure water might not be for Othello the transmitter of divinity. Rainy England, with its rural polluted wells and its erratic urban water systems, drank fermented brews at every meal, and almost never does Shakespeare focus on Matthew's and Mark's reference to Jesus' supreme praise for anyone who gives water to another:

I thursted, and ye gave me drinke . . . in as muche as ye have done it unto one of the least of these my brethren, ye have done it to me. (Matt. 25:35, 40)

To appreciate water truly, one must be from a dry part of the Mediterranean: Judea, or the land of an Othello or Caliban, where bubbling springs and water storage are absolute essentials to life. Othello, as we have already seen, refers to Desdemona as:

> where I have garnered up my heart
> The fountain from the which my current runs,
> Or else dries up—to be discarded thence!
> Or keep it as a cistern for foul toads
> To knot and gender in! (4.2.58–63)

Scholarship (Honigmann, 339) has correctly identified here a likely allusion to the Tudor *Homilies*, where whoredom is identified as a filthy collection of water, and to Proverbs 5, where husbands are exhorted to be faithful to their wives, and not to resort to "strangers with thee" or a nearby "dore." Instead,

> Drinke the water of thy cisterne, and . . . thine owne
> well. Let the fountains flowe for the [and] . . . be
> blessed, and rejoyce with the wife of thy youth. (15–18)

But is it not also likely that Shakespeare simultaneously has in mind the most extended biblical discussion of drinking water; the episode of the Samaritan woman at the well? This much-married alien, whose thirst is more for earthly water than heavenly, asks:

> from whence . . . hast thou that water of life? . . . [and] Jesus answered. . . .
> whosoever drinketh of the water that I shal give him, shal never be more
> athirst: but the water that I shal give him, shal be in him a well of water,
> springing up into everlasting life. . . . he that beleveth in me, shal never
> thurst. (Jn. 4:11-14, 7:35)

The woman, like Othello, was an alien concerned with whatever comforts marriage can bring, and yet trying to privilege the virtue of generosity to fellow humans. Memory of Jesus' encounter with the Samaritan woman could well have helped spectators organize the meaning of Othello's mistaken and twisted acts of love and selflessness—actions caused by his troubling experiences reconciling marriage, earthly survival, and eternal salvation. Tudor education fostered the ability to see almost any question from a multiplicity of sides (Jones). More than other dramatists, the author of such plays as *Lear*, *Antony*, and *All's Well* could be expected to permit a supposedly heterodoxical reading of Othello's fate after his suicide (Hubler). For many in the audience, killing oneself to die upon a kiss would be, as it is for Lodovico and Gratiano, a "bloody period" that "mar[s]" . . . "All" (5.2.357). But for many other spectators, Cassio's judgment must have seemed the more godly: Othello was "great of heart" (361). And it is the heart of a humble and charitable Cordelia or Samaritan woman that can make forgivable omissions in tact, emotional maturity, cultural habituation, or intellectual acumen. Such a judgment fits better with a God who is love, and a play that decenters the teachings of the official Calvinist-leaning church in Shakespeare's England.

NOTES

1. Interestingly,Henry Niclaes, the founder of Familism (a.k.a. The Family of Love or *Familia Charitatis*), invited conversions from a great diversity of religions: "Christian, Jews, Mahomites or Turks, and Heathen" (Bainton).

   The sexual customs of this faith were scarcely proven but widely rumored—a source of fear to late sixteenth-century governmental and ecclesiastical authorities, and a source of humor to dramatists (cf. Marston's *Dutch Courtesan*; Middleton's *Family of Love*). Because the sect was Dualist, dissociating the life of the body from that of the soul, they were often classified with the Libertines (Williams 535, 724–28, 1209–11). Like the Cathars of various earlier centuries (Weber), Familists supposedly resorted to immoral ways to release that sexual libido which they so strongly disapproved of.

   The connection of sects like the Familists with the Bosch painting is equally speculative, according to Portús, 57 and Larsen, 17–21. Again, intriguingly, the Bosch painting foreshadows *Othello*'s themes of not only nudity and sexual activity in general but 'perversion' and naked interracial interaction and even the hints of alchemical "coitus"/"coniunctio" (Dixon).

2. Ham "saw the nakedness of his father" (Gen. 9:22). According to a further tradition that was recorded by George Best in Hakluyt, and that was available also in Leo Africanus, Ham ignored his father's command that there be no intercourse in the Ark—behavior that led the Lord to dye Ham's son "blacke and lothsome" as a warning against "disobedience to all the worlde" (Neill 141).

3. I am grateful to Philip C. Kolin for his correspondence with me, calling my attention to this so typically Shakespearean quibble.

WORKS CITED

Abraham, Lyndy. *A Dictionary of Alchemical Imagery*. Cambridge: Cambridge University Press, 1998.

Ashe, Geoffrey. *The Virgin*. London: Routledge, 1976.

Bainton, Roland Herbert. "Familists." *Encyclopaedia Brittanica*. 14th ed. 1973.

Battenhouse, Roy. W. *Shakespearean Tragedy: Its Art and Christian Premise*. Bloomington: Indiana University Press, 1969.

Bethell, S. L. "Shakespeare's Imagery: The Diabolic Images in *Othello.*" *Shakespeare Survey* 5(1952): 62–80.

Coursen, Herbert R., Jr. *Christian Ritual and the World of Shakespeare's Tragedies*. Lewisburg: Bucknell University Press, 1976.

Dixon, Laurinda S. *Alchemical Imagery in Bosch's* Garden of Delight. Ann Arbor: University of Michigan, 1981.

Frye, Roland Mushat. *Shakespeare and Christian Doctrine*. Princeton: Princeton University Press, 1963.

The Geneva Bible. 1560 facsim. Madison: U of Wisconsin P, 1969.

Hankey, Julie, ed. Shakespeare's *Othello*. Bristol: Bristol Classical Press, 1987.

Hecht, Anthony. "*Othello.*" *Oblligati: Essays in Criticism.* New York: Atheneum, 1986. 51–84.

Honigmann, E. A. J., ed. *Othello.* 3rd ed. The Arden Shakespeare. Walton-on-Thames: Nelson, 1997.

Hubler, Edward. "The Damnation of Othello" *Shakespeare Quarterly* 9 (1958): 295–300.

Hunt, Maurice. "Predestination and the Heresy of Merit in *Othello.*" *Comparative Drama* 30 (1996):346–76.

Hunter, Robert G. *Shakespeare and the Mystery of God's Judgments.* Athens: University of Georgia Press, 1976.

Jones, Emrys. *The Origins of Shakespeare.* Oxford: Clarendon, 1977

Larsen, Erik. *Hieronymous Bosch.* New York: Smithmark, 1998.

Lehmkuhl, Aug[ust?]. "Sacrament of Marriage." *The Catholic Encyclopedia.* New York: Appleton, 1910.

Lupton, Julia Reinhard. "*Othello* Circumcised: Shakespeare and the Pauline Discourse of Nations." *Representations* 57 (1997): 73–89

Manzanas Calvo, Ann. "Conversion Narratives: Othello and Other Black Characters in Shakespeare's and Lope de Vega's Plays." *Sederi* 7 (1996): 231–36.

Milward, Peter, S. J. *Biblical Influences in Shakespeare's Great Tragedies.* Bloomington: Indiana University Press, 1987.

Neill, Michael. "Unproper Beds: Race, Adultery, and the Hideous in *Othello.*" *Shakespeare Quarterly* 40 (1989): 383–412. Rpt. *Shakespeare's Middle Tragedies: A Collection of Critical Essays.* E. David Young. Upper Saddle River, NJ: Prentice-Hall, 1993. 117–145.

Noble, Richmond. *Shakespeare's Biblical Knowledge and Use of the Book of Common Prayer in the First Folio.* New York: Macmillan, 1935.

Portús, J. *El Bosco.* Trans. Alicia Lewin. [Madrid]: Aldeasa, 1995.

Rice, Julian C. "Desdemona Unpinned: Universal Guilt in *Othello. Shakespeare Studies* 7(1974): 209–26.

Shaheen, Naseeb. *Biblical References in Shakespeare's Plays.* Newark: University of Delaware Press, 1999.

Shakespeare, William. *The Arden Shakespeare: Complete Works.* 3rd ed. Ed. Richard Proudfoot, Ann Thompson, and David Scott Kastan. Walton-on-Thames: Newton, 1998.

Siegel, Paul S. "The Damnation of *Othello*" *PMLA* 48 (1953): 1068–78. *A Visitors' Guide to York Minster.* London: Pitkin, 1975.

Vitkus, Daniel J. "Turning Turk in *Othello*: The Conversion and Damnation of the Moor." 48 (1997): 145–76.

Weber, N. A. "Cathari." *The Catholic Encyclopedia.* New York: Appleton, 1910.

West, Robert. "The Christianness of *Othello.*" *Shakespeare Quarterly* (1964) 15 (1964): 333–43.

Williams, George Huntston. *The Radical Reformation.* 3rd ed. Sixteenth Century Essays & Studies 15 Kirksville, MO: Sixteenth Century Journal Pub., 1992.

Representing Othello
Early Modern Jury Trials and the Equitable Judgments of Tragedy

NICHOLAS MOSCHOVAKIS

> *. . . I was, unhandsome warrior as I am,*
> *Arraigning his unkindness with my soul,*
> *But now I find I had suborned the witness*
> *And he's indicted falsely.*
>
> —OTHELLO, 3.4.152–55[1]

> *When we shall meet at compt*
> *This look of thine will hurl my soul from heaven*
> *And fiends will snatch at it.*
>
> —OTHELLO, 5.2.271–73

Othello is both a tragedy of judgment and an occasion for judgments. Its world turns on the ways in which people, presented with unwelcome facts or suspicions, will inquire into and infer each other's motives, weigh one another's deserts and demerits, accuse each other and defend themselves, and convict and finally punish each other for perceived transgressions. Its audience also faces challenges to judge and to discriminate, as readers may gather from the critics' disparate verdicts on Othello as a moral agent. Ultimately it even provokes us to judge the value of tragic art itself, or at least to decide the criteria of success and failure in the form. The author of the play's most notorious condemnation, Thomas Rymer, asked us to doubt whether an egregiously unjust event like Desdemona's murder can make for good tragedy at all, or just for a bad experience—one without redeeming artistic value, a crime against the order of "poetic justice."[2] These aspects of *Othello* and our responses to it have been under scrutiny for decades, and at one time we may have felt that the play's saturation with judicial episodes, language and implications was a theme too familiar to need reemphasizing. At the moment, however, it is one with a special and novel claim to our attention. During the mid-1990s, the tragedy's concern with justice was brought home to us by a living, politically urgent instance of courtroom drama: O. J. Simpson's murder trial.[3]

It is not difficult to see why, for audiences alert to the historical presence of racism within an ostensibly liberal society, the face of Shakespeare's Moor today could seem always about to morph into the ubiquitous visage of Simpson under his murder indictment. For all the vast disparities between the two cases, each poses similar, hard questions about the right to judge and condemn—about how the claim of any established power to act justly may be undercut by perceptions of its complicity in systematic injustice. Differences of both gender and color define positions from which authority itself can appear unjust in this domestic tragedy. Desdemona's complaint, "A guiltless death I die," not only protests her innocence of adultery, but indirectly indicts the biblical (if not legal) grounds for Othello's belief that if actually cuckolded he might "proceed upon just grounds/ To this extremity" (5.2.121, 136–7).[4] Yet her "kind lord" later pleads his own innocence of intent much as Christ might on behalf of fallen humanity, originally gulled by faith in the honest-seeming authority of a white devil: "Will you, I pray, demand that demi-devil/ Why he hath thus ensnared my soul and body?" (5.2.123, 298–99). As they weigh the degree of Othello's own culpability, Shakespeare's auditors may also find themselves passing judgment—like trial jurors, or a critical public—on their community's investment in the structures of domination (gendered, racial or otherwise) that the spectacle has staged to view.[5]

Like Shakespeare's other tragedies, then, *Othello* depicts the act of judgment as profoundly complicated by our awareness of the limitations of human justice. Othello's apprehension that, at "compt" or Doomsday, his wife's accusing "look" will be enough to convict him before the heavenly judge (5.2.271–72), encourages audiences to reflect on their judicial relationship to the tragic tableau before them; yet it reminds them too how imperfectly their verdicts adumbrate those of the last day, which will "correct mistaken earthly judgments" (Marshall, 29). Intimating at once the necessity and the difficulty of judgment, Shakespeare's scene of justice in *Othello* is finally more idealistic and optimistic than a critic like Rymer would allow—not because the Moor is noble, but because for all the ignobility in his recent history he is summoned to our judgments as a candidate for our sympathy.

So far, the prominence of judicial discourses in the play has prompted little consideration of how Othello might have faced justice in early modern England, had he lived to be tried as a felon rather than to strike himself down in the playhouse. The main instance of an attempt to apply a knowledge of early modern criminal-legal practices to *Othello* is that of Katharine Eisaman Maus (1991), who, stressing discursive contexts rather than legal process, and tending primarily to articulate broader questions about epistemology and subjectivity, cites early modern sources dealing with the prosecution of suspected witches and traitors.[6] Lacking from her account, however, is any substantial discussion of that far more common phenomenon in early modern society as in our own, the murder trial.[7] Murder, after all, is the felonious category most directly relevant to the judgments made by audences and readers of the play;[8] though Brabantio haughtily accuses Othello of witchcraft (1.3), yet it is murder of which Shakespeare more plausibly, if ambiguously, prepares us to convict the Moor at last.[9] We can learn still more about the design of Shakespeare's drama of judgment by bringing our own society's fascination with the courtroom, trial procedure, and in particular the crime of murder, to bear on *Othello* in its early social contexts. Though our association of Othello's case with that of a modern celebrity may result from an uncanny coincidence, the convergence in our understandings of what may be at stake in a great tragedy and in a televised jury trial is not due to mere historical chance. The analogy has a much older history, one beginning with the earliest criticism of tragedy itself and extending, through the theories of forensic and deliberative rhetoric which valued oratory and poetic fiction alike as frameworks for equitable judgment, into the ideology of liberal societies.

TRIAL PROCEDURE: JUDGING OTHELLO

Othello, critics have long recognized, "advances by a series of scenes analogous to trials or court actions" (Heilman, 129; cf. 129–36, 152–68). These include Brabantio's arraignment of Othello before the Senate (1.3), Cassio's dismissal from office for night-brawling (2.3), and Othello's prosecution and sentencing of Desdemona to death for adultery (3.4–5.2).[10] Last is the Moor's great speech before Lodovico, Gratiano, Montano, Cassio, the officers, and the captive Iago near the end of 5.2; here Othello voices a bold, if unlikely, appeal for the hearers to judge him in the future by these words, rather than according to the mute indictment now brought against him by Desdemona's corpse. His ambitious plea has variously struck modern critics either with wonder or with revulsion, and indeed many have been prone to judge Othello specifically *for* daring to express such hopes at all. Whether his speech inspires sympathy or not, however, we recognize in it his admission that others will sit in judgment on him at the last; their impressions will be those of record, as preserved in his biography.[11]

Seen as Othello's last chance to represent himself, this moment in 5.2 is illuminated by a knowledge of the proceedings which an accused murderer would normally face in a Tudor or Stuart court. The suspect's own performance, notably, was central to the process. One accused could not be convicted unless present: "Thieves are not judged but they are by to hear/ Although apparent guilt be seen in them" (*Richard II*, 4.1.123–4). Moreover, unlike a defense against felony charges today, "[t]he case for the defense was put by the accused, for himself and by himself. No one interceded on his behalf to influence the impression he made upon the jurors. . . . All of the pressure was brought to bear on a single point: the jurors waited to hear the accused speak for himself" (Green, 135, 137; cf. Herrup, 141–42). The self-representation of the accused in cases like Othello's is, as we shall see, only one of several elements in virtue of which the design of a Shakespearean tragedy and the conduct of a criminal trial might be compared. In this and the following section of this essay, I take into account what historians are able to tell us about the English trial by jury, and about the kinds of conditions within which it may actually or possibly have impinged upon Shakespeare's life.

It seems important to ascertain, for instance, that Shakespeare enjoyed significant opportunities for the direct observation of felony trials. The external evidence of biography can help here, though only up to a point.[12] Most Shakespeareans, for instance, are probably inclined to discount the anecdote of young Will's prosecution for deer-poaching, which might (if true) have concluded in his trial and sentencing by a justice of the peace (Schoenbaum, *Shakespeare's Lives*, 68–72). More reliably attested are the repeated instances of litigation that would have brought his father John before juries during the 1580s and 1590s; these, however, were civil suits (Eccles, 31–36; Schoenbaum, *William Shakespeare*, 37–39). Still other circumstances of the playwright's life do offer grounds for supposing that he had personal experience of the criminal courts, where the dramas that were recounted and enacted might have mortal consequences. John Shakespeare, having been a Stratford constable in 1558–1559, was in 1567 elected to the bailiff's office, becoming both justice of the peace and coroner of the borough. In 1571, when William was old enough to be in grammar school, John again served as deputy to the bailiff (Schoenbaum, *William Shakespeare*, 29, 34). Justices of the peace were legally bound to appear at the semiannual county Assizes, where capital crimes including murder were normally prosecuted.[13] Even if in practice many of these magistrates stayed home, it was more vital to the functioning of these courts that the bailiff and coroner should be in attendance.[14] Probably John, even if he never brought William to a murder trial, was able to tell him stories of several, from the perspective of a vital participant in the prosecution of the case.

William Shakespeare, for his own part, did business after the Globe's 1599 opening in a neighborhood where legal process was a striking feature of ordinary life. In John Taylor the Water Poet's words, "Five Iayles or Prisons are in Southwarke plac'd"—the Counter, Clink, White Lion, King's (or Queen's) Bench, and Marshalsea (from *The Praise and Vertue of a Jayle and Jaylers,* quoted in Dobb, 87). The location of these gaols is important evidence for Shakespeare's familiarity with criminal procedure—not just because of the daily spectacles that they would have afforded of arrests, incarcerations, and the begging or buying of food by and for prisoners at windows or in the street (Dobb, 96; Cockburn, *Calendar,* 40; Salgādo, 180), but also because of their association with court proceedings. Except for the Clink, all of these gaols were situated "in Long Southwarke," the "continual street" extending from London Bridge "straight towards the south" (and southwest); one, the Counter (distinguished from others of this name as the "Compter in Southwark"), shared space in a former parish church with "a court, wherein the assizes and sessions be kept, and the court of admiralty is also there kept" (Stow, 359, 365).[15] Another prison along this jailhouse row, the White Lion, was "the appointed gaol for the county of Surrey," of which the borough of Southwark was a part (Stow, 366). Southwark was the regular site of the winter Assizes in this Home Circuit county; once a year, a gaol delivery would be followed here by a session lasting "at least three days," and replete with what we would call courtroom drama (Cockburn, *Calendar*, 42 n. 1, 2–3).[16]

Sir Thomas Smith in *De Republica Anglorum,* his treatise on English government written circa 1565, described the questioning of accuser, accused, and witnesses during a felony trial (the charge in his example being one of theft) as a strikingly dramatic event:

> The Judge . . . asketh first the partie robbed, if he knowe the prisoner, and biddeth him looke upon him: he saith yea, the prisoner sometime saith nay. The partie pursuivant giveth good ensignes *verbi gratia,* I knowe thee well ynough, thou robbest me in such a place, thou beatest mee, thou tookest my horse from mee, and my purse, thou hadst then such a coate and such a man in thy companie: the theefe will say no, and so they stand a while in altercation, he telleth al that he can say: after him likewise all those who were at the apprehension of the prisoner, or who can give any *indices* or tokens which we call in our language evidence against the malefactor . . . there is nothing put in writing but the enditement onely. All the rest is doone openlie in the presence of the Judges, the Justices, the enquest [i.e., petty jury], the prisoner, and so manie as will or can come so neare as to heare it, and all depositions and witnesses given aloude, that all men may heare from the mouth of the depositors and witnesses what is saide. (Smith 114–15)

Smith's influential record of a trial as an "altercation" is consistent with representations of judgments as settings for dialogue and debate throughout the Shakespearean canon, and offers us a valuable point of reference for the analysis of *Othello*'s progression of "quasi-trials" (Kerrigan, 151). Othello's indictment in 1.3, his first occasion for a speech in his own defense, is the closest of these to a proper English jury trial; significantly this is also the only judgment scene to be resolved comically, as Brabantio drops the witchcraft charge following Desdemona's testimony. The judgment of Cassio in 2.3 takes place in a summary examination by a superior military officer rather than a criminal court, yet even here the accused is invited to defend himself, though he "cannot speak" for drunkenness and shame (2.3.185). Conversely, the most harrowing trial scenes are surely those comprising Othello's prejudiced inquisition into his wife's chastity, a judgment which Shakespeare represents with terrible irony as a parody of due process: "[w]hen Othello decides to follow Iago . . . he adopts . . . a new code: he will 'see' the facts, get the 'evidence,' 'prove' his case, and execute 'justice'" (Heilman, 226; cf. 131-35, 152–54). When Desdemona comes by her rare opportunities to speak on her own behalf, she fails to recapture her husband's ear.[17] These scenes depict a cautionary *exemplum* not just of jealous male passion, but of the potential for abuse inherent in the prosecution of early modern felony suspects, a context to which I will return.

The tragedy's culminating judicial episode, however, is that of Othello's suicide. It is we who judge him here; critics of the play, even those who differ over the import of this passage, have tacitly agreed that Othello actively invites and anticipates his auditors' struggle to reach a verdict. While preferring to die at once and by his own hand rather than languish as a "prisoner . . . Till that the nature of [his] fault be known/ To the Venetian state" (5.2.333–35), he also makes this his last, best chance at a partial self-exoneration, one directed towards the audience as much as at his adoptive countrymen. When Lodovico orders them to "bring him away," and the Moor begs for "a word or two before you go" (5.2.335–36), he not only stalls for an occasion to draw his blade, but enables Shakespeare to postpone his exit from the stage, and from our view, until after he has made his plea. How well he uses those dearly bought moments has been a perennial topic of critical disagreement; the speech is perhaps most fairly described as a mixture of "disparate self-judgments . . . a balanced composition of condemnation and qualification . . . [depicting] foolishness and perplexity mitigated by love and honor" (Kerrigan, 194–95).[18] If it is this, however, it is also telling how deftly Othello skirts the less forgiving proposition that he has committed felonious homicide, "a malicious, premeditated or deliberate killing" (Baker, 429).

The suicide speech is Othello's rhetorical defense, and as such it completes a sequence of apologies for his behavior, as that of a man "more dupe than engineer, more victim than self-victimizer" (Cartwright, 164), which Emilia began earlier when she chided him charitably as a "gull" and a "dolt" (5.2.159). As though this were not enough, it is also an encomium—according to Henry Peacham, a "forme of speech by which the Orator doth highly recommend to his hearers, some person or thing in respect of their worthy deserts & virtues" (Peacham, 155)—in which Othello narrates his past so as to highlight those qualities of character that have stood him best with the Venetians until now (Altman, 100–101).[19] While this self-portrayal as unwise, yet nobly inclined, contributes to the growing "latticework of 'judgment' about the victimized Othello," its apologetic structure on one common view "wobbles like thin planking in a high wind" (Cartwright, 164). Peacham cautions of the "praises" in an encomium "[that] they be not too great for meane desertes," and "that they be not perversly applied, that is to say, where rebuke and shame is rather due" (Peacham, 156). However admirable Othello's values were in the eyes of Venice when he smote the Turk, it is less clear what sort of fame he deserves for his suicidal resolution, and both contrast with his reasons (though possibly they furnish us with clues to his motives) for killing Desdemona. That Othello's appeal to character, coming so late, is nonetheless of such weight in our understanding of him shows how far the measure of his accountability has yet to be unraveled in our judgments. As E. A. J. Honigmann writes, the introduction here of new facts about the protagonist's life reminds us that "much of Othello's past remains a closed book" (5.2.350 n.).

The play's end puts us in the position of a judge or a trial jury, with nothing left to do but to render a verdict; yet it compels us to do so on a near stranger. In this our relationship to Othello accords with trends in the history of criminal process in late medieval and early modern England. On the one hand, observations of character were considered a most desirable form of evidence in trials, as well as in the justice of the peace's examinations of suspects before indictment (Herrup, 86–87); on the other, witnesses to character might be hard to procure on the date and at the location of the county Assizes, and more importantly the Crown regarded them as highly subject to bias by local interests. Since "the presumption of innocence had not yet been formulated" at this time, the gathering of testimony was viewed by magistrates in their concern with enforcement as a means of "buttressing a presumption of guilt," rather than of proving it in the modern sense (Cockburn, *Calendar*, 107). During this period, bent on enforcing order, the Crown was attempting to overcome the obstacles to conviction by expanding the scope of its role as prosecutor. Its case would likely include affidavits sworn beforehand as result of previous investigations in the county.[20] Jurors who had once been supposed to inform themselves through communal networks became increasingly dependent on courtroom testimony (Herrup, 132), in a "shift from a trial dominated by a self-informing jury to a trial based mainly on evidence produced by the prosecution" (Green, 119).

Petty juries increasingly reached their verdicts on the basis of information introduced at the trial by officers of the Crown, concerning lives which they had never before heeded or investigated. At the same time, as Smith's account implies, the less information jurors brought with them to the proceedings, the more events in the courtroom itself took on a agonistic, suspenseful character, as the performances of accuser, accused, and witnesses took on more weight. Trials called for radically artificial practices of narrative and characterological representation, since jurors were rendering verdicts on cases that they were hearing about for the first time. The urbanite's sense of the impersonal, the familiarity with unfamiliarity gained in the flux of London's "heterogeneous crowd" (Twyning, 124), is perhaps relevant to both the judicial and theatrical settings for such rhetorical compositions of history and identity.[21] At the Surrey winter Assizes, criminal suspects from far off in the country would be tried, along with a diverse assortment of Southwark residents whose faces might or might not be familiar from Bankside. In a comic scene from *Measure for Measure,* approximately contemporary with *Othello,* Escalus sits in judgment on Pompey for the first time and must be informed by the constable of his character (*Measure for Measure,* 2.1); in a criminal trial conducted under such circumstances, jurors as well as justices who did not already know the defendants might similarly have to rely on the efficiency and integrity of the constabulary.

In this context Othello's last speech evokes that of a defendant at the bar of an Assize court or of London's Old Bailey, pleading his own cause without counsel to an audience of jurors, against a plaintiff and whatever witnesses the Crown can muster. It also echoes the situation in 1.3, where, however, he was able to turn his rhetorical skills of self-characterization to better account.[22] The manner in which Brabantio there called Desdemona to witness, only to behold his own case collapsing under her testimony, reflects the play's debt to the drama of the courtroom as Shakespeare knew it. And the fact that at the play's end, Desdemona can no longer be questioned about the meaning of her dying words—which might conceivably wreck any prosecutor's case against Othello, were he not to have followed by indicting himself with a plain admission of his deed—is one of its ironies.[23]

TRIAL PROCEDURE: OTHELLO JUDGING

If we hear Othello's defense from the responsible position of a jury, or indeed of a judge, then in his relation to the slandered Desdemona—in the protagonist's performance as accuser, rather than accused—we instead find ourselves helplessly observing an utter miscarriage of justice. It is a proceeding, moreover, that is disturbingly reminiscent of the magistracy's enhanced prosecutorial powers. Before Othello will pronounce his wife's guilt in what he defines as a capital offence, he holds himself responsible with grimly ironic formality for investigating it through what Maus has called "quasijudicial inquisitory procedures" (45). The bedchamber of 5.2 is a courtroom in which Desdemona cannot call on others for testimony to her innocence, just as she most likely would not have been able to do so were she actually on trial for a felony; early modern defendants were "only grudgingly" allowed to call witnesses of their own (Green, 137). In his self-appointed judicial role, Othello considers it right to reach a verdict solely on the information of Iago and his own mind.[24]

In contrast to the manner in which Othello presided over Cassio's case in 2.3, and in this instance against the rules of English criminal procedure, Othello confronts Desdemona only with his own demands, and never with the personal testimony of her original accuser Iago (which might have resulted in a dramatic "altercation"of the kind Smith described). It has been suggested—though evidence is slight, and this opinion is disputed—that many English defendants pleading not guilty were in fact rendered mute and ineffectual before the court, out of a sense of intimidation or humiliation like Cassio's, or in the consciousness of their own ignorance (Cockburn, *Calendar,* 108; cf. Green, 136–37). Certainly suspects who defended themselves were at a disadvantage; whereas "the accused was not allowed counsel" after indictment, the Crown could and did provide itself with legal counsel in the courtroom (Green, 135; cf. Cockburn, *Calendar,* 107–108). Though Desdemona seems a more accomplished pleader than other Shakespearean heroines like *Measure for Measure*'s Isabella (Kliman, esp. 142–43), she proves unable to ensure her defense a fair hearing in the 'cause' that is both initiated and judged by her husband. This is partly because until 4.2, she is uncertain of the charge against her, and once it is heard she is unsure how to defend herself from it before her judge except with her sworn testimony to the contrary: evidence that Othello considers worthless (5.2.54–56).25

The jurors were in theory responsible for "finding fact" (Maus, 33), yet in practice, as explained above, the amassing of information was increasingly in the hands of the Crown and the justices who served it, reflecting the Assize judges' need for evidence with which to provide an increasingly non-self-informing jury. Historically, the Crown's increasing aggressiveness and sophistication as prosecutor appeared particularly in treason cases (Maus, 31–35; Parker, *Shakespeare,* 233–34); Othello reflects this as he inquires into Desdemona's alleged adultery, a transgression which he seems to define (against English law) as the capital crime of domestic treason or treason against the rule of man: "she'll betray more men" (5.2.6).26 In other ways, and especially with reference to the nature of the charge, his procedure may be comparable not so much to that of an Assize justice as to that of the ecclesiastical courts, which were inquisitorial.27 Yet in ruling Desdemona's case a capital one rather than one of morals, and by abusing the powers of prosecutorial investigation proper to the Crown in a criminal trial, Othello comes near to incarnating the conventional early modern figure of the unjust judge.28 Surely this play did make apprehensible a possible criticism of early modern judicial institutions which citizens of liberal societies today would predisposed to see as fundamental: that the failure to separate the offices of prosecutor and magistrate effectively creates kangaroo courts, in which the government is both plaintiff and judge in its own cause. It is a conflict of interest ominously foreshadowed in the privilege which the Duke earlier extended to Brabantio (1.3.66–71), and one which the Venetian Senate then nearly came to regret.29

It is hard to know whether more people in Shakespeare's audiences would have bridled at Othello's prosecution of his "cause" against Desdemona out of a politically conservative revulsion at its unjust transgressions of extant legal boundaries (between vice and felony, and between the roles of plaintiff and judge), or more radically because they detected fearsome affinities between the play's travesty of justice and the established institutions and procedures of English criminal law. To make either argument would be to beg a so far unanswered historical question: that of how far it is correct to say that early modern jurors felt "passive," or morally bound to acquiesce in the authority of prosecuting officials and magistrates. On the one hand, the petty jury possessed, as it always had, the legal authority to acquit any suspect—against the Crown's case for conviction, and even against the urgent admonitions of Assize judges who were concerned to set examples and deter crime. On the other, the extent to which juries exercised this power in practice was probably minimal, and indeed they might face Star Chamber's wrath for doing so (Cockburn, "Twelve," 179 and n. 105). Such pressures could not obviate the respect due to juries' consciences in more ordinary cases. Indeed, after 1590, jurors apparently began increasingly to exercise discretion in felony trials through "partial verdicts," or convictions on lesser charges than those technically warranted by the evidence (Cockburn, "Twelve," 179–180).[30]

Although we must confess ignorance as to the degree to which English people regarded the deliberations of petty jurors as possessing ultimate authority, and hence about the quality of audience response to Desdemona's conviction without benefit of trial, in the fictional realm we need not doubt the initiative attributed to the spectators as judges in the case against Othello. "Nor set down aught in malice," Othello urges us at last (5.2.341): a revealing choice of words, since "malice," or *mens rea,* was the essential criterion for conviction on charges of felonious homicide (Green, 126). Here Othello's diction seems meant to insinuate that to report badly of his life would be tantamount to killing him. The imprecation to us *not* to do so, coming from a man who has just calumniated and killed his wife, may seem brazen; yet if his hope is not to be found not guilty of murder, it may really have some legal justification. By Shakespeare's time a homicide committed "in hot blood" was not murder but simple homicide or manslaughter, and was clergiable on the first offense—meaning that it was punishable by branding, rather than hanging, for any offender who could claim "benefit of clergy" by reading a verse from the Psalms aloud. Even before the later fifteenth and sixteenth centuries, when the categories of "manslayer" and manslaughter were introduced and formalized, a practical distinction between capital and noncapital killings had been applied by petty jurors who simply concocted "self-defense" rationalizations for incidents of fatal violence (Cockburn, 117–21; Green, 118–24).[31] If Othello then is asking for something like such a "partial verdict" (Green, 138 –50), is this benefit of the doubt one of which we must convict him of having denied to Desdemona? Is he merely requesting equitable judgment, or is he, like Shylock according to his Christian adversaries (*Merchant of Venice,* 4.1.374 ff.), asking for a mercy which he himself has maliciously withheld?

That such a deed could be perpetrated with the self-righteousness Othello brings to it is an anomaly, one which defies us either to pronounce on his malicious intent or to accept the merciful fiction of a non-felonious explanation. Still, one might compare his last speech with Hamlet's apology for his killing of Polonius as a case of manslaughter, not murder. If we are tempted to accept such excuses, or even to invent others for Othello, we are at least not alone; even after complaining of the injustice of her death, Desdemona too decides to revert to her husband's cause, testifying with her last words to his guiltlessness (5.2.122). In effect this is her witness to the audience, and must serve—depending on how her character is portrayed on stage—as a persuasive appeal to us to judge his case equitably and taking all factors into account. Shakespeare in fact invented the whole resolution in *Othello,* 5.2, substituting it for the more definitive and stringent judgments of his narrative source; in Cinthio's tale, the Moor had resisted interrogation without confessing, and later died miserably but justly at the hands of Desdemona's kindred—a death which, it is said, he "richly deserved" (Honigmann, 385). At the close of Shakespeare's version there is no such narrator to dictate and authorize the spectator's sentiments, but only the words of a few laconic Venetians. The audience is guided mostly by its own perceptions of Othello in action, and by its preexisting beliefs and principles, as it retires from the theater of his life to evaluate him in death.

Shakespeare's characters themselves alert us to the possibility of judging tragedy, as I have been suggesting that we judge *Othello,* as the trial of a protagonist's motives and actions. After the "handkerchief" confrontation, Desdemona says hopefully—too hopefully—of her husband:

> Beshrew me much, Emilia,
> I was, unhandsome warrior as I am,
> Arraigning his unkindness with my soul,
> But now I find I had suborned the witness
> And he's indicted falsely.
> (3.4.151–55)

The irony of her fate is that it results in part from this innocent faith in Othello's good intentions, as well as from his awful judgment that her death will fulfill a higher law: "the justice of it pleases" (4.1.206). Whether we can excuse him for having made such an error depends on our persuasion by his rhetorical defense of his character at the end, by our own judgment of whether any positive account of his motives is an equitable one, and by Shakespeare's and the players' capacity for representing such a case as one that could conceivably justify such a verdict.

TRAGEDY AND EQUITY IN THE RHETORICAL TRADITION

Joel Altman has written of sixteenth-century humanist tragedies that "[a]lthough the audience is granted a wide and generous view of the tragic plight—which is examined from many perspectives . . . [t]he best it can achieve is an equitable judgment of the hero" (*Tudor,* 230). Concomitantly with the trend in English criminal procedure that I sketched in the preceding sections, English tragedy came more and more delicately to exploit the adjudicatory aspect of theatrical spectatorship. Through learned tradition, and independently of contemporary developments in the justice system, Shakespeare and his contemporaries were culturally well-placed to create works that would set a modern standard for explorations of the analogy between courthouse and playhouse: one in which the crucial term, as Altman suggests with reference to the imitation of ancient drama, was equity.

Classically educated audiences or readers of *Othello* would not have been surprised by the suggestion that their task, at the end of 5.2, was to debate whether Othello's motives were in fact predominantly good or bad, and to judge the extent of his culpability and its deserts. Indeed, ancient writers, seeking to define the conditions of probable knowledge in areas of experience that did not admit of infallible demonstration,[32] analyzed poetic fiction in both forensic and deliberative rhetorical terms. The "hypothesis"—represented by the plot or argument of a drama, or by the forensic orator's narration of a probable account of the history of events that resulted in this particular case—was distinguished from the "thesis" proposed for deliberation, where judgment was seen to depend on a more general issue or philosophical question. Wesley Trimpi has crystallized the relevance of this parallel between poetry and rhetoric to Shakspearean tragedy, citing an influential example from Quintilian's *Institutio Oratoria*:

> There are some, Quintilian [writes], who regard questions "which have reference to persons and particular cases" as theses: "for instance, if Orestes be accused, we shall have a *cause;* whereas if it is put as a question, namely 'Was Orestes rightly acquitted?' it will be a *thesis"* (3.5.11). One might rephrase the example: if we simply ask how it can be proved that Hamlet killed Claudius, we can expect a dramatized trial or detective story, but if we ask whether he is justified in killing Claudius, we include more of the materials of the completed play. (Trimpi, 33–34)[33]

Kathy Eden expands this hint in her exemplary reading of *Hamlet's* judicial and forensic themes (176–83), concluding that "Shakespeare presents us with the image of an action readied for judgment, not only for our artistic judgments . . . but also our ethical and, as it were, legal judgments" (182).[34] In *Othello* as in *Hamlet,* Shakespeare created both a probable representation of tragic actions, and ample matter for moral argument and adjudication of the actors' causes.

Rhetorical theory itself had begun with fifth-century Athenian efforts to systematize and teach practices of forensic oratory that were basic to the legal institutions of the *polis* (Kennedy, 8–9). The courts of Athens, in this respect like those described by Sir Thomas Smith, made "litigants . . . speak for themselves" against one another; homicide cases, for instance, were tried by setting the accuser against the defendant "twice, in the order plaintiff, defendant, plaintiff, defendant" (Fine, 425–26, 419). Sophistic rhetoric, the art of crafting opposing arguments for these forensic purposes as well as for political occasions, became a model for "the formal debates of the *agon*" in classical tragedy (Goldhill, 232).[35] Work by Trimpi, Altman, Eden, and others has affirmed that this generic association of tragedy with issues of justice became the basis for a vital continuity in European poetics over the centuries. Not only the agonistic element, the dialectic temper, in Athenian tragedy, but the whole repertory of concepts used in Aristotelian and later theory to analyze its representations of causation, character, probability, and intention—concepts derived from the analysis of legal representation—were successfully adapted in postclassical times. These ideas, at least, may be truly said to have survived from antiquity through Augustinian poetics and, later, the scholastic assimilation of Aristotle, into the poetic theory and revived tragic art of the Renaissance (Eden, 7–8, n, 1).[36]

English tragedy flourished at a time when English law was attributing an increasing significance to intention, as seen in its formalization of manslaughter—a category opposed to murder, much as rhetorical theory distinguished two objects of judicial concern: physical agency on the one hand, and on the other *mens rea* or culpability. Equity was the principle that dealt with the discrimination between these, and had been articulated by the time Aristotle produced his *Rhetoric,* as well as what has come down to us as his treatment of tragedy in the *Poetics.* He recognized that equity or "fairness" is at times contradicted by the "written law," so that "one must use common law and arguments based on fairness as being more just . . . fairness always remains and never changes nor does the common law (for it is in accordance with nature) but written laws often change" (*On Rhetoric,* 110 [1.15.4–6]). Crucial to the task of equitable judgment were determinations of intention and of character:

> . . . it is fair not to regard personal failings [*hamartēmata*] and mistakes . . . as of equal seriousness with unjust actions. Mistakes are unexpected actions and do not result from wickedness; personal failings are not unexpected and do not result from wickedness . . . And to be forgiving of human weaknesses is fair. And [it is also fair] to look not to the law but to the legislator and not to the word but to the intent of the legislator, and not to the action but to the deliberate purpose . . . and not to the part but to the whole, not [looking at] what a person is now but what he has been always or for the most part. (*On Rhetoric,* 106 [1.13.16–18])

The interpretation of this reference to *hamartēmata* (more generally translatable as "errors") in relation to Aristotle's account of tragic "*hamartia*" in the *Poetics* is a highly controversial business which, fortunately, need not concern us here.[37] Whatever our view of the precise ethical force of this notion, or of an agent's legal liability for "missing the mark," the Aristotelian analysis of equity and its tradition is significant for tragedy in two ways: first, in the model that forensic debate afforded for the idea of representing character, and second, in its encouragement to poets to test the limits of sophisticated discrimination among degrees of guilt and innocence. As manslaughter was recognized in English law to enable more precise distinctions in these degrees, so tragedy acquired the legal subtlety and moral ambiguity of cases like Othello's.

From these legalistic and controversial elements derives our own widely shared experience of the Shakespearean theater as a form ideally tending to challenge our prejudices, provoking complex moral assessment and argument, rather than the unconsidered passions and summary judgments of mere melodrama.[38] We may perhaps say that Othello intended, meaning that he thought that he had made the decision, to kill a "whore": terrible, if no more terrible than the law of *Measure for Measure*'s Vienna, which Shakespeare represented as inequitably harsh yet not unthinkable or universally abominated (like the malice of Iago or of Shylock). However, Othello's action fails to correspond even to his dubiously grounded intention, simply because Desdemona is not what he is led to believe about her. He misses the mark, such as it is, that he has set for himself. An equitable judgment might or might not conclude that the malice was all Iago's, not Othello's; the judicial point of tragedy is in the intricacy, if not indeed the mystery, of the processes whereby we arrive at our convictions in real cases of this kind.

Of equity's comparable prominence in classical poetics and in rhetorical theory, Trimpi has written that "[b]oth the dramatist and the orator . . . persuade their respective listeners to regard such and such a particular action as just or unjust by removing the discussion to the most generic questions involved in the controversy. . . . Permanently free of historical circumstances, the fictional imitation presents an individual situation in which the assertion of existence, the conditions of formal coherence, and the deliberations of moral choice may be rhetorically analyzed for the judgment of an audience" (Trimpi, 76–77). This formulation of the uses of fiction according to the canons of rhetoric reminds us that we have only the playwright's representations, and no more, by which to judge the "truth" of his invented history; Othello's intention is precisely as ascertainable or obscure as Shakespeare's intent in writing the part.[39] As Luke Wilson has asserted of *Hamlet,* authorial intention is performed rather than realized by a Shakespearean tragedy, in the sense that textual and theatrical performances, the products of poetic and histrionic art, are merely the materials for our equitable (re)construction of what we find to be the work's genuine meaning.[40] Our ability to practice this equity is defined by the coherence of the play's and the players' performance, but it also requires a prior faith that artificial representations, like arguments, can reveal unanticipated truths—that our equitable interpretations, those which satisfy the criterion of consistency with our moral intuitions, may take precedence over strict judgments of conformity to accepted laws and grow "to something of great constancy," however "strange, and admirable" (*Midsummer Night's Dream,* 5.1.26–27).

Othello himself assents to the revelations of rhetoric, yet in doing so fails another test of faith, unready to resist Iago's alleged probabilities with contrary arguments from his knowledge of Desdemona's character (or, in the play's shorter time scheme, from her lack of opportunity). His failure is ominous, most obviously in gesturing towards our own potential unfitness for true judgment in his or in any other case. In his role as judge he has been supplied by Iago as prosecutor, not with "proof" of the indubitable kind that he imagined he would require, but instead with a tissue of rhetorical arguments from probability (Altman, 132–44; Trousdale, 162–67). Indeed, it is because Iago's use of the handkerchief is wholly subordinate to his skill at eliciting supposed probabilities that his advancement of the hypothesis of Desdemona's adultery meets Aristotle's standards of artistic excellence, in oratory as in tragedy.[41] The persuasiveness of drama is akin to that of rhetoric; the tragedian, like the rhetorician, biases our disposition towards or against Othello so long as his heroic speeches entertain us, or while the wordless stare of his wife's corpse appalls us.[42] Nonetheless, just as his quest for arguments of guilt ends with the paltry fact of her handkerchief's misplacement (or her denial of its loss), so we ourselves are free to take even the least signs as proof of whatever our prior impressions, within or outside the theater, have prepared us to believe. After what missing handkerchiefs might we ourselves chase, in the hope of producing a plausible justification for a verdict originally dictated only by our own prejudices?

What might save us from despairing of our power to find truly when we judge a play, is simply that the imagination is more indulgent than life to our errors in judgment; the stage allows, and in effect imposes on us, more leisure and latitude of response than a court in which final verdicts must be rendered. In the luxury of our contemplations, we feel that "no reductive judgement . . . can encompass the complexity of a character" like Othello (Danson, 133). Still, the play confronts us with the ubiquity of such reductive judgments in life, and with their ramified import in every case. A trial likely arouses diverse and incompatible feelings, just as the play incites tension among the inevitably various intuitions of its audience—which in *Othello* 5.2 is especially jurylike, since, in its eyes, the protagonists do in effect "meet at compt" (5.2.271). Here, without portraying a just world, the poet grants to unjust worldlings unusually favorable conditions for the exercise of equity. Othello's prophecy of his strict condemnation by God's law challenges us to prove him wrong, even while impressing us with the gravity of the distinction between equitable judgment and a pardon granted freely, or for mere pity's sake.[43]

The gaps in our knowledge that remain signal the imperfection of mortal judgment, even from our relatively privileged vantage point as spectators, as Maus has pointed out (46–47). After all, human motives have never yet been reduced to empirically perceptible, scientifically demonstrable causes, but must in part be formulated as reasons, the representation of which is almost invariably rhetorical. Within these limits of our nature, our information concerning the killing of Desdemona is as reliable as a court could desire. How much we blame Othello for missing the mark is as much a reflection of our own judgments as it is of the character's intention, which is, after all, a fiction: one invented in Shakespeare's sources (in the broadest sense of this term), but reinvented by him, in productions of the play, and in the judicious minds of its audiences and of its critics. *Othello* therefore communicates neither "the unfathomable darkness of human motives" nor, on this view, "their terrible transparency" (Greenblatt, 251), so much as the wondrous cognitive artifice involved in our invention of motives themselves, as objects for rhetorical representation and judicial evaluation.

CONCLUSION

I have postulated two relevant historical perspectives on the significance of judicial themes in *Othello*: that of the criminal courts, and also that of the rhetorical literacy which was founded on Latin and Greek models, yet which helped to make a new vernacular tragedy possible. To do justice to tragedy as a Renaissance art is to be concerned with the one as much as the other, with Shakespeare's London (and its liberties) as well as with the Attic and Roman heritage of early modern humanism. In some important respects the conception of *Othello*—and, it might reasonably be urged, of tragedy as an English genre—resulted from an accomodation between the cultural forms of those two urban settings, the matrices in which European tragedians found two of their finest opportunities to flourish. For both Sophocles and Shakespeare, the theater implied an analogy with a law-court; its spectators might often feel like the audience at a forensic contest. The ideas of persuasion and legal representation in classical rhetorical theory were somewhat at odds with the old English idea of the criminal trial in which jurors brought their prior information and impressions into the courtroom, but as juries became less self-informing and more dependent on the prosecution, this gap between Elizabethan and Athenian trials narrowed.

Perhaps especially in the social flux of suburban London, significant changes were occurring in the relative roles of juries, judges, and suspects which made a trial resemble an oratorical competition between plaintiff and the accused rather more than it had. This favored an approximation, in tragedy, between the two formal approaches to establishing probability and discovering culpability that were most familiar to educated poets in a contentious and crime-ridden metropolis: the methods that were supplied, on the one hand by the native institution of the trial by jury, and on the other by the imitation of Greco-Roman literature. Early modern English tragedians, I am speculating, responded to the latter and to the rhetorical composition of ancient tragedy in light of their familiarity with a justice system which had always been oral and performative, but which in addition had now begun to operate under conditions altered by the greater impersonality of public roles and interactions.

The basis was thus laid for modern assertions of tragedy's universal significance only when playwrights began treating particular actions in ways less and less determined by the unspoken contingencies of preexisting communal relationships, and marked instead by an effort to discover the grounds of true judgment in individual cases, through a radically rhetorical representation of motives which to us connotes incipient social atomization.[44] Lawrence Manley has related "the quest for radical justice" in seventeenth-century English society to the Tudor emergence of a literature "in which the city was fully institutionalized," making "the anomalous mobility of urban life" the basis for a new order based on "a system of open circulation . . . a realm forgetful of hierarchy and distinction" (Manley, 76, 96). Shakespeare's Venice, in *Othello* as in *Merchant,* is another such city of man; a market of skills and money familiar to the Londoner in his guise as *homo economicus,* while at the same time home to "ideals of fairness and justice . . . a mirror of what England aspired to be" (Vaughn, 16). That is how Shylock, though ostracized in spirit by Christians for making from within the marginalized space of his faith and culture a profitable religion of "thrift" (*Merchant of Venice,* 1.3.90), is still permitted to make claims on our sympathies, and it is why Othello, having made his "fortune" (1.2.23) despite the stigma of his color, may seek first Desdemona's hand and then forgiveness in her death. As audiences balance Othello's homicidal act against the disposition to violence that he has acquired in his vocation, his experience of racial prejudice (or, if the audience is itself racist, the presumption of his race's passionate temperament), the weight of misogynistic norms in many spheres of early modern life, and above all Iago's consummate craft—which plays on the bestialization of his blackness by white society—they are moved to distinguish between such possibly mitigating factors, and that essential guilt of intention which alone can make a free agent wholly culpable, in a society founded on equitable judgment.[45]

A. C. Bradley was thus at pains to prove that "Othello's race . . . in regard to the *essentials of his character* . . . is not important," and that his character itself is not that of "the *essentially* jealous man" (157, 162, my emphases).[46] Bradley's modern apology for Othello may suggest how Shakespeare's tragedies had, in their own way, begun to exercise the spectator in a style of adjudication that would at length be promoted for universal application as the foundation of political theory in the liberal era. Thomas Hobbes wrote in *Leviathan* that "if *a man be trusted to judge between man and man,* it is a precept of the Law of Nature, *that he deale Equally between them. . . .* The observance of this law, from the equall distribution to each man, of that which in reason belongeth to him, is called EQUITY . . . the violation, *Acception of persons.*" He asserted, moreover, that the very first requirement for "a good Judge, or good Interpreter of the Lawes," was "*A right understanding* of that principall Law of Nature called *Equity*" (Hobbes, 108, 195 [chs. 15, 26]). Behind his claim lay an old and complex debate (Ziolkowski, 163–67), yet we may remark that equity, so necessitated by distributive justice, became central to Hobbes' newly atomistic conception of the state—in which laws were fundamentally "deduced . . . from the single principle of individual self-preservation" (Sommerville, 47–48, 49).[47] The acceptance of that individualistic axiom in liberal responses to Hobbes, from Locke onward, is critiqued today by radicals and reactionaries alike as part of the apparatus of capitalist ideology: the mystifying discourse of the free, "humanist" subject, who exists "in reason" and is essentially undetermined by the historical contingencies of his or her "person" (e.g., by class interests).[48] Yet it may still be valued by progressives as the commitment to a law favoring equitable verdicts, open to rhetorical articulations of the moral difference between accidental or circumstantial causes and the motions of a free will.[49]

Ironically the vehicle for Shakespeare's challenge to us to judge equitably, to discriminate essence from accident, and an intention from its consequences, is itself a history of misjudgments. Othello's belief in the truth of a slander, and the extreme injustice of the event, are made credible (as critics commonly remark) by a slanderer's appeal to the forms of prejudice most integral to the roles of political supremacy assumed by men in early modern European communities: misogyny, xenophobia, and racism.[50] Is Venice, then, on trial for these? If so, is London also named in the indictment? To press these charges would be to project a potentially utopian unrest on Shakespeare's part, a discontent with some conditions in the play's imagined Venice—perhaps those which reflect inequities in his own society. He reminds us of how social and ideological hierarchies conduce to misjudgments of culpability as serious as that prompted by Othello's jealousy, and thus of how prone we ourselves are in reality, however sensitive our consciences and thorough our information, to miss the mark of equity as we hear cases like his.

Both trials and tragedies may provoke revisions of our customary judgments. In a modern state devised to assure individual autonomy, each of us is called on to become what the eighteenth-century liberal philosopher Adam Smith termed (in his *Theory of Moral Sentiments*) a "judicious spectator": one whose rulings, as Martha Nussbaum explains, are free of partiality, while also ensuring "that emotions . . . play the valuable role they ought to play in public life." The deliberations of this ideal citizen will admit the equitable influence of "empathetic participation," while conversely affirming the law's indifference to persons by rigidly excluding "the personal bias of the interested participant" (Nussbaum, 72, 73. 75). Tragedy, with its rhetorical composition of imaginary cases, trains us well—from some perspectives, too well—in the discipline of inventing such equitable, compassionate arguments for and against conviction. For when a verdict in the courtroom is called for, the idealism that underlies our contemplative responses in the theater or the study may not be sufficient. Both Othello's incapacity to judge, and the complications that we encounter in judging his case are disheartening indications of the failures of even the most enlightened magistrates to guarantee, under the pressure of historical interests, the perfected judgment that a liberal polity would desperately require of them.

NOTES

1. Citations of *Othello* refer to the line numbering in Honigmann.

2. Rymer thought it proper to ask "what unnatural crime *Desdemona,* or her Parents had committed, to bring this Judgment down upon her; to Wed a Black-amoor, and innocent to be thus cruelly murder'd by him. What instruction can we make out of this Catastrophe? Or whither must our reflection lead us? Is not this to envenome and sour our spirits, to make us repine and grumble at Providence; and the government of the World? If this be our end, what boots it to be Vertuous?" (466). The play has since been paradigmatic of the violation of what Rymer called "poetic justice," even if more recent generations have been less inclined to judge Shakespeare by the rule than to judge the rule by Shakespeare.

3. Cf. discussion in Pechter (1–2). At least one new work for the stage, John Leerdam's *O. J. Othello,* takes the coincidences between the two as its premise; an Edinburgh Fringe Festival first-winner, it came in early 2000 to London's Riverside Studios. In the summer of 2000, Theatre West in Los Angeles produced *The Trial of Othello* by Sherwood Schwartz—"creator of 'Gilligan's Island' and 'The Brady Bunch'" (Brandes).

4. Death was the sentence imposed on adulterers in *Leviticus* 20:10, but not by Jesus (Foakes, n. to *Lear,* 4.6.109–10); attempts to institute the penalty in England during the mid-sixteenth century, and again under the Commonwealth, were unsuccessful (Archer, 253–53; Ingram, 151–53). Cf. below, n. 26.

5. Peter Stallybrass has written of the tragedy as a revelation of discourses of domination; on his account, "Iago is the projection of a social hierarchy's unease" over the legitimation of ambitious transgressors like Othello, whose initial marriage "up" in Venetian society represents "a particular form of class aspiration through romance," whereas the final "cost of rescuing Desdemona's 'honor' is her transformation into aristocratic enclosure" (Stallybrass, 271–72). In this exemplary instance of 1980s Marxist criticism, the discourses of justice that pervade the tragedy are scarcely evident, perhaps because of their inherent idealism. I would point out, however, that this idealism is in the warp and weft of the play, an indispensable part of Desdemona's character, of Othello's, and even, arguably, of Iago's (a malcontent, nursing his injured merit—though one whose sense of injustice prompts him very early, even instantaneously, to convert his virtues into amoral Machiavellian *virtù*).

6. In another recent discussion of *Othello,* Patricia Parker refers for her very particular purposes to the Tudor prosecution of treason (Parker, *Shakespeare,* 229–52). Other critics have considered the relevance of legal contexts to *Othello;* their

interest, however, has tended to focus on the ideological implications of laws as written, rather than on their application in practice. With the partial exception of Maus, they have tended to neglect the analogy between the theater and the early modern English criminal courtroom, as scenes of dramatic and rhetorical action before an audience. Since my aim is to explore the unappreciated significance of felony cases, and of murder trials in particular to the play's conception, I will avoid the issue of Desdemona's defamation – admirably investigated a decade ago by Lisa Jardine (Cunningham; Eggert; Jardine, 19–34; cf. Kornstein, 157–65)— as well as the play's evocations of other instruments of legal or extra-legal social discipline, such as the public shaming of cuckolds and fornicators through the practice of "rough music" (cf. Ingram, 163–65, with references cited in n. 140; McIntosh, 69–74). Actions for defamation were in any case civil, not criminal actions; moreover, charges of defamation involving sexual allegations were reserved for the ecclesiastical courts (which did not employ juries) even after the common law admitted other types of slander cases into the temporal courts (Baker, 364 ff.;Ingram, 295–98).

7. Maus's discussion, grounded in an interpretive tradition established in part by the work of Parker and Altman (with such others as Helen Gardner, Winifred Nowottny, and Stanley Cavell), is addressed to the theme of knowledge in *Othello* – in particular to the question of what it means to desire knowledge of other minds, with the problems of such desires' psychic expression and metaphysical implications (problems articulated in *Othello* through the gendered languages of desire and sexual possession). Maus characterizes the play's representation of inwardness as one reflecting contemporary forms of criminal investigation, while suggesting their unstable epistemological foundations; thus in Othello's suspicion that Desdemona has been secretly, monstrously unchaste, "the activities of evidence gathering and of interpreting others are intimately tied up with a process of projection" (Maus, 45). Maus makes her legal point of reference the handling of allegations of witchcraft and treason, as the sorts of crime most likely to prompt inquiry not only into criminal acts, but even into criminal *thoughts,* so that a jury might be made to render a verdict on the accused's inward state of mind. Yet despite Brabantio's allegations of the Moor's witchcraft (1.3.61ff.) and the effectively treasonous deeds of Iago, it is the idea of murder that is most crucial to the play's design, and murder that is most often named in the text. On the legal contexts for murder in *Hamlet,* cf. Watkin.

8. Early modern audiences were, furthermore, accustomed to the exploitation of murders as subject matter for sensationalistic and didactic pamphlets and plays. The most comprehensive survey of early modern English murder literature is Marshburn, though of the thirty stories Marshburn records for these two decades, some concern witchcraft rather than murder. For historical analyses cf. Lake ("Deeds," "Popular") and Walsham, *Providence.*

9. Joel Altman explains some of the relevance of the witchcraft charge by showing that rhetoric's persuasive power was commonly described in magical terms (Altman, "prophecy," 104–105).

10. I would not, *pace* Heilman, count Desdemona's advocacy of Cassio's suit for reinstatement (3.3.42 ff.) as a fully developed instance of the trial pattern. It does, however, significantly anticipate her later forensic failures; in fact her apologies

for Cassio are more fulsome, if no more effectual, than such speeches as she is able to make to Othello in her own defense (4.2.82 ff., 5.2). There, because of his interruptions or her own agitation, she never gets in more than five lines at a time —except when the patient Iago, not Othello, is her audience (4.2.147–63).

11. As Robert B. Heilman put this, "[t]he judge and prosecutor becomes, in the end, his own defense attorney, accepting the ultimate legal penalty but throwing himself morally on the mercy of the court of public opinion" (Heilman, 165). The allusion to a "defense attorney" is anachronistic (see below), and the claim that Othello's heroic suicide is precisely equivalent to a "legal" punishment is questionable; still, there is insight in the notion that he submits himself to his hearers' judgments. It has been argued that what is important here, no less than his final self-glorification, is his subsequent, belated surrender of this identity to others' evaluations: "What the world says is that Othello is a murdering fool. And Othello—what does he say? . . . The speech is a monologue of sorts, an attempt to redefine himself . . . Yet it is also open-ended, not merely acknowledging but relying on the subsequent speech of others" (Calderwood, 70).

12. Qualifications are necessary here, as on any occasion when we call on social history to supply an interpretive framework only partly manifest in the text itself. I am not about to venture into speculative debates over Shakespeare's putative "legal background" or the peculiar intensity of his interest in juridical matters. With regard to internal evidence from the plays, it is aptly observed that in Shakespeare's works, despite countless allusions to the law and to questions of justice, "an English jury-trial is never depicted" as such (Ives, 86).

13. Though this general rule is subject to qualification, J. S. Cockburn affirms on the basis of data from Essex and Kent that "the overwhelming majority of serious felonies were, as contemporary authorities assert, tried at assizes" (*Calendar*, 24) and Herrup that "the Assizes did monopolize prosecutions for violent death".

14. I generalize from Cockburn's remarks about Assize attendance on the Home Circuit (*Calendar*, 32–33) Herrup notes that in eastern Sussex "coroners . . . reported directly to the Assizes" (Herrup, 47). On the coroner's duties see Smith (108) and below, n. 20.

15. The King's Bench, a debtor's prison, housed the poet and playwright Thomas Dekker for seven years during the early seventeenth century (Twyning, 99, and refs.). The Clink was situated on Bankside close to the Globe, and was a local gaol "for such as should brabble, frey, or break the peace on the said bank, or in the brothel houses" as well as for growing numbers of recusants at the beginning of James's reign (Dobb, 90; Stow, 362). The building occupied by the Counter and its court was "once *S. Margrets* Church defac'd," as Taylor put it (from *The Praise and Vertue of a Jayle and Jaylers*, quoted in Dobb, 87); Stow briefly explained the history of this church's dissolution (Stow, 365). The Court of Admiralty existed "to deal with matters arising on the high seas" Baker, 107).

16. For accounts of gaol deliveries see Smith (110 ff.) and Cockburn (*Calendar*, 19 ff.).

17. See above, n. 10 on Desdemona's efforts at self-defense. On Desdemona's comparative silence and Othello's monologism see (Calderwood, 48–50, 67–70).

18. Opinions have ranged from T. S. Eliot's dour averral that Othello is "*cheering himself up*," and F. R. Leavis's milder charge of "self-dramatization," to Helen

Gardner's "noble moor" and more recent appreciations of the speech as "a necessary prelude to the self-judgment of his heroic suicide" (Eliot, 111; Leavis, 152; Gardner; Kerrigan, 194, citing Braden, 168–69).

19. Cf. Peacham's remark that "this is the only forme of speech, which both speaketh while the vertuous man doth live, and also liveth when the vertuous man is dead" (Peacham, 155). As an encomium of past deeds, the speech finally deals in what Aristotle called character (*ēthos*): "Encomium . . . is concerned with deeds . . . The deeds are signs of the person's habitual character" (*On Rhetoric* 84–5 [1.9.33]). Cf. Desmet: "In Aristotle's anatomy of drama, plot or action is analogous to the rhetorical hypothesis; it is a specific case to be judged. When dealing with plot we ask, for instance, whether or not Orestes is guilty of matricide. But when character is factored into the equation, we are in that middle area between judging a case and arguing an issue. The action is over, the verdict rendered: What remains to judge the quality of the act by evaluating the principal actor's *ēthos*. In this situation we do not put Orestes on trial but ask after the fact whether he was justly acquitted of matricide" (Desmet, 84–85). By abridging his legal case through suicide, Othello tries to ensure that *ēthos* (rather than fact) is the basis of any judgment that the Venetian public or Shakespeare's audience might pronounce.

20. These might be organized by justices of the peace (Langbein, 45–54, cited in Cockburn, *Calendar* 97, n. 92; cf. Herrup, 86–87), or by Assize clerks (Cockburn, *Calendar*, 97–98, 102–104). Justices of the peace relied on constables and the community at large for their information "in routine felonies" (Herrup, 68); at Assizes the coroners, who took the initiative in prosecutions for homicide, would submit certified examinations of witnesses whom they had personally bound over to testify against murder suspects (Cockburn, *Calendar*, 91–92, 96). In east Sussex and Kent, at least, constables were employed as grand jurors (cf. Cockburn, *Calendar*, 48; Herrup, 103–104); on the work of London constables, see Archer, 221–23.

21. Twyning refers to St. Paul's Walk, but crowds were also in Southwark, which "gathered many of those who came, willingly or otherwise, from Kent, Surrey, and Sussex" (Twyning, 2). Shakespeare sometimes registers this sense explicitly; cf. Antony's lines, "Tonight we'll wander through the streets and note/ The qualities of people" (*Antony and Cleopatra*, 1.1.53–54).

22. The rhetorical composition of Othello's suicide speech has been described as recapitulating that of his defense in 1.3 (Elliott, 107 ff).

23. Desdemona's dying assumption of the guilt for her own death (5.2.122–23), while imitating Christ's act of satisfaction for the sins of his murderers, thus also prepares us to appreciate the desperate agony of the conscience which would make Othello then turn witness against himself as well as her—"She's like a liar gone to burning hell:/ 'Twas I that killed her" (5.2.127–28). Debora Shuger remarks on the play's resonance with devotional discourses figuring Christ's passion as a womanish suffering at the hands of torturers, who, however, were themselves tortured in conscience by the pangs of their feminized victim (Shuger, 99,112–17, 120, 232 n. 79). At the same time, Othello's spontaneous acceptance of responsibility for his wife's death—which, Emilia concedes, he might avoid by calling her to witness her mistress's last words—confirms the proverbial wisdom that "mur-

der will out" (Tilley, M1315; Walsham, "Aspects," 84–86), recalling the expression of providential judgment by means of Vindice's bragging tongue in *The Revenger's Tragedy* (5.3.100).

24. Parker brings out this strategy's totalitarian associations for us: "In *Othello,* the coincidence of dilation with delation—of amplification with accusation—comes something closer to what Derrida calls the demand for narrative as the power of the police, that form of disclosure or bringing to light which Shakespeare elsewhere links with comic representatives of the law, but which here becomes something much more powerful, and sinister, in its effect" ("Shakespeare," 69).

25. In a criminal trial, any witnesses who might (exceptionally) be allowed to testify for the accused would not in fact be sworn—though evidence for the Crown was given under oath (Cockburn, *Calendar*, 106–107).

26. Even if Desdemona had committed adultery, this would not fall into the class of violent acts constituting "petty treason" (Baker, 428). "Othello has assumed the role of both prosecutor and judge; he also acts as lawmaker, establishing with Iago's help ad hoc punishments for marital infidelity" (Desmet, 97). Cf. above, n. 4.

27. On this distinction cf. Eden 14, n. 5. For an outline of ecclesiastical court proceedings in English cases of misbehavior, see Ingram (47–52); Othello's interrogation of Desdemona on what becomes her deathbed recalls the "notorious oath *ex officio*" (Ingram, 51), and in trying to make her confess he appears to combine the roles of an inquisitorial torturer and an ecclesiastical judge imposing "penance," though without offering her life in return (Ingram, 53–54). For us, more obviously perhaps than for Shakespeare, the church courts represent a troubling confusion between the offices of judge and jury; so far as I am aware, this was not itself at issue in the context of early modern preoccupations with social regulation.

28. Such "corrupt judges" in Tudor drama had included "All for Money in the play of that name, Sisamnes in *Cambises,* and Appius in *Appius and Virginia*" (McCune, 180); Shakespeare evoked this stage tradition in the figure of Angelo from *Measure for Measure.*

29. As Parker puts this, "the dilation which here takes place in the context of wooing, winning, and acquittal from the law becomes, after the 'close dilations' of the great temptation scene, a witching of the ear by 'circumstances' which prove an accusation or 'delation' rather than dismissing it, and in which the accuser father becomes that instrument of 'Justice' (V.ii.17) who is Othello himself" ("Shakespeare," 60).

30. The relative roles of judge and jury changed during the medieval and early modern periods in complex ways that have been obscured so far by the difficulty of research. Historians agree that the relationship was characterized by increased tension during Shakespeare's time, but differ on the balance of power between the two; Green insists, contrary to Cockburn, that the principle of a petty jury's authority to acquit was continuously acknowledged (Green, 138–150 and 150–52, n. 179; cf. Herrup, 158–59). One complicating feature in felony prosecutions towards the end of the sixteenth century was the rise of offers to plea bargain as an unofficially accepted judicial practice, whereby Assize justices could dispense with a jury trial entirely and proceed to sentencing (Cockburn, *Calendar*, 68–69).

31. Green accounts for the latter, thirteenth- and fourteenth-century stratagem as the "jury nullification" of harsh felony laws: "In order to justify killing in self-defense . . . the man attacked had to retreat until retreat was no longer possible. At the trial the jurors always alleged such a predicament, and though it was sometimes true, a comparison of the coroners' rolls and the trial rolls reveal that it often was not and that a petty jury had so altered the facts as to make pardonable what the law considered nonpardonable" (Green, 38; cf. 32–46, 76–97). For a comparative perspective on English and French pardons for homicide, which also touches on Shakespeare's *Romeo and Juliet,* see Davis (36–76, esp. 70–76) and references therein cited. Our legal fictions of self defense. cf, Wilson, *Theatres,* 55.

32. Kathy Eden observes that according to Aristotle, "[a]s an imitator of human action, the tragic poet shares with the orator [a] reliance on probability. It distinguishes him from the historian (*Poetics,* 9.1–3); it determines his construction of the incidents of the plot (7.2, 8.3, 9.11–12, 10.4, 11.1); it controls his development of character and thought (15.10, 19.5); and . . . it is responsible for the best recognitions (16.11)" (19). On probability in poetic fiction cf. Trimpi, 287–95.

33. See also Trimpi, 252–58 (esp. 256–57), and cf. Desmet citation above, n. 19.

34. Eden, however, goes so far as to portray Shakespeare as counsel for the defense: "the image of murder in Denmark serves as evidence . . . that Hamlet deserves not the more severe judgment associated with the law but a milder, more equitable judgment, pity and even pardon" (182). To me this seems a partial reading, based on too prescriptive an understanding of the historical parallel between poet and rhetorician (perhaps based on Gorgias's defense of Helen).

35. See Eden (25–32) on Gorgias's anticipations of the Aristotelian "analogy between poetry and equity" (28).

36. Altman has demonstrated at length how rhetorical pedagogy gave Tudor dramatists a dialectical paradigm for plays on controversial questions, one modelled on the oratorical debate *in utramque partem* (on both sides of an issue), which humanists already found integral to Roman comedy and which they also employed within the declamatory structures of Senecan tragedies like *Gorboduc* (Altman, *Tudor,* 26–30, 64 ff., 130–47, 229 ff., 255). Similarly, a scholar of French medieval drama has advanced the claim that scholastic legal training in debate and disputation, based on the ancient rhetorical curriculum, helped foster parallel reinventions of theatrical form during the Middle Ages, since "drama . . . emerges as the most logical literary outcome for the histrionics of forensic delivery" in that period (Enders, 128). cf. also Ziolkowski, 144–86, *passim* (esp. 167–86).

37. Whereas Aristotle's works variously articulate a "three-way distinction of intentional wrongdoing, error, and accident with equity and pardon applied to the latter two," the use of the terms *hamartia* and *hamartéma* for is not fully consistent; *hamartiai* in the *Nichomachean Ethics* are "errors" arising "from ignorance of what is right and wrong . . . warranting neither pity nor pardon," but in "the early un-Aristotelian *Rhetoric to Alexander*" they include "mitigating circumstances of error" resulting from a plain ignorance of facts, as in the example of "Mereope mistaking his son for the enemy" (Sherman, 185). In her attempt to reconcile these definitions, Sherman cites Aristotle's definition of *hamartéma* in the *Nichomachean Ethics* (1135b10–25) as an "injury" that "is not contrary to rea-

sonable expectation . . . but does not imply vice" (translating Aristotle's word for "unexpected" *[paralogos]* as "contrary to reasonable expectation"). On her account, the distinguishing significance of *hamartia* in the *Poetics* may thus be that "[w]hy things turned out unexpectedly can . . . be explained by what is predictable and repeatable. This, though, does not commit us to saying that the agent ought to have been in a position to see this as he was acting or to have been able to prevent it. . . . Tragedy is about action that is causally probable and coherent. . . . What happens is contrary to [the character's] belief [at the time of the action] but not contrary to reason . . . our prevailing response to tragedy is . . . pity for the failure to see what in principle, in optimal conditions (and sometimes only in hindsight), is accessible to human light. And it is pity for the undue suffering that must be endured" (Sherman, 186–88).

38. If this generalization should strike some as an endorsement of venerable, but lately suspect doctrines asserting Shakespeare's benign impartiality and transcendence of ideology (from "negative capability" to New Critical "irony"), I might respond that these opinions have prevailed in the post-Enlightenment criticism of Shakespeare precisely because—historically—the contestation of at least the simplest ideological prejudices has always been an effect of tragedy's forensic and controversial aspects. On the "universality" of *Othello* cf. Pechter (21 ff.).

39. "To speak of Othello as he is, without special pleading on either side, would require nothing less than the re-enactment of the play itself" (Danson, 133).

40. As Wilson shows, *Hamlet* "is permeated with legal conceptions of a typically criminal subjectivity that implicitly conceives interiority in terms of *mens rea* " or malicious intent; observing that this notion of intention is "the key component of practical strategies of action in the theater and in the law, and of a type of fictionality in which such conceptualizations are narrativized," Wilson concludes that "this fictionality partakes in *Hamlet* of the conceptual resource of the legal principle of equity, which derives fictional hypotheses from retroactive constructions of the intentions of the legislator and defendant" (27–28). (Wilson, "Hamlet," 27–28). On legal fictions of agency in Othello, cf, Wilson, Theatre, 260–62, in the phrase "Hum—I have heard/ That guilty creatures sitting at a play . . ." [2.2.584–85], seems to me to bear an excessive burden of demonstration.)

41. Iago's ability to conjure imagined adulteries within the void in Othello's faith left by a lost handkerchief exemplifies the rhetorical association between the use of visual signs as proofs and the creation of affective mental images, as developed from Aristotle's discussion of *enargeia* (vividness) in the later tradition of Cicero and Quintilian (cf. Eden, 11–20, 86–92, 179–83). This facet of Iago's forensic strategy has inspired influential commentary in Parker ("Shakespeare," 64–65) and in Altman ("'Preposterous'"), where it is seen to reveal an analogy between Iago's rhetoric and Shakespeare's tragic art (cf. Parker, "Shakespeare," 58–59, 66 –69). Interestingly, whereas Marion Trousdale has also drawn this connection, she and Altman follow it to opposite epistemological and metaphysical conclusions —Trousdale finding a cautionary reminder of the distinction between words and things, just where Altman perceives this difference collapsing into a world of imaginary contingencies (Altman, " 'Prophetic,'" 101; Altman, " 'Preposterous,' " 151; Trousdale, 167). Christy Desmet discovers what is perhaps a common ground

between these positions—finding the lesson of these episodes in Iago's ability to desensitize Othello to rhetoric's "subjunctive mood, in which truth and falsehood coexist," so that he is no longer capable of comprehending rhetorical speech except as either literal fact or hyperbolic untruth.

42. In the terms of classical rhetoric, the spectacle of Desdemona's corpse would belong to the order of "nonartistic" (or "inartificial") proofs, the use of which Aristotle contrasted in *On Rhetoric* with that of the "artistic" (or "artificial") proofs of speech (37 [1.2.2]), as well as to the sort of visible "sign" which in the *Poetics* he characterizes as the "least artful" device for the production of tragic recognitions (21 [4.3.1]).

43. Shakespeare often investigates both the grounds and the proper limits of mercy in his other plays, e.g., in *Measure for Measure* (Bradshaw, 167–69 and 164–218, *passim*).

44. The trajectory in the English theater to which I allude is that whereby, according to Robert Weimann's now classic account, "the extradramatic dimension of the *platea* tradition was increasingly integrated into Elizabethan dramaturgy," and "the significance of the conventions of speech and action associated with the *platea* was considerably diminished by more self-contained modes of dramatic composition" (237, 241). Weimann's analysis of the functions of pre-Shakespearean and Shakespearean drama alike into the "*platea* and *locus*" or, respectively, the spaces of direct address and of "illusion" (74–75), might also describe court proceedings.

45. On the significance of the interrelated concepts of equity, intention (or "good faith"), and the freedom of the will in Western legal theory through the nineteenth century, see Pound, 77–80. Classical Greek notions of justice (apart from Aristotle), while not oblivious to questions of intention, were far from granting the priority that modern liberalism accords to willed responsibility; see Dover (158–59).

46. Having cleared Othello's essence from the charges of (metaphorical) blackness and of jealousy, but still needing to take some account of the horror of Desdemona's murder, Bradley could only maintain his uncompromisingly sympathetic reading by simply refusing to pass judgment on the act itself, declaring that "the play is a tragedy, and from this point we may abandon the ungrateful and undramatic task of awarding praise and blame" (163).

47. Cf. Somerville (100–104) on the tension in Hobbes between the imperative to equitable judgment and subjects' contractual obligation to submit to the sovereign.

48. C. B. Macpherson thus argued that the emergence of "a system of obligation that is, or can become, morally binding on all individuals in a society" requires that society to be "one in which individuals are capable of seeing themselves as equal in some respect more important than all the respects in which they are unequal. . . . Hobbes grasped this. . . . In Hobbes's model, which in this respect coincides with the model of possessive market society, everyone is subject to the determination of the competitive market for powers". Hobbes, however, "did not allow for the existence of politically significant unequal classes. . . . Since he left class division and class cohesion out of his model, there was no place in his conclusions for a sovereign body tied to one class. Yet that is the kind of government

most agreeable to the model of a possessive market society" (Macpherson, 93–94). On the strong arguments against Macpherson's reading of Hobbes as the founder of capitalist ideology, cf. Sommerville (180, n. 58). Notably, those for whom equity was of the greatest practical priority in Hobbes's time were closer to communism than capitalism; whereas believers in England's ancient constitution asserted with comparative complacency "that the body of the English common law possessed an inherent rationality . . . Equity was not something outside the law, but something within it," it was the Levellers for whom "[r]eason and equity were the guiding considerations . . . not antiquity or legality as defined by positive law alone" (Burgess, 86, 224).

49. Hobbes recognized, and was much troubled by, rhetoric's importance to issues of justice (Skinner 45 and 250–326, *passim*, esp. 283–84, quoting *De Cive* XIV. xvii).

50. Of these, the latter two at least may be regarded as partly metaphorical for class anxieties. Although Venice (here as in *Merchant of Venice)* seems to have replaced distinctions of status with meritocracy, abridging the exclusive rights of birth whenever this proves convenient in the pursuit of material interest, yet Shakespeare does not exclude the psychological effects of a hierarchy of birth but displaces them (in both plays) onto ethnic difference (cf. Stallybrass and above, n. 5).

WORKS CITED

Altman, Joel. *The Tudor Play of Mind: Rhetorical Inquiry and the Development of Elizabethan Drama.* Berkeley: University of California Press, 1978.

———. "'Preposterous Conclusions': Eros, Enargeia, and the Composition of Othello." *Representations* 18 (1987): 129–57.

———. "'Prophetic Fury': *Othello* and the Economy of Shakespearean Reception." *Studies in the Literary Imagination* 26.1 (1993): 85-113.

Archer, Ian. *The Pursuit of Stability: Social Relations in Elizabethan London.* Cambridge: Cambridge University Press, 1991.

Aristotle. *Poetics.* Trans. Richard Janko. Indianapolis: Hackett, 1987.

———. *On Rhetoric: A Theory of Civic Discourse.* Trans. George A. Kennedy. New York: Oxford University Press, 1991.

Baker, J. H. *An Introduction to English Legal History.* 2nd ed. London: Butterworths, 1979.

Braden, Gordon. *Renaissance Tragedy and the Senecan Tradition: Anger's Privilege.* New Haven: Yale University Press, 1985.

Bradley, A. C. *Shakespearean Tragedy.* 1904. Greenwich, Conn.: Fawcett, n.d..

Bradshaw, Graham. *Shakespeare's Scepticism.* Ithaca: Cornell University Press, 1987.

Brandes, Philip. "Othello's on Trial in Shakespeare Sequel." *Los Angeles Times* 28 July. 2000: 28.

Burgess, Glenn. *The Politics of the Ancient Constitution: An Introduction to English Political Thought, 1603–1642.* University Park: Pennsylvania State University Press, 1992.

Calderwood, James L. *The Properties of* Othello. Amherst: University of Massachusetts Press, 1989.

Cartwright, Kent. "Audience Response and the Denouement of *Othello*." *Othello: New Perspectives*. Ed. Virginia Mason Vaughan and Kent Cartwright. Rutherford: Associated University Presses-Fairleigh Dickinson University Press, 1991. 160–76.

Cockburn, J. S., ed. *Calendar of Assize Records: Home Circuit Indictments, Elizabeth I and James I: Introduction*. London: Her Majesty's Stationery Office, 1985.

———. "Twelve Silly Men?: The Trial Jury at Assizes, 1560–1670." *Twelve Good Men and True: The Criminal Trial Jury in England, 1200–1800*. Ed. J. S. Cockburn and Thomas A. Green. Princeton: Princeton University Press, 1988. 158–81.

Cunningham, Karen. "Female Fidelities on Trial: Proof in the Howard Attainder and *Cymbeline*." *Renaissance Drama* N. S. 25 (1996): 1-31.

Danson, Lawrence. *Shakespeare's Dramatic Genres*. Oxford: Oxford University Press, 2000.

Desmet, Christy. *Reading Shakespeare's Characters: Rhetoric, Ethics, and Identity*. Amherst: University of Massachusetts Press, 1992.

Dobb, Clifford. "London's Prisons." *Shakespeare Survey* 17 (1964): 87–100.

Dover, K. J. *Greek Popular Morality in the Time of Plato and Aristotle*. Berkeley: University of California Press, 1974.

Eccles, Mark. *Shakespeare in Warwickshire*. Madison: University of Wisconsin Press, 1961.

Eden, Kathy. *Poetic and Legal Fiction in the Aristotelian Tradition*. Princeton: Princeton University Press, 1986.

Eggert, Katherine and M. Lindsay Kaplan. "'Good queen, my lord, good queen': Sexual Slander and the Trials of Female Authority in *The Winter's Tale*." *Renaissance Drama* N. S. 26 (1996): 89–118.

Eliot, T. S. "Shakespeare and the Stoicism of Seneca." 1927; rpt. *Selected Essays, 1917–1932*. New York: Harcourt, Brace and Company, 1932: 107–20.

Elliott, Martin. *Shakespeare's Invention of* Othello*: A Study in Early Modern English*. New York: St. Martin's Press, 1988.

Enders, Jody. *Rhetoric and the Origins of Medieval Drama*. Ithaca: Cornell University Press, 1992.

Fine, John V. A. *The Greeks: A Critical History*. Cambridge: Harvard University Press, 1983.

Foakes, R. A., ed. Notes to *King Lear*. 3rd Arden ed. Walton-on-Thames: Thomas Nelson and Sons Ltd., 1997.

Gardner, Helen. "The Noble Moor." 1955; rpt. *Othello: Critical Essays*. Ed. Susan Snyder. New York: Garland Publishing, 1988. 169-88.

Goldhill, Simon. *Reading Greek Tragedy*. Cambridge: Cambridge University Press, 1986.

Green, Thomas Andrew. *Verdict According to Conscience: Perspectives on the English Criminal Trial Jury 1200–1800*. Chicago: University of Chicago Press, 1985.

Greenblatt, Stephen. *Renaissance Self-Fashioning from More to Shakespeare*. Chicago: University of Chicago Press, 1980.

Heilman, Robert B. *Magic in the Web: Action & Language in* Othello. Lexington: University of Kentucky Press, 1956.

Herrup, Cynthia B. *The Common Peace: Participation and the Criminal Law in Seventeenth-Century England.* Cambridge: Cambridge University Press, 1987.

Hobbes, Thomas. *Leviathan.* 1651. Ed. Richard Tuck. Cambridge: Cambridge University Press, 1991.

Honigmann, E. A. J., ed. *Othello.* 3rd Arden ed. Walton-on-Thames: Thomas Nelson and Sons Ltd., 1997.

Ingram, Martin. *Church Courts, Sex and Marriage in England, 1570–1640.* Cambridge: Cambridge University Press, 1987.

Ives, E. W. "The Law and the Lawyers." *Shakespeare Survey* 17 (1964): 73–86.

Jardine, Lisa. *Reading Shakespeare Historically.* London: Routledge, 1996.

Kennedy, George. "Introduction." *On Rhetoric: A Theory of Civic Discourse.* New York: Oxford University Press, 1991. 3–22.

Kerrigan, William. *Shakespeare's Promises.* Baltimore: Johns Hopkins University Press, 1999.

Kliman, Bernice. "Isabella in *Measure for Measure*." *Shakespeare Studies* 15 (1982): 137–48.

Kornstein, Daniel J. *Kill All the Lawyers?: Shakespeare's Legal Appeal.* Princeton: Princeton University Press, 1994.

Lake, Peter. "Deeds Against Nature: Cheap Print, Protestantism and Murder in Early Seventeenth Century England." *Culture and Politics in Early Stuart England.* Eds. Kevin Sharpe and Peter Lake. Stanford: Stanford University press, 1993. 257–83.

———. "Popular form, Puritan content? Two Puritan appropriations of the murder pamphlet from mid-seventeenth-century London." *Religion, culture and society in early modern Britain: Essays in honour of Patrick Collinson.* Eds. Anthony Fletcher and Peter Roberts. Cambridge: Cambridge University Press, 1994. 313–334.

Langbein, J. H. *Prosecuting Crime in the Renaissance: England, Germany, France.* Cambridge: Harvard University Press, 1974.

Leavis, F. R. *The Common Pursuit.* London: Chatto and Windus, 1952.

Macpherson, C. B. *The Political Theory of Possessive Individualism: Hobbes to Locke.* Oxford: Oxford University Press, 1962.

Manley, Lawrence. *Literature and Culture in Early Modern London.* Cambridge: Cambridge University Press, 1995.

Marshall, Cynthia. *Last Things and Last Plays: Shakespearean Eschatology.* Carbondale: Southern Illinois University Press, 1991.

Maus, Katherine Eisaman. "Proof and Consequences: Inwardness and Its Exposure in the English Renaissance." *Representations* 34 (1991): 29–52.

McCune, Pat. "Order and Justice in Early Tudor Drama." *Renaissance Drama* N. S. 26 (1996): 171–96.

McIntosh, Marjorie Keniston. *Controlling misbehavior in England, 1370–1600.* Cambridge: Cambridge University Press, 1998.

Nussbaum, Martha C. *Poetic Justice: The Literary Imagination and Public Life.* Boston: Beacon Press, 1995.

Parker, Patricia. "Shakespeare and rhetoric: 'dilation' and 'delation' in Othello." *Shakespeare and the Question of Theory.* Ed. Patricia Parker and Geoffrey

Hartman. New York: Methuen, 1985. 54–74.

———. *Shakespeare from the Margins: Language, Culture, Context.* Chicago: University of Chicago Press, 1996.

Peacham, Henry. *The Garden of Eloquence.* 2nd ed. London, 1593.

Pound, Roscoe. *An Introduction to the Philosophy of Law.* 2nd ed. New Haven: Yale University Press, 1954.

Rymer, Thomas. *A Short View of Tragedy* (excerpted passages). 1692. *Four Centuries of Shakespearian Criticism.* Ed. Frank Kermode. New York: Avon, 1965. 461–69.

Salgādo, Gāmini. *The Elizabethan Underworld.* 1977. London: Alan Sutton, 1984.

Schoenbaum, S. *William Shakespeare: A Documentary Life.* New York: Oxford University Press in association with the Scolar Press, 1975.

———. *Shakespeare's Lives: New Edition.* Oxford: Oxford University Press, 1991.

Sherman, Nancy. "Hamartia and Virtue." *Essays on Aristotle's* Poetics. Ed. Amelie Oksenberg Rorty. Princeton: Princeton University Press, 1992. 177–96.

Shuger, Debora. *The Renaissance Bible: Scholarship, Sacrifice, and Subjectivity.* Berkeley: University of California Press, 1994.

Skinner, Quentin. Reason and *Rhetoric in the Philosophy of Hobbes.* Cambridge: Cambridge University Press, 1996.

Smith, Sir Thomas. *De Republica Anglorum.* 1583. Ed. Mary Dewar. Cambridge: Cambridge University Press, 1982.

Sommerville, Johann P. *Thomas Hobbes: Political Ideas in Historical Context.* New York: St. Martin's Press, 1992.

Stallybrass, Peter. "Patriarchal Territories: The Body Enclosed." 1986. *Othello: Critical Essays.* Ed. Susan Snyder. New York: Garland Publishing, 1988. 251–77.

Stow, John. *The Survey of London.* 1603. Ed. H. B. Wheatley. London: Dent, 1987.

Tilley, Morris Palmer. *A Dictionary of the Proverbs in England in the Sixteenth and Seventeenth Centuries.* Ann Arbor: University of Michigan Press, 1950.

Trimpi, Wesley. *Muses of One Mind: The Literary Analysis of Experience and its Continuity.* Princeton: Princeton University Press, 1983.

Trousdale, Marion. *Shakespeare and the Rhetoricians.* Chapel Hill: University of North Carolina Press, 1982.

Twyning, John. *London Dispossessed: Literature and Social Space in the Early Modern City.* Houndsmills: Macmillan Press Ltd., 1998.

Vaughan, Virginia Mason. Othello*: A Contextual History.* Cambridge: Cambridge University Press, 1994.

Walsham, Alexandra. "Aspects of Providentialism in Early Modern England." Diss. University of Cambridge, 1994.

———. *Providence in Early Modern England.* New York: Oxford University Press, 1999.

Watkin, Thomas Glyn. "Hamlet and the Law of Homicide." *Law Quarterly Review,* 100 (1984): 282–310.

Weimann, Robert. *Shakespeare and the Popular Tradition in the Theater: Studies in the Social Dimension of Dramatic Form and Function.* Ed. Robert Schwartz. Baltimore: Johns Hopkins University Press, 1978.

Wilson, Luke. "*Hamlet*: Equity, Intention, Performance." *Studies in the Literary Imagination* 24.2 (1991): 91–113.

————. *Theaters of Intention: Drama and the Law in Early Modern England.* Stanford: Stanford University Press, 2000.

Ziolkowski, Theodore. *The Mirror of Justice: Literary Reflections of Legal Crisis.* Princeton: Princeton University Press, 1997.

Othello Among the Sonnets

JAMES SCHIFFER

> *Therefore I lie with her, and she with me,*
> *And in our faults by lies we flattered be.*
>
> (SONNET 138.13-14)[1]

> *Do you know, sirrah, where Lieutenant Cassio lies?*
>
> (OTHELLO.3.4.1)[2]

Recent computer-based, rare-word studies of the Sonnets suggest that Shakespeare was either writing or revising at least some sonnets during the first decade of the 1600s, the same time that he was writing his major tragedies, among them *Othello*, though we also know that at least two of the sonnets (138 and 144) were written as early as 1599 (and perhaps much earlier in the 1590s), since that year versions of these two poems were published in *The Passionate Pilgrim*.[3] In any case, it seems quite possible that the Sonnets were on Shakespeare's mind when he wrote *Othello*, given the many thematic similarities between the two works: the unstable balance between love, work, and self-esteem; the insecurities caused by differences in race, age, class, culture, and gender; the predominance of black and white imagery in both the sonnet sequence and the play, and the relation of such imagery to racism depicted in these works—and embedded in the English language; the tension of same-sex friendship against heterosexual love and the link between homosociality, homoeroticism, and misogyny; the dialectic of idealized love and degraded sexuality; the pain of unfulfilled desire and the humiliation of sexual jealousy; and the gradual silencing (in the case of *Othello*) or the complete elision (in the case of the Sonnets) of women's voices, to name just a few.[4] In fact, *Othello* seems to offer a kind of photographic negative of the Sonnets' triangulated relationship between the poet, the fair friend, and the dark lady. In the play, the older protagonist rather than the lady is black, the woman is "right fair" and virtuous, and the male friend is a demi-devil, while Cassio, another male friend, is at best an innocent victim and at worst a gull.[5]

Perhaps the only thing more striking than these parallels is that so few critics have seemed to comment upon them, a fact that might be explained by the assumption of most scholars (until the last two decades) that the Sonnets were composed much earlier than the play.[6] Yet even this neglect by critics points to yet another interesting parallel: the ways criticism of both works over the last four hundred years has so often been deformed by the racism, sexism, and (in the case of the Sonnets) homophobia of those who have commented.[7] Perhaps such critical distortion is to be expected when works touching on such controversial themes as sexual jealousy, miscegenation, homoeroticism, and misogyny are discussed. Whatever the cause of such critical myopia in the past, there have been important studies in the past few decades on both works, particularly on race and gender in *Othello* and on homoeroticism in the Sonnets.[8] Much of that valuable criticism of each work has clear relevance to the other. In these postmodern times, *Othello* and the Sonnets are ripe for comparative analysis.

"SUCH CIVIL WAR IS IN MY LOVE AND HATE"

Central to each work is the experience of triangulation, jealousy, and radical uncertainty. The Sonnets poet is torn between two loves:

> of comfort and despair,
> Which, like two spirits, do suggest me still;
> The better angel is a man right fair,
> The worser spirit a woman coloured ill. (Sonnet 144.1-4)

Othello is led by Iago, "egregiously" like an "ass" (2.1.310), to believe that his Lieutenant Cassio and Desdemona "hath the act of shame / A thousand times committed" (5.2.218–19). In fact, the actual triangulation in the play, though Othello does not realize this, is between Othello, Desdemona, and Iago; the homosocial/homoerotic bond between Iago and Othello comes at the expense of Othello's bond with Desdemona, and leads to the deaths of the Moor and his innocent wife. The protagonists' experience of jealousy in both works is greatly exacerbated, furthermore, by uncertainty. The Sonnets poet states with misogynistic spite the epistemological hell he suffers in sonnet 144:

> And, whether that my angel be turn'd fiend,
> Suspect I may, yet not directly tell;
> But being both from me both to each friend,
> I guess one angel in another's hell.

> Yet this shall I ne'er know, but live in doubt,
> Till my bad angel fire my good one out. (9–14)

For Othello as well, the worst aspect of his suffering comes from his experience of doubt. What Iago advises him to do:

> I speak not yet of proof.
> Look to your wife; observe her well with Cassio.
> Wear your eyes thus, not jealous nor secure. (3.3.210–12),

is the one thing the general cannot do:

> Why, why is this?
> Think'st thou I'd make a life of jealousy,
> To follow still the changes of the moon
> With fresh suspicions? No! To be once in doubt
> Is once to be resolved. (3.3.190–94)

In *Othello*, the experience of internal division is by no means restricted to the protagonist. Desdemona admits to a "divided duty" (1.3.183) between her father and her new husband, while Emilia is torn through the last acts of the play by her desire to please her husband and her deep loyalty to her mistress. In the Sonnets, perhaps mainly because we get just a single point of view, the only way the young friend—and in some sonnets, like 131, the dark lady— seem divided is between their outward semblance of beauty and virtue (apparently more true of the friend's semblance than the dark lady's), and their alleged devious behavior.

The Sonnets poet is divided in complex ways, not only between two loves, but also between rival versions of the young friend and dark lady, as well as of himself. In relation to the young friend, the poet vacillates between hyperbolic praise ("Fair, kind, and true" [105.9, 10, 13]) and recrimination of the friend's "sensual fault[s]" (35.9; see also, for example, 33, 34, 57, 94, and 95). Even when the poet faces up to the friend's infidelity, the poet's inclination is to defend the offense rather than accuse the offender, except in an oblique, passive-aggressive way:

> For to thy sensual fault I bring in sense—
> Thy adverse party is thy advocate—
> And 'gainst myself a lawful plea commence.
> Such civil war is in my love and hate,
> That I an áccessary needs must be
> To that sweet thief which sourly robs from me. (35.9–14).

There is a curious parallel to the judicial metaphors of Sonnet 35 in Desdemona's comments to Emilia in act 3, scene 4:

> Beshrew me much, Emilia,
> I was, unhandsome warrior as I am,
> Arraigning his unkindness with my soul;
> But now I find I had suborned the witness,
> And he's indicted falsely. (152–56)

In a later scene, we hear the same tone of loving forgiveness (or even denial) of Othello's faults when Desdemona remarks to Emilia, "My love doth so approve him / That even his stubbornness, his checks, his frowns—/ . . . have grace and favor in them" (4.3.20–22). Desdemona's tendency to put Othello's interests above her own reaches a remarkable conclusion when Emilia asks her mistress "who hath done this deed?" (5.2.127), and Desdemona, dying, responds, "Nobody; I myself. Farewell. / Commend me to my kind lord. O, farewell" (5.2.128–29).

The internal battles the Sonnets speaker endures are sometimes conveyed in images of contesting parts of the body, as in sonnets 46 and 47, where "eye and heart are at a mortal war" (46.1). This motif of the disunited self also appears in the dark lady sequence where the poet's reason and emotions, judgment and will, common sense and behavior, often seem irrevocably at odds. Thus, the sonnet on lust ends with the disturbing observation:

> All this the world well knows, yet none knows well
> To shun the heav'n that leads men to this hell.
> (129.13–14),

while sonnet 137 begins with a lament prompted by the speaker's awareness of his own cognitive dissonance:

> Thou blind fool love, what dost thou to mine eyes,
> That they behold and see not what they see?
> (137.1–2).

In sonnet 147, the speaker's "reason, the physician to [his] love, / Angry that his prescriptions are not kept, / Hath left" him (5–7). Here psychological allegory conveys the speaker's fragmented self.

Othello's internal division, long dormant because of his suppressed pain and rage at the racism of Venetian society, emerges when he thinks he discovers a disjunction between how Desdemona appears and how she is in horrid deed:

OTHELLO: Ay, let her rot and perish, and be damned tonight, for she
                shall not live. No, my heart is turned to stone; I strike it, and
                it hurts my hand. O, the world hath not a sweeter creature!
                She might lie by an emperor's side and command him tasks.

IAGO:	Nay, that's not your way.
OTHELLO:	Hang her! I do but say what she is. So delicate with her needle! An admirable musician! O, she will sing the savageness out of a bear. Of so high and plenteous wit and invention! (4.1.181–90)

He cannot endure the seeming doubleness of her being, the "whore" who underlies what he takes to be her angelic surface:

> Yet I'll not shed her blood,
> Nor scar that whiter skin of hers than snow,
> And smooth as monumental alabaster.
> Yet she must die, else she'll betray more men. (5.2.3–6)

In the broken syntax of the following lines we can trace the splintering of Othello's identity, his constructed illusion of a coherent self and world:

> Haply, for I am black
> And have not those soft parts of conversation
> That chamberers have, or for I am declined
> Into the vale of years—yet that's not much—
> She's gone. (3.3.279-84)

Earlier he had boasted, "My life upon her faith!" (1.3.297); now that her faith has been cast in doubt, "Chaos is come again" (3.3.100).

"OTHELLO'S OCCUPATION'S GONE"

Both works explore a range of complex relationships between love and work, the two main sources of self-worth and satisfaction in life. While these themes play out differently in the Sonnets and in *Othello*, the preoccupation with how "occupation" affects and is affected by love is a central concern of both works. Often in the sonnets to the young friend, love is a compensation or consolation for the disappointments of fortune, as in sonnet 29:

> When in disgrace with fortune and men's eyes,
> I all alone beweep my outcast state,
> And trouble deaf heav'n with my bootless cries,
> And look upon myself and curse my fate,
> Wishing me like to one more rich in hope,
> Featured like him, like him with friends possessed,
> Desiring this man's art, and that man's scope,
> With what I most enjoy contented least;
> Yet in these thoughts myself almost despising,

> Haply I think on thee, and then my state,
> Like to the lark at break of day arising
> From sullen earth, sings hymns at heaven's gate;
> For thy sweet love rememb'red such wealth brings,
> That then I scorn to change my state with kings.

A similar theme is sounded in sonnet 91, where the speaker pronounces:

> Thy love is better than high birth to me,
> Richer than wealth, prouder than garments' cost,
> Of more delight than hawks or horses be;
> And having thee, of all men's pride I boast;
> Wretched in this alone, that thou mayst take
> All this away, and me most wretched make.
> (9–14)

Yet in the couplet of 91, one glimpses the other side of the equation: if the beloved has power to compensate the speaker for what he lacks in the way of worldly fortune, those things the speaker lacks (wealth, fame, status) make him vulnerable to abandonment by the friend, who may at any time reappraise the speaker's worth. This is the poet's fear, for instance, in sonnet 87:

> Thyself thou gav'st, thy own worth then not knowing,
> Or me, to whom thou gav'st it, else mistaking;
> So thy great gift, upon misprision growing,
> Comes home again, on better judgment making.
> (9–12)

Though the cause of the poet's lack of self-worth (at least in relation to the beloved) is not always clear, it seems related in some poems to a difference in social class as well as to a sense of shame about the speaker's profession. Many scholars, for example, have taken the following lines from sonnet 110 to be a Shakespearean autobiographical reference to working in the theater:

> Alas 'tis true, I have gone here and there,
> And made myself a motley to the view,
> Gored mine own thoughts, sold cheap what is most dear,
> Made old offenses of affections new.
> (1–4),

Similar interpretations have been offered of sonnet 111:

> O for my sake do you wish fortune chide,
> The guilty goddess of my harmful deeds,
> That did not better for my life provide
> Than public means which public manners breeds.

> Thence comes it that my name receives a brand,
> And almost thence my nature is subdued
> To what it works in, like the dyer's hand.
> (1–7)

The speaker's apparent shame about his profession creates an imbalance of valuation within the relationship, an imbalance that makes "mutual render" (sonnet 125.12) difficult, if not impossible.

Yet if one thinks of the speaker as a poet (rather than as a playwright or actor), then his occupation becomes not a source of shame, but instead a powerful means of winning and preserving love (and perhaps patronage), and of compensating for loss. This is, of course, the thrust of the many sonnets in which the speaker promises the beloved immortality through verse, as he does in sonnet 18:

> But thy eternal summer shall not fade,
> Nor lose possession of that fair thou ow'st,
> Nor shall death brag thou wand'rest in his shade,
> When in eternal lines to time thou grow'st.
> So long as men can breathe or eyes can see,
> So long lives this, and this gives life to thee.
> (9–14)

Beyond this theme of immortality, there may well be yet another twist to the love/poetry-as-profession relationship in the Sonnets, if, as Arthur Marotti and others have maintained, these are love poems written for patronage. There is even the possibility of their being genuine love poems and patronage poems at the same time, with love interests and economic interests coinciding. We speak here not with certainty, but to acknowledge the complexity of ways in which love and work are intertwined in so many of these poems.

In *Othello*, a crisis in the realm of work or of love has the effect of contaminating the other realm. The play begins with Iago's bitter complaint to Roderigo about Cassio's promotion to the lieutenancy: "Micahel Cassio, a Florentine, / . . . That never set a squadron in the field" (1.1.21, 23). Though Iago maintains he knows his "place" is "worth no worse a place" (1.1.12), it is clear from the villainy that ensues that Iago has grave doubts about his worth and that Cassio's promotion above him has deeply threatened his sense of self. His boast to Roderigo—"I am not what I am" (1.1.67)— expresses much more about the emptiness and negation at the core of his being than he perhaps means to reveal (one might note here as well the curious echo and reversal of the confident lover-poet's claim of "I am that I am" in sonnet 121 [9]). Furthermore, the professional envy and resentment Iago feels are paralleled in his marriage by feelings sexual jealousy and misogyny. The vocabulary of work spills into his paranoid fantasies of Emilia's infidelity:

> I hate the Moor;
> And it is thought abroad that twixt my sheets
> He's done my office. I know not if 't be true;
> But I, for mere suspicion in that kind,
> Will do as if for surety. He holds me well;
> The better shall my purpose work on him.
> Cassio's a proper man. Let me see now:
> To get his place and to plume up my will
> In double knavery—How, how?—Let's see:
> After some time, to abuse Othello's ear
> That he is too familiar with his wife. (1.3.387–97)

It is not just that Iago fears Othello has done his "office," but Iago also chooses to gain Cassio's place and "plume up [his] will" by destroying Othello's marriage. The two spheres are confused and entangled in Iago's mind; therefore, he determines to infect Othello's mind with a similar confusion:

> For that I do suspect the lusty Moor
> Hath leaped into my seat, the thought whereof
> Doth, like a poisonous mineral, gnaw my innards;
> And nothing can or shall content my soul
> Till I am evened with him, wife for wife,
> Or failing so, yet that I put the Moor
> At least into a jealousy so strong
> That judgment cannot cure. (2.1.296–303)

In the relationship between Othello and Desdemona, the realms of work and love initially seem to coexist in nurturing harmony. Desdemona, after all, is drawn to Othello because of his work: "She loved me for the dangers I had passed, / And I loved her that she did pity them" (1.3.169–70), and she is determined to accompany him to Cyprus:

> That I did love the Moor to live with him
> My downright violence and storms of fortunes
> May trumpet to the world. My heart's subdued
> Even to the very quality of my lord.
> I saw Othello's visage in his mind,
> And to his honors and his valiant parts
> Did I my soul and fortunes consecrate.
> So that, dear lords, if I be left behind
> A moth of peace, and he go to the war,
> The rites for why I love him are bereft me,
> And I a heavy interim shall support
> By his dear absence. Let me go with him. (1.3.251–62)

From the first, however, Othello understands that yielding to love means a potential loss of personal and professional autonomy:

> For know, Iago,
> But that I love the gentle Desdemona,
> I would not my unhousèd free condition
> Put into circumscription and confine
> For the sea's worth. (1.2.24–28).

It is his awareness of the danger of mixing love and soldiering that leads him to deny that he seeks to "please the palate of [his] appetite" (1.3.265) and to reassure the Venetian senators:

> And heaven defend your good souls that you think
> I will your serious and great business scant
> When she is with me. No, when light-winged toys
> Of feathered Cupid seel with wanton dullness
> My speculative and officed instruments,
> That my disports corrupt and taint this business,
> Let huswives make a skillet of my helm,
> And all indign and base adversaries
> Make head against my estimation! (1.3.269–77)

Yet it is not long after his arrival in Cyprus that Iago tells Cassio that "Our general's wife is now the general" (2.3.308–309); while this is clearly an exaggeration, the contamination of Othello's love and work lives has begun, and it is not long before belief in Desdemona's infidelity leads him to abandon his life as a soldier as well:

> O, now, forever
> Farewell the tranquil mind! Farewell content!
> Farewell the plumèd troops and the big wars
> That makes ambition virtue! O, farewell!
> Farewell the neighing steed and the shrill trump,
> The spirit-stirring drum, th'ear-piercing fife,
> The royal banner, and all quality,
> Pride, pomp, and circumstance of glorious war!
> And O, you mortal engines, whose rude throat
> Th' immortal Jove's dread clamors counterfeit,
> Farewell! Othello's occupation's gone. (3.3.363–73)

As Patricia Parker observes, there is sexual double meaning here on "occupation," as in occupation of Desdemona, for Othello believes Cassio has taken his "place" in his bed as later he will succeed the Moor his military command.[9] As with Iago, the language of work and the language of sexuality have become fatally confused and intertwined.

For the working women in the play, Emilia and Bianca, the lines between love and work also get tangled and confused. Emilia, as we have seen, is torn between obligation to her husband and concern for her mistress. At first she betrays Desdemona by giving the spotted handkechief to her "wayward husband" (3.3.308) in order "to please his fantasy" (3.3.315) and later by keeping silent when Desdemona asks if Emilia has seen it. At the end of the play, however, Emilia reveals her husband's treachery. When Iago charges her, "get you home," she responds:

> Good gentlemen, let me have leave to speak.
> 'Tis proper I obey him, but not now.
> Perchance, Iago, I will ne'er go home. (5.2.201–04)

Her love for her mistress overpowers her duty to her husband, and as a result Iago murders her—in an interesting twist on this theme, she dies for love of her employer. Bianca, whose profession is to sell her love, has the misfortune of falling in love with a customer, Michael Cassio. Thus, Iago describes her:

> A huswife that by selling her desires
> Buys herself bread and clothes. It is a creature
> That dotes on Cassio—as 'tis this strumpet's plague
> To beguile many and be beguiled by one. (4.1.96–99)

Though Bianca survives the bloodshed of the play's conclusion, she is called a "strumpet" by Iago and Emilia, and is charged by Iago for complicity in the murder of Roderigo and the wounding of Cassio. Her ironic words to Emilia and Iago, "I am no strumpet, but of life as honest / As you that thus abuse me" (5.1.124–25) remind us that it is best to keep love and work separate, but that it is often impossible to do so. The subtle shadings between professions of love, the profession of love, and love of profession are as rich here as they are in the Sonnets.

"AS BLACK AS HELL, AS DARK AS NIGHT"

By giving a "huswife" of questionable repute the name "Bianca," which means "white," Shakespeare calls attention to the pervasive imagery of white and black in *Othello,* and ironically challenges the conventional associations of black with physical and moral foulness, and of white with physical beauty and moral purity. In many other passages in the play, however, these conventional associations are invoked, so that Bianca's name seems not to undermine the racialist dualities but to confirm them by becoming a kind of exception to the symbolic rule, just as the Duke regards Othello as an exception when he says to Brabantio:

> And, noble signor,
> If virtue no delighted beauty lack,
> Your son-in-law is far more fair than black. (1.3.291–93)

To praise Othello's virtue, the Duke slanders his race. As Ania Loomba explains, Othello is granted the status of "honorary white," with all the privileges and insults that term suggests (181).

The Sonnets and *Othello* share this disturbing reliance on conventionally racialist images of white and black, with black almost always connoting the negative term, suggesting physical ugliness, filth, moral corruption, and even demonic depravity. In both works this reliance on conventional associations at times appears to be in the service of unconventional ends, yet finally readers must struggle to decide whether either work is itself racist or if it interrogates the effects of racism as it is built into Western social structures, thought, and language.

Discussions of the blackness of the so-called dark lady, her race, though not as frequent as discussions of Othello's race, are nevertheless reminiscent of that debate; all too often such discussions shed more light on the prejudices of the commentators than they do on the dark lady's race.[10] It could be that she is Negro, of African or West Indian descent, as Margreta de Grazia, Marvin Hunt, and others have recently maintained. It is also possible that the dark lady is Caucasian but has dark hair, eyes, and complexion. The evidence seems inconclusive (whereas there is ample evidence that Othello is black). The phrase "a woman colored ill" in sonnet 144 (in contrast to the male's friend's fairness) suggests the lady is not white, and one can read the details of sonnet 130 as describing a black person: "her breasts are dun" (3), "black wires grow on her head" (4), but these are features that can sometimes be observed on both Caucasians and people of color. Furthermore, the couplet to sonnet 131 seems to deny a dark physical appearance: "In nothing art thou black save in thy deeds, / And hence this slander as I think proceeds," as does —perhaps—the couplet to sonnet 147. In his references to blackness, the speaker shifts equivocally back and forth between physical and moral description.

The praise of black beauty in sonnet 127 does challenge conventional standards of beauty:

> Therefore my mistress's eyes are raven black,
> Her eyes so suited, and they mourners seem
> At such who, not born fair, no beauty lack,

> Sland'ring creation with a false esteem.
> Yet so they mourn becoming of their woe,
> That every tongue says beauty should look so.
> (9–14)

The same perhaps can be said of the conclusion to sonnet 130, though here the emphasis seems to be more on mocking the unrealistic descriptions of mistresses that come from other poets:

> And yet by heav'n I think my love as rare
> As any she belied with false compare.
> (13–14)

More often in the Sonnets, the speaker emphasizes the power of love to blind a lover's eyes. This is the theme of sonnet 137, "Thou blind fool love," as it is of sonnet 148:

> O me! what eyes hath love put in my head,
> Which have no correspondence with true sight!
> Or if they have, where is my judgment fled,
> That censures falsely what they see aright?
> If that be fair whereon my false eyes dote,
> What means the world to say it is not so?
> If it be not, then love doth well denote,
> Love's eye is not so true as all men's: no.
> How can it? O how can love's eye be true,
> That is so vexed with watching and with tears?
> No marvel then though I mistake my view;
> The sun itself sees not till heaven clears.
> O cunning love, with tears thou keep'st me blind,
> Lest eyes, well seeing, thy foul faults should find.

In the Sonnets we never hear directly or indirectly from the dark lady (except perhaps in sonnets like 138 and 145), so we have no way of measuring the effect upon her of the speaker's comments about her physical and moral blackness. In *Othello*, by contrast, the effects of racism are inescapable. The slurs that open the play have been analyzed by many critics, and there is little need to repeat what has been said by others about Iago's racism or Roderigo's, the references to "thick lips" (1.1.68), to the "old black ram . . . tupping your white ewe" (1.1.90–91), and to "your daughter covered with a Barbary horse" (1.1.113–14). Many critics have also commented upon Brabantio's hypocrisy and racism—Brabantio, who had so often invited Othello to his home:

> O thou foul thief, where hast thou stowed my daughter?
> Damned as thou art, thou hast enchanted her!

> For I'll refer me to all things of sense,
> If she in chains of magic were not bound
> Whether a maid so tender, fair, and happy,
> So opposite to marriage that she shunned
> The wealthy curlèd darlings of our nation,
> Would ever have, t' incur a general mock,
> Run from her guardage to the sooty bosom
> Of such a thing as thou—to fear, not to delight. (1.2.63–72)

I have already mentioned the subtle racism of the Duke in recommending Othello's virtue despite the blackness of his skin. Even more subtle, and at the same time perhaps more troubling, are the implications of Desdemona's claim that she "saw Othello's visage in his mind" (1.3.255), a claim that suggests she had to overcome an initial repugnance to his physical appearance. As in the dark lady sonnets, the love of a black person requires explanation.

One of the lasting impressions of Othello's character is the calm dignity with which he withstands so many insults before the inevitable psychic damage begins to surface. Yet surface it inevitably does, for "haply" he is black. Thus, he says to Iago,

> And yet, how nature erring from itself—(3.3.243),

a half-formed thought that Iago happily completes:

> Ay, there's the point! As—to be bold with you—
> Not to affect many proposèd matches
> Of her own clime, complexion, and degree,
> Whereto we see in all things nature tends—
> Foh! One may smell in such a will most rank,
> Foul disproportion, thoughts unnatural.
> But pardon me. I do not in position
> Distinctly speak of her, though I may fear
> Her will, recoiling to her better judgment,
> May fall to match you with her country forms
> And happily repent. (3.3.244–54)

The sign of Iago's success is that from hereon Othello uses the same racialist images of blackness as do the other characters in the play:

> My name, that was as fresh
> As Dian's visage, is now begrimed and black
> As mine own face. (3.3.402–04).

Later in the same scene Othello will refer to "black vengeance, from the hollow hell" (462) and to "marble heaven" (476), a phrase that anticipates his description of Desdemona's "whiter skin . . . than snow, / And smooth as alabaster" (5.2.4–5).

In that final scene, Emilia invokes the same imagery, "O, the more angel she, / And you the blacker devil!" (5.2.134–35). The problem is that her words could be taken as the play's final verdict, in effect reinforcing the racial stereotypes that the earlier depiction of the Moor seemed to refute. As Martha Ronk has written, "the character Othello is disturbing to the audience precisely because he does not totally break a slanderous stereotype: a black man, he is both sexually obsessed and threatening to the white world, a murderer" (66). In his introduction to his edited collection of essays on *Othello*, Anthony Gerard Barthelemy makes a similar point: "the play undoes what it does: it turns the heroic Moor into a villainous Moor, it challenges the racist stereotypes of the sixteenth-century English stage even as it confirms them" (2). Yet as Ronk and Barthelemy would perhaps agree, the fact that Othello comes to confirm a racist stereotype is itself the chief effect of racism on his character.

"PRITHEE, KEEP UP THY QUILLETS"

In both *Othello* and the Sonnets Shakespeare uses puns as a way to figure forth significant polarities, particularly the internal divisions of the protagonists. Just as the Sonnets speaker and Othello are single subjects split along various fault lines, so the pun is a verbal sign split into various meanings—in Richard III's memorable phrase, to pun is to "moralize two [or more] meanings in a word" (*Richard III*; 3.1.83). The instability of self is reflected in both works in the instability of language (in *Othello*, of course, not all the punning language, or even most of it, comes from the protagonist). Of the many puns in both works, perhaps the richest is the play of meanings on the word "lie" and its variants. Coincidentally, the word "lie" appears thirteen times in each work. More significantly, the nuances of meaning that emerge from "lie" are similar in the Sonnets and in *Othello*. In sonnet 138, the punning on "lie" reveals a complex, detached awareness of self- and mutual deception:

> When my love swears that she is made of truth,
> I do believe her though I know she lies,
> That she might think me some untutored youth,
> Unlearnèd in the world's false subtleties.
> Thus vainly thinking that she thinks me young,
> Although she knows my days are past the best,
> Simply I credit her false-speaking tongue:
> On both sides thus is simple truth suppressed.
> But wherefore says she not she is unjust?
> And wherefore say not I that I am old?
> O love's best habit is in seeming trust,

> And age in love loves not to have years told.
> Therefore I lie with her, and she with me,
> And in our faults by lies we flattered be.

The tone here is at once cynical, humorous, bawdy, desperate, and smugly triumphant ("O"!). As Stephen Booth explains, "The fact of impossible but undeniable fusion manifests itself in puns (e.g., the various and variously contradictory significances fused together in the word *lie*), in syntaxes that simultaneously indicate two distinct logical relationships among parts of sentences . . . , and in the fact that every assertion in the poem is demonstrably true and also a lie. . . . The poem as poem is like the relationship it describes; every quality or identity the poem has or presents is fused with its opposite" (477). Unlike Othello, the speaker in sonnet 138 is able to live with, or even luxuriate in, such multiplicity of contradictory meanings and feelings. In addressing his point, Edward A. Snow has eloquently written, "the speaker of the sonnet resides comfortably in the language that destroys Othello's faith; his paradoxes convey not confusion but an almost Montaignian lucidity and composure" (473). In other sonnets, of course, this comic acceptance of paradox and multivalence is absent; sonnet 147 ends with the tragic disillusion of an Othello or a Hamlet or a Troilus: "For I have sworn thee fair, and thought thee bright / Who art as black as hell, as dark as night" (13–14). The situation for the speaker in 147 is if anything even more desperate than that of these tragic protagonists since the realization of duplicity does not allow the speaker to disengage himself from what he feels. His love is "as a fever, longing *still*, / For that which longer nurseth the disease" (1–2; emphasis added). My point is not that sonnet 147 tells the entire story any more than sonnet 138 or sonnet 143 with its very different kind of realistic accommodation (see Wheeler, 195). The Sonnets present each of these moods, and many others as well, each bumping against and often contrasting with the others lying around it. The effect of these poems read together in sequence is obviously very different from, if not greater than, any single lyric moment.

Honesty—or rather, dishonesty—is an issue with all the major characters in *Othello*, as are the many other meanings of "lie." It is with the word "honest" that "honest Iago" first baits the hook that lures Othello:

OTHELLO:	Is he not honest?
IAGO:	Honest, my lord?
OTHELLO:	Honest. Ay, honest.
IAGO:	My lord, for aught I know. (3.3.112–15)

Even though Othello is credulous, Iago (perhaps sincerely) tells Roderigo that the general won Desdemona by "bragging and telling her fantastical lies" (2.1.225). Desdemona, so falsely maligned by Iago, is herself guilty of deceiving her father, as Iago is quick to remind Othello:

> She did deceive her father, marrying you;
> And when she seemed to shake and fear your looks,
> She loved them most. (3.3.220–22).

When Desdemona asks where she lost her handkerchief, Emilia lies: "I know not, madam" (3.4.24), and moments later Emilia lies by her silence when Othello interrogates her mistress. The brief exchange between Desdemona and the Clown at the beginning of act 3, scene 4 pivots on various meanings of "lie": as in "lodge" or "be dishonest," obviously, but given Cassio's relationship with Bianca (at whose lodging he sometimes lies), and given the free-floating idea of Cassio's adulterous relations with Desdemona, there is a strong sexual resonance in the punning as well:

CLOWN: I dare not say he lies anywhere.

DESDEMONA: Why, man?

CLOWN: He's a soldier, and for me to say a soldier lies,
                'tis stabbing. (3.42–6)

The word "lie" here and elsewhere in the play also suggests the issue of hierarchy, that is, the issue of where Cassio, as well as Iago, lies in relation to others. It is Cassio's promotion to the lieutenancy that initially provokes Iago's villainy, and one of Iago's goals, which he achieves, is to supplant Cassio as the officer who lies closest to the Moor in the chain of command. Iago's revenge, then, against Cassio for lying closest to Othello and perhaps for lying with Emilia ("For I fear Cassio with my nightcap too" [2.1.308]) is to fabricate a lie about Cassio's and Desdemona's lying together; thus, Iago supplants both Cassio and Desdemona and becomes the one who lies closest to Othello: "Now art thou my *lie*utenant" (3.3.494). Each sense of "lie" is closely related to the others; each meaning—dishonesty, sexuality, and hierarchy—is a token easily substituted or exchanged for the others.

The sexual/falsehood meanings of "lie" drive Othello to distraction, and then to murder. Once he has introduced the thought of Desdemona's lying with Cassio, Iago knows the general will not be able to let things lie, and thus Iago torments him:

OTHELLO: What hath he said?

IAGO: Faith, that he did—I know not what he did.

OTHELLO: What? What?

IAGO:	Lie—
OTHELLO:	With her?
IAGO:	With her, on her; what you will.
OTHELLO:	Lie with her? Lie on her? We say "lie on her" when they belie her. Lie with her? Zounds, that's fulsome. (4.1.32–37)

In the final scene, Emilia courageously reveals Iago's vile falsehood: "You told a lie, an odious, damnèd lie! / Upon my soul, a lie, a wicked lie" (5.2.188). Her courage costs her her life, and she dies asking those assembled to "lay [her] by [her] mistress' side" (5.2.245). Soon thereafter Othello uses his sword upon himself, his suicide the ultimate expression and the ultimate resolution of internal division, one part of him enacting vengeance on another. He too requests the chance to lie with Desdemona, "to die upon a kiss" (5.2.370). Upon the "tragic loading" of the marriage bed, Othello and Desdemona lie at last in peace.

TENTATIVE CONCLUSIONS

The instability of the word "lie" is a figure for the instability of emotional experience and identity that must be negotiated in both works. In *Othello* the ambiguous puns are finally resolved into tragic clarity by violence and death. In the Sonnets, by contrast, there is no final tragic—or comic—resolution. Neither is there lyric stasis. Instead, the Sonnets as a collection present the juxtaposition of, and sometimes the logical movement between, various lyric moods and matrices of thoughts and emotions. Instead of tragic progression resolved by death, we get sequential variation, variation that often involves significant incremental repetition. The differences between the Sonnets and *Othello* in this regard of resolution or irresolution may reflect a difference between the times they were written and corresponding stages of Shakespeare's artistic development. This is the opinion, for example, of Richard P. Wheeler, who assumes the Sonnets are the work of a younger Shakespeare (relative to the author who wrote *Othello*). Wheeler contends that "the *Sonnets* repeatedly seem to respond to conditions of experience that are never fully taken into the realm of artistic expression" (192). Later in his essay Wheeler concludes that unlike the Sonnets (or *The Merchant of Venice*), "but building on trends already present but selectively suppressed, displaced, or disguised in these earlier works, *Othello* dramatizes an inclusive quest for independent identity, identification with the source of nurture and security, and sexual fulfillment. This inclusiveness, characteristic of Shakespeare's later work, engenders conflicts that seek resolution in death" (206). Although Wheeler acknowledges that such differences obviously reflect differences in genre

(193), his assumption that the Sonnets belong to an earlier stage of development may well need to be reexamined in light of recent work on the dating of the Sonnets, as does his apparent privileging of tragedy over lyric sequence.

In his important essay on sonnet 138, for example, Edward A. Snow contends that the 1599 version of sonnet 138 published in *The Passionate Pilgrim* is Shakespeare's early draft of the poem (rather than an imperfectly remembered version) that he later revised into the poem that appears in the 1609 Quarto; furthermore, unlike Wheeler, Snow believes the 1609 version was probably revised *after* Shakespeare wrote *Othello*. The poem's "paradoxes and its elusiveness of tone," he asserts, "locate a crucial threshold within the world of the plays; on the one side *Hamlet, Troilus and Cressida*, and *Othello*, with their disgust with sexuality, their distrust of women, and their cynical, disillusioned, and/or subjectively isolated male protagonists; on the other *Antony and Cleopatra*, with its intermingling of male and female selves, its acceptance of the realities of sexual relatedness, and its chastened yet visionary reaffirmation of the romantic idealism of *Romeo and Juliet*" (462). Published in 1980, Snow's conclusion is indeed compatible with recent studies of the dating of the Sonnets' composition mentioned at the start of this essay. While I think Snow overlooks the strong element of cynicism in the 1609 version, his perception of a "quixotic generosity" in the speaker that is closer to the tone of *Antony and Cleopatra* than to that of *Othello* is, I believe, persuasive (474). Less persuasive, perhaps, is his argument that the 1599 version of sonnet 138 is an early draft rather than "an imperfectly remembered transcript" (463). Still, even the possibility that many of the Sonnets were written or revised at a time contemporaneous with or even after Shakespeare's composition of *Othello* should make us hesitate to say which work marks an advance upon the other. We would not wish to lose either. Since such questions of date of composition may never be resolved with absolute certainty, it may be wisest to view these works together, *Othello* lying among the Sonnets.

NOTES

1. All references to the Sonnets are to Stephen Booth's edition.
2. All references to Shakespeare's plays are to David Bevington's edition.
3. I am indebted to Peter C. Herman for first calling my attention to recent studies of the Sonnets' date of composition by Hieatt, Hieatt, and Prescott and by Donald Foster. Such studies lend support to the arguments of John Kerrigan and Katherine Duncan-Jones that the publication of the 1609 Quarto was authorized. See also my introduction to *Shakespeare's Sonnets: Critical Essays*, "Reading New Life into Shakespeare's Sonnets" 7–11. Helen Vendler notes that "sonnet 138 [published in Quarto, 1609] has seemed to some a place where we can see Shakespeare reworking an earlier draft"; Vendler favors the theory that the "version in *The Passionate Pilgrim* was reconstructed by someone with a faulty memory" (587).

4. The similarities between the Sonnets and *Othello* do not on their own establish that these works were written around the same time. Authors often return many years later to the same themes, as Shakespeare, for example, returned to twins and shipwrecks in *Twelfth Night* long after he wrote *The Comedy of Errors*.

5. Of course, the friend in the Sonnets turns out not to be as fair as the Sonnet speaker initially—and at times even later—believes; and the perfidy of the dark lady is in a very real sense open to dispute, since it is unconfirmed by other voices; our only evidence of her infidelities comes from the poet; she never gets the chance to defend herself or speak in her own voice (see Feinberg).

6. In the *Variorum* edition of the Sonnets, Rollins does cite scholars who have noted parallels between the two works, most often verbal echoes. In recent times Susan Snyder, Edward A. Snow, and Richard P. Wheeler have written extended comparisons of the two works. I briefly examine the readings of Wheeler and Snow at the end of this essay.

7. For a useful summary of the racism that has distorted criticism of *Othello*, see Barthelemy. For discussions of the effect of homophobia on the reception of the Sonnets, see Pequigney, Stallybrass, de Grazia, and Schiffer.

8. For recent discussions of race and gender in *Othello* see Loomba, Parker, and Hall; for discussions of homoeroticism in the Sonnets, see Pequigney, Sedgewick, and Fineman; for recent discussions of homoeroticism in *Othello*, see Matz and Bland; for recent discussions of race in the Sonnets see de Grazia and Hunt.

9. Parker's comments are worth quoting: "hidden within the visual language of this informer's advice to 'scan this thing no farther' is the 'thing' which elsewhere is the 'common thing' (3.3.301–302) Emilia offers to her husband, the female privity or res that Iago vulgarly sexualizes when she intrudes to offer him what he terms a 'trifle' (l. 322). Advice that appears to speak only to epistemological hunger to 'see' and 'know' introduces into the lines that follow the double meanings of a 'place' Cassio 'fills up' with 'great ability', a 'place' whose sexual inference is joined by the threat to Othello's 'occupation' (3.3 .357) through the obscener sense of 'occupy'. What is secret or unseen here is the ambiguous sexual 'place' of all the double-meaning references to the place Cassio might occupy as Othello's place-holder or 'lieu-tenant'" (177).

10. On the dark lady's color, see Rollins, Vol. 2: 242–75 (Rollins himself is dismissive of the idea of a black mistress [272]); see also de Grazia and Hunt; for a recent discussion of the theatrical tradition of representing Othello's color, see Kaul.

WORKS CITED

Barthelemy, Anthony Gerard, ed. "Introduction." *Critical Essays on Shakespeare's Othello*. New York: G. K. Hall, 1994. 1–18.

Bland, Shelia Rose. "How I would Direct *Othello*." Othello: *New Essays by Black Writers*. Ed. Mythili Kaul. Washington, DC: Howard University Press, 1996. 29–41.

Booth, Stephen, ed. *Shakespeare's Sonnets*. New Haven: Yale University Press, 1977.

de Grazia, Margreta. "The Scandal of Shakespeare's Sonnets." *Shakespeare Survey* 46 (1994): 35–49.

Duncan-Jones, Katherine, ed. *Shakespeare's Sonnets*. The Arden Shakespeare. Nashville: Nelson, 1997.

———. "Was the 1609 *Shake-speares Sonnets* Really Unauthorized?" *Review of English Studies* 34 (1983): 151–71.

Feinberg, Nona. "Erasing the Dark Lady: Sonnet 138 in the Sequence." *Assays* 4 (1987): 97–108.

Fineman, Joel. *Shakespeare's Perjured Eye: The Invention of Poetic Subjectivity in the Sonnets.* Berkeley: University of California Press, 1986.

Foster, Donald W. "Reconstructing Shakespeare Part 2: The Sonnets." *The Shakespeare Newsletter* (Fall 1991): 26–27.

Hall, Kim F. "Beauty and the Beast of Whiteness: Teaching Race and Gender." *Shakespeare Quarterly* 47 (1996): 461–75.

Hieatt, A. Kent, Charles W. Hieatt, and Anne Lake Prescott. "When Did Shakespeare Write *Sonnets* 1609?" *Studies in Philology* 88 (1991): 69–109.

Hunt, Marvin. "Be Dark but Not Too Dark: Shakespeare's Dark Lady as a Sign of Color." *Shakespeare's Sonnets: Critical Essays.* Ed. James Schiffer. New York: Garland, 1999.

Kaul, Mythili, ed. "Background: Black or Tawny? Stage Representations of *Othello* from 1604 to the Present." *Othello: New Essays by Black Writers.* Washington, DC: Howard University Press, 1996. 1–19.

Kerrigan, John., ed. *The Sonnets and A Lover's Complaint.* Harmondsworth: Penguin, 1986.

Loomba, Ania. "Sexuality and Racial Difference." *Critical Essays on Shakespeare's Othello.* Ed. Anthony Gerard Barthelemy. New York: G. K. Hall, 1994. 162–86. [Rpt. from *Gender, Race and Renaissance Drama.* Manchester: Manchester University Press, 1989.]

Marotti, Arthur F. "'Love is not love': Elizabethan Sonnet Sequences and the Social Order." *ELH* (1982): 396–428.

Matz, Robert. "Slander, Renaissance Discourses of Sodomy, and *Othello*." *ELH* 6 (1999): 261–76.

Parker, Patricia. "Fantasies of 'Race' and 'Gender': Africa, *Othello*, and Bringing to Light." *Shakespeare's Tragedies.* Ed. Susan Zimmerman. New York: St. Martin's, 1998.

Pequigney, Joseph. *Such Is My Love: A Study of Shakespeare's Sonnets.* Chicago: University of Chicago Press, 1985.

Rollins, Hyder Edward, ed. *A New Variorum Edition of Shakespeare: The Sonnets.* 2 vols. Philadelphia: Lippincott, 1944.

Ronk, Martha. "Recasting Jealousy: A Reading of *The Winter's Tale*." *Literature and Psychology* 36 (1990): 50–57.

Schiffer, James. "Reading New Life into Shakespeare's Sonnets." *Shakespeare's Sonnets: Critical Essays.* New York: Garland, 1999. 3–71.

Shakespeare, William. *The Complete Works of Shakespeare.* Updated 4th ed. Ed. David Bevington. New York: Addison Wesley Longman, 1997.

Sedgwick, Eve Kosofsky. *Between Men: English Literature and Male Homosocial Desire.* New York: Columbia University Press, 1985.

Snow, Edward A. "Loves of Comfort and Despair: A Reading of Sonnet 138." *ELH* 47 (1980): 462-81.

Snyder, Susan. *The Comic Matrix of Shakespeare's Tragedies.* Princeton: Princeton University Press, 1979.

Stallybrass, Peter. "Editing as Cultural Formation: The Sexing of Shakespeare's Sonnets." *Modern Language Quarterly* 54 (1993): 91–103.

Vendler, Helen. *The Art of Shakespeare's Sonnets*. Cambridge: Harvard University Press, 1997.

Wheeler, Richard P. "' . . . And my loud crying still': The *Sonnets, The Merchant of Venice*, and *Othello*." *Shakespeare's "Rough Magic": Renaissance Essays in Honor of C. L. Barber*. Eds. Peter Erickson and Coppélia Kahn. Newark: University of Delaware Press, 1985. 193–209.

The "O" in *Othello*:
Tropes of Damnation and Nothingness

DANIEL J. VITKUS

Othello: O! O! O!—(5.2.197)

The figure "O" is inscribed as the ruling rhetorical trope in many of the texts that bear Shakespeare's name. Its rich significance for Renaissance writers, and for Shakespeare in particular, has been eloquently deciphered by Edward Tayler in his analysis of "Negation in *King Lear*;" by Paul Jorgenson in his reading of "nothing" in *Much Ado*; and by Rosalie Colie in her study *Paradoxia Epidemica*. Joel Fineman, in a lecture originally delivered at a 1987 colloquium on Lacan's *Television*, attends to "The Sound of 'O' in *Othello*" and perceives the hollow ring of a "kind of materialized absence of self to self"—"the substantialized emptiness that motivates and corroborates . . . that psychologistic interiority for which and by means of which Shakespeare's major characters are often singled out" (109).[1] According to Fineman, the "O" in *Othello* is the expression, not only of a Shakespearean signature, but also of a historically specific form of collective consciousness ("early modern subjectivity"), which is encoded in the text. Fineman's eccentric analysis teasingly refers to the oxymoronic trope objectified in Othello's name but stops short of a thorough circumspection of the "O" in *Othello*. Focusing further attention on the "O" will allow us to perceive a tropical pattern that is present, not only in the formal mechanisms of "literary characterology" or the allegories of subjectivity that obsess Fineman, but also at other levels of signification that refer to sexual and religious forms of conversion or "turning."

For Shakespeare, the "O" is a transcendent signifier, the first and final trope summed up in a single sound and solitary letter. It is the end-all and be-all of figures, sometimes implying fullness and plenitude and at other times denoting complete emptiness. When spoken at the center of the theater's "wooden O," the "O" can be the most powerful of performative enunciations. Bruce R. Smith points out in his marvelous book, *The Acoustic World of Early*

Modern England, that the O-sound is "the most intense phoneme the human voice can make in English speech" (225). Smith's description of early modern language as "the embodiedness of an oral performance" corroborates the more specific analyses of Maurice Charney and Terence Hawkes, both of whom discuss the "O-groans" that appear at the end of *Hamlet* and throughout Shakespeare's plays. In separate essays, Charney and Hawkes comment extensively on the last words given to Hamlet in the Folio version of the play: "the rest is silence. O, o, o, o. [Dyes]." These so-called O-groans, like those emitted by Lear when Cordelia dies, by Lady Macbeth while sleepwalking, and by the Moor in act five of *Othello*, are not (as J. Dover Wilson and other textual editors have claimed mere "players' tricks of speech" without authorial legitimacy (quoted in Charney, 110). As Charney and Hawkes demonstrate convincingly, these O-groans are more than just "shorthand' indications for the director or actor, suggesting a range of action and concomitant verbal sound" (Charney, 110). Smith, Charney, and Hawkes all make great claims for the way that these "O"s function, and Hawkes goes so far as to say that Shakespeare's use of "O" "subvert[s] words," expressing a "paralinguistic," nondiscursive meaning that cannot be attained by textual editors seeking a stable, authoritative version of Shakespeare's playtext (Hawkes, 79). According to Hawkes, "they offer an orthographical blank, a vacancy, a disconcerting sign which invites a dialogical 'improvised' response" (89). The "O," for Hawkes, is an ejaculatory, Barthian paradox of "writing aloud"—a moment of jouissance referring to both sex and death but cut loose from any text-bound correspondence of signifier to signified.

Hawkes's reading of the "O" in *Hamlet* serves as a powerful demonstration of the principles of both structuralism and the new textualism, but the "O" in *Othello* is not only the marker of an oral performance: it also takes on a iconic, symbolic resonance. Its circular shape implies a "turning" or a "conversion"—the orbital movement of a point through space that produces a recurvate line as it loops back and rejoins that line at its point of origin. The written or printed form of the circle represents the open orifice of the mouth, emitting apostrophic invocation, lovelorn lamentation, a moan of horror—or simply gaping in silent, slack-jawed wonder at a tragic scene that "poisons sight" (5.2.360). The "O" is a paradox in a single symbol—the ultimate primal word signifying nothingness and absence but also suggesting the circle of wholeness and perfection.

As a "cipher" the "O" is the key to any secret method of writing that uses coded symbols, but it also stands for a nonentity: a person or thing of no power or importance. It is used by Shakespeare in this sense when the Nurse demands of Romeo, "Why should you fall into so deep an O?" (3.3.90). In this latter sense, it signifies nothing, and refers to the full range of meanings implied by "nothing" from feminine sexual anatomy to ontological enigma.[2]

An analysis of this figure in *Othello* might begin at the level of phonetic iterance, by looking at the occurrence of the isolated "O" in the text.[3] Printed either as "Oh" or simply as "O," and sometimes followed immediately by an exclamation point, the "O"–sound appears in *Othello* as a single-figure word 154 times. Seventy-five of those occurrences are in act five, a striking intensity of appearance that is unparalleled in the Shakespearean canon.[4] The word "O" or "Oh" clearly holds a place of great rhetorical importance in *Othello*, and its function can only be described as emphatic. By means of repetition and force of expression, it demands the attention of audience or reader.

The meaning of a specific "O" depends, of course, on the performative context, and to some degree its rhetorical function is indicated by syntactic placement. At the beginning of a line or sentence, it tends to have an apostrophic, invocative meaning, but at the end of a line, it usually signifies a howl or a groan. It can indicate a sigh (Juliet's "O Romeo"), physical pain (Falstaff burnt by candle flames at the end of *The Merry Wives of Windsor* and crying, "Oh, oh, oh" [l. 2584]), or Cleopatra's autoerotic death throes ("O Antony!"). Multiple "O"s represent deep emotion, passion, grief, pain, or the sound of dying.

The "O" is used frequently in Othello's early speeches, which are rhetorically rounded out with "bombast circumstance,/Horribly stuffed with epithets of war" (1.1.13). This grandiose orotundity, that of the romance hero, swells to bursting in the second act, climaxing at the reunion of Othello and Desdemona on Cyprus ("O my soul's joy" [2.1.176]), but Othello's apostrophic exclamations of happiness are soon transformed by Iago to moans of bestial anguish. In the play's final scene, the "O"–sound becomes the departing howl of a hell-bound soul. Othello's cry of "O! O! O!" (5.2.197) punctuates his tragic anagnorisis, when he learns the truth at last and feels the annihilating pain that accompanies that knowledge.

Shakespeare employs the "O" shape, not only as rhetorical figure or open-mouthed sound, but also as an archetypal image, developing several hieroglyphic meanings of the "O" as symbol, including the perfect circle as an image of the round world or all-encompassing, concentric universe that turns in ordered harmony. That the "wooden O" of Shakespearean theater is a microcosmic world is part of the play's adherence to the morality play tradition and its development of the *theatrum mundi* trope. Between heaven and earth, on the stage of the Globe theater, all the world is epitomized in the struggle between Iago as Vice and Othello as Everyman. Building on the generic conventions of early modern tragedy, the "O" in Othello also refers to the *de casibus* wheel of fortune that raises the tragic protagonist high (the Moor's successful elopement and command of the Venetian forces) and then suddenly turns 180 degrees—"as low as hell's from heaven" (2.1.180–81)—to the depths of misfortune. In the play's first scene, Roderigo acknowledges the Moor's ascent on the wheel of fortune: "What a full fortune does the thick-lips owe/If he can carry it thus!" (1.1.67–68), and Cassio declares that Othello has

F<small>IGURE</small> 16. A seventeenth-century example of the symbolic use of an "O" as "an Emblem, of Mortality" from George Wither's Collection of Emblems (London, 1635), p. 45. Image courtesy of the Strozier Library Rare Books Collection at Florida State University.

married "most fortunately" (2.1.61). Othello himself feels a pride and confidence that comes before his fall. He tells Iago, "my demerits/May speak unbonneted to as proud a fortune/As this that I have reached" (1.2.23-24). By the final lines of the play, Othello's fortune is brought to naught by his "unlucky deeds" (5.2.337), and Lodovico instructs Gratiano "to seize upon the fortunes of the Moor" (5.2.362).

A third version of the "O" in *Othello* is the incurvate form of the monster Jealousy that turns back on itself like the worm Ouroboros, swallowing its own tail. (Figure 16) It is an emblem of Jealousy, the "monster/Begot upon itself, born on itself" (3.4.155-56) and also feeding on itself—"the green-eyed monster which doth mock/The meat it feeds on" (3.3.166). This self-consuming monster of the mind is the archetype for what Fineman describes as "an anorectic, homophagic economy of subjectifying self-cannibalization" (109). Iago notes the onset of self-consuming jealousy and comments, "I see, sir, you are eaten up with passion" (3.3.392). The patriarchal imagination furiously reproduces and consumes the poisonous image of infidelity and then, needing to purge this hateful picture, devours the internal malignancy which it has produced from nothing. This version of the "O" is a vicious circle, created out of nothing: "jealousy/shapes faults that are not" (3.3.149), says Iago. Iago's account of jealousy repeats the "O"–sound with an assonance that replicates the concept of a recurring mental loop, turned over and over in the mind:

IAGO: O, what damned minutes tells he o'er
               Who dotes, yet doubts, suspects, yet fondly loves?
               (3.3.171-72)

"O misery!", answers Othello. A few lines later, the Moor compares the constant mutability of the jealous mind to "the changes of the moon." He describes the orbiting moon as a self-converting body that cannot maintain the form of perfection, but changes from full round to crescent to nothing and then reappears, an image suggesting the jealous monster's relentless neurosis, lunatic self-consumption, and unnatural autogenesis. Othello's invocation in act three of the lunar image prefigures the "huge eclipse/Of sun and moon" (5.2.100-101) that he will imagine just after killing Desdemona.

Each of the three versions of the figure "O" just mentioned (planetary sphere, wheel of fortune, self-consuming monster) develops the play's central conceit, that of a turning or revolving movement forming an "O."[5] It is also the character of Othello that is "turned" or transformed. The play's circular pattern is epitomized in the fate of Othello himself, who is converted from a faithful, "noble" condition to infidelity, damnation, and nonentity. Death, for Othello, is the necessary effect caused by his loss of identity or "good name": once the hollow bubble of his being is burst, he becomes the "nobody" who kills Desdemona. In the end, "th'affrighted globe" opens its (hell) mouth, "yawn[s] at alteration" (5.2.101-2), and swallows Othello whole.

The annihilation of the Moorish other is mirrored by another other's coming to nothing: that second other is woman, embodied in Desdemona, who is reduced to a sexual nothing. The "O" in *Othello* has a great deal to do with the patriarchal joke about female sexual anatomy as "nothing," as opposed to a man's "thing."[6] This usage of "nothing" appears in the following dialogue between Hamlet and Ophelia:

HAMLET: Do you think I meant country matters?

OPHELIA: I think nothing, my lord.

HAMLET: That's a fair thought to lie between maid's legs.

OPHELIA: What is, my lord?

HAMLET: Nothing.

Iago puns on "nothing" in a similar sense when he tells Othello, "Nay, but be wise: yet we see nothing done/She may be honest yet" (3.3.429).

The tragedy of *Othello*, as Thomas Rymer and others have pointed out, is born of something insignificant.[7] It is much ado about nothing, that "nothing" being, in one sense, Desdemona's sex. The play sustains a running joke founded on the dramatic irony of Othello's baseless jealousy, made from nothing. "Says Emilia to Desdemona, "jealous souls . . . are not ever jealous for the cause,/But jealous for they're jealous" (3.4.152-55). Like Emilia, the audience knows that Othello has not been cuckolded. Othello knows nothing but the bittersweet nothings whispered in his ear by Iago—and there is nothing to know, yet the Moor still searches for material evidence and "ocular proof." "You have seen nothing then?" (4.2.1), Othello asks Emilia. It is a nothing worth more than anything to Othello, and in this regard, his jealousy is like that of Leontes in *The Winter's Tale*, who sees Hermione and Polixenes converse and asks, "Is this nothing?/Why then all the world and all that's in't is nothing, . . . /My wife is nothing, nor nothing have these nothings,/If this be nothing" (1.2.292-96). Like that of Leontes, Othello's jealousy is driven by an all-or-nothing absolutism. For Othello, the lost handkerchief is an object of absolute significance, a symbolic substitute for his wife's maidenhead: "To lose't or give't away were such perdition/As nothing else could match" (3.4.63-64). This "nothing" (according to the patriarchal discourse of masculine presence and feminine absence) is Desdemona's lack. Her purportedly absent hymen—and the resulting hole, the hymenless orifice—becomes the central, imaginary object of Othello's "bloody thoughts," thoughts of bloody revenge for the blood spilled by Cassio in the supposed deflowering of Othello's wife. Othello kills Desdemona over nothing—because of a missing handkerchief, because of a missing hymen, because of (her) "nothing."

The text develops the theme of Othello's tragic ignorance by playing upon the ideas of carnal ignorance and knowledge. Knowledge of nothing is what destroys the fullness and symmetry of Othello and Desdemona's love. Desdemona's sexual condition becomes Othello's world: in other words, his world is contracted into her "nothing." Desdemona's "honour"—the "essence that's not seen" (4.1.15)—becomes the center and axis around which all of Othello's thoughts revolve. Iago turns Othello's mind to this object with devious circumlocution and brings about Othello's temptation through a series of rhetorical twists and verbal turns that evade the physical truth at the center— that she is "honest," and that "honest Iago" is not.

Two aspects of the play's circular troping come together here—the "O" as world/all is measured against the "O" as vagina/nothing in what serves both as an obscene joke and as a comment upon the obsessive nature of jealousy. After killing Desdemona, Othello seems convinced that she has been damned, a "liar gone to burning hell," but he admits that her pure body was once worth the world:

> Nay, had she been true,
> If heaven would make me such another world

> Of one entire and perfect chrysolite,
> I'd not have sold her for it (5.2.143-44)

This notion of female sexual wholeness as something that is worth every-thing is also developed in the dialogue between Emilia and Desdemona, in which Desdemona asks Emilia if she would commit adultery "for all the world" (4.3.61). "Not the world's mass of vanity," claims Desdemona, could make her "To do the act" (4.2.163-64), but Emilia says she would "do such a deed" and then "undo't when I had done it" (4.3.68). It is an irresistible bar-gain to give "nothing" and receive "all the world" in exchange. "All the world" is shrunk to comparison with a mere "joint-ring", and, by implication, to the "ring" of the female sexual opening. But Emilia's "common thing" is con-stricted into oblivion by Desdemona, who cannot conceive of such a "wrong." Desdemona's innocent inability to conceive of carnal sin reduces the female "O" to nothing: "I do not think there is any such woman" (4.3.79).

The concept of a sexual "nothing" and of "knowing the thing" in *Othello* is linked to further quibbling about nothing and knowledge that is not only of the body but also refers to the soul. The text emphasizes the notion of essen-tial identity being reduced to nothing. "Not to be" is to be damned, or to be eternally lost and unknown.[8] Thus, the language of "nothing" is connected to the play's concern with the nature of evil and damnation.[9] Iago's "I am not what I am," the opposite of God's self-denomination, is a negation of being and identity. He fills the abyss with words, but they are empty signifiers, a thin veneer covering evil as absence, silence, non-being. In a parody of God's cre-ation by the Word, Iago performs an *ex nihilo* destruction, declaring Othello "nothing of a man" (4.1.87), and casting the innocent Desdemona into a pit of incomprehension. Accused of being a whore, she pleads to Iago, "I do not know, I am sure I am none such" (4.2.122). When Emilia declares that some-one must be deceiving Othello, Iago responds: "Fie, there is no such man; it is impossible" (4.2.133).

If love is fullness (the catechism teaching that God, the source of all cre-ation, is love) and evil or sin are deprivation (the absence of the divine), then to be damned is to be forgotten by God and thus to cease to be. This is summed up by Othello in the words he speaks when his faith in Desdemona is first shaken. Balanced precariously between love and hatred, between being and nothingness, he declares, "Perdition catch my soul/But I do love thee; and when I love thee not,/Chaos is come again" (3.3.90-92). Later, Desdemona will declare, "All's one" (4.3.22), as Othello's identity collapses into a chaos. Rosalie Colie's elaboration on the Renaissance logic of existence and noth-ingness may serve as a gloss to those lines of Othello's: "Morality's universe is a plenum: 'nothing' and 'nobody' may not exist, but their nonexistence destroys all order and reduces constructions to chaos" (251).

Othello's love and his faith in Desdemona are turned to hate because he believes that she has been unfaithful to him: "she turned to folly, and she was a whore" (5.2.133), he tells Emilia. Othello speaks of Desdemona's alleged infidelity as a "turning" when he says to Lodovico, " . . . she can turn, and turn, and yet go on,/And turn again" (4.1.243). Here, Othello conceives of a physical, sexual turning of her body taking place in the imaginary bed where "she with Cassio hath the act of shame/A thousand times committed" (5.2.210-11). To kill Desdemona is to put a stop to this image of perpetual sexual motion: "Ha! No more moving./Still as the grave"(5.2.94-95), says Othello, satisfied that her adulterous turning has been stopped.

As the tragic action moves toward Desdemona's murder and Othello's suicide, the trope of turning or conversion occurs frequently as the effects of Iago's evil are felt.[10] In the play's opening scene, Iago tells Roderigo, "I follow [Othello] to serve my turn upon him" (1.1.42). It is not long before Iago brings Othello around to see Desdemona, who was his "soul's joy," as a "fair devil." Othello accepts the circumstantial evidence against Desdemona, and thus Iago makes good his boast that his insinuations will "turn her [Desdemona's] virtue into pitch" (2.3.328). "I see you're moved" (3.3.226) declares Iago, and later Othello tells Iago, "My heart is turned to stone" (4.1.173). Once Othello is moved from love to hate, doubt and retreat are unthinkable. Othello is seduced by Iago's claim that avoiding a direct approach to the question of Desdemona's fidelity is the best course: Iago says to Othello, "If imputation and strong circumstances, /Which lead directly to the door of truth/Will give you satisfaction, you might have't" (3.3.407). Iago keeps Othello moving away from the truth at the center. "Once wrought," Othello refuses to turn back.

Act three, scene three, is the turning point of the play, and it is during that grueling dialogue that Othello is "moved" or converted by Iago. In that scene, Othello's initial reaction to the idea of Desdemona's betrayal is to cry, "Death and damnation! O!" (3.3.396); words that point with proleptic irony to the tragic ending—to death, suicide, damnation, and the annihilation of the self. Othello threatens Iago with damnation if he "dost slander her and torture me" (3.3.368), which Iago does. Othello's threat, "For nothing canst thou to damnation add/Greater than that," is empty and absurd because Iago is already a devil damned, and perdition, according to Protestant theology, is not a matter of degree. There are no purgatorial circles in the Protestant version of hell, no hierarchy among the damned. To compare damnation to damnation is thus to measure nothing against nothing.

Desdemona's imagined sexual transgression is emphatically presented by Othello as a mortal sin resulting in damnation. "Damn thyself," he tells Desdemona, "Lest, being like one of heaven, the devils themselves/Should fear to seize thee. Therefore be double-damned" (4.2.33-36). When Emilia learns that Othello has killed her mistress, she tells him, "O, the more angel she,/And you the blacker devil!" (5.2.132). Othello believes Desdemona to have been converted by lust from angel to devil, and repeatedly justifies his own certainty of her sexual transgression in terms of divine judgement: for example, when he tells Desdemona, "Heaven truly knows that thou art false as hell" (4.2.38). These and other references to devils and angels, heaven and hell, damnation and salvation, form a pattern in the text that prepares the audience for the fifth act's tightening focus on eschatology.[11]

Foreshadowing Othello's damnation, Gratiano imagines how Brabantio would have reacted to Desdemona's murder, had he lived to see it:

> Did he live now,
> This sight would make him do a desperate turn,
> Yea, curse his better angel from his side
> And fall to reprobance. (5.2.205-208)

"Pure grief" has already killed Brabantio, but his imagined suicide is projected onto Othello. Othello does, indeed, "fall to reprobance," and for his impure grief he will pay the price of eternal damnation which Gratiano describes as a "turning."

Once he begins to doubt the justice of what he has done, Othello is, typically, "perplexed in the extreme": If he is not a divine minister, then he must be a devil damned: "O, I were damned beneath all depth in hell/But that I did proceed upon just grounds/To this extremity" (5.2.138-40). Othello's first doubt is turned swiftly to despair (repeating the pattern of his jealousy—"to be once in doubt/Is once to be resolved" [3.3.181-82]). He then asks the question, "Where should Othello go?", and the speech that follows registers Othello's recognition of his new identity. At this point, he realizes that he is not a righteous executor of God's just "cause." Othello recognizes himself as an irredeemably guilty soul and asks for divine punishment:

> O cursèd, cursèd slave! Whip me, ye devils,
> From the possession of this heavenly sight!
> Blow me about in winds! Roast me in sulphur!
> Wash me in steep-down gulfs of liquid fire!
> (5.2.275-78)

Othello links his death and damnation to the death of Desdemona, prefiguring the payment of his moratory "compt" with the moaning moras of the "O": "O Desdemon! Dead Desdemon! Dead! O! O!" (5.2.279).

Othello's damnation is the culmination of the process of his self-annihilation, which involves an erasure of name, reputation, identity, and, finally, of being itself. The text reiterates this idea of becoming nobody: Cassio ceases to "exist" when his name and reputation are destroyed; Desdemona speaks of Othello's loss of self, telling Emilia, "Who is thy lord? . . . I have none" (4.2.99-101). Just after killing Desdemona, Othello cries, "My wife, my wife! What wife? I have no wife?" (5.2.98); and Desdemona confirms their loss of identity with her last words, "Nobody, I myself."

Othello is displaced from being to nothingness. At the beginning of the play, the Moor is powerfully present, the self-declared possessor of a "perfect soul" (1.2.31); by the end he becomes an absent cipher who sighs, "Let it go all" and then "retires" (5.2.244, 269). What Gratiano says about the fleeing Iago applies also to Othello: "He's gone, but his wife's killed" (5.2.236). Othello's identity is not merely decentered; it is displaced to the point of removal. This movement reduces Othello's selfhood to an absence: he becomes a thing that is not. This is the ultimate "alteration"—a change beyond change: to be annihilated is to be transformed from being to its opposite, a non-being that is terribly and eternally stable and free from change.

When Lodovico asks, "where is this rash and most unfortunate man?", he fails to recognize the Moor who stands before him because Othello no longer exists—he is already on his way to hell. Othello confirms and acknowledges this when he answers Lodovico, "That's he that was Othello: here I am" (5.2.281). The "I" of this declaration is the damned, devilish Moor. Othello leaves his former "self" behind—the "noble Moor of Venice" or the "Othello that was once so good"—as he falls into the pit of hell.

Othello's final speech appears at first to recapture the dignified, apostrophic mode of the noble Moor, but its high-sounding rhetoric ends in a silent gesture that undoes speech once and for all. Othello's desire to have the truth come to light, and to clarify past events and motives, contrasts with Iago's sealed lips and his refusal to cooperate in the Venetians' attempts to know all.

Iago's last words affirm the annihilating power of evil: "Demand me nothing; what you know, you know./From this time forth I will never speak word" (5.2.300-301). Although Othello's attempt, in spite of Iago's silence, to restore a moral equilibrium may succeed in serving "the state" of Venice, it does no good for Othello himself. Othello ultimately joins Iago in silence and in "the time, the place, the torture" of hell.

In the pathetic anangeon of his final speeches, Othello turns away, first from the divine judge toward his adversary, Iago, and then when that adversary is revealed to be the Devil, Othello turns upon himself. This "turning" is a form of apostrophe:

> . . . in Aleppo once
> Where a malignant and a turbaned Turk
> Beat a Venetian and traduced the state,
> I took by the throat the circumcisèd dog
> And smote him thus. (5.2.347-52)

The language here suggests a circular cutting, another version of the circular form that structures the text.

The text of the last scene juxtaposes the image of castration with that of circumcision, so that Othello's loss of identity is figured as a physical loss of manhood. Symbolically castrated by Montano, Othello is told by Gratiano of his impotence: "Thou hast no weapon . . ." (5.2.254). The suicidal cut that Othello gives himself also suggests castration. When Othello declares, "Behold, I have a weapon:/A better never did itself sustain/Upon a soldier's thigh" (5.2.258-60), these words are a last attempt to assert his virility and his phallic ability to make his way "through more impediments/ Than twenty times your stop" (5.2.261-62). But Othello realizes that this is a "vain boast," and that he has only enough strength left to turn this sword upon himself.

Othello's suicide is an emblematic moment embodying the conclusion of a cycle and the conversion of Othello to infidelity. The circle is closed and completed in the physical form, on stage, of the actor playing Othello, who plunges a Spanish sword (perhaps a curved, Moorish scimitar?) into his own bowels, the weapon turned back and thrust into his own body. At this moment, his body articulates the play's central figure and trope, forming a deadly "O."[12] The wheel comes full circle for Othello as he does himself "a desperate turn." The responses of Lodovico and Gratiano to Othello's undoing—"O bloody period!" and "All that's spoke is marr'd" (5.2.353)—encourage us to read Othello's suicidal gesture as the final closing of the circle, a fulfillment that reduces all to silent nothing. The Moor's words are canceled out by his fatal act of despair. He has reached his alpha and omega: lifeline and plotline are completed in the form of tragic closure.

The closing of this circle in suicide and damnation is a tragic version of death as a completion that releases the soul into eternal life. Othello's death in suicide and his consequent damnation comprise a negative image of the death by Christian martyrdom that John Donne describes in the following passage from one of his sermons:

> So consider man's life aright, to be a Circle . . . In this, the circle, the two
> points meet, the womb and the grave are but one point. . . . Their death was
> a birth to them into another life, into the glory of God; It ended one Circle,
> and created another; for immortality and eternity is a Circle too; not a Circle
> where two points meet, but a Circle made at once; This life is a Circle, made
> with a Compasse, that passes from point to point; That life is a Circle
> stamped with a print, and endlesse, and perfect Circle, as soon as it begins.
> (*Sermons on the Psalms and Gospels,* 10)

Thus, Othello's death is a birth into the blackness of eternal nonbeing.

The play's recurrent references to heaven and hell, salvation and damnation, point to the consequences of Othello's suicide for his soul, and encourage the audience to consider the tragedy in terms of the afterlife. James Calderwood has suggested that Othello's self-punishment succeeds as a transcendently signifying gesture: "Only death can represent and define a perfection so great that desire is consumed by its own consummation" (80), but the pathetic irony of the play's ending is in the suicide's meaning as a final "fall into reprobance," assuring Othello's place in hell. Suicide, for a Christian, is an infidel act of despair, bringing certain damnation. Having told Desdemona, "I would not kill thy soul" (5.2.32), Othello goes on to kill his own soul by taking his own life. In the commission of this act, Othello usurps God's power over life and death ("Vengeance is mine, saith the Lord"), a repetition of his crime committed in acting as Desdemona's confessor, judge, and executioner. While the Moor believes that he is acting justly, his suicidal despair merely confirms his status as a damned reprobate.

As Shakespeare's play draws to a close, the well rounded phrases and verbal plenitude uttered by Othello in the first two acts are finally and utterly emptied out. By the fourth act, he is "much changed," no longer the perfectly composed commander described by Lodovico in imagery suggesting an invulnerable and essential fullness:

> Is this the noble Moor whom our full senate
> Call all-in-all sufficient? Is this the nature
> Whom passion could not shake? Whose solid virtue
> The shot of accident nor dart of chance
> Could nether graze nor pierce?
> (4.1.255-59)

He is no longer the same man: Othello's former identity has been annihilated, and this ontological shift is marked with an "O."

The repeated "O"–sounds of the final scene serve as rhetorical pointers, introducing emphatic declarations and apostrophic epithets that point to the "strange truth" (5.2.188) of the damnable crimes committed by Iago and Othello. As his "power and command is taken off" (5.2.327), Othello's speech becomes reduced to a bestial utterance emitted by an animal hunted and cornered, howling in pain and rage. These spoken "O"s are bodily signifiers expressing horror and emptiness in both sound and shape. From Montano's "O monstrous act!" (5.2.188) to Lodovico's "O bloody period!" (5.2.353), a series of emphatic "O"–sounds forms a loud prelude to the silent, speechless gape of death.

As Othello falls on the bed, still seeking resolution and symmetry in that final Judas "kiss," his last utterance gives way to the open mouth of death. The last embrace of Othello and Desdemona becomes an image of the absolute nothing at the center of the whole world.[13] Their lifeless bodies form a microcosmic emblem situated within the synechdochic concentricity of the text's circular troping. This silent circle, including Desdemona's "nothing," is the bodily shell left after Othello's essence is annihilated. In other words, the nothingness, the abyss of hell to which the Moor has gone, is indicated by this "object" which must be hid. It is an emblem of the terrifying absence of identity which remains like a sucking vortex or black hole at the center of all the other circles.

The evidence of Othello's monstrous act is concealed and covered in the central "discovery" space of the Globe theater, with the bed-curtains drawn. Commands Lodovico, "The object poisons sight;/Let it be hid" (5.2.360-61); for hell is kept hidden at the center. The central location of this force is described by Donne: "The heavens containe the Earth, the Earth, Cities, Cities, Men. And all these are Concentrique; the common centre to them all, is decay, ruine, . . . Annihilation." (*Devotions Upon Emergent Occasions,* 51). If God is a sphere whose center is everywhere and whose circumference is nowhere, then hell is the fixed point at the center of the turning world. This bloody point is the "butt/And very sea-mark" of Othello's "utmost sail" on Middle Earth, between heaven and hell. The Moor, that great traveler of the Mediterranean Sea, is moored at last in "steep-down gulfs of liquid fire." Shakespeare's play leaves its audience with a *memento mori*—we are called upon to remember the death of the Moor. Shakespeare, like Sir Thomas Browne, has "enlarged that common *Memento mori,* into a more Christian memorandum, *Memento quatuor novissima,* those foure inevitable points of us all, Death, Judgement, Heaven and Hell" (51).[14]

All of these concentric "O"s form a synechdochic pattern which gives structure to the text, but also converts all to nothing. The opposition contained in the "O" of Othello, everything and nothing, is the ultimate oxymoron, and it is one which collapses, taking all the others with it. Othello's love is converted from all to nothing, bringing mortal time to an end and beginning eternal "perdition." The "O" in *Othello* is the circle formed by Othello's movement from apostrophic fullness and perfection to apostasy, damnation, and emptiness. Othello is one who turns away from a firm standing in faith (Greek "apostasia" is derived from the words for "away" and "a standing"). Thus, the reiterated "O" of the play's last scene is an articulation of the abyss. At the same time, Othello's hollow "O" retains some of the rhetorical function of apostrophe. Brian Vickers explains the meaning of "apostrophe" in the Renaissance, a meaning so important for our understanding of the "O" in *Othello*:

> . . .'apostrophe' meant to classical rhetoricians simply the orator's turning away from the judge in order to address the adversary directly, their medieval successors equated it with 'exclamatio', which the *Rhetorica ad Herennium* describes as 'a figure which expresses grief or indignation by means of an address to some man or city or place or object' [i. e. "complaint"] . . . the medieval interpretation persisted into the Renaissance. (32-33)

Othello's self-slaughter is suicide as rhetorical gesture. It is a turning away from God the judge and a turning back upon himself, the Venetian turned

Turk. He faces his adversary, the damned villain that he has become, and expresses his indignation by killing that enemy, the "malignant . . . and turbaned Turk."

The meaning of "O" is transformed during the course of the play, turned from fullness to emptiness, and as this metamorphosis occurs, Othello himself is reduced to nothing, annihilated and cast out from the world of love and being. Othello's "content so absolute" (2.1.189) is converted, first to "tyrannous hate" (3.3.450), and finally to absolute despair. "He who was Othello" is thrown into the pit and consumed in hellfire, and his own blackness is absorbed into the infernal blackness of privation and absence. His name, beginning and ending in "O," becomes a cipher signifying nothing.

NOTES

This essay is dedicated to Professor Edward W. Tayler, with my thanks and admiration.

1. Fineman "understand[s] the sound of 'O' in *Othello* both to occasion and to objectify in language Othello's hollow self" in addition Frank Kermode observes that "The voice of the Moor has its own orotundity, verging . . . on hollowness" (110-11).

2. Tayler's article shows how, in *King Lear*, Shakespeare develops a wide range of significances of the "O"/"nothing" by returning again and again to a related set of words and ideas: "This kind of reiteration, accentuating the negative in varying though often parallel contexts, establishes subterranean associations, especially between negation and knowledge, no-ing and knowing, that are again and again released toward the surface in quibbling dialogue" (28).

3. All citations from *Othello* will refer to the New Cambridge Shakespeare text edited by Norman Sanders (Cambridge University Press, 1984).

4. This frequency of occurrence is matched by only one other play, *Romeo and Juliet*, in which it appears 151 times (with a higher relative frequency of .631 to *Othello*'s .579). *Antony and Cleopatra* follows with 97 occurrences and a relative frequency of .408. The average relative frequency of "O/oh" in the Shakespearean canon is .224. Relative frequencies are given for each play in Marvin Spevack's *Complete and Systematic Concordance to the Works of Shakespeare*.

5. One could add to these three versions of "O" the "several senses of 'O' as sign and sound and symbol" listed in David Wilbern's excellent article "Shakespeare's Nothing."

6. For further discussion of bawdy wordplay involving the word "nothing," consult E. A. M. Colman, *The Dramatic Use of Bawdy in Shakespeare* 15-18.

7. Thomas Rymer complained about *Othello* in 1693: "So much ado, so much stress, so much passion and repetition about an Handkerchief!" Rymer's critique of *Othello* can be found in his "A Short View of Tragedy" (1693), reprinted in *Critical Essays of the Seventeenth Century*, ed. J. E. Spingarn.

8. See John Donne's sermon, in which he describes the damned as those from whom God has turned away: "when all is done, the hell of hells, the torment of torments is the everlasting absence of God, and the everlasting impossibility of returning to his presence" (*The Sermons of John Donne* 5: 266).

9. On damnation in *Othello*, see the articles by Bethell, Siegel and Hubler.
10. Jonathan Dollimore, in an essay on "The cultural politics of perversion: Augustine, Shakespeare, Freud, Foucault," comments on the Augustinian sense of evil as "perversion," and cites a passage from Augustine that aptly describes Othello's turning to evil: "when the will leaves the higher and turns to the lower, it becomes bad not because the thing to which it turns is bad, but because the turning is itself perverse" (13).
11. See Bernard Spivak's *Shakespeare and the Allegory of Evil*, a study of the play's rootedness in the morality play tradition and the drama of salvation/damnation.
12. Calderwood reads Othello's suicide, the repetition of his killing the Turk in Aleppo, "as a crowning instance of the role of repetition in Othello" (107). " . . . Othello reverts at the end to the same unifying/repeating mode that has characterized him from the beginning. In this final exemplification of it, his passion for unity and repetitive selfsameness is seen to be not self-creative but self-destructive" (111). It also repeats and returns to the image of the self-destroying monster Jealousy.
13. Here, as elsewhere in the play, "the ideas of perfection and totality connected with *omnis* and the image of the circle combine with the nihilisms of the idea of nothing" (Colie, 225).
14. Parts of Browne's *Religio Medici*, especially 1:49-53, serve as a useful gloss to the eschatalogical language of *Othello*.

WORKS CITED

Bethell, S. L. "Shakespeare's Imagery: The Diabolical Image in *Othello*." *Shakespeare Survey* 5 (1952): 62–80.

Browne, Sir Thomas. *Sir Thomas Browne: Selected Works*. Ed. Geoffrey Keynes. University of Chicago Press, 1968.

Calderwood, James. *The Properties of Othello*. Amherst: University of Massachusetts Press, 1989.

Charney, Maurice. "Hamlet's O-Groans and Textual Criticism." *Renaissance Drama* 9 (1978): 109-19.

Colie, Rosalie. *Paradoxia Epidemica: The Renaissance Tradition of Paradox*. Princeton: Princeton University Press, 1966.

Colman, E. A. M. *The Dramatic Use of Bawdy in Shakespeare*. London: Longman, 1974.

Dollimore, Jonathan. "The cultural politics of perversion: Augustine, Shakespeare, Freud, Foucault." *Sexual Sameness: Textual Differences in Lesbian and Gay Writing*. London: Ed. Joseph Bristow. Routledge, 1992. 9-25.

Donne, John. *Devotions Upon Emergent Occasions*. Ed. Anthony Ragsa. Montreal: McGill-Queen's University Press, 1975.

———. *John Donne's Sermons on the Psalms and Gospels*. Ed. Evelyn M. Simpson. Berkeley: University of California Press, 1963.

———. *The Sermons of John Donne*. Ed. George R. Potter and Evelyn M. Simpson. 10 vols. Berkeley: University of California Press, 1962.

Fineman, Joel. "The Sound of 'O' in *Othello*: The Real of the Tragedy of Desire." *Critical Essays on Shakespeare's "Othello."* Ed. Anthony Gerard Barthelemy. New York: G. K. Hall, 1994.

Hawkes, Terence. *That Shakespeherian Rag: Essays on a Critical Process*. London: Methuen, 1986.

Hubler, Edward. "The Damnation of Othello: Some Limitations on the Christian View of the Play." *Shakespeare Quarterly* 9 (1958): 295-300.

Jorgenson, Paul A. "Much Ado About Nothing." *Shakespeare Quarterly* 5 (1954): 287-95.

Shakespeare, William. *Othello*. Ed. Norman Sanders, Cambridge University Press, 1984.

Siegel, Paul. "The Damnation of Othello." *PMLA* 68 (1953): 1068-78.

Smith, Bruce R. *The Acoustic World of Early Modern England: Attending to the O-Factor*. Chicago: University of Chicago Press, 1999.

Spevack, Marvin. *A Complete and Systematic Concordance to the Works of Shakespeare*. 9 vols. Hildesheim: Georg Olms, 1968-80.

Spivak, Bernard. *Shakespeare and the Allegory of Evil*. New York: Columbia University Press, 1958.

Spingarn, J. E., ed. *Critical Essays of the Seventeenth Century*. Bloomington: Indiana University Press, 1957.

Tayler, Edward. "King Lear and Negation." *ELR* 20:1 (Winter 1990): 17-39.

Vickers, Brian. *Classical Rhetoric in English Poetry*. New York: St. Martin's Press, 1970.

Wilbern, David. "Shakespeare's Nothing" in *Representing Shakespeare: New Psychoanalytic Essays*. Eds. Murray M. Schwartz and Coppélia Kahn. Baltimore: Johns Hopkins University Press, 1980. 252-54.

Trumpeting and "seeled" Eyes
A Semiotics of [Eye]conography in *Othello*

LARUE LOVE SLOAN

Although virtually every discussion of *Othello* must at some point contend with the play's references to sight and seeing, no study that I know of—Karen Newman's observations about the play's "scopic economy" notwithstanding—has explored Iago's manipulation of the iconic sign system that privileges male eyes. While Steven Baker's "Sight and a Sight in *Othello*" describes the play as "a history of seeing, looking, and watching" (302), Baker is more interested in exploring how the play's references to sights and seeing construct the literally hoodwinked Othello as an emblem of Blind Love than in investigating a semiotics of vision. In her exploration of the "sights" in *Othello*, Katherine E. Maus focuses on the relationship between the legal "visibility" of invisible evidence in English witchcraft trials and Iago's attempts to convince Othello that he can see what cannot be seen. Newman's essay on "Femininity and the Monstrous in *Othello*" argues that Desdemona's desire is punished precisely because it is "non-specular." Newman identifies the "orality/aurality" of Desdemona's sexuality "as frightening and dangerous," even monstrous, to the "male-dominated Venetian world of *Othello*," a world "dominated by a scopic economy which privileges sight" (152).

It is the semiotics of this representational culture's [eye]conic sign system that I wish to explore further. With a casual reference to the female eye, Iago evokes patriarchal fear of woman's insatiable sexuality, while his male eye references figure a patriarchal order enforced by male surveillance and custody of the potentially unruly female. Central to his construction of Desdemona as a dangerous temptress, an Eve of insatiable sexual appetites who pretends to modesty while sending clear sexual signals, is Iago's insistent linking of her eye with her sexual appetite. "Her eye must be fed," he insists, "and what delight shall she have to look on the devil?" (2.1.220–21). "What an eye she has!" he exclaims in mock admiration; "Methinks it sounds a parley to provocation" (2.3.20–21).[1] The ability to evoke and manipulate what I shall call

[eye]conography—a sign system that implies mutually exclusive spaces of male authority and female sexual desire—is at the very heart of Iago's power to produce "reality" for his male victims. This eyeconography figures eyes as gendered, occupiable spaces which encode the female's most private space² as well as enclosure—the space in which female desire is contained and circumscribed by the custodial male's field of vision. Bolstered by cultural assumptions that privilege female obedience and condemn female desire, Iago manipulates the play-world's eyeconography to transform Desdemona's autonomous gaze into "an index and prologue to the foul history of lust," her "inviting eye" into a consuming pudendum, and Othello's eye into a blind ("seeled up") space, emptied of masculine authority, credibility, or substance.

Like the misogynistic tenets on which it is based, the sign system Iago employs is not peculiar to Shakespeare's Venice. The eroticism of the female eye has experienced a long and persistent history, with the "relation between vision—the seduction of a gaze—and the erotic [lying] at the source both of an idealization of women in literary texts and a corresponding antifeminism [. . .] not only for the church fathers but for the classic misogynists of the High Middle Ages as well" (Bloch, 15). Classical, scholastic, and popular texts insisting that women were driven by their appetites typically warned men to beware of women's eyes. One twelfth-century proverb from the anonymous *Proverbia quae dicuntur super natura feminarum* equated the woman's "lustful eye" with that of the poisonous basilisk: "The basilisk kills with its poisonous look; the lustful eye of a woman brings scandal to man and dries him out like hay. It is a mirror of the devil; woe be unto even the most religious man who looks in it too often" (Uitz, 156). Marbod of Rennes, a twelfth-century bishop, expressed similar sentiments in his *De muliere mala*: "But I warn you not to look back at [a beautiful woman], since anyone who toys with desire can be turned to stone by the very sight of the Gorgon" (71). The thirteenth-century author of *Ancrene Riwle* advised anchoresses not to "peep out" of their cells if they hoped to avoid the catastrophic consequences of female "looking" (Blamires, 95). Renaissance conduct books insisted that a woman stay in the house, safe not only from the unlicensed gazing of males, but from the dangers elicited by her own "wand'ring" eye. Typical is the 1619 *Description of a Good Wife: or A Rare One Amongst Women* which advises men to wed a woman with a "fixt eye," content to remain "still" (always) in her house (quoted in Parker, *Literary Fat Ladies,* 103). Submitting to surveillance by the custodial male, or literally allowing him to "keep an eye on her," was thought to be necessary to protect a woman from her natural desire to let her eye wander, as well as from the threat posed by the unlicensed male gaze. Brabantio's exclamation "O heaven, how got she out?" (1.1.170) when he discovers that Desdemona "had eyes and chose" Othello implies this view of the male custodian as a woman's defense against the appetite of her own eye.

That the sign system Iago manipulates is not his creation is evidenced by the other characters' casual use of it. Though only Iago and his pupil Othello use traditional, misogynistic female eyeconography, male eyeconography— not least because it lacks the obscene connotations of the female eye—is introduced and used freely by other characters. Desdemona herself explicitly links male eyes to the status quo, surveillance, and custody. To the Duke's suggestion that she remain with her father, Desdemona responds, "Nor would I there reside / To put my father in impatient thoughts / By being in his eye" (1.3.241–43). The phrase "being in his eye" not only implies the physical space surveyed *by* Brabantio's eye, it also figures the male eye *as* a physical space that can be inhabited. This isn't as outrageous an implication as it might first appear. The *Malleus Malificarum* cites numerous examples of the eye's vulnerability to literal inhabitation by uninvited guests, and anthropologist Andrew P. White has identified a "medieval prescription for a salve against 'nocturnal goblin visitors' that when applied to the eyes [. . .] becomes an efficacious weapon against inhabitation" (quoted in Moss and Cappanari, 3). Brabantio's eye fails not because it is assailed by would-be inhabitants, but because his daughter steals out of it, leaving empty the chamber where she has been safely stowed: "O thou foul thief," he accuses Othello, "where hast thou stowed my daughter?" (1.2.63). Having confidently assumed his eye to be as impenetrable as his house, which he protests "is not a grange," Brabantio must finally confront not only the unpleasant fact that his daughter is no longer "in his eye," but worse, that she herself—not an unlicensed male—has penetrated it from the inside out in a "gross revolt" (1.1.135). Having failed to exert sufficiently rigorous surveillance of the female in his custody, Brabantio loses his right to dispose of her, a right on which his "authority" and "masculine identity" depend (Drakakis, 79).

The culturally-approved transaction that releases a female from her father's custody into her husband's is implied in *Othello* by her transfer from the father's eye to the husband's—from one approved custodial eye chamber to another. The eye images suggest that a woman who displeases her custodial male will be banished from his eye, which will "hold her loathed." Whether she displeases her husband or her father, the fault lies in her wandering eye, "for," as Othello ingenuously informs Iago in the temptation scene, "she had eyes, and chose me." With the male eye figuring the natural patriarchal order and the female eye its subversion, Iago's insistent positioning of Desdemona's eye at the center of his discourse constructs her "eyeing" of Othello, as well as her "slipperiness" in escaping undetected from her father's eye, as a dangerous undermining of male authority and masculine identity. Such women must be "looked to," as both Brabantio and Iago warn Othello. Consistently, the males in the play depend on the authority exercised by the male eye to validate their manhood. This construction of male eye and masculine identity as synonymous reappears in Brabantio's warning to Othello: "Look to her Moor, if thou hast eyes to see, / She has deceived her father, and may thee"

(1.3.291–92). With its implication that to lose the eyes is to lose the identity, Brabantio's bitter eyeconography will provide Iago with a significant portion of his script when he begins to refashion Desdemona as Eve and Othello as the hapless Adam.

Desdemona also unwittingly participates in her own refashioning when she describes her decision to elope in terms of "downright violence." Her words simultaneously suggest a military action—complete with violence, storming, and trumpeting—and unruly Nature herself: "That I did love the Moor to live with him, / My downright violence and storm of fortunes / May trumpet to the world" (1.3.247–49). Before he yields to Iago's insinuations, Othello does not find this female violence troubling. Indeed, he values Desdemona precisely because of her autonomous desire, a desire awakened by the same eyes that "saw Othello's visage in his mind" (1.3.250) and "spurned the wealthy curled darlings of her nation" for him (1.2.69). Othello's conviction that he can safely wager his life upon her fidelity is based on the knowledge that she looked with her own eyes, not with her father's: "for she had eyes and chose me" (3.3.193).[3] That firm conviction is easily undermined, however, once Othello incorporates the assumptions of male eyeconography into his own thought and discourse—when he begins to fear, not approve, Desdemona's desiring eye.

In act 2, the men's reaction to a macrocosmic reenactment of Desdemona's "downright violence and storm of fortunes"—a violent storm through which Desdemona's ship glides mysteriously unimpeded—reinforces the dominance of male eyeconography even in the remote outpost of Cyprus. As the "foul and violent tempest" threatens to swallow up Othello, Montano vows that he and his men will "throw out our eyes for brave Othello,/ Even till we make the main and th' aerial blue / An indistinct regard" (2.1.37–41). The striking eye image figures male eyes as lifelines (thrown out) and implies the importance of homosocial ties in combating unruly Nature, historically represented as female. The insistence on watching until their eyes blur, rendering the sea and sky indistinguishable, echoes Brabantio's insistence on rigorous male surveillance. Like Desdemona's self-described sexual desire, the unruly storm threatens not only to engulf Othello's "tall ship" (2.1.80), which Cassio's prayer for Othello's safety links to male sexual potency,[4] but, like Desdemona herself, to confound, or blur, the male gaze. Both Brabantio's warning and Montano's insistence on unremitting watching imply the patriarchal assumption that the male eye must impose order, or culture, on unruly female nature.

Into this shared discourse of male eyeconography, Iago introduces traditional, misogynistic female eyeconography. Practicing on Roderigo and Cassio before he attempts to abuse Othello's ears, Iago uses the female eye to identify even "the divine Desdemona" as depraved by her "very nature." He begins working on Roderigo as soon as he sees an opportunity (in 2.1), following Desdemona's intimate conversation with Cassio as they await Othello's arrival. Using Desdemona's own words ("violence" and "loved the Moor"), Iago begins to construct an Eve who, having been driven "unnaturally" into desire through her ear, must "naturally" revert to desiring through her eye. The Desdemona Iago creates here can be expected to indulge her wandering eye simply because she is a woman: "Very nature will instruct her in it." She is, in effect, defined by her hungry eye:

> Mark me with what violence she first loved the Moor, but for bragging and telling her fantastical lies. To love him still for prating?—let not thy discreet heart think it. *Her eye must be fed,* and what delight shall she have to look on the devil? When the blood is made dull with the act of sport, there should be again to inflame it, and to give satiety a fresh appetite, loveliness in favour, sympathy in years, manners, and beauties, all which the Moor is defective in. Now, for want of these required conveniences, her delicate tenderness will find itself abused, begin to heave the gorge, disrelish and abhor the Moor. Very nature will instruct her in it and compel her to some second choice. (2.1.214–29, emphasis added)

Because the appetite (stomach) Iago attributes to Desdemona's eye is sexual, the eye that must be fed inevitably implies both the mouth and the pudendum. Eye, stomach, and "tenderness" are thus collapsed into what the *Malleus Maleficarum* identifies as "the mouth of the womb" (47), a *mouth* because it is never satisfied.[5] Iago's defining of Desdemona by her insatiable pudendal eye confirms the opinions of women he expresses in 2.1: "Come on, you are pictures out of door" ("silent and well-behaved in public") but "hussies [huswives] in your beds" ("busy" in bed when you shouldn't be, and "unduly thrifty in dispensing sexual favors" to your husbands) (2.1.113–16).[6]

Using much the same technique on Cassio, Iago once again plays on Desdemona's words ("my downright violence . . . may trumpet to the world") to figure her eye as a trumpet that "sounds a parley to provocation." This remarkable image constructs the female eye as impudently male in its military trumpeting of desire, predictably "female" in its deliberate attempt to provoke male desire, and monstrous in its combination of phallic bugle and female pudendum:

IAGO: What an eye she has! Methinks it sounds a parley to provocation.

CASSIO: An inviting eye, and yet, methinks, right modest. (2.3.20–22)

Like the prelapsarian Othello, however, Cassio can imagine a wife who is simultaneously desiring and chaste. Initially thwarted by Cassio's courtly responses, Iago is forced to withdraw in temporary defeat. Within moments, however, Cassio proves vulnerable through his own eye. Earlier, when cautioned by Othello to "look to" the guards during the night's festivities, Cassio's response is eyeconographically correct, with the male eye figuring order, enforced by surveillance, on the unruly: "Iago hath direction what to do, / But notwithstanding, with my personal eye / Will I look to't" (2.3.1–6). Because Cassio has no investment in Desdemona, Iago's attempt to blur Cassio's eye with a "counterfeit" image of the lady is unsuccessful. The ensign's original plan to blur the eye of the watch with liquor, however, works perfectly. Easily convinced that his refusal to drink with the men will damage his reputation, Cassio shortly becomes incapable of "looking to" anything with his "personal eye" and after "discourse[ing] fustian with [his] own shadow" (2.3.261), finds himself "cashiered." Having lost the authority of his eye, Cassio loses his command and with it his reputation—his masculine identity, "the immortal part" of himself (2.3.247). This loss of identity through the eye—a fate shared by Brabantio, Cassio, and Othello—makes the eye/I quibble irresistible.

The crude female eye references Iago employs with Roderigo and Cassio have no place in his delicate manipulation of what Othello's eye "sees." However, while he dare not slander Desdemona directly, she is implicated in his every eye reference. Even his striking image of jealousy, the green-eyed monster that mocks the meat it feeds on, must inevitably summon up the time-worn image of the unfaithful wife who, with her wandering and wanton eye, "cunningly" betrays her credulous husband. In response to Iago's first and most tentative insinuations, Othello initially insists on Desdemona's fidelity, expressing approval of her free speech and love of company with his own eyeconography, which allows that a woman can be, as Shakespeare's merry wives put it, "merry and honest, too": "'Tis not to make me jealous / To say my wife is fair, feeds well, loves company, / Is free of speech, sings, plays, and dances well. / Where virtue is, these are more virtuous. / Nor from mine own weak merits will I draw / The smallest fear or doubt of her revolt, / For she had eyes and chose me" (3.3.187–93). But is it coincidence that, in defending Desdemona, Othello introduces the word "eye" into his discourse, a word he has managed to avoid for two and one-half acts? And is his omission of Desdemona's "inviting," yet "right modest" eye from his list of her virtues an "oversight"? Whether Othello is unconsciously supplying what has been left out of Iago's discourse or his choice of words is purely coincidental, that Desdemona "has eyes" is precisely what Iago wants to suggest—eyes that wander, as well as a pudendal eye that must be fed. Latching on to Othello's insistence that he "will see before [he] doubt[s]," Iago introduces the male eye into their exchange by echoing the first half of Brabantio's warning ("Look to her, Moor, if thou hast eyes to see"): "Look to your wife. Observe her well with Cassio. / Wear your eyes thus: not jealous, nor secure" (3.3.202–04). Othello's express approval of Desdemona's "free" looks prompts Iago to suggest that Othello "wear" his eyes like spectacles to improve and "correct" his myopic male gaze. As Brabantio's warning implies, any man who fails to use his eyes risks his own manhood. Authorizing this "moral theology of patriarchy"[7] by using the eye of God to represent the perfect male gaze, Iago informs Othello that Venetian women are infamous for eluding the custodial eye of their lords, leaving their adulterous acts visible only to the all-seeing eye of the deity:

Iago: In Venice they do let God see the pranks
                   They dare not show their husbands; their best conscience
                   Is not to leave't undone, but keep't unknown.

OTHELLO: Dost thou say so? (3.3.201–209)

In response to Othello's guileless question, Iago echoes the second half of Brabantio's warning ("She has deceived her father and may thee"):

IAGO: She did deceive her father, marrying you,
                   And when she seemed to shake and fear your looks,
                   She loved them most.

OTHELLO: And so she did. (3.3.210–12)

Othello is forced to concede that Desdemona has already deceived the first male responsible for her custody and that, by her own admission, she was driven to do so by her own sexual desire. If female eyes figure unlicensed female desire, Desdemona unquestionably "has eyes." But does Othello, the custodial male, have "eyes to see"? It remains for Iago to identify Desdemona conclusively as one of these same Venetian women who elude the husband's eye. The existing sign system figures any woman who is not "fixed" in her proper place as indulging her "wandering" eye. In her proper place—the custodial male's eye—she is "sealed up" for consumption only by licensed males. Once out of the male eye, she is cheapened, if only by being the object of the unlicensed male gaze.[8] Returning to that same moment in the Senate to cull another example of male eyeconography used by the lady herself, Iago reminds Othello not only of Desdemona's resistance to "being in [her] father's eye," but her astonishing proficiency at slipping out of that eye while appearing to be safely stowed within it: "Why, go to, then. / She that so young could give out such a seeming, / *To seel her father's eyes up close as oak,* / He thought 'twas witchcraft!" (3.3.212–15, emphasis added). Edward Snow points out that Iago's use of "seel" here "echoes Othello's earlier, strenuously disavowed image of the emasculating effects of married love: 'When light-wing'd toys / Of feather'd Cupid seel with wanton dullness / My speculative and offic'd instruments'" (229). As Iago uses it, the term insinuates that both father and husband have been hoodwinked, their eyes "seeled" by a Venetian strumpet (of "country disposition") who not only slips out of the custodial eye, but seals it up behind her, leaving an empty eye/I, void of masculine identity. Having seized on Othello's avowal that Desdemona "had eyes, and chose me," Iago reestablishes the vigilant male eye as the proper seat of autonomous action and refashions the female eye as a subtle unsealer of the custodial male's private property. The resulting impossibility of reconciling Desdemona's desire—figured in her eyes that chose Othello—with the male eyeconography of containment dislocates Desdemona from her father's eye and threatens to dislodge her from Othello's.

Iago's persistent manipulation of the mutually exclusive spaces figured by male and female eyes reduces Desdemona to the space of her desiring eye and re-figures her legitimate desire for Othello as wantonness. Coming as close as he dares to making a direct reference to her eye, Iago attributes her "seeming" tractability to witchcraft: "She that so young could give out such a seeming, he thought 'twas witchcraft" (3.3.215). A Desdemona who could bewitch her father's eye into dullness might well be expected to bewitch her husband's. Perhaps because it involved "seeling up" the husband's eye as well as bewitching the eye of the complicit male, female adultery was commonly believed to be a kind of witchcraft. The fascination, or literally bewitching quality, of the female eye appears to have been linked with the "cultural equation" of witchcraft and adultery found in "marriage manuals, religious treatises, legal handbooks, and other didactic writings" of the Early Modern period (Gutierrez, 9). David Kaula notes the irony in "Othello's own eyes [being] too closely seeled up for him to catch the subtle untruth that not Desdemona but he himself was the one Brabantio had accused of practising witchcraft" (120). Indications that Othello has forgotten the original charge and readily yielded to Iago's suggestion appear not only in his failure to question the ensign's revisionist history, but in his act 5 description of Desdemona's eyes as "charms" that he must "blot" from his mind's eye.

If Othello's eye, like Brabantio's, has indeed been sealed up, Desdemona has once again slipped out of proper custody, driven by the appetite of her hungry eye. Iago's challenge remains to indict Desdemona by "showing" her pudendal eye without naming it. His ability to do this may be the most impressive instance of his "double knavery":

> My lord, I would I might entreat your honour
> To scan this thing no farther. Leave it to time.
> Although 'tis fit that Cassio have his place—
> For sure he fills it up with great ability—
> Yet, if you please to hold him off a while,
> You shall by that perceive him and his means.
> Note if your lady strain his entertainment
> With any strong or vehement importunity.
> Much will be seen in that. (3.3.249–57)

"By entreating Othello to 'scan this thing (Desdemona's supposed infidelity) no farther'—indeed, by mentioning 'this thing' at all—Iago in effect forces his general to question Desdemona's honesty" (Ryding, 195). The "place" that Cassio "fills up with great ability" is a transparent reference to the "eye [that] must be fed," the "private place" that, according to patriarchal codes, rightfully belongs to Othello. Early Modern conduct books made clear that a wife's private parts were not hers, but her husband's. A typical text describes adultery as breaking, entering, and occupying private property, "very heinous in respect of our Neighbour, whose hedge we break down, and whose enclosure we lay wast . . . and defile and dishonour that which is his most proper possession" (quoted in Parker, *Literary Fat Ladies*, 105). By positioning Desdemona's unnamed "eye" at the center of their discourse, Iago in effect exposes her "enclosure" in a common, public space. That the sexual innuendo is clear enough to Othello is obvious in his subsequent lament that, because husbands can own but not control their wives' appetites, cuckoldry is the inevitable fate of "great ones."

Under the influence of Iago's obscene eyeconography, Othello demands "ocular proof" of Desdemona's infidelity: "Villain, be sure thou prove my love a whore. / Be sure of it. Give me the ocular proof . . . / Make me to see't" (3.3.364–69).[9] In her exploration of the English trial jury's "process of discovery" and its relationship to *Othello*, Maus explains that the juridical process "was usually represented as the unveiling of something that nonetheless remained invisible, beyond sight. This visible invisibility was called the 'prodigious', the 'unnatural', the 'unspeakable', the 'monstrous'" (167). She contends that Iago "encourages Othello to imagine adultery as an essentially invisible crime, in the same category with treason or witchcraft, fully displayed only before the omniscient eye of God [. . .;] tantalizes Othello by reminding him of the limitations of his 'mortal eyes'[;] and then . . . encourages him to imagine them as overcome" (171). Indeed, the chain of eye references Iago uses here in response to Othello's demand for ocular proof seems to bear out Maus's analysis, for even as Iago insists on the impossibility of witnessing the act—having already established that supersubtle Venetian females routinely slip unobserved from the male eye—he creates it, using the coded language of male eyeconography: "Would you, the *supervisor*, grossly *gape on*? / *Behold* her topped? [. . .] Damn them then / If ever *mortal eyes* do *see* them bolster / *More than their own [eyes]* [. . .] It is impossible you should *see* this [. . .]" (3.3.403–407, emphasis added). In creating this scenario for Othello's mind's eye, Iago here situates Othello as the patriarchal God whose eye penetrates all. Consistent with the use of male eyes elsewhere in the play, the passage constructs the act of seeing into the heart of a mystery as both a licensed penetration and an exclusively male privilege.

As evidence that the act he has just fabricated is "real," Iago turns Othello's eye to the unarguably substantial and material handkerchief. Now positioning himself as "the supervisor," Iago uses the handkerchief to "show" the "common thing" he has made of Desdemona's most private space. In his description of Cassio wiping his beard with the token, Iago substitutes the

handkerchief for the pudendal eye he dare not name: "such a handkerchief—
I am sure it was your wife's—did I today / See Cassio wipe his beard with"
(3.3.437–43). That he is successful in substituting the token for the "forfended
place" is evident when, in the next scene, Othello takes the analogy one step
further, once again supplying the word that Iago leaves out. In his narrative of
the handkerchief's history, Othello makes explicit his suspicion that
Desdemona has either given away her chastity or is contemplating doing so.
He describes the handkerchief as visible evidence of the wife's (his mother's)
sexual fidelity: if she "kept it," it would make her husband "amiable" and
"subdue him" to her love. But if she " lost / Or made a gift of it," she would be
expelled from her husband's eye: "my father's eye / Should hold her loathed,
and his spirits should hunt / After new fancies" (3.4.59–61). The male eyeconography Othello employs—"my father's eye should hold her loathed"—
reiterates his Iago-induced conclusion that Desdemona is "gone," he himself
is "abused," and his "relief must be to loathe her" (3.3.271–72), for the
"father's eye" that in Iago's narrative was "seeled up close as oak" becomes in
Othello's narrative the husband's eye that loathes the erring wife and seals
itself against her return. The climax of the narrative, Othello's warning to
Desdemona, identifies the handkerchief not with Desdemona's sight—her
(plural) "eyes," which cannot logically be "given away"—but with her pudendal "eye" (singular and therefore "precious") which can: "Therefore take heed
on't. / Make it a darling, like your precious eye. / To lose't or give't away were
such perdition / As nothing else could match" (3.4.53–66, 74). Just as the eye
images are obviously Iago's, so is the handkerchief's revisionist history an
obvious fabrication,[10] a thinly veiled warning designed to frighten Desdemona
into fidelity or confession. One of the play's greatest ironies is that, after
demanding ocular proof, Othello is content to take Iago's word that the handkerchief he sees in Bianca's hand is Desdemona's ("Was that mine?"). Iago's
language constructs the reality that Desdemona is "but the sign and semblance
of her honor" and that Othello, who has failed to interpret her signs "correctly," is a "horned monster and a beast."

The measure of Iago's success in reducing Desdemona to an O is evident
in Othello's adopting of a new discourse. Before the temptation scene,
Othello's sole reference to eyes is quite indirect: he refers to his own eyes as
"speculative and officed instruments," which he assures the Senate he will turn
away from Desdemona to focus on his military obligations. After Iago's
lessons in patriarchal eyeconography, however, Othello insists on making Desdemona the object not only of his gaze, but of Iago's and Emilia's. Quite suddenly, references to eyes and watching begin to pepper his discourse. By act
4, he suspects that Desdemona's eyes are the source of her power. Convinced
that Desdemona has sealed up Brabantio's eyes, trumpeted her lust to Cassio,
and bewitched her own husband, Othello determines to confront her by looking into those fatal eyes. In the same way that he later looks for proof of Iago's

diabolical origin in the villain's feet—"I look down at his feet [. . .] but that's a myth"—Othello looks for proof of Desdemona's witchcraft in her eyes: "Let me see your eyes!" he demands. "What horrible fancy's this?" she responds (4.2.27–29). Does he expect to find in Desdemona's eyes the "sweating devil" of lust he previously detected in her palm? His subsequent treatment of Desdemona as a prostitute in a brothel seems to confirm that what he sees in her eyes is indeed the devil of sexual desire—the same desire she later identifies as "the loves I bear to you" and her "sins." That Desdemona "had eyes and chose" Othello is "not so good now," for he is convinced that her lustful eyes are charms that lure other men, just as she lured him, to the common space of her pudendal eye. Having given away her "precious eye," Desdemona can no longer "subdue [Othello] to her love." Following the formula in his revisionist history of the handkerchief, his eye now, like that of "the fathers" (his own, Brabantio, the Church Fathers) will "hold her loathed." Much of Othello's energy in act 5 is then directed toward avoiding Desdemona's gaze, partly to keep her hated image from "being in his eye," and partly to avoid being bewitched anew by her lustful female gaze.

Moving toward her chamber with the intention of acting as her judge and executioner, Othello breathes to himself a counter-charm against Desdemona's fascination: "Forth of my heart those charms, thine eyes, are blotted" (5.1.36). His careful avoiding of her gaze throughout the murder scene suggests the usual precaution of having the witch brought into court "backwards so that her evil eyes might not rest on the judge and bewitch him" (Zilboorg, quoted in Baring and Cashford, 529). Othello's insistence on blotting out the "charms" of Desdemona's eyes, together with his accusation that she has turned his heart to stone ("O perjured woman! Thou dost stone my heart" [5.2.68]) indicates his conviction that Desdemona, like the lustful woman depicted in the twelfth-century proverb, possesses the basilisk's fatal gaze. Her uncontrolled lust is a "mirror of the devil" that robs Othello of his rightful identity and licit "occupation" of her most private space. What Linda Charnes has said of *Troilus and Cressida* seems to apply here as well: "controlling beauty is crucial, since the accompanying fear is that female beauty not appropriated by male agency [. . .] carries with it the threat of the Medusa: that which turns men to stone (rendering them at once rigidly 'erect' and incapable of the use of that erection)" (95). Perhaps it is this fear of Desdemona's sexual power that leads Othello to prefer looking at her when her eyes are closed ("Be thus when thou art dead, and I will kill thee / And love thee after" [5.2.18–19]). The rolling of his eyes to which Desdemona refers ("And yet I fear you; for you're fatal then / When your eyes roll so" [5.2.39–40])—particularly in its implication that the person who averts his eyes is "fatal"—may allude to the belief that a person who sees the basilisk but avoids its gaze can kill without being killed: "In evil eye beliefs, it is the eye looking at the victim that kills. In the case of the Medusa, it is the victim looking at Medusa that kills. In the case of the fabulous basilisk or cockatrice, it is the basilisk looking at the victim while the victim is looking at the basilisk that kills" (Woodbridge, 222). Under no threat of literal death at Desdemona's hands, Othello seeks to avoid the death of sexual climax, provoked by those "charms, [Desdemona's] eyes." In this version of the Fall, the tempter convinces Adam to rewrite the primal temptation scene by killing Eve, and thus preventing the betrayal of "more men" (5.2.6).

At the same moment that Othello is justifying the murder of his wife with culturally-privileged eyeconography, Iago is attempting to implicate Bianca in the attempted murder of Cassio: "What, *look you pale*? [. . .] *Look you pale*, mistress? / Do you perceive the *ghastness* of her *eye*? / Nay, an you *stare*, we shall hear more anon. / *Behold her well*; I pray you, *look upon her*. / *Do you see*, gentleman? Nay, guiltiness / Will speak, though tongues were out of use (5.1.106–112, emphasis added). Cautioning the men to "behold her well" and "look upon her," Iago interprets Blanca's "stare" and the "ghastness of her eye" as guilt, just as he previously interpreted Desdemona's "inviting eye" as an orifice that "must be fed." He is prevented from fatally inscribing Bianca within male eyeconography by his wife's insistence that she will speak, first in spite of Othello's threats, and then in spite of Iago's. It seems particularly appropriate that Emilia chooses to defend Desdemona with an eye reference, describing her as "the sweetest innocent / That e'er did lift up eye" (5.2.206–207). Emilia's redemption of her mistress's eye reconstructs Desdemona as Cassio originally described her: "the divine Desdemona," with eye "inviting," yet "right modest." Othello also confirms Desdemona's innocence by referring to her gaze, which "goes from being damned to damning; from being judged to offering the final judgment on Othello's soul" (Callaghan, 93): "Now, how dost thou look now? O ill-starr'd wench, / Pale as thy smock! When we shall meet at count, / This look of thine will hurl my soul from heaven, / And fiends will snatch at it" (5.2.279–82). His eyes now unsealed in his tragic recognition of Desdemona's innocent eye, Othello reconstructs himself not only as the husband who, according to his narrative of the handkerchief, willingly "subdues" himself to his wife's love, but in terms of a new, inclusive eyeconology. Among the four items Othello insists must be included if report is to "Speak of me as I am" is his self-description as "one whose subdu'd eyes, / Albeit unused to the melting mood, / Drops tears as fast as the Arabian trees / Their medicinable gum" (5.2.357–60). This final image implies an eye/I with both feminine ("subdu'd" and "melting") and masculine ("unused to the melting mood") attributes. No longer a patriarchal space of containment and surveillance, the eye becomes a space where both male and female desire can be accommodated. Even as this new eye space is introduced and the object that "poisons sight" is "hid" under Lodovico's direction, the reader/observer is left to consider Iago's unsettling ability to manipulate eyeconography in such a way that his constructed "characters" participate in "real" murder.

The coding of male eyes as custodial spaces and female eyes as sexual organs is central to the *Othello* eyeconography, with custody and surveillance of the sexually insatiable woman whose eye must be fed at its core. Othello's abrupt and unprecedented use of eye references, evoked by Iago during the temptation scene and continuing into the last two acts, testifies to the efficacy of Iago's technique in employing a discourse so commonplace as to be invisible, and so powerful as to be unchallengeable. In fact, Othello's fall is encapsulated in his own, perhaps self-conscious, use of eyeconography. His initial defense of Desdemona early in the temptation scene allows for female sexual desire: "For she had eyes and chose me." His conviction that she is false converts those eyes he has praised to one pudendal eye that he warns her to control: "make it a darling like your precious eye." His girding for murder and attempts to elude the fascinator are evident in "Forth of my heart those charms, thine eyes, are blotted." Finally, his tragic recognition as he sees Desdemona's innocence in her dead gaze is expressed in the image of male eyes no longer "seeled up" by patriarchal moral theology, but "subdued" by the "medicinable" tears that melt the cruel male eye/I: "one whose subdu'd eyes, / Albeit unused to the melting mood, / Drops tears as fast as the Arabian trees / Their medicinable gum" (5.2.357–60).

NOTES

1. All quotations from *Othello* are from the Norton Shakespeare.
2. Eric Partridge, *Shakespeare's Bawdy*, identifies *eye* as slang for the pudendum (102).
3. Compare *MND*'s Hermia, who wishes "I would that my father looked but with my eyes."
4. "Great Jove, Othello guard,/ And swell his sail with thine own pow'rful breath,/ That he may bless this bay with his tall ship, / Make love's quick pants in Desdemona's arms,/ Give renewed fire to our extincted spirits" (2.1.78–82).
5. Historians Anderson and Zinsser point out that "the specter of the voracious mouth, the Hell of a woman's lusting body, was repeated endlessly, translated in one form or another into stories in English, French, and German. [. . .]" (435).
6. I prefer Bevington's use of "huswives" here, as well as his notes, which I have quoted. They best capture the paradox of the proverbial wife who "husbands" her sexual riches from expense on her husband.
7. The phrase is John Drakakis's.
8. In her exploration of how women spectators in the early modern theatre were regarded, Jean Howard seems on the verge of making the connection between patriarchy and the male eye as literal custodial space. She describes the female playgoer in Stephen Gosson's *The Schoole of Abuse* as being passed "not from lip to lip," like Cressida, but "from eye to eye, her value as the exclusive possession of one man cheapened, put at risk, by the gazing of many eyes" (224).
9. Howard Marchitello suggests that, like Vesalius, Othello is seduced by a "masculinist belief" in the authority of "ocular proof," which Marchitello explains as

"the conviction that women's bodies are, or contain, stories." He adds that "it is by stories [. . .] that both Vesalius and Othello are seduced" (14).

10. Othello later reports the more plausible history that the handkerchief was a gift from his father to his mother.

WORKS CITED

Anderson, Bonnie S. and Judith P. Zinsser. *A History of Their Own: Women in Europe from Prehistory to the Present*. Volume 1. New York: Harper & Row, 1988.

Anonymous. *The Ancrene Riwle*. Trans. M.B. Salu. London: Burns & Oates, 1955.

Baker, Steven. "Sight and a Sight in *Othello*." *Iowa State Journal of Research* 61.3 (1987): 301–309.

Baring, Anne and Jules Cashford. *The Myth of the Goddess*. London: Arkana, 1993.

Bevington, David. ed. *The Complete Works of Shakespeare*. Updated Fourth Edition. New York: Longman, 1997.

Blamires, Alcuin, ed. *Woman Defamed and Woman Defended: An Anthology of Medieval Texts*. Oxford: Clarendon, 1992.

Bloch, R. Howard. "Medieval Misogyny" in *Misogyny, Misandry, and Misanthropy*. Ed. R. Howard Bloch and Frances Ferguson. Berkeley and Los Angeles: University of California, 1989. 1–24

Callaghan, Dympna. *Woman and Gender in Renaissance Tragedy*. Atlantic Highlands, NJ: Humanities Press International, 1989.

Charnes, Linda. *Notorious Identity: Materializing the Subject in Shakespeare*. Cambridge: Harvard University Press, 1993.

Drakakis, John. "The Engendering of Toads: Patriarchy and the Problem of Subjectivity in *Othello*." *Shakespeare Jahrbuch*, 1988. 62–80

Gutierrez, Nancy. "Witchcraft and Adultery in *Othello*." *Playing with Gender: A Renaissance Pursuit*. Ed. Jean Brink, Maryanne Horowitz, Allison P. Coudert. Chicago: University of Illinois, 1991. 3–18.

Howard, Jean E. "Scripts and/Versus Playhouses: Ideological Production and the Renaissance Public Stage." *The Matter of Difference: Materialist Feminist Criticism of Shakespeare*. Ed. Valerie Wayne. Ithaca: Cornell University Press, 1991. 221–36

Kaula, David. "Othello Possessed: Notes on Shakespeare's Use of Magic and Witchcraft." *Shakespeare Studies II*. Ed. J. Leeds Barroll. The Center for Shakespeare Studies, 1967.

Kramer, Heinrick and James Springer. *The Malleus Maleficarum*. Trans. Montague Summers. New York: Dover, 1971.

Marbod of Rennes. *Liber decem capitulorum*. Trans. Alcuin Blamires. Ed. Rosario Leotta. Rome: Herder, 1984.

Marchitello, Howard. "Vesalius' *Fabrica* and Shakespeare's *Othello*: Anatomy, Gender, and the Narrative Production of Meaning." *Criticism*. 35.4 (1993): 529–59.

Maus, Katherine Eisaman. "Proof and Consequences: Inwardness and its Exposure in the English Renaissance." *Materialist Shakespeare: A History*. Ed. Ivo Kamps. London: Verso, 1995.

Moss, Leonard W. and Stephen C. Cappannari. "*Mal'occhio, Ayin ha ra, oculus fascinus, Judenblick*: The Evil Eye Hovers Above." in *The Evil Eye*. Ed. Clarence-Maloney. New York: Columbia University Press, 1976.

Newman, Karen. "'And Wash the Ethiop White': Femininity and the Monstrous in *Othello.*" *Shakespeare Reproduced: The Text in History and Ideology*. Ed. Jean Howard and Marion F. O'Connor. New York: Methuen, 1987. 143–62

Parker, Patricia. *Literary Fat Ladies*. London: Methuen, 1987.

———. "Shakespeare and Rhetoric: 'Dilation' and 'Delation' in *Othello.*" *Shakespeare and the Question of Theory*. Ed. Patricia Parker and Geoffrey Harman. New York and London: Methuen, 1985.

Partridge, Eric. *Shakespeare's Bawdy*. London and New York: Routledge, 1968.

Ryding, Erik S. "Scanning This Thing Further: Iago's Ambiguous Advice." *Shakespeare Quarterly*. 40.2 (1989): 195–96.

Shakespeare, William. *The Tragedy of Othello. The Norton Shakespeare*. Ed. Stephen Greenblatt, Walter Cohen, Jean E. Howard, Katherine Eisaman Maus. New York: Norton, 1997.

Snow, Edward A. "Sexual Anxiety and the Male Order of Things in *Othello.*" *English Literary Renaissance*. 10 (1980). Reprinted in *Othello: Critical Essays*. Ed. Susan Snyder. New York: Garland, 1988.

Uitz, Erika. *The Legend of Good Women: Medieval Women in Towns and Cities*. New York: Moyer, 1988.

Woodbridge, Linda. *The Scythe of Saturn: Shakespeare and Magical Thinking*. Chicago: University of Illinois Press, 1994.

"Work on my medicine"
Physiologies and Anatomies in *Othello*

MARY F. LUX

Othello is a body-intensive text. At the core, *Othello* is a study of gross anatomy and physiology, an investigation into how bodies both condition and restrict desire. The play connects body fluids, anatomies, and physiologies with specific characters and action (Pechter). In fact, the script is a prescription for understanding the strong role Elizabethan medicine played in the anatomy of plot and characters: their physiological markers, so to speak (Kolin). These markers have all too often been ignored or glossed over from a scientific, etiological point of view. Contemporary literary theory, which has focused on representation in and of the text as body and the body as text, affords me an aperture with which to explore the physiological dimensions of the play.

By training, I am a biologist and not a literary theorist, but the medical contexts of *Othello* are palpably discernable. Unquestionably they alerted Renaissance audiences to the representation and consumption of the physical on stage. In this essay I want to explore *Othello* as an anatomical chart and an aesthetic prescription for the ways in which bodies are translated into the anatomies of texts, including plots, characters, and script.

First performed 1604, *Othello* stands amidst some of the leading scientific breakthroughs in the history of medicine. Medicine was evolving from the province of the medieval barber-surgeon to the domain of trained practioners who studied the recent discoveries of researchers like Paracelsus and Vesalius. Shakespeare knew many physicians, and often wrote them into his plays without changing their names. Dr. William Butts, the name of a character in Henry VIII, was the actual physician to Henry VIII (Lienhard).

Phillippus Aureolus Paracelsus (Theophratus Bombastus von Hohenheim), a military surgeon between 1517 and 1524, practiced in Strasbourg 1526 through 1527, and in Basel after 1527, where he lectured at the university. He addressed a number of medical, philosophical, and theological issues, including the cure for venereal disease, the cause of the plague, and the chemotherapeutic use of mercurial-and sulfur-containing compounds for the treatment of disease (McGuinn). Iago's reference to the power of sulfur: "Dangerous conceits . . . Burn like the mines of sulfur" (3.3.332) and Othello's: "Blow me about in winds, roast me in sulphur, Wash me in steep-down gulfs of liquid fire" (5.2.277–78) indicate that Shakespeare had a cursory knowledge of the properties of sulfur. Mercury would easily fit Iago's description of "a poisonous mineral" (2.1.295), as mercurial compounds are highly toxic substances.

An anatomist, Andreas Vesalius was well-known for his work in dissection during the sixteenth century, and was instrumental in ending the unchallenged authority of Galen. Galen had written extensively during the second century from his experience as a military surgeon (Pearcy). Galen's errors were perpetuated until Vesalius and Harvey dispelled Galen's authority. Vesalius promoted investigation from nature, and questioned Galen's domination in the field of anatomy. He was appointed professor of surgery at Padua and published the *Tablulae Anatomicae* in 1538. This work revolutionized medicine by focusing on clear and specific sketches based on his dissections of apes (Senfelder).

William Harvey was born in 1578, earned a degree from Cambridge in 1598, and studied in Padua until 1602. His *Anatomical Study of the Motion of the Heart and of the Blood in Animals* was published in 1628, at least two decades after Shakespeare wrote *Othello* (Johnson). The thirty-three references to the heart in *Othello* consistently refer to the heart as a seat of passion, desire, and emotion, but give no evidence of the heart's function as a pump, since this fact was not yet known. Galen, the authority of the medieval period, had not discovered the complete function of the heart, believing that blood seeped through invisible pores in the heart to connect the venous and arterial flow. Harvey himself questioned how Galen could have been so close to the discovery of circulation without determining the concept (Johnson, Galen).

Othello's insistent reminders of the human body are relevant to the plot, which concentrates on a woman's fidelity, but is also reflective of the contemporary fascination with and renewed discovery of human anatomy and physiology, and the covert role of disease in the functioning of these systems. *Othello* is filled with metonymic references to numerous parts of human anatomy and to several physiologies, all of which have a bearing on the medical subtext of *Othello*. Fluids in particular are a vital part of the *Othello* script: blood is referred to 18 times and tears 14, demonstrating the juxtaposition of violence and suffering of both male and female in the body of the text. Not surprisingly, the most frequently cited anatomical parts are the heart (33), the hand (25), the eyes (19), the ear (11), the lips (10), and the tongue (8). Each of these body sites has immense symbolic and functional value emphasizing the physical in a play about jealousy, slander, and ocular proof.

Othello demands of Iago "give me the ocular proof" (3.3.363), and so emphasizes the necessity of visual proof; his desire to see with his own eyes indicates his reluctance to accept only the cognitive and insubstantial word of Iago. Othello is later horrified as Iago questions whether the Moor has an interest in watching Cassio bedding Desdemona (3.3.398) in order to imprint and amplify Othello's vision of Cassio with Desdemona. Iago detects Bianca's horror at viewing the wounded Cassio as "the gastness of her eye" (5.1.106). The image of Bianca's pale, horrified face indicates the level of shock she experiences at the scene before her. As Iago paints a picture for Roderigo, so Iago describes Desdemona with Cassio: "They met so near with their lips and their breaths embraced together" (2.1.257). Roderigo can almost feel her lips and hear her breath as he envisions Desdomona joined to Cassio, and not to him. Othello touches his heart and proclaims "it is too much of joy" (2.1.195–97). Even though the heart is a mechanical organ of circulation, elucidation of the heart's function has not lessened its place as the symbol of love and seat of emotion. Truly, the fullness in the chest that comes from great joy and emotion, and the racing of the heart that accompanies excitement continues to symbolize and physicalize the heart as an organ of love and promise. When Othello sees the wounded Cassio and Roderigo, he resolves "Forth of my heart those charms, thine eyes, are blotted, thy bed, lust-stained, shall with lust's blood be spotted" (5.1.35–36), again carrying the audience back and forth in physiologies. Othello defends Desdemona to Iago by proclaiming: "I found not Cassio's kisses on her lips" (3.3.344), once more foregrounding desire and denial in the dynamic terms of bodily fluids.

Not only do fluids carry emotions, so do various body parts, all symbolic. Iago would "rather have this tongue cut from my mouth" (2.3.217) as a pledge of his honesty. The tongue is primarily a sensual organ with a generous supply of nerves to provide for the experience of sensation. The taste buds which are found on the tongue, and the salivary glands which are located in the mouth cooperate to produce the sense of taste because the flavor elements of food must be dissolved in saliva for the taste bud to function. The tongue assists in chewing and swallowing, and, together with the sense of taste, enhances not only the pleasure of food and drink, but makes the process of ingestion possible. The tongue is also an essential organ for normal human speech and to lose the tongue is to risk dehumanization.

The hand, like the tongue, is that anatomical part of the body that differentiates human beings from other animals. It is a miracle of evolution, and consists of skin, muscle, and bones, as well as numerous nerves and nerve endings which allow for the high levels of coordination and sense of touch. This appendage provides for many practical functions as well as for countless representational roles. The strength of Othello's hand is found in 5.2.83, as he smothers Desdomona. The hand as alternate weapon is mentioned by the Duke in 1.3.175. The functional role of a hand holding a handkerchief provides the ocular proof demanded by Othello: "By heaven, I saw my handkerchief in's hand (5.2.62). The hand of friendship is extended to Cassio by Desdemona as reported by Iago in 2.1.167. In 3.3.423, Iago relates that Cassio in his sleep, "would gripe and wring my hand," as the hand becomes an instrument of passion. When Cassio tries to demonstrate his sobriety with "this is my right hand, and this is my left" (2.3.110), he attempts to use the hand as a strategic tool. Iago uses his hand in a pledge in 2.1.255, "by this hand." Othello believes that Desdemona has a nervous, guilty hand when he states, "Give me your hand.' This hand is moist, my lady" (3.4.36). In times of stress, as well as with emotional reactions, the sweat glands in the hands overproduce sweat in the same manner that sweat glands under the arms react to stress and emotion.

Desdemona's tears which flow through the text signifying her fluctuating emotional states. During courtship Othello "did beguile her of her tears" (1.3.157), as if stealing them the way Brabantio accused him of stealing his daughter. After being struck by Othello (4.1.239) Desdemona weeps in a normal response to an undeserved blow. The powerful emotion of loss, desperate experience of betrayal, and the grievous sensation of pain, in combination or in isolation, stimulate the flow of adrenaline, a powerful hormone. Adrenaline affects the entire body in a multitude of different organs and body systems including the lacrimal glands. These glands, located above the eyes, produce tears as both an emotional and a physiological response.

Lodovicio pleads: "Make her amends, she weeps" (4.1.243). Othello believe her tears to be contrived, as false as the mythical tears shed by crocodiles as they consume their prey (4.1.244–45). Desdemona is emptied of her tears, seemingly resigned to whatever fate awaits her: "I cannot weep, nor answers have I none"(4.2.105). Tears, which are formed in the lacrimal gland to bathe the eye, can be produced in greater amounts in an emergency, but after the immediate crisis has past, there is a refractory period before the continuation of normal tear production. During this period, even a very sorrowful person may truly have no tears. Later as Iago gives false comfort to Desdemona because "all things shall be well" (4.2.173), she prepares for bed. Her eyes itch and she wonders "Doth that bode weeping" (4.3.58). The itching sensation does not predict weeping, but rather is a result of it. Due to her excessive weeping, she is experiencing the refractory period before normal tear production can resume. The scarcity of tears prohibits the smooth movement of the eyelids over the eye, leading to irritation and the sensations of itching and dryness. After confessing his error in the murder of Desdemona, Othello acknowledges her rightful tears had been spilled "as fast as Arabian trees shed their medicinable gum" (5.2.348), which stresses that Desdemona had, indeed, shed copious tears. Othello also reacts with tears in times of great emotion. After Othello accuses Desdemona of being false, he weeps and she asks, "Am I the motive of these tears, my lord" (4.2.43-44). As he enters the bedchamber, determined to murder Desdemona, he bends to kiss her as she sleeps and says mournfully, "I must weep, But they are cruel tears." (5.2.20–21). Tears are one of the mechanisms of the body for releasing great tension and emotion. Tears of joy are as common as tears of grief, yet in this tragedy, the tears are those of grief, loss, betrayal, and guilt. Desdemona's lack of tears as she prepares for her final night, singing the song she associates with death, foretells of her greater loss, her loss of breath and life.

The most basic life fluid, however, is blood, which was known as essential, life-giving fluid long before the fundamental and diverse functions of blood had been identified. Loss of blood was known to cause death even in primitive cultures. (Uthman). The flow of blood through the body is critical to life. Blood carries red blood cells which bring oxygen to every living cell; white blood cells protect the body systems from microbial invasion and platelets stop the flow of blood after injury, (Rodak). Blood also carries a multitude of dissolved chemicals, hormones, and minerals that influence every aspect of the body. Blood is used throughout *Othello* to signify vices (1.3.125), sensuality (1.3.329), curses (3.3.454), emotions (4.1.275), and lust (5.1.36). Physiologically, these references to blood are valid in the sense that hormones, which are synthesized in glands but distributed through the bloodstream, influence every aspect of the human condition, from sexual desire to anger. More traditional aspects of blood as the underlying source of life are found denoting the injuries suffered by Montano (2.3.160), Iago (5.2.285) Roderigo and Cassio [implied by a stab wound] (5.1.26), and Othello's reluctance to draw blood from Desdemona's pale skin even as he prepares to kill her (5.2.3). There has been controversy about the ultimate cause of Desdemona's death. Some researchers believe that after attempts to suffocate her, Othello panics, forgets his oath to "not shed her blood," and stabs her to accomplish his murderous intent (Furness).

Even as the play overflows with fluids, the characters show numerous signs and symptoms of their diseased states. Cassio's reluctance to drink alcohol and his excuse of "poor and unhappy brains for drinking" is consistent with Renaissance lore and a recent (1996) decree by the Institute of Medicine (IOM), in which alcohol addiction was classified as a brain disease. The effects of alcohol on the brain, and more specifically, the neurons, or brain cells, have been the object of substantial research. Neurons communicate with other neurons through neurotransmitters following the consumption of alcohol (Hunt). Some researchers believe that a deficiency of neurotransmitters contributes to the development of alcoholism and causes significant and extended changes in the neurons which affect the brains response to alcohol (Fils-Aime et al, IOM).

The first drink after a period of abstinence, as in Cassio's situation before he took his first drink, reactivates the altered response in the brain and increases the desire to consume large quantities of alcohol (Stockwell). Cassio, whose brain had now been primed by a previous drink taken in the mood of celebration, states: "I have drunk but one cup tonight, and that was craftily qualified, too, and behold what innovation it makes here! I am unfortunate in the infirmity and dare not task my weakness any more" (2.3.36–39). His later declaration that: "every inordinate cup is unblest, and the ingredience is a devil" (2.3.302), indicates his awareness of the dangers alcohol held for him. Cassio is aware of the risk of further drinking, and hesitates to compound the damage of the previous drink. Interestingly enough, a principal attribute of alcohol addiction is an impaired control over drinking behavior (Jellinek). However, the tendency toward loss of control is not reflected by the control shown by many former problem drinkers who achieve abstinence or a low level consumption (Miller, 1993). Cassio attempts the low level consumption strategy by drinking "but one cup" of watered-down wine, but after a period of abstinence, the effects of the wine were greater than he expected.

Peer pressure is a constant problem for alcoholics, and alcohol recovery programs usually recommend that recovering alcoholics avoid not only alcohol, but also the occasion of drinking as well as the company of others who are known to drink. Demonstrating his use of poisons and knowing of Cassio's affliction, Iago admonishes Cassio that, "good wine is a good familiar creature," and rationalizes and justifies the lieutenant's drunkedness (2.3.308). Iago establishes doubt in Cassio with "Tis pity of him:/ I fear the trust Othello puts him in/ On some odd time of his infirmity". . . . (2.3. 121–23) and continues "He'll watch the horloge a double set/ If drink rock not his cradle" (2.3, 126–27), and later declares: "If I can fasten but one cup upon him,/ with that which he hath drunk tonight already,/ He'll be full of quarrel and offence" (2.3.45-7) and encourages Cassio to partake of his particular poison as well as "Now 'mongst this flock of drunkards/ Am I to put our Cassio in some action/ That may offend the isle" (2.3.56–58). Cassio's disorientation in, "this is my right hand, and this is my left" (2.3.110) may be comic in performance, but his behavior shows Shakespeare exploring the involvement of both the right and left cerebral hemispheres as the lieutenant manifests the classic symptoms of alcoholic consumption (Martin and Bates).

Desdemona's place in the script is also physiologically positioned. While critics have debated her virtues and vices, what has remained unstudied is how carefully Shakespeare informs audiences about Desdemona's status in terms of her physiological portrait, and the ways in which we as audience visually/ verbally consume her body (text) on stage. Her medical history is crucial to an understanding of her moral one. We learn that Desdemona has been seen as "a maiden never bold" (1.3.95). Consequently, she has been historically portrayed as a young girl, approximately the same age as Juliet, though in more contemporary productions Desdemona has aged into her late 20s to early 30s. A recent production (e.g. Providence's Trinity Rep), cast her as a mature woman, nearing her mid 20s. An older Desdemona in point of fact is consistent with Shakespeare's physiological description of her as a conflicted character, and also consistent with a Jacobean audience's recognition and response to a specific body in the text. In production, she is often associated with a virginal whiteness; a coloration emblematizing virtue but which could just as easily code information about her hematopoetic function. Iago's reference to Desdemona's complexion expressly and powerfully alerts audiences to heed her skin coloration, which is a conclusive sign of anemia: "Of her own clime, complexion, and degree" (3.3.234). Othello's description of the sleeping Desdemona: "whiter skin of hers than snow/ And smooth as monumental alabaster"(5.2.4,5) may proleptically point to her demise, but it nonetheless carries a crucial physiological marker; her notable pallor. Similarly, Othello's comparison of her to the moon: "Her name, that was as fresh as Dian's visage,/ is now begrimed and black/ As mine own face." (3.3.389–91) compares Desdemona to Diana, the symbol for both the pale moon and for virginity.

Pale, white skin is a classic symptom of anemia. Other pertinent symptoms include weakness, fatigue, and mental confusion (Uthman). Anemia, from the Greek word for "without blood," was not used in medical circles until the nineteenth century. This literal translation is a misnomer, since the term only refers to the red blood cells. Yet, examination of the blood of an anemic person shows either one or a combination of the following abnormalities: reduction in the number of red blood cells or red blood cells with an abnormal shape and a reduced amount of hemoglobin, the protein in red blood cells (erythrocytes) that gives blood its characteristic red color (Rodak). Correspondingly, Desdemona's virginal whiteness may have been as much a sign of her anemia as her virtue. One cause of anemia that may help us to understand and type Desdemona physiologically is iron deficiency, which has been the traditional cause of anemia in women of child-bearing age, which Desdemona clearly is. In fact, monthly blood loss in women who do not ingest sufficient dietary iron depletes the body's iron reserves. Until modern studies in nutrition and biochemistry promoted iron supplements for women, iron deficiency anemia was very common in women. Significantly, however, the text never mentions Desdemona as a potential mother. She is wife, daughter, lady, the "general's general," and even a potential mistress. Perhaps the absence of any maternal instincts are grounded in Desdemona's physiological state.

Additional causes of anemia which may pertain to Desdemona include alcohol consumption and a food-related condition, favism. Iago's comment about Desdemona's consumption of alcohol, "The wine she drinks is made of grapes "(2.1.249), may be a comment on her human nature, but also indicates that Desdemona, on occasion, drank wine. As alcohol is metabolized in the body, the metabolites of alcohol interfere with the process of red blood cell formation, a possible explanation for her paleness (Harrington). Desdemona may have possibly suffered from favism, which is limited to people of Mediterranean origin. This hereditary disorder is linked to a deficiency of an enzyme necessary for metabolism of the fava bean (*Vicia faba*), a staple of the diet in the Mediterranean area which includes Venice, and certainly Cyprus. The enzyme deficiency gives some protection against malaria which was endemic throughout Africa, the Near East, Southern Europe, and the British Isles during the Renaissance (Desowitz). Ingestion, or even exposure to the pollen of *Vicia faba* can result in a hemolytic anemia that occurs due to an allergic-type reaction in which red blood cells are destroyed by a metabolic error due to the lack of the enzyme (Favism). In relocating from Venice to Cyprus, Desdemona may have been affected by a modification in her diet that included the addition of fava beans. The ingestion of the beans could have triggered a hemolytic reaction that would lead to anemia.

Thalassemia, or Cooley's anemia, is a most plausible diagnosis for Desdemona. This genetic disease is found predominantly among persons of Mediterranean, Asian, and African heritage, and so as a Venetian lady, Desdemona is a prime candidate (Rodak). This congenital anomaly is caused by genes that carry the code or pattern for the synthesis of abnormal hemoglobin. This defective hemoglobin, known as hemoglobin C, causes the red blood cells to have an abnormal shape. The misshapen cells are destroyed prematurely by the spleen, resulting in a reduction of the numbers of red blood cells, causing anemia. The genes for thalassemia arose in many parts of the world where malaria is common. The abnormal hemoglobin of thalassemia gives protection from the malaria parasite, which cannot reproduce in the abnormal cells of individuals who inherit the thalassemia from only one parent. It is believed that protection from malaria gives an evolutionary advantage to individuals with the heterozygous trait at the price of anemia (Rodak). Desdemona, if she carried the genetic code for either thalassemia trait or favism, would have enjoyed a measure of protection against the ever-present possibility of infection with malaria.

Shakespeare knew of malaria. In *Henry V*, Mistress Dame Quickly beseeches her bawdy associates to visit Sir John Falstaff: "He is so shaked of a burning quotidian tertian, that it is most lamentable to behold" (2.1.112–13). Shakespeare's knowledge of the risk factors for malaria are mentioned in *The Tempest* by Caliban: "All the infections that the sun sucks up/ From bogs, fens, flats, on/ Proper fall and make him/ By inch-meal a disease" (2.2.2–3). Malaria was common in London and the surrounding area after being transported to the British Isles by the Romans in the first century, and was transmitted by the mosquitoes that bred in the marshes of Kent and Essex. The mosquitoes carry the parasite that causes malaria. Quinine, a miraculous cure for malaria, was endorsed by the London College of Physicians in 1658, indicating the importance of the newly-discovered cure to the malaria-stricken population of England (Desowitz). Quinine, or "Jesuit bark," had been brought to Europe from South America by Jesuit missionaries who learned of the remedy from Indians. Shakespeare could have known only of the disease when *Othello* was written, but not of the cure.

Desdemona's anemic state may have rendered her weakened, drained, and compromised; the very hindrances Desdemona encounters in her role as mediatrix for Cassio with Othello. Her weakened physiological state, of course, renders her vulnerable to Iago's poisons, his "drugs or mineral." Desdemona is thus brought before the audience as a living personification of a debilitated state, epidemiologically speaking. Describing Desdemona as a tomb of monumental alabaster by a murderous Othello overlooking his sleeping wife may be more than a poetic contrivance; it could very likely be a physiological reminder to audiences that her genetic etiological disposition can and did play a major role in her behaviors and response to and interpretation of them by others, foes and allies alike.

Although Desdemona was protected against the ravages of malaria, Othello did not escape from serious consequences of the parasitic disease. Othello, suffers from a serious seizure disorder and headaches. That he suffers from some type of neurological disorder is obvious from both the seizure suffered on-stage and that mentioned by Iago (4.1.50–51). A seizure may be caused by a number of abnormalities that cause uncontrolled electrical activity in the brain. When he falls on-stage in 4.1, many actors have minimized or avoided the gesticulations of seizure, since this is the least attractive element of the role and in fact debases a "heroic" noble Moor. But Sir Laurence Olivier and Laurence Fishburne have unconditionally and bravely portrayed an epileptic Othello, presenting all the appropriate symptoms of a grand mal seizure.

Othello's epileptic disorder, like Desdemona's anemia, may have cultural/ geographical causes/roots. As malaria originated in Africa, Othello's homeland, his seizures may result from malaria. Malaria has always been associated with warm, moist climates as are found throughout the Mediterranean, but the endemic area extends to throughout most temperature climates. Malaria was thought to have originated in Africa and followed migration routes to the Mediterranean and the Near East, significant for the Venetian Desdemona as well as the African Othello (History). Typical symptoms for malaria include fever and chills, headache, muscle aches, and nausea. The more serious infections may also result in seizures, mental confusion, coma, and death (Bia and Barry). Cerebral malaria is the best known of the severe consequences of malaria, and the most frequent serious complication in adults (Poser and Bruyn). Othello's seizures may result from cerebral malaria. Like Desdemona, Othello lived in a region endemic for malaria. Unlike Desdemona, however, Othello did not benefit from the genetic protection that favism or thallasemia afforded Desdemona, leaving him at risk for the parasitic disease. Shortly before Othello's on-stage seizure, he proclaims: "It is not words that shakes me thus (4.1.4–42)." In addition to his rage, he may have been suffering from the rigors that accompany the characteristic chills of malaria. Headaches are one of the common symptoms of malaria, and Othello's complaint of "pain upon my forehead" (3.3.288) is consistent with a diagnosis of malaria. Desdemona's efforts to use her treasured handkerchief to "bind it hard, within this hour, It will be well" (3.3.290–91) would not have been sufficient to ease the pain caused by the parasite-infected cells that invade the blood vessels of the brain. Othello knew her efforts were doomed to failure and under the stress of pain, responds, "Your napkin is too little" (3.3.291). Desdemona, desperate to be of comfort to her ailing husband, exits with him. In her haste to soothe Othello's distress, she leaves behind the handkerchief, unwittingly providing Iago with a potent device to pursue his toxic scheme. Certainly there are many causes of headache in addition to malaria, but one common type of headache, the migraine, is not commonly found in men of African descent (Stewart et al.). The mental confusion common to victims of cerebral malaria contributed to Iago's success in targeting Othello with his poisonous plot.

Iago's venomous words and deeds course throughout the play. He poisons Desdemona in her father's eyes (1.1.114–15) and convinces Brabantio to blame all his troubles on Othello's spells and false medicines (1.3.62). Iago predicts that essential sustenance will become a purgative as Othello loses his trust in Desdemona: "The food that is luscious to him as locusts shall be to him shortly as acerb as coloquintada" (1.3.348–350). Jealousy becomes inner pain for Iago as he ponders Othello's marriage to Desdemona: "Doth, like a poisonous mineral, gnaw my inwards" (2.1.295). The vivid image of "pestilence" poured into Othello's ear signifies the power of his plan of deceit and destruction (2.3.351) as Othello begins to doubt Desdemona. Iago glories in the change his "poisons" have wrought (3.3.328–32) and the effectiveness of his "medicine" (4.1.45) as Othello suffers a seizure. Ironically, when Othello asks for poison to kill Desdemona, Iago suggests strangulation, as though poisons were his secret arsenal; his exclusive province.

Throughout *Othello* there is extensive use of anatomical and physiological references that convey significant information about the characters: their reflexive response to joy and love, to pain and betrayal; their state of health or condition of disease; their manner of interactions, and their very human behavior. The numerous references to basic fluids convey the vulnerability and the humanity of Cassio, Othello, and Desdemona. The possibility of blood loss, due to wounds or anemia, could have fatal consequences for victims during the Renaissance. Although fatal blood loss still occurs, modern medicine, with modern therapies and procedures, have greatly reduced loss of life from the threats of death from injury and disease that existed in Elizabethan England. The natural response of tears has not changed from the seventeenth century, and modern readers can sense the sadness, the loss, and the regret portrayed by the weeping of Desdemona, Emilia, and Othello.

Cassio, a victim of alcoholism, suffers from the same problems that face modern alcoholics. The physiological deficiencies of alcohol addiction are better understood in the twenty-first century, but there is no treatment better than abstinence and avoidance of temptation attempted by Cassio. Desdemona, weakened by her anemia, is an easy victim. Spared from the devastation of malaria by her genetic heredity, nonetheless, her physical condition is compromised and her judgement is impaired. Othello, infected by the parasitic scourge of the Mediterranean, is also in a debilitated state. Suffering from the symptoms of cerebral malaria, he suffers from confusion, headaches, and seizures. Othello is easily confused about his feelings for Desdemona, and in his diseased state is unable to think clearly about the apparent evidence presented by Iago. He cannot control his jealous rage toward Desdomona and ends her life before he learns that the contrived evidence was false.

Iago, with his poisons and poisonous intentions, portrays the anti-human and anti-doctor (Heilman, Kolin). His goals of destruction betray the good of human nature and the "do no harm" credo of the medical profession. Iago uses every available tool to attain his catastrophic intent. Iago poisons the world around him with his false accusations.

Othello centers on the intricate role human anatomy and physiology play in the development of plot and characters. The various anatomical and physiological references can be viewed in a new context by application of modern medical knowledge to the underlying intricacies of Shakespeare's phenomonal ability to portray human drama that still fascinates the literary world in the twenty-first century.

WORKS CITED

Bia, Frank J. and Michele Barry. "Parasites" *Prognosis of Neurological Disorders*. Ed. Randolf Evans, David Baskin, and Frank Yatsu. New York: Oxford University Press, 1992.

Desowitz, Robert S. *Who Gave Pinta to the Santa Maria: Tracking the Devastating Spread of Lethal Tropical Disease into America*. New York: Harcourt, 1997.

"Favism" http://www.rialto.com/favism/ (1 Jan. 2001).

Fils-Aime, M. L., M. J. Eckardt, D. T. George, G. L. Brow, L. Mefferd, and M. Linnoila. "Early-Onset Alcoholics Have Lower Cerebral Spinal Fluid 5-Hydroxyindolacetic Acid Levels than Late-onset Alcoholics." *Archives of General Psychiatry* 53 (1996): 211–216.

Furness, Horace Howard, ed. *Shakespeare: Othello*. Philadelphia: J. B. Lippincot, 1914.

"Galen" http://hsc.virginia.edu/hs-library/historical/antiqua/galen.htm (7 Jan. 2001).

Harrison, John T., ed. *Consultation in Internal Medicine*. St. Louis: Mosby, 1990.

Heilman, Robert B. *Magic in the Web: Action and language in Othello*. Lexington: University of Kentucky Press, 1956.

Henry V. The Oxford Shakespeare. Gary Taylor, ed. Oxford: Oxford University Press, 1984.

"History of Malaria" *RPH Laboratory Medicine*. http://www.rph.wa.gov.au/labs/haem/malaria/history.html (12 Dec. 2000).

Hunt, Walter. "Pharmacology of Alcohol." *Handbook of Substance Abuse*. Ed. Ralph E. Tarter, Robert T. Ammerman, and Peggy J. Ott. New York: Plenum Press, 1998.

(IOM) Institute of Medicine. *Pathways of Addiction: Opportunities in Drug Abuse Research*. Washington D.C.: National Academy Press, 1996.

———. *Dispelling the Myths about Addiction: Strategies to Increase Understanding and Strengthen Research*. Washington D.C.: National Academy Press, 1997.

Jellinek, E. M. *The Disease Concept of Alcoholism*. New Brunswick, NJ: Rutgers Center of Alcohol Studies, 1960.

Johnson, J, W. Hepburn, and J. Crawford. "William Harvey." http://www.sjsu.edu/dept/Museum/harvey.html (6 Oct. 2000).

Kolin, Philip C. *The Elizabethan Stage Doctor as a Dramatic Convention*. Salzburg: Institut fur Englische Sprach und Literatur, 1974.

Lienhard,   John   H.   "Shakespeare   and   Medicine."   http://www.uh.edu/engines/epi1143.htm (15 Sept. 2000).

Martin, Christopher S. and Marsha E. Bates. "Physiological and Psychiatric Consequences of Alcohol." *Handbook of Substance Abuse*. Ralph E. Tarter, Robert T. Ammerman, and Peggy J. Ott. Eds. New York: Plenum Press, 1998.

McGuinn, Marion G. "Theophratus Bombastus von Hohenheim." *The Robinson Research World of Knowledge*. http://www.robinsonresearch.com/HEALTH/PEOPLE/Paracelsus.htm (6 Oct. 2000).

Miller, W. R. "Alcoholism: Toward a Better Disease Model." *Psychology of Addictive Behaviors* 7 (1993): 129–136.

Othello. E. A. J. Honigmann, ed. The Arden Shakespeare, 3rd ed. Walton of Thames, U.K: Thomas Nelson and Sons, 1997.

Pearcy, Lee T. "Galen: A Biographical Sketch." http://webea.pvt.kias.pa/medant/gall-bio.htm (7 Jan. 2001).

Pechter, Edward. *Othello and Interpretative Traditions*. Iowa City: University of Iowa Press, 1999.

Poser, Charles M. and George Bruyn. *An Illustrated History of Malaria*. New York: The Parthenon, 1999.

Rodak, Bernadette. *Diagnostic Hematology*. Philadelphia: W. B. Sanders, 1995

Senfelder,   Leopold.   "Andreas   Vesalius"   *The   Catholic   Encyclopedia*. http://www.newadvent.org/cathen/15378c.htm< (11 Dec 2000).

Stewart, W. F., R. B. Lipton, D. D. Celanto, and M. L. Reed. "Prevalence of Migraine Headache in the United States: Relation to Age, Income, Race, and Other Sociodemographic Factors." *Journal of the American Medical Association* 267 (1992), 64–69.

Stockwell, T. "Experimental Analogues of Loss of Control: A Review of Human Drinking Studies." *Self-control and the Addictive Behaviors*. Ed. Heather, N. Miller, W. R., and Greeley, J. Botany, Australia: Maxwell MacMillam, 1991.

The Tempest. The Pelican *Tempest*. Northrup Frye, ed. Penguin Books, Inc. Middlesex, England: Penguin, 1970.

Uthman, Ed. *Understanding Anemia*. Jackson: University Press of Mississippi, 1998.

Reading *Othello* Backwards

JAY L. HALIO

Did Shakespeare write *Othello* backwards? Did he start with act 3, scene 3, and after completing act 5, did he compose acts 1–2? According to Ned B. Allen, writing in the pages of *Shakespeare Survey* more than thirty years ago, that is just what he did. Comparing Shakespeare's play with its main source in Giraldi Cinthio's seventh novella in his *Hecatommithi*, third decade (Venice, 1566), Allen noticed that the action of *Othello* that is directly indebted to the source begins with 3.3. Cinthio's account of the fateful marriage of Othello and Desdemona does not include the episodes of acts 1 and 2, which are Shakespeare's invention (Allen, 13–29).

Allen was concerned to show how this evidence explains, if it does not justify, the double time scheme that has puzzled some commentators on *Othello*. His concern is not mine here, although his basic argument is useful in other ways, as I shall try to demonstrate. Briefly stated, if acts 1 and 2 were composed *after* acts 3–5, as Allen argues very persuasively, then they serve in some important respects as a commentary on the action that Shakespeare presents in acts 3–5. I believe not only that that is the case, but that it helps to heighten the tragedy and contribute to its power as part of Shakespeare's design.

In Cinthio's tale, Othello and Desdemona have been married for some time as the story opens. Here, in the translation by J. E. Taylor done in 1855, is the way the novella begins (no English translation was available to Shakespeare, who probably read Cinthio in the original Italian [Kernan, 171]):[1]

> There once lived in Venice a Moor, who was very valiant and of a handsome person; and having given proofs in war of great skill and prudence, he was highly esteemed by the Signoria of the Republic, who in rewarding deeds of valor advanced the interests of the state.
>
> It happened that a virtuous lady of marvelous beauty, named Disdemona, fell in love with the Moor, moved thereto by his valor; and he, vanquished by the beauty and the noble character of Disdemona, returned her love; and their

affection was so mutual that, although the parents of the lady strove all they could to induce her to take another husband, she consented to marry the Moor; and they lived in such harmony and peace in Venice that no word ever passed between them that was not affectionate and kind.

The story proceeds to the Moor's advancement as commander of the Venetian forces in Cyprus, a very high honor, clouded only by his reluctance to leave his beloved wife behind in Venice. But Disdemona, spirited lady that she is, puts his qualms to rest by saying that she will go with him, and together they set sail for the island.

That's all there is for Shakespeare's act 1. Cinthio then proceeds to describe the Moor's ensign and his wife, who also accompany the Moor to Cyprus, and in the paragraph after that, the Moor's "captain" (Othello's lieutenant, Cassio, in Shakespeare). The affection Disdemona shows the captain is directly related, as Cinthio describes it, to that of the Moor's for him, and her affection thus arouses no jealousy whatsoever in her husband. On the other hand, Cinthio describes the ensign as a man "of the most depraved nature in the world," but so adept at concealing his wickedness that no one suspects his true nature. Though married to a "young, and fair, and virtuous lady," he falls desperately in love with Disdemona, who spurns his overtures. The ensign suspects that Disdemona will have nothing to do with him because she really loves the captain; he contrives, therefore, a means to get him out of her sight. "The love which he had borne the lady now changed into the bitterest hate, and having failed in his purposes, he devoted all his thoughts to plot the death of the captain of the troop and to divert the affection of the Moor from Disdemona." The means he determines is to tell the Moor that Disdemona has been unfaithful and that the captain is her paramour.

From there the action of Shakespeare's acts 3–5 proceeds. Note that there is no mention of a confrontation between the Moor and Disdemona's parents, of a midnight meeting at the Duke's court, or even the threat of a Turkish invasion against Cyprus. No storm at sea separates the Moor and wife, and no joyous reunion follows, for they travel on the same ship together. The brawl that occurs in 2.3 does not appear in Cinthio's novella, but the captain is guilty of an indiscretion in drawing a sword upon a soldier of the guard and striking him, an act that causes him to lose favor with the Moor. Seeing the captain deprived of his rank because of this, Cinthio says, "Disdemona was deeply grieved, and endeavored again and again to reconcile her husband to the man." These events give the ensign, after he conceives his hatred of Disdemona, the opening he desires, and he proceeds to poison the Moor's mind against his wife. Cinthio's plot and Shakespeare's thereafter continue on parallel lines.

What functions, then, do the actions of acts 1 and 2, peculiar to Shakespeare's play, serve? Some very important ones, I believe. To understand them properly, we may start by looking at Othello's remarks as Iago begins to incite him against Desdemona. After Iago first suggests jealousy ("the green-eyed monster which doth mock / The meat it feeds on," 3.3.168–69), and cuckoldry, Othello responds:

> Why, why is this?
> Think'st thou I'd make a life of jealousy,
> To follow still the changes of the moon
> With fresh suspicions? *No, to be once in doubt*
> *Is once to be resolved.* Exchange me for a goat
> When I shall change the business of my soul
> To such exsufflicate and blown surmises
> Matching thy inference. 'Tis not to make me jealous
> To say my wife is fair, feeds well, loves company,
> Is free of speech, sings, plays, and dances well:
> Where virtue is, these are more virtuous.
> Nor from mine own weak merits will I draw
> The smallest fear or doubt of her revolt,
> For she had eyes and chose me. No, Iago,
> *I'll see before I doubt; when I doubt, prove,*
> *And on the proof, there is no more but this:*
> *Away at once with love or jealousy.* (3.3.178–94; emphasis added)[2]

This is a very rational statement, and the procedure Othello outlines to entertain and then resolve doubts is a very defensible one. Those who think of Othello as an "erring barbarian," afflicted with uncontrollable sexual jealousy that they attribute racially, overlook this speech and much else that precedes it. Othello is not easily aroused; Iago has to work hard to move him to suspect Desdemona and then condemn her. He does this by cleverly attacking the weakest element in Othello's character—his anxiety, his inability to hang loose amidst uncertainty (181–82). Iago must also make sure that Othello's procedure, as he outlines it to him (192–94), is not followed; or, if it is followed, it is followed in some distorted or perverted fashion that brings Othello to a false conclusion. This is precisely what Iago does, more successfully now than he had done in act 1, for example, when he first tried to confound Othello's modus operandi. In act 2, however, Iago's machinations succeed, not in disrupting Othello's procedure but in using it to serve his own ends.

I have elsewhere discussed the aspect of anxiety in *Othello* (Halio, 123–31), not only as it reveals itself in the principal character, but also as it does in others. Here I shall focus mainly on Othello's anxiety and its consequences. In act 1, Iago is utterly unable to move his general to any rash action, even as the anxiety-ridden Brabantio disturbs him on his wedding night at the Sagittary. Othello is completely in command of himself and of all the contending forces arrayed against each other. His famous line, "Keep up your bright swords, for the dew will rust them" (1.2.59), demonstrates in both its cool rhetoric and its effect his control of the situation. Earlier, when Iago tries to get him to withdraw before Brabantio arrives, he calmly replies: "Not I; I must be found. / My parts, my title, and my perfect soul / Shall manifest me rightly" (1.2.31–32). Othello knows what he knows; he has perfect confidence in himself and implicitly in Desdemona and what they have done by eloping. He therefore leads Brabantio to the Duke's palace to resolve his conflict and to allay the old man's misgivings concerning Othello's use of witchcraft and "spells and medicines bought of mountebanks" (1.3.61).

Events at the Duke's court after they arrive are both illuminating and highly instructive. Again, Othello remains calm and confident, Brabantio's accusations notwithstanding. He begins by admitting what he has done:

> Most potent, grave, and reverend signiors,
> My very noble and approved good masters,
> That I have tane away this old man's daughter,
> It is most true; true I have married her;
> The very head and front of my offending
> Hath this extent, no more. (1.3.76-81)

Claiming that he is no orator, "Rude am I in my speech," he nevertheless says he will "a round unvarnished tale deliver / Of my whole course of love" (90–91) to describe what drugs or other treacherous means he has used to win Desdemona. Of course, the tale he does deliver is anything but "rude" and "unvarnished," as the Duke recognizes ("I think this tale would win my daughter too," 170); but even before he embarks on it, Othello does something very significant: he asks the Duke to send for the lady and let her testify before her father (114–20). When she arrives and speaks for herself, she confirms everything Othello has said in her absence. Consequently, Brabantio withdraws his charges and, however unhappily, gives his daughter to the Moor (187–96).

These events in act 1 establish from the outset a standard of behavior and judgment for a satisfactory and just resolution of conflict. If the action of 1.3 is in some sense a trial, its conduct is both fair and correct, one that has serious implications for what happens later on in the play. Why else did Shakespeare include it? That these procedures are not followed at the most crucial moments is what precipitates the tragedy. The question then becomes, why does Othello fail to act later according to those procedures he had followed earlier and in fact himself helped to establish?

Allow me to defer for awhile trying to answer that question and move instead to several incidents in 2.1 and 3, which also bear on subsequent events. After the storm has destroyed the Turkish fleet and Othello is once more reunited with his Desdemona, he says,

> O my soul's joy,
> If after every tempest come such calms,
> May the winds blow till they have wakened death,
> And let the labouring bark climb hills of seas,
> Olympus-high, and duck again as low
> As hell's from heaven. If it were now to die,
> 'Twere now to die most happy; for I fear
> My soul hath her content so absolute
> That not another comfort like to this
> Succeeds in unknown fate. (2.1.176–85)

Desdemona immediately corrects her husband, claiming that their "loves and comforts should increase, / Even as our days do grow," a point very well taken, as Othello quickly recognizes. But Othello's previous speech, like others in the play, indicates how "absolute" indeed his feelings are for Desdemona. Compare, for example, what he later says about her: "Excellent wretch! Perdition catch my soul / But I do love thee; and when I love thee not, / Chaos is come again" (3.3.90–92). It seems that at the end when he laments that he loved "not wisely but too well" (5.2.340), Othello knew what he was saying. He is an absolutist,[3] and that is what feeds the anxiety that ultimately undoes him.

But to return to the action of act 2. In scene 3, Iago succeeds in his plan through Roderigo (who has no counterpart in Cinthio's tale) to get Cassio drunk and foment a quarrel between him and others that results in a brawl breaking out in the town. As the alarm bell hideously sounds, Othello is once more roused from his nuptial bed and comes down to find out what has happened. Again, between Cassio's trial in this scene and Othello's in act 1, several differences emerge that have considerable significance (Halio, 127). For one thing, a key witness is absent and never sent for. For another, although again Othello shows his mastery of an emotionally fraught situation that threatens to break out into more violence (2.3.146, 150–55), he is now handicapped by what he does *not* know. He therefore must depend on others to tell him what he needs to know so that he may act appropriately. Unlike the situation in 1.3, however, none of the principals is willing to speak up and respond to questions put to them directly. Only when Othello warns that his "blood," (i.e., passion) is beginning to overtake his "safer guides" (i.e,. reason) does he finally get anyone to speak up, and that person is Iago.

Before all the witnesses present, Iago tells the truth. The theater audience is aware that it is only part of the truth, but none of those on stage knows the whole truth; hence, they are in no position to contradict what Iago says. Note also how insistent from the start Othello is to get to the bottom of things as quickly as possible ("once to be in doubt / Is once to be resolved"). It takes more than fifty lines of dialogue, however, before he gets any clear information, and then he gets it only because his anxiety to know what has happened becomes almost insupportable, causing him to demand the information in no uncertain terms:

> Give me to know
> How this foul rout began, who set it on,
> And he that is approved in this offence,
> Though he had twinned with me, both at a birth,
> Shall lose me. (2.3.190-194)

"Give me to know." Othello cannot stand uncertainty; he cannot bear to let things remain vague and undetermined. He must *know*. This is his anxiety.[4] It is the same anxiety that Iago seizes upon in the next act and plays upon for all it is worth.

Othello is not the only character plagued by anxiety, as Iago realizes. He exploits Cassio's also, so that the cashiered lieutenant brooks no delay in seeking a conference with Desdemona to obtain her help in restoring him to Othello's good graces. This gives Iago the opportunity to question his motives aloud when he sees Cassio "steal away so guilty-like" from Desdemona as Othello approaches (3.3.39). What follows is a virtuoso performance by Iago, arousing Othello's suspicions gradually but steadily in the ensuing dialogue. He is unwittingly abetted by Desdemona, who intercedes on behalf of Cassio and badgers her husband to set a day and time for their meeting, refusing to be put off until Othello agrees to let Cassio come whenever he chooses (3.3.41–89). Iago then picks up where he left off, inquiring if Cassio knew of Othello's love for Desdemona before they got married (3.3.93–94). From there on, using hints and insinuations, he throws Othello eventually into doubt about his wife's fidelity.

It is a doubt that Othello cannot abide, as Iago well knows. He says as much when he sees Othello reenter at 3.3.330:

> Look where he comes! Not poppy nor mandragora,
> Nor all the drowsy syrups in the world,
> Shall ever medicine thee to that sweet sleep
> Which thou owed'st yesterday. (3.3.331–34)

Othello thereupon professes the anguish that his uncertainty, his doubt, is causing him:

> Thou hast set me on the rack.
> I swear 'tis better to be much abused
> Than but to know't a little. (3.3.336–38)

He wishes he knew nothing at all than to know only a little, not enough to be certain one way or the other: "He that is robbed," he says, "not wanting what is stolen, / Let him not know't, and he's not robbed at all" (343–34), a false logic, however psychologically correct. He soon afterwards demands that Iago make certain that what he has suggested is in fact true:

> Villain, be sure thou prove my love a whore;
> *Be sure of it.* Give me the ocular proof,
> Or by the worth of mine eternal soul,
> Thou hadst been better have been born a dog,
> Than answer my waked wrath! (3.3.360–64; emphasis added)

He continues:

> Make me to see't; or, at the least, so prove it
> That the probation bear no hinge nor loop
> To hang a doubt onCor woe upon thy life! (3.3.365–67)

His uncertainty torments him:

> By the world,
> I think my wife be honest, and think she is not;
> I think that thou art just, and think thou art not.
> I'll have some proof. . . .
> Would I were satisfied! (3.3.384–91)

Iago then proposes the only kind of proof that could give Othello satisfaction: "Would you, the supervisor, grossly gape on? / Behold her topped?" (396–97). But this is more than Othello, the sensitive absolutist, can bear; hence, Iago alters his tactic and proposes "imputation and strong circumstances / Which lead directly to the door of truth" (407–408). These, he claims, will provide the "satisfaction" Othello demands, for he already has Desdemona's handkerchief and knows how to use it to this effect.

Proving by "imputation and strong circumstances," arriving at the door of truth, is not, however, the procedure Othello had indicated earlier he would follow when he said, "I'll see before I doubt; when I doubt, prove" (3.3.191.192). In the event, he *sees* nothing definitive. Cassio's "dream" of Desdemona, which Iago relates (3.3.414–27), is merely part of the "imputation" or "strong circumstance" he adduces, falsely, to convince Othello of his wife's infidelity. By this time, of course, Othello's anxiety is so acute that although Iago says it was only a dream, Othello accepts it as denoting "a foregone conclusion" (429), and he is ready to tear Desdemona "all to pieces" (432). Nevertheless, Iago here decides to make certain that Othello will act as he says, and so he tells him about the handkerchief. This, and the eavesdropping scene in 4.1, seals Desdemona's fate—and Othello's. "Now do I see 'tis true," Othello says, though in fact he has *seen* nothing yet:

> Look here, Iago,
> All my fond love thus do I blow to heaven;
> 'Tis gone.
> Arise, black vengeance, from thy hollow cell!
> Yield up, O love, thy crown and hearted throne
> To tyrannous hate! Swell, bosom, with thy fraught,
> For 'tis of aspics' tongues. (3.3.444–51)

Where in all this is the procedure that Othello followed in acts 1 and 2? Where is the testimony of either one of the principals in the alleged adultery? Where is the certain knowledge or the confidence that Othello had shown in act 1, or the trial that both acts 1 and 2 had dramatized? Nowhere; gone with Othello's occupation (3.3.358), one might say: self-assurance once gone, loss of self-control inevitably follows. In direct contrast to his prior behavior, Othello now acts on "imputation and strong circumstances," not direct testimony or "the ocular proof" he had earlier demanded. It is a travesty of justice he follows, punctuated by expediencies made all the more insistent by his anxiety, which permits him no respite. His "safer guides" are overthrown to the extent that at one point he falls into an epileptic fit occasioned by excessive emotion (4.1.35–41). In this unstable condition, now thoroughly under Iago's influence, he overhears Cassio and Iago talk about what he takes to be Cassio's love for Desdemona, although in reality it is Bianca who is the subject of their discussion. When she enters bearing Desdemona's handkerchief, which Cassio had given her to take out the work, Othello is more than ever convinced of his wife's betrayal. This is a travesty of the "ocular proof" he had demanded which Iago knows very well how to manipulate.

The murder plot is then set afoot. When Othello enters Desdemona's chamber, he has one more chance to relent, or rather, to change his present course of action and revert to the more sensible one he followed in acts 1 and 2. He is a reluctant murderer; for, Iago absent and Desdemona lying peacefully asleep, he once again feels the onrush of his love. But it is not enough to erase his erroneous sense of justice. He enters reminding himself that "It is the cause, it is the cause, my soul" (5.2.1); her adultery is what makes him act the way he must. When she is awakened by his kisses and discovers what Othello is about to do and why, she tries to assert her innocence. Told that she has given the handkerchief that he "so loved and gave thee" to Cassio, she cries out, tellingly, "No, by my life and soul! / Send for him and ask him" (5.2.49–50). "Send for him" echoes Othello's own words in act 1, "Send for the lady" (1.3.115), when he stands before Brabantio to answer his charges before the Duke and his court. On that occasion, his procedure proved sound and just, as it might have done here, had Othello allowed it the opportunity. Still protesting her innocence, Desdemona again begs Othello to send for Cassio and get his testimony (58–69); but Othello believes he already has

Cassio's confession (in the eavesdropping scene, 4.1.101–160), and in any case, the man is dead: "his mouth is stopped: / Honest Iago hath ta'en order for it" (5.2.72–73), he tells Desdemona. Only later, after he has killed Desdemona and Emilia reveals the truth about the handkerchief does Othello realize how Iago has duped him. He demands to know why Iago "hath thus ensnared my soul and body" (5.2.299), but Iago answers, "Demand me nothing; what you know, you know. / From this time forth I never will speak word" (300–301). Othello thus never learns what has motivated "honest" Iago to act as he has done. And despite all of Iago's rationalizations, for example, that he has been passed over for promotion, neither do we.[5]

Reading *Othello* backwards provides a means to see how tragedy might have been averted, had Othello observed the just and rational procedures he followed in acts 1 and 2. Evidently, Shakespeare invented those scenes to include a standard of behavior and justice against which the action of acts 3 through 5, the events in Cinthio's novella, might be judged. For tragedy, in my view, often includes an alternative to disaster, one that we are invited to recognize; or, as Abba Eban once said in a quite different context, "Tragedy is not what men suffer, but what they miss." The protagonist, as in *Julius Caesar*, may not glimpse his alternative action or, as in *Hamlet*, he may partly and then only obliquely see it. Othello does not see, until it is too late, if he sees it all, how he should have behaved. That is part of his tragedy; indeed, it enhances our tragic sense of events to know what acts 1 and 2 quite clearly point out for us, the audience, to see and understand, and what Othello misses.

NOTES

1. Compare Sanders 3, who claims that it is not easy to determine on the available evidence whether Shakespeare read Cinthio in the original Italian or in the French translation by Gabriel Chappus in *Premier Volume des Cents Excellentes Nouvelles* (1584).
2. Quotations are from the New Cambridge Shakespeare, ed. Norman Sanders.
3. This is how a former colleague, T. A. Hanzo, once accurately described him to me.
4. Othello's anxiety here anticipates Gloucester's in *King Lear*, once Edmond suggests Edgar's treachery. See *King Lear*, ed. Jay L. Halio, New Cambridge Shakespeare (1992), 1.2.30–90, especially 87–88.
5. Heilman (1956) perceptively comments that only in 1.1 and only to Roderigo does Iago speak of being passed over for promotion. No one else ever mentions it. Heilman argues that this may be simply an excuse he uses to help gull Roderigo.

WORKS CITED

Allen, Ned. B. The "Two Parts of 'Othello.'" *Shakespeare Survey* 21 (1968): 13–29.

Halio, Jay L. "Anxiety in Othello." *Costerus* 1 (1972): 123–31.

Heilman, Robert H. *Magic in the Web: Action and Language in* Othello. 1956; rpt. Westport, CT: Greenwood Press, 1977.

Kernan, Alvin, ed. *Othello*, The Signet Shakespeare. New York: New American Library, 1986.

Sanders, Norman, ed. *Othello*. New Cambridge Shakespeare. Cambridge: Cambridge University Press, 1984.

The Mystery of the
Early *Othello* Texts

SCOTT MCMILLIN

TEXTUAL DIFFERENCES: THE QUARTO (1622) AND THE FOLIO (1623)

No one could buy *Othello* and read it during Shakespeare's lifetime. It was not printed until 1622, six years after the author's death, and this version (called a "quarto" because its paper had been folded in four to make the pages) was the first Shakespeare play to be newly published in over a decade, since the quarto of *Troilus and Cressida* in 1609. Theatregoers interested in *Othello* had to see the play in performance before 1622, and this was true of about half of Shakespeare's plays—at least eighteen had not been published by then.

So the *Othello* quarto of 1622 was something of a surprise, the first Shakespeare play newly published in years. Then came a bigger surprise. In 1623, just a year later, virtually *all* of Shakespeare's plays were published in the collected edition that has come to be known as the First Folio (the paper was folded in two). Suddenly thirty-six Shakespeare plays were in print—eighteen of them having never been published before, seventeen having first been published before 1610, and one—*Othello*—having first been published just a year earlier.

The mystery is why the two *Othellos*, published within a year of each other, should differ on thousands of points and readings, some large, some small. The 1622 quarto (hereafter Q1) is missing about 160 lines which the Folio (hereafter F) includes. Where F has Othello say his bloody thoughts are:

> Like to the Pontic Sea,
> Whose icy current and compulsive course
> Ne'er feels retiring ebb but keeps due on
> To the Propontic and the Hellespont, (modernized, 3. 3. 454–57)[1]

Q1 lets him say nothing of the sort—the lines are not there. Hundreds of individual words are different. After the catastrophe, when both Desdemona and Othello

401

lie dead, Lodovico talks of the "tragic *loading* of their bed" in F. In Q1 he calls it the "tragic lodging of their bed." Lodging? Well, the word had an Elizabethan meaning we have lost: the remains left by a devastating storm. So Lodovico could have said "loading" or "lodging" meaningfully, but which *did* he say?

In F, as Othello approaches the sleeping Desdemona, intending to kill her, he makes up a new word for what happens when a snuffed-out candle is lit again: "relume." Actually he says of Desdemona nothing can "relume" thy light after I snuff *you* out, but he is thinking of how easy it is to light a candle, and his crazed imagination comes up with a word no one had ever heard before: "relume." Q1 gives him a banal word instead: "return." Nothing can make your light "return." No one can think Q1 has the stronger word in this case. But every now and then Q1 gives the sharper reading. In act three of F, Iago asks Othello, did Cassio know your wife in the days when he wooed her? This makes no sense—of course Cassio knew her if he was wooing her. But he didn't woo her, did he? Othello was wooing her. Q1 clears this up: did Cassio know your wife when *you* were wooing her, Othello. The question not only makes sense, it promises trouble by hinting at an early relationship between Cassio and Desdemona, exactly what Iago wants to suggest.

When Desdemona is summoned before the Venetian Senate to account for the status of her marriage, Q1 lets her sound sexy when she says that her heart's subdued "even to the utmost pleasure of my Lord." F tames this to "even to the very quality of my Lord" (1. 3. 247). F also removes over fifty examples of swearing, making the military men on duty in Cyprus sound now and then like schoolboys at a tea dance. So while F usually has the preferable text when the words differ, Q1 sometimes has a rough urgency which comes across well in the theatre.

But Q1 is disconcerting in two other ways: its punctuation seems haphazard and it frequently mislines the blank verse. Elizabethan punctuation was by no means standardized, but Q1 *Othello* seems strangely pointed nevertheless. It glides along on commas for one sentence after another, as though the period did not exist, but it also slots the odd period into the middle of a sentence. Here is an example of the comma-glide (in the original spelling and punctuation):

> Iago is most honest,
> Michael good night, to morrow with your earliest,
> Let me haue speech with you, come my deare loue,
> The purchase made, the fruits are to ensue,
> The profits yet to come twixt me and you,
> Good night. (2. 3. 7–12)

F, by contrast, uses periods and a colon to mark internal pauses:

> Iago, is most honest:
> *Michael*, goodnight. To morrow with your earliest,

> Let me haue speech with you. Come my deere Loue,
> The purchase made, the fruites are to ensue,
> That profit's yet to come 'tweene me, and you.
> Goodnight.

This is an extreme case, for Q1 does call upon the semicolon for internal pauses fairly often, but it seems determined to save the period for the end of the speech instead of the end of the sentence. Then, just when one is sure that is the system, a mistaken period pops into the middle of a sentence, as in this speech of Iago's:

> We cannot be all masters, nor all masters
> Cannot be truely followed, you shall marke.
> Many a dutious and knee-crooking knaue,
> That doting on his owne obsequious bondage, . . .

where the sentence should flow through to the direct object: you shall mark many a dutious and knee-crooking knave, . . .

As for lineation, Q1 sometimes marches to its own beat, and the beat is not pentameter. Here is the Q1 version when Desdemona tries to find excuses for her husband's mistreatment of her:

> Mens natures wrangle with inferior things,
> Tho great ones are the object,
> Tis euen so: for let our finger ake,
> And it endues our other heathfull members,
> Euen to that sence of paine; nay, we must thinke,
> Men are not gods,
> Nor of them looke for such obseruances
> As fits the Bridall: beshrew me much *Emillia*,
> I was (vnhandsome, warrior as I am)
> Arraigning his vnkindenesse with my soule;
> But now I finde, I had subbornd the witnesse,
> And hee's indited falsly. (3. 4. 138ff.)

It almost seems that the speech is trying to draw to a close several times on the short lines, then finds itself carrying on. That is exactly what is happening, I believe, but we will come to that in due course.

"GOOD" AND "BAD" QUARTOS

These differences between Q1 and F are a mystery to Shakespeareans today, and we are hard pressed to solve it. The Elizabethan playgoers who purchased *Othello* in 1622 probably never noticed that there was a puzzle when the Folio came out in 1623. Their *Othello* delivered a great play and they read it—for a fraction of the price (the Folio cost about fifteen to eighteen shillings, the Quarto six to eight pence.) They even saved some time by avoiding those 160 lines. Life is short. And it is an astonishing play in either version.

No one paid much attention to the differences between the texts for the better part of a century, when Shakespeare was gaining a reputation, especially in England, of having been an English genius. At that point, the Folio was thought to be superior to all of the quartos, for it had been assembled by two of Shakespeare's fellow actors, John Heminges and Henry Condell, who in their address to the reader implied that they had access to the "original" versions and made a disparaging remark about the earlier printed versions, calling at least some of them "stolen and surreptitious." Over the next 200 years, as Shakespeare's reputation as a genius spread to Germany and America, textual study intensified, and the mystery of why there were so many differences of so many kinds was recognized, but it produced fewer answers than questions. Then, early in the twentieth century, the revolution that now passes under the name of the "New Bibliography" occurred when the quartos were theoretically divided into two kinds, the "bad" quartos, cobbled together from the memories of actors or from the scribblings of play-pirates (these were said to be what Heminges and Condell meant by "stolen and surreptitious") and the "good" quartos, supplied by Shakespeare and the acting company and printed from manuscripts which could be imagined as having an ultimate source in the author's own papers.[2]

Q1 *Othello* has always held a special position in regard to this distinction. It gives a much fuller text than the "bad" quartos, yet it contains some inconsistencies in stage directions and speech prefixes, it is missing those 160 lines, it has some interpolations apparently originating with the actors, and its punctuation and verse-lineation seem hit-or-miss affairs. So it is not exactly "good" either. It is "in-between," a place textual theories have trouble reaching.

PLAYHOUSE "CONTAMINATION"

Let us glance at some of the "bad" quartos, to put Q1 *Othello* into perspective. *Henry V* has a quarto only about half as long as the Folio, and some of its speeches are botched. Important elements are missing entirely—the role of the Chorus for example—yet the play can be intelligibly performed. *Hamlet* exists in both a "bad" and a "good" quarto. The 1603 quarto is much shorter than the "good" text published a year later, and it has some startlingly garbled passages, such as a famous soliloquy which begins: "To be, or not to be, aye there's the point." Prior to the New Bibliography, the short garbled quartos were thought to be source plays by other writers which Shakespeare rewrote, or even first drafts by Shakespeare himself. Now the revolution reversed that idea. The short quartos did not precede the longer texts as first drafts or source plays; they followed *after* the longer texts, as what the actors or the play-pirates could remember of the performed play. They were "bad" because they had been performed and reconstructed from memory. The "good" texts came before performance and memory. They came from the author, more or less. A "fairly good" text, like the Folio *Hamlet*, came from the "prompt book" used to regulate performances in the theatre. An entirely "good" text, like the longer *Hamlet* of 1604, came from the author's manuscript without much adaptation for the playhouse. Playhouse alterations were sometimes called "contamination." Quartos were "good" to the extent they were not contaminated by the theatre, which is approximately the extent to which they could be imagined as coming from the author's manuscript.

Othello presented a special problem because Q1 could not be called "bad," yet both Q1 and F showed influences from the playhouse. It was difficult to say which more closely reflected the author's manuscript. The solution to the problem may lie before us on that very difficulty—in that neither reflects the author's manuscript, and both are playhouse scripts from different productions—but the New Bibliography was fixed on the issue of the author's "foul papers," as the manuscript was often known, and the most influential opinion on *Othello* took shape around the writings of W. W. Greg, who held that foul papers, or a scribal copy of them, lay behind Q1. The key evidence for Greg and the editorial tradition that followed after him consisted of several vague or erroneous stage directions in Q1, the theory being that only an author writing a draft would allow such imperfections to stand in a manuscript. They certainly would not be allowed to stand in a "prompt book." The "prompt book" would have had its loose ends tied up, its stage directions and speech prefixes perfected, its dialogue made accurate according to the version the actors were staging. Thus when Q1 *Othello* reveals a vague "two or three" in an exit direction at 1. 3. 121, another vague "and the rest" in an entrance direction at line 169 in the same scene, and an erroneous entrance for Desdemona early in this scene, at line 46, Greg was sure these "can only be his"—the author's—in his foul papers (360). Moreover, the "Messenger" designated in a stage direction at the beginning of this scene seemed to be inconsistent with the "Sailor" designation for the same character in two speech prefixes; and another "Messenger" in a stage direction at 2. 1. 51 seemed to be "an imaginary character." Prompt copy for Greg did not tolerate such imperfections, which were signs of the false starts and early guesswork characteristic of authorial foul papers.

F is a more secure text, relatively free from vagueness and inaccuracy in its directions. It raises fewer perplexities in its readings than does Q1. It lacks oaths and swearing, which were banned from the theatres in 1606. Why it has no calls for sound effects is a puzzle, but Greg took F's orderliness and accuracy as signs of prompt copy, and subsequent editors have usually accepted his view: Q1 was printed from foul papers, F reflects the influence of the prompt book.[3] This has been the standard view for the better part of a century, and it is probably wrong.

AUTHORIAL REVISION?

The 160 lines unique to F pose a special problem to the standard view, for they have the verbal richness of Shakespearean writing and yet they do not appear in the text which is supposed to reflect the author's manuscript. How did the 160 lines make their way into prompt copy if they did not appear on the foul papers? The simple explanation is that Shakespeare himself enlarged the Q1 version into the F version, adding the 160 lines as he revised, and making many of the smaller changes, too. This was not Greg's position. Greg thought the 160 lines were theatrical cuts, not author's revisions, and he was left with the question of why the cuts appear to have been already made on the author-ial papers behind Q1 and not on the prompt-script behind F. We will return to this question later, but the revision theory has proved to have staying power and we should attend to it.

The revision theory was influentially set forth by Nevill Coghill, a man of the theatre himself, who felt that no one in his right mind would have cut such good passages as the "Pontic sea" speech once they were written. Such speeches must have been added in revision, and Shakespeare must have been the revisor; for the revisions are brilliant, Coghill said. Look at the kneeling scenes. F adds different occasions in which either Othello or Desdemona kneels before Iago, in a superb example of visual repetition. Many of the F-only lines build up the role of Emilia, adding some humanizing touches to the "grossness of attitude" with which she was endowed in the Q1 version (Coghill, 190). The Willow Song was added not only to give Desdemona an opportunity for a moment of pathos, but also to let Emilia busy herself over her mistress during the song, fixing her hair, being tender, "endearing" herself to the audience. Thus the longer passages unique to F and many of the smaller details show a genius at work, revising his own play. (Perhaps the critic per-forming the analysis should be seen as the source of the genius being set forth, but that is not Coghill's claim.)

E. A. J. Honigmann picked up Coghill's argument and carried it to fresh lengths ("Shakespeare's Revised Plays"). A theme of sexuality runs through the F-only passages, Honigmann discovered. Shakespeare revised in order to intensify his concern with normal and abnormal sexuality. A more recent study (Jones) has found concerns of a different kind and some further strokes of genius. With the addition of a single word in F, Shakespeare "renders Othello's nature in a single impressionistic slash" (Jones, 246). The word is "portance." Othello is recalling the exotic tales he used to tell in Desdemona's hearing, which in its first draft Q1 version has an ordinary phrase, "with it all my travel's history." In revising, Shakespeare hits upon the great word and writes: "portance in my traveller's history" (1. 3. 138). The "Pontic sea" speech is added because Shakespeare sees a parallel with another line he is adding to the F version: where Desdemona begs "But half an hour, but while I say one prayer" in Q1 (5. 2. 83), Shakespeare inserts an interruption from Othello— "Being done, there is no pause"—doubling up on the "no pause" theme, which is the burden of the Pontic sea speech too. In both cases Othello is attributing his willfulness to an external momentum (240). The revising Shakespeare found new ways to express what Jones regards as "the weirdness of normal psychology, Othello's."

Thus by one revision theory or another Emilia's grossness was humanized, Othello's weird but normal psychology was increased, and Shakespeare's interest in normal and abnormal sexuality was intensified. Any or all of these effects resulted from deliberations as Shakespeare revised the Q1 version into the F version—so the revision theory maintains.

THEATRICAL CUTS

Yet a further observation can be made about the 160 F-only lines, and this rather tells against the revision theory. Most of the F lines in question fall in Acts 4 and 5, an odd place for a writer to have been lengthening a play that already ran over 3,000 lines, and more than half the 160 lines are assigned in F to two characters, Desdemona and Emilia, both played by boy actors. Possibly Shakespeare thought that the audience would be keen for more dialogue at the end of a long play, and that the boy actors would provide the necessary energy with one braiding the other's hair while the other sang a mournful song about lost love, but I doubt it. Someone in Shakespeare's company less given to the word-by-word worship of genius than we are could very well have decided that the later scenes had to be shorter.[4] At least he was careful not to cut anything that advances the plot. Desdemona's Willow Song does not advance the plot, nor does Emilia's discourse on married men, nor does Othello's big speech about the Pontic Sea. If someone had gone through the last half of the play looking for lines that could be eliminated without affecting the narrative, he would have come up with something like the passages missing from the last half of Q1. The 160 lines were probably cut from the end of a long play, with the boys being given less to do, and some of Othello's intricate passages being removed. Greg's view seems right on this point: the 160 lines are cuts, not additions.[5]

Still before us is the dilemma Greg faced. How did cuts make their way into foul papers? Perhaps someone marked these passage for *intended* cuts on the foul papers. The intentions were observed in the transmission of text to the printers, but were overlooked in the transmission to theatrical prompt copy. Perhaps Shakespeare tinkered with his foul papers in various other ways, with some of the tinkering eventually appearing in Q1, and some of it eventually passing through into the prompt book and hence into F. I am now blending Greg's theory into the nuances supplied by some of his followers, for the standard position raises many questions to which nuance is the only response.

But the "cuts" problem disappears if one gives up the notions that foul papers lie behind Q1. The foul-paper theory faces the undeniable problem that no Shakespeare manuscripts, foul or fair, are in existence today.[6] Perhaps the foul papers were not saved any longer than such things normally are. What if Q1 proceeds from theatrical copy too, a script for a production in which cuts were made, while the production reflected in F was not cut, or at least was not cut in the same way? Greg and his followers held to their belief that the touches of vagueness and inconsistency in Q1 resulted from first-draft tentativeness on the part of the author, one side of a dichotomy, the other side being that "prompt books" were marked by tidiness and completeness. But recent examinations of actual scripts from the Elizabethan playhouses show that bookkeepers (as the so-called "prompter" was known) sometimes allowed vague entrance directions to stand and could tolerate other inconsistencies too—they were not such tidy chaps after all. The bits of muddle that occur in the *Othello* Q1 stage directions could have been left in a backstage script, and are not a distinctive sign of foul papers. Our view of the bookkeeper's function has been cast in a new light by the discovery at the reconstruction of the Globe in London that prompting forgetful actors is virtually impossible in the configuration of the Elizabethan stage. He was not a "prompter" in the nineteenth-century line-by-line sense. The backstage figure was the "bookkeeper," the copy of the play he used was "book" of the play, and it contained some mistakes.[7]

In the case of *Othello*, a bookkeeper might very well have allowed a vague direction like "exit two or three" to stand, because he had no control over the actors' exits in the first place. Entrances were a livelier concern of his (actors can be cued to be ready for entrances, but they must get themselves to the exits), but the bookkeeper's script was probably not the primary text for regulating entrances: an outline of entrances, called the "plot," seems to have been posted backstage for this purpose. The error of including Desdemona in the entrance at 1. 3. 46 could have been tolerated in the playhouse script, that is, simply because another document contained the useful list of entrances. There are spots of confusion in Q1, but these do not in themselves point to foul paper origin. Even the "messenger" reports in 1. 3 and 2.1, though they seem untidy to readers of the trim arrangements at these points in F, can be played as written without difficulty and could have come from a bookkeeper's script.

The best procedure is to face up to the facts: (1) that Shakespeare's foul papers have disappeared and we have no first-hand evidence of what they looked like, and (2) that playhouse scripts contained the kinds of imperfections which the New Bibliography took as signs of foul papers. There is no way to think about the dichotomy between foul papers and prompt copy, because there are no Shakespearean foul papers and there never were any prompt copies, not in the modern sense of a word-perfect text. What can we think about instead?

THEATRE SCRIPTS

More than one *Othello* script would have been made during the two decades that elapsed between Shakespeare's composition of the play and the printed versions of 1622 and 1623. *Othello* was a popular play. It was revived several times and it was performed in various playhouses before various audiences—at the Globe, at the Blackfriars, at court on at least two occasions, at Oxford, just to name the recorded performances (most performances were not recorded). The acting company underwent changes of personnel during the two decades before the play was published. If a new boy actor for Desdemona were not as strong as the original had been, his role might have been abridged, and if his singing were weak, the Willow Song might have been cut. If the original Othello was gone, some of the more intricate passages might have been omitted from the new actor's part. (In fact, the original Othello, Richard Burbage, died three years before the Quarto of 1622.) Because new actors were taking on the roles, or because the playing conditions at the indoor Blackfriars Theatre were different from those at the outdoor Globe, or because acting in the short winter afternoons at the Globe was different from acting there in the summer, or because taking the play on tour may have required cuts, *Othello* would have been revised. Actors' parts would have been needed for each revival of the play. They would have reflected the cuts and adjustments of the revival, as would the backstage scripts or "books" that may also have been made for the revivals. Shakespeare retired to Stratford sometime around 1611 or 1612, about a decade before *Othello* was published. He died in 1616. Fresh scripts could well have been generated after the author's departure. We may desire to have printed texts which record Shakespeare's missing manuscripts, but history may give us something else—one or two printed *Othello*s representing playhouse scripts not necessarily made with Shakespeare's knowledge and cooperation.

That is what we should think about. Various sorts of script were generated during the two decades of *Othello*'s career before publication. Of those sorts, which would the acting company have preserved? And which would have been sent to the publishers?

The most important script from the company's perspective would have been the licensed copy, which was normally prepared for a new play close to the time of the first performances, and was sent to the Master of the Revels for official review and a signature of approval. A licensed script of *Othello* must have existed for the original performances, in about 1603 or 1604, and it would have been the copy worth preserving over the years. It would not have been sent to the printing houses—that is a virtual certainty. The printers marked up their copies for their own purposes, which had nothing to do with the purposes of the playhouse, and those copies were probably of no value to anyone after the printing was done. As a starting point for further thinking, we can assume that only a disposable script would have passed from the acting company to the printing house.

What sorts of script would have seemed disposable to the company? If the author's foul papers had been kept, they may have seemed disposable once the licensed copy was in hand. But why would foul papers have been kept? Theatre companies did not share the interest of modern Shakespeareans in foul papers. By the time the play was ready for staging, the foul papers would have so obviously taken on the characteristic we are looking for, "disposable," that they could well have been placed in the trash. Two decades after *Othello* was first staged, it is unlikely that the foul papers were in existence.

Yet the two actors who helped compile the First Folio, Heminges and Condell, claimed knowledge of Shakespeare's manuscripts as late as 1623. So fluent was the author in setting forth his thoughts, said Heminges and Condell, that his papers had scarcely a blot on them. Some degree of hyperbole surely resides in this comment. Scholars who think some Shakespearean manuscripts were available for the Folio solidly disbelieve the statement that the papers were unblotted (for instance, G. Blakemore Evans in Riverside, 28). Nevertheless, Heminges and Condell implied that some Shakespearean manuscripts lay behind the Folio, and if these were relatively unblotted, and thus not foul papers, they may have been the author's own copywork of his earlier drafts. The company hired scribes for doing the copywork, but that does not rule out the possibility that Shakespeare made some copies himself, and that Heminges and Condell were telling something like the truth. Let the possibility linger that some relatively unblotted Shakespearean fair copies may have been in the company's possession by the time of the 1623 Folio. It is a nice possibility, and it really does not matter very much.

TWO SCENARIOS

We are facing the likelihood that multiple *Othello* scripts were made for revivals of the play before Q1 and F were printed in 1622 and 1623. Here are two scenarios for explaining the printed texts, both independent of the possibility that Shakespeare may have copied his own play before he retired. Both also take into account the fact of playhouse procedures most often ignored by textual scholarship, that actors memorized their roles from "parts" that were copied onto individual strips of paper which took the form of "rolls." (The words "roll" and "role" are related, and the fact is that one learned one's role from a roll which contained one's own lines and a few cue words from the preceding speech in each case.) In addition to a backstage script of the overall play, in other words, each revival would also have made use of a set of individual parts either saved from previous performances or freshly copied for the new version.

Scenario 1: If the actors' parts from an earlier performance have been retained by the company, and if a current revival of the play now entails revisions, the revisions can made on the parts. The actors then memorize from the revised parts, and when the play is ready, a backstage script is copied from the best available source, the actors' memories. That is, the actors dictate the revised and memorized version of the play they are about to perform, with a scribe or scribes writing a rough but serviceable backstage script from the dictation. The resulting backstage script becomes disposable once the revival ends. It is a good candidate for being sold to the publishers.

There is evidence that plays were sometimes dictated. The dramatist Thomas Heywood, who did not appreciate the degree of error thereby introduced, said in a preface to the 1608 edition of his *Rape of Lucrece* that some of his plays were "copied only by the ear" and thus came into the printers' hands.[8] But did the companies retain the actors' rolls? Only one clear example of an actor's part from the commercial theatre (of many thousands that must have been prepared) has come down to us. They are about as hard to come by as the Shakespearean foul papers. Yet there was a reason to save the actors' parts, and this cannot readily be said of the foul papers. Popular plays (like *Othello*) were bound to be revived, and saving the actors' parts would have been an obvious economical move.

Scenario 2: The revisions and adjustments required for a revival of *Othello* are made on a *copy* of the licensed script, to prevent the licensed script from being marked up. This copy will be the backstage script, and it will eventually be just as disposable as the script in Scenario 1, but first the actors' parts are copied from it. The difference from Scenario 1 is that this time the backstage script precedes the memorization of the parts; in Scenario 1, the backstage script proceeds from the memorization of the parts, and that can make all the difference. Both scenarios result in disposable scripts which the company could turn into small bits of cash by selling them to the printing industry.

Variations on these scenarios must have occurred from time to time. At times the actors had scripts made for private patrons, for example, and either Scenario could be adjusted to fit that situation. The Scenarios are intended not as statements of fact, but as outlines of possibilities. Backstage scripts were needed for revivals, and if the licensed copy was not used for this purpose, the new script would either be copied from the memories of actors (Scenario 1), or would be copied from the licensed script to be the source for the actors' parts (Scenario 2), or would emerge from some combination of these possibilities. Even for the original performances of a new play, our Scenarios could have come into play. If a new play was being rehearsed while the Master of the Revels was still reviewing the script for licensing, a temporary backstage script may have been dictated from the actors' memories. This would be a combination of Scenarios 1 and 2—Scenario 2 turning into Scenario 1 because officialdom was not keeping to the schedule of a busy repertory company. This must have happened at times, even frequently, in the Elizabethan theatre, where the acting companies were introducing new plays every two or three weeks. (Most textual studies assume that rehearsals would not begin until the Master had returned the licensed copy, but the Elizabethan theatre had a swift commercial pace, and theatre people do not always attend to bureaucratic rhythms.)

With its apparent theatrical cuts in the later scenes, and falling some twenty years after the original production, Q1 *Othello* probably came from a script used in a revival, and we will soon see signs that actors' voices and memories left marks in the text, pointing to Scenario 1. The script was probably put together fairly close to the time of publication—its use of contractions such as "'em" for "them" and "ha" for "have" was taken by Greg as a sign of a late Jacobean date, and this point has recently been reinforced by Lake and Vickers. So the revival for which the script was made probably occurred after Shakespeare's death in 1616.

F, with its fuller and neater text, may have come from another revival or from a copy of the original licensed script. Honigmann (*Texts*, 71–77) has found some characteristics of the scribe Ralph Crane's work in F, and if this is right, a later date is suggested (Crane's known work for the King's Men begins around 1618). But the signs of Crane are not conclusive in themselves, and F could go back to earlier revivals. The absence of oaths in F suggests a script dating from after the Act to Restrain Abuses of Stage Players of May, 1606, but this does not rule out an expurgated copy of the original licensed script of 1603 to 1604. Perhaps it was printed from a copy of the licensed script, with the oaths removed. Perhaps Shakespeare made the copy himself, removing the oaths and never blotting a line. We do not know. But now we are thinking about scripts as they were used in the theatre, and I think that opens the way to make a further gain on the question of why the two earliest printed *Othello*s are so oddly different from one another.

ACCIDENT

Let us take up the most revealing aspect of the *Othello* texts: *accident*. There are hundreds of accidents in in the *Othello* texts, unintended bits of waywardness keeping the two versions in disagreement, and these may be more important than the kinds of intended differences we have so far been thinking about.

Most of the accidents happen in Q1. These can be as small as a misplaced period, as in the "you shall mark" example given earlier. The misplaced period makes nonsense of the lines, and there are dozens upon dozens of tiny accidents like this in Q1. Sometimes the accidents are not so tiny. At the end of this same speech, Iago in F says he will not wear his heart upon his sleeve for daws to peck at—he means jackdaws—but in Q1 this comes out as "for doves to peck at." It is hard to believe that Shakespeare *revised* "doves" into "daws" (or vice-versa). Someone has misread one word for the other—the two words do look alike in Elizabethan handwriting. The "tragic loading/lodging of this bed," noticed earlier, is another example of probable misreading, and there are dozens more.

The question to be asked of such Q1 errors as faulty punctuation and misread words is, who made them? The usual candidates are the scribe working in the theatre or the compositor working in the printing house. A scribe making a fresh copy from a manuscript could misread some words in his source, and the Q1 compositor setting print from a manuscript is subject to the same liability. A daw could become a dove in either pair of eyes. And either a scribe or a compositor could insert a mistaken period.

But there is another source to be considered for making mistakes in Q1: the actors. Some differences between Q1 and F are too extensive to be misreadings and yet too trivial to be revisions or cuts. They are the kind of mistake actors make when memory slips a little. Here is Emilia in Q1, refusing to hold her tongue at 5. 2. 217:

> 'Twill out, 'twill: I hold my peace sir, no,
> I'le be in speaking, liberall as the ayre,

Here is the F version:

> 'Twill out, 'twill out. I peace?
> No, I will speake as liberall as the North

This is something more than a misreading. Perhaps a "stroke of genius" can be found there to make us think Shakespeare revised this passage deliberately, but more than anything else the case looks like an actor's slip of memory. Elizabethan actors normally performed a different play each day of the week and often played more than one role in each play. Their memories must have been phenomenal, but slip-ups must also have occurred frequently—one word substituting for another, a phrase summoned from another part of this play, even a bit brought in from another play. In verse drama, a substitution of a word or phrase would cause wrinkles in the meter, which the actors might iron out by improvisation. The wonder is not that Elizabethan actors made errors but that they were right so often.

An actor's faulty memory could be the cause of many of the textual differences between Q1 and F. Cassio's Q1 hope that Othello will "swiftly come to Desdemona's arms" (2. 1. 80) seems rather flat in comparison with F: "make love's quick pants in Desdemona's arms." This is not a misreading by compositor or scribe. The revision-theory would credit Shakespeare with turning the dull line into the vivid one (and would charge him with writing the dull line in the first place)—but we do not know that Shakespeare revised the play. We do know that actors memorized the play. An actor could have changed the vivid line into the dull one through a trick of memory (or vice-versa, but memory-slips usually tend toward the flatter result). Many of Q1's substantive variations from F could have resulted from accidents of memory ("re-lume" turning into "return" for example).

So long as the foul-paper/prompt-book dichotomy ruled textual study, it was hard to imagine how actors' voices could have worked their way into written texts, but Scenario 1 above, with a script being compiled from the dictation of actors who had memorized their roles, would necessarily involve some accidents—either slips of the actors' memories, or mishearings on the part of a listening scribe.

ACTORS' INTERPOLATIONS AND SCRIBAL MISHEARINGS

Another kind of actor's addition has long been suspected in Q1.[9] Listen to Roderigo's dying line at 5. 1. 63. "O, damned Iago, O inhuman dog,—o, o, o." Did Shakespeare write those last three groans? They are not in F, and they ruin the meter of an otherwise good blank verse line. There are three cases of Q1 "O, O" groanings in all, and each does violence to the meter. Here some of Othello's famous lines, as Q1 has them:

> but alas, to make me
> A fixed figure, for the time of scorne,
> To point his slow unmouing fingers at—oh, oh,
> Yet could I beare that too. . . . (4. 2. 52–55)

"Oh, oh"? An actor's interpolation can be heard in the ruins of that line, which also has different wording in F: "To point his slow and moving finger at." The Q1 "O, O" groaning creeps into the meter again at Othello's climactic recognition:

> O Desdemona, Desdemona, dead, O, o, o. (5. 2. 279)[10]

Now listen to the first word of the play according to Q1. It is "Tush." Roderigo is complaining to Iago as they enter: "Tush, never tell me, I take it much unkindly. . . ." An actor can turn "Tush" into a pathetic whine or an angry outburst. It is a stagey reaction to whatever Iago has been saying as the two enter. Iago's response begins with "S'blood." He is having none of Roderigo's remonstrances. F has neither of these words. I submit that "Tush" and "S'blood" are actors' interpolations too, bits of impromptu fuel for intensifying the opening exchange and quieting the spectators, the sort of gambit that actors call upon to establish a presence. Roderigo comes in on "Tush" and goes out on the dying groan "O, O, O," and I doubt if Shakespeare wrote these exclamations. The actors had voices of their own.

Now consider several "mishearings" that have long been recognized in Q1. When Iago comments on how ideas become obsessions in jealous persons, according to Q1 he says that dangerous conceits:

> pon the blood,
> Burne like the mindes of sulphure. (3. 3. 329–30)

What are these "minds of sulfur"? F straightens out the reference: "mines of sulfur," sulfur mines. Someone seems to have misheard "mines" as "minds." In Q1 Iago warns Othello that the Duke could punish him for eloping with Desdemona:

> he will divorce you,
> Or put upon you what restraint, and grievance,
> That law with all his might to enforce it on,
> We'll give him cable. (modernized 1. 2. 14–17)

Q1 actually spells it "Weele giue him cable," but the line only makes sense in the F version: *Will* give him cable. He will put on all the restraints the law *will* allow. There are other possible mishearings of substantives in Q1 (Honigmann, *Texts*, 32, 175 n7). Perhaps the scribe or compositor was "mishearing" his copy text (it was common to read aloud at the time, so one could mishear one's own voice), but the errors could also come from someone listening to the actors speak the lines aloud and hearing some words incorrectly.

This possibility becomes very strong when it is realized that other kinds of mishearing run throughout Q1. The punctuation and syntax have been misheard too. That seems to be how Q1 turned "For thy Solicitor shall rather dye,/ Then giue thy cause away" (F) into:

> For thy solliciter shall rather die,
> Then giue thee cause: away. (3. 3. 27–28)

The F adverb "away" turns into the Q1 command "away" (i. e., let us depart) and the F "thy cause" turns into the Q1 "thee cause" through a trick of the ear. At 1. 1. 160 a listener cannot tell whether "now" goes with "bitternesse" as an adverb, or with "*Roderigo*" as part of a vocative, and so he has it both ways:

> And what's to come, of my despised time,
> Is nought but bitternesse now *Roderigo*,
> Where didst thou see her;

F makes a clear choice: "bitternesse. Now Roderigo". At 2. 1. 50 the scribe
hears a contracted "hope's" instead of the plural "hopes" that goes with the
verb "Stand" in the next line.

> Therefore my hope's not surfeited to death,
> Stand in bold cure.

At 2. 1. 74, Q1 reads:

> She that I spoke of, our great Captains Captaine,
> Left in the conduct of the bold *Iago*.
> Whose footing here anticipates our thoughts
> A sennights speede—great *Ioue Othello* guard[.]

The listener hears a normal sentence ending on the "*Iago*," inserts a period,
then hears the speech resume with a new interrogative on "Whose." The correct version makes "whose" a relative pronoun in a continuing sentence (as
F does):

> She that I spake of:
> Our great Captains Captaine,
> Left in the conduct of the bold *Iago*,
> Whose footing heere . . .

Then, in the same speech, the Q1 scribe twice tries to end an ongoing sentence which is actually continuing in a series of three:

> That he may blesse this Bay with his tall shippe,
> And swiftly come to *Desdemona*'s armes.
>   *Enter* Desdemona, Iago, Emillia, *and* Roderigo.
> Giue renewd fire,
> To our extincted spirits.
> And bring all Cypresse comfort,—O behold
> The riches of the ship is come ashore.

A verb at the end of one sentence followed by a noun phrase at the beginning
of the next can be misheard as a continuing syntatical unit. Thus at 2. 3. 46 the
scribe writes:

> and hee's to watch
> Three lads of Cypres,

when there should be a stop after "watch":

> and hee's to watch.
> Three lads of Cypres,

as F points it (with "else" for "lads"). Poetry of difficult syntax sometimes draws a mistaken period, like the one after "Moore" in the fifth line below:

> For tis most easie
> The inclining *Desdemona* to subdue,
> In any honest suite, she's fram'd as fruitfull,
> As the free Elements: and then for her
> To win the Moore. wer't to renounce his baptisme,
> All seales and symbols of redeemed sin,
> His soule is so infetter'd to her loue,
> That she may make, vnmake, doe what she list,
> Euen as her appetite shall play the god
> With his weake function: (2. 3. 312–21)

Periods are hard to hear correctly. A pause can be misheard as a complete stop, as in:

> Tho in the trade of warre, I haue slaine men,
> Yet doe I hold it very stuft of Conscience.
> To doe no contriu'd murther; . . . (1. 2. 1-3)

Q1 has always seemed to be oddly punctuated. The reason seems clear when it is recognized that punctuation is difficult to hear. A layer of listening seems to run through Q1, and what is being heard is, I think, the voices of the actors —sometimes correctly, as in the interpolations, sometimes incorrectly, as in the mistaken punctuation, syntax, and words.

MISLINEATION: A LISTENER'S HAZARD

The most noticeable shortcoming of Q1 is its frequent mislineation of the blank verse. Short lines intrude into blank-verse passages, blank verse breaks into passages intended as prose, prose takes over verse passages. Some examples can be explained as compositorial adjustments to correct for errors in the printing-house procedure called "casting off," by which page lengths were estimated in advance and the compositor was expected to waste or save space by misdividing lines as problems became apparent. Hinman (xiv–xvi) gives possible examples from Q1 *Othello*. Yet some of the mislineation in Q1 cannot be explained in this way. Some of the errors occur when the dialogue is alternating between verse and prose, for example, and the alternations themselves seem to be the cause of the mistakes. Here is Iago's "Work on, my medicine, work," 4. 1. 42, a blank verse passage in F which Q1 turns out as prose:

> Worke on my medicine, worke: thus credulous fooles are caught,
> and many worthy and chaste dames, euen thus all guiltlesse, meete
> reproach; What ho my Lord, my Lord I say, *Othello*,—how now
> *Cassio*.

Othello has been speaking in prose in both texts, but Q1 continues in that mode and misses the change to iambic pentameter at Iago's speech. A few lines later, Q1 corrects itself into verse—as though someone had caught the beat. This could be a scribe listening to the actors' voices and taking a moment to realize that the mode has changed to verse. An example of continuing the verse beat when in fact it has stopped occurs at 2. 3. 242, where Q1 carries on in poetry for a moment, although Cassio is lapsing into a prose lament:

> Reputation, reputation, I ha lost my reputation:
> I ha lost the immortall part sir of my selfe,
> And what remaines is beastiall, my reputation,
> Iago, my reputation.

With Iago's next speech, Q1 changes to prose, and thus falls into line with the F version. This does not look like a casting-off adjustment by the compositor. The Q1 page is otherwise tightly packed (F2 verso), and has a two-line marginal entrance direction, so the compositor appears to be saving space; yet Cassio speaks in mistaken verse, which uses space. The clear likelihood is that a Q1 listener missed the change of mode at first, felt his way for verse that is not there, and then caught on to the prose. Further examples are in McMillin, *First Quarto of Othello*, Introduction.

Short lines are a frequent kind of mislineation in Q1, and in many cases they seem to have resulted from the process of listening. Here is Othello's Q1 reply to Desdemona's hope that he esteems her honest (4. 2. 65 ff.):

> O I, as summers flies, are in the shambles,
> That quicken euen with blowing:
> O thou blacke weede, why art so louely faire?
> Thou smell'st so sweete, that the sence akes at thee,
> Would thou hadst ne're bin borne.

The compositor neither gains nor loses space in this botched speech, which runs five lines in any event. The page, K4 recto, may even be saving space with marginal entrance and exit directions on lines with dialogue. The poor lineation seems to be scribal, and the mistake that throws the meter off is the half line "That quicken euen with blowing."

There are dozens of half lines occuring in mid-speech in Q1 and they can more sensibly be attributed to a listening scribe than to a space-wasting compositor, when it is recognized that the majority of the verse speeches in Q1 *end* with half lines anyhow. The half line at the end of a speech would have been expected by anyone working for the King's men after about 1600, for Shakespeare and other writers for the company were increasingly closing their speeches on short lines. One reason for this practice is well known. A new rhythm was being created by having characters share a line between the ending of one speech and the beginning of the next (Wright, 270–73). That is the poetic reason. The other reason, not so well known, is that the ends of speeches had to be spotted quickly in the Elizabethan theatre by a scribe copying parts for the actors, and to some extent by a bookkeeper looking after cue lines. The scribe copying parts had to write a few cue words from the previous speaker before he wrote each speech of an actor's own part. He had to do this hundreds of times for each play, catching what was in effect a half line at the end of each speech for the cue, then writing the next speech on the actor's part. Bookkeepers had to be concerned about the lost cue-line in performance. Actors can improvise through mid-speech forgetfulness, but a blown cue-line disrupts the next speech and opens the way to disaster all around. The bookkeeper would not be able to do much line-by-line prompting over the space of the Elizabethan stage, as I mentioned above, but cue lines are a different matter; they are the triggers to the dialogue's continuation and the one kind of line a bookkeeper would have to be able to spot. Shakespeare and other writers for the King's Men were practicing a way to make the cue line visible at a glance by putting half lines at the ends of speeches. They were creating a new poetic rhythm *and* they were sharpening the speech-endings for the eyes of the scribe and the bookkeeper.

A scribe working for the King's Men after about 1600 would have learned to expect half lines at the ends of speeches, and if he was copying from dictation he would insert some half lines prematurely, for the same reason that he would insert some periods prematurely: he would think an ending had been reached, move to the next line, then discover that the speech continues.

It follows that some premature half lines would have been marked with periods in the manuscript—the anticipated half line falling together with the anticipated period, both of them wrong. The compositor would have seen this problem and changed the punctuation in most cases, but the combination of half line and period does occur in mid-speech several times:

> For my peculiar end. (B2 recto)
> To our extincted spirits. (D4 recto)
> I'le set her on. (F4 recto)
> O beware jealousie. (G3 verso)

Here is the oddly lined speech I quoted from Q1 near the beginning of this essay. It is an example of the scribe feeling his way for the half line ending (and finally finding it):

> Mens natures wrangle with inferior things,
> Tho great ones are the obiect,
> Tis euen so: for let our finger ake,
> And it endues our other heathfull members,
> Euen to that sence of paine; nay, we must thinke,
> Men are not gods,
> Nor of them looke for such obseruances
> As fits the Bridall: beshrew me much *Emillia*,
> I was (vnhandsome, warrior as I am)
> Arraigning his vnkindensse with my soule;
> But now I finde, I had subbornd the witnesse,
> And hee's indited falsly. (3. 4. 138 ff.)

The page, I2 recto, has no signs of wasted space other than the half lines, and the half lines do not occur in succession but over gaps of at least four complete lines. (The compositors usually divided successive lines to waste space.) The scribe appears to be listening for the expected half line ending, thinking it falls on the pause after "Tho great ones are the obiect," continuing in pentameter until he thinks he hears the half line ending again, on "Men are not gods," then returning to pentameters until he hears the true ending on "And hee's indited falsly." F has all the lines in pentameter until the final one. The Q1 scribe also writes "the obiect" for "their object" (if F is correct), "that sence of paine" for "a sense of pain" (F), "observances" for "observency" (F), and "unhandsome, warrior as I am" for "unhandsome warrior, as I am" (F). He may have been hearing the actors make these little changes, or he may have been *mis*hearing the actors, but he was hearing *something*, listening as well as he could, and this, I think, is the process by which thousands of tiny variations occured between Q1 and F.

The unusual features of punctuation, lineation, and mishearing seem to me rich in theatricality, as though the spoken play were being heard before our very eyes.

SUMMARY: TWO TEXTS FROM THE THEATRES

Both Q1 and F, in all likelihood, were printed from manuscripts which served temporary purposes in the playhouse, and then were of no permanent value to the acting company. In neither case was the manuscript directly derived from one of the two categories most often used to address Shakespearean textual problems—the author's foul papers. The other category, the "prompt book," shows more promise once the notion is cleared away that scripts used backstage were orderly and complete in all of their details. I use "script" instead of "prompt book" to avoid the nineteenth-century slant of the latter term, although "book of the play" would be historically correct. F probably comes from one of the disposable backstage scripts prepared for performances of

Othello over the two decades of its stage life before publication. Even the original performances of about 1603 to 1604 might have entailed a temporary script if the licensed copy was still being reviewed by the Master of the Revels during rehearsals, or if the licensed copy was kept safe and a copy was made for the performances. The Act to Restrain Abuses of Stage Players made its impact on F, from which swearing has been purged, so the copy in question was probably made after May of 1606. Some traces of Ralph Crane's handiwork hint at a date of about 1618 to1622.

Q1 comes from a performance which was abridged from something like the performance envisioned by F, with cuts falling especially in the later scenes and in the roles for boy actors. Moreover, Q1 comes from a different kind of theatre script than does F. Q1's strange mislineations, peculiar punctuation, evident mishearings, and actors' interpolations suggest a script taken from the voices of players who had memorized the play. It appears to be a dictated script. The unusual number of contractions suggest a date of about 1618-1622.

Dictation in the theatres has been obscured by the "bad-quarto" theory mentioned earlier, which assumed that copying from dictation was irregular or surreptitious behavior. The possibility now before us is that even a relatively "good" text like Q1 *Othello* may have come from the dictation of actors, not as an act of piracy or financial desperation, but as one of the regular playhouse procedures for putting a temporary script together. The actors delivering the Q1 version made some inadvertant substitutions, and the scribe taking their lines from dictation made errors of wording and (especially) of lineation and punctuation.

Thus the differences between Q1 and F are not primarily the differences between foul papers and prompt copy, but the differences between two kinds of theatrical script. F comes from a written script. Q1 comes from a written script that has entered into the memories and voices of actors. Both tell us much about *Othello* in early theatres. The chief value of the differences is not a matter of resurrecting Shakespeare's lost foul papers or of showing how he revised his play, but of illuminating such stage practices as how the play was abridged at some point before its first publication and how the actors spoke, and sometimes misspoke, their lines. The two texts of *Othello* are rich in theatricality, no matter their separation from the hand of their author.

NOTES
1. Act, scene, and line references are from Sanders.
2. The leading study was Pollard. For recent accounts of the New Bibliography, sometimes critical of its assumptions, see Werstine, "Narratives," Blayney, and Maguire.
3. The issue was complicated by a theory that F *Othello* was printed from a copy of Q1, with an authoritative playhouse manuscript being consulted on questionable readings, but this possibility was effectively denied by Walton. A summary of

scholarship on the question, including the studies which eventually justified Walton's opinion on *Othello*, is in Honigmann, *Texts*, 5–6.

4. The evidence is presented in McMillin, "The *Othello* Quarto" and in McMillin, *The First Quarto of Othello*, from which some parts of the present essay are derived. For evidence of similar cuts late in other plays, see Rasmussen.

5. Honigmann later changed his view and favored theatrical cuts: *Texts*, 7–21.

6. Some think a manuscript play called *Sir Thomas More* may have three pages in Shakespeare's hand, but the comparison has to be made from the six signatures Shakespeare made on legal documents and this is not firm evidence.

7. For discussion of scripts in the playhouses, see Gurr, "Maximal and Minimal Texts;" Long, '"A Bed / for woodstock'" and "Perspectives of Provenance;" Masten, Mowat, Rasmussen, and Werstine, "Plays in Manuscript;" and "McKerrow's Suggestion."

8. Quoted and discussed in Werstine, "Narratives," 84–85. Gurr, *Quarto of Henry V*, makes the case for dictation in that play. For dictation in non-Shakespearean quartos, *The Famous Victories of Henry V* and *The True Tragedy of Richard III*, see McMillin and MacLean, *The Queen's Men*, 114–20, where references to the other dictation arguments will be found.

9. See Walker, *Textual Problems*, 138–61, "The 1622 Quarto," and her edition of *Othello*, 121–35.

10. F lacks the other 'O' examples, but has it in this case, shortening the line to keep the meter: "Oh Desdemon! dead Desdemon: dead. Oh, oh!" Honigmann, "Reenter the Stage Direction," argues that such non-substantive groanings and exclamations were written by Shakespeare as "crypto-directions" for the actors, showing them where "to sigh, groan, gasp, roar, weep" (123). Honigmann does not take up the issue of the ruined meter in the *Othello* examples—indeed, he says that keeping within the meter in other examples is a sign that the dramatist did write the O's. Thus the extra-metrical *Othello* examples rather tell against the argument for crypto-instructions.

WORKS CITED

Blayney, Peter. "The Publication of Playbooks." *A New History of Early English Drama*. Ed. John D. Cox and David Scott Kastan. New York: Columbia University Press, 1997: 383–422.

Coghill, Nevill. *Shakespeare's Professional Skills*. Cambridge: Cambridge University Press, 1964.

Cox, John D. and David Scott Kastan, eds. *A New History of Early English Drama*. New York: Columbia University Press, 1997.

Gurr, Andrew. "Maximal and Minimal Texts: Shakespeare v. the Globe." *Shakespeare Survey* 52 (1999): 68–87.

———. *The First Quarto of King Henry V*. Cambridge: Cambridge University Press, 2000.

Greg, W. W., *The Shakespeare First Folio*. Oxford: Clarendon Press, 1955.

Hinman, Charlton. *Othello 1622*. Shakespeare Quarto Facsimiles No. 16. Oxford: Clarendon Press, 1975.

Honigmann, E. A. J. "Re-enter the Stage Direction." *Shakespeare Survey* 29 (1976): 117–25

———. "Shakespeare's Revised Plays: *King Lear* and *Othello.*" *The Library*, 6th Series, 4 (1982): 142–73.

———. *The Texts of "Othello" and Shakespearian Revision*. London: Routledge, 1996.

Jones, John. *Shakespeare at Work*. Oxford: Clarendon Press, 1995.

Lake, David, and Brian Vickers. "Scribal copy for Q1 of *Othello*: a reconsideration." Unpublished paper, presented at the Shakespeare Conference in Stratford-upon-Avon, August, 2000.

Long, William B. "A Bed / for woodstock: A Warning for the Unwary. *Medieval and Renaissance Drama in England* 2 (1985): 91–118.

———. "Perspectives of Provenance: the Context of Varying Speech-Heads." *Shakespeare's Speech Headings*. Ed. G. W. Williams. Newark, Delaware: University. of Delaware Press, 1997: 21–44

Maguire, Laurie. *Shakespearean Suspect Texts*. Cambridge: Cambridge University Press, 1996.

Masten, Jeffrey. "Playwrighting: Authorship and Collaboration." *A New History of Early English Drama*. Ed. John D. Cox and David Scott Kastan. New York: Columbia University Press, 1997: 357–82.

McMillin, Scott, and Sally-Beth MacLean. *The Queen's Men and Their Plays*. Cambridge: Cambridge Univ. Press, 1998.

McMillin, Scott, ed. *The First Quarto of Othello*. Cambridge: Cambridge University Press, 2001.

———. "The *Othello* Quarto and the Foul-Paper Hypothesis." *Shakespeare Quarterly* 51 (2000): 67–85.

Mowat, Barbara. "The Problem of Shakespeare's Text(s)." *Textual Formations and Reformations*. Ed. Laurie E. Maguire and Thomas L. Berger. Newark, Delaware: University of Delaware Press, 1998: 131–48

Pollard, A. W. *Shakespeare's Folios and Quartos*. London: Methuen, 1909.

Rasmussen, Eric. "The Revision of Scripts." *A New History of Early English Drama*. Ed. John D. Cox and David Scott Kastan. New York: Columbia University Press, 1997: 441–60.

Riverside Shakespeare. Ed. G. Blakemore Evans, *et al*. Second ed. Boston: Houghton-Mifflin, 1997.

Sanders, Norman, ed. *Othello*. New Cambridge Shakespeare. Cambridge: Cambridge University Press, 1984.

Walker, Alice, and J. Dover Wilson, eds. *Othello*. Cambridge: Cambridge University Press, 1957.

Walker, Alice. *Textual Problems of the First Folio*. Cambridge: Cambridge University Press, 1953.

———. "The 1622 Quarto and the First Folio text of *Othello.*" *Shakespeare Survey* 5 (1952): 16–24.

Walton, J. K. *The Quarto Copy for the First Folio of Shakespeare* Dublin: Dublin University Press, 1971.

Werstine, Paul. "McKerrow's 'Suggestion' and Twentieth-Century Shakespeare Textual Criticism." *Renaissance Drama* 19 (1988): 149–73.

————. "Narratives about Printed Shakespeare Texts: 'Foul Papers' and 'Bad' Quartos." *Shakespeare Quarterly* 41 (1990): 65–86.

————. "Plays in Manuscript." *A New History of Early English Drama*. Ed. John D. Cox and David Scott Kastan. New York: Columbia University Press, 1997: 481–98.

Wright, George T. "Hearing Shakespeare's Dramatic Verse." *A Comapnion to Shakespeare*. Oxford: Ed. David Scott Kastan, Blackwell, 1999: 256–76

"My cue to fight"
Stage Violence in *Othello*

FRANCIS X. KUHN

"Brutal," "aggressive," and "raw" is how fight director John Sipes described the violence he choreographed for the Oregon Shakespeare Festival's 1999 production of *Othello* (Sipes). "Nasty," "heinous," and "cold-blooded" characterized the Actors Theatre of Lousiville's 1998 production, according to Drew Fracher, the fight director for that production (Fracher). Mark Booher, who choreographed the violence for the California Shakespeare Festival in 1998, worked to realize the "personal," "immediate," and "awful" qualities he found in the violence described in the text (Booher, Sept.). *Othello* is a violent play. From Brabantio's call for weapons in 1.2 (Arden, 3) to the play's "bloody period" (5.2.355), the dialogue requires at least eleven deadly weapons, eight separate armed confrontations, and two instances of unarmed "domestic" brutality. The Quarto adds stage directions for another bloody armed encounter (5.2.232), and actors and directors have found other opportunities for violence in performance, from Barton Booth's early-eighteenth-century performance (Sprague, 198) to Oliver Parker's 1995 film version (Parker). Samuel Johnson thought the murder scene "not to be endured" (quoted in Hankey, 122), and the turn-of-the-century American critic William Winter suggested that when one leaves the play "you feel as if you had seen a murder or attended an execution" (quoted in Hankey, 1).

The "brutal," "cold-blooded" violence that professional fight directors mine in *Othello* was a staple of the Elizabethan playhouse and culture. Alexander Leggatt, in "Shakespeare and Bearbaiting," reminds us that "the playhouse audience paid to see what the bearbaiting audience paid to see, cruelty, suffering, and courage displayed for its pleasure." (52). Fredson Thayer Bowers observed that Shakespeare's audience found violent entertainment in daily life: "The Elizabethan who attended public executions as an amusement was used to the sight of blood and would scarcely flinch from it on the stage. Rather, he would demand it, for he was keenly interested in murders for any other motive than

425

simple robbery" (16). Thomas Dekker, writing in 1609, disparaged those "violent spirits" who were entertained by "some tearing Tragaedy full of fights and skirmishes" (quoted in Nagler, 131).

The delight *Othello*'s first audiences took in that play's violence can be read in the sensationalism of the following lines from a ballad attributed to the early seventeenth century, "The Tragedie of Othello the Moore":

> He sought his lady as she layde
> Within her virgin bed,
> And there his hands of blackest shade
> He dyed to gory red. (quoted in Furness, 398)

The interest has continued through the ages. Jonas Barish summarized the enduring theatricality of Shakespeare's violence: "Something about physical injuries inflicted on human bodies seems to exercise a kind of mesmerism, both over Shakespeare's generation and our own" (101).

Responses to performances of the title role in *Othello* have often focused on actors' skill with the stage violence required by that role. Talma created "a universal tumult" with his murder of Desdemona at the end of the eighteenth century; but the business was ultimately allowed to remain due to the power of Talma's performance (Rosenberg, 32). Nineteenth-century performances in particular were often measured by their approach to, and degree of, violence. John Keats hailed Edmund Kean's exclamation of "blood, blood, blood!" as "slaughterous to the deepest degree; the very words appeared stained and gory" (3: 231), and to some Edwin Booth seemed "not murderer enough." (Rosenberg, 81). Tommaso Salvini shocked audiences by "sawing" a blade "violently cross his throat" at his suicide (Mason, 107), and was faulted by Winter for killing Desdemona "in the most extreme violence of snorting fury" (Winter, 290).

The brutal violence of *Othello,* demanded by the Elizabethan audiences, dissected by nineteenth-century performers and critics, and staged by late-twentieth-century fight directors quoted above, has also provoked anxiety, discomfort, and revulsion during the play's history. Dr. Johnson's pronouncement of the unendurability of the murder scene found an echo in the Horace Furness's confession in the *Variorum* that he saw Othello's blow to Desdemona in 4.1 as leaving a "painful impression" (251n). Michael Neill found a "congruence between Dr. Johnson's desperately averted gaze" (383) and Lodovico's response to the corpse-laden bed, "The object poisons sight:/Let it be hid" (5.2.362–63) that "makes articulate the anxiety evident almost everywhere in the play's history" (Neill, 384).

The siren-like capacity to present itself as both attractive and unendurable is at the heart of the play's theatricality. A. C. Bradley communicated some of this interplay of attraction and unendurability in finding the play "the most painfully exciting" of Shakespeare's works (176). The work has, for its audience, a horrible seductiveness, or a seductiveness of the horrible, not unlike the "green-eyed monster" (3.3.168) of Iago's, and then Othello's imagination. Neill argues that "the object that 'poisons sight' is nothing less than a mirror for the obscene desires and fears that *Othello* arouses in its audiences" (412). Edward Pechter describes how these ambivalent desires and fears are evoked by the "temptation scene" in 3.3, where Iago is luring Othello with hints and innuendo: "If for no purpose beyond satisfying our appetite for developing the action, we continue to be complicit with Iago's schemes. As a result, the scene besets us with an excruciating contrariety of desires" (80).

In delineating the "scopophile economy" of *Othello,* Neill locates a "monstrous" interplay of sexuality and violence within those "desires and fears," finding their fulfillment on Desdemona's bed in her "eroticized murder " (412, 403). Some reference to these same desires and fears, and a yearning for Bradley's "painful excitement" can be felt in the critic Desmond McCarthy's racially charged complaint in a review for *The Theatre* in 1954, that "you felt no thrill of horror" at the slap in 4.1, because the actor playing Othello lacked "the fiery sensual Moorish side" of the character (quoted in Hankey, 277). More recently, Janet Maslin, in a 1995 *New York Times* review of Parker's film, noted that Laurence Fishburne's "voluptuous Moor" has a "hint of Ike Turner (whom he played brilliantly in 'What's Love Got to Do With It?')," an African-American rock and roll celebrity accused of beating his wife. Maslin went on to remark that the actor's performance "has a dangerous edge" (C11–12). Adina Hoffman, in *The Jerusalem Post,* felt that "from the very outset, he [Fishburne's Othello] seems like a potential wife-beater." It seems that audiences want their Othellos to be violent, bloody, horrible, thrilling, and painful.

Fight director Booher, who has also worked as a fight captain on over 600 performances, described Desdemona's death at the California Shakespeare Festival as having "a kind of horrible sensuality" (Sept.). The phrase offers an appropriate description of the violence in *Othello,* identifying it as the agent that moves the conflict, with its attendant sexual anxieties, from the rhetorical to the sensual, turning Othello's "bloody thoughts" (3.3.460) into Iago's "bloody business" (3.3.472). The expectation of that violent sensuality is what arouses the audience's appetite for Bradley's "painful excitement" and McCarthy's "the thrill of terror."

The promise of a stage fight invoked for the audience by Brabantio's call for weapons in 1.1 is ultimately frustrated by Othello's diplomacy outside the Sagittary in 1.2; but only after the possibility of a battle with the Turks has been established by Cassio (37–42), setting a pattern that maintains the audience's expectation of violence. This expectation is maintained throughout the play until the promise of nocturnal violence, established in 1.1, has its violent fulfillment in the last act. Julie Hankey observes that "the other tragedies proceed leisurely upon loose plots. *Othello* by contrast is relatively tight, a sort of thriller" (3). Like all thrillers, *Othello* engages its audience with the tension aroused by anticipated violence.

Anticipation is essential to the theatrical experience of *Othello* as in most Western drama, and opportunities to create anticipation are sought after and seized upon by directors. In the text *Backwards and Forwards: A Technical Manual for Reading Plays*, David Ball, former literary director for the Guthrie Theater, describes the importance of "forwards" to a production: "A forward is anything that arouses an audience's interest in things yet to come. Playwrights want the audience hooked not on the present but the *future*" (45). This practical piece of advice for theatre practitioners echoes Suzanne Langer's earlier, and more theoretical, proposal in *Feeling and Form*: that drama's "basic abstraction is the act, which springs from the past, but is directed toward the future, and is always great with things to come" (36). The expectations aroused in *Othello* are "forwards," "great with things to come," and essential to the relationship of the play to its audience.

The "sense of scandal" that Neill observes accompanying the play, "informs the textual strategies of editors and theatrical producers as much as it does the disturbed reactions of audiences and critics" (384). Violence, as a highly visible site of the play's sensuality, plays a key part in those strategies and reactions. In Booher's words, stage violence in *Othello* is "integral to the story, not a kinetic/callisthenic technical laminate" (Sept.).

Historical and contemporary approaches to the violence in *Othello*, specifically in 1.2 and 3.3, reveal how such strategies may control the audience's experience of the play, and how "the thrill of horror" is engendered in the gap between rhetoric and physicality, in both *Othello*'s world and its audience.

Othello is a soldiers' play, set mostly in a warrior environment on a "warlike isle" (2.1.43). As Tony Taccone, the director of the 1999 Oregon Shakespeare Festival production observed in an interview for this study: "It's a play about men whose first resource, in terms of conquering life's issues, is through warfare and being soldiers" (Taccone). The play's wartime military setting mirrors, augments, and precipitates the violence between the characters. Derek Cohen, in *Shakespeare's Culture of Violence*, offers an insight into the relationship between military violence in defense of the patriarchy, and violence put to the same use in other Shakespearean settings:

> From *Richard II* where monarchy loses its grip on the instruments of control and suppression, the plays represent a movement through difficulty and uncertainty to, in *Henry V*, a moment in Shakespeare's history where violence is finally harnessed by the patriarchal authority and used successfully to consolidate monarchy. The tragedies, *Titus Andronicus*, *King Lear*, and *Othello*, are a means of pursuing this same notion on a more domestic scale. (3)

Othello himself foregrounds the relationship between geopolitical and personal violence, with his "Are we turned Turks?" (2.3.166) after the brawl on Cyprus, equating the "domestic" brawl with the battle for Cyprus. With this question Othello also unconsciously predicts his ultimate identification of himself as enemy, the "turbanned Turk" (5.2.351) he defeats at the end of the play. The interplay of the personal and military strata of violence is neatly realized in Parker's film by setting the 2.3 brawl and parts of the Othello/Iago confrontation in 3.3 in an armory full of weapons and gunpowder, an "explosive" context for the scenes.

A number of productions at the end of the twentieth century have set the play in the relatively recent past, providing an added immediacy and accessibility for contemporary audiences. In the 1997 production he directed for the Royal National Theatre, the director Sam Mendes set the action in the mid-twentieth-century with "detailed tableaux that evoke the war-rooms and African campaigns of the Second World War" (Cannon). Jon Jory, director of the 1998 production at Actors Theatre of Louisville, in collaboration with scene designer Ming Cho Lee, set the action during the bloody conflict between the Greeks and Turks on Cyprus in the 1960s (Actors Theatre). This setting was appropriate for a play that Jory viewed as revealing "the battleground of the human soul" (quoted in Allen). In the view of the critic Rick Mattingly, the Louisville production's military environment established even more directly the link between military and personal violence: "In this staging, it [the play] reflects recent evidence that misogyny is alive and well in the military."

Michael Attenborough's Royal Shakespeare Company production of January 2000 was set in an Edwardian, colonial environment, taking advantage of what Paul Taylor, in *The Independent*, called "the militaristic maleness of its Edwardian, last-days-of-empire milieu," highlighting the personal aspects of the colonial patriarchy. The awareness of misogyny and the effect of institutionalized "maleness" noted by recent critics has been reinforced by the popular association of *Othello* with the arrest and prosecution of O. J. Simpson for the murder of his wife in 1994, an association investigated by James A McPherson in "Three Great Ones of the City and One Imperfect Soul" (46–48, 75–76), and by Edward Pechter in his *Othello and Interpretive Traditions* (1–2).

The choice of setting for a production defines, and may in part be determined by, the type of weapons to be used; a critical decision that will shape both the characters' and audience's relationship to the violence. Sipes, resident fight director for the Oregon Shakespeare Festival, described the process of making those choices: "The artistic staff and I consider the nature of the characters' personalities and the cultural, economic, and social context of the play's setting before deciding what weapons will be used." (quoted in Blackwood). According to its director Tom Markus and fight director Booher, the California Shakespeare production sought to capture the feeling of the Romantic era (Markus) without using firearms, and maintain a

Mediterranean, seaside flavor, so the principle weapon was the cutlass, used "to slash or cleave," augmented by knives for Iago, Othello, Roderigo and assorted soldiers (Booher, Sept.). Realistic productions set after the mid-nineteenth century, such as Mendes's National or Jory's Louisville productions, require weapons other than, or in addition to, swords. In 1971, Brewster Mason, at Stratford-upon-Avon, "prevail[ed] upon his fellows to put up their bright swords by firing a gun into the air" according to the critic Robert Cushman (36). In Mendes's production, Othello held a pistol against Iago's cheek as he threatened him with damnation in 3.3 (371–76, Brooklyn Academy). The Louisville production also used modern weapons: Brabantio's men held rifles in 1.2, Cassio stabbed Montano with a bayonet, and Othello broke up the 2.3 brawl by firing a pistol (Fracher). This last moment is shown in the photograph of Delroy Lindo and the cast in that scene (see Figure 17). Fracher, one of ten fight masters in the Society of American Fight Directors when interviewed, described his staging of Iago's murder of Roderigo in the Louisville production as an "execution style" shooting, with Iago firing into Roderigo's head at point-blank range, "like the photo from Vietnam." This seems an extraordinarily appropriate choice for a production in which the violence was intended to be "extremely realistic" and "cold-blooded" (Fracher).

Conversely, Taccone, in directing the 1999 Oregon production, had no interest in updating the play, because Shakespeare "was working in metaphor

Figure 17. Delroy Lindo as Othello restoring order among his troops in the Actors Theatre of Louisville's 1998 production (photograph by Richard C. Trigg).

anyway." He rejected the use of modern weapons: "Modern weaponry felt all wrong. It felt like the kind of killings . . . are hand-to-hand. It's a very personal and intimate play." In collaborating on this approach, fight director Sipes used "a standard single rapier approach combined with a great deal of unarmed fighting. The 'style' of the fighting turned out to be very aggressive, raw, and quite brutal" (Sipes). During the temptation scene in the Oregon production, Othello and Iago practiced swordplay, as "sparring" partners. According to Taccone, this interplay emphasized their relationship as "comrades-in-arms." During the fencing session, Othello "pressed Iago for information and Iago 'poured' the seeds of jealous doubt in Othello's ear. Othello eventually over-powered Iago and disarmed him, thus ending the session" (Sipes). According to Taccone, the superior soldier "beats Iago in the sparring match but loses in the mental match." The sword-"play" was also likely to emphasize the "bond-ing" of men in a production that found Iago "threatened by Othello's new life with a woman" (Taccone).

In another example of the importance of a production's weaponry, the Oliver Parker film had many of Brabantio's men wielding quarterstaffs as they charged down a street toward the Sagittary, evoking the image of a lynch mob. This image was made particularly resonant by the casting of the production: Laurence Fishburne's blackness had been foregrounded by his manipulation of a white mask in the opening sequence of the film, and his identity as an American was set off by the British Kenneth Branagh as Iago and the European-accented Desdemona played by the Swiss Irene Jacob. The image of a hastily armed mob seeking to lynch an African American for "violating" a white woman was unavoidable, and was completed by the choice of quar-terstaffs, essentially thick sticks, as weapons.

Given the violent culture in which the action is situated, the play offers productions opportunities for violence not specified in the script. For exam-ple, Markus explained that in his 1998 California Shakespeare festival Pro-duction: "When I felt there were opportunities for violent stage business that enhanced (but did not distort) the action of the scene, I invented some," in an effort to "prepare the audience for the final sequences, and to make credible the nature of the world of the play." In that production, for example, Cassio fended off Bianca when she lunged to scratch his face during their argument in 4.1, and Iago drug Bianca by the arm and back of the neck in 5.1 as he pub-licly accused her of framing Cassio (Booher, Dec.). In the Oregon production Othello brutally straight-armed a soldier who attacked him on Brabantio's "Lay hold upon him" (1.2.80) (Sipes). In a bit of brutality to rival Salvini, the Othello in a 1989 Colorado Shakespeare Festival production broke broke a soldier's neck to stop the brawl in 2.3 (Markus). Such choices must be care-fully considered, being certain that suspense isn't damaged by Othello jump-ing his "cue to fight" (1.2.83). However, added violent moments like these can make more horrible the threat/promise of violence later in the play.

This threat of violence, sustained by "forwards" predicting that violence, as much as the violence itself, is essential to *Othello*'s theatricality. Fracher described Othello's potential violence in the "brothel scene" (4.2) at Louisville: "He was extremely threatening . . . but he never hit her in the scene —that's what made it all the more scary." The threat of violence is established in the first scene of the play with Brabantio's call for weapons (1.1.179), raising the possibility of an imminent and bloody stage fight. In the Parker film, camera shots alternated between Brabantio and his men surging down one street while Iago, Cassio, and Othello were advancing down another. The scene is underscored with a tension inducing string *ostinato,* creating an expectant, dynamic atmosphere reminiscent of the sequence preceding the "rumble" in the film of *West Side Story,* offering visual and aural support for the expectation of upcoming violence.

In describing his plan for this confrontation between Othello and Brabantio, Constantin Stanislavsky placed Othello in a gondola, approached by Brabantio in another gondola, who was in turn backed by yet another gondola of soldiers: "The hostile movement increases with the din and nervousness of the crowd. Already men are drawing their swords, the officers are ready. One more minute and they will launch an attack" (44–45). Stanislavsky is creating an audience-engaging moment of great expectation. An impending sea battle in miniature lurks in the canals of Venice, creating a useful association with the next expected piece of violence; the impending engagement with the Turks already suggested by Cassio at the beginning of the scene (1.2.39–47). This association is also a foreshadowing of the Venetians, and eventually Othello himself, "turning Turks" as they participate in their own destruction.

The amount of combat that occurs in 1.2 varies among productions, but the presence of the two armed bands, along with the persistent provocation of Brabantio's fiery accusations, sustains an expectant tension throughout the scene. Stanislavsky summarizes the mood leading up to Othello's "Hold your hands" (62–81): "A clash is maturing, and it will be no joke" (47). Booher described his task in this scene at the California Shakespeare Festival as "heightening the sense of danger" (Sept.). At this early point in the play the audience is engaged by the expectation of violence.

As discussed earlier, the threat/promise of a street fight by the Saggitary is ultimately frustrated; but not until the possibility of a battle with the Turks is established, thereby maintaining the expectation of violence and the audience's engagement. While a modern audience may see these two types of fights as radically different, it must be remembered that on the Jacobean stage the weapons and staging techniques would be much the same, as we have learned from the Chorus's description of the impending battle of Agincourt in *Henry V*:

> Where—O for pity!—we shall much disgrace
> With four or five most vile and ragged foils,

(Right ill-dispos'd, in brawl ridiculous)
The name of Agincourt. Yet sit and see,
Minding true things by what their mock'ries be. (4.Prol.49–53)

"Four or five most vile and ragged foils" would serve as the instruments of what Dekker termed "fights and skirmishes" whether they were on the field of Agincourt or on a street in Venice. The difference seems to have resided solely in the text that precipitates and surrounds the violent engagement. For Dekker's "violent spirits" seeking a "tearing tragedy full of fights and skirmishes" (quoted in Nagler, 131), the confrontation outside the Saggitary and the impending battle with the Turks would have been virtually identical in terms of actual stage business.

Henkey's characterization of *Othello* as "a sort of thriller" is apt. As a thriller, the play builds a sense of impending violence for its audience, which anxiously and expectantly awaits the realization of the violence with something akin to Bradley's "painful excitement." Throughout the play, until Othello's suicide, the expectation of violence is raised, and its execution is deferred, spoiled, or incomplete: The battle with the Turks is frustrated by a change in the weather, the fight at the citadel is interrupted by Othello's entrance, both Roderigo and Cassio live beyond Iago's attack; and Desdemona lingers long after Othello thinks her dead. The audience, throughout the play, awaits an "incorporate conclusion" (2.1.260) to the expected violence.

The audience is prepared for a continuing, sequential displacement of potential violence by Brabantio's phallocentric equation of his daughter's marriage with the impending battle: "So let the Turk of Cyprus us beguile, / We lose it not so long as we can smile" (1.3.211–12); and then with disruption of the marriage itself: "She has deceived her father, and may thee" (1.3.293–94). These analogies locate and equate the three major sites of potential violence through the play, Brabantio/Othello, Venetians/Turks, and Othello/Desdemona; and predict Othello's ultimate analogizing of, and fatal confrontation with, himself as a Turk.

Although neither the Folio nor Quarto specifies any physical violence between Othello and Iago in 3.3, many Othellos have been remembered for their violent treatment of Iagos in what is known as the "collaring scene," in which Othello threatens Iago with the consequences of lying. Julie Hankey comments on a moment during a performance in the nineteenth century when "a man watching Macready once shouted out 'Choke the devil! Choke him!' . . . and most Othellos have done their best here to relieve the audience's feelings" (243). Othello's physicality at this moment is formalized in Nicholas Rowe's 1709 stage direction, "Catching hold of him" (363), retained by most editors, and Arthur Colby Sprague conjectures that Rowe's notation may simply "record the stage practice of his own time" (198). The way nineteenth-century Othellos structured or "scored" their violence in this scene is an important part of the play's performance history (Hankey, 243–47; Sprague, 98–99). For example, Edward Mason, in *The Othello of Tomasso Salvini* noted that this scene contained "the greatest display of physical force in Signor Salvini's 'Othello,' and, consequently, produces the greatest effect upon the audience" (53n), emphasizing the importance of physicality to the performance. Edwin Booth carefully described to Furness how he built to physical violence from "Villain, be sure thou prove my love a whore" (3.3.362):

> As before, with smothered intensity, not loud, gradually increasing, till "If thou dost slander her"—when the full force of Othello's wrath breaks forth in violent tones and he seizes Iago, who cowers. (Furness, 203)

The attack is often brutal: Salvini stopped just short of stomping on the prostrate Iago (Mason, 52–53); Booth threatened Iago with a knife (Furness, 204); and, as mentioned earlier, David Harewood's Othello held a pistol against Iago's cheek in the 1998 National Theatre production. In the Parker film Othello backed Iago into the sea, and held his head under the surf. In the 1999 Oregon production, Othello forced Iago's head into a moat of water, holding him submerged "for some time" (Sipes). The impact of the moment was captured in the accompanying photograph of Derrick Lee Weeden and Anthony Heald. (see Figure 18)

Surely there is more than performance tradition or Rowe's stage direction that has prompted so many Othellos to brutalize Iago in this scene. Does

FIGURE 18. Othello (Derrick Lee Weeden) and Iago (Anthony Heald) in the "collaring scene" during the Oregon Shakespeare Festival's 1999 production of *Othello* (photograph by David Cooper).

Othello, or the actor playing Othello, seize this rare opportunity to confront and torture his nemesis? Arthur Colby Sprague ascribed the business to the transition from Othello's "farewell" speech (3.3.348–60), describing Othello's violence at this juncture as "appropriate to the lines rather than implied in them. . . . The change in speed is striking and that it should be accompanied by physical action is most natural" (198). Hankey, in relaying the story about the response to Macready's performance (recounted above), implied that Othello is acting on the audience's behalf (232); while Stanislavsky felt that here Othello "begins to pay Iago back for his pain" (187).

Harley Granville-Barker suggested "it is here that, for the first time, Othello loses self-control" (43), and, indeed, Othello has often been played as if losing control at this point. The critic Joseph Knight described Salvini as being "recalled however, to reason" (quoted in Hankey, 245) after almost murdering his Iago. *The Scotsman* reported that Donald Wolfit's Othello, during the 1950s fell into a "blind rage" (quoted in Hankey, 247). Edwin Booth described himself as being "in a frenzy" in this scene, about to stab Iago, when at the last moment "the Christian overcomes the Moor" (Furness, 204), implying he had been momentarily "possessed" by an unchristian, Moorish spirit. The loss of consciousness implied by phrases such as "recalled to reason," "blind rage," and "a frenzy," if established here, and possibly reinforced in Othello's fainting in 4.1, might relieve Othello of some personal responsibility for Desdemona's death. Pechter notes how "the Collaring Scene looks forward to the 'incorporate conclusion'" of Desdemona's death, offering to the audience "the central idea of Desdemona's displacement by Iago . . . reinforced by the physical enactment" (99). Derek Cohen, in discussing the effect on Othello of Desdemona's waking during 5.2, notes that Othello's plan for a "mellifluous sacrifice" is ruined, and his "rage boils up once again" as he murders her (Cohen, 124). If Othello's rage has been established earlier as "blind" or frenzied, he may not be expected by an audience to hear Desdemona's desperate arguments, pleas, and bargaining. The approach to his violence against Iago in 3.3 could shape the audience's view of Othello's agency in the murder of Desdemona in 5.2.

In contrast to the blind rage of the above examples, Delroy Lindo, as Louisville's Othello in 1960s Cyprus, maintained, and exerted, total control as he grabbed and squeezed Iago's crotch in the collaring scene. According to fight director Fracher, "Othello didn't snap here, he knew exactly what was going on." The move dramatically addressed issues of control, masculinity, and superiority with a direct, painful, and humiliating attack on Iago's virility. Furthermore, it was an appropriate move for an Othello trained to engage an enemy in unarmed combat, and a way of saying, as Fracher described it, "I will kill you." If one accepts Stanislavsky's notion that Othello is paying Iago back for his own pain, it is appropriate that the imagined cuckold attacks Iago's testicles, the site of sexuality and source of masculinity. Such a move also effectively addresses "Desdemona's displacement by Iago" (Pechter, 99). Terry Eagleton located Othello's anxiety about Desdemona in his "phallocentric viewpoint [that] a woman appears to have nothing between her legs, which is as alarming for men as it is reassuring," both confirming the male's power and raising "unconscious thoughts of his own castration" (Eagleton, 64). The relationship between this scene and Othello's passionate relationship with Desdemona was evidently visible in Salvini's performance during the collaring scene. Pechter observes that "passionate desire . . . and murderous assault, as in the Collaring Scene, echo and merge with each other to produce the same 'shiver' in their audiences," borrowing the "shiver" from a personal reaction to Othello's greeting of Desdemona described by Clara Morris, a nineteenth-century American actor (99).

Many Othellos, including Kean, Macready, Forrest, Salvini, Wolfit and Olivier have attacked Iago's throat at this point (Hankey, 245–47). While it is a good tactic to attack Iago's throat as a vulnerable area, and it is an easy way to "collar" someone, the move also, as Pechter discusses, relates the "collaring" scene more directly to the strangling or choking of Desdemona (99). Reinforcing this pattern in the 1989 Colorado production, Othello choked Iago with the same hold he would later use to snap Desdemona's neck (Markus). In his 1998 dance version of the play, Lar Lubovitch employed a "strangling motif" that the *New York Times* critic found "an unnecessary and heavy-handed foreshadowing of the denouement" (Dunning). The attack on the throat also foreshadows Othello's own suicide, during which he acts out having "took by th'throat" (5.2.353) the enemy Turk. This relationship was highlighted by Booth's threatening Iago with a dagger, and by Olivier using the same concealed knife he will later use in the suicide (Pechter, 98–99). This moment of violence in the New York Shakespeare Festival's 1979 production foreshadowed the deaths of both Desdemona and Othello by Raul Julia's Othello grabbing Iago by the neck and holding a dagger to his throat (New York Shakespeare Festival).

Foreshadowing, however, will not motivate a character or sustain a piece of business over hundreds of years. The collaring of Iago reveals an impulse that will be fully realized in the last scene of the play. In 5.2 Othello warns Desdemona that, in spite of her pleadings of innocence, she "Cannot remove, or choke the strong conception / That I do groan withal" (5.2.55–56). Othello's use of the word "choke" here may explain the impulse to attack Iago's neck in 3.3, cutting off the words, ideas, and images; the "conception," flowing from Iago's mouth into Othello's imagination. Othello allows the "conception" only after his "marriage" to Iago in which a kneeling Iago vows fidelity, and Othello welcomes Iago's "love" "with acceptance bounteous" (3.3.472–73). Up to that point, Othello works to prevent the "conception" and gestation of what Desdemona later calls the "discourse of thought" (4.2.155). Iago's throat is a phallic source of power and engenderment, an image later reinforced at Othello's suicide by the close association of the Turk's/Othello's throat and emblematic genitalia: "I took by th' throat the circumcised dog" (5.2.353).

A desperate attempt to "choke the . . . conception," to stop the flow of words, can be seen in the various collarings of Iago, including the near drownings in Parker's film adaptation and at the Oregon Shakespeare Festival. All are physicalizations, incorporations, of the need to stop the text coming from someone characterized by Allesandro Serpieri as a "perverse rhetorician" (Serpieri, 142). Othello's ensign, his sign bearer, is spilling, in Eagleton's words "empty signifiers," which Othello, the "gullible reader," is ready to fill "with the imaginary signifieds of Desdemona's infidelity" (66–67).

Virtually begging to be brought to a place of unendurable pain, Othello, early in 3.3, encourages Iago to "give thy worst of thoughts / The worst of words" (3.3.135–36); but Othello cannot tolerate the "monster in thy thought" (3.3.110). Othello, like the audience experiencing this "thriller," demands the "monster" he fears. Neill observed that "as Othello's quibble upon the Latin root of the word suggests, a monster is also what, by virtue of its very hideousness, demands to be *shown*" (412). Both the audience and Othello demand to see what Dr. Johnson warned, and they know, is "not to be endured." That cruel paradox tortures Othello, and is the reason the "monster," Iago's text and Desdemona's (or Othello's) imagined performance of it, must be destroyed for Othello to fully experience, rid himself of, and satisfy, his painful need. The "monster" that Othello did not "choke" in Iago's throat is alive in Othello's imagination.

The desire to see what is imagined, the distance between rhetoric, "the worst of words" (3.3.135) and praxis, the sensuality of the "ocular proof" (3.3.363), is the source of suspense, pain, and excitement for Othello and the audience. Just as Iago's monstrous text creates a need/fear in Othello to witness the corporal infidelity of Desdemona, so the audience experiences the tension of anticipating the physical enactment of violent events promised by the dialogue of the play. Othello's obsessive interest in imagined, not-yet-visible corporal acts is nurtured by Iago's rhetoric, while the audience's "obscene desires" (Neill, 412) to witness the promised, deferred, and not-yet-visible physical violence is nurtured by the promise/threat of violence throughout the play. From the first scene until the last, *Othello* engages the audience with expectations of violence that are not satisfactorily resolved until Othello's suicide.

Having failed to choke the text that pours from Iago in 3.3, Othello attempts to put an end to his "discourse of thought" (4.2.155) by stifling or choking Desdemona in his murder of her. Sprague reports: "In murdering his wife the Moor from quite early times employed a pillow," and quotes a 1773 periodical that refers to "Desdemona stifled to death" (212). In an evidently rare exception, the *New York Herald* reported that Ernesto Rossi's Othello in 1881 killed Desdemona "by strangling her with his hands" (quoted in Sprague, 212). Julia's Othello, at the New York Shakespeare Festival in 1979, first strangled Desdemona, then smothered her with a pillow on "I that am cruel am yet merciful" (5.2.86; New York Shakespeare Festival). In his study of 5.2 in performance from the mid-eighteenth century to 1900, James R. Siemon concluded that most Othellos entered with a weapon but resisted its use, using a dagger "only to finish the deed" (50). In a description inclusive of both the "stifling" weapon and its choking function, Garrick listed "Desdeomna's strangling pillow" as a stage property (Sprague, 212). Just as the collaring choices made by Othellos were a physicalization of their unconscious motivations, so too does the choice to stifle or choke their Desdemonas. Othello is "over-reading" (Eagleton, 65) the text he mistakenly assumes to be issuing from Desdemona's "appetites" (3.3.274), the putative source of his obsession and pain. After trying to "choke the strong conception" (5.2.55) of Desdemona's infidelity, Othello discovers "the cause" (5.2.1) is his own horrible *mis*conception, and assaults a third and final throat, his own.

Returning to the script that won him privilege and acclaim, Othello recounts his heroic deed (5.2.336–54), inhabiting his text, and eliminating the gap between rhetoric and physicality; finally, sensually, meeting and embodying the "monster." Assuming control of the text, Othello finishes it with a "bloody period" (5.2.354) inscribed with his blade on his own body. The tension of expectation, the deferral of violence, is ended, both for Othello and the audience. With that "bloody period," the gap is closed: text and performance, rhetoric and praxis, are one.

WORKS CITED

Actors Theatre of Louisville. "'Othello' at Actors Theatre of Louisville." *Subscriber & Patron News* May 1998.

Allen, Fred. "'Othello' Offers Shakespeare's Story of Intrigue, Passion, Power." *The Kentucky Standard* 13 May, 1998: B9.

Ball, David. *Backwards and Forwards: A Technical Manual for Reading Plays*. Carbondale and Edwardsville: Southern Illinois University Press, 1983.

Barish, Jonas. "Shakespearean violence: a preliminary survey." *Violence in Drama*. Themes in Drama 13. Cambridge: Cambridge University Press, 1991. 101–121.

Blackwood, Russell. "Stage Combat: A Practical Perspective." *Callboard Magazine* 19 April 1996. 14 December 2000 http://www.thrillpeddlers.com/combat.htm.

Booher, Mark. E-mail to the author. 30 Sept. 2000.

———. E-mail to the author. 31 Dec. 2000.

Bowers, Fredson Thayer. *Elizabethan Revenge Tragedy 1587–1642*. Princeton: Princeton University Press, 1940.

Bradley, A. C. *Shakespearean Tragedy*. 1904; rpt. London: St. Martin's Press, 1960.

Brooklyn Academy of Music Presents Royal National Theatre of Great Britain Othello. Dir: Sam Mendes. Brooklyn Academy of Music 10 Apr. 1998. Videocassette. New York Public Library for the Performing Arts, 1998.

Cannon, Christopher. "Less than it seems." *Times Literary Supplement* 3 Oct. 1997: 19.

Cohen, Derek, *Shakespeare's Culture of Violence*. New York: St. Martin's Press, 1993.

Cushman, Robert. "Stratford/Mermaid Othello." *Plays and Players* Nov. 1971. 32–36.

Dunning, Jennifer, "A Drama Built More on Character Than Dancing." *New York Times* 12 June 1998: E24.

Eagleton, Terry. William Shakespeare. Oxford: Basil Blackwell, 1986.

Fracher, Drew. Personal interview. 6 Sept. 2000.

Furness, Horace Howard. *A New Variorum Edition of Othello*. Philadelphia: Lippincott, 1886.

Granville-Barker, Harley. *Prefaces to Shakespeare*. Vol. 2. Princeton: Princeton University Press, 1947.

Hankey, Julie. *Othello*. Plays in Performance Series. Bristol: Bristol Classical Press, 1987.

Hoffman, Adina. "Tongue-tied Shakespeare." *The Jerusalem Post* 13 May 1996: Arts and Entertainment, 5.

Keats, John. *The Complete Works of John Keats*. 5 vols. Glasgow: Gowars & Gray, 1901.

Langer, Suzanne K. *Feeling and Form: A Theory of Art*. New York: Charles Scribner and Sons, 1953.

Leggatt, Alexander. "Shakespeare and Bearbaiting." *Shakespeare and Cultural Traditions*. Eds. Tetsuo Kishi, Roger Pringle and Stanley Wells. Newark, Delaware: University of Delaware Press, 1994. 42–53.

Markus, Tom. E-mail to the author. 28 Aug. 2000.

Maslin, Janet. "Fishburne and Branagh Meet Their Fate in Venice." *New York Times* 14 Dec. 1995: C11.

Mason, Edward Tuckerman. *The Othello of Tommaso Salvini*. New York and London: G. P. Putnam's Sons, 1890.

Mattingly, Rick. "Modern Life." *Louisville Eccentric Observer* 13 May 1998.

McPherson, James A. "Three Great Ones of the City and One Perfect Soul: Well Met at Cyprus." *Othello: New Essays by Black Writers*. Ed. Mythili Kaul. Washington, DC: Howard University Press, 1997. 45–76.

Nagler, Alois M. *A Source Book in Theatrical History*. New York: Dover, 1952.

Neill, Michael. "Unproper Beds: Race, Adultery, and the Hideous in *Othello*." *Shakespeare Quarterly* 40 (1989): 383–412.

New York Shakespeare Festival and the Department of Cultural Affairs, City of New York, Joseph Papp, producers. *Othello*. Dir: Wilford Leach. 1979. Videocassette. New York Public Library for the Performing Arts, 1979.

Parker, Oliver, dir. *Othello*. By William Shakespeare and Parker. Prod. David Barton. With Laurence Fishburne, Irene Jacob, Kenneth Branagh. Videocassette. Castle Rock, 1995.

Pechter, Edward. *Othello and Interpretive Traditions*. Iowa City: University of Iowa Press, 1999.

Rosenberg, Marvin. *The Masks of Othello*. Berkeley and Los Angeles: University of California Press, 1961.

Serpieri, Alessandro. "Reading the signs: towards a semiotics of Shakespearean drama." Trans. Keir Elam. *Alternative Shakespeares*. Ed. John Drakakis. London and New York: Methuen, 1985. 119–43.

Shakespeare, William. *Othello*. Ed. E. A. J. Honigmann. Walton-on-Thames: Arden Shakesepare, 1997.

———. *The Life of Henry the Fifth. The Riverside Shakespeare*. Ed. G. Blakemore Evans. Boston: Houghton Mifflin, 1974. 935–71.

Siemon, James R. "'Nay, that's not next': Othello V.ii in Performance, 1760–1900." *Shakespeare Quarterly* 37 (1986). 38–51.

Sipes, John. E-mail to the author. 14 Oct. 2000.

Sprague, Arthur Colby. *Shakespeare and the Actors: The Stage Business in His Plays (1660–1905)*. Cambridge: Harvard University Press, 1948.

Stanislavsky, Constantin. *Stanislavsky Produces Othello*. Trans. Dr. Helen Nowak. London: Geoffrey Bles, 1948.

Taccone, Tony. Personal interview. 30 Nov. 2000.

Taylor, Paul. Review of *Othello* at Barbican. *The Independent* 10 Jan. 2000; rpt. in *Theatre Record* 1–28 Jan. 2000: 13.

Winter, William. *Shakespeare on the Stage*. New York: Moffat, Yard and Company, 1911.

An Interview with Kent Thompson, Artistic Director of the Alabama Shakespeare Festival

PHILIP C. KOLIN

Kent Thompson, the artistic director of the Alabama Shakespeare Festival since 1989, and I discussed his major production of *Othello* in 1994 and the problems and rewards the play holds for theatre companies and audiences alike. Thompson's credits are many and diverse. Having directed more than half of the Shakespeare canon, he is well-versed in mounting productions for a variety of theatre companies. He has directed with the Utah Shakespearean Festival, the North Carolina Shakespeare Festival, Boston Shakespeare Company, the Julliard School, and the University of Washington. He also serves on the board of directors for Theatre Communications Group. This interview was conducted on a rainy afternoon, June 14, 2000, at the Alabama Shakespeare Festival in Montgomery.

PK: How long have you been with Alabama Shakespeare Festival?

KT: This is my eleventh season at ASF, which means that I have produced about 150 plays here.

PK: And *Othello* was one of them?

KT: Yes, and I also directed the play in 1994. I particularly picked *Othello* in '94, because I had an actor who could convincingly portray Othello. Many directors won't produce the play unless they know in advance who's going to perform that role, and I was very fortunate to have Derrick Lee Weeden, who during the mid-1990s, went back and forth between the Oregon Shakespeare Festival and the Alabama Shakespeare Festival. Also, I produced *Othello* on our smaller stage, the Octagon, which seats 225. That was a very important choice for me. The choice of playing space had certain financial implications—the Octagon is one-third the size of our Festival Stage, where we normally produce

441

Shakespeare. But I thought it very important to stage *Othello* in the Octagon because of its intimacy. In my experience, the play often fails because it lacks the necessary psychological subtlety of characterization and tends towards bombast and spectacle. Perhaps this tendency has been reinforced by the Verdi opera, but whatever the reason when the play becomes grandiose or exaggerated, it deflates the actual pain of its tragedy. I wanted the contact between the actors and audience to be intimate, making the pain and anger and racism of the piece impossible to escape. In the Octagon, audience members cannot distance themselves from the action.

PK: Yes, there's a sense of claustrophobia in *Othello* and, as you point out, also in Verdi's *Otello*. You focus on a very crucial point here, that the casting of Othello is central to the whole piece. Do you think it is possible to cast a white actor in the role today?

KT: Personally, I don't think it's wise to do so at this moment in our social/cultural history unless you're prepared to do something wildly nontraditional throughout the production.

PK: Such as Patrick Stewart's photo-negative Othello?

KT: Yes. And even then, it's very hard. There have been recent productions in Europe that emphasized the Spanish-Moorish origins of the Othello story, and avoided the African issues.

PK: The tawny moor as opposed to the blackamoor?

KT: For me the challenge in casting Othello is to find an actor who can believably portray an extraordinary warrior-hero, yet clearly be an outsider. While I think there can be other Moorish or African characters in the play, Othello must be demonstrably higher in status, rank, achievement, and social interaction. He's a loner and a hero. The only way I can envision the character of Iago and the character of Othello working today is if we see Othello misinterpreting the cues he is given by Iago, Desdemona, Cassio, and others in the play. The play has a history of working primarily in one of two ways. The first is portraying Othello in a pejorative way that is now viewed as racist—the exotic African of great passion but little rational thought. This reinforces the racist stereotypes that Iago and others utter in the play, but it's insulting to today's audiences, especially to African American audiences. Second, portraying Othello as a warrior-hero but also a supremely lonely outsider opens up the complexity of the play. All of the spoken and unspoken racism of this world comes back to haunt Othello during the temptation scene (3.3) and after. What has always been implied to Othello—his racial inferiority, his worth only as an exotic fighting animal, the impossibility of deserving the love of a beautiful white woman, his fear of being made the cuckold and gull by a woman—comes back to reinforce Iago's innuendoes.

PK: In your production, Othello is wearing what looks like a World War I military costume (a Viennese general) and over it a caftan.

KT: Yes, we costumed it in modern dress; I guess you could say early twentieth century. In Cyprus we used the desert khaki dress of the twentieth-century soldier. We were not precise in our setting, either in location or date. The modern dress setting was, in part, a budgetary decision—we could better afford to buy or rent men's uniforms than to build Renaissance clothing. In part, it was a pragmatic choice, given the size of the Octagon stage—large numbers of men dressed in the huge garments of the Renaissance simply wouldn't work on that smaller stage. We also included elements of Othello's African heritage in his costumes.

PK: What were some of those items, beside the caftan over the soldier's tunic?

KT: We spent a lot of time researching a variety of things. We looked at Moorish Christians, Moorish Catholics; we looked at the various Arab religious cults and we came up with something that was vaguely Muslim. We were intentionally impressionistic in our design choices because we didn't want to offend anyone who in the audience who was a devout Muslim. Clearly, Othello was not of the same culture, and yet he had to wear the military uniform. Since he was a general, he could get away with various military additions to his uniform that reflected his cultural origins—overrobes, turbans, sashes, jewelry, and caftans.

PK: At any time did he wear a crucifix?

KT: No, he did not; we made the choice not to. We wanted to indicate a tradition of mysticism as his root religion—similar to the superstitious mysticism he uses when describing his mother's handkerchief embroidered with strawberries.

PK: One of the most interesting questions audiences ask about Othello is, "How could he succumb so quickly?" How did you prepare an audience, or better yet, what subtext did you use with your actors so that Othello's fall wasn't so precipitous that people would say Othello was foolish in the beginning and all the grandeur of the senses in 1.3 or 2.1 was simply dissipated?

KT: We worked hard to establish a society fraught with overt and covert racism. We tried to establish this racial bias in every scene, so that the audience could appreciate the cumulative pressure on Othello, especially after he defied that society by marrying Desdemona. Early on, we sought to make the relationship between Desdemona and Othello very special —sensual, romantic, intense. We hoped to demonstrate theirs was one of those extraordinary, almost magical relationships—passionate and thrilling—but also whirlwind. Their love affair was developed in small moments stolen inside the Brabantio household; their marriage was a hurried act of public defiance. The shadow side of such a relationship is that it is not based upon intimate day-to-day knowledge of each other. It is romantic rather than pragmatic. They do not know each other very well. Second, we were helped by the setting for most of the play—the military encampment at Cyprus. An interracial marriage is difficult enough, but when the setting is an isolated encampment of soldiers, the pressures can quickly escalate. Two things happened in 1994 to reinforce our work: the arrest of O. J. Simpson, and a scandal in the U.S. Marine Corps. The press broke the story that Marine Corps commandants were discouraging soldiers from marrying or even from staying married, because it would hurt their careers. This reinforced an age-old military misogyny, where women are seen as temptresses and seducers on the one hand and needy burdens on the other. This seemed to be reflected in the play, certainly by Iago and Cassio but even by Othello himself when he refers early on to the seductive if not hypnotic powers of a woman. In a male-dominated patriarchy, the presence of a wife was perceived as a burden to a soldier, psychologically zapping his social energy. We tried to reinforce this male-dominated world, where Iago seems fairly honest even though he's often a misogynist. Having a "general's general" became a credible and serious problem for Othello, regardless of his deep love and affection for Desdemona.

PK: Let me pick up here on two different things you said. Desdemona and Cassio, especially during the ninteenth and twentieth centuries, have been played as victims—sacrificial, almost as angelic creatures, whereas during the Renaissance Desdemona was more defiant, especially in light of working with an all-male cast.

KT: Yes, we stressed the defiance against Venetian patriarchy and, of course, Brabantio.

PK: In what way?

KT: It was very clear in 1.3. Her open defiance of her father's wishes was straightforward and strong, in no way submissive or fearful. Derrick Weeden played genuine surprise at her request of the Duke to follow Othello to Cypress. She was an independent woman of stature.

PK: How much passion did you see in the subtext of Desdemona's love for Othello?

KT: There was a lot of passion when they came together. We tried to have them make as much physical contact as possible. I knew that this would raise the stakes with the audience because it would tap into their own anxieties about interracial marriages. It was also important to show that Desdemona was from a different culture, that there was an exotic quality about their love, revealed in the way that he describes their courtship story. Essentially, we were trying to show that when they arrived at Cyprus, they actually didn't know each other well.

PK: So that the marriage was not consummated until Cyprus?

KT: If it was consummated, they still don't know each other well. They don't know how the other person really reacts. In a sense they are in an operatic world, but I prefer to think of it as romantic with a capital R. They are engulfed in a tremendous passion. There's this kind of star-crossed "meant to be together" character of their love because of the way that they relate. But in point of fact they have not had many conversations over the kitchen table. They have not had many conversations that deal with pressures that come with married life in sixteenth-century Venice, especially with a marriage of different races.

PK: You raise a fascinating point from the perspective of critical theory that in 1.3, we hear that she fell in love with Othello from the stories he told, so that she is the ear—the passive listener—and when she comes to Cyprus, and certainly later in act 4, she cannot be the passive listener anymore.

KT: And that's the great challenge of the role of the actor playing Desdemona. I chose *not* to cast somebody who was 22 or 23. Instead I cast an actor who looked in her late twenties and was actually in her thirties. Now that was a modern interpretation to fit in with the clash of cultures that is at the center of Othello. I wasn't looking for someone who was a young girl simply carried away by romance and passion.

PK: Smitten?

KT: Smitten, and where Daddy Brabantio is just a foolish old duffer. Suzanne Irving's Desdemona was somebody who was operating from a perspective of a few years and could have chosen otherwise.

PK: Roderigo, or one of the other "curled darlings" of patriarchal Venice?

KT: Yes, someone who was very important. Now, we also cast Iago with an actor who was a little older than the typical Iago so that he was seen as somebody (in this military world) who was on the cusp of being too old to be chosen as Othello's lieutenant.

PK: Of being passed over.

KT: This became doubly worse in the military encampment of Cyprus—an enclosed world filled with competitive men who know that you were passed over for a younger man. We made it a constant sources of injured pride for Iago.

PK: Kenneth Burke said that *Othello* is saturated with Iago's whispers. What did you do to have your Othello establish any kind of bond with the audience in terms of Iago's jocularity, in terms of proximics, in terms of just getting them to believe him?

KT: I didn't have to do much. First of all, we had Derrick Lee Weeden, surely one of the most handsome African men in American theatre. Derrick has tremendous presence. His relationship with Iago signals a message of trust and intimacy to the audience. You see a very warm and appealing Othello. He walks on stage and he's the leader of all the people up here. He has a great masculinity at 6'3" and is very muscular —but yet a close friend of Iago's. Othello appeared to have a long-time friendship with Iago—touching him on the shoulder, deferring to him in the presence of others.

PK: What about your Iago?

KT: Dick Elmore is about 5'9" or 5'10". He is a stocky character actor who at the time probably looked about 45. Like Derrick, he was from the Oregon Shakespeare Festival. He has this kind of rough-hewn quality. Interestingly enough, Dick also suffers from Tourette Syndrome. Not that we cast him for that reason, but what happens is that when his intensity grows, the side effects of his illness—occasional shrugs or sudden

FIGURE 19. Derrick Lee Weeden as Othello and Dick Elmore as Iago at the Alabama Shakespeare Festival.

gestures—will either drop away or increase. I don't know that we could always predict these gestures, but Dick played them when they happened —they gave his Iago an unpredictable and disturbing physicality.

PK: That's fascinating because after Mercutio, Iago's the most salacious character in the canon.

KT: What I kept trying to work on with the audience was to use Iago against Othello at every opportunity. We wanted them to find him disarmingly amusing up to a point. Then it would turn distasteful, even grotesque. I mean Iago is the sort of guy who sits down next to you and starts with a stereotype: "You know I like those 'green' people but you know they drive too many cheap cars with trailers." It's a kind of suggestive envy mashed in humor and false friendship that Dick captured so well—the quality of "I've got to always be putting someone down."

PK: So would you say that in the great polarization of life, it's an Othello play as opposed to an Iago play?

KT: They must always work together in the dance that they do in act 4. What Dick tried to do was to show that Iago was never, or rarely, in the lime-light. He was perfectly willing, even on stage, to let Derrick's Othello stand in the spotlight and be everywhere. He never wanted anybody to see what he was doing.

PK: Did you have light cues to reinforce that kind of shadowing of Iago's menacing mentality?

KT: Frequently. In 3.3, when Iago lays in the suspicions about Cassio's past relationship with Othello, he literally moved into darker areas each time after he dropped a hint. Othello kept pulling Iago back into the light to see his face. What was also interesting about Dick Elmore's Iago was the way he would inject so much humor into the role, particularly in his rela-tionship with Roderigo. His Iago was an incredible comedian.

PK: How was this accomplished—physically as well as verbally?

KT: There's a lot of physical cruelty that became Iago's signature, espe-cially in the way he treated Roderigo when he's injured, the way he made fun of him, the way he constantly upstaged the duped suitor. There was something about his Iago that underneath all his anger, his desire to seek power, to get revenge that affects every relationship— with his wife Emilia, Roderigo, Othello—that was nihilistic. People laughed at the things that they should have laughed at, but underneath the jokes was a darker, meaner edge to Iago. When Roderigo protested Iago's behavior in 4.2, Iago jostled him about until Roderigo recanted —very much like hazing. The other thing that's very common in *Othello* is the sense that Iago is continually trying to engineer inci-dents. The play is rushing forward. Iago can't let things stop, even to the point of being reckless. He can never stop the momentum. I remem-ber telling the cast that when Othello enters the bedroom in 5.2, it should feel like it's the first time we've taken a breath in the play, and of course it is a terrible moment.

PK: Can you describe the prop you used for the handkerchief? Was it large with the strawberries or did you use something a little different?

KT: No, we didn't use one that was particularly large; we just had a lady's handkerchief with strawberries woven into it.

PK: I guess the reason I'm asking is, was there exaggeration of any of the props?

KT: No, not really. What we exaggerated was the lighting, the mood, the atmosphere. When Othello frightens Desdemona in his description of the missing handkerchief ("That handkerchief/Did an Egyptian to my mother give . . ."), the lighting subtly shifted to shafts of light and shadow, reinforcing the mysticism of Othello's description. In keeping with our military emphasis, the fight scenes were set in the barracks—a masculine, metal and wood, hard-edged room.

PK: How did you choreograph the three fights, especially the most crucial one where Montano and Cassio attack each other in 2.3?

KT: We staged it as barracks violence with a strong, overpowering sense of men going out of control. The fight quickly turned into a brawl—men using benches, torches, anything in reach as a weapon. And the fighting style was ugly—a barroom brawl.

PK: With the small playing area, did the audience gasp, recoil in terror, at the fight scenes?

KT: Most definitely. The fight director, Drew Fracher, pushed the envelope as far as we could safely do so. By the time the fight erupted, the people in the front row occasionally stood up because they were afraid that they were going to be hit. Of course, they were not, but we did it to demonstrate the eruption of chaotic violence. The fight was an explosion of tempers from military men accustomed to blood and gore. If it had not been stopped by Othello, someone would have been badly injured or mortally wounded.

PK: You mentioned the barracks setting several times and also the Marine Corp and that whole ambience of military life. Have you ever thought of comparing *Othello* to David Rabe's *Streamers*?

KT: Yes. I have not done that play but I can see how it would be very similar, especially in the military atmosphere and the way turbulence occurs in regular explosions in *Othello* and *Streamers*. There's no way else to say it but that the violence winds itself up and then erupts.

PK: Picking up on the homoeroticism in *Streamers*, how did you address that issue in *Othello*, especially in 4.1 when Iago and Othello kneel in allegiance to each other?

KT: Yes, we actually had discussions about that idea; we didn't particularly pursue it but we certainly didn't deny it. I don't see the unholy wedding at the end of 4.1 where they kneel down as homoerotic. Rather, I wanted to take the cult of Renaissance male friendship and look at those Renaissance ideas in light of modern military testosterone-based friendship of warfare and valor. I'm not denying that some of it may be homoerotic, but it was not the aim of our interpretation, because it seemed to me that Iago was out for something else, and that was destruction.

PK: And we're right back to the critical conundrum Coleridge talks about— "motiveless malignity." When the ideal audience member for your *Othello* left the theatre, what would he or she have come away with as to why Iago did it—a morality play with Iago as vice figure, the devil himself?

KT: I think in my production they came away with the impression of an obsessive envy on the part of Iago toward Othello and Cassio, and a destructive bitterness from a life not working out the way he had hoped it would. I would characterize Iago's chief drive as a nihilistic envy.

PK: Do you think your audience saw Iago's psychology in such a direct way?

KT: Let me relate an incident that illustrates the extraordinary yet popular response of the audience. An elderly woman approached Mr. Winton Blount, the benefactor of our magnificent facility, at intermission. She said, "I just want to thank you for this theater, Mr. Blount." And he said, "How do you like the play?" He obviously knew that I was standing next to him. She said, "Oh, I love it, but I just know something terrible is going to happen by the end." As she left, she wiped away a tear. And that was pretty much the response of the audience at the end; they were shattered. What they were witnessing was in fact a profound waste. Iago had, however you define it, an evil trait that resulted in the waste of the lives of Desdemona, Othello, Emilia and others all dragged down and destroyed by his machinations. It was insidious. There was something in the whole business that was sick, and it wasn't the interracial marriage that was sick.

PK: Do you see Othello in act 5.2 as heroic, redeeming himself, loving Desdemona too much and using the murder as a sacrifice?

KT: I think that was what Othello is trying to do, to convince himself that he is doing in the last scene. Derrick was trying to be valiant, with tears falling during his final lines. I think that perhaps one of the traps in the operatic version is that Othello tips to the grand or sentimental too soon. I think the play is more horrific if you resist a "heroic" ending.

PK: How was Othello dressed in act 5.2 when he enters with the lantern?

KT: He was dressed in just the caftan, extremely simple. It could have been that he was coming to bed. He was not dressed for the world of his military duties.

PK: What kind of bed did you use—a four-poster?

KT: It was not a four-poster. It was more like a large ottoman bed, but it was clearly their bed. It had been identified earlier in 4.2 because we had seen it with Desdemona and Emilia.

PK: "The tragic loading of this bed"—did all three of them lie on the bed?

KT: Othello and Desdemona were on it. Emilia lay next to it.

PK: Was your production going on when the O. J. Simpson story broke?

KT: Yes. The O. J. business happened that summer, and of course that spiked interest in our production. The interest was already high, but after the story broke, we suddenly had long lines waiting as standbys to sold-out performances. Yet, I don't think that people necessarily reinterpreted Derrick's performance with O. J. in mind. It seems to me they wanted to see a similar story written 400 years earlier. So it was an odd time. However, it led to a lot of conversation, a lot of audience discussion about this issue. By the way, there are several African American actors who don't want to perform Othello, who doubt that we should ever produce *Othello* again. They feel that it's a white man's version of a black man's play. I don't entirely agree with that viewpoint, but it was interesting that culturally corollaries were drawn between O. J. and the Moor.

PK: Would you comment on those productions where you will have an African American Othello and an African American Iago, so that you have those anxieties played out, not just racially, but in terms of gender roles.

KT: In recent years, I've seen an African American Othello and an African American Iago in the same production. I think that can work, but you do diminish the given circumstances of Othello—the racism, the charged tension between two cultures. Perhaps it highlights the homoeroticism.

PK: Did you make any substitute cuts in script for Iago? Were there things that you took out because of contextualing or glossing for the contemporary audience?

KT: I'm sure that I did, but I cannot remember the specifics.

PK: I've just published a theatre and cultural history of *A Streetcar Named Desire* with Cambridge University Press, and while *Streetcar* and *Othello* may seem like very different scripts, they are much alike. Would you comment?

KT: We did *Streetcar* here that first or second season, and I'm sure that we will do it again. I think that there are some similarities in the emotional aspect of the plays and the male-female dynamics that are portrayed.

PK: Culturally, Desdemona has been raised in an environment which is Judeo-Christian, patriarchal, a culture of the law. Venice is law-driven and Stella DuBois certainly is raised at Belle Reve with the same kinds of patriarchal incentives. In both plays you have the "wheeling outsider" coming in (Stanley; the Moor), but in the *Othello-Streetcar* paradigm there's that sense in which the audience is both lured and frightened by Stanley's and Othello's violence. In your production of *Othello*, what was the most violent thing that Othello did before act 5? The slap in act 4.2?

KT: No. There was the slap, but there were a couple of times he manhandled Iago, not just putting hands on him but taking him down, clearly dominating him, driving him to fear. One incident came at a traditional moment (act 3, scene 3) when Othello says: "Villain, be sure thou prove my love a whore. Be sure of it, give me the ocular proof." The challenge there was, of course, for Iago to respond, but physically he was no match for Weeden's Othello.

PK: What kind of music did you use in the production?

KT: We used the music composed by Jim Conely. It developed three or four musical motifs borrowing liberally from Renaissance music (the Willow Song in act 4.2 and incidental music when in Venice), percussive modern music for the military encampment scenes in Cyprus, and African tribal music on a single wind instrument for Othello.

PK: Cassio has received much criticism for being nothing more than a dandy. In your production, do you portray him as sincere and faithful or do you envision him as a reckless, foolish young man who brings a lot of this on himself? "This is my ancient; this is my right hand, and this my left"— playing a drunk.

KT: We had an excellent actor, Ray Chambers, who's played a lot of leads here at various times, and he's also very handsome, very good-looking and could look extremely aristocratic and patrician. Cassio clearly was of higher rank and status than baser-born Iago. Yet, his faults were clear and we based very much of the confrontation in 2.3 on his alcoholism leading him down the path of destruction, egged on by Iago's manipulations. Part of Cassio deserves some reputation, but he probably doesn't deserve all of his reputation. Cassio is somebody who is deeply conflicted in his inner self, related certainly to Bianca, and to having his own worries about himself. Alcohol was the accelerant in his downfall.

PK: Bianca was listed in First Folio as a courtesan, yet Edward Petcher has argued in *Othello and Interpretative Traditions* (1999) that the descriptions in the cast list are not authorial, and since the compositor for the First Folio was under the sway of Iago, there's actually no evidence in the text that Bianca was anything but an honest woman and not a camp follower. How did you portray her?

KT: We tried to portray her as someone who was obviously from Cyprus. She was definitely not of Cassio's class. She came from a lower class.

PK: And how did you signal that to the audience? Dialect, dress?

KT: Dress and behavior more than dialect. She was dressed in a colorful peasant dress. Her public behavior—demanding and hanging onto her lover—clearly embarrassed Cassio. I didn't want to make her simply a prostitute. We tried to establish that Cassio is not being completely honest. To him she's an object of entertainment and sexual gratification, but no more. I guess you could say it was more of the relationship you would expect with a military officer in this machismo world of Cyprus. We tried to make the sexual attraction very strong. There were lots of kisses and hugs.

PK: Were there any indecent gestures in the play to account for this soldierly-like image?

KT: Some of the soldiers used indecent gestures with reactions to Bianca, and Cassio wiped his mouth after a sloppy kiss from Bianca. There was also a transformation in Cassio when he was with Desdemona. You saw his manners come back. He was from Florence and he knew her background and he knew how to play his cards.

PK: ASF has the reputation of being a theatre that takes risks. What "risks" as a director did you take with *Othello*?

KT: *Othello* is problematic because of the racial issues, and I think who
     Othello and Iago are today are problematic because of the types and ori-
     gins of anxieties that audiences bring with them into the theatre. You
     have to be very careful when you're doing the play. I don't think it is quite
     as problematic as that other play about Venice—*The Merchant of Venice*.
     The central risk we took was setting in the Octagon—the audience could
     not escape the racial/psychological/sexual tensions of the play. They
     were caught in the same room and were too close to objectify their
     responses. The other risk is that I directed it, and I'm a white man, not a
     Moor or an African. Even though *Othello* could return to our schedule
     soon, it's not a show that I would produce as frequently as the other major
     tragedies. I want to be very careful, because two out of three of our
     Shakespeare plays are heavily performed for high school students. But
     I've also been daunted in the last several years to realize that if I do it
     again and if I'm brasher about it, it should probably go back to the much
     larger Festival stage. So, I'm very concerned about pulling off a psycho-
     logically subtle *Othello* in such a large theatre. It could well be that my
     colleague, Kent Gash, who's African American, may direct it and that
     will be interesting, to see what new perspective he brings to the play.

PK: There was a time when an actor, Laurence Olivier, for example, could
     put on black paint, but those days are gone. But have we come to senti-
     mentalize the play?

KT: Do you mean, does it simply reinforce our own feelings/prejudices/val-
     ues?

PK: Yes, exactly, and for Renaissance audiences, too. Othello is a Moor, but
     he could also be a Coptic Christian, right?

KT: Yes, and we looked into the Coptic Christians and we looked into several
     African religions that had been modified by Western religions. I remem-
     ber going through that process. We carefully wanted to create an Othello
     whose religious heritage was mixed—another potent source of confusion
     in his search to establish his identity. We hoped to indicate his Moorish/
     African religious background had been put aside for a while.

PK: Suppressed?

KT: Yes, because Othello had to rise through the ranks of a different culture's
     military. Future Othellos may say, "Now I can let it hang out because I'm
     Colin Powell."

PK: And was Colin Powell part of the military complex you had in mind as you interpreted your text?

KT: Surely he was. However we wanted to show a world where there was only one Colin Powell and no other African American generals anywhere, or captains, or government leaders. So there's this extraordinary achievement on Othello's part. Sort of like Dumas Pere's father in the French court where you have an African general and no other Africans anywhere. Like Othello, General Dumas was highly praised but frequently scorned and despised.

Notes on the Contributors

Philip C. Kolin, the General Editor for the Shakespeare Criticism Series, is Professor of English at the University of Southern Mississippi.

James R. Andreas, Sr., Editor of the *Upstart Crow*, is Emeritus Professor of English from Clemson University.

David Bevington is the Phyllis Fay Horton Distinguished Service Professor in the Humanities at the University of Chicago.

Sara Munson Deats is Distinguished Professor of English and former Head of the Department of English at the University of South Florida.

Peter B. Erickson is Collections Access Librarian with Clark Art Institute, Williamstown, Massachusetts.

Joseph Fitzpatrick teaches drama at Duke University.

John R. Ford is Associate Professor of English at Delta State University.

John Gronbeck-Tedesco is Associate Dean of Liberal Arts and Professor of Theatre at the University of Kansas.

Jay L. Halio is Profesor of English at the University of Delaware.

Sujata Iyengar is Assistant Professor of English at the University of Georgia.

Francis X. Kuhn is Chair and Assistant Professor of Theatre at the University of Southern Mississippi.

Mary F. Lux is Associate Professor of Medical Technology at the University of Southern Mississippi.

Scott McMillin is Professor of English at Cornell University.

Thomas Moisan is Professor of English, and former Chair of the Department of English, at St. Louis University.

Nicholas Moschovakis is an instructor at Sewanee: The University of the South.

Bryan Reynolds is an Associate Professor of English and Comparative Literature at the University of California, Irvine, and Head of the Doctoral Studies Program.

Hugh Macrae Richmond is Emeritus Professor of English at the University of California at Berkeley.

Clifford Ronan is Associate Professor of English at Southwest Texas State University, San Marcos.

James Schiffer is Chair of the Department of English and Professor of English at Northern Michigan University.

LaRue Love Sloan is Assistant Professor of English at Louisiana Tech University.

Kent Thompson is the Artistic Director of the Alabama Shakespeare Festival.

Daniel J. Vitkus is Assistant Professor of English at The Florida State University.

Printed in Great Britain
by Amazon

52412379R00269